Ethnic America: Readings in Race, Class, and Gender

Rita Cameron Wedding
Eric Vega
Gregory Yee Mark

California State University, Sacramento

KENDALL/HUNT PUBLISHING COMPANY
4050 Westmark Drive   Dubuque, Iowa 52002

Front cover by Frank La Pena. Painting from the Collection of Mort and Marcy Friedman.

Contents

SECTION FOUR: Organizing for Social Justice 369

Preface

Ethnic studies as a discipline has existed for over three decades. During this period the number of ethnic studies departments, programs, faculty, student majors, and students enrolled has increased dramatically. During the 2002–03 academic year at California State University, Sacramento (CSUS), over 3,200 students enrolled in ethnic studies courses. New textbooks are in constant demand to meet the challenges of this continually evolving field of study. For the course Ethnic America, finding adequate readings has been a major challenge. This anthology, a collective product of ten CSUS Ethnic Studies faculty members, intends to fill this gap.

This book is divided into four thematic categories so that the experiences of Native Americans, African Americans, Asian Pacific Islanders, and Latinos-Chicanos can be examined from several viewpoints. The sections, Conceptualizing Race, Class, and Gender; Histories; Resistance and Discontent; and Organizing and Social Justice, emerged from the articles that we as faculty believe make significant contributions to the discipline of Ethnic Studies. While the chapters located within these sections might focus on one particular race or ethnic group, the lessons they teach are many. We encourage you to think and question critically the issues which emerge for you as you read this material so that you can understand both the similarities and differences between the race and ethnic group experience. We also suggest that you consider these groups not as discrete but as they affect and are affected by broader structural forces of a capitalist society. The connections we make across race-ethnic boundaries reveal the myriad ways, subtle and overt, that race and racism are constructed and preserved.

We arranged these chapters based on their ability to convey the theme of the category in which they are located and to examine and analyze these themes from a group-based perspective. U.S. race and gender categories and corresponding ideologies were established to justify and rationalize positions of dominance and subordinance. Section I *Conceptualizing Race, Class, and Gender* addresses the many ways in which social categories are renegotiated within the context of changing political and socioeconomic conditions. This section explains that definitions and connotations of social categories are not fixed, but rather fluid as they are determined largely by external political and economic forces. These forces include laws, ideological belief systems, and social practices, as well as internal forces created by social movements and demands for social justice.

The chapters in this section also examine how race as a social construction intersects with other systems of inequality such as gender, class, and sexual orientation. These systems are interdependent; therefore, how people experience "race" will depend largely on how it intersects with other social categories.

We also note that race, ethnicity, and gender are dynamic and not static systems and how they are conceptualized, defined, and understood are directly linked to prevailing socioeconomic conditions and group identities.

Section II *Histories* focuses on the historical experiences of all of the groups. Some chapters approach these discussions chronologically while others highlight key historical events.

The chapters in this section describe the experiences of oppression and subordination as constructed by laws and social practices. This section also examines how various racial and ethnic groups have historically mobilized and organized to resist subordination.

We recognize that the experiences of racial and ethnic groups are produced in large part by oppressive forces. Therefore, it is important that in Section III *Resistance and Discontent* groups self-define and describe their own responses, resistance movements, and rebellions in their efforts to claim agency over their lives.

In Section IV *Organizing and Social Justice*, we respond to the question asked time and time again by many of our students—"What can we do?" Quite often in academic literature there is a disconnect between theory and practice. Because ethnic studies emerges from a long tradition of social action, we included in this section chapters written by people on the front lines fighting for issues of social justice and equality.

While there are many ways for our students to interpret and apply these readings, we suggest that you consider a consistent theme that runs throughout this collection—how racial and ethnic group experiences are shaped by the relationship between forces of social domination and group resistance.

Finally, we hope this reader will provide you with the material needed to understand the inextricable connection between theory and practice that has brought voice to the race and ethnic experience in U.S. society.

Acknowledgments

We would like to express our deep appreciation for the departments of Ethnic Studies and Women's Studies at California State University, Sacramento, for the support that made this book possible.

About the Contributors

Steven J. Crum (Western Shoshone of the Duck Valley Reservation in Nevada) is an associate professor of Native American Studies at the University of California, Davis. He is the author of *The Road On Which We Came* (1994), which is a history of the Western Shoshone people of the Great Basin region. Crum is also the author of several journal articles. His specialty areas include the history of the Western Shoshones, Native Americans in higher education, and general twentieth century Native American history.

Alexandre Kimenyi is Professor of Linguistics, Ethnic Studies, and African Languages at California State University, Sacramento. He is the author of several books and articles on linguistics. He is former editor of *Impuruza*, an international journal of Rwandans in Diaspora, and *Wihogora Rwanda*, an international journal of the 1994 Tutsi genocide survivors. He is the coeditor of *Anatomy of Genocide: State-Sponsored Mass-Killings in the 20th Century*. He also writes poetry. His research interest includes all areas of descriptive and theoretical linguistics, the genesis and dynamism of signs and structures in all semiotic systems, genocide and holocaust studies, cultural survival of minority groups, indigenous people, folklore, and popular culture.

Nicole Lim is an assistant professor of Ethnic Studies at California State University, Sacramento. She is a staff attorney for the National Indian Justice Center and is integrally involved in the development of the California Indian Museum and Cultural Center. Ms. Lim holds a B.A. from the University of California at Berkeley and a J.D. from the University of San Francisco School of Law. She is a member of the Pinoleville Band of Pomo Indians of northern California.

Wayne Maeda is a lecturer in the Department of Ethnic Studies, California State University, Sacramento. He is one of the founding members of the Asian American Studies Program and Ethnic Studies Department. He taught the first Asian American course in 1970 and continues to teach a variety of ethnic studies courses at California State University, Sacramento, Sacramento City College, and periodically for University of California, Davis. He is the author of *Changing Dreams and Treasured Memories: A Story of Japanese Americans in the Sacramento Region*.

Eric D. Vega lectures in Ethnic Studies at California State University, Sacramento. He is the current chair of the Freedom Bound Center, a nonprofit organization working to train a new generation of social justice activists.

Rita Cameron Wedding, Ph.D., is the Women's Studies Coordinator and a professor in Women's Studies and Ethnic Studies at California State University, Sacramento. She is also a member of the California Commission on the Status of Women.

Gregory Yee Mark is Chair and Professor of the Department of Ethnic Studies at California State University, Sacramento. He is also the Director, Principal Investigator of the Asian/Pacific Islander Youth Violence Prevention Center in the John A. Burns School of Medicine at the University of Hawaii, Manoa.

Robert Munoz, Jr., Ph.D., Sociology, University of Colorado, Boulder. Dr. Munoz is a professor in the Department of Ethnic Studies at California State University, Sacramento. His areas of research include cultural competency, female-headed households, higher education, and service learning. He has spent several years in the struggle for people of color in higher education, specifically regarding issues of access, equality and diversity. He is committed to issues of social and economic justice for human beings everywhere, especially in communities of color and communities affected by globalization trends.

Introduction

Robert Munoz, Jr.

The study of race and ethnicity in the U.S. presents the possibility of understanding and negotiating the commonalities and differences of our historical experiences. A survey of race and ethnic studies reveals an extensive analysis of, and testament to, the contributions of people of color in naming—and playing an integral part in—the political, social, economic, and cultural formation and history of the U.S. The field also presents a larger analytical scope in its examination of the claims, culture, and trajectory of western civilization and the increasingly global nature of politics, culture, and economy.

Race and ethnic studies offer a more meaningful and representative view of life, of the human condition, and of different societies, regions and communities. Scholarship in the field has unearthed hidden histories—and her stories—of Mexican guest workers in the forties; of Asian immigrants braving toxic hazards in Silicon Valley; of clerical workers' contributions to the success of the civil rights movement; of the contributions of Native Americans and Filipino Americans to victory during World War II; and of so many more areas of our lives. Besides examining the impact of race and ethnicity on people's life circumstances, these studies also uncover the meaning of these experiences for people, the reasons and strategies they employ in responding to racial barriers and conditions. These studies tell the stories of our parents—many of which our parents chose to not tell us in the hope of sparing us the ugliness of the racism they experienced and any possible bitterness that might ensue from hearing these accounts.

There are important points to keep in mind regarding terms. "Race" and "ethnicity" are used interchangeably in this essay. Race represents a social demarcation of groups on the bases of physical *and* cultural differences rather than a predetermined biological ordering of human beings; the concept itself is a figment of social imagination. While "ethnicity" could be used to denote cultural different groups, rather than race, it is not free of racial thinking. For the larger part of our history, ethnicity has been racialized. In fact, the term "ethnics" originated among puritans as a parallel term for "heathens" or non-Christians, particularly Native Americans and African slaves. Finally, in regards to terms, reference to "race and ethnic relations" includes relationships between all groups, whether it is relationships among people of color and whites, or among people of color from different racial and ethnic backgrounds.

We are all in this together. Our relationships do not simply represent vertical relationships of power between dominant and minority groups; they also include horizontal relationships between groups and people who find themselves located on a similar plane, whether that is a result of structural location or the temporal social and private spaces where our lives come together along gender lines, common interests, or intimate desire. Although there are rigid societal structures that impede the full inclusion of people of color and the erasure of the color lines that separate us, we must also recognize the complexity of our social relations, the spaces where possibilities and transcendent impulses exist—where relationships, strategies, and practices are developed to solidify human relationships along different and stronger ties of values, interests, and commonalities.

Nonetheless, our relationships are not always transcendent; most often our social interaction reasserts the social structures and processes that separate us. The anatomy and architecture of desire and our relationships do not exist outside the suspension systems of the histories that structure our life circumstances; the loftiest of ideals do not escape the reaches of the social structures in which our lives our located. In fact, our oblivion to our histories and social structures blinds and binds us. We must go about the business of learning about the world we live in: who we are, how we got here, and what we can do. Otherwise we face the danger conveyed in the maxim, those who don't know their history are bound to repeat it. If anything, the study of race and ethnicity has been driven by the ambition to know our history so that we will not keep repeating it.

This essay, as any introductory chapter, is ambitious in its aim. The first section, *The Importance of a Point of View*, begins with an analogy about the way we approach knowledge and consequently our actions. For many readers, the knowledge presented here is part of a course meant to fulfill some requirement. However, many of you are reading these pages because you want to learn about your fellow Americans. Many of you, hopefully, see knowledge as a necessary part of learning about and making the world—or at least our relationships, work places, and communities—a better place. This discussion is essential because so often many people come to race and ethnic studies with assumptions that prejudice their ability to consider the full weight of the experiences and knowledge presented by scholars of race and ethnicity.

The second and third sections, *The History Behind Race and Ethnic Studies* and *Liberal Arts, Eurocentrism, and Traditional Disciplines,* discusses the history in which race and ethnic studies emerged. It underscores the conditions that have informed, engendered, and driven the development of ethnic studies. There are two main components: the heart and intellect behind ethnic studies, and the harm and limitations of eurocentric academic traditions. The aim of the third section is not to tag all things of European origin bad, but to present that which has limited and distorted the study of humanity. It's not all bad, though; nor is it simple.

Sketching the contours of history belies the messiness of real life—all that which does not fall neatly within the lines and categories we devise. In these matters, it is best to make distinctions between intention and result, between the rule and the exception. The discussion of the liberal studies curriculum makes clear a tradition that values alternative forms of knowledge and the experience of diverse ethnic groups. In reality, however, invocation of those values did not manifest itself in a curriculum inclusive of the realities and perspectives of different racial and ethnic groups; nor did it prevent the opposite: the denigration, misrepresentation, and omission of people of color (except for discussions problematizing their experience and inclusion).

Yet, the failure of many to practice and institute inclusion should not take away from those efforts that produced tangible results, whether it was via additions to the curriculum, the hiring of faculty of color, or the production of scholarship. The continued existence of a rationale in higher education for inclusion is a value that has been consistently invoked by people of color and white allies as a rationale for the establishment and continued existence of race and ethnic studies departments. Also, while limited by disciplinary constraints, the scholarship produced by traditional disciplines brought these topics into the academy and served as building blocks in the study of race and ethnicity.

We must remember, however, that these efforts were the exception to the rule. Changes did not come about until different groups of people of color engaged in the struggle to establish ethnic studies departments. Also, significant changes and growth in the knowledge of race and ethnicity did not come about until the establishment of the ethnic studies departments. Yet, this did not happen without the support and contributions of others.

The next section, *Theories on Race and Ethnicity*, examines the existing theories on race and ethnicity and race and ethnic relations to familiarize readers with the different explanations and approaches. The discussion also presents limitations of theoretical approaches.

Theories are presented in order of their emergence. Like any scholarly field, these theories represent the developmental nature of knowledge. Many of theories here account for different levels of social phenomena, given that successive theories build on previous work, especially to address areas left unexamined or inadequately explained by other theories, usually real life situations or experiences unaccounted for by other theories.

Theories also reflect the assumptions of researchers and the context of the research. For example, some theories assume that all race and ethnic groups will be eventually incorporated on an equal basis into all levels of U.S. society, based on observations about the experience of European immigrants. Theories within this perspective present U.S. history as a linear, forward-moving progress towards democracy, freedom, justice, and inclusion of all peoples.

Other theories point to the continual exclusion of racialized and ethnic groups at various levels of U.S. society. The basis of these theories is the experience of North American indigenous groups and immigrants of color. Instead of a linear evolution towards progress, these theories present U.S. history as a cycle of progressive and regressive structures and policies that make democracy, justice, freedom, and inclusion of all peoples a fluctuating principle and uncertain reality in our society.

The final section, *Current Developments and Issues in Ethnic Studies*, discusses current scholarship and issues in race and ethnic studies in the hope of making evident the challenging, complex, and promising nature of race and ethnic studies.

The Importance of a Point of View

Our view of reality can shift when we see situations in a different light. In his book, *Seven Habits of Highly Effective People*, Covey presents the experience of a naval captain to illustrate how our vantage point affects the way we view and approach the world:

Two battleships assigned to the training squadron had been at sea on maneuvers in heavy weather for several days. I was serving on the lead battleship and was on watch on the bridge as night fell. The visibility was poor with patchy fog, so the captain remained on the bridge as night fell.

Shortly after dark, the lookout on the wing reported, "Light, bearing on the starboard bow."

"Is it steady or moving astern?" the captain called out.

The lookout replied, "Steady, captain," which meant we were on a dangerous collision course with that ship.

The captain then called to the signalman, "Signal that ship: We are on a collision course, advise you change course 20 degrees,"

Back came a signal, "Advisable for you to change course 20 degrees."

The captain said, "Send, I'm a captain, change course 20 degrees."

"I'm a seaman second class," came the reply. "You had better change course 20 degrees."

By that time, the captain was furious. He spat out, "Send, I'm a battleship. Change course 20 degrees."

Back came the flashing light, "I'm a lighthouse."

We changed course. (33)

Covey uses this account to illustrate how "we can see a reality that is superceded by his limited perception—a reality that is as critical for us to understand in our daily lives as it was for the captain in the fog" (33). As we embark upon our journey across the field of race and ethnic studies and encounter the varied terrain of experience covered in these essays, we hope you can encounter realities experienced by other people situated in different vantage points that supercede previous perceptions on matters of race—that you can see the experiences and situations of people of color, and your responses and relationships to them, in a new light.

The meaning and importance of race in our society—in determining or influencing our history and geography, our historical circumstances, our social and class structure, and even our individual selves—is a highly contested matter. We approach it from different vantage points and sets of ideas and experiences. Various ideas about race exist in our society: Is race a figment of our imagination, a drawn out category we need to put out of its misery? Is it a part of a divine scheme? Is race a social category with a profound impact on the development and character of our nation; or nothing else than the pigment of skin? Is it useful or valid to talk about people as part of racial and ethnic groups, about which we can make meaningful generalizations? Is race a form of confinement or a crutch? What ideas, or mental constructions, do we have about race and ethnicity, or racial and ethnic groups? Schneider asks several questions helpful in eliciting these ideas:

How was race explained to you as a child? Was it explained to you at all?

In what ways do you organize your identity and resources around race? How consciously does race affect your choice of where to live, shop, or send your children to school?

What would be the ideal percentage breakdown for you between people of your race and others in a neighborhood in which you lived? What is the actual breakdown in your neighborhood? What would be the "tipping point," the point at which the racial balance becomes uncomfortable enough to make you want to leave your neighborhood?

How do you account for the fact that the distribution of wealth among whites, blacks, and Native Americans is nearly the same now as it was in 1866, as slavery formally came to an end? (243-244).

Most people who answered these questions realized they had more ideas about race than they thought. Often, we are unaware of the way in which friends, parents, schools, news agencies, entertainment industries, and political processes have constructed our views on race and ethnicity, our willingness and ability to learn and talk about it. Regardless of where we stand, the way our society constructs meanings and responses to race—especially, in terms of the voices and experience of people from diverse racial and ethnic backgrounds—has a monumental impact on the nature and character of our society, our communities and our own personal lives.

Thomas Kuhn utilized the concept of paradigms to explain our knowledge of the world and how transformations or shifts occurred in those paradigms, especially in the fields of science and other academic areas. He defined those paradigms as worldviews, values and techniques held in common by members of a given community. In her discussion of race relations models and theories, Hune discusses the role of paradigms in academia and general society:

Paradigms in the scientific community often become simplified as models or examples that govern its practitioners more than the subject matter itself. As "exemplary past achievements," paradigms are difficult to change. Moreover, paradigms endure outside the scientific community and reflect the dominant belief system of general society. (79)

The ideas about race and ethnicity in our society emerge from paradigms incorporated and circulated in academic and political institutions:

They become habits of mind and patterns of behavior taught to subsequent generations of scholars. Racial paradigms are also embedded in ideologies, policies, and practices and are integrated into the formal structures and institutions of U.S. society as well as our everyday lives. (79)

Hune explains that although people benefiting from the operative racial paradigms have an interest in perpetuating them, new models and definitions emerge to challenge traditional ways and understandings, thereby leading to paradigm shifts and the replacement of existing models. These paradigm shifts are typically brought about in the work of newcomers and outsiders to the field who are not as vested or encumbered by existing approaches and "whose experiences offer alternative views to established ways of examining social phenomena" (79).

The following chapters present a world of differences in disciplinary approaches and perspectives of the experiences of people of color in the U.S. Shining the light on these differences often presents a challenge for people new to ethnic studies. For many, it is difficult to believe that the large part of our national history represents a clear denial of the right to life and liberty and the pursuit of property and happiness. It is disturbing to encounter a vast body of evidence of national policies, beliefs, actions, laws, speech, and attitudes that willfully excluded, and discounted the humanity of, many of our citizens on the basis of their race. The views of U.S. President John Quincy Adams, and the little good they did, serve as an instructive example:

> *Well after he left power, John Quincy Adams became an outspoken critic of slavery and policy towards the indigenous population – policies that he described as "among the heinous sins of this nation, for which I believe God will one day bring [it] to judgement." He hoped that his belated stand might somehow aid "that hapless race of native Americans, which we are exterminating with such merciless and perfidious cruelty." But the recantation by the intellectual father of Manifest Destiny and domination of the hemisphere had no effect on the extermination, which continued in full ruthlessness (Chomsky).*

It is unnerving to encounter a history that clearly reflects a willingness to use any means necessary—brutal violence in particular—to accomplish this racial order and exclusion.

Coming upon this knowledge, people wonder why they were not taught this part of our national history; why they have not learned about the life histories of many of our citizens. Many wonder about the purpose and usefulness of this knowledge. At times, convincing people of the merits of findings produced by rigorous, systematic, and countless studies is an arduous task. Many hear the critique of U.S. societal failures in race and ethnic studies as a denial of national ideals, a dismissal of the promise of western civilization's strides toward democracy. Some scholars, such as Sean Wilentz (Harvard professor of ethnic studies) argue that ethnic studies scholars depict the U.S. chiefly in terms of racial and ethnic identities and antagonisms (Marable 47).

However, it is encouraging to discover that the motivation behind these challenges for many people is a great concern about the national ideals like democracy, equality, freedom, justice, and opportunity. It is important for them to maintain the belief that these ideals mean something—that the history of our society does in fact represent progress toward achieving these ideals. Most race and ethnicity scholars would argue that the promise of these ideals has been an important part of the struggles of people of color.

In the midst of all these contested meanings, differences in vantage points and various opinions become evident. We do not propose to settle the score here. What we hope to accomplish, however, is to create a more informed discussion that goes beyond rhetoric to create an understanding based on the many facets of racial dynamics and relations in our society, of the various facts, and the distinguishing features of ethnic studies. Our strides toward this understanding are not meant as a mere intellectual exercise. The histories and perspectives presented here concern the lives of our fellow human beings, our friends, coworkers, and community—they are real in their consequences. Your response and willingness to see the lighthouses on your journey along the beachheads we occupy, the particular peninsulas of our existential circumstances, is an essential part of the collective set of possibilities and constraints surrounding matters of race, and more importantly, race and ethnic relations.

Ethnic studies is not just about singular struggles of particular ethnic groups or people of color. A key contribution of this field is its attention to a history and society of which we are all a part. Countless Americans from racial and ethnic backgrounds different from those fighting a particular battle for the right to education, voting, property, and what not have participated in these struggles. African Americans took countless actions toward making Chinese and other Asian Americans welcome in public, private, and work spaces; Mexican American women married South Asian men, giving these immigrants the ability to establish businesses and exercise property rights (Okihiro). Today, older established Asian American groups, such as Chinese and Japanese Americans, have enlisted in the struggle of newer Asian American populations such as the Vietnamese or Hmong populations to achieve access to education and civic liberties (Mazumdar; Reisberg; Monaghan).

Many white Americans put their bodies on the line, welcomed people into their homes, held onto property of Japanese Americans in internment camps, or put up the money and took on the legal battles of African, Asian, Mexican, and Native Americans. In his debut speech as a freshman in Congress, Abraham Lincoln put his political career on the line by challenging President James Polk's declaration of war on Mexico in 1846 as unjust and an attempt to expand slavery, which Lincoln opposed (Ross). Henry David Thoreau went to jail for refusing to pay taxes in protest of what he believed to be an illegal and unjust U.S. invasion and occupation of Mexico, which was justified on the basis of a belief in Manifest Destiny, a social doctrine that held that God had chosen Anglo-Americans as the custodians of democracy and the rightful heirs of the land, from 'ocean to ocean and pole to pole' (Acuna 49).

In addition to Lincoln and Thoreau, many white Americans fought and protested against slavery and the illegal war and occupation of Mexico alongside the Mexicans and African Americans who were affected by these policies and lynched for expressing opposition. In more recent history, Frank Sinatra fought to desegregate and change inequalities in the entertainment business so that black entertainers, such as Count Basie, Duke Ellington, Sammy Davis, Jr., might get the respect they deserved (Seitz). In the summer of 1960, young students, many of them white, traveled to the South to fight for the voting rights of blacks (McAdam). Five students (three blacks, two white) were murdered for their efforts. These students put their lives on the line in the struggle for the freedom and equality of all Americans.

In the 1940s, Orson Welles, Nat King Cole, Rita Hayworth, and Anthony Quinn provided significant support to the legal defense of 17 Chicanos convicted on the basis of scant evidence in the Sleepy Lagoon Trial. Events surrounding the trial had a significant impact on Chicano communities and public perception (Chavez 118–120). Perhaps most significant was the national and international publicity. During the trial, the police and trial judge made statements depicting Mexican Americans as un-American and prone to violence and crime. Police conducted mass sweeps. Over 600 Chicano youth were arrested, many never charged, and most not convicted. In this climate, servicemen, encouraged by the press and police collaboration, went into the East Los Angeles Chicano community to beat up Zoot Suiters and, eventually, any Mexican American or minority-looking person in their path. The violence and negative press ended when troops were brought in response to the Mexican government's request for the State Department to intervene. The U.S. needed the workers Mexico was sending to make up for labor shortages created by the war. Newspapers ran stories about the necessity of treating justly the citizens of our allies. "Sadly," Chavez writes, "even as the press called for an end to further violence, it refused to admit that most of the victims were U.S. citizens" (120). The involvement of these public figures, in addition to representatives of peoples from all racial and ethnic groups, in the support of this legal case and against the public disgrace of Mexican Americans, also attests to the rich history of a resistance to racial injustice among different sectors of our society and of a desire for racial integration and racial equality.

Many of the essays herein serve to demonstrate that we are all an important part of the larger societal puzzle and processes—the actors, agents, or players that produce, sustain, and change the structure, policies, processes, behavior, and attitudes that comprise our positions in society and relationships with one another. People of color cannot achieve racial equality and harmony in a vacuum. Without faith in the existence of the commitment to freedom, equality, and justice among white people at various points in U.S. history, it would be difficult to imagine, and pointless to investigate, progress in achieving racial equality. The examples provided here reflect a commitment to the ideals among several sectors of the population to racial justice and equality, including many white Americans.

The History Behind Race and Ethnic Studies

To understand the nature, approaches, and current issues of ethnic studies, it is important to examine the historical context that has informed the development of ethnic studies. Demographic changes played a key role, particulary in terms of concentrating substantial racialized ethnic populations in almost all major U.S. cities (Marable). Marable explains:

> As Northern industrial and manufacturing jobs became available to blacks before and during World War I, millions trekked out of the South in the Great Migration. In the 1940s and 1950s several million Mexicans who frequently crossed the border to obtain work began to resettle the Southwest (49).

These changes affected the cultural landscape of American popular culture, including professional sports, music and film—all of which "began to be profoundly shaped and interpreted through the prism of minority group cultures" (Marable 49).

Several developments in the sixties created an atmosphere of faith in the promise of the grassroots struggles and government strides towards democracy and racial equality. In his inaugural speech, President Kennedy inspired a nation in his charismatic call for citizens to become activist participants of democracy—embodied in the oft-quoted words from that speech, "Ask not what your country can do for you but what you can do for your country." Under the leadership of Martin Luther King, Jr., the Civil Rights movement was gaining momentum. As television sets became a common household item, millions of Americans, and people across the world, witnessed for the first time the harsh economic circumstances and political repression experienced by African Americans in the U.S. (Gitlin). This situation challenged the image of the United States as a democratic nation. Domestically, it reflected the reality of the unfulfilled democratic ideals. Internationally, it undermined the rhetoric of U.S. claims about its necessary political and military involvement in global affairs to ensure democracy; consequently, President Kennedy was compelled to give public support to the civil rights movement (Umemoto).

The publicity surrounding the efforts of African Americans in their struggle for civil rights, and the words of Dr. Martin Luther King Jr., also served as an inspiration for many citizens across the U.S. Umemoto elaborates:

> The Civil Rights Era profoundly impacted the racial ideology of the nation, particularly Third World youth. The dreams of Martin Luther King, Jr., and unsung heroes inspired actions for equality, dignity, and self-respect. The African-American movement clearly revealed the deep-rooted, institutionalized nature of racial oppression. Although protests resulted in reforms limited to the legal arena, their impact was felt in all other sectors of society. (50)

The sector in which this impact became most evident was higher education. The struggle for ethnic studies also took place in the midst of rising social movements among young people, students, women, antiwar activists and Asian American, Chicanos, Native American, and Puerto Rican communities. Marable draws the connection between the Civil Rights movement and the emergence of ethnic studies:

> The civil rights campaigns of the 1950s and the 1960s helped give shape and impetus to other new protest movements, reflecting the demands and agendas of Chicanos and Puerto Ricans, feminists, lesbians and gays, American Indians, and many other groups. These profound movements for social reform, in turn, pressured predominantly White colleges and universities to open their doors to racialized minorities for the first time. (49)

In addition to the Civil Rights movement, the struggle for ethnic studies occurred during a historical period of mass movements in Third World countries. The ideas and lessons forged in the struggles of Third World countries in Asia, Africa, and Latin America to overthrow American and European colonialism inspired and influenced these movements (Omatsu). The influence is evident in the names students attached to their struggles and demands, e.g., the

Third World Liberation Front at San Francisco, the Third World College at University of California, Berkeley, and the Third World Center at the University of Colorado, Boulder.

Of significant influence was the articulation of a need to define the history and culture of their country and people in their own terms (Okihiro). Moreover, the framework of colonization provided a provocative and fruitful form of analysis for relationships between the white majority and respective racial and ethnic groups (Barrera). In fact, the socioeconomic circumstances and political relationships affecting their respective positions and experiences in our society paralleled the historical relationship and foreign policy of the U.S. with respective nations, despite the fact that many of these people were native-born U.S. citizens (Umemoto). Consequently, the revolutionary and liberating forms of structural responses and cultural expressions resonated with many of our citizens.

This historical context—Kennedy's call to action, the Civil Rights Movement and the larger societal emergence of a counterculture among young people, women, and communities of color—created an atmosphere of faith among many Americans, students in particular, in the struggle against colonialism and the promise of democracy and racial equality in the face of oppression. Umemoto argues that these movements:

> had a profound impact on the culture and ideology of America Though these movements did not produce major changes in the economic and political structure, they strongly affected popular ideology and social relations. They also resulted in the formation of mass organizations and produced a cadre of activists who continue to pursue their ideals. (49)

The visible impact occurred in the realm of human values. Omatsu explains that these struggles redefined the values that shape how we live our daily lives, especially our interactions with each other.

In the struggle for civil rights on college campuses, a common set of demands emerged for increased accessibility of higher education to respective ethnic groups and the development of an education that was relevant to the experiences, needs, values, perspectives, and approaches of their communities. In November of 1968, students at San Francisco State University began a five-month-long struggle, known as the San Francisco College Strike, to make their university more accessible and relevant to their education. Umemoto succinctly describes the essence of the students' struggles:

> Their tenacity engaged the university, the police, and politicians in a five-month battle giving birth to the first School of Ethnic studies in the nation. Batons were swung and blood was shed in the heat of conflict. But this violence was only symptomatic of the challenge made by activists to fundamental tenets of the dominant culture as manifested in the university. African America, Asian American, Chicano, Latino, and Native American students called for ethnic studies and open admissions under the slogan of self-determination. They fought for the right to determine their own futures. They believed that they could shape the course of history and define a "new consciousness."

For Asian American students in particular, this also marked a "shedding of silence" and an affirmation of identity. (49)

The larger struggle of people of color was characterized by more than just the traditional civil rights demand for inclusion. The importance of the right to self-determination in terms dictated by different racial/ethnic groups—African Americans, Asian Americans, Chicana/os, Latina/os, and Native Americans—became a central element of these movements and a signature feature of the origin and development of ethnic studies:

The Third World movement was and continues to be a demand of colonized peoples for freedom and self-determination—for the right to control and develop their own economic, political and social institutions. (Murase, 1976, quoted in Umemoto)

Consequently, rather than resulting in a homogeneous course, the trajectory of ethnic studies reveals an incredibly heterogeneity in the disciplinary, epistemological, methodological, and institutional development of Black Studies, Asian American Studies, Chicano Studies, and Native American studies. These developments are also reflective of the particular political and historical conditions of respective racial/ethnic groups and race relations in different parts of the U.S., especially at the regional, city, and campus level. Thus, as Hune explains, shifts in our understanding of "race" and "ethnicity" occurred as the result of the entrance of new voices of outsiders "whose experiences offer alternative views to established ways of observing" racial dynamics and the experience and perspectives of people of color in the U.S. (49). However, before examining the contributions of ethnic studies scholars, it seems pivotal to explain commonalities and differences with the traditional course and scope of the university and traditional disciplines.

Liberal Arts, Eurocentrism, and Traditional Disciplines: Possibilities and Constraints

Of course, none of these endeavors, projects, or trajectories occurs outside the historical context of our political and economic structures and relationships and the larger historical trajectory of western civilization. Despite differences in our group histories and positions in American society, we also share many historical, structural, and cultural frames of references. In the midst of cultural differences and contested meanings, parallels and commonalities also exist. Outside legislative changes and political efforts renouncing racism in our society, our society has increasingly recognized the importance of the diverse make-up, and the contributions of multicultural heritage, of the American people, especially at the level of mainstream culture, via such efforts such as public service announcements and educational curriculum changes.

Nonetheless, some scholars argue that the inclusion of the perspectives and values of people of color in higher education undermines the contributions of western civilization, particularly the role of western civilization in the development of the U.S. (Bloom; D'Souza; Schlesinger). They argue that the traditional liberal arts education represents a legacy of the universal values and principles of western civilization—'the sacred and immutable underpinning of liberal education.' Aside from overlooking evidence of our country's violation of the values and principles, these authors also misrepresent the history and substance of liberal arts education:

> Far from being a transhistorical value as traditionalists would have us believe, liberal education should exemplify what universities do best, which is to study "currents and crosscurrents of change over time." Most often forgotten or ignored by the critics is the rationale that Harvard University President Charles William Eliot employed in the late 19th century to replace a fixed curriculum with a free elective system as the underpinning of a modern liberal education. Eliot wanted to ensure a flexible curriculum that could incorporate new subjects and thereby expand the existing body of knowledge to "enlarge the circle of the liberal arts." Just as he believed that within the liberal arts, different subjects should be held in equal regard, so he believed that the many cultures immigrants brought to America should be equally respected. (24)

Fundamental changes in the curriculum leading to the emergence of a liberal arts education occurred during the largest and most diverse influx of immigrants into the U.S., including southern, eastern, and western Europeans from Jewish, Catholic, and Protestant religious backgrounds (Hu-DeHart). Notably, our historical and contemporary diversity involves more than statistical growth in the racial-ethnic diversity of the American people; it must include recognition of diverse populations, cultures, experiences, and perspectives. Liberal arts play an important role towards the possibility of a more pluralistic democratic multicultural society. Hu-Dehart explains:

> Liberal education, based since its inception on an expanding curriculum that prepares students to "reflect on habits of thought and familiar frameworks in the light of new subjects, critiques and alternatives" becomes ever more crucial in the pluralistic democratic multicultural America strives to honor. Since its inception, liberal education in a democracy also has been conceived of as necessary for laying the foundations for active citizenship. That is why the predecessors of western civilization courses, considered by triumphalists to be the sacred and immutable underpinning of liberal education, bore names such as "Problems of Citizenship" when they were introduced between World Wars I and II. Even at Columbia University—one of the few institutions that retain a traditional western civilization course—the original liberal education core was entitled "Contemporary Civilization." The first syllabus contained this timely statement: We are living in a world in which there are great and perplexing issues on which keen differences of opinion have arisen; and it is important now, not less during the war, that men should understand the forces which are at work in the society of their own day. (25)

However, the mere articulation of 'the importance of the many cultures immigrants brought to America' did not result in the actual manifestation of a curriculum that fully implemented their contributions and experiences with 'equal regard.' The progress of people of color in all sectors of U.S. society has been born of hard-fought struggles initiated and orchestrated by communities of color and immigrants. Nowhere is this more evident than in the struggles to establish ethnic studies as an academic discipline.

Significantly, the curriculum changes brought about by the struggle for and development of ethnic studies have not been a simple continuation of the course and scope of western civilization studies. The beginning of ethnic studies occurred in the context of a centuries-long struggle against a eurocentric worldview that excluded or subordinated people of color in its definitions of civilization, culture, humanity, and progress, thereby functioning not only to propel and justify their enslavement, colonization, exploitation, and disappearance, but also serving to deny their rights, needs, values, perspectives, and contributions. Elements of this worldview also permeated the academy, particularly in approaches to knowledge that discounted the experiences and perspectives of people of color. These traditional disciplines were informed by ideas about the inferior or cultural deficiency among people from non-European origins, i.e., people of color.

Okihiro discusses the approaches of traditional disciplines to the study of people of color prior to the emergence of ethnic studies. Anthropology studied non-European cultures within a limited view of them as primitive, tribal, and static. Political, economic, and cultural change was assumed to begin upon European contact. In the field of history, Africa and the people of its different nations were deemed as lacking in any history because "they were bound by tradition and were thus changeless" (19). One prominent philosopher wrote, "Africa is no historical part of the world; it has no movement or development to exhibit"; while an Oxford historian described Africa's past as "only the unrewarding gyrations of barbarous tribes in picturesque but irrelevant corners of the globe" (Wilks 7 quoted in Okihiro 19).

Coincidentally, the prevailing view was that "history" in Africa did not occur until European contact and consisted only of the vast and dynamic actions, institutions, processes, and changes initiated by whites; apparently, according to these scholarly treatments, this vast continent of nations was populated solely by passive, indistinguishable, and undifferentiated people, namely blacks. We can also see the limitations of a Eurocentric liberal tradition in the study of Asians. Okihiro explains:

> Asians posed a problem for whites who saw America as a "melting pot" that fused diverse peoples into a homogeneous whole; . . . physically and culturally distinct from whites, [they] could not blend into the mainstream, and thereby comprised a problem for both the American identity and for the "unmeltables" . . .

Several Eurocentric elements are evident in the analysis presented by the approach of traditional disciplines.

First, although discrimination on the basis of skin color was a real fact encountered by Asian immigrants and natives to the U.S., it is an artifact of a nation and civilization in which skin color had become racialized. That is, skin color came to be known as a marker of differ-ent races among human beings. This classification was not simply an indicator of difference among peoples from different cultures, nations, or regions of the world. Europeans increasing-ly ordered these physical differences within a racial classification scheme constructed by its "scholars" and "scientists" in a manner representative of a hierarchical natural and social order. Thus, the supposed problem presented by the physical and cultural distinctiveness of Asians was, in fact, a problem created by a eurocentric view of differences in skin color (not white) and cultures (not European) as aberrant and deviant. A signature feature of many of these studies is the tendency to blame Asians—and other racial and ethnic groups—for the prob-lems, discrimination, prejudice and oppression they experienced as a result of the actions of white Americans:

> [U]nlike Europeans, went the argument, Asians came with a sojourner mentality, per-sisted in keeping their culture, and, accordingly must shoulder some of the blame for anti-Asian sentiment . . . [Asians] remaining uninvolved in the life around them, were easily exploited and became targets for anti-Asian sentiment. It was only after humanitar-ian and American ideals converted them from sojourners to immigrants did [they] enjoy and participate in the promises of democracy. (Okihiro 19)

One wonders how these results can emerge from a tradition of scholarship that claimed to be objective and scientific.

Second, these studies fail to reflect any sense of agency among Asian Americans and immi-grants or their right to cultural maintenance or their own traditions—especially in a nation in which both groups arrived as immigrants during the same historical period. There is only one culture assumed to be valid, representative, and correct. Only conversion and conformity to American culture and ideals would make democratic promise of the right to pursue life, liber-ty, happiness, and property possible—a democratic right which apparently precluded the right of Asian Americans and immigrants to make independent and valid existential and cultural choices that differed from the presumably dominant culture. According to these historical accounts, their culture choices necessitated the humanitarian intervention and rescue of American ideals, which coincidentally happened to represent the ideals, aesthetics, values, and principles of western civilization.

Third, these studies reflect a Eurocentric preference for glorifying and emphasizing success-es of western civilization and the U.S., while minimizing failures and blemishes (Hu-DeHart). Inherent in this preference is the presupposition that the existential and historical circum-stances, choices, and possibilities available to people of European origins are representative of the experiences and evolution of all peoples, and thereby universally beneficial and supremely preferable for all. Notably, this scholarship has often overlooked or minimized the role and harm caused by institutions, laws, ideologies, and citizens of American society and western civ-ilization. Until the early 1950s, Asian immigrants were prevented from becoming citizens. In the case of Chinese, U.S. immigration laws for the most part only allowed men to immigrate. With few Chinese women in the U.S., and laws prohibiting intermarriage between Chinese men and white women, those who decided to stay were deprived of the ability to start and maintain any sense of family life. Female companionship was mostly limited to prostitutes. Asians were also subjected to mob violence and extreme animosity. Laws also prevented them from owning property.

Given these circumstances, the ideas present in these studies—that their lot had something to do with a sojourner mentality, the refusal to give up their culture, or an unwillingness to become involved in American life—either represent a neglect, obliteration, or distortion of historical fact and circumstance. There was little incentive and few opportunities for Asian immigrants to become a part of American life. In fact, there were severe limitations and impediments. Thus, everything considered progressive and liberating about American society and western civilization was unavailable for these people. A brief examination of this period reflects a much different reality, one in which Asian American and immigrants faced "enormous individual prejudice, frequent mob violence, and extreme forms of institutional discrimination" (Fong 13). The range of opportunities and choices—and the democratic and humanitarian benefits—available to European immigrants were unavailable to Asian immigrants.

Fourth, what perhaps makes the eurocentrism of the traditional disciplines so manifestly evident—prior to the emergence of ethnic studies, the countercultural revolution of the 1960s, and the rebellion of third world nations—particularly in the examples above, is all that is imperceptible and invisible from the products of their scholarly work about history and contributions of people of color. It is not as if the expansive history and contributions of both Africa and Asia were unknown. In fact, they are known historical realities. Africans, namely Egyptians, brought mathematics, science, agriculture, and science to the world (Okihiro). Moreover, the development of western civilization is indebted to all that Chinese civilization has contributed to the world: mechanical clocks, modern agriculture, modern shipping, modern oil industry, modern astronomical observatories, modern music, decimal mathematics, paper money, umbrellas, fishing reels, wheelbarrows, multistage rockets, guns, gun powder, underwater mines, parachutes, hot-air balloons, manned flight, brandy, whisky, chess, the design of the steam engine, nautical and navigational improvements such as ship rudders, the compass, and multiple masts—which made travel to the Americas and European colonialism possible—the stirrup, paper, moveable type, the printing press, the first law of motion (Temple).

The omissions of the contributions of non-European cultures to human civilization have been the product of a conscious effort to promote European civilization at the expense of other people, cultures, nations, and civilizations:

African and Asian civilizations contributed much to the dawning of European civilization in the Greek city-states . . . [They] brought not only devastation but also religion, culture and science. That intimacy would later be denied by the Europeans, who, after crusades to expel the "infidels" from Christendom and after the rise of nationalism and mercantile capitalism, conceived of an ideology that justified their expansion and appropriation of land, labor, and resources in Africa, Asia, and the Americas. That ideology, in the name of religion and science, posited the purity and superiority of European peoples and cultures, unsullied by the anti-Christian, uncivilized non-Europeans—the

Other—and found expression in European colonization of the Third World. (Okihiro 65)

The impact of Eurocentrism in academia served to discount the value, legitimacy, and contributions of people of color. This aim has not been one simply of omission or neglect; nor has it been the result of some historical trajectory that resulted in an inadvertent, unintentional, misguided view of different peoples and cultures. A large part has been the result of a conscious belief in the superiority of Western Civilization and its European progenitors and heirs as evidenced in the doctrine of Manifest Destiny in the U.S.

Theories on Race and Ethnicity

This section is an overview of the way people have thought about race and ethnicity, sufficient to develop a basic understanding of relevant concepts, theories, and approaches. The study of race and ethnicity, and race relations, can be easily understood by examining the different classifications of human beings developed over the last four centuries. It is also helpful to examine the different levels of social life concerning race and ethnic relations in the United States. To begin, let us distinguish between race and ethnicity. It is important to note in making this distinction that race is a socially defined concept; no scientific evidence exists to establish the existence of different races.

The idea of race as a distinctive category of human beings with physical characteristics transmitted by descent did not emerge until European expansion in the sixteenth century; prior to that, race was used to describe descendants from a common ancestor (Feagin and Feagin). Subsequently, Europeans grouped according to physical characteristics thought to be hereditary and biologically distinct. The association of certain personality and social traits with different races has been used to rationalize subordination and inequality on the basis of presumptions about the superiority and inferiority of certain "races" and cultures. "Races" were believed to be a part of a natural, hierarchical order. Ethnicity, on the other hand, is a concept used to group people according to cultural and national-origin characteristics.

The distinction between race and ethnicity is complicated by the tendency of people at all societal levels use the terms loosely. Some, hoping to overcome notions of different races of human beings, refer to African Americans or Mexican Americans as ethnic groups. The difference is also made complex by the fact that some groups, Chinese Americans, for example, have been considered both a "race," Asian—presumably, a distinctive biological group with inherent traits—and an ethnic group, Chinese—a group with distinctive cultural characteristics associated with national origins. Moreover, many groups—Mexican Americans for example—can be described as racialized ethnic groups, that is, a group whose ethnicity is defined in relation to ideas about their racial status and characteristics.

Terms and concepts have important implications for the study of race and ethnicity and race and ethnic relations. For example, understanding race as a socially defined or socially constructed concept allows us to see that the history of ideas about "race" and race relations and characteristics associated with race are not fixed; in fact, they have not always been pejorative or injurious. This comprehension presents possibilities and hope. These terms and concepts also affect what we can uncover or silence in our study of race and ethnic relations. Some scholars refuse to acknowledge the existence of a race to such a degree that they refuse to even consider it as a category of a study or classification. Consequently, they argue there is no essential difference between European immigrants and Asian or Mexican immigrants. The only differences that exist are cultural or national in origin. With time, they argue, all groups will adapt and integrate into American life. This denies the reality of the way these groups have been racialized, that is, seen and treated as belonging to distinctive races with inborn characteristics. It prevents us from examining the way in which states and institutions make policies and decisions on the basis of race, or ideas about racialized groups, that adversely affect the lives and livelihood of millions of Americans of color, particularly in terms of getting a chance for decent work, housing, education, and the ability to pursue life, liberty, and happiness in a just and democratic fashion.

Treating race as a socially constructed category thus allows us to see the workings of race in the history of our society and the lives of human beings without giving credence to its existence as a biological marker of an inherent and hierarchical fact of human life. It allows us to uncover the definitive historical and cultural circumstances that have shaped our social position and identity, our cultural thought and frameworks, without attributing to the social structure and individual person a definitive, permanent, and immutable racial order in which compassionate, creative, transforming, or transcendent relationships among people and communities would be impossible.

In reading the essays herein, it is useful to have a basic sense of the theories on race and ethnicity and race and ethnic relations. These theories examine the origin, emergence, continuation, and changes in racial-ethnic diversity and stratification. Theories focus on individual attitudes and behavior (symbolic interaction theories), group interaction (assimilation and adaptation theories), and the larger societal structures (conflict theories, racial formation theory).

Symbolic interaction theories examine individual-level phenomena, mainly interpersonal relations. These theories explain different social phenomena concerning race, such as racism or racial inequality, by reference to the individual interaction. Race and ethnic relations are explained by reference to the meanings individuals give to their social interactions—particularly their interpretation of social situations and behavioral negotiation—with individuals from different racial and ethnic groups, or in matters involving issues of race, ethnicity and immigration.

For example, racial inequality in housing, education, and employment are explained as a result of the prejudices that affect people's choices in their interactions with people of color. Yet, this decision is not solely affected by individual choice, but other factors, also. In the case of housing, a certain individual may wish not to act on racially prejudiced views but still does so because choosing otherwise—e.g., allowing someone who is black to move into an all-white neighborhood—may affect the property value of the homes, the size of the client base, or one's employment position in a company. According to this school of thought, it is in this reassertion or renegotiation of meaning in our interactions—instead of any existing structure or regularity created by society—that the societal patterns and structures that affect racial and ethnic stratification are recreated and created anew. In its most radical form, this theory suggests that there is no objective reality, only the subjective interpretations of reality that emerge from our social interactions. It seems implausible to believe that property values, client bases, and employment positions are solely our interpretation of social interactions and not a part of a larger social reality.

Despite limitations present in their discussion of larger social structure(s), symbolic interaction theories are helpful in understanding how race and ethnicity affect our perspectives. For example, the discussion of racial socialization in symbolic interaction theories sheds some light on how people can see and experience race relations differently. Fong and Shimigawa explain:

> One interactionalist approach focuses on how racial socialization contributes to feelings of solidarity with one's own racial-ethnic group. Racial socialization is a process of social interaction relative to one's personal and group identity, intergroup and individual relationships, and position in the social stratification system. In other words, a person of the dominant majority group may see race relations as smooth, while a person of a minority group may see nothing but problems. (3)

While we may see fundamental differences in our social lives, there are also points of commonality that result in more harmonious race and ethnic relations at the interpersonal level. Symbolic interaction theories are helpful in explaining the different possibilities in the meaning and form of relationships between people from different racial-ethnic groups.

Nonetheless, symbolic interaction theories have been criticized for failing to discuss the impact and influence of culture and social structure on social interactions. Individual decisions to discriminate may be affected by larger social factors, as evident in the example above: it is not just a matter of perception or interpretations, but also the systemic practices and social structures that are a part of the society in which we live. Theories at the level of social groups (assimilation and adaptation) and social structure (conflict and racial formation) address this level of race and ethnic relations. Although theories may differ, they are helpful in explaining the developments in different areas of social life. They both tell the story of what happens when people from different nations and cultures come together, particularly in terms of the distribution of resources, from attempts to coexist peacefully, to attempts at genocide, to attempts to redress social inequalities.

The difference in these theoretical approaches lies in divergent analyses of the nature of racial and ethnic diversity and stratification. Assimilation and adaptation theories point to eventual incorporation of race and ethnic groups into all levels of U.S. society based on observations about the experience of European immigrants. Race and ethnicity are seen more as temporary statuses on the road to achieving American ideals. U.S. history is presented as a linear, forward-moving progress towards democracy, freedom, justice, and inclusion of all peoples.

The definitive analytical framework for assimilation theories is represented by Robert E. Park's concept of the race relations cycle, which all immigrant groups are believed to "progress" through (Park). This cycle consists of four stages: contact, competition, accommodation, and assimilation. Feagin and Feagin present a succinct overview of these stages:

> In the contact stage migration and exploration bring peoples together, which in turn leads to economic competition and thus to new social organization. Competition and conflict flow from the contacts between host people and the migrating groups. Accomodation, a critical condition in the race relations cycle, often takes place rapidly. It involves a migrating group's forced adjustment to a new social situation . . . Most scholars working in this tradition have argued that there is a long-term trend toward assimilation of subordinated racial groups in modern societies. "Assimilation is a process of interpenetration and fusion in which persons and groups acquire the memories, sentiments, and attitudes of other persons or groups, and, by sharing their experience and history, are incorporated with them in a common cultural life." (36–37)

Essentially, the successful incorporation of people of color, according to this theory, is associated with assimilation to Anglo-Protestant culture. Assimilation can be represented by the equation, $A + B + C = A$, where "A" represents Anglo-Protestant culture, and "B" and "C" equal other cultures.

There are several problematic assumptions in assimilation theories. Assimilation and adaptation theories proceed from the assumption of voluntary migration or contact. The colonization of North America and the institution of slavery and forced labor made contact involuntary for Native Americans, Native Mexicans, Africans, and many Asian and some European immigrants. There is also an assumption about the desirability of assimilation. For example, the opportunity of assimilation was not present for black slaves. It is implausible to imagine that a black person could break from the shackles of slavery by merely assimilating to the Anglo-Protestant culture of the slaveholders.

These theories assume that people of color have not assimilated or do not want to assimilate. There is also an assumption that U.S. society has always been ready and willing to include all immigrants and people of color. This assumption conveys what Feagin and Feagin (2002) describe as an establishment bias that does not distinguish between the ideals conveyed by our society and the actual conditions and practices of our society, between what should have happened and what has happened. The existence of racism and racial inequality has often been explained by these theorists as a result of the failure of immigrant groups or U.S. citizens of color to assimilate to the structure and culture of the dominant group. In fact, the origin of the term occurred during a particularly fervent anti-Asian period in U.S. society discussed earlier, in which Asians were criticized and physically attacked for not being like the "good groups" who assimilated to Anglo-Protestant culture (Feagin and Feagin). In essence, people are blamed for the violent and exclusive actions of others.

Adaptation theories look beyond the obstacles to, and desirability of, assimilation. They present two other alternatives, the melting pot and cultural pluralism. In attempting to describe the rich diversity brought by the constant tide of immigrants in New York City, Frenchman J. Hector de Crevecoeur originated the concept of the melting pot theory, the idea that the formation and character of the United States is best described as a combination of all cultures (Parillo). That is, all cultures are mixed to form a new culture.

The melting pot theory can be presented by the equation, $A + B + C = D$, where D represents the common culture emerging from a blending of different cultures. Although racial and ethnic groups have definitely made a contribution to the formation of U.S. society—e.g., the extensive borrowing of our federal government and constitution from the Iriquois form of governing; the ranching and mining expertise of Mexicans, and local forms of government (mayors, councils, counties); the tradition of music and the spiritual sense of struggle and redemption that emerged from African American culture—our society's social and economic structure and culture does not represent a respect for, inclusion of, or clear articulation of the importance of people of color (their work and ideas) to the formation and development of the U.S.

Looking beyond the melting pot, another possible pattern of inclusion is articulated in the idea of cultural pluralism, the idea of the coexistence of different racial-ethnic groups and cultures. Here the representative equation is $A + B + C = A + B + C$. The idea of cultural pluralism was articulated as early as the 1900s by Horace Kallen who argued that cultural diversity can exist within the context of a unified nation (Craig). Kallen argued that people have a right to exist on their own terms and a democratic right to maintain their ethnic heritage (Feagin and Feagin). The current manifestation of cultural pluralism is multiculturalism, especially in curriculum and programming. Within this school of thought, social structures, policies, and relationships reflect the existence of different cultures and cultural perspectives and approaches. People can exist on their own terms in their interactions with each other.

Competition theory, on the other hand, argues racial stratification and inequality emerge from a competition between different racial-ethnic groups over economic and political resources such as jobs, houses, political office, funding sources, college acceptance, tax dollars, and other forms of economic and political power (Fong; Feagin and Feagin). Conflict, protest, and social movements are seen as emerging as a result of these conflicts. Policies benefiting one group lead to political mobilization by other excluded groups, in this case, people from different racial and ethnic groups. In most cases, racial stratification and inequality is seen as emerging from the competition that results when groups migrate and come into contact with other groups.

The limitation of competition and multicultural—and all assimilation and adaptation—theories lies in the omission of a discussion of the national historical context of race and ethnic groups and relations, particularly the power imbalances and racial inequalities present throughout the history of the U.S. People do not compete on equal terms; there is differential access to economic and political resources. Moreover, the cultures of people of color are not given equivalent weight in the decision making, inclusion, and respect in our social structures, policies, curricula, and programming.

The theories that examine the historical, political, and economic context of race and ethnic relations are conflict theories and racial formation theories. These theories point to historical exclusion of racial and ethnic groups at various levels of U.S. society; their basis is the experience of non-European immigrants and the indigenous groups of North America. Like competition theory, conflict theories begin with the assumption that people compete over limited resources in social structures. However, conflict theories argue that the racial stratification has more to do with the inequality created by capitalism, economic subordination, and institutional discrimination. Here, groups do not merely compete with each other. Instead, one group exploits others. The story of racial inequality begins with European enslavement and genocide of people from Africa and the Americas. Racism, an ideological framework privileging one group at the expense of another, develops afterwards to rationalize the treatment of other human beings in this manner. In other words, race and racism are simply part of a larger ideology that seeks to subjugate and divide workers for the benefit of the capitalist classes.

Rex examines the role of class analysis in the study of race relations. He argues that race relations arise from imperial and colonial systems that have left a long-lasting impact on the stratification of colonial and metropolitan (advanced capitalist) societies:

> The imperialist system . . . has generated . . . numerous class and ethnic groups which, whatever their sources of conflicts are, which arise from sheer cultural difference, find their dynamic in the fact that the groups concerned have differing degrees of power in a complex economic and political order. (73–74)

Lest it sound as if he is giving emphasis solely to the means of production, Rex does give central emphasis to ethnic or cultural factors:

> [W]hile the economy and polity provide the dynamic for inter-group relations, actual bonding of the groups internally depends upon cultural factors. The multi-faceted class struggle is also an ethnic struggle. (74)

Here, Rex is not referring to mere differences arising from variant cultural perspectives but rather the differential allocation and control of the means and relations of production on the basis of race or ethnicity.

It is clear that Rex is referring to an expanded use of the term 'class' to include access to and control of political and legal resources. Such a conceptualization of class entails an analysis that looks at the historical circumstances that have placed a group in their position relative to the means and relations of production. Nonetheless, Rex does not depart from the Marxist view of that which constitutes the central element of class formation: relationship to the means of production. The relevancy of his argument is his clarification of the fact that class positions are often assigned along race or ethnic lines:

> I would suggest that groups or individuals have been placed in different relationships of access to and control of the political apparatus and are united or divided by interests which they are forced by their situations to pursue . . . The resultant groupings are bonded by ethnicity . . . This does not mean . . . that ethnicity and cultural differences are the sole or main basis of the dynamics of their interaction. (77)

Obviously, Rex also gives the politics an important role in the formation of class. This emerges from a reference to a Weberian sense of class dynamics. Whereas Marxists give centrality to the means of production in explaining the basis of class formation, Weberians add to the basis of class formation one's relative position to the control of political and legal power. Rex, however, gives primacy to a group's relationship to the means of production:

> *Once political status determines a position in the production system, it is the production system which generates patterns of conflict of interest and gives rise to collective actions. Black workers in South Africa . . . are assigned to production as a result of the political system, but having been so assigned operate as a class. (79)*

Thus, if we are to understand the status of people of color in the scheme of race relations, we must examine their position in capitalist modes and relationships of production.

Some theorists have argued that the situation of people of color in the United States can be explained best by a theory and condition of internal colonialism (Blauner; Barrera). Here, racial and class stratification are a part of related systems of oppression (Feagin and Feagin). People of color have been subjugated and displaced by the U.S. through forced entry or annexation, unfree labor, and physical and cultural destruction. Native Americans were killed and removed from their lands. Slaves were brought from Africa to serve as a cheap source of labor. Asian and Pacific peoples were exploited as slaves, indentured servants, and contract workers. Referring to Blauner's work, Feagin and Feagin explain:

> *Agriculture in the South often depended on black labor; in the Southwest, Mexican agricultural development was forcibly taken over by European settlers, and later agricultural development was based substantially on cheap Mexican labor coming into what once was northern Mexico. In exploiting the labor of non-European peoples, who were made slaves or were paid very low wages, white agricultural and industrial capitalists reaped enormous profits. From the internal colonialism perspective, contemporary racial and ethnic inequality is grounded in the economic interests of whites in low-wage labor— the underpinning of capitalistic economic exploitation. (46)*

In short, people of color have been subordinated because of the desires of European settlers in the United States for labor, land, wealth, and political power.

However, the limitation presented by a class analysis is the fact that workers do not share the same interests, even when both are part of a laboring class that must sell their wages to earn a living. The split-labor market theory argues that there are really two sectors of employment, primary and secondary. The primary labor market, which is predominantly white, has better wages, working conditions, and benefits, while the secondary labor market, in which most people of color work, is characterized by low wages, poor working conditions, and a pervasive lack of benefits (Fong).

Racial stratification and conflict are said to emerge from the different allocation of people of color in these different labor markets: Owners and primary labor market workers—mostly white—discriminate against people of color and relegate them to the secondary labor market in their efforts to protect their positions and privileges (Feagin and Feagin). The resulting division amongst black and white workers impedes unionization and mobilization around important worker interests and issues. White workers' unions have restricted the access and advancement of African Americans by not allowing them to become members of local chapters. Although white workers benefit from restrictions against blacks in that there is less competition for jobs categorized in such a way that they privilege whites, the existence of another pool of labor that can be trained and paid lower wages places them at a disadvantage. For example, most recently the Dominican Republic has made programmers available at much lower wages. A lack of interest in the plight of, and solidarity with, workers in Third World countries, makes professionals in a previously high-paying sector of the labor market vulnerable to the flight of capitalists across the world in search of lower wages.

However, even though this theory accounts for divisions within the working classes, it does not account for the fact that some people of color have achieved a modicum of economic status, security, and means. That is, they address the reality that not all people of color are located in the working class. Although the opportunity structure may be limited by racial stratification, people of color have achieved economic means and security as owners of small businesses such as car lots, restaurants, and grocery stores.

Two theories examine entrepreneurship among people of color, middleman minority theory and enclave theory. Both theories begin from the observation that people of color are excluded from mainstream business and the surrounding community as a result of racial discrimination. Their entry into the primary labor market may also be impeded by language fluency, lack of experience, and recognized credentials (e.g., academic credentials from another country). Consequently, in order to rise above the low-level positions and wages of lower economic classes, these groups open small businesses, usually in retail or service industries. Examples of these businesses would include mom and pop stores, dollar stores, restaurants, gardeners, painters, and labor contractors.

The middleman theory addresses racial and ethnic groups who occupy the position between those who own the means of production and those who must sell their labor for wages, between producers and consumers, between those who have power and resources and those who do not have much of either, between owner and renter, between employer and employee (Feagin and Feagin; Bonacich and Modell). In class theory, these people are referred to as the *petite bourgeoisie,* or merchants who own their own business (Fong and Shinigawa 5). These groups act as a go-between in the movement of goods and services as small-scale traders, merchants, labor contractors, landlords, brokers, and other areas of self-employment and business ownership. They provide services and merchandise that people in low-income areas do not typically have easy access to. Often, these neighborhoods lack large supermarkets such as Safeway or Albertsons. Classic examples include Chinese-American-owned stores in Mississippi catering to black customers and Korean-American-owned stores in black neighborhoods. This theory is helpful in explaining interaction and antagonism between (and sometimes within) racial and ethnic groups.

Ethnic enclave theory addresses the existence of successful ethnic economic enterprises and entrepreneurs within racial and ethnic communities (Fong and Shinigawa). This theory focuses on autonomous social and economic enterprises in ethnic communities that operate apart from, and in competition with, the mainstream economy and surrounding society (Fong and Shinigawa 6). The focus here is on the social spaces, especially in terms of the labor market, in which racial and ethnic groups can create their own avenues of success. Entrepreneurs in these communities create their own labor markets in which they achieve the levels of economic benefit and advancement unavailable, inaccessible, or too costly for them in the labor market of the larger society (Feagin and Feagin). However, these economic entities are also segmented. While some achieve the benefits offered in the primary labor market, such as higher wages, employee benefits, and career advancement, for lower-level employees the work is harder, the hours longer, and the pay lower. The ability to pay lower wages is due to the fact that these workers are excluded from the primary labor market due to language fluency or immigration status (Fong and Shinigawa). However, some argue that the low pay is a temporary part of an apprenticeship that will make the same entrepreneurial opportunities available to these workers (Fong and Shinigawa). In addition to helping explain the social spaces and mechanism whereby racial and ethnic groups can maintain strong cultural ties rather than assimilating, ethnic enclave theory also provides insight into the exploitation that occurs within racial and ethnic groups.

While middleman minority and enclave theories are helpful in explaining some features and dynamics of racial and ethnic relations, stratification, and inequality, there are some shortcomings. Feagin and Feagin argue that Korean and Chinese Americans have not in fact occupied a middle position between poor and richer racial and ethnic groups. Nor do these theories explain how middleman groups like Jewish Americans have become a dominant part of the mainstream economy. In addition, several researchers point to the continued existence of exploitative wages and the lack of long-term opportunities (Fong and Shinigawa). Also, this theory fails to account for the fact that men benefit more than women from ethnic enclaves; specifically, women face greater exploitation.

Where most theories above fail to account for the gender dynamics that serve to further stratify the economy, politics, and property ownership, the theory of gendered racism addresses the simultaneous and added exploitation and inequality experienced by women. The level of exploitation, exclusion, and prejudice addressed by this theory is not simply a combined consequence of being a woman and a person of color. Instead, it is an exponential effect brought about by being a woman of color. That is, it is a specific consequence of ideas doubly weighted by both racist and sexist conceptualizations of women of color. The limitations, the exclusion, and the harm experienced by these women came at the hands of whites, men, and men of color. In the case of poor women of color, and immigrant women of color, classist and nationalist prejudices also came to play, what feminists have adroitly termed, described and theorized—what some have called *theory in the flesh*—as the triple (quadruple if we include immigration status) or multiple jeopardy of oppressive systems (Moraga and Anzaldua; Davis; King).

This gendered racism manifests itself in specific ideas attached to particular human bodies according to race and gender. For example, black women were weighted with stereotypes of an oppressive matriarchy that cripples men; or an inherent laziness that made them prone to want to live off welfare. American companies, in countries like Mexico, prefer to hire women because they are seen as passive and pliant and thereby more easily exploitable (Davidson). The line of thinking is that men would strike against such conditions. Some managers argue that women are hired because they have more nimble fingers and are "better suited" for certain types of exacting labor. But often problems encountered with these women are dealt with by discussions with their fathers. Moreover, the globalization of low-paying factories across the world has brought an unprecedented growth of female employment in rates that surpass those of men, many of whom face equally unprecedented rates of unemployment (Pena). Andersen and Collins describe this gendered racism as part of a matrix of domination:

> In this matrix of domination, interlocking levels of domination stem from the societal configuration of race, class, and gender relations. This structural pattern affects individual consciousness, group interaction, and group access to institutional power and privileges. (xi)

In essence, the experience of women of color took a whole other dimension that could not be understood without examining the way in which gender and racial status came together to inform and limit their social position, experiences, and outcomes.

These theories examine the importance of race in several areas of our social lives. The trajectory of the development of theories on race and ethnicity demonstrate that many of these theories overlook or underemphasize certain aspects or realities of the phenomena they examine. As with any field of knowledge, new discoveries emerge from areas previously unexamined or new theoretical developments. Racial formation theory has opened up widespread examination of the relationship between societal ideas about race, government policy, and research approaches. In fact, there is an uncanny parallel between popular ideas about race and supposedly objective academic theories about race. The concept of gendered racism points to the complexity of race relations, especially in terms of its connection to the larger nexus of social relations in which several dynamics operate simultaneously. Middleman minority and ethnic enclave theories have pointed out racial dynamics that exist between and within racial and ethnic groups. The contributions of scholars working in these theoretical traditions inform many of the current developments in race and ethnic studies.

Current Developments and Issues in Ethnic Studies: Contributions and Challenges

In discussing the dynamics and factors leading to shifts in our paradigms regarding "race" and ethnic dynamics and relations, Hune concludes that it is no surprise that "Ethnic Studies as a new field would begin to transform existing modes of thought and contribute to recent shifts in theoretical orientation" (79). Her basis for arguing this point lies within the context of Thomas Kuhn's discussion of paradigms, particularly his belief that "as exemplary achievements," paradigms are difficult to change (Hune). My discussion of the contributions of ethnic studies will begin by examining the contributions and limitations of a traditional discipline, sociology, in the hopes of highlighting the different and more developed approach towards racial dynamics and relations in U.S. society.

Traditional approaches in academia have also circumscribed the possibilities present in our responses and remedies. This is evident if we examine a prevalent theory on racism in the field of sociology that holds that racism is a result of prejudice and discrimination. Despite limitations, this theory provided great insights into the workings of racism at the interpersonal level, thereby explaining and accounting for views and actions that led to racist views and behavior. However, there are key limitations to this approach towards understanding racism. First, this approach is based on a view of America as a melting pot in which individual people of color can succeed on an individual basis once they are provided with an opportunity: the focus is one of individual acceptance and acceptability (Vander Zanden). This approach to racism coincides with "American values sanctifying the importance of individual democracy, equality, tolerance and ameliorative views on social reform" (Lowy 7). Lowy summarizes the net effect of this approach on the discourse on race:

> The modern ideology favors locating racism at the level of autonomous individual so as to minimize the degree to which racist discourse and practice must be viewed as even more fully embedded in the rational and discursive practice of various social institutions in an ever-changing historical political context . . . The underlying assumption is that if prejudice can be eliminated at the individual level then individuals will be able to gain entrance into any sector in society. (6)

The error in assumption here is that prejudice results from a personal or character disorder that needs to be eliminated by psychological help and more contact with people of color. Vander Zanden explains:

> . . . the picture that has emerged is that of prejudice as some sort of little demon which comes to characterize people because they are depraved and suffering from some psychological "hang up" . . . or a sick personality structure. (38)

There is a focus in this approach on attitudes as opposed to actions.

Moroever, the approach used in this research consisted of surveys of attitudes. The use of the survey method, while maybe methodologically sophisticated and unarguably empirical, does not suffice for a theory that provides an explanation for the sources and workings of racism (Vander Zanden; Baca-Zinn). It is not very insightful or useful in studying the manner in which people of color are systematically oppressed, exploited, and excluded by institutions that are controlled by whites, a process known as institutional racism:

> . . . decisions are made, agendas structured, issues defined, beliefs, values, and attitudes promulgated and enshrined, commitments entered into, and/or resources allocated, in such a way that non-whites are systematically deprived or exploited. It should be emphasized that . . . intentions of the actors, or the formal statements of the relevant

norms, laws and values are irrelevant to the question of whether an institution is acting in a structurally racist manner. What counts is whether its actions in fact distribute burdens and rewards in a racially biased fashion or defend or support other actors who are making biased distributions (Vander Zanden 39).

The focus on prejudice limits the discourse on race because it detracts attention from the fact that prejudice is not a result of mentally deranged personalities but rather the result of being socialized in a society whose very structure is racist:

> *Institutions structure, shape, and restrict the experiences that people will have. Prejudices, accordingly, are acquired from concrete social experiences in a racist social order . . . And it follows that discrimination is not primarily an expression of prejudice but rather a byproduct of purposive striving to attain or hold social, economic, and political disadvantage and privileges. We need, then, to recognize that minority-dominant relations are group relations; a study of prejudice does not suffice (Vander Zanden 39).*

Racism conceptualized as a result of prejudice and discrimination does not provide a sophisticated theoretical framework that accounts for the centrality of race in the discourse, processes, and structures perpetuating racism. Thus, this research approach presents limitations on discourse and research guided by praxis:

> *A consequence of defining racism in terms of prejudice was that [it] . . . could be further used . . . to invalidate racial thinking, promote a non-racial agenda, and at the same time uphold both an assimilationist social philosophy while delegitimizing any prior racist practices through which present racial privilege would have been historically created.*
> *. . . [It] served to retard the ongoing use of popular racial thinking to justify social prejudice and institutional discrimination but without meaningfully impacting the decades and centuries of accrued inequality and social accumulation that had already been produced because of the racist discourse and practice that upheld previous social formations in which non-Europeans were victimized and treated as less than equal and not fully human (Lowy 7)*

This critique demonstrates the effect of the traditional sociological approach to the discourse of race: it undermines a discussion of the impact of racial dynamics at the structural and social levels on one's identity, social relationships, political rights, geographic and economic location. Lest we think much has changed, in a more recent analysis of the sociological study of race and ethnicity, Espiritu concludes:

> *Paradoxically, even as sociologists wrestled with issues of power, conflict and inequality, they have largely neglected or subordinated race and thus have missed the manner in which race has been "a fundamental axis of social organization in the U.S. . . . . By treat-*

ing race as a property of individuals instead of a principle of social organization, sociologists saw "difference" but failed to "see differently." (512)

Thus, we can see the way in which the approach of a traditional discipline presents theoretical limitations to research attempting to locate and explain the systemic, social, and symbolic sources and operations that sustain and perpetuate racism.

Several developments and trajectories in ethnic studies provide a much more complex and developed approach to ethnic studies. The theory of racial formation examines the totality of social relations in the explanation of racial stratification and inequality. Race is not seen as being a limited aspect of American life, but rather a central feature of U.S. society. Omi and Winant explain:

> *Although no one factor, no single causative principle, can adequately account for the contemporary crisis, there is an aspect of recent U.S. history whose political importance is overlooked. We refer, of course, to the racial dimension of American life. In contrast to much existing political and racial theory, the present work has emphasized the centrality of race in American society. We have sought to explain the process by which race has shaped, and been shaped by, U.S. politics. (138)*

> *We have approached race as a phenomenon whose meaning is contested throughout social life. Race is a constituent of the individual psyche and of relationships among individuals; it is also an irreducible component of collective identities and social structures. In American history, racial dynamics have been a traditional source both of conflict and division and of renewal and cultural awareness. Race has been a key determinant of mass movements, state policy, and even foreign policy. Racial meaning systems are contested and racial ideologies mobilized in political relationships. (138)*

> *From the 1960s to the 1980s, racial politics profoundly transformed personal identity, collective action, the state, and American society as a whole. (144)*

Here, race is seen as a persistent yet dynamic social marker, reflected in the structural, social, cultural, and individual impediments to full inclusion of people of color in race and ethnic relations. Race is not seen as a fixed category or static concept. Race relations are a dynamic process constantly in flux in social struggles over the meaning and workings of racial dynamics, and the concomitant inequality, and the necessity of policies to address race matters. Thus, an important contribution of this theory is its focus on the way in which the state, and the government, have played a key role in racial policies and developments. However, people of color also have a sense of agency, a voice, in the racial structures, policies, and meanings that affect their lives, which according to the theory are both a source of "conflict and division and of renewal and cultural awareness" (138).

Also, instead of a linear evolution towards progress, U.S. history is seen as representing a cycle of progressive and regressive structures and policies—sometimes leaps and bounds (Civil

Rights movement), sometimes one step forward, two steps back (ballot issues to eradicate affirmative action policies or divest naturalized citizens of the rights of citizenship)—that make democracy, justice, and inclusion of all peoples an unsteady principle or reality in our society. These excerpts attest to the power Omi and Winant give race as an explanatory variable for social phenomena. Their work demonstrates that race has always been a strong determinant of one's identity, social relationships, political rights, and location in the labor market. The development of research, policy, and social action must take these racial structures and contested meanings into account. The matter of racial identity and categorization is not an academic exercise—it affects employment, housing, publicly and privately valued goods, public policy, disbursement of local, state, and federal funds, and the organization of elections. Thus, Hune recommends that policies and programs understand the centrality of race, stay current on the existing racial dynamics, and understand the connection between race and the quality of their neighborhood (80).

Another important development is a definitive move towards and growth of research examining race relations beyond a black-and-white model (Hune). A large part of the study on "race" has been informed and shaped by studies of blacks in comparison to and in relation with whites. The experience and perspectives of other people of color have also been studied overwhelmingly in the context of their groups' relations with white Americans. On the other hand, their efforts to resist, to create alternatives, to struggle for justice, to resolve conflict, and to empower their communities, have been framed in comparison to African Americans. To get beyond this limiting dichotomy, ethnic studies scholars have begun to examine other points of reference and power dynamics besides relationships with European Americans and positions of subordination. There are important dynamics present in relationships between and within ethnic groups that inform and shape the dynamics of ethnic relations, racial inequality, and social mobility. Hune lists different examples of groups and areas to examine: 'relations between Asian American owners and non-Asian employees and clientele,' 'new multiracial and multiethnic residential patterns,' 'biracial families,' [and] 'the growing disparities within racial/ethnic groups' (80). Marable stresses the importance of comparative approaches in order to get beyond 'the narrow terrain of our experiences.' The danger is that "in our own separate languages, from the vantage point of our respective grievances . . . we trust only in ourselves, cursing the possibility that others unlike ourselves share a common destiny (56)—to which we can attach common origins. A comparative approach allows a "comparative, historical awareness about the commonalities of [our] oppression and resistance" (56). Examining commonalities and differences make us more aware of the intricate racial structures and processes in the U.S.

In addition to developing comparative analyses between racialized ethnic groups is the importance of examining the diversity and heterogeneity that exists within groups. A consequence of developing the respective place of each group's historical experiences and perspectives in the university curriculum at the beginning of ethnic studies resulted in a monolithic and homogeneous representation of each group, what has commonly been referred to as a cultural nationalism. In fact, this scholarship was intensely nationalistic as early scholars attempted to define distinct differences from European American society (Espiritu):

Writing from an anti-assimilationist stance, many scholars sought to unearth a buried past, to chronicle traditions of protest and resistance, and to establish that racialized populations have been absolutely crucial to the making of history. (511)

These histories consisted of the experience of males and earlier immigration waves. Drawing on these broad outlines, experience was confined to certain areas of life. Differences, especially along gender and class lines, were minimized (Espiritu). Consequently, they overlooked variations and distinctions that represented the heterogeneity of the group. Espiritu discusses the important dynamics overlooked in a cultural nationalist approach:

These complex realities—the products of uneven histories and unequal power relations—challenge the binaries implicit in the cultural nationalist paradigm, and they demand that Ethnic Studies scholars pay attention to the complicated, conflicted, and composite nature of all social identities, particularly to the inseparability and mutually constitutive realities of race, class, gender, and sexuality. (511)

People experience racial dynamics differently depending on their class and their gender. In addition to an examination of the role of class, gender, and sexuality, any examination of the experience of particular groups must also take into account the differences in generational experiences and perspectives, political and economic dynamics, particular historical situations—especially in terms of difference in political and economic eras and circumstances—regional factors, and national or immigrant status (Hune 82). Also, in examining points of commonalities and divergence in experience, position and perspective, we must also look for strengths and weaknesses in terms of political strategy and identification as discrete racialized ethnic groups.

Research on the heterogeneity within groups also points to another emergent and promising area of research, the differential structures of access, power, and agency (Hune). Communities of color have not passively accepted their position in the U.S. social structure. They have been active agents in the circumstances of their lives. Many have maintained their right to determine their existence rather than passively accept mainstream U.S. racial and ethnic views. This resistance is part of a several-centuries-old tradition of living their lives according to the beliefs and principles of the group, regardless of the threat presented by the tradition of exclusion and brutality in U.S. society towards those who do not fall in line or appear as legitimate citizens or worthy human beings. Although many have learned the ways of mainstream American culture, this does not mean they have given up their culture. Respective ethnic groups have power as communities (Hune). Rather than waiting for politicians or policy changes these groups develop their own strategies and agendas that reflect their strengths, needs, and resources. These community efforts take place within the context of a struggle for decision-making power or influence in the allocation of resources. Research in this area allows us to examine the strengths, needs, and resources of these communities, in addition to the strategies that work and the obstacles and limitations presented to them.

Another rapidly emerging paradigm is research at the international level examining the factors affecting racial dynamics and ethnic relations. The two main areas of study are global studies and diasporic studies. A key factor here is the growing importance of immigration. The fourth wave of immigration to the U.S. between 1961 and 1990 brought an estimated 18 million legal immigrants (Pedraza and Rumbaudt) and an estimated 5 million undocumented immigrants (Marable). These immigrants settled in major urban areas. This migration has brought many groups in contact. Often, the result has been competition for resources in the areas of employment, education, and business ownership that has resulted in conflict. In California, contact between these groups manifested itself in anti-immigrant sentiments evident during the Los Angeles Rebellion/Riots and Proposition 187, which would have denied undocumented immigrants and their children access to health care and education. The growth in immigration has changed the make-up of our society and the major cities. Research in this area is examining the factors that lead to negative and positive developments and consequences.

However, there is also a larger focus on the transnational dynamics and factors that are creating this migration. The involvement of the U.S. in these countries via foreign and economic relations has been associated with these developments. Important differences—and thereby the points of interest in research—in the situations between and within these countries have led to different life conditions and possibilities for the migrants. Also, the home country, or the country of origin, continues to inform and shape the experiences, approaches, and perspectives of these populations and their relationships with other groups in the U.S. In a sense, the borders of ethnic studies have been expanded. The developments in our understanding of racial dynamics have taken on a much larger and more complex character. The challenge to ethnic studies lies in the complexity and the amount of work ahead in the expansive areas and tasks of research at hand for our discipline. The essays here represent further work in these areas. We hope they convey the unique, rich, and complex factors that inform the racial dynamics and ethnic relations that present limitations and inform possibilities in our efforts to surmount racial inequality and create more just, fulfilling, engaged, integrated, and sustainable relationships, communities, and societies.

The road we embark upon is about accounting, analyzing, challenging, and understanding difference, and acting in the name of a greater good only we ourselves can choose to define, cherish, commit and cultivate. To be human is to be different; differences abound; differences are constant; difference—along with commonalities—makes the world go around. Difference only becomes the source of racism when we assign or allow ourselves—without consciousness, conscientiousness, conviction or calling into question—advantage and privilege in the name of an alleged superiority of a group of a human beings that is gained by disregarding, differentiating, degrading and stigmatizing another group; by believing, invoking, perpetuating and letting lie destructive and divisive myths about their physical and cultural being (Memmi). We make meaning of difference; we must decide what difference will mean to us and what we will make of it; what differences we will value sufficiently to endure and understand and embrace; what differences we will discard or put aside to discover meaningfully unique ways of living and to find meaningful points of connection; and, to decide how we, ourselves, will make a difference.

Bibliography

1. Acuna, Rodolfo. Occupied America: A History of Chicanos. Addison-Wesley Publishing Company. 1999.
2. Andersen, Margaret L. and Patricia Hill-Collins. Race, Class, and Gender: An Anthology. Wadsworth Publishing Company. 1995.
3. Baca-Zinn, Maxine. "Sociological theory in emergent Chicano perspectives." Pacific Sociological Review, Vol. 24: 255–272. 1981.
4. Barrera, Mario. "A Theory of Racial Inequality." Latinos and Education: A Critical Reader. Eds. Antonia Darder, Rodolfo D. Torres, Henry Gutierrez. 1997. pp. 3–44.
5. Blauner, Bob. Racial Opression in America. Harper and Row. 1972.
6. Bloom, Allan. The Closing of the American Mind. Touchstone Books. 1988.
7. Bonacich, Edna and John Modell. The Economic Basis of Ethnic Solidarity: Small Business in the Japanese American Community. University of California Press. 1980.
8. Chomsky, Noam. "Introduction: Contours and Context, Section 2: Military Science and Spirit." Rethink Camelot: JFK, the Vietnam War, and U.S. Political Culture. URL: http://www.zmag.org/chomsky/rc/rc-intro-s02.html (5 June 2003).
9. Covey, Stephen. Seven Habits of Highly Effective People. Simon & Schuster. 1990.
10. Craig, R. Philosophical and Educational Foundations in a Multicultural Society. Waterbury, CT: Emancipation Press. 1999.
11. Davidson, Miriam. Lives on the Line: Dispatches from the U.S.-Mexico Border. University of Arizona Press, 2000.
12. Davis, Angela. Women, Race, and Class. Vintage. 1983.
13. D'Souza, Dinesh. Illiberal Education: The Politics of Race and Sex on Campus. Free Press. 1998.
14. Espiritu, Yen Le. "Disciplines unbound: Notes on sociology and ethnic studies." Comparative Sociology, Vol. 28, No. 5, pp. 510–514. 1999.
15. Feagin, Joe R. and Clairece Booher Feagin. "U.S. Racial and Ethnic Relations." Prentice Hall. 2002.
16. Fong, Timothy. "Introduction." Asian Americans: Experiences and Perspectives. Eds. Timothy P. Fong and Larry H. Shinagawa. Prentice Hall. 2000. pp. 1–10.
17. Fong, Timothy P. and Larry H. Shinigawa (Eds). Asian Americans: Experiences and Perspectives. Prentice Hall. 2000.
18. Gitlin, Todd. The Whole World Is Watching: Mass Media in the Making and Unmaking of the New Left. 2003. University of California Press.
19. Hu-DeHart, Evelyn. "Reconceptualizing liberal-education: The importance of ethnic studies." Educational Record. Vol. 76., no. 2/3, p. 22. 1995.
20. Hune, Shirley. "Rethinking Race: Paradigms and Policy Formation." Asian Americans: Experiences and Perspectives. Asian Americans: Experiences and Perspectives. Eds. Timothy P. Fong. and Larry H. Shinagawa. Prentice Hall. 2000. pp. 79–85.
21. King, Deborah K. "Multiple Jeopardy, Multiple Consciousness: The Context of a Black Feminist Ideology." Signs, 14, 42–73. 1988.

22. Kuhn, Thomas. The Structure of Scientific Revolutions. University of Chicago Press. 1970.
23. Lowy, Richard F. "The limitation of liberal theories of racism and prejudice: A historical, political and cultural critique of the paradigm of assimilation and tolerance building on David Theo Goldberg's discussion of racist culture." Paper presented at Western Social Science Association, April, 1994.
24. Marable, Manning. "We Need New and Critical Study of Race and Ethnicity." The Chronicle of Higher Education, vol. 46, no. 25, February 25, 2000.
25. Mazumdar, Sucheta. "Asian American Studies and Asian Studies: Rethinking roots." Asian Americans: Comparative and Global Perspectives. Eds. Shirley Hune, Hyung-chan Kim, Stephen S. Fugita, and Amy Ling. Washington State University Press. 1991.
26. McAdam, Doug. Freedom Summer. Oxford University Press. 1990.
27. Memmi, Albert. Racism. University of Minnesota Press. 2000.
28. Monaghan, Peter. "A new momentum in Asian American Studies." Chronicle of Higher Education, Vol. 45, No. 30. April 2, 1999.
29. Moraga, Cherie L. and Gloria E. Anzaldua. This Bridge Called My Back. Kitchen Table/Women of Color. 1984.
30. Okihiro, Gary. "African and Asian American Studies: A Comparative Analysis and Commentary." Asian Americans: Comparative and Global Perspectives. Ed. Shirley Hune. 1991. pp. 17–28.
31. Okihiro, Gary Y. "Is Yellow Black or White?" Asian Americans: Experiences and Perspectives. Eds. Timothy P. Fong. and Larry H. Shinagawa. Prentice Hall. 2000. pp. 63–77.
32. Omatsu, Glenn. "The Four Prisons" and the Movements of Liberation: Asian American Activism from the 1960s to the 1990s." Contemporary Asian America: A Multidisciplinary Reader. (Eds.) Min Zhou and James V. Gatewood. New York University Press. 2000. pp. 80–115.
33. Omi, Michael and Howard Winant. Racial Formation in the United States: From the 1960s to the 1990s. Routledge. 1994.
34. Parillo, Vincent. Strangers to These Shores: Race and Ethnic Relations in the United States. Allyn & Bacon. 1997.
35. Park, Robert E. Race and Culture. Free Press. 1950.
36. Reisberg, Leo. "As Asian enrollments diversify, so too do students demands." Chronicle of Higher Education, Vol. 45, No. 37. May 12, 1999.
37. Rex, John. Race and Ethnicity. Open University Press. 1986.
38. Schlesinger, Arthur M. The Disunity of America: Reflections on a Multicultural Society. W.W. Norton and Company. 1998.
39. Schneider, Bart (Ed.). race: an anthology in the first person. Three Rivers Press. 1997.
40. Seitz, Matt Zoller. "Sinatra: A Voice that could touch anyone." NJ.com: The Star Ledger. http://www.nj.com/sinatra/stories/0518tribute.html. 1999.
41. Temple, Robert. "The West's Debt to China." Readings for Sociology. Ed. Massey, Garth. W.W. Norton. 1996.

42. Umemoto, Karen. ""On Strike" San Francisco State College Strike, 1968–69: The Role of Asian American Students." Contemporary Asian America: A Multidisciplinary Reader. (Eds.) Min Zhou and James V. Gatewood. New York University Press. 2000. pp. 49–79.
43. Vander Zanden, James W. "Sociological studies of American blacks." The Sociological Quarterly Vol. 14: 32–52. 1973.

SECTION ONE

Conceptualizing Race, Class, and Gender

Introduction

Section I discusses the various ways in which race, class, and gender are conceptualized and how interpretations, legal definitions, and ideological standpoints all shift according to prevailing social conditions. But even with these shifting paradigms of race, one thing has remained constant throughout U.S. history, and that is the persistent use of race particularly as it interacts with identities of class and gender as a mechanism to organize status arrangements in social and economic life.

Many chapters in this reader address the intersectionality of race, gender, and class. Conceptualization of these categories can directly or indirectly determine social class outcomes. In bell hooks's *Class Matters*, she speaks to class and how it serves as the subordinating mechanism that cuts across all intersections. This chapter provides an opportunity to examine social-economic class as both a cause and a consequence of social status arrangements.

The complexities associated with identifying and clarifying multiracial identities are discussed in Wayne Maeda's *Ties That Bind*. This chapter reminds us that "historically all means—both legal and extralegal—have been used to categorize people for the purposes of maintaining political, economic, and social privileges of the dominant group."

In *The Genesis of Ethnicity and Collective Identity,* Alexandre Kimenyi differentiates ethnic studies' prescriptive approach, which is motivated by social justice concepts, from the descriptive study of ethnicity predominant in other disciplines. Through the examples of numerous case studies and references, he points out that the concept of ethnicity is best understood as flexible and "always emerging" in relation to nationality, race, class, and gender formations.

In Michael Moore's *Stupid White Men*, we see how language interacts with racial ideologies to construct meanings of race that are so persuasive that they can create social consensus that preserves racial protections.

Gender, when examined from a social perspective, must be seen as prescriptive and not neutral. Like race, the use of gender is not incidental and as such can be used as an intentional and explicit form of social control. In *Race, Gender, and Social Control*, Luana Ross illustrates the significance of gender and class in the incarceration experiences of Native American Women.

Racial discourses, as they are reiterated wittingly and unwittingly throughout classrooms, playgrounds, churches, and in all aspects of social life, underscore the embedded cultural assumptions about racialized minorities and white privilege. The failure to critically analyze, question, and intervene against these assumptions results in the intransigence of race and racism that is self-perpetuating.

The intersectionality of race, gender, and class is a mechanism used and even appropriated to reproduce and preserve status arrangements in major social institutions such as labor, education, social welfare, and criminal justice. The chapter by Rita Cameron Wedding, *Colorblindness: Challenging the Discourse of U.S. Racism,* discusses how systems that preserve and reinscribe racial hierarchies are as intact today as they were during the height of U.S. racial apartheid.

In *Hiring Immigrant Women*, Karen Hossfeld describes how race and gender ideologies as well as the ideologies of nationality are sometimes appropriated by institutions as rational and "legitimate" justifications for exploitation. For example, one manager used "a simple hiring formula," ". . . small, foreign, and female. You find those three things and you're pretty much automatically guaranteed the right kind of work force. These little foreign gals are grateful to be hired—very, very grateful—no matter what." Such formulas constructed as "race logic" and "gender logic" create inflexible employment hierarchies that position employees not according to ability but according to race-gender identities.

How Jews Became White Folks describes how Jews, as they came to occupy statuses previously held only by whites, could take advantage of race preferences in the redistribution of societal resources. Ideological redefinitions of whiteness allowed the advantages accrued to them to be framed as the result of hard work and "pulling themselves up by their bootstraps" while masking the role of government sanctioned programs such as the GI Bill and FHA loan programs. Author Karen B. Sacks refers to this phenomenon as affirmative action for whites, and describes how it facilitated their emergence into the "white" middle class.

This section on conceptualizing race, class, and gender examines the utilization of race and the consequences of racism particularly as they intersect with other systems of oppression.

1

Class Matters

bell hooks

Everywhere we turn in our daily lives in this nation we are confronted with the widening gap between rich and poor. Whether it is the homeless person we walk by as we go about daily chores in urban areas, the beggars whose cups tinkle with the sound of a few coins, the middle-class family member or friend who faces unemployment due to cutbacks, plant closings, or relocation, or the increased cost of food and housing, we are all aware of class. Yet there is no organized class struggle, no daily in-your-face critique of capitalist greed that stimulates thought and action—critique, reform, and revolution.

As a nation we have become passive, refusing to act responsibly toward the more than thirty-eight million citizens who live in poverty here and the working masses who labor long and hard but still have difficulty making ends meet. The rich are getting richer. And the poor are falling by the wayside. At times it seems no one cares. Citizens in the middle who live comfortable lives, luxurious lives in relation to the rest of the world, often fear that challenging classism will be their downfall, that simply by expressing concern for the poor they will end up like them, lacking the basic necessities of life. Defensively, they turn their backs on the poor and look to the rich for answers, convinced that the good life can exist only when there is material affluence.

More and more, our nation is becoming class-segregated. The poor live with and among the poor—confined in gated communities without adequate shelter, food, or health care—the victims of predatory greed. More and more poor communities all over the country look like war zones, with boarded-up bombed-out buildings, with either the evidence of gunfire everywhere or the vacant silence of unsatisfied hunger. In some neighborhoods, residents must wear name tags to gain entrance to housing projects, gated camps that are property of the nation-state. No one safeguards the interests of citizens there; they are soon to be the victims of class genocide. This is the passive way our country confronts the poor and indigent, leaving them to die from street warfare, sugar, alcohol, and drug addiction, AIDS, and/or starvation.

The rich, along with their upper-class neighbors, also live in gated communities where they zealously protect their class interests—their way of life—by surveillance, by security forces, by direct links to the police, so that all danger can be kept at bay. Strangers entering these neighborhoods who look like they do not belong, meaning that they are the wrong color and/or have the appearance of being lower class, are stopped and vetted. In my affluent neighborhood in Greenwich Village, I am often stopped by shopkeepers and asked where I work, whose children do I keep, the message being you must not live here—you do not look like you belong. To look young and black is to not belong. Affluence, they believe, is always white. At times when I wander around my neighborhood staring at the dark-skinned nannies, hearing the accents that identify them as immigrants still, I remember this is the world a plantation economy produces—a world where some are bound and others are free, a world of extremes.

Most folks in my predominately white neighborhood see themselves as open-minded; they believe in justice and support the right causes. More often than not, they are social liberals and fiscal conservatives. They may believe in recognizing multiculturalism and celebrating diversity (our neighborhood is full of white gay men and straight white people who have at least one black, Asian, or Hispanic friend), but when it comes to money and class they want to protect what they have, to perpetuate and reproduce it—they want more. The fact that they have so much while others have so little does not cause moral anguish, for they see their good fortune as a sign they are chosen, special, deserving. It enhances their feeling of prosperity and well-being to know everyone cannot live as they do. They scoff at overzealous liberals who are prone to feeling guilty. Downward mobility is a thing of the past; in today's world of affluence, the message is "You got it, flaunt it."

When longtime small family businesses close down because the rents are too high and yet another high-priced gift shop or hair salon opens, they may feel regret but understand this to be the price of economic progress—the price of real estate constantly zooming upward in cost. They have no memories of the days when the West Village was the home of struggling artists, musicians, and poets, a sanctuary for the sexually free and transgressive, a place of rebellion. They have no memory of days when black females could not rent a room or flat here because white folks saw us all, no matter our class, as prostitutes—as bad news. Nowadays we can have the keys to the big house as long as we are coming to clean and do childcare. Neighbors tell me the lack of diversity has nothing to do with racism, it's just a matter of class.

They really believe all black people are poor no matter how many times they laugh at Bill Cosby, salute Colin Powell, mimic Will Smith, dance to Brandy and Whitney Houston, or cheer on Michael Jordan. Yet when the rich black people come to live where they live, they worry that class does not matter enough, for those black folks might have some poor relatives, and there goes the neighborhood. Like the taxi drivers who won't stop because blackness means you are on your way out of the city to Brooklyn—to places that are not safe. They lump all black people together. If rich black people come into the neighborhood, then poor black people will not be far behind.

Black folks with money think about class more than most people do in this society. They know that most of the white people around them believe all black people are poor, even the ones with fancy suits and tailored shirts wearing Rolex watches and carrying leather briefcases. Poverty in the white mind is always primarily black. Even though the white poor are many, living in suburbs and rural areas, they remain invisible. The black poor are everywhere, or so many white people think.

When I am shopping in Barneys, a fancy department store in my neighborhood, and a well-dressed white woman turns to me even though I am wearing a coat, carrying my handbag, and chatting with a similarly dressed friend—seeking assistance from the first available shopgirl and demands my help, I wonder who and what she sees looking at me. From her perspective she thinks she knows who has class power, who has the right to shop here; the look of the poor and working class is always different from her own. Even if we had been dressed alike she would have looked past attire to see the face of the underprivileged she has been taught to recognize.

In my neighborhood everyone believes the face of poverty is black. The white poor blend in, the black poor stand out. Homeless black males entertain, sing songs, tell jokes, or court attention with kind phrases hoping for money in their cup. Usually white homeless men mumble to themselves or sit silent, a cardboard sign naming their economic pain, separated when they seek help in the mainstream world. At the end of the day black and white indigents often pool earnings, sit side by side, sharing the same bottle, breaking the same bread. At the end of the day they inhabit a world where race and class no longer mean very much.

My other home is in a small midwestern town, a liberal place in the conservative state of Ohio, a state where the Nazi party is growing strong and flags hang in the windows of the patriotic haves and have-nots. It is a racially integrated town, a town with a progressive history, and there is still a neighborly world of caring and sharing. Here, class segregation has been imported from the outside, from a professional-managerial academic class who have come in from northern cities and west coast states and have raised property values. Still, neighborhoods in our small town have greater class and racial diversity than most places in the United States. Racism and sexism exist here, as everywhere. A changing class reality that destabilizes and in some cases will irrevocably alter individual lives is the political shift that threatens. Like everywhere in the Midwest plants are closing; small universities and community colleges are cutting back; full-time employees are "let go" and part-time help is fast becoming a national norm. Class is the pressing issue, but it is not talked about.

The closest most folks can come to talking about class in this nation is to talk about money. For so long everyone has wanted to hold on to the belief that the United States is a class-free society—that anyone who works hard enough can make it to the top. Few people stop to think that in a class-free society there would be no top. While it has always been obvious that some folks have more money than other folks, class difference and classism are rarely overtly apparent, or they are not acknowledged when present. The evils of racism and, much later, sexism, were easier to identify and challenge than the evils of classism. We live in a society where the poor have no public voice. No wonder it has taken so long for many citizens to recognize class—to become class conscious.

Racial solidarity, particularly the solidarity of whiteness, has historically always been used to obscure class, to make the white poor see their interests as one with the world of white privilege. Similarly, the black poor have always been told that class can never matter as much as race. Nowadays the black and white poor know better. They are not so easily duped by an appeal to unquestioned racial identification and solidarity, but they are still uncertain about what all the changes mean; they are uncertain about where they stand.

This uncertainty is shared by those who are not poor, but who could be poor tomorrow if jobs are lost. They, too, are afraid to say how much class matters. While the poor are offered addiction as a way to escape thinking too much, working people are encouraged to shop. Consumer culture silences working people and the middle classes. They are busy buying or planning to buy. Although their fragile hold on economic self-sufficiency is slipping, they still cling to the dream of a class-free society where everyone can make it to the top. They are afraid to face the significance of dwindling resources, the high cost of education, housing, and health care. They are afraid to think too deeply about class.

At the end of the day the threat of class warfare, of class struggle, is just too dangerous to face. The neat binary categories of white and black or male and female are not there when it comes to class. How will they identify the enemy. How will they know who to fear or who to challenge. They cannot see the changing face of global labor—the faces of the women and children whom transnational white supremacist capitalist patriarchy exploits at home and abroad to do dirty work for little pay. They do not speak the languages of the immigrants, male and female, who work here in the meat industry, in clothing sweatshops, as farmworkers, as cooks and busboys, as nannies and domestic workers. Even though the conservative rich daily exploit mass media to teach them that immigrants are the threat, that welfare is the threat, they are starting to wonder about who really profits from poverty, about where the money goes. And whether they like it or not, one day they will have to face the reality: this is not a class-free society.

Oftentimes I too am afraid to think and write about class. I began my journey to class consciousness as a college student learning about the politics of the American left, reading Marx, Fanon, Gramsci, Memmi, the little red book, and so on. But when my studies ended, I still felt my language to be inadequate. I still found it difficult to make sense of class in relation to race and gender. Even now the intellectual left in this nation looks down on anyone who does not speak the chosen jargon. The domain of academic and/or intellectual discourse about class is still mostly white, mostly male. While a few women get to have their say, most of the time men do not really listen. Most leftist men will not fully recognize the left politics of revolutionary feminism: to them class remains the only issue. Within revolutionary feminism a class analysis matters, but so does an analysis of race and gender.

Class matters. Race and gender can be used as screens to deflect attention away from the harsh realities class politics exposes. Clearly, just when we should all be paying attention to class, using race and gender to understand and explain its new dimensions, society, even our government, says let's talk about race and racial injustice. It is impossible to talk meaningfully about ending racism without talking about class. Let us not be duped. Let us not be led by spectacles like the O. J. Simpson trial to believe a mass media, which has always betrayed the cause of racial justice, to think that it was all about race, or it was about gender. Let us acknowledge that first and foremost it was about class and the interlocking nature of race, sex, and class. Let's face the reality that if O. J. Simpson had been poor or even lower-middle class there would have been no media attention. Justice was never the central issue. Our nation's tabloid passion to know about the lives of the rich made class the starting point. It began with money and became a media spectacle that made more money—another case of the rich getting richer. The Simpson trial is credited with upping the GNP by two hundred million dollars. Racism and sexism can be exploited in the interests of class power. Yet no one wants to talk about class. It is not sexy or cute. Better to make it seem that justice is class-free—that what happened to O. J. could happen to any working man.

It has been difficult for black folks to talk about class. Acknowledging class difference destabilizes the notion that racism affects us all in equal ways. It disturbs the illusion of racial solidarity among blacks, used by those individuals with class power to ensure that their class interests will be protected even as they transcend race behind the scenes. When William Julius Wilson first published *The Declining Significance of Race*, his title enraged many readers, especially black folks. Without reading the book, they thought he was saying that race did not matter when what he was prophetically arguing, albeit from a conservative and sometimes liberal standpoint, was that our nation is fast becoming a place where class matters as much as race and oftentimes more.

Feminist theorists acknowledged the overwhelming significance of the interlocking systems of race, gender, and class long before men decided to talk more about these issues together. Yet mainstream culture, particularly mass media, was not willing to tune into a radical political discourse that was not privileging one issue over the other. Class is still often kept separate from race. And while race is often linked with gender, we still lack an ongoing collective public discourse that puts the three together in ways that illuminate for everyone how our nation is organized and what our class politics really are. Women of all races and black people of both genders are fast filling up the ranks of the poor and disenfranchised. It is in our interest to face the issue of class, to become more conscious, to know better so that we can know how best to struggle for economic justice.

I began to write about class in an effort to clarify my own personal journey from a working-class background to the world of affluence, in an effort to be more class conscious. It has been useful to begin with class and work from there. In much of my other work, I have chosen gender or race as a starting point. I choose class now because I believe class warfare will be our nation's fate if we do not collectively challenge classism, if we do not attend to the widening gap between rich and poor, the haves and have-nots. This class conflict is already racialized and gendered. It is already creating division and separation. If the citizens of this nation want to live in a society that is class-free, then we must first work to create an economic system that is just. To work for change, we need to know where we stand.

2

Ties That Bind or Ties That Blind: Crossing Historically Forbidden Borders of "Race"[1]

Wayne Maeda

The **Ties That Bind** project was initiated by *Movimiento de Arte y Cultura Latino Americana* of San Jose, to explore the complex worlds of California Asians and Latinos who chose to cross the historically forbidden borders of "race." The Census of 2000 for the first time collected data on America's multiracial population: respondents had the choice of marking multiple "boxes" to indicate their racial or ethnic identity. Thus, we now know that in California in the year 2000, more than one in ten Asians and more than three in every fifty Latinos identified themselves as multiracial.[2] A total of forty self-identified Asian-Latino families and individuals answered the call to publicly explore the emotional, cultural, social, economical, religious, and culinary tensions as they tried to understand, negotiate, and capture what, in many cases, turned out to be not only fluid but contingent multiracial identities. The experiences of these multiracial families and individuals in the Silicon Valley, in all likelihood, mirror the larger shifts across California and the nation.

Paradoxically, at the very period when interracial unions are on an upward trajectory and increases in diversity across California and other states, we now hear the clarion call to become a "color-blind" society by ridding ourselves of these racial and ethnic markers. One might be tempted to proclaim that the once forbidden racial frontiers have been conquered. One could

From *MACLA/Movimiento de Arte y Cultura Latino Americana*. Reprinted by permission of the author.

just as easily, though, raise the more troubling question: why have there been so few interracial individuals, given the long history of these groups in the United States. When the white majority was, in fact, the numerical majority in California, there was little or no discussion of doing away with "racialized categories." The notion that merely eliminating these "racial categories" would lead to a nondiscriminatory society is not only disingenuous but flies in the face of actual historical experience. For those, even with "good intentions," advocating this color blindness is a moral sense of justice and fairness without a history. Historically, all means—both legal and extralegal—have been used to categorize people into various quanta of racial origins for the purposes of maintaining political, economic and social privileges. Race did and does matter today and how the meaning of race was constructed may help contextualize these stories and prove insightful to understanding that while "race mixing" has always occurred, it has occurred infrequently, unevenly, and affected various groups differently across America.[3]

The Shirakawa family trilogy, one of the 15 oral histories collected by the **Ties That Bind** project, helps us to understand the changing meanings of "race mixing." George Shirakawa Jr. begins the Shirakawa narrative with his Nisei (second-generation Japanese American) grandfather Masaji who, in the 1930s, married a Mexican American woman from the Esparza family. They were married halfway across the country in Minnesota, which unlike California was one of a few states that did not have anti-miscegenation laws prohibiting marriage between "Mongolians" and whites.[4] In their attempt to cross racial borders, the Shirakawas also had to cross literal state borders. Masaji Shirakawa and his Mexican American wife had no idea that the construction of "race" that necessitated their travel to Minnesota to marry because she was legally "white" and he was a "Mongolian" began long before America became America.[5]

The American South was the first to enact (and last to end) the prohibition against interracial marriages between whites and blacks. Maryland began in 1661, followed by Virginia (1662), to construct anti-miscegenation laws. In that same year Virginia embarked upon a course to create a dual society: matrilineal for African Americans and the traditional patrilineal system for whites. Not only did the South construct different lineage systems based on race, but also moved to construct racial groups differently.[6]

During the early colonial period, marriage between colonists and Native Americans was a fairly common occurrence. Localities constructed whiteness by determining the minimum quantum of "Indian blood" one could have and still retain the privilege of being "white" (if there were no privileges, why the construction of "white"?). For example, in Virginia, it was not the absence of Indian blood but rather the minimum that was set. "One-sixteenth or less of the blood of the American Indian and . . . no other non-Caucasic blood" would qualify one as "white"; this was often referred to as the "Pocahontas' rule."[7] The question of who qualified as an African American, in contrast, was dealt with differently by constructing, over time, the "one-drop" rule.

The "one-drop" rule dictated that anyone with so much as a trace of African ancestry was black and lineage was traced through the mother's side.[8] So of course race did not matter: it was just that a white mother could give birth to a black or white child but a black mother could only give birth to a black child no matter who the father might be. The implications are clear as to why these two groups were constructed differently and how each construction worked to preserve not only a racial but a gender hierarchy as well.[9] The racial landscape and prohibition against interracial marriage became more convoluted, one might even argue, "elegantly constructed" in its ingenuity, as settlers continued their Westward expansion.

Similar to the Native American/white experience east of the Rockies, in the West, this pattern continued with white men and Mexican women in the Southwest and what was to become California. No doubt some of these unions were for intimate personal reasons and, without a doubt, some marriages were for the purposes of acquiring Mexican land grants.[10] In any event, what emerges is the curious anomaly that no anti-miscegenation laws passed in the United States were written against Mexicans. In fact, according to the Treaty of Guadalupe Hidalgo (ending the Mexican American War in 1848) Mexicans were granted, among other things, citizenship conferring on them the legal status of white. Of course, the legal status of being constructed "white" did not always translate into being treated or accepted as "white" in everyday life. Let us not forget "Remember the Alamo!" Nevertheless, it is in the West, paradoxically because of its diversity, that race and intermarriage take on an ever-widening exclusive policy.

It is ironic that it was in the West—Frederick Jackson Turner's last frontier that shaped the "democratic character" of Americans—that the definitions of "white," "citizenship," and "interracial marriage" were elegantly linked together to exclude Asian groups from joining mainstream America.[11] Racial engineers constructed Chinese, Japanese, Koreans, "Kanakas" (Hawaiians), "Hindus" (the other Indians), and Filipinos but not Armenians or Mexicans as non-white.[12] Once the Supreme Court determined that Asians were not eligible for citizenship based on a 1790 naturalization law (one had to be "free white"), the next step was for various states to enact anti-miscegenation laws preventing marriages between Mongolians and whites.[13]

In California, for example, Chinese were added in the 1880s to the list of Black and mulatto, who could not marry whites, and by extension each successive group of immigrant Asians was added to this laundry list of prohibited groups.[14] The arrival of large numbers of Filipinos in the late 1920s created a curious and novel problem. The existing anti-miscegenation law in California prohibited "Mongolians" from marrying white persons and some Filipinos, denied marriage certificates, argued in court that they were not of Mongolian lineage but rather fit into the "Malay" race. The California courts agreed that Filipinos were not Mongolians but Malay; therefore, they were not covered under the existing prohibition against marrying whites. The California legislature, in 1934 in its infinite wisdom, added "Malay race" to the list of those prohibited from marrying whites.[15]

Those from India (mistakenly referred to as Hindus) faced the most elegant solution of all. While the anthropological "experts" were in agreement that Indians belonged to the Caucasian (Aryan) race, thus making them eligible for citizenship, the Supreme Court later deemed them not "white" as understood by the ordinary person. Of course, race did not matter, but how does one come to terms with the legal gymnastics of the Supreme Court defining a group as Caucasian but not white?[16] In everyday life, however, these artificial racial borders were crossed by the Sikhs from India, who were Caucasians but not "white." In California, the Sikhs were allowed to marry Mexican women in the 1920s and 1930s, in all likelihood, because they did not really look white.[17] Oregon's list, during this same period, included Chinese,

Kanaka (Hawaiian) and Indian, while South Dakota added "Corean"[Korean], Malayan or Mongolian to those prohibited from marrying whites.[18]

California was not finished with constructing race as Masaji Shirakawa, his Mexican American wife and their American children would find out. As World War II began, their story becomes even more convoluted with President Franklin Roosevelt's decision to incarcerate Japanese Americans on the West Coast into concentration camps. The Mexican American mother was faced with the prospect of accompanying her "half-Japanese, half-Mexican" American children into the camps because they "looked like the enemy." The United States government defined a Japanese as anyone with "one-sixteenth blood" Japanese blood and made the Shirakawa children eligible for incarceration as their Japanese American father volunteered for the United States Army, Military Intelligence Service.[19]

The complexities of negotiating a biracial relationship did not end with Masaji Shirakawa but continued into the next generation. George Shirakawa Sr., the son of this biracial relationship, continued the tradition of crossing racial lines and married a white woman in the 1960s. But this time, he did not have to cross state borders. Unlike his father Masaji, George Sr. was able to marry in California because of changes made to anti-miscegenation law by the Supreme Court of California in 1948.[20] Ironically, while it was California that had created such twisted categories of racial groups, preventing mixed marriages, California in 1948 was the first state to dismantle these laws (through the judicial process) that led the way for the United States Supreme Court to declare anti-miscegenation laws unconstitutional across the land in 1967.[21] The legacy of crossing racial borders continued with George Sr.'s son, George Jr.

George Jr. grew up in the 1970s and 1980s in the Santa Clara Valley, presumably in a more enlightened period. Yet he still faced the legacy of racial categories and meanings attached to census "boxes." At times he subverted these racial meanings by allowing others to define him as "Hawaiian" in high school and as a "Native American" while serving in the Army.[22] He continued the Shirakawa tradition of crossing racial borders when he married a Mexican American woman. They had three children, part Japanese, white, and Mexican American: a lineage created over a span of three generations in California where the democratic frontier clashed with the racial frontier.

We hope that this all too brief overview of how "races" were kept separate in America has provided a context to understand the difficult terrain those involved in multiracial relationships have had to navigate in the past. Furthermore, this snapshot of the past has yielded a picture with no simple formula of maintaining separation of the "races" or even the definition of "race." The complexities and variations of this attempt to create and maintain separateness, however, are a testament that "race" mattered for most our history and one cannot help but conclude that these socially constructed barriers were erected to preserve hierarchies of power and privilege. One has to wonder whether the latest move to socially construct a "color blind" society is another attempt to maintain these hard won privileges over the centuries for the white majority.

For Latinos and Asians who are multiracial in America, the controversy of whether to rid society of census" boxes" and, by implication, "race," seems oddly misplaced or at the very least creates a false dichotomy. Either they or their parents have moved beyond the socially constructed racial divide and are becoming increasingly a category that eludes simple classification and, in all likelihood, will become even more complex.[23] The **Ties That Bind** project moves into uncharted territory by creating a public space for Latino and Asian multiracial couples and individuals who are situated at the intersections of the various forces in play—the legacy of anti-miscegenation, segregation, intimacy, continued discrimination and privilege, and the unintended influences of mass media—to begin the conversation with the rest of us.

Notes

1. This article first appeared as "Ties that Bind or Ties that Blind," in *Ties That Bind: Exploring the role of intermarriage between Latinos and Asians in the making and transformation of Silicon Valley.* (San Jose: Movimiento de Arte y Cultura Latino Americana, 2002), 7-9. The article is reprinted with minor additions and revisions by the author.
2. 6.42% (704,531) of Latinos out of a total of 10,966,556 have self-identified themselves as being multiracial. 11.73% (507,111) out of 4,321,585 Asian American and Pacific Islanders have so identified themselves. Compiled from *Census 2000.*
3. Peggy Pascoe, "Race, Gender, and Intercultural Relations: The Case of Interracial Marriage," 12 *Frontiers* (1991): 5-6. See also Paul R. Spickard, "Who is an Asian? Who is a Pacific Islander?: Monoracialism, Multiracial People, and Asian American Communities," in *The Sum of Our Parts: Mixed Heritage Asian Americans*, eds. Teresa Williams-Leon and Cynthia L. Nakashima (Philadelphia: Temple University, 2001), 17.
4. Paul R. Spickard, *Mixed Blood: Intermarriage and Ethnic Identity in Twentieth-Century America* (Madison: The University of Wisconsin Press, 1989), 374-375. States which never had anti-miscegenation laws: Connecticut, New Hampshire, New Jersey, New York, Vermont, Kansas, Illinois, Iowa, Minnesota, Wisconsin, Alaska, Hawaii, Washington and District of Columbia.
5. Contrary to popular misconception, Mexican Americans in California were legally defined as being "white"; hence a person of "obvious color" (Japanese) could not marry another person of "obvious color" (Mexican) because of the way race had been constructed. Tomás Almaguer, *Racial Fault Lines: The Historical Origins of White Supremacy in California* (Berkeley and Los Angeles: University California Press, 1994), 58.
6. A. Leon Higginbotham, Jr. *Shades of Freedom: Racial Politics and Presumptions of the American Legal Process* (New York: Oxford University Press, 1996), 34-45.
7. Rachel F. Moran, *Interracial Intimacy: The Regulation of Race and Romance* (Chicago: University of Chicago Press, 2001), 49. See also, Gary Nash, "The Hidden History of Mestizo America," in *Sex, Love, Race: Crossing Boundaries in North American History,* ed. Martha Hodes (New York: New York University Press, 1999), 11, for discussion on Patrick Henry's attempt in 1784 to convince the Virginia legislature to offer a bounty for white-Indian marriages.
8. Sharon M. Lee, "Racial Classification in the U.S. Census: 1890-1990," *Ethnic and Racial Studies* 16 (1993): 75, 77.

9. Higginbotham, 34–45.

10. Almaguer, 54–56.

11. Nash, 15.

12. See Robert Mirak. "Armenians" in *Harvard Encyclopedia of American Ethnic Groups,* ed. Stephan Themstrom (Massachusetts: Harvard University Press, 1980), 139, 141, 143.

13. Ronald Takaki, *Strangers From A Different Shore: A History of Asian Americans* revised (New York: Little, Brown and Company, 1998), 14.

14. Moran, 31.

15. Sucheng Chan, *Asian Americans: An Interpretive History* (Boston: Twayne Publishers, 1991), 60. See Salvador Roidan v. L.A. County.

16. U.S. v. Bhagat Singh Thind (1923). See Chan, 94.

17. Karen Isaken Leonard, *Making Ethnic Choices: California's Punjabi Mexican Americans* (Philadelphia: Temple University Press, 1992), passim.

18. Spickard, 375.

19. Japanese American Citizens League National Education Committee, *The Japanese American Experience: A Lesson in American History* (2002), 6–7.

20. Perez v. Sharp. See discussion of this case in Moran, 84–88.

21. Loving v. Virginia as cited in Moran, 95–99.

22. Interview of George Shirakawa, Jr., February 28, 2002.

23. Teresa Williams-Leon and Cynthia L. Nakashima, eds. *The Sum of Our Parts: Mixed-Heritage Asian Americans* (Philadelphia: Temple University Press, 2001), passim.

The Genesis of Ethnicity and Collective Identity

Alexandre Kimenyi

thnicity, like other concepts, is defined and understood differently depending on the academic discipline and the school of thought. The reasons of scientific inquiry into its formal and functional properties also differ according to the discipline as well. For anthropologists and sociologists, for instance, the scope of study is only descriptive and explanatory. For ethnic studies scholars, however, the inquiry goes beyond. The three levels of analysis (observation, description and explanation) are met, but a prescriptive element is also added. The study of ethnicity is not done for pure knowledge's sake but to improve the minority rights and social justice. This essay shows that it is not easy to draw the line between ethnicity and other social categorizations such as nationality, race or class in pluralistic societies.

It is also shown that ethnicity is dynamic, ever changing because of paradigm shift in scholarship and public policy and other socioeconomic factors. Examples drawn from different societies support the view that ethnicity is both essentialist and a social construct.

Factors responsible for the genesis of ethnicity are space movement and movement of the people as illustrated by nation-building processes, colonization, diaspora phenomena and migration. Using the conflict model, it becomes clear that ethnicity and collective identity are created for solidarity purposes and mutual support because of shared existential experiences.

1. Defining Ethnicity

Pluralism and ethnicity mean the same thing in pluralistic societies. For political scientists, a pluralistic society is one which allows people to belong to a party of their choice or tolerates different political persuasions. In ethnic studies, however, pluralism refers to a complex social organization which is diverse in its ethnic make-up. There is thus lack of homogeneity. Within the discipline of ethnic studies itself, ethnicity acquires different meanings depending on the theoretical bias. There are two competing theories, namely, the functionalist model and the conflict model. Like many others, I will use the term "equilibrium" for the former, because it creates ambiguity or assigns a new meaning to the term functionalist. In both hard sciences and social sciences, the term functionalist is used in opposition to formalist which is mainly interested in the architectural organization of the subject under study, namely, how paradigmatic elements interact with the whole structure.

In the equilibrium model's point of view a true pluralistic society is one in which a peaceful coexistence of ethnic diversity exists. These groups have reached a consensus that to live in harmony, to insure society's survival and progress, it is necessary to tolerate each other. According to this theory, pluralism is a prerequisite to true democracy since democracy means to accept the rules of the game, to compromise, to accept the decision that has been agreed upon. Democracy means diversity of opinions, groups, etc. Homogeneity doesn't therefore create a good ground for democracy. To illustrate this concept, social scientists cite Switzerland, Belgium and Canada as examples. They also call their respective governments consociative democracies. They assert that in these three countries, ethnic groups live in harmony.

The three are not good examples, however. Switzerland happens to be a federated state where four groups, namely French, Germans, Italians and Romanche live in four separate cantons. Switzerland doesn't have a national language or culture. It is very clear that if one language were to be imposed, there will be without any doubt a conflict. Belgium like Switzerland is a federation also where two groups, two languages and two separate spaces are found, namely Flemish and Walloons. It is true that Canada is more liberal as far as its immigration policy is concerned. Despite its huge size, twice the United States, its total population which numbers around 30 million is lower than that of California. Canada also allows symbolic ethnicity by aiding, with generous grants, different groups to organize ethnic festivals. This has resulted in Canada being assigned the label of a true exemplar of a multiculturalist nation par excellence. The dominant group is still Anglo-Saxon, however, just like in the United States. As far as the largest minority is concerned, the French, there is always a conflict. There is a powerful separatist movement which has been trying to secede but lost in successive referendums. For true pluralism to exist, people of diverse ethnic backgrounds have to live harmoniously in the same space. If there are no tensions among the various groups in Switzerland, Belgium and Canada, it is because, as we have noticed, they live in separate spaces. The equilibrium model is fundamentally flawed because it is not supported by any empirical data.

True pluralist societies lend support to the conflict model. Social unrests, civil wars, separatist movements, nativist reactions, forced removal of individuals to areas far from their homelands, destruction of minority cultures and mass killings are endemic in multiethnic societies. There is a civil war pitting Hutus against Tutsis in Burundi right now which has killed more than 200,000 in the last few years. In Northern Ireland, the war has been going on for a long time between Catholics and Protestants. Belfast is literally a war zone. Separatist movements are operating right now in Sudan, Sri Lanka, India, in the Basque territory, in Chechnya just to name a few. The Chechens want to be independent from the Russians who they see as colonialists or occupiers. In France and Spain, Basques want their own homeland. In Sri Lanka, the Tamils want to secede from the Sinhalese majority. The Muslim Kashmir state wants to separate from the Hindu India. Southern Sudanese are fighting the federal government because it is dominated by the northerners who are Muslims whereas the southerners are Christian or animists. In the early 1960s, more than one million ethnic Ibos died during the Biafra war when they tried to secede from the federal Nigerian government. The Berbers in Algeria are complaining about the Arabization of their language and culture by the Arab majority. This also explains the disintegration of the Soviet Union and the collapse of Yugoslavia and the failed modern states of Liberia, Sierra Leone and Somalia.

Not only are minority groups segregated but they are also sometimes forcibly removed to undesirable areas and hostile environments such as the infamous Trail of Tears, when thousands of Cherokee together with the Seminoles, the Creeks, the Choctaws, and the Chicasaws were relocated to Oklahoma and later this forced relocation became the law of the land, forcing all Native Americans to move to reservations in compliance with the Manifest Destiny doctrine. A similar experience happened to Blacks in South Africa during the apartheid regime. They were forced to move to Bantustans or Homelands which were really unfertile lands that Whites didn't like. The relocation of Tutsi to Nyamata, a tsetse fly infected area by the Parmehutu regime of Gregoire Kayibanda follows the same pattern.

Nativist reactions are increasing in many parts of the world because of the economic downturn. In Malaysia, the government is deporting Indonesians and Filipinos. The current troubles that the West African country Ivory Coast is experiencing right now are due to the current government policies which discriminate and exclude Northerners from participating in the national affairs, accusing them of being aliens. This xenophobic attitude is seen in many European countries where Middle Easterners and African immigrants are being scapegoated for all social ailments. In Uganda under Idi Amin's regime all Indians were expelled and left behind their businesses, farms and properties. A similar fate affected Chinese in the United States in the late 19th century with the 1882 Chinese Exclusion Act when the Chinese were expelled from the United States. During the Great Depression bona fide U.S. citizens of Mexican descent were repatriated (a euphemism for forced mass deportation), leaving behind everything they cherished.

The most extreme behavior in multi-ethnic societies is the total extermination of the minority by the majority, such as the Jewish Holocaust by Nazi Germany, the 1994 Tutsi genocide in Rwanda by the Hutu government, the ethnic cleansings in the Balkans, the Albanian massacres in Kosovo. The massacre in Srebrenka, a Muslim enclave in Serbia by Bosnian Serb troops and Serbian police and the killings in Sarajevo were an attempt by President Slobodan Milosevic to create an enlarged state for Serbs only by driving out non-Serbs. This man's inhumanity to man by the majority is usually rationalized with moral justification by demonizing and dehumanizing the victim. These subordinate groups are not only aliens, they are also believed to be inferior, parasites, sub-humans and responsible for all types of evil. In pluralistic societies, subordinate groups are always denied their basic rights: civil liberties, civil rights, human rights and constitutional rights. The disaffection and disenfranchisement of victimized groups creates tension which oftentimes explodes into violence. It is with the conflict model that the terms *majority*, meaning dominant group, and *minority*, subordinate group, and also the concepts of "us" and "they" find meaning.

Ethnicity and Phenomenological Awareness

Phenomenological awareness is used in Edmund Husserl's sense. Members of the minority and majority groups have to discover this "otherness." A good example which illustrates this view is the newly persecuted minority, namely Arab Americans. Arab Americans were formerly classified among Caucasians and nobody paid attention to them but because of the 9/11 terrorism attacks the situation has changed. In Russia, the Cossacks have recently "discovered" that they are a distinct minority, different from Russians. There are also members of minority groups who distance themselves from their group and join only when a wake-up takes place, such as being treated differently because of specific group membership. Blacks in Brazil, for instance, since they lack this phenomenological awareness and therefore don't show any group solidarity, cannot be described as an ethnicity according to this view. The two most important movements which have put ethnicity at the forefront are the 18th century Enlightenment philosophy of Voltaire, Rousseau and Montesqieu and the 1960s American Civil Rights movement. The genesis of ethnicity requires social consciousness.

Ethnicity and the Existential Otherness

Phenomenology and existentialism are closely linked. The phenomenological awareness is responsible for the awareness of the "us" and "they." The discovery of the existence of the other is a terrible experience. It proves the existentialist credo "Hell is others." This doesn't mean that human beings should let this "absurd world" keep its course. True human beings have a responsibility to keep fighting for equality and social justice even if this life doesn't seem to have meaning.

2. Essentialist and Social Construct Ethnicities

There is a big debate in social sciences as to whether ethnicity is essentialist, that is, natural, biologically based or a social construct, that is, artificial or manmade. Ethnic or racial classification in the United States, South Africa, Brazil and Rwanda would support the social construct thesis. In the United States as far as race is concerned, there are two groups, whites and blacks. A mixed person with 90% white blood and 10% black blood is automatically classified in the black category. There is nothing in between. In South Africa, however, there are three distinct groups, whites, blacks and coloreds. The latter group consists of people with mixed blood between white and black. A colored cannot be white or black. Brazil presents a different situation. It has the fifth largest population in the world with 174 million people, coming after China, India, United States and Indonesia. It also has the second largest black population in the world, around 80 million, after Nigeria which counts 120 million. The latest census, however, found out that there are only 6% of the population who recognize themselves as blacks. This is due to the practice of the Brazilian government of classifying people according to the degree of skin color from the lightest to the darkest. There are around 40 categories. In the conflict model of ethnicity, black ethnicity doesn't exist in Brazil since there is lack of consciousness and black group solidarity. In Rwanda, ethnicity is determined by the father. A child from a Tutsi father and a Hutu mother is a Tutsi and a child from a Hutu father and a Tutsi mother, even if she comes from the highest aristocracy, is a Hutu. Since Hutu and Tutsi share the same language and culture, and had a very high intermarriage rate, it was possible for a Tutsi to change his or her identity when he or she moved to an area where people didn't know who the parents were. It is the reason why during the anti-Tutsi regimes from 1959 to 1994, to enforce the discrimination policies, everybody in the country had to carry an identity card which mentioned whether the ID carrier was a Hutu or a Tutsi. It is also important to note that this type of categorization has been ingrained in Rwandans' minds. When asked about their ancestry and genealogy the majority know only about their father's side. This is the opposite of what happens among the Seneca and some other Iroquois groups. It is the mother who determines ethnicity. This classification, as examples eloquently indicate, seems to be arbitrary and is indeed socially constructed.

The majority of ethnic groups, however, are natural because members of the group share the same culture, the same history, the same language. They have characteristics which set them apart from other groups. The Gypsies in Europe are different from other Europeans, the Kikuyu in Kenya are different the Luya. The Xhosa in South Africa are different from the Zulu. The Hopi are not the same as the Navajo. Essentialism as a theory was very popular in the 1970s in many social sciences such as feminist theory, took the back seat in the 1980s in favor of social construct, but came back in the 1990s. The existence of socially constructed ethnicity doesn't preclude the existence of an essentialist ethnicity, as the existence of genetically engineered crops doesn't preclude the existence of natural ones. Essentialism versus social construction is the same old debate under different names, namely culture versus nurture, as to whether concepts, perception and social behavior are innate, biologically programmed or are shaped by culture and environment. Essentialism is back in full force and has been resurrected, among many others, by the MIT linguist Steven Pinker in his latest book *The Blank Slate and the Modern Denial of Human Nature*. Theories like ideologies sometimes blind the practitioners by preventing them from seeing the whole picture. The Balkanization of academic theories does not advance a true intellectual debate.

3. The Genesis of Ethnicity

Ethnicity or the creation of a multi-ethnic state comes from both the movement of space and movement of the people. Traditional states such as city-states or tribes were homogeneous and believed in a common mythical ancestry. However, modern nation-states have been created through space expansion. This expansion occurs either through annexation using brutal force or federation through mutual agreement. Those whose territory has been annexed by force, most of the time become automatically the subordinate group. The United States has used both annexation and federation to be what it is today. Many states joined the thirteen colonies through federation but the southwestern states were acquired by force when Mexico was forced to sign the Treaty of Guadalupe Hidalgo in 1848 making californios, nuevos mexicanos, tejanos a subordinate group in their native land. In modern times, Tanzania was formed after both Tanganyika and the Indian Ocean island, Zanzibar, became independent. Nation-building creates ethnicity because people from different cultural, religious, linguistic or racial backgrounds start sharing the same space for the first time.

In the 19th century, the factor mostly responsible for the creation of multi-ethnic states was colonialism. The purpose of colonialism is the maximum exploitation of both natural and human resources of the conquered nations. Colonialists sometimes brought with them indentured workers to help in this exploitation. These indentured workers were initially sojourners but later on settled permanently thus becoming another minority in the new land. Examples of indentured workers who became settlers are Indians in Fiji and the West Indies.

The reason why post-independence African nations have ethnic conflicts is because many states were created artificially without respect to geographical, national, linguistic, historical and cultural boundaries. In the 1885-6 Berlin Conference on the Partition of Africa, European powers carved the map of Africa according to their own colonialists' interests thus separating families and destroying nations and for the first time dumping together people from different nationalities. For instance, the kingdom of Congo was divided into three parts one going to the Portuguese (Angola), another to the Belgians (Democratic Republic of Congo) and the other one to the French (Republic of Congo). The Massai saw themselves separated into groups, one group being annexed to Kenya and another one to Tanzania. Some nations ceased to exist altogether, such as the Kurds. They have now become minorities in countries that they have been attached to: ethnic Kurds in Iran, ethnic Kurds in Turkey and ethnic Kurds in Iraq. Migrant states such as the United States, Australia and New Zealand reduced the indigenous people to an invisible minority.

Because of the end of the cold war, there are many instabilities in developing countries. This situation has created a new wave of economical and political refugees who automatically become minorities in the host countries where they become targets of xenophobic treatment.

4. Race, Class, Clan, Nationality and Ethnicity

In a pluralistic society, a racial group, a class, a clan, a religious or national group can be either a minority or majority, thus dominant or subordinate.

It is sometimes difficult in the conflict model to draw the line between ethnicity and these other types of social groups. Although some scientists dispute the existence of race, race is a reality. They do so in reaction to those who espouse a racist ideology, the belief in the superiority of certain races and the inferiority of others. It is true that pure races are hard to find because of a very high racial degree of inter-group mixture but this doesn't erase its presence. The fact that certain types of diseases target specific groups is already evidence of the existence of race. Skin color, hair texture differentiate certain groups from others. Five different groups are usually recognized, namely Caucasians (Europeans, North Africans, Middle Easterners and Indians), Blacks (Sub-Sahara Africa), Asians, Pacific Islanders and Native Americans.

Class is defined as a social group which shares the same values and lifestyles. It is characterized by either social demotion or promotion. There is a possibility of both horizontal and vertical mobility, being able to be elevated to a higher social status and moving to better neighborhoods, being accepted into private clubs and facing less discrimination and segregation.

It also happens that in pluralistic societies, a great number of the minority groups belong to the low class and the majority of the upper class belong to the dominant group. In Latin American countries such as Honduras, Guatemala, El Salvador, the lowest class found at the bottom of the society is the landless and jobless Indians. In the U.S. the majority of Blacks, Mexican Americans and Asian Americans live in the inner city slums.

Caste is an inherited social status, there is no possibility of mobility or moving out, as illustrated by Burachumin of Japan and the Untouchables of India. The term caste is usually used to refer to the low caste, the pariahs of the society. These people are usually marginalized, ostracized, do the dirty work that other citizens refuse to do and are totally dehumanized. In both India and Japan, they are indeed "untouchables." They cannot mix with other groups. Marrying them is a social demotion. A caste is clearly a social construct since there are no distinctive physical, cultural or behavioral features which distinguish caste members from the mainstream society.

A clan is a social organization found mostly in traditional societies. Its formal features are totems and taboos. The totems in many societies which have clans are mostly birds and animals. Rwanda has around 14 clans and some of the totems are frogs, royal cranes, wagtails, hyenas, etc. (Kimenyi, 1988).

Among the Ndebele of Zimbabwe, some of the totems are "the monkey," "the leopard," "the crocodile." It is the same with Native Americans as well—where we find the "fox" clan, the "crow" clan, "eagle" clan, the "turtle" clan, etc. There are certain things that clan members are not allowed to do such as eating certain types of foods. A clan member cannot kill and eat the meat of the animal which is his or her totem. There are certain groups that they cannot marry from, either. Strict rules of endogamy and exogamy exist in those societies.

Ethnicity is, as examples show, connected to some of these other social groups. In many parts of the world, people are being persecuted because they are a religious minority, as in Northern Ireland for Catholics, Muslims in India, Shiite Muslims in Iraq by the ruling minority Sunni Muslims. Women are discriminated against in many parts of the world; like other minorities they are victims of glass ceilings and glass walls, these invisible barriers which prevent them from getting social promotion or preventing them from having access to private clubs or other areas. The French revolution, the Bolshevik revolution and the Cambodia "killing fields" by the Khmer Rouge led by Pol Pot were class conflicts. The French peasants didn't only kill the royal family but the whole French aristocracy. The Bolshevik revolution massacred the czar's family and the upper class as well. In Cambodia, Pol Pot targeted the whole bourgeoisie or elite. It is possible for some individuals to belong to more than one of these oppressed and powerless groups. Since women regardless of class, race, ethnicity, religion, are already discriminated against in many societies, those who belong to the ethnic minority are being victimized twice. This type of treatment is referred to as double-jeopardy, triple-jeopardy or multiple jeopardy.

5. The Illusion of Ethnic Homogeneity

The majority always has a tendency to lump together minority groups who are not related in any way whether it be culture, language or nationality. This ignorance is due to the lack of interest in knowing who these subordinate groups truly are because they are seen as irrelevant in social, economic and political national affairs because of their marginal status. This essay will limit itself to Asian Americans and Native Americans as examples, only for illustration purposes.

Asian Americans are labeled the model minority by the media and politicians because unlike other minorities, they are seen as very close to the majority by their work ethic, family values, success in business and education and as law-abiding citizens. Far from being a compliment, not only is this perception a myth, a distortion of the reality, but it is also harmful to this group because the majority fails to recognize and acknowledge problems rampant in the Asian communities. Romanticized Chinatowns are like other ethnic ghettos, where misery and crimes are found. This assertion also implies that Asian Americans are the same. The truth of the matter is that it is the most diverse group second only to Native Americans. Take the countries of Indonesia and the Philippines, for instance. Their respective nationals were already multi-ethnic before migrating to the United States. Indonesia, the largest archipelago in the world with around 1400 islands, is very diverse linguistically and culturally. The Philippines, another archipelago with approximately 700 islands also has many ethnic groups, languages and cultures. Thus the Asian-American diversity is seen in national origin, race, ethnicity, class, language, religion, experience here in the United States and period and purpose of migration. Asian Americans are separated by religion, namely Buddhism, Shintoism, Islam, Catholicism and animism. The oldest immigrants, the Chinese, came from rural areas and were sojourners. They initially came to make money and go home. The immigrants who come in the 1960s after the passage of the 1965 Immigration and Naturalization Act were mostly middle class who came as university students or businessmen whereas the 1970s immigrants, the "boat people" were political refugees from Laos and Cambodia. The majority were poor and illiterate.

The difficulty in finding the right term to refer to Native Americans is already an indication that we are dealing with a very heterogeneous group. The only thing that Native Americans have in common is the shared existential experience, being uprooted, degraded, humiliated, alienated and being the only indigenous people of the American continent. They are a very diverse group, with different histories, cultures, languages and nationalities. Although they numbered 1.9 million people in the 1990s census, they were at least more than 10 million when Whites came to this country. The dramatic reduction which is attributed to diseases for which they didn't have any immunity with their contact with Europeans, was definitely due to genocide. There are now 558 federally recognized Indian tribes. Scientists classify them into seven geo-cultural groups, namely the Arctic Indians, the Subarctic Indians, Northwest Indians, Plateau Indians, Great Basin Indians, Plains Indians, Northeast Indians, Southeast Indians, Southwest Indians, Pacific Indians and California Indians. The Arctic Indians (Inuit and Aleut) are found in Canada and are physically and culturally different from the other groups. Northwestern Coast Indians (*Chinook, Makah, Nookta, Kwakiutl, Haida, Tlingit, Shimshian*, etc.) were known for their totem poles, woodwork and sophisticated fishing techniques. The Subarctic Indians (*Carrier, Chipewyan, Cutchin, Cree, Mountagnais, Naskapi, Beothuk*) also found mostly in Canada. Plateau Indians: *Spokan, Yakama, Walla Walla, Klamath, Modoc, Nez Perce* lived mostly on fish. Great Basin Indians such as the *Paiute, Ute, Shoshone, Washoe, Chemehuevi* and *Bannock* lived in a poor area unsuitable for farming and animal domestication and therefore subsisted on wild fruits and small animals. Plains Indians such as the *Sioux* (*Dakota, Lakota, Nakota*), *Osage, Omaha, Apache, Comanche, Cheyene, Arapaho, Blackfoot,* . . . are probably the most known in the mainstream society because of Hollywood with their horse-riding mastery and their relation with the Plains icon, the buffalo.

The Northeastern Indians were sedentary. These include, among others, the *Pequot, Chippewa, Illinois, Ottawa, Miami, Menominee, Massachusetts, Winnebago, Shawnee, Algonkin, Narragansett, Mahican* and the famous League of Six Nations: *Cayuga, Seneca, Mohawk, Onondaga, Oneida,* and *Tuscarora*, from whom the United States borrowed the concept of federation and representative government. The Southeast Indians were very much advanced in agriculture. Among them are found the five Civilized Nations: *the Cherokees, the Chicasaws, the Choctaws, the Creeks,* and *the Seminoles* as well as other groups such as *Alabama, Apalachee, Caddo, Calusa, Catawba, Coushatta,* and *Yamasee*. Indians in the Southwest had also developed farming techniques and had domesticated many crops and animals. Their architecture was also spectacular. These are *Apache, Hopi, Mojave, Navajo, Pueblos, Yaqui, Zuni*. California or Pacific Coast Indians were hunter gatherers. These include

Hupa, Chumah, Pomo, Yahi, Shasta, Salinas, Diegueno, Maidu, Miwok, Wintun, Yokuts, and *Mission Indians.*

Like other nations, Native Americans also had different political systems, different social organizations, waged wars against each other, signed treaties and many didn't have contacts with others because the distance, lack of communication and means of contact were very much limited at that time. To call this diverse group one ethnic group is clearly an aberration and one fails to see interethnic problems that exist between these groups. The Navajos and Hopis, for example, are always having disputes over land and respective boundaries. This ignorance is due to the fact that ethnicity is defined from the top, the distance that exists between the dominant and the subordinate group and the lack of interaction between the majority and the minority.

6. Identity Shift

Ethnic identity shift occurs because of shift of space boundaries or because of paradigm shift. To illustrate the former, I will use myself as an example.

In Rwanda, when I was there before the extermination of my family in the 1994 Tutsi genocide, I was known as a Tutsi in my home village, but in the capital Kigali, I was recognized as either a southerner or a Butarean (from Butare prefecture). During Habyarimana's regime, southern Hutus were also subjects of discrimination. Their Hùtuism was being questioned. They were believed to have a lot of Tutsi blood. When I am in any African capital such as Kampala, Nairobi, Bamako, Dakar, and so on, for the first time I am called Rwandan. Nobody knows or cares about my ethnicity. All Rwandans living in other African countries are called ethnic Rwandans. Hutus and Tutsi mix freely. In Europe, however, when I am in Paris, Rome, London, Brussels or Frankfort, I became African. Nobody cares to know about my nationality. It is in the U.S. that I become Black. This observation supports the idea that indeed ethnicity has to do with group solidarity because of shared experience in a hostile environment.

Paradigm shifts and government policies also affect the changing definition and understanding of ethnicity. If African-Americans are so labeled today, it is the consciousness that they are indeed connected to their motherland. The previous successive names, namely Negroes, Coloreds, Blacks and Afro-Americans, reflected the attitudes of the time. During the Civil Rights movement, Mexicans were divided into two camps, Mexican Americans and Chicanos. Chicanos wanted to reclaim their identity whereas Mexican Americans wanted to assimilate. Today there is a movement to make all of them Hispanics. There was a time in the United States when Jews, Irish and Italians were treated as non-whites. They were discriminated against because they represented the urban underclass. But because of attitude change and the move from their ethnic enclaves and the subsequent gentrification of housing, they have now melted into and been accepted into mainstream white society.

Society's systemic changes such as family structure, political regime, religion, economic system, education, etc., affect this ethnic dynamism. Minority status doesn't differ from colonialism, either. Colonized people and minority groups share the fact that they cannot determine their destiny. Groups which find themselves in this type of situation are denied their right to be who they want to be. They are even stripped of their names, like in the case of Native Americans who had to abandon their names and were given European names. Even names of their leaders and heroes such as Sitting Bull, Crazy Horse, Red Cloud, Black Hawk are obviously calques, loan-translations from Native American languages. It is the reason why former European colonies are redefining their identities and renaming their post-colonial countries after their pre-colonial names. The giant Central African nation, the Democratic Republic of Congo's capital, Kinshasa, was called Leopoldville, after the name of Leopold, the Belgian king who held it as a personal property. Other Congolese towns such as Kisangani, Lubumbashi were also named after Europeans, Stanleyville and Elizabethville, respectively. This led the late dictator Mobutu Sese Seko, the ruler of Congo, to introduce the policies of *authenticity*: the abolition of Christian European names. All Congolese wherever they happened to be had to get rid of their European names and go back to African names. Under the colonial Belgian rule, the Rwandan university town of Butare was called Astrida, a Belgian queen. The country of Burundi became Urundi and its capital Bujumbura became Usumbura. The Southern African countries, Zimbabwe and Zambia, were called Southern Rhodesia and Northern Rhodesia, respectively after Cecil Rhodes, who became a billionaire by monopolizing the exploitation of gold and diamonds of these countries. There are two polar opposite forces at work. The dominant group always wants to define the subordinate group whereas the minorities keep redefining and reinventing themselves.

7. Conclusion

Historical and comparative studies show that there is no homogeneous society. This notion seems to be a utopia. Social harmony is not found anywhere among pluralistic societies. As it has been illustrated in this article, ethnicity overlaps with other social categorizations especially with gender, class and caste because members of these groups inherit the subordinate status and have difficulty moving out of it.

Ethnicity, like culture, to which it is symbiotically related, is not static. It is dynamic, ever changing. The change is not necessarily Darwinian, that is evolutionary, linear and unidirectional. It can also be cyclic. The Jewish Holocaust was planned and executed in a country which was most advanced scientifically, intellectually and artistically. The architects of the 1994 Tutsi genocide in Rwanda were graduates of some the best universities of Europe and North America.

In-group changes, mainstream social trends and transformations and revolving-door paradigm shifts, such as the move from melting pot to multiculturalism, shape and define ethnicity. The best way to understand it, define it and explain it is through a panchronic approach instead of studying it either diachronically or synchronically like a specimen in a laboratory, frozen in space and time. Like language and culture, ethnicity is always emerging, real but ideal, looking for its teleological structure and function.

The dichotomy between essentialism or nature versus social construction or nurture is not necessary. The whole phenomenon has to be looked at holistically to be able to provide a satisfactory account.

References

Hochschild, Adam. 1998. *King Leopold's Ghost: A Story of Greed, Terror and Heroism in Colonial Africa.* Houghton Mifflin.

Kimenyi, Alexandre. 1989. *Kinyarwanda and Kirundi Names: A Semiolinguistic Analysis of Bantu Onomastics.* Newiston: New York. The Edwin Mellen Press.

Kimenyi, Alexandre and Otis L. Scott, eds. 2001. *Anatomy of Genocide: State-Sponsored Mass Killings in the 20th Century.* Newiston: New York. The Edwin Mellen Press.

Lind, Michael. 1995. *The Next American Nation: The New Nationalism and the Fourth American Revolution.*

Pinker, Steven. 2002. *The Blank Slate: The Modern Denial of Human Nature.* Viking.

Wilson, O. Edward. 1980. *Sociobiology.*

Wynter E. Leon. 2002. *American Skin, Pop Culture and the End of White America.* Crown Publishers.

4

Kill Whitey

Michael Moore

I don't know what it is, but every time I see a white guy walking toward me, I tense up. My heart starts racing, and I immediately begin to look for an escape route and a means to defend myself. I kick myself for even being in this part of town after dark. Didn't I notice the suspicious gangs of white people lurking on every street corner, drinking Starbucks and wearing their gang colors of Gap Turquoise or J. Crew Mauve? What an *idiot!* Now the white person is coming closer, closer—and then—*whew!* He walks by without harming me, and I breathe a sigh of relief.

White people scare the crap out of me. This may be hard for you to understand—considering that I *am* white—but then again, my color gives me a certain insight. For instance, I find *myself* pretty scary a lot of the time, so I know what I'm talking about. You can take my word for it: if you find yourself suddenly surrounded by white people, you better watch out. *Anything* can happen.

As white people, we've been lulled into thinking it's safe to be around other white people. We've been taught since birth that it's the people of that *other color* we need to fear. *They're* the ones who'll slit your throat!

Yet as I look back on my life, a strange but unmistakable pattern seems to emerge. *Every* person who has ever harmed me in my lifetime—the boss who fired me, the teacher who flunked me, the principal who punished me, the kid who hit me in the eye with a rock, the other kid who shot me with his BB gun, the executive who didn't renew *TV Nation*, the guy who was stalking me for three years, the accountant who double-paid my taxes, the drunk who smashed into me, the burglar who stole my stereo, the contractor who overcharged me, the girlfriend who left me, the next girlfriend who left even sooner, the pilot of the plane I was on who hit a truck on the runway (he probably hadn't eaten in days), the other pilot who decided to fly through a tornado, the person in the office who stole checks from my checkbook and wrote them out to himself for a total of $16,000—every one of these individuals has been a white person! Coincidence? I think not!

I have never been attacked by a black person, never been evicted by a black person, never had my security deposit ripped off by a black landlord, never *had* a black landlord, never had a meeting at a Hollywood studio with a black executive in charge, never seen a black agent at the film/TV agency that used to represent me, never had a black person deny my child the college of her choice, never been puked on by a black teenager at a Mötly Crüe concert, never been pulled over by a black cop, never been sold a lemon by a black car salesman, never *seen* a black car salesman, never had a black person deny me a bank loan, never had a black person say, "We're going to eliminate ten thousand jobs here—have a nice day!"

I don't think I'm the only white guy who can make these claims. Every mean word, every cruel act, every bit of pain and suffering in my life has had a Caucasian face attached to it.

So, um, why is it exactly that I should be afraid of black people?

I look around at the world I live in—and, folks, I hate to tell tales out of school, but it's not the African-Americans who have made this planet such a pitiful, scary place to inhabit. Recently a headline on the front page of the Science section of the *New York Times* asked the question "Who Built the H-Bomb?" The article went on to discuss a dispute that has arisen between the men who claim credit for making the first bomb. Frankly, I could have cared less— because I already know the only pertinent answer: "IT WAS A WHITE GUY!" No black guy ever built or used a bomb designed to wipe out hordes of innocent people, whether in Oklahoma City, Columbine, or Hiroshima.

No, my friends, it's *always* the white guy. Let's go to the tote board.

- Who gave us the black plague? A white guy.
- Who invented PBC, PVC, PBB, and a host of chemicals that are killing us? White guys.
- Who has started every war America has been in? White men.
- Who is responsible for the programming on FOX? White men.
- Who invented the punch card ballot? A white man.
- Whose idea was it to pollute the world with the internal combustion engine? Whitey, that's who.
- The Holocaust? That guy really gave white people a bad name (that's why we prefer to call him a Nazi and his little helpers Germans).
- The genocide of Native Americans? White man.
- Slavery? Whitey!

- So far in 2001, American companies have laid off over 700,000 people. Who ordered the layoffs? White CEOs.
- Who keeps bumping me off the Internet? Some friggin' white guy, and if I find him, he's a dead white guy.

You name the problem, the disease, the human suffering, or the abject misery visited upon millions, and I'll bet you ten bucks I can put a white face on it faster than you can name the members of 'N Sync.

And yet when I turn on the news each night, what do I see again and again? *Black* men alleged to be killing, raping, mugging, stabbing, gangbanging, looting, rioting, selling drugs, pimping, ho-ing, having too many babies, dropping babies from tenement windows, fatherless, motherless, Godless, penniless. "The suspect is described as a black male . . . the suspect is described as a black male . . . THE SUSPECT IS DESCRIBED AS A BLACK MALE . . ." No matter what city I'm in, the news is always the same, the suspect always the same unidentified black male. I'm in Atlanta tonight, and I swear the police sketch of the black male suspect on TV looks just like the black male suspect I saw on the news *last* night in Denver and the night before in L.A. In every sketch he's frowning, he's menacing—and he's wearing the same knit cap! Is it possible that it's the same black guy committing every crime in America?

I believe we've become so used to this image of the black man as predator that we are forever ruined by this brainwashing. In my first film, *Roger & Me*, a white woman on Social Security clubs a bunny rabbit to death so that she can sell him as "meat" instead of as a pet. I wish I had a nickel for every time in the last ten years someone has come up to me and told me how "horrified" and "shocked" they were when they saw that "poor little cute bunny" bonked on the head. The scene, they say, made them physically sick. Some had to turn away or leave the theater. Many wondered why I would include such a scene. The Motion Picture Association of America (MPAA) gave *Roger & Me* an R rating in response to that rabbit killing (which compelled *60 Minutes* to do a story on the stupidity of the rating system). Teachers write me and say they have to edit that part out of the film so they won't get in trouble for showing my movie to their students.

But less than two minutes after the bunny lady does her deed, I included footage of a scene in which the police in Flint opened fire and shot a black man who was wearing a Superman cape and holding a plastic toy gun. Not once—not *ever*—has anyone said to me, "I can't believe you showed a black man being shot in your movie! How horrible! How disgusting! I couldn't sleep for weeks." After all, he was just a black man, not a cute, cuddly bunny. There is no outrage at showing a black man being shot on camera (least of all from the MPAA ratings board, who saw absolutely nothing wrong with that scene).

Why? Because a black man being shot is no longer shocking. Just the opposite—it's *normal*, natural. We've become so accustomed to seeing black men killed—in the movies and on the evening news—that we now accept it as standard operating procedure. *No big deal, just another dead black guy!* That's what blacks do—kill and die. Ho-hum. Pass the butter.

It's odd that, despite the fact that most crimes are committed by whites, black faces are usually attached to what we think of as "crime." Ask any white person who they fear might break into their home or harm them on the street, and if they're honest, they'll admit that the person they have in mind doesn't look much like them. The imaginary criminal in their heads looks like Mookie or Hakim or Kareem, not little freckly-faced Jimmy.

How does the brain process a fear like this, when everything it sees says the opposite? Are white people's brains hardwired to see one thing but believe the opposite because of race? If that's the case, then do all white people suffer from some shared low-grade mental illness? If every time the sun was out it was nice and bright and clear, but your brain told you to stay inside because it definitely looked like a storm was brewing, well, we might encourage you to seek some professional help. Are white people who see black boogeymen around every corner any different?

Obviously, no matter how many times their fellow whites make it clear that the white man is the one to fear, it simply fails to register. Every time you turn on the TV to news of another school shooting, it's always a white kid who's conducting the massacre. Every time they catch a serial killer, it's a crazy white guy. Every time a terrorist blows up a federal building, or a madman gets four hundred people to drink Kool-Aid, or a Beach Boys songwriter casts a spell causing half a dozen nymphets to murder "all the piggies" in the Hollywood Hills, you know it's a member of the white race up to his old tricks.

So why don't we run like hell when we see whitey coming toward us? Why don't we ever greet the Caucasian job applicant with, "Gee, uh, I'm sorry, there aren't any positions available right now"? Why aren't we worried sick about our daughters marrying white guys?

And why isn't Congress trying to ban the scary and offensive lyrics of Johnny Cash ("I shot a man in Reno/just to watch him die"), the Dixie Chicks ("Earl had to die"), or Bruce Springsteen (". . . I killed everything in my path/I can't say that I'm sorry for the things that we done"). Why all the focus on rap lyrics? Why doesn't the media print rap lyrics like these and tell the truth?

I sold bottles of sorrow, then chose poems and novels.

—Wu-Tang Clan

People use yo' brain to gain.

—Ice Cube

A poor single mother on welfare . . . tell me how ya did it.

—Tupac Shakur

I'm trying to change my life, see I don't wanna die a sinner.

—Master P

5

Race, Gender and Social Control: Voices of Imprisoned Native American and White Women

Luana Ross

They keep me at a level here where they can control me. They think if they keep me drugged up all the time, that everything's going to go just dandy. But I've tongued my meds before and went and puked them up. I wasn't thinking straight in my head; I couldn't figure out what was going on. So much has happened; I feel like they already broke me.

(Native Woman Prisoner, Women's Correctional Center)

There is a dearth of empirical data on incarcerated females. Especially neglected in the literature are imprisoned women of color, who represent 60% of the total population of women incarcerated in state prisons (Greenfeld & Minor-Harper, 1991). Whereas imprisoned women of color have been ignored in sociological studies of female criminality (Lewis, 1981; Mann, 1984), the subject of imprisoned Native American women is virtually an unexplored area. There is little systematic research on how women experience prison. The majority of studies on women in prison refer to women as a homogeneous group and ignore the interaction of race, gender, and class. There is scant recognition of special problems women of color may face while incarcerated, thus there is an underlying assumption that all women are equally afflicted.

I conducted the first study of imprisoned Native American women in 1990–1991 (Ross, 1992). The purpose of this study was to give voice to these subgroups of women by describing and defining their experiences as prisoners. One way in which imprisoned women can resist oppression and facilitate social change is by telling their own stories. In the words of bell hooks (1989, p. 43), "oppressed people resist identifying themselves as subjects, by defining their reality, shaping their new identity, naming their history, telling their story." Incarcerated women need to tell their own stories. In this study, I let the women speak for themselves.

Furthermore, I am interested in systems of oppression and issues of equality in Euro-American society. Because our society is stratified by race, class, and gender, different categories of people experience life in unequal ways. Racism, classism, and sexism exist outside prison in Euro-American society. I was interested in how they functioned within a state prison, and how they affected the experiences of incarcerated Native American and white women.

The data suggested that experiences of women incarcerated in Montana's Women's Correctional Center varied according to race and location of confinement. Native women experienced prison differently than white women. Women imprisoned in the general-population building, with medium and minimum security classifications, experienced incarceration differently from those classified as close and maximum, who were confined in the maximum-security unit or isolation cells. Moreover, the study concluded that control was exerted in this prison over the prisoners not only as women, but also as Native Americans. The prisoners experienced multiple forms of control (see the original study for a thorough examination); however, this paper will focus on relationships between prisoners and guards, sexual intimidation, mind-altering drugs, and prisoners' responses to control.

Methodology

This study was designed to focus on women from two different races—Native American and white—who were incarcerated in a state prison located in Montana. A comparison allowed me to examine race as a critical variable. The research design was qualitative using unstructured interviews. Nonparticipant observation, informal conversations with prisoners and staff, and reports and letters from the American Civil Liberties Union (ACLU) were used to supplement data gathered from the interviews. The study focused on the subjective experiences of women in prison. These accounts are useful in that they uncover aspects of social life that had been previously invisible, and interpret social reality from a new point of view. When the experiences of invisible groups are not exposed, their voices are not heard and the status quo is maintained (Collins, 1991). In an interactional exchange with the prisoners, we gained knowledge from each other. I listened to the voices of the imprisoned women—to their own explanations of their lives as prisoners. The stories presented are unique and rare, and they need to be respected and treated as such.

For analysis, I compared the accounts of women on the basis of race/ethnicity, reservation status, length of sentence, location of confinement, and number of children. The sample consisted of a total of 31 participants: 27 imprisoned women—14 Native women out of a total of 17 and 13 white women out of a total of 48. The total population of the prison was sixty-five. The prisoners were questioned concerning: the prison's social environment, their major concerns as imprisoned mothers, and the prison support offered to them as imprisoned mothers. Additionally, I interviewed the prison's warden, the treatment specialist who was the primary counselor, the parenting-class facilitator, and the state social worker who worked with foster and adoptive placements for imprisoned mothers. The prisoners ranged in age from 18 years to 45 years old; the average age was 30.1 years old.

Prisoner Profile

The following is a profile of the incarcerated Native female drawn from the sample: She is 30 years old, single or divorced, with 2 children. The number of living children would be higher, however, several Native women had children who were deceased. Prior to incarceration she was not employed and had an eighth grade education. "Her crime was alcohol- or drug-related and she was convicted of a "male-type" crime (murder, robbery, assault, escape, etc.). The sentence length for Native women ranged from 5–60 years; the average was 19.1 years.

The following is a profile of the incarcerated white female drawn from the sample: She is 30 years old, most likely divorced with 2 to 3 children. She either completed high school or received her GED. If she was employed prior to incarceration, she held a low-level, low-paying position. Her crime was alcohol- or drug-related and she was convicted of a "female-type" crime (bad checks, shoplifting, prostitution, etc.). The sentence length for white women ranged from 5–20 years; the average was 9 years.

Clearly, Native women were given longer sentences. It must be taken into account, however, that they were convicted more for "male-type" crimes (e.g., robbery, assault, etc.) than white women, which could account for longer sentence lengths. Thus, there was a qualitative difference in crime-type. Despite this, sentence length demands investigation because when the crimes were the same, Native women still received longer sentences.

Native women were 25% of the total prison population in a state in which they were approximately 6% of the total state population. Native women were significantly overrepresented in the prison population. A factor that complicates the position of imprisoned Native women is the jurisdictional maze created by the Federal Government. In Montana, all Indian reservations, except one, are subjected to Federal control over criminal matters; the exception is under state control concerning criminal matters. This means that, on all reservations (excluding the one under state control), Natives sentenced to prison are incarcerated in out-of-state Federal prisons; only those arrested on the state-controlled reservation and off the reservation are sent to the state prison. Therefore, it is safe to assume that most Native women in Montana state prison come from one specific reservation or are landless Native Americans. Montana has a relatively large number of landless Natives—descendants of those Natives who refused to sign a treaty and thus were left out when reservations were formed in the state of Montana by the Federal Government.

Next, I will present the concept of social control and how race and gender affected the experiences of imprisoned Native American and white women. I've given the women names to humanize them and, when appropriate, I identify their race.

Social Control in Women's Prisons

Race, gender, and class play critical roles in the responses of both informal and formal agents of control. The use of arrest statistics as evidence of the relative involvement of different social groups has been criticized by both labeling theorists and Marxist theorists, who argue that individuals do not come to the attention of the criminal justice system solely on the basis of their behavior. The definition of behavior as criminal, in addition to the course of action taken in response to it, depends upon contextual features (Kitsuse, 1962). Thus, factors independent of the behavior of the *criminal* individual enter into official statistics. Responses by others to *criminal behaviors* are influenced by expectations regarding race and gender-specific behavior. In this way, the labeling of *criminal behavior* can be seen as a form of social control. Crime is thus defined as such by powerful individuals in American society (Chambliss & Seidman, 1982; Quinney, 1970). Definitions of crime and the criminal justice system operate as systems of social control; and race, gender, and class biases in the criminal justice system operate to put more women of color in prison. Nichole Rafter (1990, p. 157) defines *social control* as "the mechanisms by which powerful groups consciously or unconsciously attempt to restrain and to induce conformity, even assent, among less powerful but nonetheless threatening segments of society."

Rafter (1985, 1990) suggests that extra-legal factors, such as race and gender, influence not only incarceration rates but also prison treatment of women as well. Racism and sexism appear to affect the treatment of people of color and women when they encounter the criminal justice system. *Racism* can be defined as a "system of domination" which contains "a complex of beliefs and attitudes" (Blauner, 1972, p. 112). *Institutional racism* refers to the interaction of the various spheres of social life used to maintain a pattern of oppression (Blauner, 1972). Mechanisms of exclusion are built by Euro-American society to maintain a pattern of subordination. In this way, privilege becomes institutionalized and embedded in informal rules and social positions. This pattern is characterized by its indirect method and by the salience it ascribes to the institutional or structural roles over individual attitudes (Blauner, 1972). *Sexism* can be defined in the same manner; however, rather than race as the crucial factor, gender becomes paramount. Racism and sexism have emerged in the United States as systems of oppression used to control people of color and women.

Prisoner/Guard Relationships
"[A guard] invites it; she entices it, and that's part of her control."

Daily life in women's prisons is somewhat different from that found in male correctional institutions. Incarcerated women, compared to incarcerated men, generally do not present a threat to the staff or fellow prisoners. Given this, and that women's prisons are typically smaller than men's prisons, it is the belief of some scholars that they operate in a less rigid fashion (Bowker, 1981; Giallombardo, 1966; Ward & Kassebaum, 1965). However, Rafter (1985,1990) suggests that, despite the benign appearance of women's prisons there is still strict control of their behavior; and that, indeed, one function of prisons is to control not only crime but also gender.

Two qualitative studies conducted in Scotland (Carlen, 1985; Dobash, Dobash, & Gutteridge, 1986) show that relationships inside the prison—especially the nature of contacts with prison guards—are an important part of the lives of incarcerated women. Many of these incarcerated women feared their relationships with the guards and lived in constant dread of being formally sanctioned for supposed *bad* behavior. In addition, in these studies some women felt that guards purposely picked on certain prisoners. Generally, prison rules are those which do not apply in ordinary life and are exercised with wide discretion to give staff much power and control. In these prisons, there was a tendency to punish women for things that imprisoned men would normally do, such as swearing; and, consequently, women were more closely controlled than men.

The prison staff members most exposed on a continual basis to prisoners confined in Montana's Women's Correctional Center, were the guards. Prisoner/guard relationships, thus, were an important part of the daily lives of the prisoners. The prison employed 21 full- and part-time guards; 7 were male and 14 female. All the guards were white. As argued by Carlen (1985, p. 11), I found the Women's Correctional Center, "organized to respond" to prisoners who did not comply with rules. Indeed, this prison's environment exposed itself as a violent, mean game in which the rules were arbitrarily enforced by those in authority. Many prisoners, Native and white, insisted that the prison rules and regulation manual, which prisoners referred to as "the joke book" was unevenly adhered to by prison staff. The women described an environment in which the enforcement of the rules changed depending upon who was on duty. The prisoners experienced a prison staff that never followed the rules; they claimed that staff made up the rules, hence the joke book label. Moreover, the ACLU's letter to the director of corrections cited inconsistency in staff enforcement of rules and particularly the arbitrary enforcement of the rules associated with multiple write-ups (formal complaint filed by the prison against the prisoners) given to prisoners, and their subsequent removal from the general population to lockup.[1]

In agreement with previous research (Carlen, 1985; Dobash et al., 1986), many women in the Women's Correctional Center lived in fear of the guards and worried constantly about being written-up for *bad behavior*. Concurring with Carlen (1985) and Dobash et al. (1986), in the Women's Correctional Center many women believed the guards purposely picked on them; this was particularly true for the Native women who maintained that, because they were a cohesive group, they were threatening to prison staff.

In a fictional account of incarcerated Euro-American women, Patricia McConnel (1989), who has been in jail several times and in Federal prison, writes about the relationships between the guards and the prisoners. Her experiences echo those of incarcerated women in Scotland (Carlen, 1985; Dobash et al., 1986) and those of incarcerated women in Montana. McConnel details the physical and emotional abuse found in jails and prisons—abuse which McConnel believes is a policy that is approved of throughout the criminal justice system. Furthermore, McConnel relates this kind of cruelty to the subsequent low self-esteem found in many prisoners. In describing a power relationship between prisoner and a guard named Garth, McConnel acknowledges that the following interaction actually happened to her:

> Garth is a specialist at the power/humiliation game. She knows that every instinct in the marrow of my bones is rebelling . . . I've been insubordinate and she can throw me in the hole, and there goes some of my time off for good behavior . . . She's ordering my every movement as if I were a robot. I'm dammed if I do and dammed if I don't. It isn't a decision I can take time to ponder over, and the main thing in my life right now is to get out of here on the earliest possible day If Garth doesn't get my self-respect today she'll get it tomorrow anyway so what's the use? (McConnel, 1989, pp. 180–181)

Regardless of race, women in Montana's prison reported the same belittling experiences from prison guards, that McConnel (1989) described.

Most guards were characterized by prisoners in the Women's Correctional Center as stirring up trouble in the prison:

> [A guard] invites it; she entices it, and that's part of her control. She'll come up to you and you'll be reading the newspaper, and she'll rip it out of your hand. And, if you do anything, you can get written up for it.

Other women described some guards as "evil" and were fearful of them. These women very much felt intimidated by these guards. In the words of one woman,

> and this one officer, the minute she hits the floor [arrives on the job] everybody heads to their rooms because she's just on the prowl. She's like what the Bible describes—the devil as an angry lion ready to pounce on you at any minute. That's the way she is. She's angry about the whole world.

Some prisoners I interviewed experienced guards as petty. For instance, one prisoner said she was issued a write-up for running up the stairs two at a time. Additionally, many prisoners said some guards on occasion engaged them in tedious tasks. For example, Dorine remarked that one guard was "real demeaning." Dorine explained, "She had us moving furniture back there—first you put the table over there, then you put it back over there." Dorine said menial tasks of this sort gave prisoners the feeling that everything they did was wrong. Furthermore, some women said when prisoners did these tasks without getting angry, the guards then became angry. The guards seemed to be deliberately provoking prisoners and perhaps baiting them to justify time in lockup. Dorine offered another example: She stated she and other prisoners had worked for days to get the prison ready for a visit from the state legislators. A guard came in and said the prison was not clean enough; that they needed to work harder. At this point, Dorine "blew it":

> I said [to the guard], "What? What did you say? I've been working my ass off on this place, and now you're telling me after I've done all this for my 50 cent pay today, to get my ass in there and scrub those bathroom walls? I'm not going to do it unless you give me a direct order." I was crying and I said [to the guard], "You can't look at the good that we've done, and say you guys did a good job? You have to pick out the bullshit and say you didn't do enough? You gotta do more? Or you gotta do this or that? Why can't you just once say, 'you did a damn good job.'" I was crying, embarrassed, humiliated. It was like the last straw. The girls looked at me like ooh. I got mad and grabbed the rags and the Purex fell and I said, "Furthermore, they don't give you anything to clean it with; that piss has been on those walls for years, and you give me one bottle of disinfectant!" I got in there and took my anger out on the wall [laugh].

Prisoners realize that if they try to save their self-respect they could possibly end up in maximum security. On the other hand, guards generally do not respect prisoners no matter what they do—even if they comply with prison staff.

One prisoner stated that many male guards were especially hard on women who were assertive because the guards demanded that, as women, they be submissive:

> If anybody that's got a little bit of heart and backbone, as far as projecting that—holy jeez! [The guards will] ride you; they'll make sure your room get shook-down. They'll make sure you get write-ups; they'll follow you around the institution. They'll stand outside your door and listen to what you're talking about.

Some women portrayed guards as "cold." For instance, Joan said when she was first incarcerated she thought she could relate to several guards in a mutually respectful way. It was not long, however, when Joan discovered that she was wrong:

> Another [guard], she violated my trust. I was just hurt the other night; she discounted me. I was talking with her, and then she got a phone call and I sat there for about 10 minutes. She was still on the phone and she says, "Oh, you can go now." It was like, "goodbye, and I think we will keep on the basis that we're on—cop and inmate. You be the cop that you are and watch me wax my floors when I get extra duty, and you be the cold one." I put her on a pedestal.

All prisoners described only one guard as "respectful," "humorous," and a "good Christian man." They claimed he would write-up prisoners for infractions but in a "respectful" and consistent way; and, in turn, they respected him for his behavior. Several guards, generally lower-ranked, were described by prisoners as "okay" or "nice" and "respectful." Joan stated that there were two guards that she felt she could talk to; nonetheless, she knew she had to manipulate them in order to be heard. For example, one night when Joan was too stressed out to perform her in-house job, she asked the guard for time-out in the gym:

> [I'll tell the guard] "I'm so glad you're on." I will butter them up so much after they give me something. I will thank them, "Thank you from the bottom of my heart" because I feel it. It's the truth—if they give you something be thankful for it . . . hang onto them and praise them because otherwise if you say it was something little—no, you'd better expect that it is one of the big things.

The preceding quotation describes the deference required of Joan in order to get something she desperately needed. Although Joan told me the guard was "good," she was still being manipulated by the guard and she definitely learned how to play the game, which included stereotypic ladylike behavior—one of deferring. Moreover, it is descriptive of an emotionally abusive relationship in which the prisoner was forced to beg for a favor and to be thankful for it when it was delivered. Even the "good" guards were aware of the us/them attitude that existed in this prison. The strict separation conclusively divided guard and prisoner, and the line was not to be crossed. Hence, prisoners experienced that they were generally discounted by guards and not treated with the respect human beings deserve.

Previous work (Kruttschnitt, 1983) suggests that the race of the prisoner affects treatment by prison staff. Native women in this prison claimed race influenced the white guards' treatment of them. For example, Agnes, a Native woman, told me that the prison's administration had pegged her as a *troublemaker* and, because of this, most guards treated her harshly. Agnes viewed both the labeling and subsequent treatment as racist. Agnes said that some guards purposely baited her in order to lock her up in maximum security. Furthermore, Agnes stated the guards were alarmed that she might be affiliated with legal groups, since she had been corresponding with the state's ACLU. Agnes had been documenting the prison's treatment of Native prisoners and sending the information to the ACLU. This proved threatening to the prison. According to Agnes,

> some of the officers go through my mail to see if I'm getting any kind of mail from Native American groups—who's corresponding with me. I don't know what they're afraid of. Why are they so afraid to address these issues? What scares them? What's so threatening about it?

Agnes had written multiple letters to Native American newspapers and organizations expressing the negative treatment Native women were receiving in this prison. She described the prison's reaction to her:

So, therefore, I was labeled a radical; like I discriminate against white people. And, of course, they don't even understand that term, yet they hear someone else say it so they say it. They say I'm prejudiced in some ways because I want to help the Native American.

The treatment specialist had warned me about Agnes, whom she described as "a manipulator—even the Indian women hate her" and as one who "hates white people." Agnes felt it odd that she was labeled as a *racist*: "I mean, they call me a *racist* and here I am in a white prison, run by white people, based on white values."

Other Native women wrote letters to local newspapers criticizing the prison system and offering cost-effective alternatives to imprisonment and to existing prison conditions. These women declared they were subsequently perceived as troublemakers by prison staff, and thus treated harshly. Dorine, who had written several letters to newspapers, said the treatment specialist told her to "either knock it off or you're going to be here for the rest of your life." The above examples illustrate the threatening environment produced by prison staff, including the guards, when Native prisoners were assertive and tried to help other Native prisoners.

Sexual Intimidation
". . . he was touching her and he's not supposed to."

Rafter (1985, 1990) argues that another way to control incarcerated women is through sexual abuse. Incarcerated women of all races have been victims of this kind of violence. All women that I interviewed, both Native and white, discussed being sexually intimidated by male guards. They all related this specifically to male guards on night duty "peeking" at them in their room when they were undressing for bed. Regular bed checks were a part of prison policy and were to occur at scheduled times. Nevertheless, prisoners maintained that some guards would come early and surprise the prisoners. This was alarming to the women because most of them would be in the middle of undressing and not fully clothed. Many white women had an attitude very different from that of Native women concerning this violation. White prisoners would generally say, "Oh, so what—if he wants a show, let him look. I ain't got nothing anyway." Although both Native and white women felt sexually intimidated, Native prisoners were generally modest and had a particularly difficult time coping with this violation. Their solution was to undress in the closet and many wore sweatpants and T-shirts to bed. Prisoners also reported that, in one of the bathrooms, there was a window with no curtain and some male officers frequently watched them when they were sitting on the toilet. Again, an unneeded stressful situation was created—a situation that smacked of control and Peeping Tomism.

All prisoners mentioned an incident that had recently taken place regarding sexual intimidation. Whereas several prisoners, both Native and white, maintained that the prisoner enticed the guard and was a willing participant, other prisoners were incensed that it had occurred at all. Delphina witnessed this sexual assault: "He [the guard] just put his hands all over her; he kissed her. He didn't screw her or whatever you call it, but he was touching her and he's not supposed to."

Delphina said this particular guard was either fondling prisoners or "roughing them up."

>*He's really rough with us girls. He'll either completely ignore you, like I said to him, "Can I ask you a favor?" He says, "No, you're not going to ask me nothing all night long." So, I can't. So, I'm sitting back here in a cell all by myself, and he's abusing girls—like kicking them, pulling their hair. Then when you say something to him, he'll say, "Well, I had to do it to defend myself." Jesus, come on. We're girls—there's no reason for him to do that to us.*

The guard was found not guilty of sexual assault by an investigative team from outside the prison. The prisoner involved was represented by a local county attorney. Several days after the investigation was completed, this prisoner was transferred to maximum security. Prisoners said prison staff argued she was not moved because she filed charges against this guard, but for other reasons. Several prisoners, however, said they knew she was transferred to maximum security specifically because she filed charges. In Delphina's words, "She's sitting in max. We all know where that stems from; we're not stupid. We know that their reasons for max are not the reasons they give!" Whereas the guard had his hands slapped for his behavior, the prisoner was punished by lockup in maximum security. Surely, this punishment for reporting the guard's behavior will deter any prisoners from pressing charges against guards or prison staff for sexually assaulting or intimidating them.

The case of Joan Little, an African American who killed a white jailer who attempted to rape her, is not typical. Although molestation by guards may be typical, few incarcerated women kill their attackers (Feinman, 1986). Rural jails in the southern part of the U.S. are known to be "target for sexual abuse" of incarcerated women, especially African American women (Sims, 1976, p. 139). African American women, as well as other women of color, are targets for sexual abuse because of racist attitudes. From a study conducted in Great Britain (Hall, 1985), a statement by an African American woman depicts a racist stereotypic image and the subsequent treatment with which many women of color must contend:

>*There's a particular fear of white men that Black girls grow up with. We know they think we're hot, sexual animals, that we're always available. It goes back to slavery. What they think about us sexually is a part of the racism. (Hall, 1985, p. 48)*

While none of the white women discussed being raped while incarcerated, two Native women said they were raped in jail by white, male jailers. One of the women, Agnes, was raped twice by the same jailer. This occurred just prior to her conviction and subsequent transfer to prison. The other woman, Dorine, was raped several years ago when she was in a county jail. Both women maintained that the rapes happened because they were Native American. Although Dorine decided to eventually bring her rapist to the attention of the authorities, Agnes was intimidated by the criminal justice system and only wanted to process her rape emotionally, not legally. Agnes's attorney told her not to press charges against the jailer because she had "slept with" many men and was "no angel." Furthermore, Agnes said that, because she was raped as a child and then later as an adult in jail, the sexual intimidation which occurred in this prison sickened her.

Several prisoners, both Native and white, mentioned that when the prison had a smaller population, prisoners would trade sex with guards for marijuana and alcohol. Agnes agreed this had happened but insisted only white women prisoners were involved in that activity with guards. Citing cultural differences she explained:

> To me it's a violation of your being. I guess it's just a different type of raising. With these white women sitting here, you know probably because they roamed the streets so many years, it doesn't bother them—they've become immune to it.

When I asked the warden what the most common issue was for prisoners, without hesitation he announced, "sexual abuse." Both he and the treatment specialist estimated that 90% of the prisoner population suffered from sexual abuse. That some male guards sexually intimidated prisoners is, therefore, paramount. These women did not feel safe with male guards "lurking" around the halls at night and possibly looking into their rooms. This clearly created a stressful situation for all prisoners, but possibly affected those who had been sexually abused more significantly.

Medication as Control
"They keep me at a level where they can control me."

Studies in the U.S. indicate that incarcerated women are more heavily medicated than incarcerated men (Resnik & Shaw, 1980). By prescribing drugs, many women may become addicted to the medication thus compounding their problems—especially if they came into prison with addiction problems. It has been argued that there is a sexist bias to psychiatric diagnoses in the criminal justice system (Smart, 1976). The basic assumption is that women are more vulnerable to emotional disturbances and thus imprisoned females require more psychiatric treatment services (especially psychotropic drugs). And, in some cases, this has led to women serving longer sentences so that they will have time to *benefit* from the treatment (Haft, 1980). A study conducted in a women's prison (Carlen, 1985) found that the drugs psychiatrists prescribe actually can threaten a prisoner's survival. These drugs were perceived by some imprisoned women as a way to control them. Furthermore, some women experienced negative side effects from the drugs, such as weight gain and not being able to think clearly—or what Pat Carlen (1985, p. 160) called being reduced to "zombies."

The Women's Correctional Center had a contract with a doctor from the nearby mental institution, but had a nurse on staff full-time (5 days a week). Additionally, the prison employed one psychologist, who worked in the prison 5 1/2 hours per week, and a psychiatrist who was retained by the prison for 3 hours per week. The prisoners called the psychiatrist "Dr. Feel Good" due to the amount of mind-altering drugs he prescribed to prisoners.

Prescription medications and over-the-counter remedies were obtained from the nurse or guards. Prisoners alleged that medication and mind-altering drugs, prescribed by the psychiatrist, were given to the wrong prisoners by unqualified guards dispensing medication. When asked about health care, a Native women revealed the following: "When I got sick, I couldn't get them to do anything. I didn't know what was happening. They ended up giving me somebody else's meds." And, when asked if the prison simply made a mistake, she replied:

> *No! They knew what they were doing; it was to make me numb. And, they said that they called the doctor and he told me to take them, but I don't like to take things unless I hear it from the doctor.*

In the Women's Correctional Center, women complained not only about the large number of prisoners receiving prescribed mind-altering medications, but that they were given to the wrong prisoners. This was confirmed by a report issued by the ACLU. Although some prisoners were worried that this would compound their addiction problems, other were more concerned that, as the Carlen (1985) study indicated, this was a way to control and thus break prisoners. The idea of being broken, according to prisoners in the Women's Correctional Center, was the process of control used by the prison to produce compliant women or model prisoners. Part of this process was humiliation, lowering self-esteem, multiple times in lockup, and mind-altering drugs.

Native women believed their behavior was misinterpreted by white staff, and that this led to the prescribing of drugs. Several Native women talked about what an alien environment prison was compared to the familiarity of life in Native communities. The way Native women chose to respond to this was to become quiet and observe how things were conducted. These women said that their behavioral reaction, one of quietness, was misinterpreted by the prison psychologist as a type of suppression of their anger and bitterness. Agnes clearly believed that because the prison did not know how to relate to Native Americans they then wanted to control them:

> *So, in order for white society to deal the Native American, they give them a type of dependent. And, I fought with this when I first got here because they told me that they felt I should go on antidepressants. So I said—and this was a psychologist talking to me— I said, "My sentencing papers say that one of the conditions are that I deal with my alcohol problem. I have an alcohol problem." And, I said, "So now I'm dealing with it. I'm going to groups and participating, but yet you people are telling me that I need antidepressants. You're going to take me off one dependent and put me on another, so when I leave here I'm going to have two dependents." I said, "That don't make sense, so this is your rehabilitation to me? This is what your offering me?"*

Fortunately, the psychologist, according to Agnes, was dumbfounded that she spoke up so readily; he never prescribed any medication for her, and never asked to see her again. Agnes insisted that the overuse of mind-altering drugs was just another way the prison controlled prisoners and characterized this as "totally outrageous."

Agnes, similar to other prisoners, talked about one Native woman who had been on Thorazine since her arrival. This woman was at the point of hallucinating and the staff continued to medicate her. This woman was described as "extremely mentally disturbed" by institutional personnel. I wanted to interview this particular woman but she was too drugged to talk to me, and other prisoners maintained she had been broken by the prison. Another Native prisoner, who had been in maximum security for nearly one year, insisted that lengthy lockup time in combination with drugs had broken her:

> They keep me at a level here where they can control me. They think if they keep me drugged up all the time, that everything's going to go just dandy. But I've tongued my meds before and went and puked them up. I wasn't thinking straight in my head; I couldn't figure out what was going on. So much has happened; I feel like they already broke me.

Prisoners were thus subjected to too much social control and, consequently, broken. Furthermore, several prisoners I talked to mentioned they were on Prozac or Tranzine, and several others were on "sleeping pills" they could not identify. Additionally, several prisoners remarked it was easier to get drugs legally in prison than it was illegally out on the streets.

Prisoners in Maximum Security
"They call it the hell-hole."

Montana's Women's Correctional Center presented a benign appearance. There were no high barbwire-fences around the general-population building, no bars on the windows, no required prisoner uniforms, and minimum-status prisoners could be seen walking around the grounds accompanied by the recreational director. Although the general-population building presented a benevolent appearance, the maximum-security setting strongly resembled a fortress. All doors were locked and prisoners were constantly watched. The women in this unit were there not for certain crimes, but for behavioral problems. Behavioral problems included prisoners talking back to a guard or other staff, causing fights within the general-population facility, sexual misconduct, or general insubordination. Isolation cells were reserved for those women who could not mix either in general population or maximum security. Again, confinement in isolation did not hinge on the specific crimes the women may have committed, but on their behavioral problems. Prisoners in maximum security were allowed out once a day for one hour, with a guard, to get fresh air; however, some prisoners said this did not happen every day.

Most women housed in maximum security can be described as women who were pushed to their emotional edge, and were consequently rendered extremely angry and vulnerable. Native women were disproportionately represented in maximum security: out of 11 women, 6 were

Native. Three women were in isolation cells: two prisoners were white and one was Native. This overrepresentation of Native women in maximum security and isolation related directly to Native prisoners' relationships with white guards because generally the guards issued write-ups. Additionally, the warden, treatment specialist, and recreation director had the authority to issue write-ups.

Whereas a typical day in general population and on the floor of maximum security started at the 6:30 a.m. count, with the freedom for prisoners to go back to bed if they did not have GED (general equivalency diplomas) classes or in-house jobs, the typical day in a lockup cell in maximum security started at 5:00 a.m.[2] At this time, prisoners were to arise and three times a week they were permitted to shower. These prisoners were allowed outside for fresh air ranging from 1 hour to 10 minutes per day. Although prisoners said prison policy specified that the length of stay in maximum was not to exceed 6 months, the duration ranged from 1 month to 15 months. The length of stay in isolation ranged from 3 days to 6 months.

Confinement in maximum security was difficult for Native prisoners primarily because they were refused the opportunity to pray with other Native women on Sunday's group day, and were not allowed to see the Native woman counselor. Both Native and white prisoners had restricted visitation and were denied access to any programming, with the exception of GED classes. With little programming available, it was nearly impossible to get any good-time credit in this unit.[3] Several women specifically mentioned the need for sexual-abuse counseling, although they were denied access. Furthermore, women in maximum security and isolation were not permitted religious services of any kind and not allowed to talk to each other.

Confinement appeared to be most difficult for prisoners in isolation. Not only was their regime strict, but also they were not allowed visits from family and friends. This treatment further pushed these prisoners to their emotional edge. Delphina, for example, felt the prison was trying to break her. In regard to this treatment, she related her confinement to her sexual preference:

> They put me in a max cell where I can't see nobody; can't talk to nobody but the guards. Come on [crying]—what are they trying to do? Destroy me? And that's what's going to happen. You know, if they're trying to kill what I have going for me and people think that being gay is wrong, and a lot of people don't agree with it but it's just the way I feel. And, I don't push it on anybody, so they shouldn't push back. It's not like I'm pushing to hurt anybody. Yeah, this place reminds me of [the drug treatment center] where they take you and tear you apart and build you back up. Only this place don't build you back up—they just tear you down.

Delphina related the breaking process to severe readjustment problems once prisoners were released. She maintained that because their self-esteem was pushed to such a low level by lock-up time and general prison treatment, it would be impossible to survive on the outside.

One recently incarcerated Native women was in maximum security not because of any write-ups she received, but because the general-population building was full. She felt the prison staff had lied to her because they told her she would only be in maximum security "a few days," and she had been there for over one week. When asked why she was being kept in maximum security, she discussed being lied to by prison staff concerning the length of time she would be in that unit, and the consequences of the *tough Indian* image she believed she projected to prison staff:

> *I'm taking it personally. Maybe they think I'm a bulldog, but I'm not. I've never lied to these people and I won't lie to them . . . But they think, probably because of my size and tattoos or something, that I'm a bulldog—I don't know. I don't appreciate being lied to. If they want a reason to keep me over here, I'll give them one; that's stupid to think that way but I don't like being lied to. People say they don't think you're going to make it. Why do they have to lie to you? Why can't they just say, "We don't think you're going to do very well so we're going to keep you here for a couple of months."*

When I asked her about appealing her classification, she said that prisoners seldom win their appeals so it was "a hopeless battle." One Native woman, who had been in maximum security for nearly one year, was afraid to appeal her lengthy stay. As one prisoner insisted, "The whole thing [the appeal process] is to help them [the prison staff], not us. So, why try to do anything?"

Dorine was in maximum security because of multiple write-ups, which she did not consider valid. The prison did a shakedown (investigation) of her room and found a pair of scissors she had used for her beadwork. Although the scissors had been previously approved and met prison regulations, she received a write-up for possession of the scissors. Dorine received another write-up for contraband, which turned out to be acne medication belonging to another prisoner. The write-up that landed her in maximum security was the threat of a *hex* on an officer (i.e., "threatening another person with bodily harm"). Feeling pushed to her emotional edge by a guard during the shakedown of her room, Dorine, in retaliation, told the guard that because she was a Native she had the power to "put a spell" on her. Dorine perceived this as a joke and maintained she said it to relieve her anger. Although the guard did not hear the remark, a white prisoner told prison staff what Dorine had said. This incident increased already existing tension between Native prisoners and white guards, and between Native and white prisoners. Dorine was subsequently confined to lockup for 4 days without the privilege of a shower or soap to cleanse herself. When she asked the guards if she could file a grievance, she was told it was too late because it had to be filed within 24 hours. Dorine eventually was permitted by the prison to file a grievance, however, her hearing was canceled because the hearing officer was not present. The prison then moved her from the lockup cell to the maximum-security floor for 6 months. Dorine insisted that she was sent to maximum security because she was a Native, articulate, and questioned the rules.

Native women in the general-population building were a close-knit group, and had formed a spiritual organization to further that bond. Several Native women told me that their unity appeared threatening to prison staff. The consequence was that several Native women, who prison staff perceived as *bulldoggers* or troublemakers, were reclassified as close status and transferred to maximum security under what the women considered trumped-up charges.[4] For example, one Native prisoner was transferred to maximum security for calling a white prisoner a "used-up whore." This was interpreted as sexual misconduct by prison staff.

Sometimes a transfer to this unit was in the guise of health reasons. One traditional Native woman was transferred from the general-population building to maximum security because she had been in an accident prior to incarceration and walked with a cane. The prison staff decided that living in maximum security would be easier for her because this building did not contain stairs. In the opinion of the Native women, this was done to break up the closeness of the Native women. Although most white prisoners were not aware of this racism, Joan (a white prisoner) viewed this transfer in the same way as Native women:

> [The prison staff] has been real shitty too about the Native Americans. I know somebody that's prejudiced that's up there [in prison administration]; somebody's gotta be prejudiced because that lady [with the cane] would not be over there—she did not deserve it. She never had a write-up or anything. To deserve to go over to hell; that is hell over there. They call it the hell-hole.

Interviewing women in maximum security and isolation was particularly problematic. Oppressive conditions produced rambling, unfocused conversations. Additionally, many women in these units were medicated. This proved to be important because women incarcerated in these units could not concentrate on my questions. The fact that it was difficult to keep these women focused was telling in itself. These women were more concerned with their personal survival of the prison experience and, therefore, were not afforded the occasion of thinking about other issues. Or, perhaps, these women were too medicated to keep a focus and not afforded the luxury of concentration.

Prisoner Responses to Control
"She cut her arms and nothing was done."

The study conducted by Carlen (1985) argues that prison life is a violent game in which the rules are arbitrarily decided by others. According to Carlen (1985) and Dobash et al. (1986), this kind of cruelty may lead to violence on the part of the prisoner who is trying to maintain some form of self-respect. Thus, this type of violence can be seen as a response by the prisoner in order to survive a socially sick environment. The response to prisoner violence by the staff? Lockup in the maximum-security unit where prisoners are isolated in order to learn their lesson. Additionally, Carlen (1985) argues that, knowing that they will be thrown into lockup, if they do not comply, usually keeps prisoners in their places.

Moreover, according to Carlen (1985), officer violence and lockup are only one kind of threat. Other threats to survival include isolation, provocation by guards, institutionalization and boredom and the use of mind-altering drugs to control imprisoned women. Carlen (1985) and Dobash et al. (1986) maintain that guards deliberately manipulate and force imprisoned women to their emotional edge. Some imprisoned women are pushed to that edge earlier than others because they are extremely vulnerable when they enter prison. Thus, prison guards have complete control over prisoners. Consequences of this kind of control, other than prisoner violence, include suicide, self-mutilation, and insanity. It is no wonder that some opt for compliance with prison staff in order to survive. Other survival tactics, according to Carlen (1985), include humor, forming close friendships with fellow prisoners, and attaining a "top-dog" position in which the prisoner learns to manipulate the system to ensure that nobody, neither prison staff nor prisoner, will bother them.

One consequence of the cruelty prisoners experienced was suicide attempts. Dobash et al. (1986) found that suicide attempts were defined as assaults; one could be written up for this behavior and put in isolation as punishment. Moreover, this behavior was viewed by prison staff as attention-seeking rather than symptomatic of stress and anxiety; thus, Dobash et al. (1986) found that suicide attempts were rarely taken seriously by prison staff. Suicide attempts, as also revealed by Dobash et al. (1986), were not taken seriously in the Women's Correctional Center. When I asked the treatment specialist about suicide attempts, she insisted they seldom occurred and, when they did, they were attention-seeking behavior. The treatment specialist offered the example of a young Native woman who had swallowed a piece of plastic and placed a rubber band around her neck "just to get attention—she was not serious." However, when I asked the prisoners about suicide attempts, they said attempts were frequent and they also said that the staff responded to suicide attempts by dispensing write-ups to the prisoners for this behavior. In addition, prisoners claimed that those who attempted suicide were often transferred to maximum security. One prisoner explained:

My friend came and said, "I'm going to kill myself and you can't stop me." She's a tough con; I'd never seen her even cry. So, she told the guard she was going to kill herself. He just sat there. She tried to kill herself; she cut her arms and nothing was done. Plus, she got wrote up for it.

Although some prisoners received write-ups for suicide attempts, in some cases they were transferred to the forensic ward of the state mental hospital.

When I questioned the director of Montana's only women's prerelease center about suicide attempts, she informed me they were frequent in the prerelease center—especially among Native women. This woman placed the blame directly on depression that resulted from being in a foreign, white environment. She suggested the need for cultural differences to be incorporated into all aspects of the criminal justice system, particularly prisons and prerelease centers.

Another way prisoners coped was to take the prescribed mind-altering drugs. Although not all prisoners were required to take these drugs, some did so because many were not strong enough to refuse them or some took them to cope with the "evil" prison environment. For instance, one Native prisoner, who had been in maximum security for over one year, said she initially took a drug called Haldol to cope with her experiences in lockup:

Haldol is a drug they give to people who can't cope with lockup. It makes you feel dead, paralyzed. And then I started getting side effects from the Haldol. I wanted to fight *anybody, any of the officers. I was screaming at them and telling them to get out of my face, so the doctor said we can't have that. And, they put me on Tranzine. I don't take pills; I never had trouble sleeping until I got here. Now I'm suppose to see [the psychiatrist] again because of my dreams. If you got a problem, they're not going to take care of it; they're going to put you on drugs so they can control you.*

In Carlen's (1985) view, another survival tactic for prisoners is learning to manipulate the system. Several prisoners in the Women's Correctional Center, both Native and white, talked about "playing the game" in order to survive prison. One prisoner explained how she used the game to her advantage:

In prison I call all the male officers, sir; I call all the female officers, ma'am. I'd like to call them what they act like, but I don't. Other prisoners say, "You're kissing their ass." I'm going to play their game to get out of here and I don't care what other inmates say.

Although this prisoner did not like the guards, she knew she could not reveal her true feelings. To do so would possibly land her in maximum security. Thus, she, like others, played the game to benefit herself.

Dorine said she refused to manipulate the system because she believed that ultimately it would prove to be detrimental to her. She stated that she was in prison because she played games on the outside. Whether playing the game outside prison or inside, the core of the game was dishonesty and manipulation. Dorine said, "There's a time when a person's got to be honest with themselves. If you don't have that you don't got nothing . . . [prisoners who manipulate] are going to fail."

Dorine stated that the penal system theoretically insisted upon truthfulness from prisoners, yet lied to the prisoners and manipulated them. The following words of a Native prisoner expressed what many prisoners said:

It's all a game and it don't make sense to me, because they want you not to be manipulative to get what you want. They don't want you to play games but they're playing games with you, so you have to be a good player. It doesn't make sense. This place doesn't make sense.

In turn, many prisoners did the same in order to survive; however, once released from prison, many had difficulty unlearning the same behavior that saved them in prison. This behavior would, according to Dorine, then return them to prison. Dorine and others felt trapped in a sick environment, and they believed that this alone made many prisoners mentally and physically ill. Moreover, Dorine claimed that when prisoners rejected and fought, which she labeled as a reaction to a "sick" environment, prison officials would then label prisoners as troublemakers, bulldoggers, or manipulators and then try to break the prisoners. This was a serious threat to prisoner survival, and the other option was to conform to staff expectations.

I never interviewed any prisoners who said they conformed to staff expectations. However, I talked to prisoners who would comment about prisoners who conformed and were called "snitches." This was different from prisoners seen as "pets" of the prison staff. Snitches were seen as allying themselves with prison staff and would tell prison staff about the rule infractions that other prisoners allegedly committed. Generally, both Native and white prisoners detested the snitches. Nevertheless, Dorine had a different perspective:

> *There are a couple of girls in here who are having a hard time because they run to the guards and tell them everything. One of the girls that does that has never had anybody that really stood up for her, or with her. She has a real low self-esteem—worse than most of us. I feel sorry for her.*

Prisoners who were seen as staff pets were not seen by other prisoners as totally conforming. This type of behavior appeared to be more problematic for white prisoners, rather than for Native prisoners. For instance, when we would be discussing in-house jobs, white prisoners would frequently mention that a certain prisoner was favored by prison staff. Regarding another prisoner, one white prisoner said, "Oh, she's just the warden's little pet; she was in reform school when he was working there." These statements were generally made about prisoners who held the coveted jobs in the prison. Native prisoners did not make these comments. The consequence, from these prisoners' view, was that the prisoners who conformed, that is the snitches, were not liked by other prisoners. I imagine that this behavior increased the already existing tension between white prisoners, and further prevented any possibilities for prisoner solidarity.

Carlen (1985) suggests that another way to survive prison is through the formation of close friendships with other prisoners. While Native women presented themselves as cohesive, white women were not unified. Following the Kruttschnitt (1981) study, although these women were not a cohesive group, they were still in opposition to prison staff. Furthermore, when some of the white women conformed to prison-staff expectations, they made it clear that they did so to benefit themselves. As one white woman said, "I'm in here to do my time and get out; I ain't taking any of these women with me."

This, I believe, reflects on white prisoners' loneliness and isolation from each other, as well as prisoners' conforming to reap any rewards possible in a bleak situation. I was overwhelmed by the loneliness that most white prisoners experienced. They were cut-off not only from their families, but also from each other. White prisoners were especially vulnerable and felt it best not to openly express any emotion. The prison environment was, indeed, a hostile environment and prisoners were intimidated not only by the prison environment in general but also by other prisoners, prison staff, and the guards. Thus, they were afraid most of the time, which may have contributed to their low self-esteem. Many white prisoners claimed that in this environment it was difficult, if not impossible, to show support for other prisoners. Trust between white prisoners was at an extremely low level and, when victimized by other prisoners, the last people they wanted to contact was the guards. Prisoners contended that the guards, similar to some prisoners, were abusive and unpredictable.

Conclusion

Previous studies on experiences of imprisoned women (Carlen, 1985; Dobash et al., 1986; O'Dwyer et al., 1987) disregard race as an important factor. This study suggests that race was a critical variable and that, although all women encountered problems specific to them as women, they did not experience prison in the same way. The experiences of imprisoned women varied according to race and location of confinement. Incarcerated Natives experienced prison differently than white prisoners; and prisoners housed in maximum security, where Natives were disproportionately represented, experienced prison differently than prisoners in the general-population building.[5]

The personal experiences of imprisoned women, both Native and white, reflect the structure of Euro-American society in which certain subgroups are not only disadvantaged because of their race and gender, but controlled as well. The data suggests that, although all women were subjected to horrendous treatment, Native women were additionally discriminated against because of their race and culture. The racism was direct, indirect, and institutionalized. Prison staff and white prisoners made racist comments to me and Native prisoners about Indians *and* Indian culture. Direct and subtle racism not only contributed to the low self-esteem of Native prisoners, discriminatory practices added to an already stressful environment.

In this prison, I found strict control over prisoners' behavior. Part of the regime was the overuse of mind-altering drugs, sexual intimidation, and lengthy stays in maximum security and isolation. Generally, prisoners responded to the prison's social environment in several ways: suicide attempts, conformity to prison staff expectations, unity or self-imposed isolation, or they would rebel and subsequently spent lengthy time in maximum security or isolation. Native prisoners in the general-population building coped with the social environment by forming a solid group among themselves. White prisoners were not a cohesive group and, accordingly, were isolated from each other. The cohesiveness of Native prisoners was utilized in a therapeutic manner and was a means to successfully survive the prison's social environment. This unity was perceived as a threat by prison staff and they continually worked to split the cohesiveness of Native prisoners. One solution was to transfer Native prisoners to maximum security. Native prisoners who spent lengthy time in lockup were more likely than others to attempt suicide.

Prison staff continually focused on the concept of *rehabilitation* during my interviews with them. Nonetheless, to all prisoners, regardless of race, this concept was not operating in this prison. The prisoners perceived the prison to be punitive. Prisoners felt forced to survive in a sick environment. The use of manipulation and games by staff and prisoners contributed to the sickness of the prison's social environment. Many prisoners, Native and white, believed this alone affected recidivism because, to a certain extent, everyone must play the game—a game in which only the guards knew the rules. Moreover, all prisoners discussed the inconsistency of staff enforcement of prison. Prisoners experienced an arbitrary enforcement of rules and numerous write-ups, and subsequent transfers to maximum security. These actions added to the feeling of control, rather than rehabilitation, in the prison.

Most prisoners suffered belittling and humiliating experiences. Most important was the survival of the prison experience and maintenance of one's sanity. Prison appears to be a powerful, dehumanizing process which is clearly not conducive to rehabilitation. Indeed, it is no wonder that some prisoners rebel as a way to maintain their integrity as human beings; and, in addition, it is no wonder that others comply in order to do "easy time" as a way to survive. The conditions in women's prisons many times result in women fending for themselves, in whatever way they see best. The data reflected that in this small, underfunded, understaffed, and overcrowded state prison, the concept of rehabilitation appeared to be operating in theory only. Rehabilitation, in my opinion, means the reintegration of the transgressor into the community; the restoration of balance and transformation into a whole human being again. Women in this prison were not made whole; they were controlled and this control was affected by the race, gender, and sexual preference of the prisoner.

I never met any woman in this prison whose prior *deviant* behavior warranted incarceration. When I was sitting in prison observing, I remember thinking that the prison system seemed to be flawed by design. The criminal justice system in the United States needs a new approach. Of all the countries in the world we are the leader in incarceration rates; even higher than South Africa and the former Soviet Union—countries which are perceived as oppressive to their own citizens. Euro-America builds bigger and bigger prisons and fills them up with *criminals*. I believe the incarceration of nonviolent offenders is self-defeating. We need to focus on alternatives such as probation, halfway houses, community service, house arrest, electronic surveillance, and treatment programs. The goal should be rehabilitation, not punishment. We need to redefine what is *criminal*; we need to reintegrate true transgressors back into our communities. The criminal justice system, as it is presently designed, brings destruction. Indeed, the Euro-American prison system demands a new approach.

Notes

1. The state's ACLU office had written a letter to the director of corrections and submitted a report concerning the conditions of the female prisoners in Montana. The director of the ACLU gave me copies of both and permission to use them in the study. Due to issues of confidentiality, and the protection of the prisoners, I am unable to cite the source.
2. Count refers to the process in which prisoners lined up outside their rooms. The guards then count the prisoners to ensure that no one has escaped. This occurred 4 times a day: at 6:30 a.m., 10:45 a.m., 4:00 p.m., and 10:30 p.m.
3. Good-time credit refers to a reduction in the actual time that must be served by the prisoner. For example, if someone was given a 5-year sentence, she may actually serve only 3 years due to the good-time credit given for participation in various prison programs.
4. Bulldogger was a term used in the Women's Correctional Center to describe a prisoner who intimidated other prisoners, physically and emotionally, to get what she wanted.
5. The larger study (Ross, 1992) fully details the differences in experiences between Native and white women, and between reservation and landless Natives.

References

Blauner, R. (1972). *Racial Oppression in America.* New York: Harper & Row.

Bowker, L. H. (1981). "Gender Differences in Prisoner Subculture." In L. H. Bowker (Ed.), *Women and Crime in America* (pp. 409–419).

Carlen, P. (1983). *Women's Imprisonment: A Study in Social Control.* London: Routledge & Kegan Paul.

Carlen, R (Ed.). (1985). *Criminal Women: Autobiographical Accounts.* Cambridge, Great Britain: Polity Press.

Chambliss, W., and R. Seidman (1982). *Law, Order, and Power* (2nd ed.). Reading, MA: Addison-Wesley.

Collins, P. H. (1991). *Black Feminist Thought: Knowledge, Consciousness, and the Politics of Empowerment.* New York: Routledge.

Dobash R. P., R. E. Dobash and S. Gutteridge (1986). *The Imprisonment of Women.* New York: Blackwell.

Feinman, C. (1986). *Women in the Criminal Justice System* (2nd ed.). New York: Praeger.

Giallombardo, R. (1966). *Society of Women: A Study of a Women's Prison.* New York: Wiley.

Greenfeld, L. A. and S. Minor-Harper (1991). *Women in Prison* (Bureau of Justice Statistics Special Report No. NCJ-127991). Washington, DC: U.S. Department of Justice.

Haft, M. (1980). "Women in Prison: Discriminatory Practices and Some Legal Solutions." In S. K. Datesman and F. R. Scarpitti (Eds.), *Women, Crime, and Justice* (pp. 330–338). New York: Oxford University Press.

Hall, R. E. (1985). *Ask Any Woman: A London Enquiry into Rape and Sexual Assault. Report of the Woman's Safety Survey Conducted by Women Against Rape.* Bristol, England: Falling Wall Press.

hooks, b. (1989). *Talking Back: Thinking Feminist, Thinking Black.* Boston: South End Press.

Kitsuse, J. I. (1962). "Societal Reaction to Deviant Behavior: Problems of Theory and Method." *Social Problems*, 9, 247–256.

Kruttschnitt, C. (1981). "Prison Codes, Inmate Solidarity, and Women." In M. Q. Warren (Ed.), *Comparing Female and Male Offenders* (pp. 123–141). Beverly Hills: Sage.

Kruttschnitt, C. (1983). "Race Relations and the Female Inmate." *Crime and Delinquency*, 29, 577–591.

Lewis, D. (1981). "Black Women Offenders and Criminal Justice: Some Theoretical Considerations." In M. Q. Warren (Ed.), *Comparing Male and Female Offenders* (pp. 89–105). Beverly Hills: Sage.

Mann, C. R. (1984). *Female Crime and Delinquency.* Tuscaloosa: University of Alabama Press.

McConnel, P. (1989). *Sing Soft, Sing Loud: Scenes From Two Lives.* New York: Athenaeum.

O'Dwyer, J., J. Wilson, and P. Carlen (1987). "Women's Imprisonment in England, Wales and Scotland: Recurring Issues." In P. Carlen and A. Worrall (Eds.), *Gender, Crime, and Justice* (pp. 135–148). Milton Keynes, England: Open University Press.

Quinney, R. (1970). *The Social Reality of Crime.* Boston: Little, Brown.

Rafter, N. H. (1985). *Partial Justice: Women in State Prisons, 1800-1935.* Boston: Northeastern University Press.

Rafter, N. H. (1990). *Partial Justice: Women, Prisons, and Social Control* (2nd ed.). New Brunswick, NJ: Transaction Publishers.

Resnik, J. and N. Shaw (1980). "Prisoners of Their Sex: Health Problems of Incarcerated Women." In I. P. Robbins (Ed.), *Prisoners' Rights Sourcebook* (pp. 328-330). New York: Clark Boardman.

Ross, L. (1992). *Mothers Behind Bars: A Comparative Study of the Experiences of Incarcerated American Indian and White Women.* Unpublished dissertation, University of Oregon, Eugene.

Sims, P. (1976). "Women in Southern Jails." In L. Crites (Ed.), *The Female Offender* (pp. 137-148). Lexington, MA: Heath.

Smart, C. (1976). *Women, Crime, and Criminology: A Feminist Critique.* London: Routledge & Kegan Paul.

Ward, D. A. and G. C. Kassebaum (1966). *Women's Prisons: Sex and Social Structure.* Chicago: Aldine.

6

Colorblindness: Challenging the Discourse of Contemporary U.S. Racism

Rita Cameron Wedding

The purpose of this article is to explore the methods by which race is reproduced in the twenty-first century. In the past, commonplace social practices of discrimination such as segregation in schools, restrictive covenants and redlining in housing, "whites only" drinking fountains, blacks in the back of the bus, and the KKK left no question about the role of racism in the control and regulation of society. However, in a post-civil rights society racism is often covert so people can choose to be oblivious as to how it is manifested.

Racial politics *encompasses the role of social construction of race and race differences in formal, institutional politics as well as in the political interpretations of everyday life* (Hanchard 1999, 1). In the U.S., racial politics was established and secured through a formalized, legally constituted racial caste system with a nearly rigid color line. But racial politics that protected centuries-old policies of white entitlements were threatened by the passing of civil rights laws and affirmative action programs. The elimination of rigid laws of exclusion, which seems to have eradicated the most overt signs and symbols of racism, implies that we are living in a racial democracy. But the fact is that systems that preserve and reinscribe racial hierarchies are as intact today as they were during the height of U.S. racial apartheid.

Consider the example of affirmative action. Debates about the legitimacy of affirmative action are fought on the basis of its potential to destabilize the status quo because with its passing emerged the possibility that racial entitlements for whites would be lost. As a consequence, such laws intended to provide redress of historic social inequalities were targeted by so-called colorblind laws such as California's Proposition 209 and the current Racial Privacy Initiative.

Proposition 209 outlawed California's affirmative action program by asserting that the "State would not discriminate on the basis of race and gender." Entitled "The Civil Rights Initiative," this law was promoted as pro-civil rights, antidiscrimination law. The use of the word *discriminate* was very strategic. I think most would agree that the State should not *discriminate*, but this new use of the word did not hold the same meaning as the old antidiscrimination language. Now it meant that the State would not recognize historically oppressed groups in order to adjust for structural discrimination. In other words, by eliminating affirmative action, the State would be stripped of any potential redistributive power. By taking no "affirmative action," the [State] *law masks as natural what is chosen; it obscures the consequences of social selection as inevitable* (C. Harris 1995, 287). The structural forces of a racist, capitalist, and patriarchal society that selects and ranks white men above all other groups, when left undisturbed by "social manipulations" of affirmative action, will be enough to deliver the same racial arrangements as those of more historically overt and rigid racial regimes.

If the *Racial Privacy Initiative* is passed, it will be a tremendous boon to the colorblind culture. This initiative that calls for the elimination of racial classifications results in the inability to measure racial inequality in employment and other critical areas of social life. Eliminating racial classifications and suppressing the public discourse on race will not produce neutral outcomes, nor will it result in hiring and selection processes free of bias. The systems that produced oppression in the pre-civil rights era were not eliminated, just transformed. Without any regulatory oversight and standards for affirmative action, we revert to U.S. racial politics of the past. The new ethos of colorblindness that emerged as the so-called solution to ending race-based politics is instead a strategy to preserve and protect racial hierarchies. In the Supreme Court's review of the constitutionality of affirmative action programs, the Court determined that race should be narrowly construed to mean skin color, devoid of any historical, political, or economic value, or determination or history. This "colorblind" ruling disavowed any knowledge of the historic meanings of race and established a precedent that "nobody's skin color should be taken into account in government decision-making" (Crenshaw 1998, 284).

> *When a previously degrouped group begins to fight back, the dominant group steps up its restrictive controls. Therefore, it is not surprising that when there are increasing numbers of people of Color in the United States, as well as increasing awareness of how "race" is socially constructed—that is, at the very moment when race is on the verge of taking center stage in the analysis of oppression—all of a sudden, race doesn't matter and we should be colorblind. (Hurtado and Stewart, 304)*

Whiteness is defined by its relationship to racial subordination. It is more than just skin color; it is the embodiment of race entitlements. The government's apparent divestment in the "property" interest in whiteness is only a decoy. The argument that government should not play a role in offsetting historic inequality with programs like affirmative action underscores its commitment to preserving the status quo. By not actively deconstructing systems of oppression and their inevitable racially stratified outcomes, the government gives its consent to the continuation of race politics in America. Although Trent Lott was censored for nostalgic comments about segregation, it is almost certain that the values and attitudes that underscored these comments were a keynote of his career as a lawmaker.

Within a colorblind culture, individual attitudes as they inform and permeate institutions can maintain racial hierarchies when the following conditions are met: (1) the conscious or unconscious conviction that whites are superior; (2) the mobilization of social, political, legal and economic structures; (3) the masking of the omnipresent oppressive forces by redefining the terms of racial discourse; (4) the collective and social acts of individuals who utilize racial codes and symbols in ways that produce patterned outcomes within private life as well as in major social institutions; and (5) the collaboration of social institutions in reproducing outcomes that support and reinforce status arrangements of race, gender, and class.

Though each of these five conditions will be discussed separately, in practice they operate simultaneously and interdependently. Ideologies frame how we interpret private and public interactions.

The Conscious or Unconscious Conviction That Whites Are Superior

Andrew Hacker, in his 1992 book *Two Nations,* recounts the results of a classroom exercise in which he probed the value of whiteness according to the perceptions of whites. The study asked a group of white students how much money they would seek if they were changed from white to black. "Most students seemed to feel that it would not be out of place to ask for $50 million, or $1 million for each coming black year" (C. Harris 1995, 286).

If asked, many people would deny that they believe whites are superior. In the pre-civil rights era, white supremacy was openly expressed through word and deed, but today such beliefs must remain discreet because direct links to whiteness and privilege contradict colorblind ideology. Ideologies that once showed direct correlations to whiteness, privilege, and power have been replaced by those which reiterate the neutrality of whiteness.

Convictions of white superiority are produced by racial ideologies. Racial ideologies are essential in normalizing relationships of dominance and subordinance. They are inextricable from the racialization process as they reiterate negative and stigmatizing images of nonwhites that serve as a constant reminder of their "racialness" (C. Harris 1995, 283). Whites, on the other hand are seen as normative, a baseline against which all other groups are compared.

Prowhite ideology underscores the "conscious and unconscious conviction that white Euro-American cultural patterns and practices, as reflected in values, language, belief systems, interpersonal styles, behavior patterns, political, social roles, economics, music, art, religious tenets, and so forth, are superior to those of other visible racial/ethnic groups (Asian, Black, Hispanic, Indian)" (Carter 1997, 200). Because these assumptions are not associated with anti-group sentiments they can easily conceal racial biases that support white privilege. Such attitudes can not be seen as neutral because they rank cultural patterns, practices, and values of other groups based on how closely they approximate those of the privileged class (Jewell 1993, 6).

As long as there is congruency between the ideological constructions and how people are positioned in the social hierarchy, the work of ideologies can go undetected. Because white men as a race-gender group are systematically portrayed in popular culture and in intellectual sources as good, meritorious, and competent leaders—as Americans and as men—positive assumptions accrue to them. For example, at our university a few years back, we hired three deans to head the newly configured colleges. All three deans were white men. Their pictures appeared in a campus newspaper announcing their appointments. The ideological belief of white men as competent, deserving, and in positions of power required no imagination, whereas hiring three black women would be absolutely unimaginable. Consider hiring three black women who are stereotyped as loud, aggressive, and hostile—images totally counter to the ideologies needed to support such appointments as college deans. Despite impeccable qualifications, the appointment of three black women would be met with a great deal of scrutiny as well as charges of reverse discrimination. As a matter of fact, the appointment of any three people of the same race-gender configuration would challenge our understanding of who's deserving, meritorious, and qualified. These jobs, though held by women and men of color in increasingly large numbers, are still the domain of whites, specifically white men. Only they can occupy such roles disproportionately without any suspicion of social manipulation. Beliefs about "the most qualified person for the job" might require that we deconstruct ideological constructions of whites as inherently superior.

Consequently, the strategic locations of whites in positions of power, in leadership posts as CEOs in corporations, social institutions, and heads of state, has resulted in the adoption of their values and cultural patterns as the universal standard. As a result of their seemingly "natural fit" for positions of status, their disproportionate representation is difficult to politicize.

Mobilization of a Formidable Defense: White Privilege Can Still Deliver

Even though white privilege has been somewhat undermined by social justice movements, it still has the power to deliver.

> *Even as the capacity of whiteness to deliver is arguably diminished by the elimination of rigid racial stratifications, whiteness continues to be perceived as materially significant. The property interest in whiteness has proven to be resilient and adaptive to new conditions. Over time it has changed in form but it has retained its essential exclusionary character and continues to distort outcomes of legal disputes by favoring and protecting settled expectations of white privilege (C. Harris 1995, 286).*

White privilege is a highly contested system, but a brief examination of the socioeconomic indices reveal that whites fare consistently better on most quality of life indices—including wealth, education, occupation, and health—more than any other group.

One of the best measures of white privilege to deliver is its ability to mobilize the necessary institutional systems for its preservation and survival. This is possible because whites are in charge of these systems and therefore they have the power to pass laws, build institutions, and influence public opinions. In *Fighting Words,* Patricia Hill Collins states "elites have the means to manufacture consent . . . This does not mean that all opinions of elites are always adopted by the public at large, but only that their opinions are well known, that they have the most effective means of public persuasion and the best resources for suppressing or marginalizing alternative opinion" (Hill Collins 1998, xi).

The terms of modern-day racism were established on the basis of colorblindness. Colorblind discourse reframed the discussion on race by asserting the following: (1) race is just skin color and not a marker for status, history, or power, but a false phenotype; (2) race is made up and treating people differently on the basis of "made up" categories is unacceptable; and (3) racism lacks any nexus to power and therefore must be treated as a personal, not a governmental concern (Guinier 2002, 39). It is important to note that the colorblind idea that race is "made up" overlaps with critical race theory's idea that race is socially constructed. Critical race theory insists on historical knowledge of discrimination based on legally produced racial categories, while colorblind ideologies deny the importance of this history, asserting instead that we are all now "on a level playing field." The shift in the political race discourse suppresses the historic relevance of race as well as its continued social, political, and economic consequences.

Co-opting colorblind ideology, the State argues that it cannot interfere to redistribute racial value because to do so is an illegitimate end that would upset the natural outcomes of the market (Crenshaw 1998, 283). Therefore, in a colorblind culture any historical or structural conditions that institutionalize injustice such as inadequate education or poverty are considered irrelevant. Racial disparities in employment and housing and in other spheres are simply the consequences of a private market—the fact that whites are more competitive. Programs designed to target outreach and support to people of color, such as bilingual education programs, are considered out-of-bounds because such activities could upset the "natural" order of things. The same government that authorized and legitimized historical social injustice now abdicates its authority to intervene.

Colorblindness employs yet another innovative strategy—reverse discrimination. Allen Bakke, whose application for admission to the University of California Davis Medical School was rejected in favor of supposedly less deserving minority applicants, was one of the first to initiate a legal case defending the inherent value of white entitlements under the banner of reverse discrimination. This defensive strategy gave whites an opportunity to suppress increasing attempts to diminish their property interest in whiteness.

Nowhere are the unmentioned assumptions of the "inherent" merit of whiteness more clear than in the legal battles on reverse discrimination. The increasingly openly expressed response to charges of racism is the assertion that whiteness is a legitimate criterion of resource allocation because merit is colorblind and it is a coincidence (or inher-

ent *superiority) that most meritorious persons happen to be white and male (Hurtado and Steward 1997, 304).*

Ideologies are probably the most essential tool of a colorblind culture as they provide the themes around which all social institutions can be mobilized.

Media

Racial ideologies have long been a media staple. At the end of the year, one television station was "looking back" on their news reporting and bragging that viewers got breaking stories more often from them than any other news outlet. As they showed a collage of news stories reported throughout the year, they used an image of a black male in an orange jail jumpsuit to introduce the segment on crime reports. This image was self-explanatory, black men symbolize criminal activity and having them in custody makes our communities safe. Could the same message have been as easily conveyed with an image of a white man in an orange jumpsuit? The ideological connections between black men and criminal behavior are a part of our collective awareness. In Michael Moore's *Stupid White Men*, he states:

> *when I turn on the news each night, what do I see again and again? Black men alleged to be killing, raping, mugging, stabbing, gangbanging, looting, rioting, selling drugs, pimping, ho-ing, having too many babies, dropping babies from tenement windows, fatherless, motherless, Godless, penniless. I believe we've become so used to this image of the black male predator that we are forever ruined by this brainwashing. (p. 59)*

> *Despite the fact that more crimes are committed by whites, white men are not pathologized as a threat to society. Black faces, on the other hand, are usually attached to what we think of as a crime.*

Law Enforcement and Racial Profiling

Racial profiling is a strategy that treats blacks and other minority groups as criminal suspects based on the assumption that doing so will increase the odds of catching criminals. This strategy, adopted by law enforcement and used throughout the retail industry and in the war on terrorism, has helped to forge the relationship of blacks and other nonwhites with criminal behavior. Contrary to what the "rational" law enforcement justification for racial profiling would predict, the hit rate for drugs and weapons in police searches of African Americans is the same as or lower than the rate for whites (D. Harris 2002, 14). Racial profiling of all white males as criminals would be unthinkable. But in the aftermath of the Oklahoma City bombing, when the attack was first assumed to be the work of "terrorists," ideological constructions that targeted men of Middle Eastern descent were employed. When it became clear that white men were responsible, race became irrelevant. Timothy McVeigh and his accomplices were not treated as "white terrorists" but as individual men who bombed the Oklahoma City Federal Building. Crimes for which white men are the suspects become focused and specific, as they should, so that all white men are not treated as potential terrorists. Thus, white men have escaped the racial profiling that many argue is an essential law enforcement tactic.

Education

Education is one of society's primary agents of socialization and it plays a pivotal role in shaping the discourse on race and gender differences in our society. Education informs and at once is informed about the meaning of race by all other major social institutions (such as the media and law enforcement). Knowledge produced in education is pervasive in its scope and influence because of its ability to preserve white entitlements through the reproduction and legitimation of knowledge. Education reproduces knowledge based on the interests of those in charge. It determines what information is worth producing. The teaching of history from a male and Eurocentric perspective is considered objective and accurate; what great works are considered "classics," and what constitutes history are all decisions of the "dominant class." This ethnocentric history typically omits discussions about the genocide of Native Americans, the enslavement of Africans, or the impact of the exploitation of the labor, land, and resources on Indians and people of African, Mexican, and Asian descent. Traditional educational paradigms reinscribe the power and privilege of the "dominant group" by rendering all other groups invisible, weak, incidental, and irrelevant. Their tenuous statuses and their invisibility create distortions in our history that support hegemonic standards of education. Knowledge emerging from these systems normalizes whiteness and marginalizes and reinforces the status of "other" for everyone else.

Masking by Redefining the Terms of Race Discourse

Colorblind culture has redefined the meaning of race and the terms by which race can be discussed and negotiated. Integral to this redefinition are the ways in which race and racism have been renamed, reframed, and redefined.

Who is a racist? Conservatives associate racism with the actions of skinheads, white supremacist hate groups, and the KKK, while making off-limits the use of the terms racism and racists as they might apply to the actions of everyday people that make modern-day oppression possible.

According to colorblind discourse, it is racist to talk about race, so the one who mentions race first is the racist. In the popular film *Color of Fear,* David, the white, former vineyard owner from Ukiah, California, states with regard to racism: "there are no problems if people don't make them." For many people, the real race problem is that people complain about it.

Aspersions cast upon those who raise the specter of racism and sexism often result in their being vilified as "femi-nazis" and militants or discredited for "playing the race card." The conservative spin made "political correctness," an ideological framework based on tolerance and inclusivity, the fodder of jokes on late night TV, and made cultural sensitivity a laughing matter. These have been effective tools for the suppression of critical thinking, activism, and problem solving; it seems that anyone and anything that challenges the oppressive forces of discrimination risks being seen as a problem greater than the problem of racism itself.

A tricky aspect of racism is the way in which it has been transformed from that which was incontrovertible to systems that are equivocal and chameleon-like. But as long as actions can be understood in a racial context, they offer the possibility that racism can be promoted even though the intention or action can be argued as not being at all linked to race. Modern-day oppression rarely uses race or gender as the subordinating mechanisms (Carter 1997, 200). In other words, we'll rarely hear "we don't hire blacks." Instead, opportunities are structured so that they are disproportionately inaccessible to nonwhites.

Ideologies mask the ways blacks and other nonwhites are foreshadowed by omnipresent racial signs and symbols that have no meaning other than pressing them to the lowest level of the social hierarchy (hooks 1995, 3). Media depictions offer broad representations of whites. Where imbalances in media portrayals exist, they favor consistent and widely held assumptions of whites as model citizens. In contrast, portrayals of black men as drug addicts and drug dealers are consistent with widely held assumptions of their criminality. As we saw in the discussion on racial profiling, even criminals who are white and male benefit from the positive ideological constructions of their group. Conversely, all members of racialized groups are disadvantaged because they are judged first by negative assumptions and then required to prove that they are the "exception" to the rule.

Ideologies are not neutral. They are by definition distortions that when shared, applied, and reproduced throughout society can rationalize and reconcile dramatic inconsistencies in the ways race-gender groups experience social life. Ideologies often work on a subliminal level. We often unconsciously accept the ideological interpretations of the most inexplicable social facts. Perhaps this explains why the fact that the U.S. incarcerates a higher percentage of black men by a factor of six than did South Africa's Botha government during apartheid goes virtually unnoticed (Guinier 2002, 263).

Daily, students of color express the myriad ways race and, more specifically, race-gender ideological constructions influence their assumptions about the social status and intelligence of others. In one example, a black female student very new to the job introduced herself at an employees' gathering to someone she had not met. The other employee, who was white, asked her "Are you on the housekeeping staff?" and my student responded, "No, I'm the new auditor." In another example, a white student in my Ethnic Studies 100 class rushed up to me to express her embarrassment. She explained that she had just left a statistics class. Having no idea as to what was being discussed, she automatically turned to an Asian woman sitting next to her in class (assuming that because this student was Asian she would be able to help her). The Asian woman responded: "I don't know what the hell the teacher is talking about." This interaction resulted in my student confronting the model minority stereotypes of Asians, as well as cultural ideologies that construct Asian women as docile and submissive.

It's important to note that ideological constructions are commonly understood by most members of society. As they are woven into the fabric of American life, their influence is pervasive but not inevitable. People can learn to deconstruct ideological constructions by being more conscious and critical (like my student in the Ethnic Studies 100 class) about the ways in which ideologies are used and internalized. But regardless of how these constructions are operationalized and by whom, they have but one objective and that is the reification of white superiority.

The silencing around race has resulted in tension, discomfort, anger, distrust, and ignorance. The compromise within colorblind culture was a framework for addressing "differences." The reframing of the discussion of racism-sexism as it is subordinated to broader, more palatable discussions of diversity and multiculturalism can occur in the absence of any authentic discussions of the power dynamics. Many individuals and institutions concerned with managing diversity use devices that work like Cliff Notes or a cheat sheet to understand "what these groups are like." These checklists or grids are used as simple descriptions of cultural characteristics, "Asians are like this and Mexicans are like this," to understand groups that are dynamic and constantly changing. As a result of this diversity model for teaching cultural competence, groups are understood within the context of simplistic characteristics that depict them as single- rather than multidimensional. Assimilation patterns, mobility shifts, social class adaptations, and occupational arrangements all result in groups deviating from these static characteristics. But these changing dynamics are often overlooked because they are too complex and cannot be taught by using fixed social-cultural maps and grids.

Therefore, some diversity models can do more harm than good because these approaches

- result in an over-reliance on the sameness or homogeneity of group members, as if all Asians have the same beliefs and want the same things more than all whites do,
- create frameworks that are inflexible and nonresponsive to social change,
- compare all other groups to whites, reinforcing whiteness as normative,
- provide little insight into existing power relations of dominance and subordinance,
- mask race biases on a private and public level.

Indeed, diversity models can be useful, and all forms of "diversity," including religion and sexuality, are significant, but it is the way in which they intersect structural arrangements of race, gender, and class that has the potential to situate people in certain locations of the hierarchy.

The Collective and Social Acts of Individuals

The relationship between ideological constructions and individual and institutional transactions is crucial to a colorblind culture, as it is the collective acts of individuals who create and apply standards and procedures within institutions that reproduce racist outcomes (Carter

1997, 200). Colorblind culture requires more or less the cooperation of every individual. Even those disadvantaged by such systems are pressed into service unwittingly to protect the very system that results in disadvantages to them. Individuals ratify and replicate social arrangements of race in every major social institution. Whether the individuals in these institutions are members of the dominant group is irrelevant to the fact that their ability to do their job as a teacher, counselor, social worker, politician, or correctional officer is linked to their ability to uphold the wishes of the dominant group; thus, many assimilate, acculturate, and embrace the dominant values upon which criteria for good employees are expected. In this way we all become agents of a race-gendered and classed system that we are taught to view as neutral or "professional" and void of power relations. The practices by which individuals operate must comply with value systems that emerge from the cultures of those in charge. The individual-institutional relationship results in the reproduction of social arrangements in the broader society. The attitudes that reproduce these arrangements in all institutions reflect the tension between values of equality and allegiance to a racial order.

Individuals will apply their interpretation of race and gender in every private and public interaction unless they consciously and intentionally work against it. Ideological belief systems infused into laws, customs, and social practices produce intentional and unintentional race and gender inequalities. "In turn, these inequalities become a part of the established and accepted patterns of social life, and an aspect of the socialization of every member of society. Few can escape the cultural and cognitive forces that promote racial bias" (Gaertner 1997, 18).

Teachers, like social workers, bring their interpretations of race and gender to the workplace. To the extent that racial biases and attitudes are consistent with the cultural values of the dominant group, they seem normal and go unchallenged. Fannie's story is an example of the relationship between ideological constructions and individual-institutional transactions. A fourth grade teacher determined that Fannie's inconsistent academic performance was caused by some type of "disability." Despite the fact that there was nothing to support this determination, the teacher recommended retention. The data on school retention and expulsion show that black children are disproportionately labeled with Attention Deficit Hyperactivity Disorder (ADHD) and Emotionally Behaviorally Disturbed (EBD). This child was one of only a few black children in the entire school. In the absence of any other conclusive data to support the teacher's assumptions, it was indeed very possible that belief systems that rationalize and link the experience of black children to school failure created a framework within which this baseless decision was normalized. The school's test results yielded no information to confirm ADHD or any disability or deficiency that would warrant making this child repeat the fourth grade. Yet the teacher, who was adamant that this was the only correct action, told the child, "Holding you back is the best thing for you to have a good life." What caused her to believe, over the objections of the parents and in the absence of more conclusive evidence, that this decision was in the best interest of the child? What was her belief based on? If you set aside the racial stereotyping for a moment, all other data would support the fact that she should be performing at least at grade level in all areas, if not higher. While the majority of students had English as a second language, this child did not have to negotiate language barriers. Moreover, she came from a family in which at least one parent and two grandparents had advanced educational degrees.

Influences of race and racism in this case are unmistakable. There seemed to be a greater commitment on the teacher's part to see this child fail than to succeed. Because Fannie's parents both worked, she frequently went to her grandmother's home after school. The teacher told the child that because her grandmother was an immigrant, she was probably incapable of giving her the after-school support she needed with her homework. The grandmother, who has been in this country since the 1940s, speaks perfect English. Upon what did the teacher base this assumption, and would she have felt the same way if the grandmother (who had emigrated from an Afro-Caribbean country) had emigrated from a European country?

In response to an incident in which Fannie took a piece of candy from a candy dish that sat on the teacher's desk, the teacher informed the child's mother that she could file a police report for this incident. This was an extreme position to take over a piece of candy. Apparently the candy dish was there as a reward system. Many educators would question the prudence of these kinds of reward systems that invariably set up conditions in which the "loser's" losses are further magnified by the fact they don't get any candy. The fact that the child "stole" the candy should not be overlooked, but the incident is more appropriately understood within context. What could be considered typical and childlike, and therefore dealt with as a "teachable moment" was instead perceived as criminal behavior that would warrant a police report. In contrast, the same teacher had a white male student who stole the school picture money from the teacher's desk. This theft, which is far more serious than the piece of candy, was not reported by the teacher to the school administration nor to the authorities.

The teacher's authority to label, criminalize, and construct a path of failure and deviance, which conformed to cultural depictions of black kids, had the potential to do irreparable damage to this child and even change the course of her life. Contrary to the teacher's belief that "holding her back was the best thing for her to have a good life," data show that there is a direct relationship between school failure and school alienation. A report entitled "Racial Profiling and Punishment in U.S. Public Schools" (1999) indicates that "because racial profiling of students of color operates within certain boundaries of accepted normal practices in our public education system, it is difficult to define, identify, and root out, yet the outcomes are irrefutable." Institutional racism and sexism is embodied in school policies, practices, and teacher attitudes. Stereotypes and assumptions about student abilities on the basis of race and gender can influence teacher recommendations in matters of promotion, retention, and suspension.

These biases can also influence routine grading practices. Such biases can be an impetus for decisions that result in the systematic sorting, selecting, or tracking of students. In Fannie's case, she was determined to be a problem. The overemphasis on a "disability" or failure became the centerpiece of her education in this teacher's class. In effect, the teacher constructed a disorder and then proceeded to teach according to her assumptions about her student's abilities. This required that she reject any evidence that conflicted with her construction, such as family input and test scores. The student was performing below grade level in some areas but at grade level and above in others. The evidence to support behavioral problems outside the realm of normal kid stuff was weak and specious at best. Some of the examples the teacher used to support her actions were not based on her experience with the child but on second-hand accounts about incidents that had occurred in a prior school year. In the student's presence the teacher spoke of her alleged disorders, with utter disregard to her feelings or the impact such labeling might have on the student academically or emotionally.

A study of 200 girls in four California detention facilities found that the vast majority (91 percent) of the female detainees had experienced between one and three school failures. More than four in five girls reported being suspended or expelled from school on one or multiple occasions, nearly one in three had been forced to repeat one or more grades. The link between school failure and delinquency is indisputable. Nationally, the number of female juvenile offenders has grown to the point where some states like Florida have built their first maximum security prisons for girls. Studies indicate that a critical developmental turning point for girls occurs between 8 and 11 years old (Acoca 200, 4). The arbitrary decisions of teachers and others in helping professions can place children on a trajectory of failure. Individual acts, despite claims of colorblindness, can nonetheless contribute to racial consequences in which Fannie and others like her are added to the roster of the disproportionate number of black children who fall through the cracks.

A postscript to this story: Testing conducted by the school and an independent educational testing center paid for by Fannie's parents confirmed that there was no evidence of a learning disability. Fannie's family successfully challenged the decision of retention that was upheld by the principal, but reversed at the superintendent's level. In the following academic year, while attending the same school with a different teacher, Fannie was named student of the month and recommended for a citywide black achievement award. Such success would not have been possible under the classroom conditions of her previous teacher.

Like all other social institutions, discrimination practices in education are covert and often indiscernible. But evidence of persistent discrimination is revealed in outcome measures of retention, expulsion, drop-out, college-going, and graduation. Differential student achievement outcomes, often assumed to be the result of biological or cultural differences of race and/or gender, can in fact be caused by educational practices such as institutional racism embedded in school policy, culture, curriculum, pedagogy, and teacher attitudes rather than academic ability of children. Thus race and gender bias in schooling is an aspect of the hidden curriculum that communicates behavioral norms and individual status in school culture. This is the process of socialization that cues children into their place in the hierarchy of larger society.

The 2002 report *Building a Culture of Fairness and Equity in California's Child Welfare System (CWS)* states that:

> *Whatever the contributing factors may in fact be, the disturbing fact is that there is an enormously disproportionate number of African American children who are placed in foster care (Roberts 2002, 8). National indicators suggest that African Americans represent as much as 42 percent of children in foster care despite the fact that they are only 17 percent of the U.S. population. Disproportionality exists when there is a difference*

between the proportion of children of a particular racial or ethnic group in the child wel-fare system and the proportion of children in that particular racial or ethnic group in the general population (156).

There is strong support in the child welfare literature that systemic and attitudinal forces are responsible for the geographic disparity as well as the disproportionate involvement of large numbers of minority children at all stages of child welfare decision making. Roberts, for exam-ple, has written that the child protection process is designed and operates in a way that prac-tically invites bias and encourages unfair habits, "Vague definitions of neglect, unbridled dis-cretion, and lack of training form a dangerous combination in the hands of caseworkers charged with deciding the fate of families" (157).

Racial discrepancies at all levels of the process from intake to disposition are reported. Obviously, the numbers of blacks in the system, their experiences once they are in the system such as longer stays in foster care, less likelihood for reunification, and greater frequency of removal from foster care homes, underscore disparities. The role of the social worker at each intersection is pivotal to the outcome. It is at the discretion of these individuals that decisions relating to placement, removal, foster care, and reunification are made. The idiosyncratic val-ues and beliefs of social workers, supervisors, court personnel, legislators, and bureaucrats frame the discussion, policies, and practices of the child welfare system that either produce out-comes of fairness and equity or reproduce systems of injustice.

Collaboration of Social Institutions in the Reproduction of Raced Outcomes

Social institutions, such as education, social welfare, the criminal justice system, reproduce social arrangements based on race and gender because the individuals who staff and run these institutions bring to them a consciousness informed by ideological belief systems that ration-alize racial disparities. Pervasive ideological constructions of race create preconditions for how individuals are perceived and treated. The extent to which institutional arrangements mirror those of the broader society can be seen as normal and inevitable outcomes.

Uniformity in managing these tensions of race is found among all major social institutions. The ability of the criminal justice system to absorb the individuals who fall through the bot-tom in education or social welfare is predictable and predetermined. For example, by investing more money in corrections than education, our expectations for the attainment of future gen-erations has been sealed. "For the cost of imprisoning one person for one year, California could educate ten community college students, five California state university students, or two University of California students" (Guinier 2002, 267). The role of institutions to formalize, document, and label individual status (such as college graduate or felon), to function as track-ing systems that influence and possibly even determine status arrangements, and to obfuscate any arbitrariness within the culture is essential to colorblind culture.

Conclusion

Colorblind culture prescribes the conditions and terms of the public and private discourse on race. The individual-institutional relationship has replaced the old political regimes in which racism was centralized through rigid laws of visible exclusion with one that is tightly and invisibly woven into all aspects of social life. Under the guise of a colorblind culture, race stratification remains intact.

Instead of perceiving racism as an unfortunate "symptom" of current institutional arrangements, it should be interpreted as a set of tools that produces and sustains social hierarchies. This article attempts to illuminate some of these tools in the hope that they are rendered more discernable and therefore criticized and resisted.

References

Acoca, Leslie. 2002. "Educate or Incarcerate," National Council on Crime and Delinquency *Building a culture of fairness and equity in California's child welfare system.* California Welfare Services Stakeholders Group.

Carter, R. T. 1997. Expressions of racial identity. In *Off white: Readings on race, power and society,* ed. M. Fine, L. Weis, et al., 198–209. New York: Routledge Press.

Collins, P. H. 1998. *Fighting words: Black women and the search for justice.* Minneapolis: University of Minnesota Press.

Crenshaw, K. W. 1998. Color blindness, history and the law. In *The house that race built,* ed. W. Lubiano, 280–288. New York: Vintage Books.

Gaertner, S. L. 1997. Does white racism necessarily mean anti-blackness: Aversive racism and pro-whiteness. In *Off white: Readings on race, power and society,* ed. M. Fine, L. Weis, et al., 167–178. New York: Routledge Press.

Guinier, L. 2002. *The miner's canary: Enlisting race, resisting power, transforming democracy.* Cambridge, MA: Harvard University Press.

Hanchard, Michael. 1999. "Introduction," *Racial Politics in Contemporary Brazil,* ed. Michael Hanchard. Durham, NC: Duke University Press.

Harris, C. 1995. Whiteness as property. In *Critical race theory,* ed. K. Crenshaw, et al. New York: New York Press.

Harris, D. 2002. *Profiles in injustice.* New York: The New press.

hooks, b. 1994. *Teaching to transgress.* New York: Routledge Press.

hooks, b. 1995. *Killing rage.* New York: Henry Holt and Company.

Hurtado, A. and Stewart, A. 1997. Through the looking glass: Implication of studying whiteness for feminist methods. In *Off white: Readings on race, power and society,* ed. M. Fine, L. Weis, et al., 297–311. New York: Routledge Press.

Jewell, K. S. 1993. *From mammy to Miss America and beyond.* New York: Routledge Press.

Moore, Michael. 2001. New York: Regan Books. "Kill Whitey." In *Stupid White Men,* Michael Moore.

Racial profiling and punishment in U.S. public schools. 1999. Applied Research Center (ARC).

Roberts, D. 2002. *Shattered bonds: The color of child welfare.* New York: Basic Civita Books.

7

Hiring Immigrant Women:
Silicon Valley's "Simple Formula"

Karen J. Hossfeld

I have a very simple formula for hiring. You hire right, and managing takes care of itself. Just three things I look for in hiring [entry-level, high-tech manufacturing operatives]: small, foreign, and female. You find those three things and you're pretty much automatically guaranteed the right kind of workforce. These little foreign gals are grateful to be hired—very, very grateful—no matter what.

—a White male production manager and hiring supervisor in a
Silicon Valley printed circuit board assembly shop

Trainers and employment agencies around town have this story we tell that explains why we prefer to invest our resources in groups with a good track record.

If you tell people that there's a job call Monday morning downtown at nine, this is what happens: the Chinese and the Koreans show up the night before and camp outside the door, so they'll be the first in line. The Iranians used to show up at seven, but now they own everything so they don't need the jobs. Between eight and nine, the Whites

*show up. The Mexicans come in the afternoon, after their siesta, and the Blacks roll by—
maybe—sometime the next day.*

—a White male industrial training program and
employment agency director in Silicon Valley

California's famed high-tech industrial region, Silicon Valley, is renowned for the great opportunities it has provided to live out the American dream. Since the 1970s, thousands have flocked there in hopes of getting rich quick by hitching their wagons (computerized ones, of course) to the lucrative high-tech revolution. In fact, thousands have indeed become millionaires in the process. Thousands more have successfully turned to the industry in search of new and exciting professional careers, at a time when most other industries in the country are declining. But not every group has had equal access to the preponderance of riches fueled by the region's rapid industrial growth. In fact, shoring up the simple formula of the American dream is another "simple formula" that is actually quite complex: many employers' predilection for basing hiring on gender, race, and nationality. This chapter examines this predilection on the "low-tech" side of high-tech industry: manufacturing assembly work. I explore the factors that peg workers who are "small, foreign and female" in the lowest paid jobs—factors that are not quite as obvious as they might appear.

The findings draw from my larger study of the lives and labors of Third World[1] immigrant women workers in Silicon Valley's semiconductor manufacturing industry (Hossfeld 1988, 1992). Empirical data come from conversations I had between 1982 and 1990 with over 200 workers, as well as with many of their family members, employers, managers, labor organizers, and community leaders. Extensive in-depth inter-views were conducted with eighty-four immigrant women representing twenty-one nationalities, and with forty-one employers and managers who represented twenty-three different firms. All but five of these management representatives are white men born in the United States. All of the workers and managers are employed at Santa Clara County, California, firms engaged in some aspect of semiconductor chip manufacturing assembly. I directly observed production at fifteen of these firms.

Silicon Valley's high-tech production labor force includes immigrants from at least thirty Third World nations. The primary informant sampling in the study reflects this diversity. Approximately 40 to 50 percent of the workers, in both the study and the larger labor force, are from Mexico, with other sizable groups representing Vietnam, the Philippines, South Korea, and Taiwan. Smaller numbers come from Cambodia, Laos, Thailand, Malaysia, Indonesia, India, Pakistan, Iran, Ethiopia, Haiti, Cuba, El Salvador, Nicaragua, Guatemala, and Venezuela. There is also a very small group of Southern European workers, mainly from Portugal and Greece, who are not considered in this study.

All of the women workers were first interviewed informally, in small groups, and then individually, following a formal interview schedule that lasted at least three hours. None of the workers were approached on the job or interviewed at the job site. Additional in-depth, open-ended interviews were conducted with thirty-six of the women at their homes, and were accompanied by group interviews with their household members. Access to worker informants was gained by three methods: through my established contacts in immigrant communities; by attending social, church, and neighborhood functions within these communities; and by attending advertised job calls at high-tech manufacturing firms. Many of my initial informants introduced me to their friends and coworkers. In order to ensure a broad sample, I did not interview more than five people who were introduced by the same source or who worked at the same plant.

In addition to interviews, many worker informants were also visited several times over an eight-year period. During these visits, I participated in household functions and helped deal with family, immigration, and work concerns. By far the most revealing data, from managers and workers alike, were gathered during informal conversations in homes or other social environments.

Managers and employers were identified and approached through personal contacts in the local high-tech industry. The three largest semiconductor manufacturing firms that dominate the industry are all represented in the management sample, as are the majority of the middle-sized firms that employ assembly workers. Managers and employers were formally interviewed for a minimum of one hour at their work site; most also were interviewed informally away from the work site for at least an hour.

Hiring Dynamics: The Continuing Significance of Race

Silicon Valley high-tech manufacturing companies' propensity to recruit and hire primarily Asian and Latina women for operative jobs has been documented by several researchers (Green 1980; Katz and Kemnitzer 1984; Siegel and Borock 1982; Snow 1986). It is well recognized that this pattern is not exclusive to the region but applies to the high-tech industry globally (Ehrenreich and Fuentes 1981; Grossman 1979; Lim 1978; Women Working Worldwide 1991). The microelectronics industry is, in fact, at the forefront of corporate capital's trend to relocate manufacturing production in peripheral and semi-peripheral areas where cheap, often state-controlled, women's labor is plentiful, particularly in Southeast Asia but also in Mexico, Puerto Rico, and other locations in Asia, Central America, South America, and Europe (Siegel 1980). Since the 1960s, large U.S. microelectronics manufacturers have been shifting the bulk of their production facilities to offshore locations but have maintained factories in core regions, such as Silicon Valley, in order to facilitate prototypic, custom-design, and short-term manufacturing.

Employers and labor market analysts frequently argue that individuals who are women and/or people of color and/or immigrants take low-paying jobs either because they are content with them, or because they are unqualified for and sometimes even undeserving of better-paying jobs. I refer to these ideologies—and the hiring strategies that accompany them—as racial, immigrant, and gender "logic." Whether employers are conscious of it or not, each of these logics serves as a form of "capital logic," that is, as strategies that increase profit maximization. Specifically, hiring patterns that are informed by racism, national chauvinism, and sexism increase class stratification and labor control, and decrease potential unity among workers.

White employers' use of racism to help establish a hierarchical and exploitative division of labor is not a new phenomenon, nor is it specific to high-tech industry. The contemporary textile industry, for example, also draws heavily on Third World women workers, an increasing trend in global capitalist development. In textiles, as in high-tech industry, employers have used sexist and racist stereotypes to help establish an international division of labor. For example, textile employers tell indigenous textile workers in Western Europe and North America that wage cuts and layoffs should be blamed on Third World women who are "naturally" willing to work for less and to tolerate more exploitative conditions than workers in the core, not on the skewed capitalist international division of labor (Chapkis and Enloe 1983).

Another aspect of racism and the division of labor is explored by Ralph Fevre in his case study of wool textile firms in West Yorkshire, Britain (Fevre 1984). He found that Indians and Pakistanis were recruited and hired in this low-paid manufacturing sector mainly because their labor had already been categorized by a racially discriminatory society as being worth less than White workers'—before they were ever hired. Employers set low wages not only because of cost and profit dictates but also because they "regarded low wages as the basic, immutable condition of wool textile production" (Fevre 1984:11), and as all that Asian workers deserved. Employer respondents in Fevre's study believed that Indian and Pakistani male workers were "intellectually limited," and that they possessed racially specific characteristics suiting them to the monotonous work. As one of these British employers put it: "Asians are plodders so you put them in combing where you need plodders" (Fevre 1984:111). These same groups of workers were denied the opportunity to demonstrate other work abilities because employers refused to hire them for "non-plodding" jobs.

William Julius Wilson, one of the most widely read sociological scholars of contemporary racial dynamics, argues that since World War II, race has played a diminishing role in the structuring of the aggregate capitalist labor force in the United States (Wilson 1978, 1988). Wilson's work focuses specifically on Black Americans, but his thesis that class has replaced race as the most significant determinant of Blacks' economic condition in the United States has influenced the way sociologists look at race and racism in general. Critics such as Manning Marable have challenged Wilson's emphasis, arguing that although socioeconomic class may indeed have an increasing significance for middle-class Blacks, this does not decrease the significance of race and racism for most Blacks in the United States, who are not middle class. Part of the danger of Wilson's insistence on the diminishing impact of racism, Marable argues, is that it legitimates social policy aimed at cutting affirmative action, and implies that capitalist economic development, left unhindered, can and will rid itself of racism (Marable 1980:215–217). My research in Silicon Valley suggests that at least within the particular industrial sector I studied, capitalist economic development utilizes and thrives on racism as a method of labor division and control. Precisely because it is a major indicator of class, race remains a significant determinant in the Silicon Valley division of labor.

Two other contemporary scholars of racism's relationship to employment, Michael Omi and Howard Winant, argue that racism was actually resurgent in the 1980s, and that race relations have the capacity to shape class relations in the contemporary United States (Omi and Winant 1983, 1986). They note that most traditional sociological interpretations of the relationships between workers and employers, such as those of Marx, were based on White males. Thus, these theories do not fully consider how women and people of color may be treated differently by employers and managers. In fact, Omi and Winant argue, racism serves employers as an effective tool to divide workers, and the class system functions to serve White privilege (1983:40).

"Model minority" theory is another interpretation of race-employment dynamics currently in vogue both in mainstream social sciences (Wong 1985) and in many corporate personnel offices. The findings of my study challenge model minority theory's explanation of why different racial minority groups have had different economic "success" rates, and the theory's corollary prescription for how "less successful" minority groups might better succeed. Model minority theory posits that lifestyle patterns and cultural values of some racial minority groups (Asians) are more conducive to successful integration into the mainstream U.S. economy than those of other groups (African Americans and Latinos). Model minority theorists in previous decades took Japanese and Chinese Americans as models for other groups to emulate. In the 1980s, model minority theorists pointed to Vietnamese and Koreans as economic success models.

Model minority theory tends to overlook structural barriers, such as institutionalized racism, that restrict economic opportunities for people of color. One of its dangerous implications is that it facilitates blaming the comparatively low income levels of African Americans, Latinos, Native Americans, and unaffluent Asians on their cultural values. The theory also has been used to argue that affirmative action and equal opportunity programs are unnecessary, because "some" racial minorities have "made it on their own." It can be used to validate excluding all Asians from affirmative action, including the many Asians and Pacific Islanders who are not wealthy or privileged (Wong 1985).

The idea that all Asians have "made it" in the United States, and that they have done so because of racial or cultural superiority, is, as Eugene Wong points out, a true American myth (Wong 1985). It is also a myth that is damaging to all minority groups, including Asian ones, who are now being lumped together and attacked by Whites for being "too successful" (Omi and Winant 1986). Omi and Winant have argued against simplistic explanations that posit Asians as lesser victims of racism because they are seen by Whites as "closer" to Whites in color and culture. It is not that Whites are "less racist" to Asians than to other people of color but, rather, that racism against different groups takes different forms in different historical periods.

Asian workers have historically been among the most exploited in the United States, which may make it appear that employers have preferred to hire Asians. But Whites' designation of Asians as favored workers has been conflictual and frequently hostile, as California's anti-Filipino riots of the 1930s and long history of anti-Chinese legislation illustrate. More recently, in the mid-1980s, a nationwide anti-Japanese backlash, blaming the Japanese for loss of American jobs and cheaper foreign products, helped create the climate for a series of violent racial hate crimes (including murder) by Whites against anyone the perpetrators thought "looked Japanese." Since the 1980s, Asian immigrants and their U.S.-born children have become disproportionately high achievers in American schools. If this trend continues, and if

U.S. Asian populations continue to grow dramatically, Whites' professed admiration for Asians' cultural values as a path to upward mobility may turn increasingly to resentment.

Silicon Valley's Division of Labor

Silicon Valley, as California's Santa Clara County is commonly referred to, is famed for its microelectronics industry and for the technological revolution it helped to generate. The region is renowned for its computer wizards and for the high-tech fortunes made and lost by venture capitalists and entrepreneurs. But behind Silicon Valley's celebrity is a less-known feature both of the specific region and of the world's fastest-growing industry in general. The microelectronics industry is predicated on a division of labor that is more sharply stratified by class, gender, race, and nationality than almost any other contemporary industry. The high-profile, high-paid engineers, executives, and investors are overwhelmingly White, male U.S. citizens. On the opposite end of the occupational spectrum, the majority of low-paid manufacturing workers are Third World women.

Close to 200,000 people, or 25 percent of employees in the San Jose Metropolitan Statistical Area labor force, work in Silicon Valley's microelectronics industry.[2] There are over 800 manufacturing firms that hire ten or more people each, including 120 large firms that each count over 250 employees. In addition, an even larger number of small firms hire fewer than ten employees apiece. Approximately half of this high-tech labor force—100,000 employee—are in production-related work.[3] An estimated one-quarter of all high-tech industry employees, or half of production-related workers (50,000–70,000), work in semiskilled operative jobs (Siegel and Borock 1982). This contrasts sharply with the majority of other manufacturing industries, where the workers directly engaged in production average from 70 to 80 percent of total employees (Gregory 1984). Semiconductor manufacturing, the industrial sector that is the focus of this study, involves the production of integrated circuits, the silicon "chips" that serve as the basic building block of microelectronics technology. Production includes a complex combination of engineering processes that are performed by highly skilled technicians, as well as finishing and assembly work that is classified as unskilled or semiskilled work. The division of labor within the industry is highly skewed by gender and race. Although women account for close to half of the total Santa Clara County paid labor force both within and outside the industry, only 18 percent of managers, 17 percent of professional employees, and 25 percent of technicians in the industry are female. Conversely, women account for at least 68 percent, and by some reports as much as 85–90 percent, of the operative jobs in high-tech work (California Department of Development 1983).

Similar disparities exist vis-à-vis minority employment, although there are established bourgeoisies among the immigrant communities in the region who have achieved financial prosperity.[4] According to the 1980 census, 73 percent of all employees in Santa Clara County are non-Hispanic White; 15 percent are Hispanic (all races); 7.5 percent are Asian or Pacific Islander; 3 percent are Black; and 0.5 percent are Native American (California Department of Development 1983:96–97). These work force figures are roughly equivalent to each group's regional population percentage, according to census estimates. However, the census does not adequately measure the county's thousands of undocumented residents. In addition, since the census, the region has seen a steady increase in the number of Third World immigrants arriving each year, due in part to influxes of refugees. The number of Indochinese living in Santa Clara County is thought to have quadrupled between 1980 and 1984 alone. It is in these groups of recent immigrants that high-tech employers find much of their production labor force.

Within the microelectronics industry, 12 percent of managers, 16 percent of professionals, and 18 percent of technicians are minorities, mainly concentrated at the lower-paying and less powerful ends of these categories. An estimated 50–75 percent of operative jobs are held by racial minorities, according to state estimates (California Department of Development 1983). Employers and industry analysts estimate that in the industry as a whole, approximately half of all operatives are Third World immigrants.

Findings

Findings indicate that race, national origin, and gender have major significance in determining the class structure and division of labor of Silicon Valley's high-tech industry. High-tech industry managers still use race and nationality, in addition to gender, as primary categories in designating the division of labor. At each of the subcontracting firms I observed, between 80 and 100 percent of workers are Third World immigrants. These firms tend to specialize primarily in unskilled and semiskilled assembly work, which is subcontracted out from other firms. Subcontractors usually pay lower wages and offer fewer benefits than the larger, more vertically integrated, better-known semiconductor firms, such as Silicon Valley's "Big Three": Intel, National Semiconductor, and Advanced Micro Devices. Subcontractors provide an easily expandable and expendable labor force for the very volatile industry. These assembly shops, where immigrant women were the most highly concentrated, have the lowest job security in the business.

Both employers and workers interviewed in this study agree that the lower the skill and pay level of the job, the greater the proportion of Third World immigrant women tends to be. Assembly work, which is classified as the lowest skilled and is the lowest-paid production job, has the highest concentration of these workers. Entry-level electronics production workers, in job categories such as semiconductor processing and assembly, earn an average of from $4.50 to $5.50 an hour; experienced workers in these jobs earn from $5.50 to $8.50. At each of the small (less than 250 employees) subcontracting assembly plants directly observed, immigrant women account for at least 75 percent and up to 100 percent of the assembly labor force. At only one of these plants do White males account for more than 2 percent of the production workers. By contrast, 90 percent of managers and owners at these businesses are White males. The proportion of nonimmigrant women of all races and of immigrant and nonimmigrant minority men increases in skilled production work. Men are concentrated in higher-paying specialties, such as machine and tool operating and technician work. The nonimmigrant women who work in production tend to do semiskilled labor, such as semiconductor processing. This pays slightly more than assembly work but less than jobs where men are concentrated.

The large nonsubcontracting firms I observed have higher percentage of male and nonimmigrant women assemblers and operatives than do smaller subcontracting firms. But even at the big firms, Third World immigrant women typically account for at least 50 percent of the workers. Men are always in a minority on the assembly line, and White men are rare. The presence of some men, however, and of larger numbers of nonimmigrants at larger firms is probably related to the greater opportunities for advancement there. A personnel manager who had worked both at a subcontracting firm and at one of the Big Three told me that the larger, vertically integrated semiconductor firms, unlike subcontractors, try to hire "a certain percentage of 'regular' American workers." This, he says, enables personnel departments to have "an educated, more permanent, in-house work force that we can draw on for training and promotion for more skilled work."

Gender Logic

The employers interviewed indicated that they prefer to hire immigrant women, as compared to immigrant men, for assembly work because of beliefs shared by workers and employers alike that women can afford to work for less. None of the employers had any concrete knowledge about their workers' families or arrangements. Yet almost all of the employers stated that they assumed that their women workers were attached to male workers who were earning more than the women were. In fact, 80 percent of the women workers I interviewed were the main income earners in their families.[5]

Approximately 75 percent of the managers and employers interviewed stated that immigrant women are better suited to high-tech assembly work than immigrant men. Their jobs are characterized by assembly line-style repetition of a small set of tasks. According to workers, the work is extremely tiring because it requires constant concentration and intensive eye-hand coordination to manipulate the tiny, intricate circuitry. Employers and managers consistently claimed that Third World immigrant women are particularly suited to the work because of their supposedly superior hand-eye coordination and their patience. One male manager claimed that the "relatively small size" of many Asian and Mexican women "makes it easier for them to sit quietly for long periods of time, doing small detail work that would drive a large person like [him] crazy." The workers this man supervised, however, thought he preferred to hire physically small women because he could then feel superior and intimidating, "more like a big man," as a Filipina employee put it.

"Immigrant Logic" in Hiring

If I had to pay higher wages, I wouldn't stay in business here. It's not that I couldn't "afford" it per se, but the profit margin would be smaller, obviously. In Singapore, labor costs one-fifth of what it does here.
                                   —a White male employer, subcontracting assembly plant

According to employers, low-level production jobs in Silicon Valley probably would not exist unless there were workers available to work cheaply at insecure nonunionized jobs. Without such a reserve army of labor to call on, manufacturers might very well have developed the industry differently, with an even greater emphasis on automation and overseas location. An engineer in charge of production technology at a semiconductor manufacturing firm observed: "We already have the technology to fully automate everything we do here—it's just more expensive. We could definitely automate every step of the process if it ever becomes cheaper to do that than use human labor. Because of the large supply of unskilled immigrants in the area, labor is still cheaper for doing certain jobs than machines are." He later commented that two major factors could tip the balance in this equation: a curtailed immigration flow and unionization.

Employers interviewed in Silicon Valley electronics plants explain their penchant for hiring large numbers of immigrants in terms typical of employers everywhere who hire immigrants: they are more willing than nonimmigrants to work for low pay in "bad" jobs (i.e., jobs that are unsafe, monotonous, uncomfortable, and unsteady). Immigrants are seen—and see themselves—as being more desperate for work at any wage, because of lack of language, employable skills, or education.

Fifty percent of the employers interviewed offered some form of unsolicited moral legitimation for why they pay such low wages. The following remark from an assembly shop owner typifies this: "I don't want you to think I'm some kind of heartless ogre—my people really do seem to manage quite well on what they earn." The remaining 50 percent offered no personal legitimation: they simply indicated that their wage structures are the result of market supply and demand. This comment from an employer at a subcontracting assembly plant is unusually straightforward:

Beats me how [entry level operatives] survive: they can't possibly do much more than eke by on these wages. But if they don't know the language, and some of them are illiterate even in their own language, and let's suppose, hypothetically of course, that they're not exactly here [in the U.S.] legally—just how many options have they got? We [employers] take advantage of this, but I'm not here to apologize for capitalism.

Employers (as well as the nonimmigrant White and African American workers with whom I talked) argue that immigrants from industrializing countries are better able to survive on very low wages than nonimmigrants. They surmise this is for two reasons. First, people from poor countries are viewed as skilled at and "used to" living on scant resources. Several employers and managers believed that "poverty management skills," as one assistant personnel manager termed it, are one of the "cultural values" that render certain minority groups more likely to succeed. A White male owner of a disk drive manufacturing facility reported:

> These people from Third World countries really are incredible: they're so resourceful! I have this one woman who works for me—she's Filipino, or from somewhere around there—and she supports three kids and her parents on $5.65 an hour. Not only that, but she always makes the best of the situation, and she's always bringing in cakes and things for everyone. We only have one kid, and my wife says she can't make ends meet. And believe me, I make more than $5.65 an hour!

A second explanation several employers offered in explaining immigrant workers' willingness and ability to live on low wages is that such workers' family members are probably still living in their countries of origin, to which the immigrants themselves are planning to return. What might seem like meager savings in the United States, these employers pointed out, stretch much farther in poorer countries.

Historically, employers and the public in the United States have viewed Third World immigrant workers as being able to survive on substandard wages because the immigrants' families were living "back home," where U.S. dollars went farther. Immigrants are seen as people—usually men—who live frugally now in order to live well when they return to their countries of origin. For some immigrants, this scenario is indeed true, but the majority of immigrants to the United States never return to their native countries to live. Today's immigrants to Silicon Valley are rarely planning to save money in order to return home: over 95 percent of the immigrant workers I interviewed reported that they plan to stay in the United States permanently. The great majority also came with families: the low wages they earn must support them on U.S., not Third World, prices. And although many are helping to support relatives in their countries of origin, all had immediate family members living in the United States.

Employers stressed that they are doing immigrant workers a favor by supplying them with any job at all, as the following quotes from two board shop owners reveal:

> I don't really prefer to hire immigrants, but they're usually the only ones willing to do the job. Most Americans would find it kind of boring work, but the Mexicans and the rest of them are grateful for whatever they can get. It beats welfare—both from their point of view, and from ours.

> Actually, it's a good deal all around. A lot of these people were starving before they came to the States, so to them this job is a real step up. They haven't got many skills and they don't speak much English, so they can't expect to be paid much. They're grateful for whatever they get, and I feel we're providing a service by employing them.

In general, employers feel that immigrants are not taking jobs away from U.S. citizens, because relatively few citizens apply for such low-paid and "boring" jobs. That U.S. citizens do not, by and large, take these jobs does indeed suggest that they do not want them, as long as they can get better-paying ones. Yet White North American workers of both sexes, and often men of color, are discouraged by management from applying for entry-level manufacturing jobs, and are more likely to be denied such jobs when they do apply. This was openly confirmed by the majority of hiring personnel interviewed, who claim that most men and White women are not well suited for these jobs.

All of the subcontracting employers interviewed think American-born workers, and particularly American men, would be so frustrated at the lack of mobility opportunity in assembly shops that they would soon quit. One of them explained: "I've had White guys come in here— mainly college kids on breaks wanting to pick up money for the summer. One of them I put in management, but I won't put them on the line. They wouldn't last a week, it's so boring."

When I applied for assembly jobs at various plants, I was repeatedly told by personnel directors that the work wouldn't suit me and that I'd be much happier at a professional job or in a training program, because I was "an American." Naomi Katz (like me, a college-educated, White, North American woman) told me she had the same experience when she looked for assembly work during her study of Silicon Valley workers (Katz and Kemnitzer 1984). While investigating *maquiladora* work in southern California, Maria Patricia Fernandez-Kelly, who speaks both Spanish and English fluently, found that when she made phone inquiries for production jobs in Spanish, she was told there were openings, but when she inquired in English, she was told there were not (Fernandez-Kelly 1985).

Adapting Fernandez-Kelly's technique, I had a team of nationally diverse male and female students call plants and inquire about entry-level production job openings. Female students with Asian, Pacific Islander, or Latino "accents" were told there might be jobs available for them three times more often than male students with Anglo accents.[6] One of the reasons for this bias, a personnel director told me, is that managers think the only educated Americans who would take such jobs must be either journalists or union organizers who were trying to get a story or stir up trouble.

Managers typically exclude American workers of color from their rationale that U.S. citizens are not appropriate for assembly jobs. The hiring personnel I interviewed tended to lump all applicants within a broad racial or ethnic grouping together in their hiring evaluation, whether the individuals were U.S. citizens, native-born or not, especially if the applicants speak with any kind of accent that managers perceived as "foreign." Thus, a third-generation Chicana worker who speaks with a "Spanish" accent may be classified with recent Mexican immigrants in terms of managers' racial and nationality categorizations about who is appropriate for a job.

One of the central reasons that employers "prefer" to hire immigrants rather than available nonimmigrants for low-skill, low-paid, and precarious jobs is that their worth is less valued in society in general. This is clearly expressed by one of the factory owners I interviewed: "This industry is very volatile: the market demand is constantly fluctuating. One month I may have to let a third of my production people go, and the next month I may need to double my work force. Let's face it, when you have to expand and contract all the time, you need people who are more expendable. When I lay off immigrant housewives, people don't get as upset as if you were laying off regular [sic] workers."

Employers also prefer Third World immigrants because they are often newly proletarianized, with little organizing experience in an industrialized setting. And as people who are insecure in their residential status, whether documented or not, immigrants are seen as unlikely to "make waves" against any part of the American system for fear of jeopardizing their welcome. Many of the production processes in semiconductor manufacturing involve the use of highly toxic chemicals, and the rate of reported occupational illnesses in the industry in California is three times the average for all industries (Olson 1984:71). Labor organizers interviewed believe that one of the reasons management prefers to hire immigrants is that they are less familiar with occupational health and safety laws than other workers, and less likely to seek their enforcement.

Racial Logic

As the quote about job trainers' racial hiring preferences at the beginning of this paper suggests, Silicon Valley employers and their colleagues distinguish not only between immigrants and nonimmigrants but also between different immigrant groups. A clear racial, ethnic, and national pecking order of management's hiring preferences emerges from interview findings. Most employers have a difficult time clearly distinguishing the myriad diverse races, ethnicities, and nationalities represented in their labor force. Yet this did not prevent many of them from making stereotypic assumptions about very broadly and usually incorrectly categorized groups. The two such broadly defined "groups" most prevalent in the immigrant work force, and thus most often compared by employers, are Asians and Pacific Islanders, to whom employers variously refer as "Asians" or "Orientals"; and Latinos, to whom employers variously refer as "Hispanics," "Latins," "South Americans," or, generically, "Mexicans." Asian immigrant women are clearly management's preferred production workers. Eighty-five percent of the employers and 90 percent of the managers interviewed stated that they believe Asian women make the best assembly-line workers in high-tech manufacturing.

Because employers tend to ascribe specific work characteristics to entire groups, they assign each group to jobs that emphasize these characteristics, thereby fulfilling their own prophecies. I observed hiring practices that appeared to be based on employers' racial and gender pecking orders. The training and employment agency director quoted at the beginning of this article assumes that different work characteristics exist according to race, and that members of some racial groups always show up late, and some always early, to job calls—not only to job calls, he implies, but also to work. Yet at none of the five large job calls I attended at high-tech manufacturing plants was this the case: Blacks, Whites, Latinos, and Asians all showed up early.

At the two job calls where I was able to obtain the relevant data, Asians were the most likely to obtain entry-level assembly jobs requiring no previous experience, and Whites and Blacks the least likely, regardless of nationality. Of those applying, approximately 20 percent of Asians, 12 percent of Latinos, 5 percent of Whites, and 5 percent of Blacks were hired.

Although over 25 percent of the applicants for entry-level assembly jobs were male, they received only approximately 10 percent of the jobs. Three men who came specifically to apply for assembly jobs were hired as technicians, jobs for which they did not originally apply. Although data collection at these job calls did not control for other important factors—such as age, education, immigration status, language skills, and job experience—the heavily skewed hiring preferences clearly suggest racial discrimination.

Most managers interviewed consider African Americans to be the least desirable workers, not because they are believed to be too good for the jobs, as Whites are generally considered, but because they are not considered dependable enough for employment in general. Managers were mixed in their evaluation of Black immigrants: one production manager commented that Black Caribbean immigrants are "not usually as cocky" as African Americans. Management attitudes toward entry-level African American applicants are more negative than toward any other group. For working-class African Americans in Silicon Valley, this suggests, Wilson's prognosis of the declining significance of race in the labor market is not applicable. However, Silicon Valley hiring personnel repeatedly commented that there is a shortage of African American applicants at the professional level. I was told by several that they would like to find and hire well-credentialed African American engineers or programmers.[7] This suggests that White racism against Blacks may indeed be partially mitigated by Blacks' class and educational status, as Wilson proposes (Wilson 1978), but I was unable to find African American high-tech professionals who could confirm or deny this. My impression from talking with both managers and workers is that White racism against Blacks is a strong factor in the structuring of the Silicon Valley labor force but that, unsurprisingly, it is more intensely (although certainly not exclusively) experienced by and directed toward working-class Blacks.

Three of the firms I talked with were considering opening plants in U.S. localities with large Mexican populations (Brownsville, Texas; Albuquerque, New Mexico; and Watsonville, California). When I suggested locations characterized by large reserve labor pools of Black workers, such as nearby Oakland and East Palo Alto, spokespersons at all three firms indicated that these areas did not have suitable labor climates. Black workers are hired by high-tech production facilities in North Carolina's Research Triangle, however. An organizer whose union was conducting an organizing campaign in the high-tech manufacturing industry at the time suggested that Silicon Valley firms would not consider locating in Oakland because of union strength in that largely Black area. A leader in a different union that was targeting a large local semiconductor manufacturing company believed the industry's avoidance of the region was directly rooted in racism.

Four employers who had no direct experience—either negative or positive—with hiring Blacks and Latinos in skilled positions told me that they would prefer not to do so unless no one else was available. Their preferences, according to the respondents, were not based on comparative productivity reports from colleagues but on what they had personally concluded about these groups outside of the workplace. "Blacks are troublemakers," explained one administrator. "I found that out when I was at [the University of California at Berkeley]. They don't like Whites and they don't like authority—and I'm both." Only two of the employers interviewed reported that they had no racial preferences in hiring for entry-level jobs. Only one of the two claimed to have absolutely no racial preference for hiring at any level, but even he amended his claim by adding, "as long as the secretaries are pretty, and personally, I don't find most Black women that attractive."

I was told several times by employers and managers that they prefer not to put Blacks and Hispanics in jobs that require much training, because, as one White manager worded it, "that would be throwing good money after bad—they tend to quit faster, so why invest in them?" Yet at none of the companies I observed was management able to provide me with a racial break-down of turnover rates. A Black Jamaican woman who worked in the plant of the manager just quoted confided: "More Blacks would be likely to stick around if they gave us a chance at the better jobs, but they never do. So of course you're going to leave if you find a better offer, or if you just get tired knowing you'll stay at the bottom, no matter what you do."

Guadalupe Friaz's in-depth study of a large Silicon Valley electronics firm provides another example of how what appears to be a race distinction between workers may actually be a result of managers' racism. Friaz found that Asians had the lowest turnover rate of any group at the firm, and that Blacks and Latinos had the highest. She suggests that one possible explanation for this difference is the bias of racist supervisors, who treat workers differently and recom-mend promotions according to race (Friaz 1985).

Certainly not all employers and managers I interviewed and observed displayed blatant racism. Even those who admitted to personal racial preferences in hiring typically indicated that they knew it was illegal to institutionalize such preferences, as this executive's words illus-trated: "It would be fine with me if I could simply advertise that I only wanted to hire certain groups. But nobody's that stupid—you'd get your butt sued off. But it's not against the law to choose where you post jobs—and where you don't. . . . I resent anybody telling me who I should hire, regardless of who does the best work, but I'm a stickler about doing everything by the law."

Less than 10 percent of the managers and employers in my study reported that they were aware of the Equal Employment Opportunity Commission (EEOC) investigating or reviewing their firms' hiring practices. One employer, however, pointed out that if his firm were being investigated, he probably would not admit it. An EEOC staff worker who was contacted for this study clarified that the agency mainly dealt with professional-level jobs and/or firms with government contracts. Even if someone filed a discrimination complaint, she explained, the regional office was backlogged well over a year in its investigations.

Interviews with White employers and administrators suggested that they are most comfort-able when their workplace colleagues and office staff are also White, and their production work force is not. This makes it easier for management to construct an "us" and a "them" to help solidify the division of labor. It protects the white-collar Whites from having to confront their own racism, enabling them to view work relationships as occupationally, rather than racially, based. This is certainly not a unique situation. As a union organizer phrased it, "Historically, it has always been easier for bosses to exploit people they don't identify with."

Are Asians "Better" Workers?

Over 80 percent of employers and managers interviewed referred to Asian immigrant workers as one collective category, rarely distinguishing between ethnic and nationality groups. All but one thought Asians make the best production workers. The reasons Silicon Valley employers and managers gave for preferring Asian workers typically paralleled model minority theory analysis. The theory was directly applied in several Silicon Valley personnel offices, and was mentioned by name by personnel staff at three different plants. A personnel director at one of the fifteen largest semiconductor manufacturing firms in Silicon Valley said she approaches her job (making most of the firms' hiring decisions) with the assumption that Asians are "better" production workers than other racial groups. She explained that the basis for her assumption was theoretical, not experiential: her master's thesis in industrial psychology was a review of model minority literature about "the Asian success story." She cited "uniquely Asian cultural values" as being "especially well-suited to the American free market system." According to this manager, these Asian values explain comparatively high income levels for Asian Americans and Asian immigrants, and include the following traits: investment in and commitment to higher education, even at the cost of financial hardship; dedication to hard work and willingness to work unusually long hours; a frugal lifestyle; putting aside small sums of capital until investment in a small business is possible; employing [apparently unpaid or low-paid] family members to keep labor costs down; and "a cultivated tradition of perseverance, coupled with cultural identification with, and a strongly positive feeling towards, the American dream."[8]

Employers' explanatory schemata for why Asians are the best workers ignore two interrelated critical factors: class origins and racism. In terms of class origins, several of the earlier waves of Indochinese, Koreans, and Chinese who worked in Silicon Valley production shops were originally from college-educated, middle-class, professional backgrounds. Although they temporarily lost that status upon immigration, particularly in the case of political refugees, who frequently fled with only the clothes they wore, eventually many of them were able to reestablish it, at least to some extent. White American employers who saw this reestablishment of upper-middle-class origins often seemed to confuse it with some innate racial ability. By comparison, few Mexican immigrant workers come from middle-class, college-educated backgrounds. Because earlier waves of Asian immigrants, particularly from Indochina, include substantial numbers of the ruling class and professionals, later groups of immigrants from these countries, who are from poorer backgrounds, have had both role models and, often, sponsors. This is another reason why Asians are perceived as working harder than Mexicans: they may in fact work faster and more carefully because they believe there will be a payoff greater than their paycheck. They have more examples in their communities who suggest that hard work can indeed result in class mobility. In addition, employers, trainers, educators, and social service workers may have formed opinions of Asians based on interaction with or exposure to the middle- and upper-class sectors of the population.

Today, the class background of Asian immigrant communities is rapidly shifting. The later waves of Indochinese refugees are not entrepreneurs and professionals fleeing socialist nationalization of private property but "boat people" who are poor, destitute, unskilled at industrialized jobs, and comparatively unlikely candidates for upward mobility. With this class and demographic change, the dominant White culture's perception of Asian communities may also change, and with it employers' preference for Asian workers. Social service workers I interviewed in Asian communities suggest this is already occurring. Vietnamese residents of Silicon Valley report that an escalating racist backlash is accompanying the growth in the number of Vietnamese-owned businesses and the political and religious clout of the Vietnamese population in the Silicon Valley city of San Jose. San Jose's Vietnamese population grew from an estimated 11,700 in 1980 to 75,000 in 1987. Jim McEntee, director of human relations for the Human Relations Commission of Santa Clara County, reports that racism against the Vietnamese is on the rise, due to "paternalistic" attitudes in the mainstream population about the proper place of minority groups. "It was fine as long as [the Vietnamese] were nice and quiet. Then they were 'nice' people" (*San Jose Mercury News*, July 26, 1987:1B).

In general, although employers and managers express resentment of upper- and middle-class Asians and Asian Americans whom they view as competitors, they continue to prefer Asian workers. One manager, who refers to his Mexican workers as "bean eaters," said, "I've just never liked Mexicans. They rub me wrong." He explained that he finds Mexicans both lazy and insubordinate on the job. When asked for specifics, he replied: "Well, it's not anything they do or don't do. It's not like there have been any incidents. I just pick up on their attitude. Once a grape picker, always a grape picker."

Many of the White managers interviewed resent Mexicans and Chicanos because they think Mexican immigrants are "ripping off" the United States. Several of the production and other midlevel managers grew up in California agricultural regions where battles between White farm owners and the predominantly Mexican United Farm Workers have been bitter. They interpret the union's organizing as a racial problem, not as class struggle. Most seem to have no idea that similar battles had been waged between Whites and Asians in earlier generations (Filipino farm workers, for example, were also active in forming the United Farm Workers), and that White hostility to Asian workers was once just as vehement.

Although employers claim that certain racial groups are more productive or responsible workers, none of the employers or managers interviewed could provide any comparative productivity data to back up such claims. Categorical judgments about particular racial groups may indeed be borne out in reality, but they also may be based on stereotyping that results in self-fulfilling prophecy. One employer, for example, admitted that since the start of his company, he has channeled Blacks and Latinos into monotonous and dangerous jobs where high turnover is expected and comparatively unimportant, since "those people have a propensity to quit sooner and be less reliable workers anyway." As to why he hires workers he believes are inferior, he commented, "I'm not prejudiced—I hire every color of the rainbow here. We're a regular affirmative action paragon of virtue." Indeed, his production force is composed entirely of minority groups. In contrast, his office staff is entirely White, which he explains by saying that race is not a factor; he simply hires the most qualified who apply for each job. His company, he claims, passed EEOC guidelines with "flying colors," and thus is eligible to obtain government contracts.

Another example of self-fulfilling racist prophecies is shown in the story of two neighbors who, unbeknownst to each other, called about the same job openings as packers (typically a job filled by men) at a high-tech manufacturing assembly plant. One, a Chinese immigrant who speaks English with a very discernible Chinese accent, was told to show up on the following morning at 8 A.M. sharp. The other, a U.S. citizen whose voice patterns as an African American are also very discernible, was told to "come by sometime tomorrow morning." When the Black man arrived at 9 A.M., he was told the job had already been filled, on a first-come, first-served basis. The Chinese man, who got one of the positions, later reported that at the end of the first day of work, employees were told that there were still two openings available, in case they knew anyone who might be interested. He told the White employer that his neighbor, who was "like a brother" to him, might want the job and was told, "Chinese are good workers; bring him by." The neighbor, the same Black man who had tried earlier to apply, accompanied the Chinese man to work the next day, where he was again told there were no openings. The employer later told the Chinese employee, "I thought you said you were bringing your brother." The next week, two other Asian immigrants were hired. On a separate occasion, the White personnel director at this firm told me that the reason so few Blacks worked at her firm was because so few applied. "Personally, I think because [Blacks] have lived here longer [than Asian immigrants] they know how to scam better." She added, "They don't need to get regular jobs in order to survive."

Immigrant Women Workers' Consciousness

It takes time . . . sometimes even years, before many Third World immigrants realize that racism stands in their way. . . . They tend to think their slow economic progress is just because they are new in this country, just as the Irish and the Italians and the Jews once were. It takes a while for them to realize the ramifications of the fact that although accents and citizenship and cultural customs can change in one or two generations, skin color does not. That is the main way that today's immigrants differ from yesterday's. When their newness wears off, they will still be non-Whites in a world dominated by Whites.

—a Chinese American social worker in
San Francisco's Asian immigrant communities

Cross-nationally, working-class immigrants interviewed for this study concurred with employers' "immigrant logic" that all immigrants who arrive in the United States with little or no material wealth, and with little or no English or easily transferable job skills, will have to work their way up from near the bottom of the job and class ladders. Even those who arrive with transferable job skills do not expect to compete on an equal footing with nonimmigrant workers in the short run. There is a strong sense that as new immigrants, they must pay their dues by taking unpreferred jobs and living close to the poverty margin. Most do not view this as unfair or exploitative. It does not make them like their jobs, but they see their situation as something every family or ethnic group must go through upon immigration. They view their position in the U.S. labor force as part of a cycle of economic assimilation. They believe that any new immigrants who work hard and pay their dues will eventually move into the middle or upper middle class, or at least the stable working class, and that their low-level jobs will be filled by new waves of immigrants, who in turn can work their way up and be replaced by even newer waves. This is described by many as the "American way." Almost all believe that their families will be economically assimilated by their second generation in the United States, if not sooner.

The ideology that Third World immigrants "deserve less" is cut from a cloth similar to the ideology that devalues women's labor, and the two are often intertwined in the workplaces where immigrant women are employed. There is a major difference between the two ideologies, though. Immigrant status can be overcome, at least within one generation, but gender status is more permanent. And even in terms of immigrant status, the reality of U.S. society is that not every immigrant group has made equal inroads into the middle- and upper-class strata, even with time. Although most White groups have done so, many Third World groups have not.[9]

Many of the immigrant informants confirmed that they are indeed better off than they would be if they had stayed in their countries of origin. A Vietnamese community leader explained that my questions about the "quality of work" and "standard of living" are not very relevant to refugees who have brushed death so closely. The majority of immigrants interviewed were grateful to the United States and to their employers, an attitude I did not expect to find among such a low-paid work force. Even the immigrant workers who did not feel particularly grateful, mainly Latinos but also some Asians, agreed that whatever the shortcomings of their lives in the United States, they were economically worse off before they came here. A Mexican woman told me: "I don't earn enough here to support my family. If there weren't three of us working in our household, we wouldn't get by. But what choice do I have? [In Mexico] I had no job at all, and three babies to feed."

Regardless of how long they have been at their current jobs, all of the women workers interviewed believed that they would move on to better jobs within a few years. I found numerous workers who had been doing the same or similar work for over five years, yet still maintained that their jobs were temporary. Even individuals who had been on the job for as long as ten years still tended to view the job as a temporary stop, as a stepping-stone to somewhere else. Although this may prove to be the case, they have spent a substantial portion of their work lives "not getting involved" in trying to change unfavorable conditions because of this view. A union organizer commented:

> Six years ago, when we approached workers at [a large semiconductor firm], I met this very bright, articulate Mexicana who seemed pretty feisty, who I thought would be an excellent union advocate on the floor. I approached her about it, and she said no, that she believed in unions but she was going to be out of that place soon and didn't want to make any commitments there. This year I ran into her again—she's now at [a competitor

firm] doing the same job, and she said the exact same thing. Maybe she'll go for it in another five years—if there's any jobs left here to be "about to quit" in the first place.

Excerpts from an interview with a young Filipina fabrication operator also illustrate this predicament. Asked about her attitudes toward unions, she replied: "Most of the women here are not interested in organizing a union. The work is pretty bad for the health, and we'd like to see that changed, and better benefits, but most of us don't expect to be here too long. Union drives take a long time—sometimes a couple of years—and I'll be gone by then." This statement takes on a new perspective when juxtaposed to an earlier part of the interview:

Interviewer (I): How long have you been in this line of work?
Respondent (R): Four years.
I: How long did you plan on staying when you took the job?
R: A year.
I: When do you plan on leaving?
R: Within a year. (laugh) This time I mean it!
I: What kept you from leaving sooner?
R: I was trying to save up enough to go to school to get a beautician's license.
I: Have you saved almost enough?
R: No, nothing. I spent it all on things my family needed.
I: What will you do when you leave?
R: Something more interesting—I don't know. Maybe we'll win the lottery! (laughter)

I later showed this woman her two sets of statements, and asked her to compare them. After reading her own words, she explained:

You're probably thinking that in four years I could have worked to organize a union, or at least filed a grievance about the allergies I developed from the [processing chemicals]. But even though I didn't leave, I was ready to at any time, in case something else came along. And I want to stay ready to leave at any time—I don't want to feel committed and sucked in at a job I don't like. . . . this year I'm leaving for sure.

Two years later, this same woman was working at another semiconductor plant after being temporarily unemployed due to a layoff at her old plant.

Although small groups of immigrants suffered racial or ethnic oppression in their homelands, most of the immigrant workers interviewed were accustomed to being members of the majority racial group in their countries of origin. Thus, most of them did not grow up subject to internalized racial oppression, as Erica Sherover-Marcuse (1986) suggests is the case for people of color born and raised in the United States. This may help to explain why managers often make a pretense of disguising their racism as immigrant logic when dealing directly with workers. Many of the more recent immigrants deny the existence of discrimination and prejudice against their racial or national group in the United States. Informants who have been in the

United States five years or less are much more likely to explain their experiences with discrimination as being based in their ignorance as, or others' ignorance of, foreigners rather than as race related. This is true for close to 70 percent of the Asian immigrants interviewed but for only 30 percent of the Mexican immigrants. Mexican immigrants are more likely to have heard explicit accounts of racism in the United States before immigrating, from friends and relatives who migrated back and forth between the two countries. A recently arrived, undocumented Mexican worker commented: "I already knew that 'gringos' don't like Mexicans before we came here, because my cousin lived in the States. But I also knew they would hire us for certain jobs, so we came anyway." Her observation is typical of those made by her compatriots. Latinos in general, as well as the few Black immigrants among the informants, are more likely than Asians to expect racism to deter their access to equitable jobs and incomes.

Most of the Asian immigrants were not very knowledgeable about U.S. racism when they immigrated, or at least did not realize it extends to Asians. A woman from India commented: "I knew that Americans [sic] did not like the Blacks, but I was surprised they don't like Indians too much, either." Remarks from a recently immigrated Chinese worker suggest that she is shocked by derogatory racial slurs when they are directed at her own national/racial group, but not when they are directed at certain others: "Why do they say these things to us?" she asked. "People treat us bad, like they do the Blacks or Mexicans. I don't understand. I thought Chinese culture is very respected here."

Conclusion

The main source of legitimation of both gender and racial hierarchy within the high-tech industry in Silicon Valley lies, obviously, in the existence of occupational and social stratification. Every day workers and managers view the gender-, class-, and race-tiered structure of the industry, and although some may consider it unfair, most believe that it is inevitable. As a Chicana who worked as a bonder in a large firm said of the company's racial and gender hierarchy: "Of course I don't like it, but there's nothing I can do about it—it's like that everywhere." An African American woman coworker agreed: "It's a White man's world—just look around the plant. I take the job I can get and I do it." The few who did challenge the hierarchy, during conversation, were mainly not immigrants: some of the White women workers questioned sexual hierarchies, and some nonimmigrant women of color questioned both sexual and racial boundaries. In general, though, as with sexism, employers can use "immigrant-specific" logic because it corresponds to workers' own consciousness of their limited options.[10]

In conclusion, the racial division of labor in the Silicon Valley high-tech manufacturing work force originates in the racially structured labor market of the larger economy, and in the "racial logic" that employers use in hiring. This "racial logic" is based on stereotypes—both observed and imagined—that employers have about different racial groups. One of the effects of this racial logic, vis-à-vis workers, is to reproduce the racially structured labor market and class structure that discriminates against minorities and immigrants. Another effect is that within the workplace, racial categories and racism become tools for management to divide and control workers. These are dynamics that individuals and organizations interested in social change must become more familiar with—not just in Silicon Valley but elsewhere. As for the situation in highly "innovative" Silicon Valley itself, to date, neither labor, women's, nor ethnic organizations have made major inroads in challenging the hiring hierarchy (Hossfeld 1991). But challenge it we must. Equality of opportunity, both at work and away from it, cannot be achieved unless we learn to recognize and reject practices that are based on "simple formulas" about gender, race, and nationality.

Notes

1. As many recent scholars and activists have noted, the term "Third World" is problematic and imprecise. Yet so, too, are currently available substitute terms such as "postcolonial," "industrializing," and "developing." For references to the terminology debate from a feminist perspective, see Mohanty, Russo, and Torres, 1991. In this article, the term "Third World immigrants" refers to individuals who have immigrated (in this case to the United States) from world regions with a history of colonial domination.

2. Statistical references in this study have not been updated to reflect the 1990 census because the research was conducted, and refers to conditions, during the 1980s.

3. These production jobs include the following U.S. Department of Labor occupational titles: semiconductor processor, semiconductor assembler, electronics assembler, and electronics tester. Entry-level wages for these jobs in Silicon Valley are $4.00–$5.50; wages for workers with one to two years' experience or more are $5.50–$8.00 an hour, with testers sometimes earning up to $9.50. California Department of Employment Development 1983.

4. This is especially true of Asian communities. The Vietnamese, for example, have founded several business associations, and own several blocks of businesses in downtown San Jose. Hispanic groups have a much smaller business ownership base, although there is a Hispanic Chamber of Commerce in the area.

5. For a more extensive discussion of how gender ideologies are used as the basis of both labor control and labor resistance in this work force, see Hossfeld 1990.

6. The student team was composed of University of California at Santa Cruz undergraduates, aged eighteen to twenty-five.

7. In Silicon Valley, the low proportion of Black workers correlates to the low proportion of Blacks in the overall county labor force, 3.11 percent.

8. The association of a "frugal lifestyle" with the consumeristic American dream is perplexing.

9. Japanese Americans are among the top income earners in the United States, while Blacks and Hispanics are among the lowest in income. For evidence that Japanese and other Asian Americans have had to work harder for relatively lower economic status than whites, see Woo 1985.

10. For discussion of how immigrant women workers resist managers' efforts to use racism and sexism as forms of labor control, see Hossfeld 1990. For discussion of barriers to labor organizing around these issues, see Hossfeld 1991.

References

California Department of Employment Development. 1983. *Annual Planning Information: San Jose Standard Metropolitan Statistical Area 1983-1984.* San Jose.

Chapkis, Wendy, and Cynthia Enloe. 1983. *Of Common Cloth: Women in the Global Textile Industry.* Amsterdam: Transnational Institute.

Ehrenreich, Barbara, and Annette Fuentes. 1981. "Life on the Global Assembly Line." *Ms.,* January, pp. 52-59.

Fernandez-Kelly, Maria Patricia. 1983. *For We Are Sold, I and My People: Women and Industry in Mexico's Frontier.* Albany: State University of New York Press.

____. 1985. "Advanced Technology, Regional Development and Hispanic Women's Employment in Southern California." Paper presented at the Women, High Technology and Society Conference, University of California, Santa Cruz, June 1.

Fevre, Ralph. 1984. *Cheap Labour and Racial Discrimination.* Aldershot, U.K.: Gower.

Friaz, Guadalupe. 1985. "Race and Gender Differences in Mobility and Turnover in a Large Electronics Firm." Paper presented at the Women, High Technology and Society Conference, University of California, Santa Cruz, June 1.

Green, Susan S. 1980. *Silicon Valley's Women Workers: A Theoretical Analysis of Sex-Segregation in the Electronics Industry Labor Market.* Honolulu: Impact of Transnational Interactions Project, Cultural Learning Institute, East-West Center.

Gregory, Kathleen. 1984. "Signing-up: The Culture and Careers of Silicon Valley Computer People." Ph.D. dissertation, Northwestern University. Ann Arbor, Michigan: University Microfilms International.

Grossman, Rachel. 1979. "Women's Place in the Integrated Circuit." *Southeast Asia Chronicle* 66 and *Pacific Review* 9 (joint issue): 2-17.

Hossfeld, Karen. 1988. "Divisions of Labor, Divisions of Lives: Immigrant Women Workers in Silicon Valley." Ph.D. dissertation, University of California, Santa Cruz. Ann Arbor, Michigan: University Microfilms International.

____. 1990. "'Their Logic Against Them' Contradictions in Sex, Race and Class in Silicon Valley." In Kathryn Ward, ed., *Women Workers and Global Restructuring.* Ithaca, N.Y.: ILR Press.

____. 1991. "Why Aren't High-Tech Workers Organized?" In Women Working Worldwide, eds., *Common Interests: Women Organizing in Global Electronics.* London: Women Working Worldwide.

____. 1992. *Small, Foreign, and Female: Immigrant Women Workers in Silicon Valley.* Berkeley: University of California Press.

Katz, Naomi, and David S. Kemnitzer. 1984. "Women and Work in Silicon Valley: Options and Futures." In Karen Brodkin Sacks and Dorothy Remy, eds., *My Troubles Are Going to Have Trouble with Me: Everyday Trials and Triumphs of Women Workers*. New Brunswick, N.J.: Rutgers University Press.

Lim, Linda. 1978. *Women Workers in Multinational Corporations: The Case of the Electronics Industry in Malaysia and Singapore*. Michigan Occasional Papers in Women's Studies no. 9. Ann Arbor: University of Michigan.

Marable, Manning. 1980. *From the Grassroots: Social and Political Essays Toward Afro-American Liberation*. Boston: South End Press.

Mohanty, Chandra, Ann Russo, and Lourdes Torres, eds. 1991. *Third World Women and the Politics of Feminism*. Bloomington: Indiana University Press.

Olson, Lynne. 1984. "The Silkwoods of Silicon Valley." *Working Woman* (July): 71–72, 106, 108, 110–111.

Omi, Michael, and Howard Winant. 1983. "By the Rivers of Babylon: Race in the United States." *Socialist Review* 13, no. 5 (September–October): 31–66.

____. 1986. *Racial Formation in the United States from the 1960's to the 1980's*. New York: Routledge and Kegan Paul.

Sherover-Marcuse, Erica. 1986. *Emancipation and Consciousness*. London: Basil Blackwell.

Siegel, Lenny. 1980. "Delicate Bonds: The Global Semiconductor Industry." *Pacific Research* 1.

Siegel, Lenny, and Herb Borock. 1982. *Background Report on Silicon Valley*. Prepared for the U.S. Commission on Civil Rights. Mountain View, Calif.: Pacific Studies Center.

Snow, Robert. 1986. "The New International Division of Labor and the U.S. Workforce: The Case of the Electronics Industry." In June Nash and Maria Patricia Fernandez-Kelly eds., *Women, Men and the International Division of Labor*. Albany: State University of New York Press.

Wilson, William Julius. 1978. *The Declining Significance of Race: Blacks and Changing American Institutions*. Chicago: University of Chicago Press.

____. 1987. *The Truly Disadvantaged*. Chicago: University of Chicago Press.

Women Working Worldwide, eds. 1991. *Common Interests: Women Organizing in Global Electronics*. London: Women Working Worldwide.

Wong, Eugene F. 1985. "Asian American Middleman Theory: The Framework of an American Myth." *The Journal of Ethnic Studies* 13, no. 1 (Spring): 51–88.

Woo, Deborah. 1985. "The Socioeconomic Status of Asian American Women in the Labor Force: An Alternative View." *Sociological Perspectives* 28, no. 3 July): 307–338.

8

How Did Jews Become White Folks?

Karen B. Sacks

> *The American nation was founded and developed by the Nordic race, but if a few more million members of the Alpine, Mediterranean and Semitic races are poured among us, the result must inevitably be a hybrid race of people as worthless and futile as the good-for-nothing mongrels of Central America and Southeastern Europe.*
>
> (Kenneth Roberts, qtd. in Carlson and Colburn 1972:312)

It is clear that Kenneth Roberts did not think of my ancestors as white like him. The late nineteenth and early decades of the twentieth centuries saw a steady stream of warnings by scientists, policymakers, and the popular press that "mongrelization" of the Nordic or Anglo-Saxon race—the real Americans—by inferior European races (as well as inferior non-European ones) was destroying the fabric of the nation. I continue to be surprised to read that America did not always regard its immigrant European workers as white, that they thought people from different nations were biologically different. My parents, who are first-generation U.S.-born Eastern European Jews, are not surprised. They expect anti-Semitism to be part of the fabric of daily life, much as I expect racism to be part of it. They came of age in a Jewish world in the 1920s and 1930s at the peak of anti-Semitism in the United States (Gerber 1986a). They are proud of their upward mobility and think of themselves as pulling themselves up by their own bootstraps. I grew up during the 1950s in the Euroethnic New York suburb of Valley Stream where Jews were simply one kind of white folks and where ethnicity meant little more to my generation than food and family heritage. Part of my familized ethnic heritage was the belief that Jews were smart and that our success was the result of our own efforts and abilities, reinforced by a culture that valued sticking together, hard work, education, and deferred gratification. Today, this belief in a Jewish version of Horatio Alger has become an entry point for racism by some mainstream Jewish organizations against African Americans especially, and for their opposition to affirmative action for people of color (Gordon 1964; Sowell 1983; Steinberg 1989: chap. 3).

It is certainly true that the United States has a history of anti-Semitism and of beliefs that Jews were members of an inferior race. But Jews were hardly alone. American anti-Semitism was part of a broader pattern of late-nineteenth-century racism against all southern and eastern European immigrants, as well as against Asian immigrants. These views justified all sorts of discriminatory treatment including closing the doors to immigration from Europe and Asia in the 1920s.[1] This picture changed radically after World War II. Suddenly the same folks who promoted nativism and xenophobia were eager to believe that the Euro-origin people whom they had deported, reviled as members of inferior races, and prevented from immigrating only a few years earlier were now model middle-class white suburban citizens.

It was not an educational epiphany that made those in power change their hearts, their minds, and our race. Instead, it was the biggest and best affirmative action program in the history of our nation, and it was for Euromales. There are similarities and differences in the ways each of the European immigrant groups became "whitened." I want to tell the story in a way that links anti-Semitism to other varieties of anti-European racism, because this foregrounds what Jews shared with other Euroimmigrants and shows changing notions of whiteness to be part of America's larger system of institutional racism.

Euroraces

The U.S. "discovery" that Europe had inferior and superior races came in response to the great waves of immigration from southern and eastern Europe in the late nineteenth century. Before that time, European immigrants—including Jews—had been largely assimilated into the white population. The twenty-three million European immigrants who came to work in U.S. cities after 1880 were too many and too concentrated to disperse and blend. Instead, they piled up in the country's most dilapidated urban areas, where they built new kinds of working-class ethnic communities. Since immigrants and their children made up more than 70 percent of the population of most of the country's largest cities, urban America came to take on a distinctly immigrant flavor. The golden age of industrialization in the United States was also the golden age of class struggle between the captains of the new industrial empires and the masses of manual workers whose labor made them rich. As the majority of mining and manufacturing workers, immigrants were visibly major players in these struggles (Higham 1955:226; Steinberg 1989:36).[2]

The Red Scare of 1919 clearly linked anti-immigrant to anti-working-class sentiment—to the extent that the Seattle general strike of native-born workers was blamed on foreign agitators. The Red Scare was fueled by economic depression, a massive postwar strike wave, the Russian revolution, and a new wave of postwar immigration. Strikers in steel, and the garment and textile workers in New York and New England, were mainly new immigrants. "As part of a fierce counteroffensive, employers inflamed the historic identification of class conflict with immigrant radicalism." Anticommunism and anti-immigrant sentiment came together in the Palmer raids and deportation of immigrant working-class activists. There was real fear of revolution. One of President Wilson's aides feared it was "the first appearance of the soviet in this country" (Higham 1955:226).

Not surprisingly, the belief in European races took root most deeply among the wealthy U.S.-born Protestant elite, who feared a hostile and seemingly unassimilable working class. By the end of the nineteenth century, Senator Henry Cabot Lodge pressed Congress to cut off immigration to the United States; Teddy Roosevelt raised the alarm of "race suicide" and took Anglo-Saxon women to task for allowing "native" stock to be outbred by inferior immigrants. In the twentieth century, these fears gained a great deal of social legitimacy thanks to the efforts of an influential network of aristocrats and scientists who developed theories of eugenics—breeding for a "better" humanity—and scientific racism. Key to these efforts was Madison Grant's influential *Passing of the Great Race*, in which he shared his discovery that there were three or four major European races ranging from the superior Nordics of northwestern Europe, to the inferior southern and eastern races of Alpines, Mediterraneans, and, worst of all, Jews, who seemed to be everywhere in his native New York City. Grant's nightmare was race mixing among Europeans. For him, "the cross between any of the three European races and a Jew is a Jew" (qtd. in Higham 1955:156). He didn't have good things to say about Alpine or Mediterranean "races" either. For Grant, race and class were interwoven: the upper class was racially pure Nordic, and the lower classes came from the lower races.

Far from being on the fringe, Grant's views resonated with those of the nonimmigrant middle class. A *New York Times* reporter wrote of his visit to the Lower East Side:

> *This neighborhood, peopled almost entirely by the people who claim to have been driven from Poland and Russia, is the eyesore of New York and perhaps the filthiest place on the western continent. It is impossible for a Christian to live there because he will be driven out, either by blows or the dirt and stench. Cleanliness is an unknown quantity to these people. They cannot be lifted up to a higher plane because they do not want to be. If the cholera should ever get among these people, they would scatter its germs as a sower does grain (qtd. in Schoener 1967:58)*[3]

Such views were well within the mainstream of the early-twentieth century scientific community. Grant and eugenicist Charles B. Davenport organized the Galton Society in 1918 in order to foster research and to otherwise promote eugenics and immigration restriction.[4] Lew Terman, Henry Goddard, and Robert Yerkes, developers of the so-called intelligence test, believed firmly that southeastern European immigrants, African Americans, American

Indians, and Mexicans were "feebleminded." And indeed, more than 80 percent of the immigrants whom Goddard tested at Ellis Island in 1912 turned out to be just that. Racism fused with eugenics in scientific circles, and the eugenics circle overlapped with the nativism of WASP aristocrats. During World War I, racism shaped the army's development of a mass intelligence test. Psychologist Robert Yerkes, who developed the test, became an even stronger advocate of eugenics after the war. Writing in the *Atlantic Monthly* in 1923, he noted:

> *If we may safely judge by the army measurements of intelligence, races are quite as significantly different as individuals. . . . [and] almost as great as the intellectual difference between negro and white in the army are the differences between white racial groups. . . .*
>
> *For the past ten years or so the intellectual status of immigrants has been disquietingly low. Perhaps this is because of the dominance of the Mediterranean races, as contrasted with the Nordic and Alpine. (qtd. in Carlson and Colburn 1972:333–334)*

By the 1920s, scientific racism sanctified the notion that real Americans were white and real whites came from northwest Europe. Racism animated laws excluding and expelling Chinese in 1882, and then closing the door to immigration by virtually all Asians and most Europeans, in 1924 (Saxton 1971, 1990). Northwestern European ancestry as a requisite for whiteness was set in legal concrete when the Supreme Court denied Bhagat Singh Thind the right to become a naturalized citizen under a 1790 Federal law that allowed whites the right to become naturalized citizens. Thind argued that Asian Indians were the real Aryans and Caucasians, and therefore white. The Court countered that the United States only wanted blond Aryans and Caucasians, "that the blond Scandinavian and the brown Hindu have a common ancestor in the dim reaches of antiquity, but the average man knows perfectly well that there are unmistakable and profound differences between them today" (Takaki 1989:298–299). A narrowly defined white, Christian race was also built into the 1705 Virginia "Act concerning servants and slaves." This statute stated "that no negroes, mulattos and Indians or other infidels or jews, Moors, Mahometans or other infidels shall, at any time, purchase any christian servant, nor any other except of their own complexion" (Martyn 1979:111).[5]

The 1930 census added its voice, distinguishing not only immigrant from "native" whites, but also native whites of native white parentage, and native whites of immigrant (or mixed) parentage. In distinguishing immigrant (southern and eastern Europeans) from "native" (northwestern Europeans), the census reflected the racial distinctions of the eugenicist-inspired intelligence tests.[6]

Racism and anti-immigrant sentiment in general and anti-Semitism in particular flourished in higher education. Jews were the first of the Euroimmigrant groups to enter colleges in significant numbers, so it wasn't surprising that they faced the brunt of discrimination there.[7] The Protestant elite complained that Jews were unwashed, uncouth, unrefined, loud, and pushy. Harvard University President A. Lawrence Lowell, who was also a vice president of the Immigration Restriction League, was openly opposed to Jews at Harvard. The Seven Sisters schools had a reputation for "flagrant discrimination." M. Carey Thomas, Bryn Mawr president, may have been a feminist of a kind, but she also was an admirer of scientific racism and an advocate of immigration restriction. She "blocked both the admission of black students and the promotion of Jewish instructors" (Synott 1986:233, 238–239, 249–250).

Anti-Semitic patterns set by these elite schools influenced standards of other schools, made anti-Semitism acceptable, and "made the aura of exclusivity a desirable commodity for the college-seeking clientele" (Synott 1986:250; and see Karabel 1984; Silberman 1985; Steinberg 1989: chaps. 5, 9). Fear that colleges "might soon be overrun by Jews" were publicly expressed at a 1918 meeting of the Association of New England Deans. In 1919 Columbia University took steps to decrease the number of entering Jews by a set of practices that soon came to be widely adopted. The school developed a psychological test based on the World War I army intelligence tests to measure "innate ability–and middle-class home environment" and redesigned the admission application to ask for religion, father's name and birthplace, a photo, and a personal interview (Synott 1986:239–240). Other techniques for excluding Jews, like a fixed class size, a chapel requirement, and preference for children of alumni were less obvious. Sociologist Jerome Karabel (1984) has argued that these exclusionary efforts provided the basis for contemporary criteria for college admission that mix grades and test scores with criteria for well-roundedness and character, as well as affirmative action for athletes and children of alumni, which allowed schools to select more affluent Protestants. Their proliferation in the 1920s caused the intended drop in the number of Jewish students in law, dental, and medical schools and also saw the imposition of quotas in engineering, pharmacy, and veterinary schools.[8]

Columbia's quota against Jews was well known in my parents' community. My father is very proud of having beaten it and of being admitted to Columbia Dental School on the basis of his sculpting skill. In addition to demonstrating academic qualifications, he was asked to carve a soap ball, which he did so well and fast that his Protestant interviewer was willing to accept him. Although he became a teacher instead because the dental school tuition was too high, he took me to the dentist every week of my childhood and prolonged the agony by discussing the finer points of tooth filling and dental care. My father also almost failed the speech test required for his teaching license because he didn't speak "standard"–that is, nonimmigrant, nonaccented–English. For my parents and most of their friends, English was a second language learned when they went to school, since their home language was Yiddish. They saw the speech test as designed to keep all ethnics, not just Jews, out of teaching. There is an ironic twist to this story. My mother was always urging me to speak well and correctly, like her friend Ruth Saronson, who was a speech teacher. Ruth remained my model for perfect diction until I went away to college. When I talked to her on one of my visits home, I heard just how New York-accented my version of "standard" English was now that I had met the Boston academic version.

My parents' conclusion is that Jewish success, like their own, was the result of hard work and of placing a high value on education. They went to Brooklyn College during the depression. My mother worked days and started school at night, and my father went during the day. Both their families encouraged them. More accurately, their families expected this effort from them. Everyone they knew was in the same boat, and their world was made up of Jews who advanced as they did. The picture of New York–where most Jews lived–seems to back them up. In 1920, Jews made up 80 percent of the students at New York's City College, 90 percent of Hunter College, and before World War I, 40 percent of private Columbia University. By 1934, Jews made up almost 24 percent of all law students nationally, and 56 percent of those in New York City. Still, more Jews became public school teachers, like my parents and their friends, than doctors or lawyers (Steinberg 1989:137, 227). Steinberg has debunked the myth that Jews advanced because of the cultural value placed on education. This is not to say that Jews did not advance. They did. "Jewish success in America was a matter of historical timing. . . . [T]here was a fortuitous match between the experience and skills of Jewish immigrants, on the one hand, and the manpower needs and opportunity structures, on the other" (1989:103). Jews were the only ones among the southern and eastern European immigrants who came from urban, commercial, craft, and manufacturing backgrounds, not least of which was garment manufacturing. They entered the United States in New York, center of the nation's booming garment industry, soon came to dominate its skilled (male) and "unskilled" (female) jobs, and found it an industry amenable to low-capital entrepreneurship. As a result, Jews were the first of the new European immigrants to create a middle class of small businesspersons early in the twentieth century. Jewish educational advances followed this business success and depended upon it, rather than creating it (see also Bodnar 1985 for a similar argument about mobility).

In the early twentieth century, Jewish college students entered a contested terrain in which the elite social mission was under challenge by a newer professional training mission. Pressure for change had begun to transform the curriculum and reorient college from a gentleman's bastion to a training ground for the middle-class professionals needed by an industrial economy. "The curriculum was overhauled to prepare students for careers in business, engineering, scientific farming, and the arts, and a variety of new professions such as accounting and pharmacy that were making their appearance in American colleges for the first time" (Steinberg 1989:229). Occupational training was precisely what drew Jews to college. In a setting where disparagement of intellectual pursuits and the gentleman's C were badges of distinction, it was not hard for Jews to excel.

How we interpret Jewish social mobility in this milieu depends on whom we compare Jews to. Compared with other immigrants, Jews were upwardly mobile. But compared with that of nonimmigrant whites, their mobility was very limited and circumscribed. Anti-immigrant racist and anti-Semitic barriers kept the Jewish middle class confined to a small number of occupations. Jews were excluded from mainstream corporate management and corporately employed professions, except in the garment and movie industries, which they built. Jews were almost totally excluded from university faculties (and the few that made it had powerful patrons). Jews were concentrated in small businesses, and in professions where they served a largely Jewish clientele (Davis 1990:146 n. 25; Silberman 1985:88–117; Sklare 1971:63–67).

We shouldn't forget Jews' success in organized crime in the 1920s and 1930s as an aspect of upward mobility. Arnold Rothstein "transformed crime from a haphazard, small-scale activity into a well-organized and well-financed business operation." There was also Detroit's Purple Gang, Murder Incorporated in New York, and a host of other big-city Jewish gangs in organized crime, and of course Meyer Lansky (Silberman 1985:127–130).

Although Jews were the Euroethnic vanguard in college and became well established in public school teaching, as well as being visible in law, medicine, pharmacy, and librarianship before the postwar boom, these professions should be understood in the context of their times (Gerber 1986a:26). In the 1930s they lacked the corporate context they have today, and Jews in these professions were certainly not corporation based. Most lawyers, doctors, dentists, and pharmacists were solo practitioners and were considerably less affluent than their postwar counterparts.

Compared to Jewish progress after the war, Jews' prewar mobility was also very limited. It was the children of Jewish businessmen, not those of Jewish workers, who flocked to college. Indeed, in 1905 New York, the children of Jewish workers had as little schooling as children of other immigrant workers.[9] My family was quite modal in this respect. My grandparents did not go to college, but they did have a modicum of small-business success. My father's family owned a pharmacy. Although my mother's father was a skilled garment worker, her mother's family was large and always had one or another grocery or deli in which my grandmother participated. It was the relatively privileged children of upwardly mobile Jewish immigrants like my grandparents who began to push on the doors to higher education even before my parents were born. Especially in New York City—which had almost 1.25 million Jews by 1910 and remained the biggest concentration of the nation's 4 million Jews in 1924 (Steinberg 1989:225)—Jews built a small-business-based middle class and began to develop a second-generation professional class in the interwar years.[10] Still, despite the high percentages of Jews in eastern colleges, most Jews were not middle class, and fewer than 3 percent were professionals, compared to somewhere between 20 and 32 percent in the 1960s (Sklare 1971:63).

My parents' generation believed that Jews overcame anti-Semitic barriers because Jews are special. My belief is that the Jews who were upwardly mobile were special among Jews (and were also well placed to write the story). My generation might well counter our parents' story of pulling themselves up by their own bootstraps with, "But think what you might have been without the racism and with some affirmative action!" And that is precisely what the postwar boom, the decline of systematic public anti-immigrant racism and anti-Semitism, and governmental affirmative action extended to white males.

Euroethnics into Whites

By the time I was an adolescent, Jews were just as white as the next white person. Until I was eight, I was a Jew in a world of Jews. Everyone on Avenue Z in Sheepshead Bay was Jewish. I spent my days playing and going to school on three blocks of Avenue Z, and visiting my grandparents in the nearby Jewish neighborhoods of Brighton Beach and Coney Island. There were plenty of Italians in my neighborhood, but they lived around the corner. They were a kind of Jew, but on the margins of my social horizons. Portuguese were even more distant, at the end of the bus ride, at Sheepshead Bay. The schul, or temple, was on Avenue Z, and I begged my father to take me like all the other fathers took their kids, but religion wasn't part of my family's Judaism. Just how Jewish my neighborhood was hit me in first grade when I was one of two kids in my class to go to school on Rosh Hashanah. My teacher was shocked—she was Jewish too—and I was embarrassed to tears when she sent me home. I was never again sent to school on Jewish holidays. We left that world in 1949 when we moved to Valley Stream, Long Island, which was Protestant, Republican, and even had farms until Irish, Italian, and Jewish exurbanites like us gave it a more suburban and Democratic flavor. Neither religion nor ethnicity separated us at school or in the neighborhood. Except temporarily. In elementary school years, I remember a fair number of dirt-bomb (a good suburban weapon) wars on the block. Periodically one of the Catholic boys would accuse me or my brother of killing his God, to which we would reply, "Did not" and start lobbing dirt-bombs. Sometimes he would get his friends from Catholic school, and I would get mine from public school kids on the block, some of whom were Catholic. Hostilities lasted no more than a couple of hours and punctuated an otherwise friendly relationship. They ended by junior high years, when other things became more important. Jews, Catholics, and Protestants, Italians, Irish, Poles, and "English" (I don't remember hearing WASP as a kid) were mixed up on the block and in school. We thought of ourselves as middle class and very enlightened because our ethnic backgrounds seemed so irrelevant to high school culture. We didn't see race (we thought), and racism was not part of our peer consciousness, nor were the immigrant or working-class histories of our families.

Like most chicken and egg problems, it's hard to know which came first. Did Jews and other Euroethnics become white because they became middle class? That is, did money whiten? Or did being incorporated in an expanded version of whiteness open up the economic doors to a middle-class status? Clearly, both tendencies were at work. Some of the changes set in motion during the war against fascism led to a more inclusive version of whiteness. Anti-Semitism and anti-European racism lost respectability. The 1940 census no longer distinguished native whites of native parentage from those, like my parents, of immigrant parentage, so that Euroimmigrants and their children were more securely white by submersion in an expanded notion of whiteness. (This census also changed the race of Mexicans to white [U.S. Bureau of the Census, 1940:4.] Theories of nurture and culture replaced theories of nature and biology. Instead of dirty and dangerous races who would destroy U.S. democracy, immigrants became ethnic groups whose children had successfully assimilated into the mainstream and risen to the middle class. In this new myth, Euroethnic suburbs like mine became the measure of U.S. democracy's victory over racism. Jewish mobility became a new Horatio Alger story. In time and with hard work, every ethnic group would get a piece of the pie, and the United States would be a nation with equal opportunity for all its people to become part of a prosperous middle-class majority. And it seemed that Euroethnic immigrants and their children were delighted to join middle America.[11]

This is not to say that anti-Semitism disappeared after World War II, only that it fell from fashion and was driven underground. Micah Sifry's (1993) revelations of Richard Nixon's and George Bush's personal anti-Semitism and its prevalence in both their administrations indicate its persistence in the Protestant elite. There has also been an alarming rise of anti-Semitic and anti-African American hate groups and hate crimes in recent years. While elites do not have a monopoly on anti-Semitism, they do have the ability to restrict Jews' access to the top echelons of corporate America. Since the war, the remaining glass ceilings on Jewish mobility have gotten fewer and higher. Although they may still keep down the number of Jews and other Euroethnics in the upper class, it has been a long time since they could keep them out of the middle class. However, a 1987 Supreme Court ruling that Jews and Arabs could use civil rights laws to gain redress for discrimination against them did so on the grounds that they are not racial whites. As historian Barbara Jeanne Fields (1990:97) notes, "[T]he court knew no better way to rectify injustice at the end of the twentieth century than to re-enthrone the superstitious racial dogma of the nineteenth century."[12]

Although changing views on who was white made it easier for Euroethnics to become middle class, it was also the case that economic prosperity played a very powerful role in the whitening process. Economic mobility of Jews and other Euroethnics rested ultimately on U.S. postwar economic prosperity with its enormously expanded need for professional, technical, and managerial labor, and on government assistance in providing it. The United States emerged from the war with the strongest economy in the world. Real wages rose between 1946 and 1960, increasing buying power a hefty 22 percent and giving most Americans some discretionary income (Nash et al. 1986:885–886). U.S. manufacturing, banking, and business services became increasingly dominated by large corporations, and these grew into multinational corporations. Their organizational centers lay in big, new urban headquarters that demanded growing numbers of technical and managerial workers. The postwar period was a historic moment for real class mobility and for the affluence we have erroneously come to believe was the U.S. norm. It was a time when the old, white and the newly white masses became middle class.

The GI Bill of Rights, as the 1944 Serviceman's Readjustment Act was known, was arguably the most massive affirmative action program in U.S. history. It was created to develop needed labor-force skills, and to provide those who had them with a life-style that reflected their value to the economy. The GI benefits ultimately extended to sixteen million GIs (veterans of the Korean War as well), included priority in jobs—that is, preferential hiring, but no one objected to it then—financial support during the job search, small loans for starting up businesses; and, most important, low-interest loans and educational benefits, which included tuition and living expenses (Brown 1946; Hurd 1946; Mosch 1975; *Postwar Jobs for Veterans* 1945; Willenz 1983). This legislation was rightly regarded as one of the most revolutionary postwar programs. I call it affirmative action because it was aimed at and disproportionately helped male, Euro-origin GIs.

GI benefits, like the New Deal affirmative action programs before them and the 1960s affirmative action programs after them, were responses to protest. Business executives and the general public believed that the war economy had only temporarily halted the Great Depression. Many feared its return and a return to the labor strife and radicalism of the 1930s (Eichler 1982:4; Nash et al. 1986:885). "[M]emories of the Depression remained vivid and many people suffered from what Davis Ross has aptly called "depression psychosis"—the fear that the war would inevitably be followed by layoffs and mass unemployment" (Wynn 1976:15).

It was a reasonable fear. The eleven million military personnel who were demobilized in the 1940s represented a quarter of the U.S. labor force (Mosch 1975:1, 20). In addition, ending war production brought a huge number of layoffs, growing unemployment, and a high rate of inflation. To recoup wartime losses in real wages caused by inflation as well as by the unions' no-strike pledge in support of the war effort, workers staged a massive wave of strikes in 1946. More workers went out on strike that year than ever before, and there were strikes in all the heavy industries: railroads, coal mining, auto, steel, and electrical. For a brief moment, it looked like class struggle all over again. But government and business leaders had learned from the experience of bitter labor struggles after World War I just how important it was to assist demobilized soldiers. The GI Bill resulted from their determination to avoid those mistakes this time. The biggest benefits of this legislation were for college and technical school education, and for very cheap home mortgages.

Education and Occupation

It is important to remember that prior to the war, a college degree was still very much a "mark of the upper class" (Willenz 1983:165). Colleges were largely finishing schools for Protestant elites. Before the postwar boom, schools could not begin to accommodate the American masses. Even in New York City before the 1930s, neither the public schools nor City College had room for more than a tiny fraction of potential immigrant students.

Not so after the war. The almost eight million GIs who took advantage of their educational benefits under the GI bill caused "the greatest wave of college building in American history" (Nash et al. 1986:885). White male GIs were able to take advantage of their educational benefits for college and technical training, so they were particularly well positioned to seize the opportunities provided by the new demands for professional, managerial, and technical labor. "It has been well documented that the GI educational benefits transformed American higher education and raised the educational level of that generation and generation to come. With many provisions for assistance in upgrading their educational attainments veterans pulled ahead of nonveterans in earning capacity. In the long run it was the nonveterans who had fewer opportunities" (Willenz 1983:165).[13]

Just how valuable a college education was for white men's occupational mobility can be seen in John Keller's study of who benefited from the metamorphosis of California's Santa Clara Valley into Silicon Valley. Formerly an agricultural region, in the 1950s the area became the scene of explosive growth in the semiconductor electronics industry. This industry epitomized the postwar economy and occupational structure. It owed its existence directly to the military and to the National Aeronautics and Space Administration (NASA), who were its major funders and its major markets. It had an increasingly white-collar work force. White men, who were the initial production workers in the 1950s, quickly tranformed themselves into a technical and professional work force thanks largely to GI benefits and the new junior college training programs designed to meet the industry's growing work-force needs. Keller notes that "62 percent of enrollees at San Jose Junior College (later renamed San Jose City College) came from blue-collar families, and 55 percent of all job placements were as electronics technicians in the industrial and service sectors of the county economy" (1983:363). As white men left assembly work and the industry expanded between 1950 and 1960, they were replaced initially by Latinas and African-American women, who were joined after 1970 by new immigrant women. Immigrating men tended to work in the better-paid unionized industries that grew up in the area (Keller 1983:346–373).

Postwar expansion made college accessible to the mass of Euromales in general and to Jews in particular. My generation's "Think what you could have been!" answer to our parents became our reality as quotas and old occupational barriers fell and new fields opened up to Jews. The most striking result was a sharp decline in Jewish small businesses and a skyrocketing of Jewish professionals. For example, as quotas in medical schools fell the numbers of Jewish doctors mushroomed. If Boston is an indication, just over 1 percent of all Jewish men before the war were doctors compared to 16 percent of the postwar generation (Silberman 1985:124, and see 118–126). A similar Jewish mass movement took place into college and university faculties, especially in "new and expanding fields in the social and natural sciences" (Steinberg 1989:137).[14] Although these Jewish college professors tended to be sons of businesspersons and professionals, the postwar boom saw the first large-scale class mobility among Jewish men. Sons of working-class Jews now went to college and became professionals themselves, according to the Boston survey, almost two-thirds of them. This compared favorably with three-quarters of the sons of professional fathers (Silberman 1985: 121–122).[15]

Even more significantly, the postwar boom transformed the U.S. class structure—or at least its status structure—so that the middle class expanded to encompass most of the population. Before the war, most Jews, like most other Americans, were working class. Already upwardly mobile before the war relative to other immigrants, Jews floated high on this rising economic tide, and most of them entered the middle class. Still, even the high tide missed some Jews. As late as 1973, some 15 percent of New York's Jews were poor or near-poor, and in the 1960s, almost 25 percent of employed Jewish men remained manual workers (Steinberg 1989:89–90).

Educational and occupational GI benefits really constituted affirmative action program for white males because they were decidedly not extended to African Americans or to women of any race. White male privilege was shaped against the backdrop of wartime racism and postwar sexism. During and after the war, there was an upsurge in white racist violence against black servicemen in public schools, and in the KKK, which spread to California and New York (Dalfiume 1969:133–134). The number of lynchings rose during the war, and in 1943 there were antiblack riots in several large northern cities. Although there was a wartime labor shortage, black people were discriminated against in access to well-paid defense industry jobs and in housing. In 1946 there were white riots against African Americans across the South, and in Chicago and Philadelphia as well. Gains made as a result of the wartime Civil Rights movement, especially employment in defense-related industries, were lost with peacetime conversion as black workers were the first fired, often in violation of seniority (Wynn 1976:114, 116). White women were also laid off, ostensibly to make jobs for demobilized servicemen, and in the long run women lost most of the gains they had made in wartime (Kessler-Harris 1982). We now know that women did not leave the labor force in any significant numbers but instead were forced to find inferior jobs, largely nonunion, parttime, and clerical.

Theoretically available to all veterans, in practice women and black veterans did not get anywhere near their share of GI benefits. Because women's units were not treated as part of the military, women in them were not considered veterans and were ineligible for Veterans' Administration (VA) benefits (Willenz 1983:168). The barriers that almost completely shut African-American GIs out of their benefits were more complex. In Wynn's portrait (1976:115), black GIs anticipated starting new lives, just like their white counterparts. Over 43 percent hoped to return to school and most expected to relocate, to find better jobs or new lines of work. The exodus from the South toward the North and far West was particularly large. So it wasn't a question of any lack of ambition on the part of African-American GIs.

Rather, the military, the Veterans' Administration, the U.S. Employment Service, and the Federal Housing Administration (FHA) effectively denied African-American GIs access to their benefits and to the new educational, occupational, and residential opportunities. Black GIs who served in the thoroughly segregated armed forces during World War II served under white officers, usually Southerners (Binkin and Eitelberg 1982; Dalfiume 1969; Foner 1974; Johnson 1967; Nalty and MacGregor 1981). African-American soldiers were disproportionately given dishonorable discharges, which denied them veterans' rights under the GI Bill. Thus between August and November 1946, 21 percent of white soldiers and 39 percent of black soldiers were dishonorably discharged. Those who did get an honorable discharge then faced the Veterans' Administration and the U.S. Employment Service. The latter, which was responsible for job placements, employed very few African Americans, especially in the South. This meant that black veterans did not receive much employment information, and that the offers they did receive were for low-paid and menial jobs. "In one survey of 50 cities, the movement of blacks into peacetime employment was found to be lagging far behind that of white veterans: in Arkansas 95 percent of the placements made by the USES for Afro-Americans were in service or unskilled jobs" (Nalty and MacGregor 1981:218, and see 60–61). African Americans were also less likely than whites, regardless of GI status, to gain new jobs commensurate with their wartime jobs, and they suffered more heavily. For example, in San Francisco by 1948, Black Americans "had dropped back halfway to their pre-war employment status" (Wynn 1976:114, 116).[16]

Black GIs faced discrimination in the educational system as well. Despite the end of restrictions on Jews and other Euroethnics, African Americans were not welcome in white colleges. Black colleges were overcrowded, and the combination of segregation and prejudice made for few alternatives. About twenty thousand, black veterans attended college by 1947, most in black colleges, but almost as many, fifteen thousand could not gain entry. Predictably, the disproportionately few African Americans who did gain access to their educational benefits were able, like their white counterparts, to become doctors and engineers, and to enter the black middle class (Walker 1970).

Suburbanization

In 1949, ensconced at Valley Stream, I watched potato farms turn into Levittown and into Idlewild (later Kennedy) Airport. This was a major spectator sport in our first years on suburban Long Island. A typical weekend would bring various aunts, uncles, and cousins out from the city. After a huge meal we would pile in the car—itself a novelty—to look at the bulldozed acres and comment on the matchbox construction. During the week, my mother and I would look at the houses going up within walking distance.

Bill Levitt built a basic 900–1,000-square-foot, somewhat expandable house for a lower-middle-class and working-class market on Long Island, and later in Pennsylvania and New Jersey (Gans 1967). Levittown started out as two thousand units of rental housing at sixty dollars a month, designed to meet the low-income housing needs of returning war vets, many of whom, like my Aunt Evie and Uncle Julie, were living in quonset huts. By May 1947, Levitt and Sons had acquired enough land in Hempstead Township on Long Island to build four thousand houses, and by the next February, he'd built six thousand units and named the development after himself. After 1948, federal financing for the construction of rental housing tightened, and Levitt switched to building houses for sale. By 1951 Levittown was a development of some fifteen thousand families.

Hartman (1975:141–142) cites massive abuses in the 1940s and 1950s by builders under Section 608, a program in which "the FHA granted extraordinarily liberal concessions to lackadaisically supervised private developers to induce them to produce rental housing rapidly in the postwar period." Eichler (1982) indicates that things were not that different in the subsequent FHA-funded home-building industry.

At the beginning of World War II, about 33 percent of all U.S. families owned their houses. That percentage doubled in twenty years. Most owned their houses. Levittowners looked just like my family. They came from New York City or Long Island; about 17 percent were military, from nearby Mitchell Field; Levittown was their first house; and almost everyone was married. The 1947 inhabitants were over 75 percent white collar, but by 1950 more blue-collar families moved in, so that by 1951, "barely half" of the new residents were white collar, and by 1960 their occupational profile was somewhat more working class than for Nassau County as a whole. By this time too, almost one-third of Levittown's people were either foreign-born or, like my parents, first-generation U.S. born (Dobriner 1963:91, 100).

The FHA was key to buyers and builders alike. Thanks to it, suburbia was open to more than GIs. People like us would never have been in the market for houses without FHA and VA low-down-payment, low-interest, long-term loans to young buyers.[17] Most suburbs were built by "merchant builders," large-scale entrepreneurs like Levitt, who obtained their own direct FHA and VA loans (Jackson 1985:215). In the view of one major builder, "Without FHA and VA loans merchant building would not have happened" (Eichler 1982:9). A great deal was at stake. The FHA and VA had to approve subdivision plans and make the appraisals upon which house buyers' loans were calculated. FHA appraisals effectively set the price a house could sell for, since the FHA established the amount of the mortgage it would insure. The VA was created after the war, and it followed FHA policies. Most of the benefits in both programs went to suburbs, and half of all suburban housing in the 1950s and 1960s was financed by FHA/VA loans. Federal highway funding was also important to suburbanization. The National Defense Highway Act of 1941 put the government in the business of funding 90 percent of a national highway system (the other 10 percent came from states), which developed a network of freeways between and around the nation's metropolitan areas, making suburbs and automobile commuting a way of life. State zoning laws and services were also key. "A significant and often crucial portion of the required infrastructure—typically water, sewer, roads, parks, schools—was provided by the existing community, which was in effect subsidizing the builder and indirectly the new buyer or renter" (Eichler 1982:13).[18]

In residential life as in jobs and education, federal programs and GI benefits were crucial for mass entry into a middle-class homeowning suburban life-style. Indeed, they raised the U.S. standard of living to a middle-class one.

It was here that the federal government's racism reached its high point. Begun in 1934, the FHA was a New Deal program whose original intent was to stimulate the construction industry by insuring private loans to buy or build houses. Even before the war, it had stimulated a building boom. The FHA was "largely run by representatives of the real estate and banking industries" (Jackson 1985:203–205; Weiss 1987:146). It is fair to say that the "FHA exhorted segregation and enshrined it as public policy (Jackson 1985:213). As early as 1955, Charles Abram blasted it:

A government offering such bounty to builders and lenders could have required compliance with a nondiscrimination policy. Or the agency could at least have pursued a course of evasion, or hidden behind the screen of local autonomy. Instead, FHA adopted a racial policy that could well have been culled from the Nuremberg laws. From its inception FHA set itself up as the protector of the all white neighborhood. It sent its agents into the field to keep Negroes and other minorities from buying houses in white neighborhoods. (1955:229; see also Gelfand 1975; Lief and Goering 1987)

The FHA believed in racial segregation. Throughout its history, it publicly and actively promoted restrictive covenants. Before the war, these forbade sale to Jews and Catholics as well as to African Americans. The deed to my house in Detroit had such a covenant, which theoretically prevented it from being sold to Jews or African Americans. Even after the Supreme Court ended legal enforcement of restrictive covenants in 1948, the FHA continued to encourage builders to write them against African American. FHA underwriting manuals openly insisted on racially homogeneous neighborhoods, and their loans were made only in white neighborhoods. I bought my Detroit house in 1972 from Jews who were leaving a largely African-American neighborhood. By that time, after the 1968 Fair Housing Act, restrictive covenants were a dead letter (although blockbusting by realtors was rapidly replacing it).

With the federal government behind them, virtually all developers refused to sell to African Americans. Palo Alto and Levittown, like most suburbs as late as 1960, were virtually all white. Out of 15,741 houses and 65,276 people, averaging 4.2 people per house, only 220 Levittowners, or 52 households, were "nonwhite." In 1958 Levitt announced publicly at a press conference to open his New Jersey development that he would not sell to black buyers. This caused a furor, since the state of New Jersey (but not the U.S. government) prohibited discrimination in federally subsidized housing. Levitt was sued and fought it, although he was ultimately persuaded by township ministers to integrate. There had been a white riot in his Pennsylvania development when a black family moved in a few years earlier. West Coast builder Joe Eichler had a policy of selling to any African Americans who could afford to buy. But his son pointed out that his father's clientele in more affluent Palo Alto was less likely to feel threatened. Eichler's clients tended to think of themselves as liberal, which was relatively easy to do because there were few African Americans in the Bay area, and fewer still could afford homes in Palo Alto (Eichler 1982; see also Center for the Study of Democratic Institutions 1964).

The result of these policies was that African Americans were totally shut out of the suburban boom. An article in *Harper's* described the housing available to black GIs. "On his way to the base each morning, Sergeant Smith passes an attractive air-conditioned, FHA-financed housing project. It was built for service families. Its rents are little more than the Smiths pay for their shack. And there are half-a-dozen vacancies, but none for Negroes" (qtd. in Foner 1974:195).

Where my family felt the seductive pull of suburbia, Marshall Berman's experienced the brutal push of urban renewal. In the Bronx in the 1950s, Robert Moses's Cross-Bronx Expressway erased a dozen solid, settled, densely populated neighborhoods like our own; . . . something like 60,000 working- and lower-middle-class people, mostly Jews, but with many Italians, Irish and Blacks thrown in, would be thrown out of their homes. . . . For ten years, through the late 1950s and early 1960s, the center of the Bronx was pounded and blasted and smashed" (1982:292).

Urban renewal made postwar cities into bad places to live. At a physical level, urban renewal reshaped them, and federal programs brought private developers and public officials together to create downtown central business districts where there had formerly been a mix of manufacturing, commerce, and working-class neighborhoods. Manufacturing was scattered to the peripheries of the city, which were ringed and bisected by a national system of highways. Some working-class neighborhoods were bulldozed, but others remained (Greer 1965; Hartman 1975; Squires 1989). In Los Angeles, as in New York's Bronx, the postwar period saw massive freeway construction right through the heart of old working-class neighborhoods. In East Los Angeles and Santa Monica, Chicano and African-American communities were divided in half or blasted to smithereens by the highways bringing Angelenos to the new white suburbs, or to make way for civic monuments like Dodger Stadium (Pardo 1990; Social and Public Arts Resource Center 1990:80, 1983:12–13).

Urban renewal was the other side of the process by which Jewish and other working-class Euroimmigrants became middle class. It was the push to suburbia's seductive pull. The fortunate white survivors of urban renewal headed disproportionately for suburbia, where they could partake of prosperity and the good life. There was a reason for its attraction. It was often cheaper to buy in the suburbs than to rent in the city (Jackson 1985:206). Even Euroethnics and families who would be considered working class based on their occupations were able to buy into the emerging white suburban life style. And as Levittown indicates, they did so in increasing numbers, so that by 1966 50 percent of all workers and 75 percent of those under age forty nationwide lived in suburbs (Brody 1980:192). They too were considered middle class.

If the federal stick of urban renewal joined the FHA carrot of cheap mortgages to send masses of Euros to the suburbs, the FHA had a different kind of one-two punch for African-Americans. Segregation kept them out of the suburbs, and redlining made sure they could not buy or repair their homes in the neighborhoods where they were allowed to live. The FHA practiced systematic redlining. This was a system developed by its predecessor, the Home Owners Loan Corporation (HOLC), which in the 1930s developed an elaborate neighborhood rating system that placed the highest (green) value on all-white, middle-class neighborhoods, and the lowest (red) on racially nonwhite or mixed and working-class neighborhoods. High ratings meant high property values. The idea was that low property values in redlined neighborhoods made them bad investments. The FHA was, after all, created by and for banks and the housing industry. Redlining warned banks not to lend there, and the FHA would not insure mortgages in such neighborhoods. Redlining created a self-fulfilling prophecy. "With the assistance of local realtors and banks, it assigned one of the four ratings to every block in every city. The resulting information was then translated into the appropriate color [green, blue, yellow, and red] and duly recorded on secret 'Residential Security Maps' in local HOLC offices. The maps themselves were placed in elaborate 'City Survey Files,' which consisted of reports, questionnaires, and workpapers relating to current and future values of real estate" (Jackson 1985:199).[19]

FHA's and VA's refusal to guarantee loans in redlined neighborhoods made it virtually impossible for African Americans to borrow money for home improvement or purchase. Because these maps and surveys were quite secret, it took the 1960s Civil Rights movement to make these practices and their devastating consequences public. As a result, those who fought urban renewal or who sought to make a home in the urban ruins found themselves locked out of the middle class. They also faced an ideological assault that labeled their neighborhoods slums and called those who lived in them slum dwellers (Gans 1962).

The record is very clear that instead of seizing the opportunity to end institutionalized racism, the federal government did its best to shut and double seal the postwar window of opportunity in African Americans' faces. It consistently refused to combat segregation in the social institutions that were key for upward mobility: education, housing, and employment. Moreover, federal programs that were themselves designed to assist demobilized GIs and young families systematically discriminated against African Americans. Such programs reinforced white/ nonwhite racial distinctions even as intrawhite racialization was falling out of fashion. This other side of the coin, that white men of northwestern and southeastern European ancestry were treated equally in theory and in practice with regard to the benefits they received, was part of the larger postwar whitening of Jews and other eastern and southern Europeans.

The myth that Jews pulled themselves up by their own bootstraps ignores the fact that it took federal programs to create the conditions whereby the abilities of Jews and other European immigrants could be recognized and rewarded rather than denigrated and denied. The GI Bill and FHA and VA mortgages were forms of affirmative action that allowed male

Jews and other Euro-American men to become suburban homeowners and to get the training that allowed them—but not women vets or war workers—to become professionals, technicians, salesmen, and managers in a growing economy. Jews' and other white ethnics' upward mobility was the result of programs that allowed us to float on a rising economic tide. To African Americans, the government offered the cement boots of segregation, redlining, urban renewal, and discrimination.

Those racially skewed gains have been passed across the generations, so that racial inequality seems to maintain itself "naturally," even after legal segregation ended. Today, in a shrinking economy where downward mobility is the norm, the children and grandchildren of the postwar beneficiaries of the economic boom have some precious advantages. For example, having parents who own their own homes or who have decent retirement benefits can make a real difference in young people's ability to take on huge college loans or to come up with a down payment for a house. Even this simple inheritance helps perpetuate the gap between whites and nonwhites. Sure Jews needed ability, but ability was not enough to make it. The same applies even more in today's long recession.

Notes

This is a revised and expanded version of a paper published in *Jewish Currents* in June 1992 and delivered at the 1992 meetings of the American Anthropological Association in the session *Blacks and Jews, 1992: Reaching across the Cultural Boundaries* organized by Angela Gilliam. I would like to thank Emily Abel, Katya Gibel Azoulay, Edna Bonacich, Angela Gilliam, Isabelle Gunning, Valerie Matsumoto, Regina Morantz-Sanchez, Roger Sanjek, Rabbi Chaim Seidler-Feller, Janet Silverstein, and Eloise Klein Healy's writing group for uncovering wonderful sources and for critical readings along the way.

1. Indeed, Boasian and Du Boisian anthropology developed in active political opposition to this nativism; on Du Bois, see Harrison and Nonini 1992.
2. On immigrants as part of the industrial work force, see Steinberg 1989:36.
3. I thank Roger Sanjek for providing me with this source.
4. It was intended, as Davenport wrote to the president of the American Museum of Natural History, Henry Fairfield Osborne, as "an anthropological society . . . with a central governing body, self-elected and self-perpetuating, and very limited in members, and also confined to native Americans who are anthropological, socially and politically sound, no Bolsheviki need apply" (Barkan 1991:67–68).
5. I thank Valerie Matsumoto for telling me about the Thind case and Katya Gibel Azoulay for providing this information to me on the Virginia statute.
6. "The distinction between white and colored" has been "the only racial classification which has been carried through all the 15 censuses." "Colored" consisted of "Negroes" and "other races": Mexican, Indian, Chinese, Japanese, Filipino, Hindu, Korean, Hawaiian, Malay, Siamese, and Samoan. (U.S. Bureau of the Census, 1930:25, 26).

7. For why Jews entered colleges earlier than other immigrants, and for a challenge to views that attribute it to Jewish culture, see Steinberg 1989.

8. Although quotas on Jews persisted into the 1950s in some of the elite schools, they were much attenuated, as the postwar college-building boom gave the coup-de-grace to the gentleman's finishing school.

9. Steinberg (1989: chap. 5), challenging the belief that education was the source of Jewish mobility, cites Gutman's comparison of a working-class Jewish neighborhood on Cherry Street and a business and professional one on East Broadway in 1905, showing that children of Jewish workers did not go to college.

10. Between 1900 and 1930 New York City's population grew from 3.4 million to 6.9 million, and at both times immigrants and the children of immigrants were 80 percent of all white household heads (Moore 1992:270, n. 28).

11. Indeed, Jewish social scientists were prominent in creating this ideology of the United States as a meritocracy. Most prominent of course was Nathan Glazer, but among them also were Charles Silberman and Marshall Sklare.

12. I am indebted to Katya Gibel Azoulay for bringing this to my attention

13. The belief was widespread that "the GI Bill . . . helped millions of families move into the middle class" (Nash et a]. 1986:885). A study that compares mobility among veterans and nonveterans provides a kind of confirmation. In an unnamed small city in Illinois, Havighurst and his colleagues (1951) found no significant difference between veterans and nonveterans, but this was because apparently very few veterans used any of their GI benefits.

14. Interestingly, Steinberg (1989:149) shows that Jewish professionals tended to be children of small-business owners, but their Catholic counterparts tended to be children of workers.

15. None of the Jewish surveys seem to have asked what women were doing. Silberman (1985) claims that Jewish women stayed out of the labor force prior to the 1970s, but if my parents' circle is any indication, there were plenty of working professional women.

16. African Americans and Japanese Americans were the main target of wartime racism (see Murray 1992). By contrast, there were virtually no anti-German American or anti-Italian American policies in World War II (see Takaki 1989:357–406).

17. See Eichler 1982:5 for homeowning percentages; Jackson (1985:205) found an increase in families living in owner-occupied buildings, rising from 44 percent in 1934 to 63 percent in 1972; see Monkkonen 1988 on scarcity of mortgages; and Gelfand 1975, esp. chap. 6, on federal programs.

18. In the location of highway interchanges, as in the appraisal and inspection process, Eichler (1982) claims that large-scale builders often bribed and otherwise influenced the outcomes in their favor.

19. These ideas from the real estate industry were "codified and legitimated in 1930s work by University of Chicago sociologist Robert Park and real estate professor Homer Hoyt" (Jackson 1985:198–199).

References

Abrams, Charles. 1955. *Forbidden Neighbors: A Study of Prejudice in Housing.* New York: Harper.

Barkan, Elazar. 1991. *The Retreat of Scientific Racism: Changing Concepts of Race in Britain and the United States between the World Wars.* Cambridge: Cambridge University Press.

Berman, Marshall. 1982. *All That Is Solid Melts into Air: The Experience of Modernity.* New York: Simon and Schuster.

Binkin, Martin, and Mark J. Eitelberg. 1982. *Blacks and the Military.* Washington, D.C.: Brookings.

Bodnar, John. 1985. *The Transplanted: A History of Immigrants in Urban America.* Bloomington: Indiana University Press.

Brody, David. 1980. *Workers in Industrial America: Essays of the Twentieth Century Struggle.* New York: Oxford University Press.

Brown, Francis J. 1946. *Educational Opportunities for Vetrans.* Washington, D.C.: Public Affairs Press, American Council on Public Affairs.

Carlson, Lewis H., and George A. Colburn. 1972. *In Their Place: White America Defines Her Minorities, 1850-1950.* New York: Wiley.

Center for the Study of Democratic Institutions. *Race and Housing: An Interview with Edward P. Eichler, President, Eichler Homes, Inc.* 1964. Santa Barbara: Center for the Study of Democratic Institutions.

Dalfiume, Richard M. 1969. *Desegregation of the U.S. Armed Forces: Fighting on the Fronts, 1939-1953.* Columbia: University of Missouri Press.

Davis, Mike. 1990. *City of Quartz.* London: Verso.

Dobriner, William M. 1963. *Class in Suburbia.* Englewood Cliffs, N.J.: Prentice-Hall.

Eichler, Ned. 1982. *The Merchant Builders.* Cambridge, Mass.: MIT Press.

Fields, Barbara Jeanne. 1990. Slavery, Race, and Ideology in the United States of America. *New Left Review* 181:95-118.

Foner, Jack. 1974. *Blacks and the Military in American History: A New Perspective.* New York: Praeger.

Gans, Herbert. 1962. *The Urban Villagers.* New York: Free Press.

____. 1967. *The Levittowners.* New York: Pantheon.

Gelfand, Mark. 1975. *A Nation of Cities: The Federal Government and Urban America, 1933-1965.* New York: Oxford University Press.

Gerber, David. 1986a. Introduction. In *Anti-Semitism in American History,* ed. Gerber. 3-56.

____. ed. 1986b. *Anti-Semitism in American History.* Urbana: University of Illinois Press.

Glazer, Nathan. and Patrick Moynihan. 1963. *Beyond the Melting Pot: The Negroes, Puerto Ricans, Jews, Italians, and Irish of New York City.* Cambridge, Mass.: MIT Press.

Gordon, Milton. 1964. *Assimilation in American Life.* New York: Oxford University Press.

Greer, Scott. 1965. *Urban Renewal and American Cities.* Indianapolis; Bobbs-Merrill.

Harrison, Faye V., and Donald Nonini, eds. 1992. *Critique of Anthropology* (special issue on W.E.B. Du Bois and anthropology) 12(3).

Hartman, Chester. 1975. *Housing and Social Policy*. Englewood Cliffs, N.J.: Prentice-Hall.

Havighurst, Robert J., John W. Baughman, Walter H. Eaton, and Ernest W. Burgess. 1951. *The American Veteran Back Home: A Study of Veteran Readjustment*. New York: Longmans, Green.

Higham, John. 1955. *Strangers in the Land*. New Brunswick: Rutgers University Press.

Hurd, Charles. 1946. *The Veterans' Program: A Complete Guide to Its Benefits, Rights, and Options*. New York: McGraw-Hill.

Jackson, Kenneth T. 1985. *Crabgrass Frontier: The Suburbanization of the United States*. New York: Oxford University Press.

Johnson, Jesse J. 1967. *Ebony Brass: An Autobiography of Negro Frustration amid Aspiration*. New York: Frederick.

Karabel, Jerome. 1984. Status-Group Struggle, Organizational Interests, and the Limits of Institutional Autonomy. *Theory and Society* 13:1–40.

Kessler-Harris, Alice. 1982. *Out to Work: A History of Wage-Earning Women in the United States*. New York: Oxford University Press.

Lief, Beth J., and Susan Goering. 1987. The Implementation of the Federal Mandate for Fair Housing. In *Divided Neighborhoods*, ed. Gary A. Tobin, 227–267.

Martyn, Byron Curti. 1979. Racism in the U.S.: A History of Anti-Miscegenation Legislation and Litigation. Ph.D. diss., University of Southern California.

Monkkonen, Eric H. 1988. *America Becomes Urban*. Berkeley and Los Angeles: University of California Press.

Moore, Deborah Dash. 1992. On the Fringes of the City: Jewish Neighborhoods in Three Boroughs. In *The Landscape of Modernity: Essays on New York City, 1900–1940*, ed. David Ward and Olivier Zunz, 252–272. New York: Russell Sage.

Mosch, Theodore R. 1975. *The GI Bill. A Breakthrough in Educational and Social Policy in the United States*. Hicksville, N.Y.: Exposition.

Murray, Alice Yang. 1992. Japanese Americans, Redress, and Reparations: A Study of Community, Family, and Gender, 1940–1990. Ph.D. diss., Stanford University.

Nalty, Bernard C., and Morris J. MacGregor, eds. 1981. *Blacks in the Military: Essential Documents*. Wilmington, Del.: Scholarly Resources.

Nash, Gary B., Julie Roy Jeffrey, John R. Howe, Allen F. Davis, Peter J. Frederick, and Allen M. Winkler. 1986. *The American People: Creating a Nation and a Society*. New York: Harper and Row.

Pardo, Mary. 1990. Mexican-American Women Grassroots Community Activists: "Mothers of East Los Angeles." *Frontiers* 11:1–7.

Postwar Jobs for Veterans. 1945. *Annals of the American Academy of Political and Social Science* 238 (March).

Saxton, Alexander. 1971. *The Indispensable Enemy*. Berkeley and Los Angeles: University of California Press.

____. 1990. *The Rise and Fall of the White Republic*. London: Verso.

Schoener, Allon. 1967. *Portal to America: The Lower East Side, 1870–1925*. New York: Holt, Rinehart and Winston.

Sifry, Micah. 1993. Anti-Semitism in America. *Nation,* January 25, 92–99.

Silberman, Charles. 1985. *A Certain People: American Jews and Their Lives Today.* New York: Summit.

Sklare, Marshall. 1971. *America's Jews.* New York: Random House.

Social and Public Arts Resource Center. 1990. *Signs from the Heart: California Chicano Murals.* Venice, Calif.: Social and Public Art Resource Center.

____. 1983. *Walking Tour and Guide to the Great Wall of Los Angeles.* Venice, Calif.: Social and Public Arts Resource Center.

Sowell, Thomas. 1981. *Ethnic America: A History.* New York: Basic.

Squires, Gregory D., ed. 1989. *Unequal Partnerships: The Political Economy of Urban Redevelopment in Postwar America.* New Brunswick: Rutgers University Press.

Steinberg, Stephen. 1989. *The Ethnic Myth: Race, Ethnicity, and Class in America.* 2nd ed. Boston: Beacon.

Synott, Marcia Graham. 1986. Anti-Semitism and American Universities: Did Quotas Follow the Jews? In *Anti-Semitism in American History,* ed. David A. Gerber, 233–274.

Takaki, Ronald. 1989. *Strangers from a Different Shore.* Boston: Little, Brown.

Tobin, Gary A., ed. 1987. *Divided Neighborhoods: Changing Patterns of Racial Segregation.* Beverly Hills: Sage.

U.S. Bureau of the Census. 1930. *Fifteenth Census of the United States.* Vol. 2. Washington, D.C.: U.S. Government Printing Office.

____. 1940. *Sixteenth Census of the United States,* vol. 2. Washington, D.C.: U.S. Government Printing Office.

Walker, Olive. 1970. The Windsor Hills School Story. *Integrated Education: Race and Schools* 8(3): 4–9.

Weiss, Marc A. 1987. *The Rise of the Community Builders: The American Real Estate Industry and Urban Land Planning.* New York: Columbia University Press.

Willenz, June A. 1983. *Women Veterans: America's Forgotten Heroines.* New York: Continuum.

Wynn, Neil A. 1976. *The Afro-American and the Second World War.* London: Elek.

Questions

1. Discuss the role the U.S. Constitution and laws have played in the changing conceptualizations of race.

2. Describe how racial categories have been used for the purposes of maintaining political, economic and social privileges for the dominant group.

3. Define ethnicity and discuss how and why it remains flexible and always emerging.

4. What is the meaning of an "invisible knapsack of unearned privileges"? Discuss how one can simultaneously benefit from race and be oppressed by gender.

5. Gender does not create a universal experience for all women. Discuss how the intersections of race and social class can influence the construction of gender.

SECTION TWO

Histories

Introduction

I t is commonly understood that appreciating history helps us to avoid unnecessary suffering in the world. History is not the mere recitation of the past. It is instead a series of political questions that have been answered by power relations and the facts on the ground. But power and facts are themselves influenced by ideas and prejudice. Thus, the forced removal of Native American people from the southeastern part of the United States was both a physical fact in time and an ideological reflection of the "common sense" prevalent in the settler community. The study of history allows us to think about some of the larger stories and myths that surround such acts. It affords an opportunity to weigh the political options available at the time and analogize to the problems confronting us today. Of course, the lessons we learn will be varied and complex. As an example, the meaning and significance of "colorblindness" has changed significantly over time. The antidiscrimination argument found in the dissenting opinion of *Plessy v. Ferguson* urged that laws be colorblind and avoid any discriminatory classifications. This can be distinguished from the more recent use of the term "colorblind" to argue against laws and programs that seek to remediate the effects of discrimination.

Other extraordinary events from history may also appear distinctly foreign, yet carry important implications for our own time. How is it that thousands of women were burned as witches in the 15th century? Could it happen again? These are difficult questions. They require us to think critically about the past and the world around us. The university is precisely the institution where you must ask why these fifteenth century women were demonized. What set of ideas supported their burning? Do all cultures need such scapegoats and does each era require new witches? Who are the scapegoats today? Undocumented immigrants? Muslims? Clones? The role of the university is to help you ask such questions. What can we learn from the past? Can we think our way through unhealthy power relations that we see dramatized in history? How do we analyze silence and omissions? Who has been marginalized and why?

In the context of ethnic studies, these questions may become even more critical. The articles in the following section review important points in the history of ethnic America. They underscore and describe a host of conflicts and an array of responses by the people who were subordinated. The readings describe both a history of oppression and the ways in which oppressed people constructed a political force in response. Disturbing questions naturally flow from these histories.

How has racial, ethnic, and gender stratification developed in this country? Is the traditional presentation of history simply an elaborate press release for empire? How do we distinguish American history from propaganda? Of course, our purpose is not to settle on some new and final truth regarding U.S. history. But these inquiries serve to challenge traditional grand narratives and universal claims that are embedded in our culture, inform our viewpoints, and shape our understanding of the problems we face in the world today.

From an ethnic studies perspective, the central features of U.S. history include the racial and ethnic subordination of labor and the social attitudes, practices, and "common sense" arrangements that perpetuated white supremacy. Although the contours of this structured ranking are complex, the story begins with the exclusion and exploitation of Native American and African peoples. Mathew Snipp's *The Changing Political and Economic Status of the American Indians* reminds us of the relationship between economic development and the treatment of Native Americans as captive nations and internal colonies. Both *Tribal Sovereignty and Governmental Authority* by Nicole Lim and *Native Americans and the United States* by Steven Crum analyze the connection between U.S. laws and policies that have deeply impacted the Native American experiences.

The recent scandal surrounding Senator Trent Lott's memories of the segregated South reminded many observers of a shift in the shape of racism in this country. The change from a state supported regime of violence and discrimination to a more benign but nevertheless racialized division of political and economic power has not gone unnoticed. Both African and Native American peoples have experienced this transition as one part of the social and political contradictions found in this country's history.

As an example, the language of the Declaration of Independence and U.S Constitution, with their emphasis on freedom and liberty, stands in stark contrast to the structured violence of slavery and the official state supported segregation of Jim Crow. It is obvious that slaves and masters saw the same words in a different light. In *Free Blacks and Resistance,* J. Cedric Robinson discusses changes in abolitionist strategy. He notes how an early emphasis on education changed into militant antislavery actions and revolutionary insurrectionism. The latter strategy was informed by a growing belief that slavery alone was not the question, but that self-determination was key. In this light, the author describes the importance of maroon communities, quilombos, and the Black-Indian alliances that emerged in opposition to colonial rule. Later, the structure of white supremacy was openly challenged by way of organized resistance to state supported segregation in the South. In *We Shall Overcome,* Harvard Sitkoff discusses the importance of nonviolent civil disobedience as both a philosophy and tactic in that struggle.

For Mexico, the moral authority of the north was less ambiguous. The U.S. was eager to engineer a "manifest destiny" on the backs of mestizo and Indian people. The growing desire for land and resources led to the Mexican-American War and the Treaty of Guadalupe Hidalgo in 1848. The Treaty formalized the exchange of land and established the contour of power relations between Anglo and Mexican residents in the Southwest. In *Legacies of Conquest,* David G. Gutierrez discusses the fate of those debased people who were acquired as a result of the war. Their subordination as a cheap labor force and the negative stereotypes associated with their social status led to both social segregation and discrimination. At the same time, this atmosphere of hostile occupation also led to the construction of an affirmative ethnic consciousness and oppositional structures like *mutualistas.* Mutual assistance and shared circumstances nurtured a unique Mexican identity in the Southwest, but equally strong pressure to assimilate emerged by the 1930s. In *American Southwest*, John R. Chavez examines the drive of Mexican American generations to minimize their Indian ancestry and emphasize their Americanization. At the same time, organizations like the League of United Latin-American Citizens were involved in testing the promise of fairness and integration in American society. Although some legal victories were achieved, long standing problems of poverty, culture, and status required a mass movement. In *Origin and History of the Chicano Movement*, Roberto Rodriguez analyzes the struggles of students, farm workers, artists, and Chicano activists within the larger anticolonial struggles of the 1960s.

Finally, in *History of Asian Americans* by Timothy P. Fong and *Filipino Americans* by Linda A. Revilla, we learn how Asian immigrants were received and incorporated into the U.S. labor market. Valued as cheap labor, they were also the object of mob violence and anti-Asian laws and policies. Although the specter of a generalized Asian threat or "Yellow Peril" has been a reoccurring theme in American history, the authors underscore the importance of more recent immigrants and the demographic changes that have resulted from the 1965 Immigration Act and the post-Vietnam War era.

9

The Changing Political and Economic Status of the American Indians: From Captive Nations to Internal Colonies

C. Matthew Snipp

No other minority group in America can claim the sovereign legal and political status traditionally occupied by American Indians. This status stems from special agreements between American Indians and the Federal Government. The broader significance of these arrangements is seldom recognized by most social scientists. Even fewer are aware that the industrialized world's growing desire for inexpensive natural resources is moving Federal-Indian relations in significant new directions.

For sociologists interested in the global expansion of modern capitalism and its by-products, the changing status of American Indians graphically illustrates the processes related to political subjugation and economic exploitation. Against the background of two major themes in development literature, this paper sketches a simple typology for describing the changing political status of Indian tribes, and the redefinition of their role in the national economy.

An exhaustive review of the development literature relevant to this typology is beyond the scope of this paper, instead, a few key ideas are highlighted for the purpose of amplifying a concept advocated by historian D'Arcy McNickle and his colleagues.[1] They characterize the historic status of American Indians in law and public policy as "captive nations." This term

From *American Journal of Economics and Sociology,* Vol. 45, No. 2, April 1986 by Matthew Snipp.

describes the limited political autonomy of tribal governments, and reflects the relative isolation and detachment of Indians from the mainstream of American society and economic life.[2] As captive nations, tribes are subject to the higher political authority of the U.S. Government but in other respects, their lands are closed enclaves outside of American society.

Resource development on tribal land *is reshaping* the authority of tribal governments as they seek to control the flow of raw materials into the national economy. The relationship they have with American society is increasingly colonial and their insularity is steadily eroding. These changes signify a new political and economic status for American Indians as "internal colonies."

American Indians and Resource Development

The enigma of American Indians juxtaposes their low economic standing with their control of scarce and potentially valuable natural resources. In addition to large reserves of energy resources, American Indians also have substantial holdings in water, fishing, lumber, and pristine recreation areas.[3] For instance, in 1974 commercial forests occupied 5.5 million acres of Indian land and produced nearly $68 million worth of lumber.[4] Yet the median family income of Indian households was $13,724 in 1979 compared to $20,835 for White households in the same year.[5] Understanding how this situation came to exist, and what the eventual impact of development will mean *for* American Indians is complicated by their diversity. Vast differences exist between tribes in terms of their history, culture, views toward development, and sophistication in dealing with non-Indians. This diversity defies broad generalizations.

Tribal differences are especially critical because they provide the context and limiting conditions for *statements* about the changing status of Indians. In relation to natural resource development, three important distinctions include (1) the type of resource to which a tribe has access, (2) the scale of development, especially in capital intensity, and (3) the historical period in which development occurs. It would be a serious mistake to expect that all reservations are equally endowed with the same resources, or that the extent of development is consistent across reservations. Indeed, some tribes have consciously resisted development in favor of a more traditional lifestyle.

In recent years, federal bureaucrats, the popular press, academics, and some major U.S. corporations have taken an especially ardent interest in tribal affairs. This attention from disparate quarters of American society is primarily directed at a small group of tribes known for their reserves of energy resources. These tribes are frequently referred to as "energy resource" tribes and are represented by an organization known as the Council of Energy Resource Tribes (CERT) through a loose cartel agreement. They control vast amounts of energy-related resources such as coal, oil, gas, shale, and uranium. Some estimates suggest that 23 tribes control 33 percent of the nation's strippable low sulphur coal, 80 percent of U.S. uranium reserves, and between 3 and 10 percent of domestic reserves in gas and oil.[6] Only a small fraction of these reserves is being actively developed, and among these twenty-three tribes are some of the poorest segments of the Indian population, the Navajo and Cheyenne for example.[7]

Another important consideration is that Indian tribes do not share equally in resource development and exemplify a state of uneven development. In terms of development, some tribes have opted for actively exploiting their resources while others have acted with more restraint.[8] In absolute value, some tribes have resources which are larger or more valuable than others; a barrel of oil is worth more than a barrel of water. Likewise, some tribes have one type of resource while other tribes are rich in another type, and some have none at all. For example, the tribes in the plains and mountain states have energy related resources while most lumbering and fishing is limited to a few groups in the Pacific Northwest. For example, fourteen reservations collect 96 percent of all Indian timber revenues.[9]

Many studies of Indian resource development, especially those concerned with energy resource tribes,[10] operate within a narrow historical focus; often limited to a single tribe or a short time period. This is misleading because it creates the impression that the discovery of energy resources on Indian land is recent. The scale and scope of development is relatively new but energy development on Indian land has been on-going since the turn of the century. A small coal lease was negotiated with the Uinta of Utah in 1941 and earlier, in 1911, large reserves of petroleum were found on the Osage reservation of Oklahoma. As early as 1884, the Cherokees of Oklahoma unsuccessfully tried to develop petroleum leases on their land.[11]

American Indians and Models of Development

A complete review of development theory is far afield but two models are especially pertinent because they have been used to analyze the impact of social change on American Indians. The early literature on Indian development is dominated by cultural diffusion models emphasizing acculturation and assimilation.[12] Cultural diffusion models embrace themes found in the literature on modernization or "convergence" theory.[13] Recent analyses adopt "critical" or neo-Marxist perspectives that are heavily indebted to the development theories of Baran and Frank.[14] Modernization and critical perspectives both strive to (1) explain the impact of development on Indian tribes, (2) anticipate the likely changes among tribes seeking to become part of this process, and (3) predict the eventual status of tribes lacking resources or declining to develop them. As accurate guides for predicting the effects of development on American Indians, the achievements of the older development theories are dismal and the prospects for the newer theories are uncertain.

Convergence theory postulates a growing similarity between developing and developed nations as an inevitable outcome of economic advancement. As lesser developed societies expand and diversify their economies, they will increasingly resemble more highly industrialized nations in other facets of their social organization—the "melting pot" on a global scale. Cultural diffusion models embrace this idea by viewing economic development as an irresistible force of acculturation and assimilation. In this perspective, western cultural practices are an accoutrement of economic advancement and material well-being.

Cultural diffusion models further stipulate that prolonged contact between distinct cultural groups will eventually result in the adoption and diffusion of cultural practices. Over time, distinct groups become increasingly similar until they are no longer distinguishable as separate cultures.[15] For American Indians, a version of this model posits that cultural exchanges are asymmetric, and over time, they will be absorbed by the dominant White culture. Prolonged contact with White society ordains the disappearance of Indian culture,[16] as its loss facilitates higher levels of social development. The ethnocentrism of this view hardly needs mentioning. Berkhofer[17] notes that it discounts the possibility of cultural adaptation. Once exposed to White society, Indians are expected to adapt their own culture by discarding it.

For decades, this model dominated theoretical anthropology, and for decades, anthropologists awaited the eventual demise and disappearance of American Indians.[18] To their surprise, American Indians did not disappear. Studies repeatedly showed that they retained a strong attachment to traditional values and lifestyles, even in otherwise alien urban environments.[19] This instigated a theoretical crisis, causing one frustrated anthropologist to question "our earlier expectations concerning the rate of American Indian acculturation and why full acculturation to White American ways of life is not occurring in the contemporary American scene."[20]

The persistence of American Indian culture eroded the influence of cultural diffusion models as guides for understanding the impact of development. Besides their inability to explain cultural persistence, cultural diffusion models invited criticism by neglecting the role of social conflict, colonial relations of domination and subordination, and struggles for political power and other societal resources.[21] In their place, development models with an explicit interest in social conflict have become popular. These models posit the existence of two discrete social systems. Initially, these bodies are culturally, economically, and politically distinct. The development of social relations between these groups creates the opportunity for one group to dominate and exploit the other. Colonial relations, for example, are expressly established for domination and exploitation. In this situation, the powerful seek out the weak for their own enrichment.

The growing interest in colonial relationships does not signify a radical departure from the intellectual concerns expressed in cultural diffusion models. Differences between highly developed urban societies and the traditional, or "folk" social structures of native populations once dominated the interests of anthropologists.[22] A focus on colonialism pays less attention to the differences between more and less developed nations, in favor of a much stronger emphasis on the exploitation and inequality in their relationship. Baran's[23] analysis of neo-colonial relations has influenced several contemporary anthropologists.[24] He argues that the developed nations sustain their advantage in the world economy through an asymmetrical exchange of resources with less developed societies. Resources essential for economic production in western nations are extracted from less developed countries that, in return, gain few benefits from their exports. In this manner, developed nations grow richer by depleting the resources of weaker countries.

To describe the structure of colonial relationships, Andre Gunder Frank coined the terms "satellite" and "metropolis."[25] According to Frank, less developed societies are economic satellites dominated by the influence of colonial powers, the "metropolis." As Jorgenson[26] points out, it is important to notice that the "satellite-metropolis" typology does not readily imply a rural-urban distinction. Jorgenson explains that "the term 'metropolis-satellite' is used here rather than 'urban-rural' in a characterization of political economy because the latter implies a city, a locational unit filled with people. 'Metropolis' implies *the concentration of economic and political power and political influence.* 'Urban' and 'metropolis' are not, of course, completely independent . . ."[27]

In his analysis of western capitalism and its impact on Latin America, Frank argues that Latin America is a satellite of capitalist interests in metropolitan North America and western Europe. In his words, this relationship has led to the "development of underdevelopment" in Latin America. The satellite-metropolis relationship not only fosters underdevelopment in the satellite; the growing impoverishment of the satellite also forces it to become increasingly *dependent* on the metropolis, especially for economic assistance. Dependency theory is also responsible for another idea: internal colonialism. Besides its global character, underdevelopment and dependency also occur between regions and locations within nations. When one area is exploited for the benefit of another, the exploited area is deemed an "internal colony."[28]

Internal colonies, also called periphery areas, are created when one area dominates another to the extent that it channels the flow of resources from the periphery to the dominant core area. Periphery economies are heavily concentrated in extractive or agricultural production that serves the development of the core area, especially by providing raw materials. Hechter[29] adds that ethnocentrism plays a role in the underdevelopment of periphery areas by offering a rationale for cultivating the disadvantaged status of periphery populations

Since its introduction, the term internal colony has been applied to conditions in developing and developed nations. Applied to the U.S., it has been used to describe the plight of minority populations, especially Blacks.[30] In the last ten years, it also has become popular for describing the situation of native populations. Andre Gunder Frank[31] was one of the first scholars to apply this framework to indigenous societies in his analysis of the status of South American Indians. He argues that the regions they inhabit are internal colonies. These Indians are caught up in the larger forces affecting Latin American underdevelopment, except they suffer disproportionate hardships because they reside within the underdeveloped areas of underdeveloped societies.

Following Frank's example, the concepts of internal colonialism and underdevelopment have found popularity among students of North American Indians.[32] Most of these applications are used for describing the impact of resource development, especially energy resources, on Indian reservations. Analyzing conditions on reservations, these discussions closely follow the standard themes of underdevelopment theory. The underdevelopment perspective makes three points about the status of North American Indians. First, reservations are the exploited satellites and American society is the exploiting metropolis. Second, the relationship between the tribes and the Federal Government has nurtured underdevelopment and dependence in Indian communities. Third, resource development is an invitation for yet greater exploitation and underdevelopment.

This perspective emphasizes that the Bureau of Indian Affairs (BIA) has been instrumental in perpetuating the subordinate, colonized status of Indian reservations. The BIA is blamed for actively cultivating Indian dependencies and for being a willing accomplice to their economic exploitation.[33] Amid these accusations, Nafziger[34] suggests that the BIA is merely an instrument for carrying out policies that serve the interests of the dominant culture in general, and industrial capitalism in particular.

At first glance, models of underdevelopment are appealing explanations for the conditions on Indian reservations. The exploitation of American Indians and their dependence on federal authorities are well known and widely documented. The extraction of natural resources from Indian lands for the greater benefit of the U.S. economy fits especially well with underdevelopment models. However, a closer examination of this perspective reveals that it does not neatly fit the circumstances of American Indians.[35] An overarching problem is that the historical specificity of underdevelopment theory limits its generality from one setting to another. Underdevelopment theory was constructed around the events leading to the conquest and exploitation of Latin America. As useful as these insights may be, they bear no necessary relation to the circumstances of North American Indians. In particular, the differences between North and South American Indians are sufficiently large that facile comparisons should be discouraged.

Frank[36] locates South American Indians in the periphery of Latin American national development because this population traditionally has been a cheap source of labor. As plantation and factory workers, Latin American Indians share with the peasants—the family and subsistence farmers—the exploitation which accompanies development. As Frank points out,[37] since the arrival of the Spanish, the Indian population of Latin America has provided a valuable source of labor either as slaves or as easily exploited peasants. Unlike their South American counterparts and especially compared to European immigrants, there is little to suggest that the labor of North American Indians, either as farmers or factory workers, made an important contribution to the development of American capitalism. After an analysis of historical data, Jacobson[38] concludes that "in the United States the corporations who benefited from colonization benefited for the most part from the exploitation of Indian lands rather than Indian labor." The mismatch between the original context of underdevelopment theory and the unique historical and political status of North American Indians can be improved by recognizing three special considerations.

Some Amendments for Underdevelopment Theory

In its present form, the literature dealing with underdevelopment and colonialism has a number of shortcomings in its view of American Indians. In part, these liabilities arise because the special circumstances of North American Indians were never considered in the original discussions of this theoretical perspective. The mismatch between the original context of underdevelopment theory and the unique historical and political status of North American Indians can be improved by recognizing several special considerations.

First, American Indian tribes have a unique status as political sovereigns within the framework of the U.S. political system; no other ethnic minority group in the U.S. enjoys a similar status. Originally, tribal sovereignty was granted in recognition of American Indians as credible military threats. As this threat diminished over time, the authority of tribal governments became embedded in law through treaty negotiations and in federal case law. The authority granted by tribal sovereignty has waxed and waned since the early 19th century but it remains an accepted legal doctrine closely embraced by tribal governments and their supporters. This authority is subordinate to federal powers, but it grants tribal governments with control over reservation development and the power to enter negotiations with non-Indians on behalf of the tribe.[39]

Second, the political separation of American Indians has been reinforced by the geographic and social isolation of Indian tribes from American society. One result of this isolation is that, historically, there has been very little American Indian participation in the U.S. economy. In the 19th century, Indians were viewed as obstacles to progress and removed to isolated reservations away from the mainstreams of economic activity.[40] The cession of tribal lands made the expansion of American capitalism possible but only recently have many tribes and reservations had a role in the American economy, making their satellite status relatively new.

Third, developing Indian lands for the purpose of industrial production confronts Indian people with potentially profound changes in their traditional lifestyles. Before they were subjugated by European powers, American Indians practiced a lifestyle based on hunting and subsistence agriculture. Yielding to the political authority of the United States did not mean that this lifestyle was abandoned. Instead, it was relocated and adapted to the confines of reservations on Indian territory, as in Oklahoma; sometimes in the face of steep opposition from authorities. More recently, resource development poses a difficult dilemma for many tribes as they struggle to reconcile desires for traditional lifestyles with demands for the economic benefits offered by resource development. The interests of traditionalists, reinforced by traditional religious beliefs about the sanctity of nature, are served through the preservation of open land and especially pristine wilderness areas—often the same sites targeted for development. This conflict has been instrumental in slowing the rate of development on several reservations.[41]

Fourth, conquest and removal did not bring revolutionary changes in the economic base of many tribes; most American Indians continued hunting and agriculture for their livelihood. However, developments in the 19th century brought about major changes in their political status. Prior to economic development and their appearance in the periphery of the U.S. economy, American Indians practiced their traditional lifestyles in the face of an increasingly complex political environment affecting their right of self-government and notably, control over the use of their land. Unlike many colonial situations, military conquest and subsequent occupation of their land did not immediately lead to economic development. Instead, many tribes spent an earlier interregnum period during which they were quarantined from White society and made dependent on the agents of the Federal Government, especially the Bureau of Indian Affairs. During this period, there was a wholesale redefinition of the political status of American Indians which established the scope of control of federal authorities over Indian land, and especially how it eventually would be developed.

This earlier phase of development in Indian-White relations is important because it foreshadows the present satellite status of the tribes involved with resource development. For these tribes, the era preceding the development of their resources is critical because it describes the antecedent political conditions that facilitate existing economic relationships between Indian satellites and non-Indian metropolises. This also reveals a significant gap in underdevelopment theory in so far as it offers few insights about the structure of Indian-White relations preceding any satellite-metropolis configuration.

There is a conceptual element needed in the underdevelopment vocabulary to express the pre-colonial status of American Indians. In this respect, a simple typology for describing the transition of Indian reservations from their isolated pre-development origins to their developing status as periphery regions fills an important gap in the conceptual framework of underdevelopment theory. Thoroughly exploring the implications of this typology is not possible in this brief discussion. However, the goal of this typology is to broadly outline how Indian-White relations are being altered by developing natural resources on tribal lands.[42]

Tribal land development, especially natural resource exploitation for consumption outside the reservation, signals a new era in tribal history and marks the end of an old one. This transition is significant because it represents a basic restructuring of the tribe's relationship with the U.S. economy. Framing this transition, the terms "captive nations" and "internal colonies" are a pair of simple, though heuristically useful, categories for delineating two major stages of tribal development. The expression "captive nations"[43] defines the status of American Indian tribes prior to the development of tribal resources for nontribal consumption. For those tribes without resources or development, "captive nationhood" reflects their existing relationship with non-Indian society. For tribes in the midst of development, their situation can be plausibly compared with the conditions associated with internal colonialism. The term "internal colony," in its conventional usage, is a new status for many tribes as the resources they *harbor become more valuable and* sought after.

Discussion

Empirical data for documenting the transition from captive nation to internal colony is not readily available. By its nature, this process gradually occurs over long periods of time. For this reason, the rationale behind this typology is based on historical developments in the relationship between Indian tribes and the United States. These developments span a long period in American history beginning in colonial times and reaching into the present. In a subsequent article, I will review the major historical developments related to the emergence of internal colonies from captive nations. However, there are several key points to remember about this typology.

The first point is that the status of "captive nation" is defined mainly in political terms. Captive nationhood describes the limited amount of self-rule that Indian tribes exercised following their submission to the authority of the Federal Government. Prior to captive nationhood, many Indian tribes were fully independent of European powers. For example, tribes such as the Iroquois regularly maintained political alliances with the French and the English, and as recently as the Civil War, the Cherokee tribe established a formal alliance with the Confederacy. The redefinition of the political status of American Indians was accomplished through military and bureaucratic actions, yet the rights of political autonomy and self-government were not completely stripped. As a result, tribal authorities still enjoy a measure of political power that is highly circumscribed, not as independent nations but as captives. Some tribes such as the Creeks and Cherokees continue to refer to themselves as "nations."

As American Indians gave up their sovereign political powers to become captive nations, they did not experience a comparable revolution in their economic life. However, the status of captive nation paved the way for internal colonization by making formerly self-sustaining Indian tribes dependent upon federal authorities. As a matter of stated policy, for good and bad reasons, American Indians were made "wards" of the State with federal authorities, primarily the BIA, assuming extensive oversight responsibilities for the management of remaining Indian lands. Since becoming federal wards, Indians have continued to rely heavily on activities such as hunting, fishing and subsistence agriculture for their subsistence. However, as the resources on their land have become more valuable, many tribes are facing a revolution in their economic life unmatched since the redefinition of their political status in the 19th century.

The nature of this revolution is characterized by the changes which accompany the transition from captive nation to internal colony. The most profound change brought about by this transition is that American Indians are subject to entirely new forms of economic dominance, in addition to the older forms of political dominance exercised by the federal government. The types of economic relations associated with internal colonialism are a relatively new set of contingencies among people accustomed to relatively simple forms of economic activity. However, as resource development intensifies on Indian lands, internal colonization is almost certain to become more prevalent as the political dominance of earlier times gives way to newer and more complex forms of economic and political relations.

Notes

1. D'Arcy McNickle, Mary E. Young, and Roger Buffalohead, "Captives Within a Free Society," in American Indian Policy Review Commission (AI PRC), *Final Report of the American Indian Policy Review Commission* (Washington, D.C.: U.S. Government Printing Office, 1977), Chapter 1, pp. 47–82.
2. McNickle, et al., are not the first scholars to use the expression "captive nation." Political scientists also use this term to describe the satellite status of Eastern Bloc nations in relation to the Soviet Union.
3. Americans for Indian Opportunity (AIO), *Indian Tribes as Developing Nations; A Question of Power*. Indian Control of Indian Resource Development (Albuquerque, NM: Americans for Indian Opportunity, Inc., 1975), pp. 1–9; Sar A. Levitan, and William B. Johnston, *Indian Giving: Federal Programs for Native Americans* (Baltimore: Johns Hopkins Univ. Press, 1975), pp. 124–150; Sam Stanley, ed., American Indian Economic Development (The Hague: Mouton Publishers, 1978), Chapter 1, "Introduction," pp. 2–14.
4. Levitan and Johnston, op. cit., p. 25.

5. U.S. Bureau of the Census, *Detailed Population Characteristics, United States Summary, Section A: United States* (Washington, D.C.: U.S. Government Printing Office, 1984).

6. Joseph G. Jorgenson, Richard O. Clemmer, Ronald L. Little, Nancy J. Owens and Lynn A. Robbins, *Native Americans and Energy Development* (Cambridge, MA: Anthropology Resource Center, 1978), p. 6.

7. Ibid, p. 5

8. Stan Albrecht, "Energy Development: prospects and implications for Native Americans," paper presented at the annual meetings of the Society for the Study of Social Problems, 1977.

9. Levitan and Johnston, op. *cit.,* pp. 25.

10. Jorgenson et al., op. cit.; Roxanne Dunbar Ortiz, *Economic Development in American Indian Reservations* (Sante Fe, NM: Native American Studies, University of Mexico, 1979); Lorraine Turner Ruffing, "Navajo Economic Development. a dual perspective," in Sam Stanley, ed., *American Indian Economic Development* (The Hague: Mouton Publishers, 1978), pp. 15-86.

11. H. Craig Miner, *The Corporation and the Indian: tribal sovereignty and industrial civilization in Indian territory, 1865-1907* (Columbia, MO: Univ. of Missouri Press, 1976), pp. 147-62.

12. J. Milton Yinger, and George Eaton Simpson, "The Integration of Americans of Indian Descent," *Annals of the American Academy of Political and Social Science,* 436, pp. 137-51, (1978).

13. W. W. Rostow, *The Stages of Economic Growth* (Cambridge: Cambridge Univ. Press, 1960); Bert F. Hoselitz, and Wilbert E. Moore, eds., *Industrialization and Society* (Mouton: UNESCO, 1966); Neil J. Smelser and Seymour M. Lipset, "Social Structure, Mobility and Development," in Neil J. Smelser and Seymour M. Lipset, eds., *Social Structure and Mobility in Economic Development* (Chicago: Aldine, 1966).

14. Paul Baran, *The Political Economy of Growth* (New York: Monthly Review Press, 1957); Andre Gunder Frank, *Capitalism and Underdevelopment in Latin America: historical studies of Chile and Brazil* (New York: Monthly Review Press, 1967).

15. Milton M. Gordon, *Assimilation in American Life: the role of race religion, and natural origins* (New York: Oxford Univ. Press, 1964).

16. Yinger and Simpson, op. cit., pp. 142-3.

17. Robert F. Berkhofer, Jr., *The White Man's Indian: images of the American Indian from Columbus to the present* (New York: Random House, 1979), pp. 28-9.

18. Ralph Linton, *Acculturation in Seven American Indian Tribes* (New York: Appleton-Century, 1940), Chapter 10, pp. 501-20.

19. Prodipto Roy, "The Measurement of Assimilation: the Spokane Indians," *American Journal of Sociology* 67, pp. 541-51 (1962); Joan Ablon, "Relocated American Indians in the San Francisco Bay Area: social interactions and Indian identity," *Human Organization* 23, pp, 296-304 (1964); Lynn C. White, and Bruce A. Chadwick, "Urban Residence, Assimilation, and Identity of the Spokane Indian," in Howard M. Bahr, Bruce A. Chadwick and Robert C. Day, eds., *Native Americans Today: sociological perspectives*

(New York: Harper and Row, 1972); Bruce A. Chadwick, and Joseph H. Strauss, "The Assimilation of American Indians: the Seattle case," *Human Organization*, 34, pp. 359-69 (1975).

20. Evon Z. Vogt, "The Acculturation of American Indians," *Annals of the American Academy of Political and Social Science* 311, pp. 137-46 (1957), p. 139.

21. Joseph G. Jorgenson, "A Century of Political Economic Effects on American Indian Society, 1880-1980," *Journal of Ethnic Studies* 6, pp. 1-82 (1968), pp. 1-2.

22. Redfield is credited with the distinction between "folk" and "urban" societies and for his work on analyzing the differences between these two types of cultures. Redfield's work was later disputed by Lewis which resulted in a major controversy in the anthropological literature. See Robert Redfield, "The Folk Society," *American Journal of Sociology*, 52, pp. 293-298 (1947) and Oscar Lewis, "Tepoztlan Revisited," *Rural Sociology*, 18, pp. 121-36 (1953).

23. Baran, op. cit.

24. Joseph G. Jorgenson, "Indians and the Metropolis," Chapter 2 in Jack O. Waddell and O. Michael Watson, eds. *The American Indian in Urban Society* (Boston: Little, Brown and Company, 1971), Jorgenson, op. cit, Nancy Oestreich Lurie, "Menominee Termination: from reservation to colony," *Human Organization* 31, pp. 257-70 (1972); Ruffing, op *cit*.

25. Gunder Frank, op. cit.

26. Jorgenson, op. cit.

27. *Ibid*, 84.

28. Gunder Frank, op. cit.

29. Michael Hechter, *Internal Colonialism* (Berkeley: Univ. of California Press, 1975).

30. Robert Blauner, "Internal Colonialism and Ghetto Revolt," *Social Problems* 16, pp. 393-408 (1969); William K. Tabb, *The Political Economy of the Black Ghetto* (New York: W. W. Norton, 1970).

31. Gunder Frank, op. cit., pp. 123-42. Although an early application, Andre Gunder Frank was not the first to use this perspective. An even earlier discussion of colonialism and American Indians is Everett E. Hagen and Louis B. Schaw, *The Sioux on The Reservation: an American colonial problem* (Cambridge, Mass.: Center for International Studies, 1960) and Everett E. Hagen, *On the Theory of Social Change* (Homewood, Ill.; The Dorsey Press, 1962).

32. Lurie Oestreich, op. cit., Nancy J. Owens, "Indian Reservations and Bordertowns: the metropolis-satellite model applied to the northwestern Navajos and Umatillas," Ph.D. Dissertation in anthropology, University of Oregon, (1976); Robert Bee, and Ronald Gingerich, "Colonialism, Causes, and Ethnic Identity. Native Americans and the National Political Economy," *Studies in Comparative International Development* 12, pp. 70-93 (1977); Mel Watkins, ed., *Dene Nation: the colony within* (Toronto: Univ. of Toronto Press, 1977); Jorgenson, op. cit.; Turner Ruffing, op. cit, Gary Anders, "The Internal Colonization of Cherokee Native Americans," *Development and Change* 10, pp. 41-55 (1979); Gary Anders, "Theories of Underdevelopment and the American Indian," *Journal of Economic Issues* 40, pp. 681-701 (1980); Gary Anders, "The Reduction of a

Self-Sufficient People to Poverty and welfare Dependence: an analysis of the causes of Cherokee Indian underdevelopment," *American Journal of Economics and Sociology* 40, pp. 225-37 (1981); Roxanne Dunbar Ortiz, *Economic Development in American Indian Reservations* (Santa Fe, NM: Native American Studies, University of New Mexico, 1979); Roxanne Dunbar Ortiz, *American Indian Energy Resources and Development* (Santa Fe, NM: Native American Studies, University of New Mexico, 1980); Richard Nafziger, "Transnational Corporations and American Indian Development," pp. 9-38 in Roxanne Dunbar Ortiz, ed. *American Indian Energy Resources and Development* (Santa Fe, NM: Native American Studies, University of New Mexico, 1980); Cardell K. Jacobson, "Internal Colonialism and Native Americans: Indian labor in the United States from 1871 to World War II," *Social Science Quarterly* 65, pp. 158-71 (1984).

33. Anders, "Internal" op. cit.; Anders, "Theories," op. cit.; Anders, "Reduction," op. cit; Nafziger, "Transnational Corporations," op, cit., pp. 9–38

34. Nafziger, ibid.

35. These numbers are illustrative but they should be regarded with caution. Even in recent censuses, federal data are notoriously inaccurate for American Indians.

36. Gunder Frank, op. cit

37. Ibid.

38. Jacobson, op. cit., p. 169.

39. It is true that petty exploitation was widely practiced by licensed traders and other agents of the Federal Government. Thomas Jefferson is generally credited with founding the trading outpost system which used a variety of deceits to keep Indians dependent on traders (De Rosier, 1970).

40. H. Craig Miner, *The Corporation and The Indian: tribal sovereignty and industrial civilization in Indian territory, 1865-1907* (Columbia, MO: University of Missouri Press, 1976).

41. Jim Richardson, and John A. Farrell, "The New Indian Wars," *Denver Post*, Special Reprint, November 20-27, 1983.

42. Another dimension of this issue concerns the wisdom of the trade-off between traditional lifestyles and economic development. According to Richardson and Farrell (1983, pp. 19-25), many tribal leaders believe that economic development is possible without sacrificing too many elements of traditional culture. Whether this belief is justified remains to be seen.

43. This term is borrowed from McNickle *et al., op. cit*

10

Tribal Sovereignty and Governmental Authority: A Historical Overview

Nicole Lim

The inherent sovereignty of North American Indian tribes, defined as the right to make their own laws and be governed by them separate and apart from the European and American governmental authorities, was recognized by foreign nations long before the United States Constitution was made the law of the land. European colonial governments used tribal sovereignty as a basis for their dealings with tribes. Tribes were treated as independent nations for the purposes of making treaties, trade agreements, and land grants.[1] To some degree the treatment of tribes as political entities was strategic on the part of the colonizing nations. Tribes were treated as sovereigns to the extent necessary to negotiate transactions.[2] To the extent that these transactions involved the cessions of Indian territories or resolved boundary disputes, they also accorded tribes a sovereign status equivalent to that of the colonial governments and affirmed their ownership of the lands they used and occupied.[3] While tribes granted certain rights to foreigners, those rights were never intended to diminish their authority over their own people and ancestral lands. After the Revolutionary War, the newly created United States federal government sustained the sovereign recognition of tribes by continuing to engage in treaty making.[4] The Commerce Clause of the U.S. Constitution[5] acknowledged that tribes had political powers separate and distinct from state governments, and the United States Supreme Court interpreted the Commerce Clause as granting Congress broad power to legislate over matters concerning Indian tribes.[6]

The Marshall Trilogy

Chief Justice John Marshall of the U.S. Supreme Court framed the legal boundaries and scope of tribal sovereignty in three early-nineteenth century cases known as the "Marshall trilogy." The first case, *Johnson v. McIntosh*,[7] was decided in 1823. The case involved the pre-revolutionary purchases of Indian land. A dispute arose between two non-Indians who claimed title to the same plot of land. McIntosh claimed his title was superior to that of Johnson because he had acquired it as a land patent from the federal government. Johnson was a successor in interest to title that had been conveyed by an Indian tribe. The validity of title transfer was a matter of whether or not Indians had the right to convey title to real property. Marshall looked to British law to decide the controversy. The British Proclamation of 1776 outlined a legal justification for colonial expansion called the Doctrine of Discovery. The doctrine entitled European nations, upon "discovery" of territories in the New World, "the exclusive right to extinguish Indian title of occupancy, either by purchase or conquest."[8] This meant that upon the declaration of discovery of the New World, Britain acquired the sole right to acquire the soil from the natives and to establish settlements within the new colony.[9] Thus the United States, as Britain's successor in interest, inherited superior rights to the land through this doctrine. Marshall used the concept of "aboriginal title" to further define tribal land rights. He argued that while discovery afforded tribes the rights to use and occupy land, it divested them of the right to own it because the federal government had preemptive rights of ownership.[10] By holding the tribes had no right to convey land title to private individuals, Marshall indoctrinated European cultural racism and discrimination into the foundation of federal Indian law.[11] This decision rendered American Indians incompetent to hold title to real property at that time and opened the door to federal bureaucratic oversight of lands to which Indians held beneficial title pursuant to the federal/tribal "trust" relationship.

The second case of the trilogy was handed down in 1831. The controversy in *Cherokee Nation v. Georgia*[12] arose out of the State of Georgia's attempts to challenge the sovereignty of the Cherokee Nation. Georgia passed a series of laws imposing state law on matters of internal tribal affairs. The Cherokee Nation took the matter to the U.S. Supreme Court. Before Marshall could consider the merits of the case he had to explore jurisdictional considerations. Article II, Sec. 3 of the U.S. Constitution defined federal judiciary powers. The Court's original jurisdiction extended to matters between state governments and another "state or citizens thereof, and foreign states, citizens, or subjects."[13] The issue before the Court was whether the Cherokee Nation fit within the constitutional definition of a "foreign state." Marshall decided that tribes did not fall within the meaning of a "foreign state" but that they were a "distinct political society." He described tribes as being "domestic dependent nations" and characterized their relationship to the federal government as that of a "ward" to a "guardian."[14] This decision and treaties with Indian tribes provide the framework for the federal/tribal "trust" relationship, a legal doctrine that still exists today.

The following year, Marshall reaffirmed federal paternalism over Indian affairs by subordinating state's rights. In *Worcester v. Georgia*,[15] the State of Georgia continued attempts to impose state authority over Cherokee affairs. Georgia required all non-Indians traveling within Indian territories to purchase a license from and swear an oath of allegiance to the State of Georgia. A missionary by the name of Samuel Worcester refused to comply with the state law. He was arrested, convicted, and sentenced to four years of hard labor. In deciding this case, Marshall stated that the "Indian nations had always been considered as distinct, independent political communities, retaining their original natural rights" and that the use of the word "nations" with reference to tribes confirmed their status as separate sovereigns.[16] Marshall further reasoned that despite this sovereign status, tribes remained in a relationship of dependence on the federal government for needed protections. He concluded that state law could not interfere with the relationship between tribes and the federal government and that attempts to do so were "repugnant to the constitution, laws and treaties of the United States."[17] Because of this decision, states cannot apply their laws to Indian territories unless so authorized by Congress.

Two fundamental aspects of tribal sovereignty are shaped by the Marshall trilogy. Vine Deloria, Jr., and Clifford M. Lytle explain that (1) "Tribes are under the protection of the federal government and in this condition lack sufficient sovereignty to claim political independence" and (2) "tribes, however, possess sufficient powers of sovereignty to shield themselves from any intrusion by the states."[18] These concepts can be summarized by the notion of quasi or limited sovereignty. Quasi sovereignty refers to the internal sovereign powers of tribes, their ability to exercise governmental authority over their own peoples and territories. The Supreme Court divested tribes of their external sovereign powers by declaring that the exercise was inconsistent with their dependent status, but shielded them from state regulation. David Getches describes "the very establishment of a reservation for the exclusive use and occupancy of a tribe is an act that preempts state authority in conflict with that purpose. Thus, most state laws controlling zoning, environmental degradation, domestic relations and child welfare do not extend to Indians in Indian country."[19]

The Doctrine of Plenary Power

In 1886, the Supreme Court invented the doctrine of plenary power, a legal fiction designed to coincide with the quasi-sovereign status of tribes. Plenary power refers to Congress's absolute authority over Indian affairs. This means that Congress may enact legislation that preempts state governments from regulating in related matters.[20] The notion of plenary power was set forth in *United States v. Kagama*.[21] The U.S. Supreme Court considered the issue of whether Congress acted outside of its legislative authority[22] in passing the Major Crimes Act of 1885.[23] The Major Crimes Act gave exclusive jurisdiction to the federal government when certain enumerated offenses occurred on Indian lands. Originally, the act specified seven enumerated offenses: murder, rape, kidnapping, arson, burglary, robbery, and aggravated assault. In 1886, a murder occurred on the Hoopa Valley Reservation in northern California. Two Indians were indicted for the murder pursuant to the Major Crimes Act. They claimed that Congress acted outside its law-making authority in creating the Major Crimes Act and that there was no federal jurisdiction in the case.[24] They argued that the constitutional basis for congressional authority over Indian affairs was limited in scope to commerce. The Court disagreed, stating that the federal government could not fulfill its duty of protection to Indians without having broad authority to act on behalf of the tribes. Justice Miller stated that "from their very weakness and helplessness, so largely due to the course of dealing of the Federal Government with them and the treaties in which it has promised, there arises the duty of protection, and with that the power."[25]

Expansion of Federal Powers

As tribes began to develop government infrastructure and exercise regulatory powers, the U.S. Supreme Court responded with decisions limiting their authority. During the 1970s and 1980s, non-Indians raised serious challenges to tribal sovereignty.[26] In *Oliphant v. Suquamish Indian Tribe*,[27] tribal police on the Suquamish tribe's Port Madison Reservation exercised criminal jurisdiction over two non-Indians. At the time, 127 tribes were exercising similar authority.[28] Mark Oliphant was arrested by the tribal police for assaulting a tribal officer and resisting arrest. Daniel Belgrade was arrested pursuant to a high-speed chase on a reservation highway. The chase resulted in a collision with a police car.[29] Both defendants argued that the tribe did not possess criminal jurisdiction over them and the U.S. Supreme Court agreed. Justice Rehnquist cited Marshall's language from *Johnson v. McIntosh* in explaining that the "inherent limitations on tribal powers stem from their incorporation into the U.S.[30] He further reasoned that it was an important duty for the U.S to protect its citizens from unwarranted intrusions upon their personal liberty." Since the power of criminal jurisdiction had the potential to restrict an individual's liberty, it was considered a power reserved for the "overriding authority of the United States."[31] In the opinion, Rehnquist gave little weight to practical considerations of policing Indian country and injected race as a factor in deciding who is subject to tribal criminal jurisdiction. Certainly race is not a factor in determining the legal criminal jurisdiction of federal and state criminal courts.

In 1990, the U.S. Supreme Court further eroded tribal sovereignty by deciding that tribal criminal jurisdiction no longer applied to nonmember Indians.[32] *Duro v. Reina*[33] involved the murder of a teenage boy on the Salt River Reservation in Arizona. Mr. Duro, a member of the Torrez Martinez Tribe of California, resided on the Salt River Reservation and worked for a tribal construction firm. He fled to California following the crime. He was captured and returned to Phoenix by the FBI; however, the U.S. attorney failed to prosecute the case and turned Duro over to the Salt Lake authorities. The Salt River tribal prosecutor charged Mr. Duro with the unlawful discharge of a firearm.[34] In the spirit of *Oliphant,* Mr. Duro argued in a writ of habeas corpus to the federal district court that the tribal court lacked criminal jurisdiction to prosecute his case. The case was eventually heard by the U.S. Supreme Court and it agreed with Duro's argument. In 1990, federal legislation referred to as the "Duro Fix" was passed to override the case and affirm the authority of tribes to exercise criminal jurisdiction over all "Indians" within reservation boundaries.[35] Although Congress legislatively overruled the U.S. Supreme Court decision in the Duro case, there is a growing trend in the present U.S. Supreme Court to compromise tribal sovereignty. Nancy Thorington and Raquelle Myers state that "by focusing on the membership status of the parties, rather than the jurisdictional boundaries of the reservation, the U.S. Supreme Court and lower courts continue to make it more difficult for the tribes to preserve the integrity of their political and social units."[36]

Another landmark decision that supported tribal sovereignty was *Talton v. Mayes*.[37] In that case, the U.S. Supreme Court decided that tribes as governments pre-dated the U.S. Constitution and unless specifically mentioned, tribes were not obligated to follow the federal mandate of the Constitution. Years after the decision, Congress responded by passing the Indian Civil Rights Act of 1968[38] to govern the actions of tribal governments. This legislation, also known as the Indian Bill of Rights, essentially subjects tribal governments to constitutional restraints.[39] Congress adopted the act to ensure that tribal governments respect the civil rights of Indians and non-Indians because the personal protections of the U.S. Constitution do not apply to tribal governments. Provisions of the act mirror the U.S. Bill of Rights in many respects. It includes the free exercise of religion, equal protection, freedom of speech, and the privilege against self-incrimination. However, Congress went further to restrict tribal governmental powers by adding a provision that limits the amount of a penalty or the duration of punishment that a tribe may impose. The original act restricted tribes to a maximum imposition of a $500 fine and/or six-month imprisonment. Today the restriction has been amended to allow tribes to impose a $5000 fine and/or one-year imprisonment.[40] Outside of a habeas corpus petition, a petition for release from unlawful detainment, persons alleging a violation under the act must use avenues of appeal available through the tribal court system.[41]

A recent assault on tribal sovereignty by the U.S. Supreme Court is the case of *Strate v. A-1 Contractors*.[42] This case involved a vehicular accident between a driver of a truck owned by a non-Indian company doing business with the tribe and the spouse of a deceased tribal member, a non-Indian. The accident occurred on a highway that runs through the Fort Berthold Reservation in North Dakota. A right of way for the highway had been granted to the state. The U.S. Supreme Court determined whether the tribe had civil jurisdiction over the case.[43] The Court modified the existing four-part test used to determine tribal civil jurisdiction by reducing it to a presumption that tribes lack civil jurisdiction in cases involving the actions of nonmembers on non-Indian land within the boundaries of the reservation. The presumption could be rebutted by two circumstances: (1) where the individual has entered into a consensual agreement with the tribe or tribal members, and (2) where the conduct of the nonmember threatens or has some direct effect on the political integrity, economic security, health, or welfare of the tribe.[44]

Affirming Tribal Sovereignty

In 1978, the U.S. Supreme Court decided the issue of whether the double jeopardy clause of the Fifth Amendment of the U.S. Constitution bars consecutive prosecution of an Indian in federal court after he has already been convicted of a lesser offense by a tribe.[45] In *United States v. Wheeler,* the Court considered the concept of "dual sovereignty." The prohibition against double jeopardy does not bar successive prosecutions by separate sovereigns.[46] The Court affirmed tribal sovereignty by concluding that the double jeopardy clause did not apply to the case. Thus, the defendant was not being tried for the same offence, because tribal and federal prosecutions originate from separate sovereigns.[47]

During the same year, the U.S. Supreme Court supported the power of tribes to determine their own membership requirements in *Santa Clara Pueblo v. Martinez.*[48] The issue arose when Mrs. Martinez, a tribal member, and her daughter sued the Santa Clara Pueblo Tribe because of a discriminatory membership ordinance. The tribe granted membership to the children of male members who married outside of the tribe but denied membership to children of female members who did the same.[49] In deciding this case, the U.S. Supreme Court recognized the sovereignty of the Santa Clara Tribe and declared that sovereign immunity generally protected its government from lawsuits. However, in the majority opinion, Thurgood Marshall went beyond the issue of sovereign immunity to reaffirm the sovereign status of tribes. He stated that intervention on the part of the federal judiciary would "substantially interfere with a tribe's ability to maintain itself as a culturally and politically distinct entity."[50] Unfortunately, this case has fueled the efforts of unsavory tribal leaders to recklessly disenroll legitimate tribal members and deny them a forum for redress.

The Federal/Tribal Trust Relationship

In creating federal paternalism over Indian affairs, the federal government has acknowledged a duty to protect the interests of Indian tribes. This duty of protection stems from the federal/tribal "trust" relationship, which describes the U.S. government's fiduciary duty to protect the interests of tribes.[51] Broadly defined, this includes the duty to protect Indian lands, resources and cultural heritage.[52] The Bureau of Indian Affairs (BIA) is the primary federal agency charged with managing these trust responsibilities.

Ideally, the federal government is held to standards of good faith and fair dealings with Indian tribes.[53] However, this is often not the case. In 1996, the Native American Rights Fund filed a class action suit against BIA officials on behalf of over 300,000 Indian trust beneficiaries for the mismanagement of tribal trust funds.[54]

Tribal Governmental Powers

Tribal sovereignty presumes the rights of self-governance. Tribes exercise these rights to the extent that they have not been diminished or extinguished by the federal government. In general, tribal governmental authority includes the power to establish a form of government, the power to determine membership, the power to administer justice, police power, the power to exclude persons from the reservation, the power to charter business organizations, and sovereign immunity.[55] Tribal sovereignty is always at great risk because there are anti-Indian interests that prefer to extinguish all tribal government powers, and since Congress has plenary authority in Indian affairs, it has the power to eliminate tribal sovereignty. The enemy of tribal sovereignty is always prodding Congress to act.

Sovereign Immunity

The U.S. Supreme Court has declared that federally recognized tribes possess sovereign immunity from suit, not unlike that possessed by federal and state counterparts. This means that the tribal government in question cannot be sued unless it makes an "unequivocally expressed" waiver of sovereign immunity. This means that a tribe, federal, or state government may waive their immunity for a particular purpose. When a tribe waives its sovereign immunity it is not waiving tribal sovereignty; it is exercising sovereignty. These are confusing but different concepts. A waiver of sovereign immunity is where the tribe lifts its protective shield from suit for a particular purpose; it is not a relinquishment of the power to govern. In some cases, Congress has the power to waive immunity on behalf of tribes. Tribal sovereignty is limited and it is constantly at risk.

Notes

1. Nancy Thorington and Raquelle Myers, *Civil and Criminal Jurisdiction over Matters Arising in Indian Country* (National Indian Justice Center, 1999), 2.
2. David Getches, Charles Wilkinson, and Robert Williams, Jr., *Cases and Materials on Federal Indian Law*, 4th ed. (St. Paul: West Group, 1998), 2.
3. The American Indian Lawyer Training Program, *Indian Tribes as Sovereign Governments: A Source Book on Federal-Tribal History, Policy and Law*, 4th ed. (AIRI Press, 1993), 4.
4. Ibid.
5. United States Constitution, art. 1, sec. 8, clause 3: "The Congress shall have Power . . . to regulate Commerce with foreign Nations, and among the several States, and with Indian Tribes."
6. David Getches, "Beyond Indian Law: The Rehnquist Court's Pursuit of States' Rights, Color-Blind Justice and Mainstream Values," *Minnesota Law Review* 86, (2) (December 2001): 269.

7. *Johnson v. McIntosh*, 21 U.S. 543, 5 L.Ed. 681 (1823).

8. *Johnson v. McIntosh*, 21 U.S. 543.

9. Ibid.

10. Ibid.

11. Getches, Wilkinson, and Williams, *Federal Indian Law*, 36–37.

12. *Cherokee Nation v. Georgia*, 30 U.S. 1, 8 L.Ed. 25 (1831).

13. *Cherokee Nation v. Georgia*, 30 U.S. 1.

14. Ibid.

15. *Worcester v. Georgia,* 31 U.S 515, 8 L.Ed. 483 (1832).

16. Thorington and Myers, *Civil and Criminal Jurisdiction*, 2.

17. *Worcester v. Georgia,* 31 U.S 515.

18. Vine Deloria, Jr., and Clifford M. Lytle, *American Indians, American Justice* (Austin: University of Texas Press, 1983), 33.

19. Getches, Wilkinson, and Williams, *Federal Indian Law*, 5.

20. David E. Wilkins, *American Indian Politics and the Political System* (Roman and Littlefield Publishers, Inc., 2002), 45.

21. *United States v. Kagama,* 118 U.S 375, 6 S.Ct. 1109, 30 L.Ed. 228 (1886).

22. Ibid.

23. 18 U.S.C. sec. 1153.

24. *United States v. Kagama,* 118 U.S 375.

25. Ibid.

26. Getches, Wilkinson, and Williams, *Federal Indian Law, 531.*

27. *Oliphant v. Squamish Indian Tribe,* 435 U.S. 191, 98 S.Ct. 1011, 55 L.Ed. 2d 209 (1978).

28. Getches, Wilkinson, and Williams, *Federal Indian Law*, 533.

29. *Oliphant,* 435 U.S. 191.

30. Ibid.

31. Ibid.

32. Getches, Wilkinson, and Williams, *Federal Indian Law,* 540.

33. *Duro v. Reina,* 495 U.S. 676 (1990).

34. *Duro v. Reina,* 495 U.S. 676.

35. Getches, Wilkinson, and Williams, *Federal Indian Law,* 540.

36. Thorington and Myers, *Civil and Criminal Jurisdiction,* 25.

37. *Talton v. Mayes,* 163 U.S. 376, 384 (1896).

38. 25 U.S.C. sec. 1301–1341.

39. Wilkins, *American Indian Politics*, 115.

40. 25 U.S.C. sec. 1302.

41. 25 U.S.C. sec. 1303.

42. *Strate v. A-1 Contractors,* 117 S.Ct. 1404 (1997).

43. *Strate v. A-1 Contractors,* 117 S.Ct. 1404.

44. Ibid at 1409–1410.

45. *United States v. Wheeler,* 435 U.S. 313, 98 S.Ct. 1079, 55 L.Ed.2d 303 (1978).

46. *United States v. Wheeler,* 435 U.S. 313.

47. Ibid.
48. *Santa Clara Pueblo v. Martinez,* 436 U.S. 49, 98 S.Ct. 1670, 56 L.Ed.2d 106 (1978).
49. *Santa Clara Pueblo v. Martinez,* 436 U.S. 49.
50. Ibid.
51. Thorington and Myers, *Civil and Criminal Jurisdiction,* 3.
52. Wilkins, *American Indian Politics,* 339.
53. Ibid.
54. Ibid. at 3.
55. The American Indian Lawyer Training Program, *Indian Tribes as Sovereign Governments,* 36–39.

---------------------------------- 11 ----------------------------------

Native Americans and the United States, 1830–2000 Action and Response

Steven J. Crum

Introduction

In this chapter, I will focus on federal government policies toward Native American people from the early nineteenth century forward. Although this story has been told numerous times, and scholars have called it an old-fashioned historical approach to the writing of Indian history—an assessment I agree with—I will work hard not to repeat the same examples others have given over the years. Instead, I will provide some new examples as much as possible. My main argument is that the history of federal government policy toward Indian people is one of action on one side and response and reaction on the other. More often than not, the federal government initiated the action and the Indians responded or reacted to it. At times, however, the Indians served as actors and persuaded the federal government what to include in its interactions with tribal people, including treaty provisions of the nineteenth century.

Indian Removal

In 1830, Congress passed the Indian Removal Act, which paved the way for the mass-scale physical removal of thousands of Native Americans who lived east of the Mississippi River. In the southeast alone, the federal government moved roughly 60,000 tribal people to the area we now call eastern Oklahoma (Indian Territory up to 1907). Those of us who study Native

American history know the historical accounts of the removed Cherokee, Choctaw, Creek, Chickasaw, and Seminole. We are fully aware of the Trail of Tears of 1838 in which thousands of Cherokee died en route from their former homeland.[1]

Although Indian removal was a case of the American government having its way, at the same time, some of the tribes made certain that favorable provisions ended up in the removal treaties. In the Treaty of Dancing Rabbit Creek of 1830, negotiated with the Choctaw of Mississippi, the Choctaw leadership persuaded the government to include a provision for the education of Choctaw people. The tribe viewed education as a means of "survival" and a way of dealing with the white Americans. With the funds coming from the treaty, the tribe eventually created the Forty Youth Fund, which helped several Choctaws pursue a higher education. Some earned college and university degrees from eastern postsecondary institutions and returned home to help maintain their Choctaw Nation. Concerning the educational provision of the 1930 treaty, it was a case of the Choctaw leadership calling the action and the treaty negotiators responding.[2]

When we read about Indian removal of the nineteenth century, we typically think about eastern Indians being removed west of the Mississippi River. What we seldom read about are the number of far western tribes who were also subjected to the same policy. In the state of California alone, the government applied its removal policy to the tribes of this state, especially in the 1860s. In 1863, California state troops gathered up roughly 400 Concow Maidu of Butte County (about 100 miles north of Sacramento) and marched them across the Sacramento Valley, over the coastal range, and placed them on the Round Valley Reservation in Mendocino County. The descendants of the Maidu still live at Round Valley.[3] In another case, the military gathered up 800 Owens Valley Paiute from eastern California and placed them at Fort Tejon in the mountains overlooking the San Joaquin Valley. Because the military did not have the strength to manage the Paiutes, every one of them eventually escaped and most returned to Owens Valley. A few ended up on the Tule River Reservation between Fresno and Bakersfield.[4]

Along with these actual removal cases in California, there were also removal proposals made by federal officials. In 1862, Senator Milton Latham of the state submitted a bill into Congress which, if passed, would have paved the way for the tribes of the state to be removed over the Sierra Nevada Mountains and placed in Owens Valley. This bill never made it out of Congress. There was also a removal proposal to colonize the tribes of California on some of the off-shore islands near Santa Barbara.[5]

The Reservation Policy

Around the mid-nineteenth century, the government created a new policy called the reservation policy. Its objective was to gather up the tribes of the North American continent and place them on reserves where they could be managed and controlled. Under the supervision of federal agents, the tribes could slowly be subjected to so-called American "civilization" since the white Americans viewed Indians as savages. The new reservation policy did not replace the earlier removal policy entirely. Instead, the federal sector carried out both simultaneously, with the tribes being removed to reservations. The only noticeable difference was that the government did not move the eastern tribes farther west.[6]

Some tribal individuals showed their extreme dislike of the reservation policy by eventually rejecting reservation life. The Office of Indian Affairs (today's BIA), the federal agency given the responsibility to run Indian affairs, required the Modoc of extreme northern California to move across the state line and settle on the newly established Klamath reservation of southern Oregon in the 1860s. At first the tribe went along with the plan. However, the Modoc felt uncomfortable living in a foreign area. Not willing to face confined reservation life, the Modoc left and returned to their ancestral homeland in northern California. The government branded the Modoc as lawbreakers and declared war against them. This led to the well-known Modoc War of 1873 in which the American military finally won.[7]

To punish the Modoc, the government carried out three forms of punishment. In the first instance, it hung the major leaders and sent their skulls to Washington, D.C., for so-called scientific study. Next, it confined two leaders on Alcatraz Island as prisoners. Third, it removed the larger number of Modoc to eastern Indian Territory, where they remained as prisoners of war of the government until 1909. Removal thus became a form of punishment for tribes that did not accept the reservation policy.[8]

Other Native Americans refused to move to newly established reservations when asked. For example, in 1877, the government created the Duck Valley Reservation, which straddles the Idaho-Nevada border. The plan was to induce all the Western Shoshones of the Great Basin region to move there in the years immediately thereafter. But this effort was largely a failure, for only one-third of the tribe moved, those tribal groups and bands that lived closest to Duck Valley. The other two-thirds publicly refused to move and used the aboriginal argument of their deep attachment to particular valleys and mountain ranges where their ancestors had lived "since time immemorial." Their form of punishment was deliberate indifference; that is, the government largely pretended that nonreservation Indians did not exist in the Basin area. Thus they received little or no services from the Indian bureau. Not until the 1930s would the BIA give these Shoshones consistent federal attention.[9]

Assimilation

Around 1880, the American government came up with a third generalized Indian policy called assimilation with the objective to Americanize those Indians living on reservation land. The assimilation campaign had several components. The Indian bureau created on-reservation police forces and tribal courts to make adult Indians give up their native ways. The police forces consisted of tribal members who were bought off by BIA agents. Agents provided them various benefits and services, which included wood-frame houses, firewood, and extra food provisions. Under the supervision of the agent, the police tried to make their own kind surrender their Indian ways and become good Americans.[10]

Many tribal individuals outsmarted the assimilation plan by pretending to become respon-sible Americans. They joined Christian churches, learned rudimentary English, and displayed different forms of American patriotism. Some reservation Indians organized Fourth of July Grounds where they camped out for days to celebrate American independence and democra-cy. But in reality these encampments were a way for the Indians to create underground cultures that allowed the participants to perpetuate native dances and social practices, including indige-nous forms of gambling. To this day, the descendants of the nineteenth-century reservation Indians still remain native to varying degrees.[11]

One of the most visible forms of assimilation for young Indians was formal schooling. The government developed three kinds of schools in the last quarter of the nineteenth century: reservation day schools, reservation boarding schools, and off-reservation boarding schools. Typically, the youngest children started their schooling in the reservation schools. As they became older, the bureau removed them from their families, kinship groups, and tribes and sent them to large off-reservation schools located hundreds or even thousands of miles away from home. In other instances, very young children spent all their schooling in distant off-reservation boarding schools.[12]

In the government schools, the government subjected the students to a detribalization process. It stripped them of their native dress and issued military uniforms for young boys and Victorian dresses for the girls. It suppressed tribal languages and required the students to speak and read English. It made the students follow American values and practices, which included the puritanical work ethic, Christian values, and die-hard individualism.[13]

As for the students, they reacted to forced schooling by expressing various forms of resist-ance, which can be classified as "overt" and "covert." Perhaps the most popular form of overt resistance was running away. Unable to cope with institutionalized schooling, an unspecified number of students ran away with the objective of returning home. Most were captured, but some succeeded in returning to their families and tribes. Covert forms of resistance included "work slow down," talking tribal languages behind the scenes, and stealing food from the cafe-teria.[14]

Although the vast majority of students ended up learning English and wearing American clothing, they still remained native to varying degrees, and most returned home to their Indian communities. There they lived out their lives by being both American and native. They built wood-frame houses and acquired horses and cattle. Yet, at the same time, they continued to speak their native languages and relied on indigenous medicinal remedies. In short, their schooling was only a partial success.[15]

Another form of assimilation was the breaking apart of Indian reservation land. To carry out this initiative, Congress passed the Dawes Act (General Allotment Act) of 1887, which allowed the federal sector to subdivide reservation land and issue individual allotments to the tribal members. For the most part, adult heads of households received 160 acres of land since this specific acreage represented the size of a nineteenth-century American homestead. The BIA expected the Indian allottees to farm the land and become American-style homesteaders. Once the government surveyed and allotted a reservation, it sold any remaining surplus land.

By carrying out these initiatives, it hoped to destroy the tribal way of life and make Indians think and act individualistically rather than communally or tribally.[16]

Many tribal people did not passively accept the allotment process. They expressed their dislike in a number of ways. One person, Lone Wolf of the Kiowa tribe in Indian Territory, took the American government to court because of his opposition to the 1887 act. In the Supreme Court decision *Lone Wolf v. Hitchcock* (1903), Lonewolf argued that the Dawes Act could not be applied to the Kiowa because of prior treaty rights. He was correct, for some years earlier, under the Medicine Lodge Treaty of 1867 made with the Kiowa and other tribes of the southern Great Plains area, the treaty specified that the only way the government could alter the landbase of the reservation given to the Kiowa was if the majority of adults agreed to any form of alteration. But years later, the Kiowa never agreed in the majority to have their reservation subdivided by the Dawes act. Thus the act violated Kiowa treaty rights. However, the Supreme Court disregarded treaty rights and argued that the federal government had superior power over Indian tribes.[17] Therefore, Congress could apply an act to Native Americans, regardless of prior treaty rights.

To show their anger over the Dawes Act, which of course led to substantial land loss, other Native Americans considered leaving the United States completely in the late nineteenth and early twentieth centuries and moving to Mexico. Several tribal individuals from Indian Territory made trips to Mexico between 1890 and 1938 to look for a new homeland where Indian tribes could be free from negative governmental laws and policies. In the opening decade of the twentieth century, Crazy Snake and his followers of Creek Indians of eastern Oklahoma talked about moving to Mexico. As late as the 1930s, some Seminoles of Oklahoma met with the president of Mexico to discuss Mexico as a future home. In the end, these delegations chose to remain in the U.S.[18]

Other aspects of the overall assimilation policy surfaced after the turn of the century. One was the BIA's in-house regulation called Circular 1665 of 1921 and 1923. This BIA regulation either suppressed or prohibited Native American religious practices. It allowed Indians to have only one monthly traditional dance, which could be held from September to February. No dances could be held from March to August. Moreover, the monthly dance could take place only during the day time. No nighttime dance could take place. Only those fifty years and older could participate in the monthly daytime dance. Lastly, Indians could no longer carry out their traditional giveaways.[19]

Most Native American people rejected Circular 1665 and found ways to maneuver around the regulation. Some tribal individuals held dances in remote areas where BIA agents could not find them. Some joined the dances of other tribes held in outlying areas where agents would not or could not visit. Others practiced public exhibition dancing for white audiences, thus enabling them to practice traditional dances throughout the year. The BIA did not prohibit exhibition dances because these dances were nonthreatening and pleased the white crowds that wanted to observe what it labeled "exotic" Indians. Some Indians performed popular forms of white dances and entertainment during early evening hours to convince watchful agents that they were becoming good Americans. Once the officials left, and late at night, the Indians resorted to their traditional dances. All these tactics allowed tribal individuals to outwit the BIA in the early years of the twentieth century.[20]

Cultural Pluralism and the Indian New Deal

As time moved forward in the twentieth century, some white people realized that the government's campaign to assimilate the Indians had largely failed. Native Americans simply could not be completely transformed because of their deep-rooted cultures and traditional beliefs. White reformists advanced the argument that because the U.S. was a democracy where people are given choices, then Indian people must be given the choice to remain native if they wanted. One of the noted reformers was non-Indian John Collier who created the American Indian Defense Association in 1923 with a two-fold purpose: that Indians must be given their religious freedom and that the Indian landbase must be preserved. Besides private individuals such as Collier, even some federal officials concluded that the BIA needed to change some of its policies toward Indian people. In response, Hubert Work, the Secretary of the Interior in 1926, authorized the establishment of a ten-member team to study the "so-called Indian problem" and make recommendations in a published report of how the BIA could be improved.[21]

In 1928, the Meriam team released its lengthy study called *The Problem of Indian Administration,* or popularly known as the Meriam report. The report pointed out the serious problems within Indian affairs, including the substantial land loss of Indian people since the passage of the Dawes Act in 1887, poor health care, and the poor quality of education and life students had received in the BIA boarding schools. At the same time, the report team made positive recommendations of how life could be improved for Native Americans. The federal government needed to provide improved health care for Indians, Indian students needed to be given a quality education in the Indian schools, and the Indian students needed to be taught native subject matter. Here was a case of reformists rejecting the half-century assimilationist policy.[22]

One of the ten members of the Meriam team was Henry Roe Cloud of the Winnebago tribe in Nebraska. After experiencing the boarding school process as a youngster, Cloud made the decision to go to college. He earned more than one college degree, including the bachelor's degree from Yale in 1910. Aware that the BIA did not give Indian students a full high school education in the early twentieth century, he established the American Indian Institute, an all-Indian high school in Wichita, Kansas, for those students who aspired to a full secondary education. Cloud encouraged his students to appreciate their Indianness, and it became obvious why the Meriam report favored the teaching of native subject matter in the Indian schools.[23]

One important end result of the reform sentiment of the 1920s and early 1930s was the Indian Reorganization Act (IRA) of 1934. The provisions of this congressional act were largely the work of John Collier, who became the new commissioner of the BIA in 1933. As a federal official, Collier put his reformist ideas into action by making sure Congress passed the IRA. Some of the provisions of the act were as follows: it ended any further allotment of Indian reservations; it returned to reservation status any remaining surplus land; it allowed tribes to organize politically with tribal constitutions and charters, or it gave tribes a kind of quasi-sovereign status; it provided loans so that tribal individuals could create business enterprises and become better off economically; it provided loans so that Indian students could pursue a college or university education; and it introduced "Indian preference," which was a measure to employ qualified Indians to work in the BIA.[24]

The majority of Indian tribes voted to become IRA tribes since they liked the provisions of the act. Specifically, 181 of them voted in favor of the act. However, 77 tribes voted against it for their own reasons.[25] As a case in point, the Paiutes of Owens Valley voted against the act in large numbers, not because they disliked the act, but because of the BIA's recent rhetoric of Indian removal. Both before and at the time of the act's passage, the BIA had considered removing the Owens Valley Paiutes completely from their ancestral valley in eastern California. The bureau used the argument that the Indians could not really make a living there because the city of Los Angeles had taken much of the water from the Owens River for its California Aquaduct, channeling the river water across the desert to Los Angeles. Thus the BIA wanted the Paiutes to move either to the Walker River Reservation in western Nevada or to move over the Sierra Nevada Mountains and settle down near Merced in the San Joaquin Valley. Insecure about possible removal, the Paiutes voted against the act. In the end, the bureau backed away from removal, allowed the Paiutes to remain, and even created three small reservations for them in the second half of the 1930s: Bishop, Big Pine, and Lone Pine.[26]

The Hupa of northern California also voted against the IRA. Unlike the Paiutes of Owens Valley, the Hupa voted against the act for completely different reasons. First, the tribal leaders favored land allotment, which the IRA ended. Secondly, the Hupa already had a tribal council in operation for some years before Congress passed the act. Thus, there was no need to create a new one under the IRA. Lastly, the Hupa, as well as other tribes of California, had impending claims against the American government. This claims matter was rooted in the eighteen treaties that the Senate did not ratify in the mid-nineteenth century, which would have set aside over seven million acres of land for California Indians. Six years before Congress passed the IRA, it had approved the California Indian Jurisdiction Act of 1928 to allow the California tribes to file suit for past injustices, including the unratified treaties. The Hupa in the mid-1930s felt that the IRA might somehow disrupt the current claims case even though the act itself specified that cases would not be affected.[27] Here was a case of government action and tribal reaction.

Since the passage of the IRA in 1934, tribal individuals have expressed a wide range of views about the act. Some leaders pointed out that despite the act's limitations, it still had some good outcomes. Tim Giago (Lakota), former editor of *Indian Country Today*, stressed that "there wouldn't be any reservations left today if it wasn't for the IRA."[28] Another Lakota, Pat Spears, leader of the Lower Brule Sioux, stated.: "It's better than what it replaced. . . . I don't think we're better off by the IRA. . . . It's been the only vehicle we had, but I think it's time we trade it in."[29] Webster Two Hawk, chairperson of the Rosebud Sioux Tribe, expressed a similar view: "I have mixed opinions regarding the IRA. I have to support it because I work for an IRA government. . . . The IRA was a child of the federal government and did not really contain Indian ideas. . . . In redoing it, I would remove many of the restrictions."[30] Some Lakota leaders were much more critical of the IRA. Robert Fast Horse, tribal judge from Pine Ridge, stressed that the IRA "wouldn't recognize our traditional form of government."[31] Bertha Chasing Hawk of Cheyenne River argued that "the tribal court is useless to us because the [IRA] tribal council can overrule the tribal court's decisions."[32] All of the above individuals are from reservations in North and South Dakota.

Regardless of the IRA's shortcomings, it did create some new directions. The Indian preference clause made it possible for more Indians to be employed by the BIA, especially those who were college educated. By the mid-1940s, the following individuals were superintendents of BIA agencies and reservations: Henry Roe Cloud (Winnebago), Kenneth Marmon (Laguna Pueblo), George LaVatta (Shoshone), Archie Phinney (Nez Perce), Frel Owl (Cherokee), and Gabe Parker (Choctaw).[33]

Termination

In the late 1940s and early 1950s. the BIA inaugurated a new Indian policy called Termination. Its basic purpose was the end of the "long-term historic relationship" the Indian tribes had with the American government. The government wanted Indians to assimilate into the larger dominant society. To carry out the new policy, the BIA and other branches of the government came out with several components of termination. The first was the congressional Indian Claims Commission Act of 1946. Under it, the government wanted to compensate the Indian tribes for all unjust acts committed against Indian people. The tribes would be given the opportunity to develop shopping lists and submit documented examples of injustices before the Indian Claims Commission. If a tribe won suit, it was awarded a monetary settlement or claims money. The BIA distributed this money in the form of per capita payments.[34]

Another component was House Concurrent Resolution (HCR) 108 in 1953, which paved the way for the elimination of various Indian reservations across the country. Under HCR 108, the Indians lost 1.3 million acres of land in the postwar period. The BIA wanted the more successful tribes to be terminated first, including the Menominee of Wisconsin and the Klamath of Oregon. But in the end, most of the tribes terminated were small and defenseless. This included forty small Indian rancherias of California and four Southern Paiute bands of southwestern Utah.[35]

Another component of termination was Operation Relocation (1952) in which the BIA induced reservation people to leave their respective reservations and move to urban areas. The BIA provided incentives, including paid transportation; rent money for the first few months; short-term educational training that included auto mechanics, welding, licensed practical nursing, and dental assistant training; and the overall promise of a better way of life, which included jobs, education, and recreation.[36]

From a statistical standpoint, relocation was extremely successful, for thousands of Indians across the nation moved to various big cities that had BIA-run relocation centers. Some of the cities included Chicago, Dallas-Fort Worth, Denver, Detroit, Los Angeles, Oakland, San Francisco, and San Jose. As a result of relocation, Native Americans became markedly urbanized from the 1950s forward. In 1950, only 13.4 percent of the Indian population lived in cities, whereas by 1980, fifty percent of them were urbanites. The Indian population of California alone skyrocketed after 1950. In 1950, only 19,000 Indians lived in the state. By 1960, it was 39,000. By 1980, it stood at 200,000 with relocation being the huge factor.[37]

The relocation component was both a success and a failure. On the success side, if the BIA's plan was to amalgamate Indians into the overall population in urban America, this effort led to urban Indians having one of the highest out-marriage rates in the nation. Those in the cities have a 50/50 chance of marrying non-Indians. On the failure side, many urban Indians did not melt into urban white America. Instead, they looked for ways to remain native. Some worked hard to live in certain neighborhoods so that families could visit one another. Christian Indians established all-Indian churches in the inner city. Those who were more traditional held sweat ceremonies in their backyards and carried out Peyote ceremonies.

Most attended intertribal pow wows. Others sponsored all-Indian sports, which included basketball and softball tournaments. Others gathered at intertribal urban Indian centers that provided various services, including job referral and social gatherings. In short, urban Indians reacted and created ways to remain native and never surrendered their identities, both tribal and intertribal.[38]

Self-Determination

After 1960, the American government came up with still another Indian policy called self-determination. This policy in certain ways was the opposite of termination. The government encouraged Indians to remain on reservations if they chose. The BIA wanted the tribes to become involved in running their own affairs with federal financial support. Like termination, self-determination had a number of components. The Department of Housing and Urban Development (HUD) helped tribal families build "self-help" houses to replace the older substandard houses that lacked indoor running water and other basic necessities. These new houses of the 1960s forward eventually became known as HUD houses, named after the federal department.[39]

Reservation Indians also benefitted from aspects of the Office of Economic Opportunity (OEO) which was intended for poor people in general, regardless of race. Young Indian students entered preschool programs called Headstart, and high school students lived on college campuses during summer months under Upward Bound. This latter program sought to encourage the high school students to consider higher education after graduating from high school.[40]

The BIA also encouraged the teaching of Indian languages and culture in reservation-based schools run by the tribes themselves. The Rough Rock Demonstration School of the Navajo reservation in Arizona was an example of the Navajos creating their own school to emphasize native culture. The school received financial support from the BIA. Several other tribes would also build their own tribally run schools to provide elementary and secondary education.

These schools received support from the congressional Indian Self-Determination and Education Assistance Act of 1975.[41]

Self-determination also encouraged tribal people to develop reservation-based higher education programs because of the shortcomings of mainstream higher education. The Navajo Nation established its Navajo Community College in 1968 (renamed Dine College in 1997). This tribally controlled college inspired dozens of other tribes also to establish tribal colleges.[42] As of 2000, thirty-three tribally run colleges existed throughout the U.S. They are run largely by college-educated tribal people, and they offer Indian courses to the students. The colleges receive funding from a number of sources, including the congressional Tribally Controlled Community College Act of 1978.

Congress supported the notion of self-determination in the late 1960s and 1970s by passing more than one act. The Indian Civil Rights Act of 1968 applied certain aspects of the U.S. Bill of Rights to Indian reservations. This meant that reservation-based Indian people possessed certain constitutional guarantees, including the freedom of religion, the freedom of the press, and the right to assemble. The Indian Child Welfare Act of 1978 provided a preference of who could adopt Indian children. First preference is given to the child's extended family, second to other members of the child's tribe, third to members of other tribes, and fourth to non-Indians if no one adopted from the three higher categories. Congress passed this law to make sure an adopted Indian child would remain connected to his native culture. In the same year, Congress passed the American Indian Religious Freedom Act which allowed Indian people to possess sacred objects (e.g., eagle feathers), overall freedom to practice traditional religions both on and off reservation, and the right to practice ceremonies at traditional places.[43]

Self-Governance

The most recent federal Indian policy is self-governance, which emerged in the late 1980s. For the most part, self-governance is an extension of self-determination but with some big differences. Under it, the BIA wants to shift its long-term functions over to the tribes themselves. One example of this action is higher education, which has been a BIA function since the early 1930s. From the 1950s forward, the BIA's regional area offices administered higher education grants and loans to Indian students pursuing a postsecondary education. But under self-governance, the tribes themselves receive BIA funds to run their own higher education programs. The BIA is no longer involved except to channel funds.[44]

Conclusion

In this brief account of the history of Indian policy, we have looked at the pattern of government action and native responses and reactions. Although this has been the prevalent pattern for almost two centuries, there are also times when the process is reversed, with the Indians as actors and the government as the reactor. For example, in 1916, the BIA began to add the higher high school grades to its off-reservation boarding schools, which went only to the eighth grade. This BIA action was in response to the Indian members of the intertribal organization Society of American Indians, which asserted that Indians should be given more education instead of being educated as simple laborers in the Indian schools.[45] More recently, in 1988, Congress passed the Indian Gaming Regulatory Act, which determines what tribal nations can do in the domain of gaming. The act designates three classes of gaming: (1) traditional gaming, which tribes can carry out without restriction; (2) gaming such as bingo and card games, which Indian tribes can have in their casinos but would be regulated by a national Indian gaming commission; and (3) Nevada-styled gaming, which the tribes can carry out but only if these forms are legal within a given state where the Indian casino is located. Congress passed the law because it wanted to regulate the rising tide of Indian gaming that started in 1979 with the Seminole tribe in Florida. As of the late 1990s, 148 tribal groups had casinos with class three gaming. They introduced them for two reasons in the 1980s. The first was to move away from the state of poverty that many tribes had lived in for decades. Second, in the early 1980s, President Reagan's administration reduced substantially federal funds for poverty programs. The tribes sought new sources of funding for tribal survival, and one means was the revenue from new casinos. But when casinos started to become too numerous, the government stepped in with its regulations.[46] Here was a case of Indian action and government reaction.

Notes

1. Philip Weeks, *Farewell My Nation: The American Indian and the United States, 1820–1890* (Arlington Heights, IL: Harlan Davidson, Inc., 1990), 22–23; Francis Paul Prucha, *The Great Father: The United States Government and the American Indians,* abridged edition (Lincoln: University of Nebraska Press, 1984), 64–93.
2. 7 Stat. 315; Grayson B. Noley, "The History of Education in the Choctaw Nation from Precolonial Times to 1830," (Ph.D. dissertation, Pennsylvania State University, 1976), 172; Clara Sue Kidwell, *Choctaws and Missionaries in Mississippi, 1818–1918* (Norman: University of Oklahoma Press, 1995), 96, 136; James D. Morrison, *Schools for the Choctaws* (Durant, OK: Choctaw Bilingual Education Program, 1978), 240.
3. Dorothy Hill, *The Indians of Chico Rancheria* (Sacramento, CA: Department of Parks and Recreation, 1978), 39–42.
4. Steven Crum, "Deeply Attached to the Land: The Owens Valley Paiutes and Their Rejection of Indian Removal, 1863 to 1937," *News From Native California,* 14 (summer 2001): 18.
5. "A bill . . ." *The Visalia (Weekly) Delta,* 5 June 1862, p. 2; "About Indian Affairs," *The Visalia (Weekly) Delta,* 17 December 1983, p. 2; James J. Rawls, *Indians of California: The Changing Image* (University of Oklahoma, 1984), 169.
6. Prucha, *The Great Father,* 116, 129–132, 181–197; Weeks, *Farewell My Nation,* 60, 159, 170, 178, 208.

7. Lucille J. Martin, "A History of the Modoc Indians: An Acculturation Study," *The Chronicles of Oklahoma,* 47 (winter 1969–70): 398–417.

8. Ibid., 420–421, 441.

9. Steven Crum, *The Road on Which We Came* (Salt Lake City: University of Utah Press, 1994), 43–84.

10. Prucha, *The Great Father,* 195–197, 218–219; Weeks, *Farewell My Nation,* 217–232.

11. Crum, *The Road,* 52.

12. David Wallace Adams, *Education for Extinction: American Indians and the Boarding School Experience, 1875–1928* (Lawrence: University Press of Kansas, 1995), 21–24, 28–59.

13. Ibid., 97–163.

14. Ibid., 232–238; K. Tsianina Lomawaima, *They Called It Prairie Light: The Story of Chilocco Indian School* (University of Nebraska Press, 1994), 115–126.

15. Adams, *Education for Extinction,* 273–306.

16. Prucha, *The Great Father,* 224–228.

17. Blue Clark, *Lone Wolf v. Hitchcock: Treaty Rights and Indian Law at the End of the Nineteenth Century* (University of Nebraska, 1994).

18. Steven Crum, "'America, Love It or Leave It': Some Native American Initiatives to move to Mexico, 1890–1940," *The Chronicles of Oklahoma,* 79 (winter 2001–02): 408–429.

19. Peggy V. Beck and Anna L. Walters, *The Sacred: Ways of Knowledge, Sources of Life* (Tsaile: Navajo Community College Press, 1977), 158–161.

20. Annette Louise Reed, "Rooted in the Land of Our Ancestors, We Are Strong: A Tolowa History," (Ph.D. dissertation, University of California, Berkeley, 1999), 155–163.

21. Kenneth R. Philp, *John Collier's Crusade for Indian Reform, 1920–1954* (Tucson: University of Arizona Press, 1977), 55–91; Peter Iverson, *'We Are Still Here,' American Indians in the Twentieth Century* (Wheeling, IL: Harlan Davidson, Inc., 1998), 58–76.

22. Prucha, *The Great Father,* 277–279; Iverson, *'We Are Still Here,'* 75.

23. Steven Crum, "Henry Roe Cloud: A Winnebago Indian Reformer: His Quest for American Indian Higher Education," *Kansas History,* 11 (autumn 1988): 171–184.

24. Prucha, *The Great Father,* 311–339; Philp, *John Collier's Crusade,* 135–186; Iverson, *'We Are Still Here,'* 77–102.

25. Philp, *John Collier's Crusade,* 163; Prucha, *The Great Father,* 324.

26. Crum, "Deeply Attached to the Land," 19.

27. Joachim Roschmann, "No 'Red Atlantis' on the Trinity: Why the Hupa Rejected the Indian Reorganization Act," paper presented at the Sixth Annual California Indian Conference, 27 October 1990; George H. Phillips, *The Enduring Struggle: Indians in California History* (San Francisco: Boyd & Fraser Publishing Company, 1981), 50, 69.

28. Quoted in "Lakotas Have Different Views on Indian Reorganization Act," *Lakota Times,* 28 November 1984, 7.

29. Ibid.

30. Quoted in "Fifty Years of IRA—Working or Not?" *Lakota Times,* 4 July 1984, 1.

31. "Lakotas Have Different Views," 7.

32. Ibid.
33. *Interior Department Appropriation Bill for 1947,* 97th Congress, 2nd session, Part I (Washington, D.C.: Government Printing Office, 1946), 822.
34. Donald L. Fixico, *Termination and Relocation: Federal Indian Policy, 1945-1960* (Albuquerque: University of New Mexico Press, 1986), 3-21; Larry W. Burt, *Tribalism in Crisis: Federal Indian Policy, 1953-1961* (UNM, 1982); Prucha, *the Great Father,* 340-356; Iverson, *'We Are Still Here,'* 103-138.
35. Fixico, *Termination and Relocation,* 91-110; Prucha, *The Great Father,* 340-356.
36. Ibid., 137-157; Donald L. Fixico, *The Urban Indian Experience in America* (University of New Mexico, 2000), 8-25.
37. Prucha, *The Great Father,* 394; Francis Paul Prucha, *Atlas of American Indian Affairs* (University of Nebraska Press, 1990), 142; Russell Thornton, *American Indian Holocaust and Survival: A Population History Since 1492* (University of Oklahoma, 1987), 227.
38. Thornton, *American Indian Holocaust,* 236; Fixico, *The Urban Indian Experience,* 74, 80, 125, 127, 133.
39. George Pierre Castile, *To Show Heart: Native American Self-Determination and Federal Indian Policy, 1960-1975* (University of Arizona Press, 1998), 23-42.
40. Ibid, 35-42.
41. Margaret Connell Szasz, *Education and the American Indian: The Road to Self-Determination,* 3rd ed. (University of New Mexico, 1999), 169-187.
42. Wayne J. Stein, *Tribally Controlled Colleges: Making Good Medicine* (New York: Peter Lang, 1992).
43. Iverson, *'We Are Still Here,'* 170-171; Prucha, *The Great Father,* 379.
44. David E. Wilkins, *American Indian Politics and the American Political System* (New York: Rowman & Littlefield Publishers, Inc., 2002), 105, 117-118.
45. "Editorial Comment," *Quarterly Journal of the Society of American Indians,* 2 (April-June 1914): 99; *Annual Report of the Department of the Interior, 1915, Vol. II: Indian Affairs and Territories* (Washington, D.C.: GPO, 1916), 7.
46. W. Dale Mason, *Indian Gaming: Tribal Sovereignty and American Politics* (University of Oklahoma, 2000), 44, 47, 64-65; Wilkins, *American Indian Politics,* 164-172.

12

Free Blacks and Resistance

Cedric J. Robinson

If any wish to plunge me into the wretched incapacity of a slave, or murder me for the truth, know ye, that I am in the hand of God, and at your disposal. . . . For what is the use of living, when in fact I am dead.
—David Walker's Appeal to the Coloured *Citizens of the World*

Beyond the immediate world of the slaves and the slaveholders, the response to slavery and racial oppression in the pre-Civil War period took many and sometimes conflicting forms. In the diverse communities where free Blacks and fugitive slaves resided, all manner of opinion was possible save indifference. The same must be said of non-Blacks, even among those who opposed slavery. The range of contradiction in these two parts of the nation's political culture was represented, at one extreme, by those free Blacks in Louisiana who themselves owned slaves and, at another, by the insurrectionary army of whites, free Blacks, and fugitive slaves gathered by John Brown at Harper's Ferry in 1859. Some Blacks supported colonization to Africa, more opposed it; some Blacks planned and executed emigration to the West Indies or Canada; more opposed it. Some antislavery northern whites endorsed the social and political equality of Blacks; a few prominent Federalists (for examples, Chief Justice John Jay, Vice President Daniel Tompkins, Treasury Secretary Alexander Hamilton) joined such associations as the New York Manumission Society dedicated to the legal defense of fugitive slaves; still others like John Quincy Adams, the former president, secretary of state, and member of Congress, assisted in the defense of the Mendi mutiny on board the *Amistad* in 1840–1841; but the majority of whites in the antislavery camp merely opposed the further expansion of slavery into the West. In short, there were only local consensus. In the absence of any more exact evidence, we can surmise that the vast majority of Blacks opposed slavery, while whites were divided by class, religion, and region on the question of support for the system. As Edmund Morgan has suggested, slavery was profoundly interwoven with the popular and public perception of the identity of the new country.

Among those opposed to slavery—the abolitionists, as they were called—one strain of thought was that the Constitution of the United States institutionally and judicially embraced slavery: William Lloyd Garrison, one of the most influential and prominent of the white abolitionists, saw the Constitution as a proslavery instrument and all political parties as necessarily proslavery parties. Generally recognized by their contemporaries as part of the extreme wing of the antislavery movement, Garrisonians dismissed political organizing and, eventually, championed the dissolution of the federal policy. According to Stephen Symonds Foster, a Garrisonian, the Constitution's encoding of slavery into its articles on representation, taxation, and interstate commerce had subordinated national power to the South:

> [The South] commands our armies. It controls our treasury. It dictates law to our judges. It expounds the gospel to our churches. It has bound the conscience of the nation by an oath to participate in its crimes, and thereby rendered its opposition impossible, or powerless. At its command we trample the law of God under our feet, and refuse to hide the outcast. Thus has it made us at once a nation of atheists and an empire of slaves.

On the other hand, there were those whom Robert Cover has called the "Constitutional Utopians." Gerritt Smith, Garrison's most ardent abolitionist critic and rival, and Frederick Douglass, the most famous fugitive slave (who did not break with Garrison until the late 1840s), argued that the Constitution outlawed slavery. Federal courts, they urged, would provide legitimacy to abolitionist activists and eventually judicial rulings would destroy slavery. That this was utopian was revealed when James Madison's notes on the Constitutional Convention were published for the first time in 1840. As Staughton Lynd puts it, the convention's records made it obvious that the delegates had deliberately manufactured "a sordid sectional compromise" with slavery. They had knowingly produced a Constitution that one of them, Luther Martin, had characterized as an "*insult to that God . . . who views with equal eye the poor African slave and his American master*." Nevertheless, in 1860, while opposing Foster's urgings of revolution and Garrison's plea for a dissolution of the Union, Douglass declared:

> I have much confidence in the instincts of the slaveholders. They see that the Constitution will afford slavery no protection when it shall cease to be administered by slaveholders. . . . [T]here is no word, no syllable in the Constitution to forbid that result. . . . There was one Free State at the beginning of the Government: there are eighteen

now . . . Within the Union we have a firm basis of opposition to slavery. It is opposed to all the great objects of the Constitution. . . . My position now is one of reform, not of revolution. I would act for the abolition of slavery through the Government—not over its ruins.

Douglass was, of course, correct that reform had been consequential: gradual abolition had been enacted successively in Vermont (1777), Massachusetts/Maine (1780), Pennsylvania (1780), New Hampshire (1783), Rhode Island and Connecticut (1784), New York (1799), and New Jersey (1804). But these triumphs were less an opposition to slavery than a resolve by merchants and manufacturers to inaugurate a purer capitalism dependent on wage labor.

Douglass was mistaken, then, to believe that it was the moral authority or even the internal logic of the Constitution that compelled these changes. The Supreme Court's Chief Justice, Roger B. Taney, for one, perceived nothing remotely like opposition to slavery in the Constitution when in 1857 he rendered his Dred Scott decision that Blacks "were not regarded as a portion of the people or citizens of the Government then formed." And Douglass and Smith, both indicted by Virginia authorities for their complicity in the John Brown affair, were not wholly candid in their public professions on behalf of legal methods. By 1860, the sectional conflict between the North and the South, at base a contest between two forms of property and commerce, required an extreme government policy. Thus, the oppositions to slavery that had earlier propelled the nation toward revolution or reform, and that were grounded on alternative and contradictory conceptions of America, had alarmed the rulers of the South to the point of revolution.

Abolition and Free Blacks

Abolitionism can be said to have manifested itself in three phases: the elitist phase, militant-populist phase, and the revolutionary phase. These transitions were not neatly chronological nor did the body of abolitionists cohere as factions metamorphosed from one tendency to another while others strengthened or dissipated. Abolitionism and abolitionists changed. In the American Revolutionary era, the most visible abolitionist societies first appeared in the urban centers of the North: Philadelphia in 1775, New York in 1785, and so on. In 1794, five of these societies coalesced into the national organization, the American Convention for Promoting the Abolition of Slavery and Improving the Condition of the African Race. This formal, organized opposition to slavery was led by an educated and largely wealthy elite drawn from the ranks of both the merchant and manufacturing capitalists. For half a century, these moderate leaders created and sought to maintain a sedate antislavery, projecting the end of slavery as the result of a gradual process of moral (that is, Christian) "suasion" rather than by force or insurrection. But, as the abolitionist movement acquired deeper and different social roots, its ideology changed. By the 1830s, the movement drew much of its white membership from the rural rather than urban areas (thus embracing small Ohio communities like that of Owen Brown's, the father of John Brown); and the numbers and resources of free Blacks in the North were sufficient for some to emerge as the movement's new leaders. The growing domination of these social elements produced a second, militant, abolitionist movement, signaled by the appearances of organizations that used the term "Anti-Slavery" to distinguish their militancy from the moderate "abolitionist" organizations of the first period.

In its rural redoubts and small towns of the North and South (Louis Filler recounts that in 1827, 106 of 130 antislavery societies were in slave states), a largely religious opposition to slavery achieved some modest impact on opinion and cultivated some rather remarkable white adherents (Benjamin Lundy, Frances Wright, Angelina and Sarah Grimke, Lydia Maria Child, John Rankin, and Elihu Embree, to name some). Some were poets, others early suffragettes, others merchants, and two (the Grimkes) the children of eminent slaveholders. More, however, were small farmers, quietly pursuing the dictates of their consciences.

Religious principles, however, pushed some of these white abolitionists into "precipitous" action; specifically, actions the laws of several slave states signified as "slave stealing." For example, in 1841 three members of the Mission Institute in Quincy, Illinois—Alanson Work, James E. Burr, and George Thompson—crossed the Mississippi River into Missouri to encourage slaves to escape. The three were betrayed and sentenced to twelve years in the state penitentiary for slave stealing (they were pardoned in 1846). In June of 1844, Charles Torrey, the editor of the *Albany Patriot* and a Congregationalist minister, was arrested in Baltimore for assisting slaves to escape. He was sentenced to six years in the state penitentiary, where he died of tuberculosis in 1846. In September of 1844, Reverend Calvin Fairbank (of the Methodist Church) and Delia Webster, the principal of the Lexington Female Academy in Kentucky, were apprehended by a Kentucky posse after the two had rescued Lewis Hayden and his family. Fairbank was sentenced to hard labor for fifteen years, Webster was given a two-year sentence. Webster was pardoned after serving two months; but Fairbank, pardoned in 1849 (Hayden led the campaign), was arrested again in 1851 for "abducting" a female slave and remained in the penitentiary for thirteen years, until 1864. Johnathan Walker, a sailor and shipwright, was also arrested in 1844 after he returned from Cape Cod to his former home in Pensacola, Florida, in order to escort his former slaves to freedom. He was imprisoned for a year (his fine of $600 was paid by abolitionists) and had the letters *SS* (slave stealer) branded on his hand. In 1848, William L. Chaplin, Torrey's successor at the *Patriot* and a lawyer, was implicated in the escape of seventy-seven slaves being transported to freedom aboard the schooner *Pearl.* The schooner was intercepted, and its captain Edward Sayres and his coconspirator Daniel Drayton were convicted and fined $20,000 (they received pardons in 1852). Chaplin was not indicted, but in August 1850, while assisting two escaped slaves from Washington, he was arrested and charged with "larceny of slaves." While their actions were short of John Brown's guerrilla war, these "fanatics," "extremists," nevertheless put their lives on the line. And the Black abolitionists honored them, along with their own: Tubman, Hayden, William Still, David Ruggles, the imprisoned Leonard Grimes, Elijah Anderson, Samuel Burris, Oswald Wright, and Samuel Green.

Johnathan Walker was reputed to have friends among his slaves with whom he behaved "on terms of perfect equality with his family"; Fairbank preached in Black churches; and Torrey attended only Black churches in Washington and was active in the Black community in

Philadelphia. But with these few exceptions, the whites who opposed slavery were not conspic-uous in their sympathies for Blacks. Leon Litwack writes, "It was possible to be both 'antislav-ery' and anti-Negro," a reality obvious to many observers. The Black Philadelphian abolition-ist, Sarah Forten, gave some contemporary evidence of this when she "recalled a white friend who told her that when walking with a Negro 'the darker the night, the better Abolitionist was I'" (139).

What was generally true of the abolition movement was, of course, even more transparent-ly present in the slaveholder aristocracy. Indeed, it was a hatred of the Black that caused some members of the Southern ruling class to hatch the most radical scheme to prolong slavery: African colonization. Not surprisingly, colonization attracted broad support and even Congressional approval.

> [In December 1816] there was a meeting in Washington, composed almost entirely of Southerners. Judge Bushrod Washington . . . presided. Present also were Henry Clay, John Randolph of Roanoke, and others of mark. They set up the American Society for Colonizing the Free People of Colour of the United States, and in the face of skepticism quickly built up impressive support.

Unlike the religious enterprise that characterized abolition, this scheme was engendered by those who despised Blacks, particularly free Blacks. Whatever the intrinsic merits of emigra-tion, it was now sullied by association with some of the most rapine racists in the nation. This backing, however, was not sufficient to doom the plan, as a federal allocation of $100,000 sub-stantiated. What scuttled colonization was that it achieved no consensus among the planto-crats, the class that had spawned it. The presence of free Blacks provided moral legitimacy to the paternalistic pretensions of the slave order, and their social and economic roles subsidized the slave economy and the ruling of slaves. Moreover, colonization offended the leadership among the free Blacks: the wealthy James Forten and his actively abolitionist daughters, Sarah and Margaret, and granddaughter, Charlotte; such prominent ministers as Absalom Jones, John Gloucester, and Peter Williams; and, among professionals, the equally impressive blind hydrotherapist, David Ruggles. Some of these spokespersons even castigated Harriet Beecher Stowe for having one of her heroic Black characters in Uncle Tom's Cabin emigrate to Liberia (220–21). Later, by the 1850s, some would be forced by circumstance into changing their minds about emigration (two of the most significant being Henry Highland Garnet and Martin Delany), but in the late 1820s and early 1830s, free Blacks were poised to make claims on their rights as American citizens.

The Black Abolitionists

According to the official census, by 1830 there were nearly 320,000 free Blacks in the coun-try (compared to over 2,009,000 slaves), almost half of them re-siding in the northern and west-ern states, which had abolished or were ending slavery. But, if the rate of increase is taken as a measure of the well-being of the free Black population, then it must be surmised that their lives were hard: over the next three decades, while the slave population nearly doubled to 3,953,000 in 1860, the free Black population only increased by 170,000 (in 1840, free Blacks numbered 386,303; in 1850, 434,495; in 1860, 488,070). Tens of thousands of Blacks, particularly the fugitives, had made their way into Canada (nearly 50,000 by 1860); still the different growth of the two Black populations was telling.

Although some free Blacks could always be found among the slave insurrectionists and conspirators, the majority of leading free Black abolitionists let considerations of property and civic gentility sway them toward reform. Thus, long after free Black workers had begun to sour on the new country, the free Black middle classes remained enchanted by the possibility of achieving equality in America. Indeed, as a token of their patriotism and expectations, Black men and women of influence rallied their communities to the defense of Philadelphia and New York during the War of 1812. Consequently, Black businessmen, clergy, professionals, and the like took to the abolitionist movement with enthusiasm. They believed that ending slavery would secure their own rights, ensure their personal security, and add dignity to their claims. When, in 1832, Garrison proposed to publish the *Liberator*, Forten the sailmaker subsidized the project and James Vashon, a well-to-do Black barber, provided timely advances of capital. By virtue of such visible endorsements, Black support was assured. Benjamin Quarles reports that "for the first three crucial years the majority of the paper's subscribers were Negroes; in April 1834 whites comprised only one-quarter of the 2300 subscribers." Indeed, Black support was Garrison's constant companion. And when, in 1833, Garrison determined to take his abolitionist message to England, Blacks rallied to him.

> Garrison had no money for the trip, but his Negro admirers took up collections, raising nearly $400. . . .
> When Garrison, after four months in England, prepared to return to America, he was again without funds. This time he turned to Nathaniel Paul, a Negro Baptist clergyman. . . . Paul advanced Garrison $200, "so that I could return home without begging," as he phrased it in a letter to Lewis Tappan. (20–21)

Garrison received sanctuary in Black homes when he was attacked by proslavery mobs, and during his travels around the country was received and domiciled by Blacks.

The sympathetic impulse among Black leaders toward the abolitionist movement continued despite the racial intolerance and paternalism so frequently exhibited by white antislave activists. Thus, when many of the abolitionist societies refused membership to Blacks, separate Black antislavery societies were formed. Nevertheless, the ambivalence of their white comrades stung: commenting on the undercurrent of racist paternalism among his white abolitionist comrades, the physician, dentist, and explorer Martin Delany wrote in 1852 that "we were doomed to disappointment, sad, sad disappointment."

With the emergence of Black antislavery associations, it was only a matter of time before the contradictions of being free and Black would become manifest in alternative and opposing political impulses among Black abolitionists. The options that matured were militant political reformism, "Negro sovereignty" (as Howard Bell characterized emigrationism), and insurrection. Even the most steadfast Black leaders found it difficult to choose the most effective means of securing the equality desired by free Blacks and the liberty pursued on behalf of the slaves. Douglass, the fugitive slave, made the most dramatic odyssey, moving from moral suasion, to militant reform, to conspiring with John Brown on insurrection, and, on the eve of the Civil War, flirting with free Black emigration (to Haiti). Delany, on the other hand, traveled a much shorter road: from militant reform in the 1840s to emigration in the 1850s. The majority of Black abolitionists, however, were committed to political reform, supporting movements like the Liberty Party (founded in 1839) and the Free Soil Party (1848), which opposed the expansion of slavery and counted on the gradual disappearance of the institution itself. Until the 1850s, it was much smaller factions of free Blacks who championed the radical proposals to emigrate or conspire for a general slave uprising. But then, most suddenly, as Leon Litwack reports, a change occurred:

> During the crucial decade of the 1850s, the Negro abolitionist grew ever more restive and impatient. The Fugitive Slave Act, the resurgence of the American Colonization Society, the unsuccessful attempts to win equal suffrage, and finally, the Dred Scott decision, impressed many Negroes with the increasing helplessness of their position in the face of the white man's apparent determination to maintain racial supremacy. (150)

The Congress, the courts, and the Constitution had failed them, and many free Blacks found themselves in agreement with Delany's sentiments: "I must admit, that I have no hopes in this country—no confidence in the American people." (152) With this growing recognition of the deep current of racism in American culture, abolitionism took on its third and revolutionary form: the pursuit of Black self-governance, on the one hand, and an insurrection of the slaves on the other.

Black Sovereignty

The resolve to move beyond the orbit of slavery and oppression was as old as slavery. As we have seen, the Spanish and other European slave entrepreneurs encountered this form of resistance as early as the sixteenth century; in the seventeenth century, English slavers and colonists wrestled with slave fugitives, maroons, and insurrectionists. In Brazil, New Spain, Florida, the British West Indies, and elsewhere, African and then Creole peoples had established and defended mountain-based *quilombos* and "nanny-towns," hill-secured free towns, and swamp-remote maroon communities in the seventeenth, eighteenth, and nineteenth centuries. In the southeastern United States, Black Indians and Black-Indian alliances had pursued liberty through an anticolonial struggle and under the authority of Indian nations. Petitions and plans for a Christian African emigration emanated from the Black communities of Newport and Boston in the 1780s; in the mid-1820s, some 6,000 Blacks reportedly left the United States for Haiti. For much of the national era, then, as the vise of slave oppression closed more securely on their brethren, free Blacks grew more acutely conscious of their own jeopardy and frustrated by their inability to end slavery. One result was that by "the eve of the Civil War," as Howard Bell reveals, "there was scarcely a Negro leader of national prominence who had not paid deference to the twin concepts of emigration and Negro nationalism." By 1861, this included Frederick Douglass, the figure who came closest to having become a national leader; William Watkins, the orator and abolitionist agitator; Martin Delany; and William Wells Brown, the former slave and author (*Narrative of William W. Brown, a Fugitive Slave,* published in 1842; *Clotel: or the President's Daughter,* 1853)—all of whom had opposed emigration for decades.

The advent of a middle class among the free Blacks in the nineteenth century added some profoundly new elements to emigrationism: namely, ambitions for the economic development of the free Black community and for self-governance. The rejection by most free Blacks of the American Colonization Society's program of transporting free Blacks to Africa was so passionate that any interest in emigration was at first only tentatively expressed in public forums. In 1838 in *The Colored American,* two letters signed "Augustine" raised the issue, suggesting that the successes of Black communities in the West Indies and Canada were a basis for questioning the general resolve to die before submitting to transportation. "Augustine" reasoned that he "rather be a *living freeman,* even in one of these places, than a 'dead nigger' in the United States." The next year, James Whitfield—poet, reporter, and editor—gave substantial space in *The Colored American* to an emigrationist plan developed by the Young Men's Union Society in Cleveland. In 1847, with Liberia's declaration of independence, the free Black middle class discovered a destination for its economic and political impulses. "By 1847," Bell notes, "the National Negro Convention at Troy, New York, was ready to listen respectfully to a plan for a commercial venture involving Negroes of Jamaica, the United States, and Africa . . . a company owned and operated by people of African descent."

In 1848, Black delegations from Ohio and Kentucky returned from Liberia and the west coast of Africa with favorable reports. The next year, there appeared the first prominent Black voice for emigrationism since Paul Cuffe's 1814–1816 Sierra Leone colonization project. In articles appearing in *The North Star* in January and March of 1949, Henry Highland Garnet nominated Liberia as a land where free Blacks might secure wealth and power. Garnet, however, felt it necessary to impose certain Black nationalist ethics on this pursuit, chastising those Africans in Liberia who were still involved in the slave trade. He advised them to take up "some other and honorable business." With the growing consolidation of free Blacks' social organization, the stock of the nationalists began to rise and with it the impulse towards emigration: "For these individuals, a nationalistic viewpoint required the acceptance of emigration as well," Floyd Miller reports.

The National Negro Convention movement had begun in 1830, fueled by a Baltimore emigrationist, Hezekiah Grice, and under the patronage of Bishop Richard Allen. From the first meeting in Philadelphia (the principal agenda was emigration to Canada), the movement spawned "annual" national and state conventions—"almost as frequent as church meetings," as *The Anglo-African* put it in October 1859—concerned with the plight of free Blacks and the slaves. Both in 1849 and 1852, at the Black state conventions in Ohio (Columbus and

Cincinnati, respectively), John Mercer Langston and W. H. Burnham supported emigration, but their proposals were defeated by a 4 to 1 margin in the 1852 meetings. In 1851, before the interested gaze of many Black abolitionists, two prominent fugitive slaves and writers, Samuel Ward and Henry Bibb, emigrated to Canada, from where Bibb agitated for an emigration meeting. Bibb's call resulted in the Toronto convention in September 1851, at which James T. Holly from Vermont presented his plan for a North American and West Indian Federal Agricultural Union to cooperatively purchase and distribute land in the Caribbean. In the same year, Blacks from Trenton, New Jersey, met to plan the purchase and settlement of lands in Canada. In July 1852, emigrationists met in convention in Baltimore, indicating a preference for Liberia but also a readiness to investigate other possible sites. The next year, 1853, a second meeting was held in Canada (at Amherstburgh), and it was proclaimed that "the American Negro owed no loyalty to the United States; that if emigration did not take place, revolution would; that if Canada were not an acceptable haven, then Haiti beckoned."

Delany had rejected emigration as late as 1851. For the most part, his objections were based on his opposition to the American Colonization Society and his belief that the society's proposed African site, Liberia, was actually a "nominal nation" dominated by white interests. Thus, the revelation of Delany's own program for a Black nation in the Caribbean was somewhat unexpected. However, in the spring of 1852, following his own emigration to Canada, Delany issued his pamphlet *The Condition, Elevation, and Destiny of the Colored People of the United States, Politically Considered.* Delany coupled his plan with a denunciation of the Colonization Society and Liberia, a scheme that had forced him, he revealed, to abandon his earlier (1836) plan for free Black emigration to the eastern coast of Africa. In the piece, Delany enveloped his concern for the fate of the slaves with Black nationalism: "The redemption of the bondmen depends entirely upon the elevation of the freeman; therefore, to elevate the free colored people of America, anywhere upon this continent, forebodes the speedy redemption of the slaves." A Black nation, Delany argued, would have a "reflex influence" on the condition of the slave. He wrote to Frederick Douglass in the same year saying, "We must have a position, independently of anything pertaining to white men or nations." Delany was more than ready, then, in August 1854, when the largest ever emigrationist convention met in Cleveland. Supported by William Monroe, Reverend William Paul Quinn, and the widow Mary Bibb (Henry had recently died in Jamaica), Delany now submitted a lengthy report, "Political Destiny of the Colored Race on the American Continent."

> *It denied both the citizenship and the freedom of the American Negro and contended that Freedom existed only where a racial group constituted a majority; it approved emigration to the Caribbean area via Canada as a way station; and it warned that the rights withheld by a majority were never freely given but must be seized.*

Delany's plan, as faithfully reported in the otherwise hostile Pittsburgh *Daily Morning Post,* was to construct empires ruled by the "nearly twenty-one millions [of] colored people of African and Indian origin" in the West Indies, Central America, Latin America, and Brazil. These empires would form the seat of "negro civilization" and to the slaves of the United States would serve as "the facility of escape, the near neighborhood of friends and aid . . . drain[ing] off from the Southern States all the most intelligent, robust, and bold of their slaves." The convention, made up in its entirety of emigrationists, approved the proposal and met again in 1856 to continue its work as the National Emigration Convention.

Paradoxically, at this point, it was the intervention of non-Blacks that propelled the movement to its next stage. In January 1858, member of Congress Frank Blair, Jr., of Missouri, proposed that the House of Representatives initiate and subsidize a colony of free Blacks in Central America. Almost immediately, leading Black emigrationists took him up on the suggestion. James Holly had been active since 1854 in negotiating with the Haitian government of Emperor Faustin I on behalf of potential settlers; James Whitfield was nearing twenty years as an emigrationist agitator. Now, Holly and Whitfield informed Blair that Blacks were already active in the field and that his best contribution would be to secure financial support for those programs. Delany, ever suspicious of whites, made certain that Blair understood that the origin of the plan was his own.

The publicity generated around Blair's intervention helped to revitalize the emigration to Haiti programs. In 1859, James Redpath—the radical Scottish journalist, abolitionist, and associate of John Brown—traveled to Haiti and secured a pledge of $20,000 for the project from A. Jean Simon, the new Haitian Secretary of State whose president (General Fabre Geffrard) was desperately searching for agricultural specialists. Redpath returned to the United States, began publishing a weekly emigrationist newspaper called *The Pine and the Palm;* enlisted the support of Holly, Garnet, Douglass ("let us go to Hayti, where our oppressors do not want us to go"), William Wells Brown, and Watkins; hired recruitment agents (one of whom was John Brown, Jr.); and organized the Haitian Bureau of Emigration. Christopher Dixon makes it clear that the material support the Haitian government provided proved decisive:

> *The first group of emigrants to leave for Haiti under the auspices of the Bureau left the United States in January 1861. By the time the final group departed in August 1862, the Bureau had despatched over two thousand African Americans to the island republic.*

The Haitian scheme, however, was aborted by a constellation of factors. Some were internal: Redpath's mercurial temperament and revolving ideology (in 1861, he renounced violence as an instrument of slave liberation, rededicating himself to religion); illness among the emigrants; mismanagement on the ground in Haiti; and opposing objectives among the emigrants and the bureau's leaders. Others were external, such as the Civil War and President Lincoln's semiliberatory proclamations on slaves as confiscated property; the threat of war between Haiti and Spain (which seized the Dominican Republic in 1861); and the criticisms of Black emigrationists like Delany (who believed himself the better organizer), Mary Ann Shadd Cary, and William Newman. The more principled opponent was Cary, an editor of the *Provincial Freeman* who had herself emigrated to Canada in the 1850s and was the daughter of Abraham Shadd, an early emigrationist. She had warned that climate and disease made Haiti a death trap and the scheme merely another permutation of the American

Colonization Society. In any case, many of those emigrants who survived returned to the United States and the Bureau closed in 1862. Holly, who was to become the first Black Episcopalian Bishop, had accompanied one colony of emigrants to Haiti and remained there until his death in 1911.

An earlier expression of organized emigrationism also matured. In 1858, the National Emigration Convention met for a third time. As president, Delany was now replaced by William H. Day (who then abandoned emigrationism) while Delany secured the position of foreign secretary. In that capacity, Delany set about planning and seeking funding for the Niger Valley Exploring Party, an expedition to western Africa (Delany would eventually include Liberia along with the Yoruba region of present-day Nigeria as a destination). And for that purpose he organized a new enterprise, the African Civilization Society of Canada, largely a paper entity. Meanwhile, in Philadelphia, Henry Highland Garnet organized a rival African emigrationist organization, the African Civilization Society of New York, with the intention of exploring the Niger River region for free Black colonies. Garnet's group was aided by sympathetic whites (such as Benjamin Coates of the American Colonization Society), and it was somewhat disturbing to Delany that this meant it achieved the funding for its Niger expedition more quickly. Even more annoying to Delany was that Garnet's group designated Robert Campbell as its leader. Campbell, a Jamaican-born chemist and a teacher in the Institute for Colored Youth in Philadelphia, had been nominated by Delany to the Board of Commissioners of the National Emigration Convention in 1858. Fortunately, they were reconciled when Delany, bowing to financial expediency, was compelled to compromise with white colonizationists in New York (194–97).

Delany disembarked in Liberia on July 10, 1859; Campbell's ship anchored off Lagos on July 21, 1859. In early November, the two met at "Abbeokuta," and from that moment they traveled together on horseback: "We proceeded to Ijaye, population 78,000, reckoned by the white missionaries and officers of the Niger Expedition of Her Majesty's service; . . . Oyo, population, 75,000; Ogbomoso, population 70,000; Illorin, population 120,000; returning back, *via* Ogbomoso to Oyo." The two departed Lagos on April 10, 1860. Delany and Campbell both wrote accounts of their expedition: Delany's entitled, "Official Report of The Niger Valley Exploring Party"; and Campbell's "A Pilgrimage to My Motherland: An Account of a Journey Among the Egbas and Yorubas of Central Africa, in 1859–60." These works constituted two of the first deliberate contributions to ethnography by New World Blacks. Delany, always mindful of the historic and moral import of Black American emigration, recorded some memorable nationalist injunctions. To the free Black emigrationists, he warned:

> *Africa is our fatherland and we its legitimate descendants, and we will never agree nor consent to see . . . the first voluntary step that has ever been taken for her regeneration by her own descendants—blasted by a disinterested or renegade set, whose only object might be in the one case to get rid of a portion of the colored population, and in the other, make money. (110)*

And, like Garnet, Delany addressed himself to the slavers, both Black and white:

> *We do not leave America and go to Africa to be passive spectators of such a policy as traffic in the flesh and blood of our kindred, nor any other species of the human race. . . . We will not live there and permit it. . . . We will bide our time; but the Slave-trade shall not continue! (114)*

Eventually Campbell returned to Liberia to settle in 1862, while Delany remained in America. In the next months, Delany began recruiting Blacks for the Civil War (joining the efforts of Tubman, Mary Ann Shadd Cary, and Garnet) and became the first Black major in the armed services. After the war, Delany emerged as a political figure in South Carolina but still held to his nationalist/emigrationist beliefs.

Emigrants both preceded and followed the expedition of Delany and Campbell. "Between 1820 and the beginning of the Civil War, some ten thousand free blacks and newly emancipated slaves sailed to Liberia," we are told by Shepard, Pollard, and Schwartz (96). Among the earliest were the former slave, Lott Cary, the first Western educator in the country, and Joseph Jenkins Roberts, a free Black who became Liberia's first Black governor and first elected president. But it would not be until long after the Civil War, Reconstruction, and the advent of American apartheid (Jim Crow) that Africa would beckon again in the form of a mass movement. Meanwhile, an even smaller minority of radical free Black abolitionists chose a different path to the ending of slavery, conspiring to provoke a general slave uprising.

Insurrection

In his Appeal, David Walker urged a general slave revolution in 1829. In 1831, Nat Turner attempted to organize such an uprising. In Florida, in the mid-1830s, the Black Seminoles prosecuted a series of slave insurrections. In 1843, Henry Highland Garnet came within one vote of winning a Black convention's endorsement of violence to end slavery. In the mid-1850s, following his second and third tours of the South, James Redpath, under the pseudonyms of "James Ball, Jr." and "Jacobius," reported in the abolitionist press on his secret interviews with free Blacks and slaves: "At Richmond and at Willmington . . . I found the slaves discontented, but despondingly resigned to their fate. At Charleston I found them morose and savagely brooding over their wrongs." In the September 8, 1854, issue of Garrison's Liberator, Redpath recounted one Charleston slave's declaration to him: "All [slaves] that I does know *wants to be free very bad*, I tell you, and *may be will fight before long if they don't get freedom somehow*." During the 1840s and 1850s in Louisiana, Mississippi, North Carolina, and Alabama, the resistances of slave fugitives, maroons, and radical white abolitionists plagued the slavers of the South, documenting Redpath's reports.

Even Harriet Beecher Stowe, disappointed by the social impact of her popular *Uncle Tom's Cabin* (over 300,000 copies sold the first year), took up the necessity of a slave uprising in her second novel, *Dred, A Tale of the Great Dismal Swamp* (published in 1856). In her nonfiction work between the two novels, *A Key to Uncle Tom's Cabin* (published in 1853), Stowe first defended the factual basis of her first novel and then proceeded to examine the laws of slavery, which progressively increased the oppression of the slaves and inspired fear among free Blacks. Propelled by the stark honesty of Judge Thomas Ruffin's declaration in *State v. Mann* (1829) that "the power of the master must be absolute, to render the submission of the slave perfect," Stowe came to accept, as Lisa Whitney concludes, that the "slaveholder's power . . . both inspires and justifies rebellion on the part of slaves." In her second novel, drawing on Nat Turner, Stowe's Dred spurred his fellow conspirators by recounting how the law legitimized the murder of slaves. In real life, Simeon Souther (*Souther v. Commonwealth*, 1851) took twelve hours to torture his slave Sam to death: "Whilst the deceased was so tied to the tree, the prisoner did strike, knock, kick, stamp, and beat him upon various parts of his head, face, and body; that he applied fire to his body . . . that he then washed his body with warm water, in which pods of red pepper had been put and steeped." Souther was convicted of only second-degree murder and sentenced to the Virginia penitentiary for five years. Stowe's fictive slaveholders exercised the same absolute rights ("Dey's all last night a killing of him"). Dred, by referring his comrades to the *Declaration of Independence*, assured them of the justice of their conspiracy to liberate themselves.

As we have seen, in the real world of slavery Nat Turner was succeeded by hundreds of Black rebels, slave and free. Their numbers swelled to nearly 200,000 during the Civil War, when self-liberated slaves and free Blacks joined the Union forces to bring slavery to the fore of the war. But nearly a century would pass before the maroons and Black-Indian warriors and their struggles were restored to American history. Meanwhile, history recorded two white figures as icons and explanators of the struggle against slavery: the madman, John Brown, and the tragic president, Abraham Lincoln. Among Blacks, however, it was never accepted that Brown was insane; nor, as we shall see later, did they believe that it was Lincoln who had ended slavery.

A week before the execution of John Brown, "some colored ladies" of New York sent a letter to his wife, Mary, announcing their intention to make contributions to her family: "Tell your dear husband then, that henceforth you shall be our own!" On the day of his execution, December 2, 1859, Blacks by the thousands congregated in northern churches to declare their debt to John Brown. In Detroit, William Lambert spoke for the crowd at Second Baptist Church: "Resolved, That we hold the name of Old Capt. John Brown in the most sacred remembrance, now the first disinterested martyr for our liberty." In Boston, the pastor at Tremont Temple, the former slave J. Sella Martin, spoke of Brown, who, "like John the Baptist, retired into the hard and stony desert of Kansas, and there, by the weapons of heroism, by the principles of freedom, and the undaunted courage of a man, wrung from that bloody soil the highest encomiums of Freedom, and the most base acknowledgments of slavery, that the one was right and the other wrong." The free Black support for John Brown's "business" was not just talk nor just after the fact.

Twelve years before the expedition against Harper's Ferry by Brown's army, he divulged his plan of attack on slavery to Frederick Douglass. Douglass recounted their 1847 discussion:

> *"These mountains [the Alleghenies]," he said, "are the basis of my plan. God has given the strength of the hills to freedom; they were placed here for the emancipation of the Negro race. . . . My plan, then, is to take at first about twenty-five picked men, and begin on a small scale; supply them with arms and ammunition and post them in squads of fives on a line of twenty-five miles. The most persuasive and judicious of these shall go down to the fields from time to time, as opportunity offers, and induce the slaves to join them, seeking and selecting the most restless and daring." . . .*
>
> *[T]hey would run off the slaves in large numbers, retain the brave and strong ones in the mountains, and send the weak and timid to the North by the Underground Railroad."*

Before divulging the plan, Douglass remembered Brown saying that "he had been for some time looking for colored men to whom he could safely reveal his secret, and at times he had almost despaired of finding such men; but that now he was encouraged, for he saw heads of such rising up in all directions." (105) By the time that Brown's men stormed the arsenal at Harper's Ferry, he had found his "colored men": the free Blacks John Anthony Copeland, Lewis S. Leary, and Osborn Perry Anderson; and the former slaves Dangerfield Newby and Shields Green.

Douglass was one of Brown's closest confidantes in the free Black and former slave communities of the North; Delany and Tubman served as his principal resources for recruitment among the 40-50,000 Black emigrants in Canada. Delany was on his African sojourn when Brown's army struck in 1859. But the year before, in Chatham, Canada, he had met with Brown and organized his meeting with other Blacks. Delany had also been at the May 1858 conclave of thirty-four Blacks and twelve whites during which Brown unveiled his plan and his Provisional Constitution. They had expected Douglass, Garnet, J. W. Loguen, and Tubman (of whom Brown had written: "*He Harriet* is the most of a *man* naturally that *I* ever met with"), but, in their absence, Brown had been elected as commander-in-chief and Osborn Anderson as a member of congress in the proposed revolutionary state. The conferees also agreed that their objective was not to dissolve the United States but to submit it to "Amendment and Repeal."

Douglass was absent again when Brown's army struck and was defeated. Once again a fugitive, now sought for his role in the conspiracy, Douglass castigated himself in his Canadian retreat:

> *In a letter to the Rochester* Democrat and American, *Douglass confessed that, "tried by the Harper's Ferry insurrection test," he was "most miserably deficient in courage . . . when he deserted his old brave captain, and fled to the mountains." . . . "Posterity will owe everlasting thanks to John Brown," for he "has attacked slavery with the weapons precisely adapted to bring it to the death." (315)*

Douglass's self-criticism is understandable: for twelve years he and Brown had been friends and confederates and he mourned for the loss of "the old captain." But in their last meeting in August 1859, they had disagreed on the merits of the proposed action. Doubtless, Douglass, the escaped slave who for decades had faced violent, hostile mobs, had shown more than sufficient courage in the struggle.

Alongside Douglass, Tubman, and Delany, the number of prominent free Black leaders linked to Brown's plan was rather impressive. In Brooklyn, there were Dr. J. Gloucester and his wife; in Syracuse, J. W. Loguen, a Black minister; and in Philadelphia, the Reverend Stephen Smith, William Still, Frederick Douglass, and Brown's old friend and fellow revolutionary, Henry Highland Garnet. Brown had held conferences with the Philadelphians in March 1858 and Brown left Philadelphia fully expecting these men to raise money and Negro recruits for the coming revolution (240–41). Their efforts at support had meager results, but without them there would likely have been a much smaller Black contingent at Harper's Ferry.

By the next year, some Blacks did make their way to Brown's farm in Maryland: in July, Newby, who hoped to free his wife; in August, Green, who hoped to free his son; in late September, Osborn Anderson, the emigrant printer; in mid-October, Copeland, the carpenter, and Leary, the harness-maker (both Oberlin-trained). When the firing began in the morning hours of October 17, "Newby was the first of the raiders to die and the last hope of his slave wife whose letter he carried in his pocket: 'Oh dear Dangerfield, com this fall without fail monny or no Monney I want to see you so much that is the one bright hope I have before me.'" (294) Leary and Jeremiah Anderson, too, were killed as were Oliver and Watson, Brown's sons; John Kagi, a reporter; Stewart Taylor; William Leeman; William Thompson; and Dauphin Thompson. One free Black, Copeland, and one fugitive slave, Green, were captured, tried, and sentenced to be hanged.

> "I am not terrified by the gallows," John Copeland, the Negro college student, wrote his parents in Oberlin. "Could I die in a more noble cause? Could I die in a manner and for a cause which would induce true and honest men more to honor me, and the angels more ready to receive me to their happy home of everlasting joy above?" Shields Green retained a quiet dignity as he waited for the gallows like the others; even some Virginians had to concede that the two Negroes were "persevering" and "manly" (although Governor Wise refused to give up the bodies of Green and Copeland after they were executed, unless "white men came after them"). (338)

Osborn Anderson escaped, surviving to fight in the Civil War and provide what DuBois considered the best account of what happened at Harper's Ferry. Of the rest of the raiders, four escaped: Owen Brown (the third of John's sons involved in the raid), Francis Meriam (to serve as the captain of a Black company during the Civil War), Charles Tidd (killed in the Civil War), and Barclay Coppoc (killed in the Civil War). Captured were Barclay's brother Edwin, Aaron Stevens, John Cook, and Albert Hazlett.

Brown, too, was captured. Despite an insufficient number of slaves coming to his aid, and the death of his sons Oliver and Watson (a third, Owen, escaped), Brown maintained that what he had done was right. Fifty-nine years old, a participant in the Underground Railroad in Ohio's Western Reserve, a veteran of the free-state war in Kansas (where his son, Frederick, had been killed), and a "slave-stealer," Brown knew only that his attempt at "Amendment" had proven inadequate. He had been ill often with "ague" in the previous three years, and at his hastily arranged trial he was carried in on a cot, his wounds still apparent. It might be reasonably expected that he would not be up to the ordeal. The trial, however, went badly for the slaveholders. First Brown rejected "as a miserable artifice" the case for insanity so carefully crafted by his friends and defense counsel (Lawson Botts and Thomas Green) from the official construction of Brown's capacity for judgment. His eloquence on that score immediately dampened his image as a madman. The American and foreign journalists took note, angered perhaps by the scent of a ruse in the authorities' characterization of Brown. But what persuaded most observers, near and afar, of his sound judgment was Brown's extraordinary rejoinder to his sentence of death. Reminding his audience that the authority for his actions was the Bible ("a book kissed here"), and describing how the Southern courts had countenanced the most heinous crimes on behalf of slavery ("had I interfered in behalf of the rich, the powerful, the intelligent, the so-called great . . . it would have been all right"), Brown stood his ground by saying:

> Now, if it is deemed necessary that I should forfeit my life for the furtherance of the ends of justice, and mingle my blood further with the blood of my children and with the blood of millions in this slave country whose rights are disregarded by wicked, cruel, and unjust enactments,—I submit; so let it be done!

On the day he was hanged, on the walk to the gallows, he handed a note to an attendant:

> Charlestown, Va, 2d, December, 1859.
> I John Brown am now quite certain that the crimes of this guilty, land: will never be purged away; but with Blood. I had as I now think: vainly flattered myself that without very much bloodshed; it might be done.

In his 1970 biography of Brown, Stephen Oates declared Brown's operation a "dismal failure." Echoing the self-deceit of Andrew Hunter, the state prosecutor at Brown's trial, Oates presumed, "No uprisings had taken place anywhere in Virginia and Maryland, because the slaves there . . . had been both unable and unwilling to join him." But sixty years earlier, DuBois had seen the event differently, mirroring the slaveholders' terrified view: "Fifteen or twenty Negroes had enlisted and would probably have been present had they had the time. Five, probably six, actually came in time, and thirty or forty slaves actively helped." The trials of Brown and his comrades had begun on October 27, nine days after their arrests. During those nine days, while the militias and the federal army marshaled thousands to stand watch over the slaves and proslavery mobs began their long terror, the slaves employed arson: "five incendiary fires in a single week after the raid," DuBois recorded. Over the next months, the slaveholders' activities testified to their understanding of the threats they faced.

In Virginia and Maryland, slave sales increased, reducing the slave population in the counties adjacent to Harper's Ferry (352–54). Throughout the South, recounts Seymore Drescher, "especially incomprehensible were the campaigns to intimidate people of color and white outsiders. . . . Motions introduced in southern legislatures to expel or enslave resident free blacks seemed signs of a society gone out of control." In the Senate, James Mason (of Virginia) chaired a special investigating committee (Jefferson Davis of Mississippi was the chief counsel) hoping to indict and punish Brown's influential supporters, the "Secret Six" who had financed much of the operation: Samuel Gridley Howe, George Luther Stearns, Garrit Smith, Thomas Wentworth Higginson, Theodore Parker, and Franklin Sanborn. Ironically, a proposed Thirteenth Amendment was passed through Congress from the House of Representatives, which would have given "a perpetual commitment to the sanctity of slave property in *states* as opposed to territories." Lincoln publicly asserted he neither would nor could raise an objection to the amendment. Four years later, the actual Thirteenth Amendment would state: "Neither slavery, nor involuntary servitude, except as a punishment for crime whereof the party shall have been duly convicted, shall exist within the United States, or any place subject to their jurisdiction."

For the masters and merchants of the slave economy, however, neither Congress nor the presidents (Buchanan and then Lincoln), neither the Federal army nor their own militias could insure them against the slaves and their allies. Thousands of abolitionists all across the nation had met to plead for Brown's life following his extraordinary performance in the trial; after his execution, they continued to meet to honor their new martyrs. In 1860, as another troubling sign, the American Anti-Slavery Society had taken the audacious step of publishing Joshua Coffin's thirty-six-page pamphlet, *An Account of Some of the Principal Slave Insurrections*, an act that reflected the new radicalism now flashing from the abolitionist camp. Besieged by what they now believed to be "the Abolitionist North" (on the evidence of Brown's connections with prominent Republicans, white abolitionists, and free Blacks), the slaveholders and their allies accelerated their movement toward secession.

There was, then, much that was true in Brown's prophetic final note; but what Douglass concluded about the matter was even truer: "if John Brown did not end the war that ended slavery, he did, at least, begin the war that ended slavery."

13

We Shall Overcome

Harvard Sitkoff

artin Luther King's determination to provoke a confrontation in Birmingham in 1963 resulted in a massive wave of nonviolent action—"the Negro Revolution." His action decisively changed both the nature of the struggle for racial justice and white attitudes toward civil rights. After more than twenty thousand blacks were jailed in hundreds of demonstrations, King's action eventuated the passage of the most comprehensive antidiscrimination legislation in American history.

The decision to launch a campaign to end segregation in Birmingham had been reached in a three-day strategy session conducted by the SCLC at its retreat near Savannah at the end of 1962. The motives were both personal and political, practical as well as philosophical. The Albany debacle weighed heavily on King and his aides. Malcolm X had said "the civil rights struggle in America reached its lowest point" in Albany, and many in the movement agreed. Albany brought into the open doubts about King's leadership and disillusionment with the established techniques of protest. The head of the SCLC wanted desperately to prove that nonviolence could still work, that "you can struggle without hating, you can fight without violence." King also believed it imperative to demonstrate his own courage and effectiveness. His reputation, and SCLC's influence, necessitated a daring, dramatic effort, especially since 1963 would be the year of the one hundredth anniversary of the Emancipation Proclamation.

King realized the need for some majestic achievement to rekindle the morale and momentum of the freedom struggle. Social movements require victories for sustenance, and civil rights gains had not kept pace with the rising expectations of blacks. Despair mounted in 1962, and King feared that if the movement faltered, blacks would turn to leaders like Malcolm X, who mocked nonviolence and had nothing but scorn for "integration"—a word, Malcolm said, "invented by a northern liberal." The SCLC leadership craved and needed a major triumph.

The time had come, moreover, to force Kennedy's hand. The President's policy of trying to show concern for blacks while at the same time avoiding action to inflame the white South, said King, had brought the movement nothing but delay and tokenism. By 1963, thirty-four African nations had freed themselves from colonial bondage, but more than two thousand school districts remained segregated in the South. Only 8 percent of the black children in the South attended class with whites. At this rate of progress, civil-rights leaders moaned, it would be the year 2054 before school desegregation became a reality, and it would be the year 2094 before blacks secured equality in job training and employment. Kennedy would have to be pushed, and pushed hard. "We've got to have a crisis to bargain with," Wyatt Tee Walker explained at the SCLC retreat. "To take a moderate approach hoping to get white help, doesn't help. They nail you to the cross, and it saps the enthusiasm of the followers. You've got to have a crisis."

Birmingham appeared to answer King's diverse needs. The Reverend Fred Lee Shuttlesworth, the head of the Alabama Christian Movement for Human Rights, a SCLC affiliate, had just invited King to conduct nonviolent demonstrations in Birmingham, the most segregated big city in America. No other undertaking would be more audacious. Absolute segregation was the rule—in schools, restaurants, rest rooms, drinking fountains, and department-store fitting rooms. Municipal officials closed down the city parks rather than comply with a federal court order to desegregate them. Birmingham abandoned its professional baseball team rather than allow it to play integrated clubs in the International League. Although over 40 percent of the population was black, fewer than ten thousand of the 80,000 registered voters were black. Despite the city's industrial prosperity, moreover, blacks remained restricted to menial and domestic jobs. Describing race relations in Birmingham, Harrison Salisbury wrote in *The New York Times*:

> *Whites and blacks still walk the same streets. But the streets, the water supply and the sewer system are about the only public facilities they share. Ball parks and taxicabs are segregated. So are libraries. A book featuring black rabbits and white rabbits was banned. A drive is on to forbid "Negro music" on "white" radio stations. Every channel of communication, every medium of mutual interest, every reasoned approach, every inch of middle ground has been fragmented by the emotional dynamite of racism, reinforced by the whip, the razor, the gun, the bomb, the torch, the club, the knife, the mob, the police and many branches of the state's apparatus.*

To crack Birmingham's solid wall of segregation would be a mighty achievement.

Birmingham was more than unyielding on segregation. It had the reputation of a danger-ous city. Blacks dubbed it "Bombingham" for the eighteen racial bombings and more than fifty cross-burning incidents that occurred between 1957 and 1963. Leading the vanguard of the brutal, last-ditch defenders of segregation was Eugene T. ("Bull") Connor. The jowly, thickset police commissioner prided himself on being as vigilant as he was cruel in "keeping the nig-gers in their place." The SCLC could count on Connor to respond viciously to any effort to alter the city's racial order, and that just might create the crisis that would force the President to act. King decided to aid Shuttlesworth, but to avoid having their nonviolent campaign used as a political football, they postponed the demonstrations until after the April 2 mayoralty runoff election. In the meantime, King and his associates prepared a top-secret plan which they called "Project C"—for *Confrontation.*

King and his task force arrived in Birmingham the day after the election. They promptly issued a manifesto spelling out the grievances of blacks in that city. It called for an immediate end to racist employment practices and Jim Crow public accommodations, and for the rapid formation of a biracial committee to plan for further desegregation. "The absence of justice and progress in Birmingham demands that we make a moral witness to give our community a chance to survive," the manifesto concluded; it reasoned that since Birmingham officials had resisted every attempt at mediation and compromise, the only recourse left to blacks was open protest. "We're tired of waiting," Shuttlesworth angrily reiterated to a packed church meeting that evening. "We've been waiting for 340 years for our rights. We want action. We want it now." As the congregation responded with feverish renditions of "Woke up This Mornin' with My Mind Stayed on Freedom" and "Ain't Gonna Let Nobody Turn Me 'Round," King rose to vow that he would lead an economic boycott and demonstrations against the downtown mer-chants until "Pharaoh lets God's people go."

The first stage of Project C began the next morning. Small groups of protesters staged sit-ins at the segregated downtown lunch counters. The anticipated arrests followed. King contin-ued this tactic for several days, patiently piquing the concern of the Kennedy Administration and the interest of the national news media while arousing the black community. He careful-ly avoided provoking the racist fury of white Birmingham until these objectives were reason-ably accomplished. To accelerate the process, King ordered Project C's second stage to start on April 6.

Some fifty blacks led by Shuttlesworth marched on City Hall that Saturday morning. Connor arrested them all. The next day, Palm Sunday, Connor similarly intercepted and jailed a column of blacks marching on City Hall headed by Martin Luther King's brother, the Reverend A. D. King. Day after day the public marches and arrests continued, all in the full glare of newspaper photographers and television cameras. King had counted on these inci-dents and the economic boycott accompanying them to activate larger numbers of Birmingham blacks, to focus national attention on the issue of civil rights, and to discomfort the city's economic elite. He had calculated right. On April 10, city officials secured an injunc-tion barring racial demonstrations. They thought it would stop the SCLC campaign in its tracks, robbing King of his desired publicity and dampening the fervor of the black communi-ty. But King announced that he saw it as his duty to violate this immoral injunction and that he would do so on Good Friday, April 12. Accompanied by Abernathy and Al Hibbler, the popular blind blues singer, King led some fifty hymn-singing volunteers on yet another trek toward City Hall. Chanting "Freedom has come to Birmingham!" nearly a thousand blacks lined their route. An infuriated "Bull" Connor, now assisted by a squad of snarling, snapping police dogs, ordered their arrest. The national spotlight illuminated Birmingham's racial crisis as never before.

King used his time in jail to compose an eloquent essay justifying the strategy of the black freedom struggle. Ostensibly written to the eight Birmingham clergymen who had condemned the SCLC campaign as "unwise and untimely," King addressed his reply to the many whites and blacks who apparently shared his goals but questioned his tactics, especially those who urged the movement to be patient, moderate, and law-abiding. Begun in the margins of news-papers and continued on bits of scrap paper smuggled to him by a prison trusty, King worked for four days on his nineteen-page "Letter from the Birmingham Jail." Soon after, several national periodicals published it in its entirety and reprints were distributed across the nation. The news media frequently quoted it and, for the most part, cited it favorably. The letter proved to be a potent weapon in the propaganda battle to legitimate the direct-action move-ment. It quieted numerous critics of civil disobedience; it won significant new support for "Freedom Now."

King's letter began with a refutation of the charge of "outside agitator," arguing that as a Christian and an American he had the duty to combat injustice wherever it existed. Then King explained how the white leadership of Birmingham left blacks no alternative but to demon-strate at this time. He detailed the broken promises and refusal to negotiate by the white elite, juxtaposing them against his portrayal of the dismal, brutal plight of black Birmingham. The advocates of civil rights, therefore, had to turn to nonviolent direct action to dramatize the issue. Something had to be done to break the crust of apathy and indifference that enabled white America to ignore such injustice; something had to be done to create a crisis so the city could no longer evade a solution. To those who asked blacks "to wait," King retorted that "wait" generally meant "never." He had never "yet engaged in a direct action movement that was 'well timed,'" King observed, "according to the timetable of those who have not suffered unduly from the disease of segregation.

> *I guess it is easy for those who have never felt the stinging darts of segregation to say wait. But when you have seen vicious mobs lynch your mothers and fathers at will and drown your sisters and brothers at whim; when you have seen hate-filled policemen curse, kick, brutalize, and even kill your black brothers and sisters with impunity; when you see that vast majority of your twenty million Negro brothers smothering in an air-tight cage of poverty in the midst of an affluent society; when you suddenly find your tongue twisted and your speech stammering as you seek to explain to your six-year-old daughter why she can't go to the public amusement park that has just been advertised on television, and see tears welling up in her little eyes when she is told that Funtown is closed to colored children, and see the depressing clouds of inferiority begin to form in her little mental sky, and see her begin to distort her little personality by unconsciously*

developing a bitterness toward white people; when you have to concoct an answer for a five-year-old son asking in agonizing pathos: "Daddy, why do white people treat colored people so mean?"; when you take a cross-country drive and find it necessary to sleep night after night in the uncomfortable corners of your automobile because no motel will accept you; when you are humiliated day in and day out by nagging signs reading "white" men and "colored"; when your first name becomes "nigger" and your middle name becomes "boy" (however old you are) and your last name becomes "John," and when your wife and mother are never given the respected title "Mrs."; when you are harried by day and haunted by night by the fact that you are a Negro, living constantly at tiptoe stance never quite knowing what to expect next, and plagued with inner fears and outer resentments; when you are forever fighting a degenerating sense of "nobodiness"—then you will understand why we find it difficult to wait.

King next turned to a philosophical vindication of civil disobedience. Because segregation laws injured the soul and degraded the human personality, he defined them as unjust. Then King cited Augustine, Thomas Aquinas, Paul Tillich, and Martin Buber in support of his contention that one has a moral responsibility to disobey unjust laws. He reminded his fellow ministers that the laws of Hitler had been technically "legal," and further emphasized the undemocratic nature of the segregation ordinances by demonstrating that blacks had been excluded from the political process which enacted these state and local laws. To those still unpersuaded of the justness of civil disobedience, King posed the alternative. "If this philosophy had not emerged I am convinced that if our white brothers dismiss us as 'rabble rousers' and 'outside agitators'—those of us who are working through the channels of nonviolent direct action—and refuse to support our nonviolent efforts, millions of Negroes, out of frustration and despair, will seek solace and security in black nationalist ideologies, a development that will lead inevitably to a frightening racial nightmare." King concluded with an expression of his disappointment with moderates who care more about law and order than about justice. He looked forward to the day when the nation would recognize its real heroes.

They will be the James Merediths, courageously and with a majestic sense of purpose, facing jeering and hostile mobs and the agonizing loneliness that characterizes the life of the pioneer. They will be old, oppressed, battered Negro women, symbolized in a seventy-two-year-old woman of Montgomery, Alabama, who rose up with a sense of dignity and with her people decided not to ride the segregated buses, and responded to one who inquired about her tiredness with ungrammatical profundity: 'My feets is tired, but my soul is rested.' They will be the young high school and college students, the young ministers of the gospel and a host of their elders, courageously and nonviolently sitting in at lunch counters and willingly going to jail for conscience's sake. One day the South will know that when these disinherited children of God sat down at lunch counters they were in reality standing up for the best in the American dream and the most sacred values in our Judeo-Christian heritage, and thus carrying our whole nation back to great wells of democracy which were dug deep by the founding fathers in the formulation of the Constitution and the Declaration of Independence.

That day had certainly not yet arrived in Birmingham. As the disinherited children of God continued to try to march to City Hall, "Bull" Connor's police acted with less and less restraint. The movement responded to police violence with larger and larger demonstrations. And Birmingham blacks reacted by tightening the economic boycott which pinched the merchants more and more. As the racial tension mounted, events outside of Birmingham heightened the sense of impending crisis.

On April 21, William L. Moore, a white Baltimore mail carrier and CORE member, set off from Chattanooga on his "freedom walk." Wearing a sandwich-board sign proclaiming "Equal Rights for All—Mississippi or Bust," Moore intended to hike to Jackson and personally deliver a letter to Mississippi Governor Ross Barnett protesting Southern segregation. On the afternoon of April 23, he walked through Gadsden, Alabama. That evening he was found murdered on a lonely road ten miles outside the city. Moore had been shot in the neck and head.

The killing of Moore embittered many in the movement. As officials throughout the nation bemoaned the outrageous crime, Diane Nash Bevel led a group of eight Birmingham blacks to Gadsden to complete Moore's pilgrimage. All were jailed. Then an interracial group of CORE and SNCC staffers left Chattanooga on May 1 to take up the freedom walk. Nearly a hundred cars filled with bottle- and rock-throwing whites followed them across the Alabama state line, shouting "Kill them!" "Throw them niggers in the river!" Alabama highway patrolmen immediately arrested the freedom walkers, repeatedly shocking them with electrical cattle prods. The CORE-SNCC contingent refused to accept bail and spent a month in prison. Two weeks later, a third attempt to resume Moore's freedom walk, organized by CORE, resulted in the arrest of another six blacks and five whites. Their incarceration, unlike the earlier arrests, barely made news. By this time King had been released from jail and had launched the third stage of his confrontation with Birmingham's establishment.

D Day, May 2, an astonished national audience, generated by the sit-ins, protest marches, police brutality, and the slaying of William Moore, watched over a thousand black children, some only six years old, march out of the Sixteenth Street Baptist Church to demonstrate and be arrested. Before the cameras, the young blacks sang freedom songs, chanted freedom slogans to the hundreds of cheering adult spectators, and knelt to pray as the police corralled them. They offered no resistance to Connor's stupefied forces, clapping, dancing, laughing, and skipping to the patrol wagons waiting to take them to jail. "Black and glad," determined yet not somber, the children stunned the nation.

Criticism of King for his "children's crusade" came from every quarter. Moderates anguished about the safety of the children. Conservatives denounced the tactic as cynical and exploitative. Radicals demeaned it as unmanly. "Real men," objected Malcolm X, "don't put their children on the firing line." King retorted that, by demonstrating, the children gained a "sense of their own stake in freedom and justice," as well as a heightened pride in their race and belief in their capacity to influence their future. He asked his white critics pointedly: Where had they been with their protective words when down through the years, Negro infants were born into ghettos, taking their first breath of life in a social atmosphere where the fresh air of freedom was crowded out by the stench of discrimination?

Words of reason no longer mattered, however. Action had taken precedence. The rules of the game had changed. Another thousand black children of Birmingham packed the Sixteenth Street Baptist Church that evening to shout their approval of King and his promise "Today was D Day. Tomorrow will. be Double-D Day."

The *New York Times* account of the May 3 demonstrations began: "There was an ugly overtone to the events today that was not present yesterday." No one would accuse the reporter of overstatement. As an enraged "Bull" Connor watched a thousand more students gather in the church to receive their demonstration assignments, he abandoned all restraint. He ordered his forces to bar the exits from the church, trapping inside about half the young protesters, and then had his men charge into those who escaped and had gathered in Kelly Ingram Park in front of the Sixteenth Street Baptist Church. The police, swinging nightsticks brutally and indiscriminately, beat demonstrators and onlookers. They sicced their dogs on the young, wounding several. When some adults in the park, horrified at the mistreatment of the children, hurled bricks and bottles at the policemen, Connor commanded the firemen with their high-pressure hoses: "Let 'em have it." With a sound like gunfire, streams of blistering water roared from the nozzles, blasting blacks against buildings and sweeping kids down slippery streets. The hundreds of pounds of pressure ripped the bark off trees; it also tore the clothes off young people's backs and cut through their skin. Those jailed that Friday brought the number of children arrested in two days to nearly thirteen hundred.

King had his confrontation, and more. On Saturday, an additional two hundred students were arrested, and several thousand adult blacks skirmished with the police, pelting them with rocks and stones. Again, scenes of clubbing, police dogs, and fire hoses appeared on the front pages of newspapers and on television sets throughout the country. The appalling pictures of snarling dogs lunging viciously at youthful marchers, of bands of policemen ganging up to beat children and women, of high-pressure hoses knocking the very young and the very old off their feet or into the air, brought a surge of anger and determination across black America and aroused the conscience, or guilt, of millions of whites. King suddenly had the support of much of the nation. Kennedy now had to act.

The pictures of violence in Birmingham made him "sick," the President admitted to a delegation from the Americans for Democratic Action that Saturday. Yet he doubted aloud that he had a constitutional mandate to act. He termed impossible the liberals' suggestion that he intervene immediately and forcefully in Birmingham, but acknowledged: "I am not asking for patience. I can well understand why the Negroes of Birmingham are tired of being asked to be patient." Privately, the President knew that the time had come to act. He had to resolve the conflict with the least possible political damage to himself. He shared the sense of national outrage at Southern white atrocities yet shrank from the prospect of using federal force to impose a new racial order. Kennedy simply wanted the quickest possible restoration of civil peace. Secretly he ordered Justice Department mediators to Birmingham to persuade the contending groups to negotiate a settlement. Concurrently, key Administration officials began an intensive campaign to pressure Birmingham's most influential businessmen, especially those connected with U.S. Steel, to accept a compromise agreement.

Until this moment in the crisis, the Senior Citizens' Committee, covertly organized by the Birmingham Chamber of Commerce to deal with desegregation problems, would not even talk with King and his associates. They were the so-called white moderates of the South—the gentlemen who said "nigra" rather than "nigger"—supposedly too busy making money to hate, yet for a month they had avoided even a hint of willingness to end the disorder and violence. Now, suddenly, they were ready to talk. They had felt the heat from Washington. They feared the city was on the verge of a major bloodletting. And they had reckoned the toll of the black boycott: sales in April had dropped more than a third in the downtown stores. So Birmingham's economic elite started to negotiate in earnest on May 4, even agreeing to hold all-night sessions. They talked and listened but would not accede. The SCLC would not back down. Deadlock. King ordered the demonstrations to continue.

The most massive black protest to date began early Monday, May 6, and police violence intensified accordingly. A flyer distributed near Negro schools urged all students: "Fight for freedom first, then go to school. Join the thousands in jail who are making their witness for freedom. Come to the Sixteenth Street Baptist Church now . . . and we'll soon be free. It's up to you to free our teachers, our parents, yourself and our country." Once again, thousands of young blacks heeded the call. In some schools, attendance dropped nearly 90 percent. Preaching to a jammed church and to the thousands more in Ingram Park listening to loudspeakers, King reminded the students of their stake in this "righteous struggle for freedom and human dignity." He reiterated the necessity for nonviolence: "The world is watching you." Violence is impractical as well as immoral; the power of nonviolence is a greater weapon.

Dick Gregory, the well-known black comedian, led the first group of demonstrators out of the church. Police hurried them into the waiting paddy wagons as the students chanted: "Don't mind walking, 'cause I want my freedom now." Then another group left the church, shouting: "Freedom! Freedom! Freedom!" They, too, were quickly herded off to jail. Out came another group of young blacks, and then another, and another. For an hour, wave after wave of twenty to fifty black students, chanting and shouting for freedom, defiantly offered themselves up for arrest. The huge crowd in the park roared their approval for each contingent leaving the church. Many sang a new ditty: "It isn't nice to go to jail/There are nicer ways to do it/But the nice ways always fail."

The audacity of the students, the contempt of the blacks, stirred Connor's fear and loathing. After more than a thousand demonstrators had been seized, he turned his police on the crowd in the park. Shoving and kicking, the men in blue now vented their fury. As the television cameras rolled and the photographers focused their lenses, snapping police dogs once again leaped at the throats of taunting children, fire hoses bowled over rock-throwing blacks, and Connor's minions indiscriminately clubbed onlookers.

A shocked nation demanded federal action to end the conflict. Kennedy's mediators redoubled their efforts. They pressed King to yield on his demands for immediate desegregation and an end to discrimination in employment. They warned him of the folly of prolonging the crisis in the expectation of intervention by federal troops. Separately, the Justice Department officials urged the city's business establishment to make real concessions, not merely promises of future action. They threatened the white elite with the probable consequences of federal action and the economic effects of a bloodbath in Birmingham. Neither negotiating team would budge. The talks resumed, and so did the confrontation.

Tuesday, May 7, the conflict peaked. A larger number of students than ever before, and far less submissive, appeared on the streets. Rather than march from the church and orderly court arrest, some two thousand young blacks suddenly converged on the downtown area at noon. Most staged sit-ins. Others picketed the major stores. Some held pray-ins on the sidewalks. Several thousand adult spectators then spontaneously joined a raucous black parade through the business section. Over and over they sang "I ain't scared of your jail 'cause I want my freedom! . . . want my freedom!" "We're marching for freedom!" others chanted. "The police can't stop us now. Even 'Bull' Connor can't stop us now."

Connor certainly tried. Adding an armored police tank to his arsenal of hoses, dogs, clubs, and cattle prods, he ordered his men to drive the protesters back into the black ghetto. Brutally, they did so, eventually penning nearly four thousand in Ingram Park. Connor commanded that the high-pressure hoses be turned on the trapped blacks. The water shot from the nozzles whacked the bark off trees. It tore bricks loose from the walls. The crowd screamed, some for mercy, some in anger. Rocks flew. Bottles and bricks were hurled at the police. SCLC aides circulating in the crowd pleaded for nonviolence. Few could even hear them over the crashing of the huge hoses; and not many who could hear wanted to listen. Soon after Shuttlesworth entered the park to try to calm his followers, a blast of water slammed the minister against the side of a building. On hearing that an injured Shuttlesworth had just been placed in an ambulance, Connor laughed. "I waited a week to see Shuttlesworth get hit with a hose. I'm sorry I missed it. I wish they'd carried him away in a hearse." Not until the crowd had been thoroughly pacified and dispersed did the dogs cease biting, the clubs stop crashing bones, and the hoses end knocking blacks down and washing them along the sidewalks. A reporter who watched in despair mumbled "God bless America."

That noon, as the blacks demonstrated tumultuously downtown, a secret emergency meeting of the Senior Citizens' Committee resolved to end the disorder that had caused Birmingham to become an international byword for unrestrained police brutality. With the din of freedom chants in their ears, the business leaders directed their negotiators to come to terms with the SCLC. That evening a three-hour bargaining session brought the two sides close to agreement. Differences remained, but the premonition of unchecked violence affected both negotiating teams. Following three more days of talk, they reached agreement.

"I am very happy to be able to announce," King stated, "that we have come today to the climax of a long struggle for justice, freedom and human dignity in the city of Birmingham." The SCLC had won its demands for the "desegregation of lunch counters, rest rooms, fitting rooms and drinking fountains"; for the "upgrading and hiring of Negroes on a nondiscriminatory basis throughout the industrial community of Birmingham"; and for the formation of a biracial committee. It accepted, however, a timetable of planned stages, relenting on its insistence that these changes take effect immediately. The SCLC, moreover, acceded to the release of arrested demonstrators on bond, giving up its demand for the outright dismissal of all charges against them. Still and all, King could well claim with pride "the most magnificent victory for justice we've ever seen in the Deep South."

King concluded his May 10 press conference with a plea for brotherhood and reconciliation, but too many in Birmingham, black and white, wanted neither. That Saturday, Connor and other leading local and state officials broadcast their denunciations of the biracial accord. In language dripping with venom, they. assaulted the Senior Citizens' Committee and the Kennedy brothers as well as King and the SCLC. At nightfall, over a thousand robed Ku Klux Klansmen met to hear further diatribes against the agreement. Shortly after the rally ended, two dynamite bombs rocked the home of A. D. King, strewing glass and timber in every direction. No one was injured, but the front porch had been replaced with a large crater and the house was a shambles. Sullen neighbors milled about, vowing vengeance. The Police and Fire Department officials inspecting the rubble were jostled and threatened. As the crowd grew, so did calls for retribution. Some angry blacks slashed the tires of police cars and fire trucks. A. D. King pleaded for peace, and only his herculean effort contained the assemblage's rage.

Minutes later, another bomb exploded, blasting a gaping hole in the Gaston Motel, the SCLC's headquarters in Birmingham. Thirsting for vengeance, the black underclass of Alabama's steel town streamed out of the bars and pool halls in the ghetto. They pelted the arriving police and firemen with stones and bottles. They stabbed one officer and assaulted several others. When some of King's aides urged them to stop throwing rocks and go home, the mob shouted back: "They started it! They started it!" "Ladies and gentlemen," Wyatt Tee Walker pleaded into a megaphone, "will you cooperate by going to your homes. Please. Please go home." "Tell it to 'Bull' Connor," came the reply. "This is what nonviolence gets you."

As police reinforcements swarmed into the area, additional rioters joined the rampaging mob. Many were parents of arrested children who had just heard tales of brutality and mistreatment in the prison. Martin Luther King, Jr., to the contrary, they would not love their enemy. Others had been so ground down by racist oppression that they wanted only to kill "whitey." They had never accepted King's talk of nonviolence, and this night they felt emboldened to display their hatred. Pandemonium reigned for several hours. Sporadic battles between the mob and the police flared. A white cabdriver, lost in the ghetto, was attacked by blacks, his car overturned and set on fire. Two grocery stores owned by whites were put to the torch. Soon an entire block was ablaze. "Let the whole fucking city burn," Walker heard a young black scream. "I don't give a good goddamn—this'll show those white motherfuckers!" Some blacks, however, struggled throughout the night to prevent bloodshed. Their exertions managed to keep the surge of violence from becoming a flood. Still, over fifty had been injured and the Birmingham *News* estimated property damage at more than $40,000.

King hurried back from Atlanta the next day to calm black Birmingham and to see that the accord held. He and other SCLC officials made the rounds of black bars and pool halls, schools, and churches, preaching the necessity of avoiding any provocation that might jeopardize the agreement. King pleaded that blacks stay on the nonviolent road to freedom. "Don't stop," he urged. "Don't get weary. There is a great camp meeting coming." How long? He was asked; not long, he promised. "We *shall* overcome." The familiar refrain reassured and comforted. The furor subsided. City officials and business leaders began to implement the desegregation pact on schedule. Order returned to Birmingham.

Further racial disorder, however, swept across much of the rest of the nation as a result of the impact of Birmingham on black America. The audacity of taking on "Bull" Connor's "Johannesburg" and vanquishing it, the unprecedented children's crusade and savage white response, the determination of all strata of black Birmingham to fight racial oppression by whatever means they chose, all combined to affect more Afro-Americans, more deeply, than any previous civil-rights protest. The black struggle had reached a new plateau.

Birmingham fully awakened blacks to a sense of their new power; it ignited a mighty confidence in the potency of mass social dislocation to overcome white intransigence. Blacks took to heart King's description of the accord as a great victory, and heard repeatedly that the lesson of Birmingham was that if such a bastion of segregation could be defeated then any other city or area could be brought to heel by an aroused and determined black community. Birmingham also spurred self-pride, a spirit of black unity, a willingness to join the struggle. James Farmer termed this optimistic assertiveness "a spiritual emancipation" and journalists trumpeted the emergence of a "New Negro," dwelling endlessly on his loss of fear, his readiness to go to jail, and his urgent quest for Freedom Now!

In part, the bravery of Birmingham's black children inspired this commitment. The image of the young, first seen on television and then seared in memory, volunteering to face down Connor's bullies and dogs and hoses, goaded thousands more to demonstrate. The same images also shamed blacks into the struggle. If children could court jail so that all blacks could be free, how could their elders do less. Simultaneously, the pictures of violence against women and kids engendered new depths of anger and widespread bitterness. The catalysts of hatred and retaliation in part dissolved black apathy and helped spark a brushfire of "little Birminghams" across the country in mid-1963.

More significantly than the increased number of demonstrators, the nature of black protest changed after Birmingham. Blacks en masse forsook gradualism for immediacy. The era of tokenism had ended. Limited gains—a handful of students in an integrated school or the desegregation of a specific public accommodation—would no longer suffice. The insistence on *Freedom Now* meant, unmistakably, sweeping basic changes without either delay or dilution. "The package deal is the new demand," wrote Bayard Rustin. Instead of accepting further protracted, piecemeal alterations in the racial system, blacks clamored now for "fundamental, social, political and economic change." The price of racial peace, they insisted, must be decent jobs and housing for blacks as well as the franchise, an end to police brutality as well as immediate desegregation of all schools and public accommodations. To underscore their determination, moreover, blacks demonstrated for these concerns in an exceedingly bellicose and relentless manner.

Birmingham also induced the previously torpid, very poorest blacks to participate in the racial struggle. Their entry into the movement both reflected and accelerated the radicalization of civil-rights strategies and goals. The unemployed and working poor had little interest in the symbolic and status gains that the college students, professionals, and religious Southern middle-class blacks, who had constituted the bulk of the movement prior to Birmingham, had centered their energies on. They had even less sympathy for, or knowledge of, the spirit of *Satyagraha*. King's talk of love left them cold. His request that they nobly accept suffering and jailing made them snicker. As the black struggle became more massive and encompassing, impatience multiplied, disobedience became barely civil, and nonviolence often a mere stratagem.

In addition, both deliberately and inadvertently, all the major civil-rights organizations further radicalized the movement. All responded to the changes wrought by Birmingham with an increasing militancy. "There go my people," King often quoted Gandhi at this time. "I must catch them, for I am their leader." And as King hurried to capitalize on the new spirit and participants in the struggle, so did James Forman and John Lewis of SNCC, James Farmer of CORE, Roy Wilkins of the NAACP, and even Whitney Young, the executive director of the National Urban League since 1961. Far more outspoken than his predecessors, Young in 1963 constantly harped on the themes that civil rights are not negotiable, that the time for compromise or delay had passed, and that the nation owed blacks a "domestic Marshall Plan." "The only fair and realistic way of closing the gap and correcting historic abuses," Young insisted, "calls for a transitional period of intensified special effort of corrective measures in education, in training and employment, in housing and in health and welfare." Although never a direct-action organization, the Urban League in 1963 publicly defended that strategy and urged blacks to demonstrate and protest.

So did the NAACP. And it backed it up with action. Wilkins, who had chided black demonstrators in Jackson in 1961, returned to that city two years later to be arrested for picketing a Woolworth store that refused to desegregate. At the NAACP annual convention in July, Wilkins demanded that the association "accelerate, accelerate, accelerate" the civil rights attack. For the first time, moreover, the national office provided all-out support for its local branches engaging in direct action, especially in the Carolinas, Mississippi, and Philadelphia, where Cecil Moore, the branch president, led blockades of the job sites of lily-white construction unions and boasted: "My basic strength is those 300,000 lower-class guys who are ready to mob, rob, steal and kill."

CORE, however, took the lead in the North in 1963. From New York to San Francisco, it organized rent strikes and school boycotts, demonstrated against job bias and for compensatory employment, and focused public attention on police brutality in the ghetto. And as CORE involved more urban blacks in the struggle, its stridency escalated. Militancy for the sake of militancy took hold, spurring ever more radical demands and tactics. At the same time, similarly responding to pressure from local blacks, CORE put forth a greater effort than ever before in the South. Often in conjunction with the SCLC and SNCC, it mounted major voter-registration campaigns in Louisiana and Mississippi and participated in massive demonstrations against segregation in Alabama, Florida, Maryland, North and South Carolina, and Virginia. All these struggles exhibited the uncompromising impatience and sweeping demands of the thousands of new active-movement adherents, which CORE field secretaries did their best to articulate and channel. The followers were leading, the leaders following.

Competition *among* the civil-rights organizations added to the militancy injected into the movement by those most recently mobilized. All the groups in the fight against racism sought the manpower and money necessary to battle successfully. Each tried to gain influence in Washington and standing in a local community, as well as the approval of the masses and the active support of true-believers. And each group, believing its solution best, sought power to affect the outcome of events. Competition among organizations in the civil-rights movement had always existed. Prior to 1963, however, it had been muted. Despite tactical differences, their goals had remained close, and their combined weakness relative to the opposition had placed a premium on cooperation or, at a minimum, absence of open opposition.

Birmingham changed the rules of the competition, and the stakes. There was a lot more to compete for, and more reason to win. The pool of prospective dues-paying members, of bodies to be utilized in demonstrations, and of committed activists willing to work full-time in the movement increased spectacularly after Birmingham. So did the potential of white backing. The door swung open to the possibilities of immense financial contributions, alliances with powerful business and political leaders, and public endorsements and assistance from the nation's major white religious, civic, and labor groups. At the same time, the probability of victory, of making real changes in the racial order, also zoomed following Birmingham, intensifying each civil-rights organization's desire to shape the future according to its light. Variances between the groups, in style and substance, once easily glossed over, now began to appear insurmountable. CORE, SNCC, SCLC, and the NAACP each hungered for the lion's share of the resources they believed would enable them to set the terms of future agreements and legislation. Each tried to outdo the others, to be more successful in its campaigns, to be more devoted to the struggle. The NAACP and CORE demonstrated that in their competing efforts in a score of cities in the North and in the Carolinas; the same was true of the rivalry of SNCC and SCLC in Danville, Virginia, and in Gadsden and Selma, Alabama; and the contest for primacy in the civil-rights struggle in Mississippi among the NAACP, SNCC, and CORE generated still further momentum and militancy within the movement.

Impatience, tactics, and demands escalated, moreover, because the civil-rights leadership recognized that the new mood in black America would not be long sustained. They feared that delay could dissipate the intense involvement generated by Birmingham. Worrying that anything smacking of "business as usual" might precipitate individual blacks' hasty withdrawal into the private struggle for a better life, the leaders pressed for "all, now!" The civil-rights organizations concertedly demanded as much as they could as quickly as possible. In tandem, the NAACP, CORE, SNCC, and SCLC schooled their followers in the politics of disorder, planning ever more provocative demonstrations.

Blacks responded with a siege of direct action. A far greater number of blacks participated in many more demonstrations against a broader array of discrimination than ever before, and with unprecedented verve. Describing the change, King indicated that prior to 1963 "the quiet sobbing of an oppressed people had been unheard by millions of white Americans." Then, starting with Birmingham, "the lament became a shout and then a roar and for months no American, white or Negro, was insulated or unaware." Nearly eight hundred boycotts, marches, and sit-ins in some two hundred cities and towns across the South occurred in the three months after the Birmingham accord. Over eighty thousand disenfranchised blacks cast ballots in a Mississippi freedom election to protest their being denied the vote. And hundreds of thousands of Northern blacks paraded to demonstrate their solidarity with their Southern brothers and sisters. In addition to staging their own school walk-outs against de facto segregation, they picketed against discrimination in employment, and conducted rent strikes against racism in housing. Indeed, vivid daily accounts of blacks demonstrating and being brutally attacked by police and white mobs became the number-one feature of the news media in mid-1963.

This onslaught of disruptive militancy forced the white South to retreat. Many Southern white leaders suddenly began bargaining for peace, as a result of fear or a sense of fairness. Further, they were concerned for business profits and they also calculated that some reform might best forestall a revolution in race relations. No longer able to count on the indifference of the North or the intransigence of their white constituents, white officials acceded to the desegregation of public accommodations in some fifty Southern and border cities in the five months from May to the end of September. Scores of localities established biracial commissions and hired their first black policemen. And demagogues who had vowed "Never" registered Afro-Americans to vote and enrolled blacks in previously all-white schools. More racial change came in these few months than had occurred in three-quarters of a century. But it did not come everywhere in the South; and even in those areas that did start to alter their racial system, numerous whites remained unreconciled to any black advance.

From southwest Georgia across the Black Belt to the delta land of Louisiana, white supremacists mobilized for a last-ditch stand. They viewed themselves as the defenders of an isolated outpost—abandoned by the rest of white America, outnumbered by blacks, and under attack by an alliance of the federal government and civil-rights agitators. Embattled and endangered, they grew desperate, anxious to go down fighting and wound the hated black movement in whatever ways they could. First they tried all manner of harassment and intimidation, especially economic coercion. When that failed to stop the civil-rights troops, they called on sheriffs and deputies, who arrested over fifteen thousand demonstrators in the Deep South during the spring and summer of 1963. In one citadel of white racism after another, police brutally clubbed protesters, teargassed them, scarred their bodies with electric cattle prods, and turned biting dogs and high-powered hoses on the volunteers in the movement. Still, the demonstrations continued.

Fearful, frustrated, angry whites turned to terrorism and murder. Fiery crosses placed on the lawns of civil-rights spokesmen and carloads of whites night-riding ominously through the black part of town served as preludes to the burning and bombing of homes and businesses owned by integrationists, or the destruction of schools due to be desegregated. In Mississippi, still the most closed society in the feudal South, where most cars owned by whites bore license-plate legends such as MOST LIED ABOUT STATE IN THE UNION, FEDERALLY OCCUPIED MISSISSIPPI, KENNEDY'S HUNGARY, whites put to the torch several NAACP leaders' homes and stores in Gulfport, demolished the cars of civil-rights workers in Biloxi, wounded five SNCC staffers by shotgun blasts in Canton, and shot and killed a young movement organizer in Tchula. In Greenwood, 1963 brought the destruction of the SNCC office, the gasoline bombing of at least a half dozen black businesses and homes, the shooting of as many voter-registration workers, and the machine-gunning of SNCC's Jimmy Travis. Not to be outdone, whites in Jackson burned a restaurant that agreed to hire blacks, ravaged the homes and churches of several integrationists, and frequently fired rifles at cars driven by civil-rights workers. Returning from a mass meeting to his home in the capital shortly after midnight on June 11, Medgar Evers, the NAACP field secretary in Mississippi, was murdered by a sniper lying in ambush. Evers had just vowed to fight to end "all forms of segregation in Jackson."

Three months later, after two dozen black youths in defiance of Governor George Wallace had desegregated several previously all-white schools in Birmingham, a bomb constructed from fifteen sticks of dynamite shattered the Sunday-morning peace of the Sixteenth Street Baptist Church, the staging center of the spring protests. Dozens of children attending a Bible class and worshipping God were injured by the explosion. Four black girls, two of them fourteen, one eleven, and one ten, who had been changing into choir robes in the basement, lay dead and buried under the debris. Later in the day, a sixteen-year-old black youth was shot in the back and killed by a policeman with a shotgun, and a black thirteen-year-old riding his bicycle was shot to death by some white boys.

Revolted by this orgy of racist violence, mainly perpetrated by members of the Klan and the White Citizens' Council, public opinion in the North swung decisively behind the demand of the movement for an effective civil-rights law. From the May demonstrations in Birmingham through the September bombing in that city, white support for the black struggle steadily mounted and grew potent. Birmingham aroused the dormant conscience and sense of justice of millions of white Americans, and subsequent protests ended the complacency of still millions more. Dozens of student associations, labor unions, and religious organizations provided financial and political backing. Hundreds of liberal groups went on record in resolutions of support for the movement, and in certain white circles, being jailed in a civil-rights demonstration became as much a badge of honor as it was in the black community. Polls and surveys in the summer of 1963 disclosed overwhelming majorities in favor of laws to guarantee blacks voting rights, job opportunities, good housing, and desegregated schools and public accommodations. For a season, at least, Birmingham had altered the minds and hearts of millions of white Americans.

Northern whites, like their Southern counterparts, responded from fright as much as from conscience. Birmingham revealed how easily black discontent could flare into rioting, and melees throughout the summer, especially in Cambridge, Maryland, in Jackson after the assassination of Evers, and in Birmingham again, highlighted the disposition of blacks to meet racist violence with retaliatory rampages. In the main, blacks in 1963 vented their accumulated hostility against whites with rhetoric, but the words were so brutally frank, so uncompromising, so filled with fury, that they constituted an act as foreboding to whites as an assault. What whites heard and read, mostly for the first time, chilled them, and forced many to acknowledge the reasonableness of the civil-rights movement's tactics and goals.

The news media accentuated such fears, popularizing many of the most apocalyptic prophets of doom and destruction. The press played up Robert F. Williams's 1962 tract, *Negroes with Guns*, which preached the necessity of armed force by blacks to gain their freedom. It stressed the growing impatience with nonviolence among the more aggressive CORE and SNCC field secretaries, and their dire warnings of race riots to come unless the demands of blacks, North and South, were fully met. It sensationalized the terrorist fantasies of quasi-Maoist black revolutionaries.

Mostly, the media focused on the black threat vividly articulated by James Baldwin and Malcolm X. Baldwin's *The Fire Next Time* forced into the consciousness of whites a new sense of the rancor of blacks and the destruction awaiting America if it did not quickly and completely change its racial ways. He described the Afro-American's past of

> *rope, fire, torture, castration, infanticide, rape; death and humiliation; fear by day and night, fear as deep as the marrow of the bone; doubt that he was worthy of life, since everyone around him denied it; sorrow for his women, for his kinfolk, for his children, who needed his protection, and whom he could not protect; rage, hatred and murder, hatred for white men so deep that it often turned against him and his own and made all love, all trust, all joy impossible.*

He evoked the bleakness blacks presently faced. "For the horrors of the American Negro's life," he wrote, "there has been almost no language." Neither religion nor reason has persuaded whites to treat blacks decently, so, not surprisingly, the appeal of the Black Muslims keeps growing. "There is *no* reason that black men should be expected to be more patient, more forbearing, more farseeing than whites; indeed, quite the contrary." Whites must expect retaliation, unless they change and accept the unconditional freedom of blacks. The price of white security, Baldwin summed up, "is the liberation of the blacks—the total liberation, in the cities, in the towns, before the law, and in the mind." Anything less, he warned in the words of a Negro spiritual: *"God gave Noah the rainbow sign/ No more water, the fire next time!"*

The popularity of the Black Muslims' incitement of violent enmity, described by Baldwin, had first been impressed on white America by CBS's inflammatory documentary in 1959, *The Hate That Hate Produced*. The Nation of Islam was depicted as an army of black fanatics planning for the inevitable race war. Little or nothing most whites read and heard informed them of Muslim success in rehabilitating blacks that others considered beyond reclamation, or of the Muslim gospel that blacks had to conquer their own shame and poverty by adhering to such traditional American virtues as hard work, honesty, self-discipline, mutual help, and self-respect. Rather, the media spotlighted Malcolm X's most extremist visions of separatism and violence; and Malcolm quickly learned that the more shocking his comments, the more white attention the Black Muslims received. He played to the media, conjuring fantasies of jet fleets, piloted by blacks, someday bombing all-white neighborhoods, and publicly thanking *his* God for answering black prayers on the occasion of a plane crash in France which killed 120 white Atlantans. Malcolm X appeared on television more than any other black spokesman in 1963, and few whites remained unaware of his expressions of contempt for all things white, his appeal to blacks to fight racism "by any means necessary," and his insistence that the "day of nonviolent resistance is over."

What often frightened whites instilled a fighting pride in blacks. An apostle of defiance, Malcolm particularly gave voice to the anger and pain of young blacks in the ghetto. His hostility and resentment toward whites epitomized their feelings, and they cheered when Malcolm preached "an eye for an eye" or when he brought "whitey down front." Such utterances expressed the rarely publicized longings of the dissident black masses. Malcolm's insistence on black unity and the right of self-defense, and especially his affirmation of blackness and his contention that blacks must lead and control their *own* freedom struggle, struck still deeper chords among the many in Afro-America who demanded faster and more fundamental changes in racial conditions and called for more forceful means to achieve these ends. To them, of all black leaders, only Malcolm seemed to understand the depth of the racial conflict; and only Malcolm appeared to view the black struggle for equality as a power struggle, not a moral one. To virtually all blacks, moreover, Malcolm X stood as an implacable symbol of resistance and a champion of liberation.

Malcolm X remained a reproach to all white hypocrites and compromising blacks. His extremism, together with the threats of violence and revolution epitomized by Robert F. Williams and *The Fire Next Time*, provided a sharp cutting edge to the black struggle. They kept the pressure on civil-rights leaders to be bolder, more militant. Simultaneously, their radicalism made the movement's leadership and objectives appear responsible and moderate. And they scared some white leaders into accepting the civil-rights demands as the only effective way to avert potential disaster. The more Malcolm loomed as the alternative that whites would have to confront if CORE, SNCC, and SCLC failed, the more white officials acceded to the stipulations posed by the established leadership of the campaign for racial equality.

The threat of black insurrection, and even of more Birminghams and the intensification of black economic boycotts, especially touched the national corporate community. Businessmen saw no profit in turbulence, and many concluded in mid-1963 that meeting the reasonable aims of the civil-rights movement was the best way to lay to rest the specter of increasing racial violence and disorder. They suddenly became, King wrote, "prepared to tolerate change in order to avoid costly chaos." Corporate leaders began to put pressure on local governments, where they had substantial plants and offices, to negotiate their differences with movement organizers; they also started to endorse and to lobby for the proposed civil-rights bill. On June 19, 1963, nearly a hundred chairmen of corporations and foundations answered the call of the president of the Taconic Foundation to aid the civil-rights movement financially. Meeting at the Hotel Carlyle in Manhattan, they pledged over a million dollars to the five major civil-rights groups. These leaders of finance and industry perhaps assumed that by assisting the established black organizations to secure their goals they could preclude the emergence of radicalism that would fill the vacuum if the movement failed. Whatever their intentions, these funds, and the sizable contributions from other whites and blacks, enabled the black struggle to expand, to reach more potential supporters, and to plan larger, more ambitious campaigns. The national staffs of SCLC and SNCC nearly trebled; scores of new field secretaries were added; the number of CORE chapters jumped from sixty to over a hundred; and NAACP membership increased by a third, to more than half a million.

As King observed: "The sound of the explosion in Birmingham reached all the way to Washington." The profound consequences of that campaign on both blacks and whites forced the President's hand, altering his perception of what needed to be done and what could be done. In response to Birmingham and the rush of spring and summer events that followed,

Kennedy traveled in fits and starts toward a commitment to civil rights, and an identification with the movement, that he had previously resisted. Although he never fully reached that destination, he moved nearer to it than any previous American President.

Kennedy began to act decisively on civil rights in the summer of 1963. He did so in part because of his personal sense of morality and in part because of his calculations as party leader and Chief Executive on how to respond to new pressures. He needed to satisfy the millions of Americans, white and black, liberal and moderate, protesting federal inaction and wanting an end to disorder. The President also had to dampen the explosive potential of widespread racial violence and to maintain the confidence of the mass of blacks in government. Additionally, Kennedy considered it necessary to assist Farmer and King and Wilkins in securing their objectives lest the movement be taken over by extremists.

Kennedy's first chance to demonstrate his new intentions came shortly after the Birmingham accord had been reached. On May 21, a federal district judge ordered the University of Alabama to admit two black students to its summer session. Governor George Wallace immediately threatened to defy the court order and to bar the entrance of any black who attempted to desegregate the university. "I draw the line in the dust and toss the gauntlet before the feet of tyranny, and I say, Segregation now! Segregation tomorrow! Segregation forever!" Wallace had announced in his inaugural address, and he now promised his white constituents, "I will not let you down." The nation braced for a repeat of the confrontation at Ole Miss. But Kennedy was determined to keep Tuscaloosa from becoming another Oxford. Unlike his behavior in the events leading to the crisis at the University of Mississippi in 1962, Kennedy in 1963 acted promptly and forcefully, leaving Wallace no doubt as to the President's resolve. The governor capitulated.

Several hours after the first black students at the University of Alabama had registered, just a couple of hours before the assassination of Medgar Evers, Kennedy spoke to the nation on the race issue in a televised address that most of his advisors had counseled him against. He had decided to assert his leadership on what he called "a moral issue . . . as old as the Scriptures and . . . as clear as the American Constitution." It ought to be possible, Kennedy intoned,

> for American students of any color to attend any public institution without having to be backed up by troops. It ought to be possible for American consumers of any color to receive equal service in places of public accommodation, such as hotels and restaurants and theaters and retail stores, without being forced to resort to demonstrations in the street, and it ought to be possible for American citizens of any color to register and to vote in a free election without interference or fear of reprisal. . . . In short, every American ought to have the right to be treated as he would wish to be treated, as one would wish his children to be treated. But this is not the case.

The President reviewed with intense emotion the plight of the American Negro, and asked:

If an American, because his skin is dark, cannot eat lunch in a restaurant open to the public; if he cannot send his children to the best public school available; if he cannot vote for the public officials who represent him; if, in short, he cannot enjoy the full and free life which all of us want, then who among us would be content to have the color of his skin changed and stand in his place?

Who among us would then be content with the counsels of patience and delay? One hundred years of delay have passed since President Lincoln freed the slaves, yet their heirs, their grandsons, are not fully free. They are not yet freed from the bonds of injustice; they are not yet freed from social and economic oppression. And this nation, for all its hopes and all its boasts, will not be fully free until all its citizens are free.

Then Kennedy warned that "events in Birmingham and elsewhere have so increased the cries for equality that no city or state or legislative body can prudently choose to ignore them. The fires of frustration and discord are burning in every city," and the moral crisis "cannot be met by repressive police action" or "quieted by token moves or talk. It is a time to act in the Congress, in your state and local legislative body, and, above all in all our daily lives."

A week later, saying that "the time has come for this nation to fulfill its promise," to "make a commitment it has not fully made in this century to the proposition that race has no place in American life or law," Kennedy asked Congress to enact the most comprehensive civil-rights law in history. A far cry from the eviscerated bill he had proposed in February, his June measure included provisions for desegregating public accommodations; granting authority to the Attorney General to initiate school-desegregation suits; establishing a Community Relations Service to prevent racial conflicts; improving the economic status of blacks; and empowering the government to withhold funds from federally supported programs and facilities in which discrimination occurred. Mississippi's Senator James Eastland termed the bill a "complete blueprint for a totalitarian state," but congressional liberals moved quickly to strengthen it further, adding provisions for a permanent Fair Employment Practices Commission and for federal registrars to enroll black voters.

On August 28, over two hundred thousand Americans, black and white, and from almost every state in the union, converged on the Capitol, chanting: "Pass that bill! Pass that bill! Pass that bill!" Joyously, harmoniously, they marched to signify their belief in equal rights. Gathered in unity before the Lincoln Memorial, the vast, exalted throng cheered the nation's religious and civil-rights leaders' concerted declarations of support for black freedom. They accepted with delight the approval offered by the scores of government officials and dignitaries crowded on the platform behind the speaker's stand. Afterward, the President stated publicly that he had been "impressed with the deep fervor and the quiet dignity" of the marchers, and he lauded the demonstration as one of which "this nation can properly be proud." In the next day's *New York Times*, Russell Baker commented: "The sweetness and patience of the crowd may have set some sort of national highwater mark in mass decency." Few newspapers depicted it any differently. It appeared to be the apogee of the civil-rights movement. But it had not been so conceived, the unanimity was deceptive, and many of those who participated in and praised the march had opposed it when first announced by A. Philip Randolph.

The legendary head of the Brotherhood of Sleeping Car Porters, Randolph had long nurtured a hope for a march on Washington. He had previously broached the idea in 1941 to get President Roosevelt to open defense jobs to blacks and in 1948 to pressure President Truman to desegregate the armed services. In December 1962, he and Bayard Rustin began to plan a march for economic justice for blacks, centered on demands for fair-employment legislation and the passage of an increased minimum wage. Desultorily, CORE, SNCC, and SCLC approved Randolph's February call "for a broad and fundamental program of economic justice" and for a mass pilgrimage to Washington to dramatize the black-unemployment crisis. The NAACP and NUL bowed out. The idea drifted until Birmingham. Then it picked up steam as Rustin oriented it toward civil rights, rather than economic legislation, and Randolph agreed to bill the demonstration as "the March on Washington for Jobs and Freedom."

The President met with the civil-rights leadership on June 22 to dissuade them from encouraging blacks to march on Washington. "We want success in Congress, not just a big show at the Capitol," he stressed, "Some of these people are looking for an excuse to be against us; and I don't want to give any of them a chance to say 'Yes, I'm for the bill, but I am damned if I will vote for it at the point of a gun.'" There had been much loose talk of demonstrations and encampments on the White House lawn and mass sit-ins in the legislative galleries. Kennedy warned that their only effect would be "to create an atmosphere of intimidation—and this may give some members of Congress an out." Vice President Lyndon B. Johnson added that to get the necessary uncommitted votes "we have to be careful not to do anything which would give those who are privately opposed a public excuse to appear as martyrs." Wilkins and the more moderate black leaders concurred. They, too, worried that a mass demonstration might erupt into violence and discredit the movement. Others were concerned that this attempt to pressure Congress might backfire and stimulate congressional resistance.

Randolph, King, and Farmer stood fast. "The Negroes are already in the streets," Randolph firmly informed the President. "It is very likely impossible to get them off. If they are bound to be in the streets in any case, is it not better that they be led by organizations dedicated to civil rights and disciplined by struggle rather than to leave them to other leaders who care neither about civil rights nor about non-violence?" Sustaining the argument, King stated that it was not a choice of a demonstration or legislation. The march "could serve as a means through which people with legitimate discontents could channel their grievances under disciplined non-violent leadership. It could also serve as a means of dramatizing the issue and mobilizing support in parts of the country which don't know the problems at first hand." "We understand your political problem in getting the legislation through," Farmer added, "and we want to help in that as best we can." Then the head of CORE reinforced the contentions of King and Randolph. "We could be in a difficult if not untenable position if we called the street demonstrations off and then were defeated in the legislative battle. The result would be that frustration would grow into violence and would demand new leadership." The President seemed almost persuaded, but he held off approving the march until he felt secure in its content and logistics. "I have my problems with the Congress," he ended the meeting, "you have yours with your own groups. We will undoubtedly disagree from time to time on tactics. But the important thing is to keep in touch."

The march organizers turned their energies, after the conference, to alleviating the qualms of the President and the moderates in the civil-rights camp who still did not back the proposed demonstration in Washington. They shelved all plans for civil disobedience in favor of staging a mass rally. Instead of laying siege to Capitol Hill, they would parade peacefully from the Washington Monument to the Lincoln Memorial. The economic demands favored by Randolph were further downgraded. By July, Rustin had the active cooperation of the NAACP, NUL, and nearly two hundred religious, labor, and civic organizations. Endorsements poured in. At his July 17 press conference, Kennedy characterized the coming demonstration as being "in the great tradition" of peaceful assembly "for a redress of grievances." "I'll look forward to being here," he added pointedly. His aides worked closely with the march leaders on arrangements. A month later, the President even worried that the march might not be massive enough, that the promised one hundred thousand people might not materialize.

The turnout exceeded all expectations. Nearly a quarter of a million attended the March on Washington to petition for black rights, including at least seventy-five thousand whites. They took heart in their numbers, and in the hundreds of celebrities who joined them. The day became a celebration. The assemblage clasped hands as Joan Baez intoned "We shall overcome," sang along with Peter, Paul and Mary when they asked "How many times must a man look up before he can see the sky?" and hushed to hear Bob Dylan sing a ballad about the death of Medgar Evers. They clapped and cried their accompaniment to "If they ask you who you are, tell them you're a child of God" by Odetta, and Mahalia Jackson's renditions of "I been 'buked and I been scorned." Good-naturedly, they endured the heat and humidity and the seemingly endless introduction of notables and repetition of clichés by speaker after speaker. As the afternoon wore on, some grew listless, and chose to nap, to play with the many children brought by parents, and to wade in the Reflecting Pool between the Washington Monument and the Lincoln Memorial. It did not matter. They had made their point by their presence and demeanor. Then Randolph introduced Martin Luther King, Jr., who had been, as Wilkins put it, "assigned the rousements."

"Five score years ago," King began to the sound of a thunderous ovation, "a great American in whose symbolic shadow we stand, signed the Emancipation Proclamation." The crowd grew quiet as King surveyed the century that had passed since that day, declaiming over and over "One hundred years later . . ." and finding that not much had changed. "So we have come here today to dramatize an appalling condition." He termed the promises of the Declaration of Independence "a sacred obligation" which had proved to be, for blacks, a bad check—"a check which has come back marked 'insufficient funds.'" But, King shouted to the standing tens of thousands who roared their agreement, "we refuse to believe that the bank of justice is bankrupt. We refuse to believe that there are insufficient funds in the great vaults of opportunity of this nation."

Melodiously, King's rich baritone praised the "veterans of creative suffering" and urged them to continue the struggle. "*Now* is the time to make real the promises of Democracy. *Now* is the time to rise from the dark and desolate valley of segregation to the sunlit path of racial justice. *Now* is the time to open the doors of opportunity to all of God's children. *Now* is the time to lift our nation from the quicksands of racial injustice to the solid rock of brotherhood." He reminded the nation that there "will be neither rest nor tranquility in America until the Negro is granted his citizenship rights," and in rising tones answered those who asked, "When will you be satisfied?"

We can never be satisfied as long as our bodies, heavy with the fatigue of travel, cannot gain lodging in the motels of the highways and the hotels of the cities. We cannot be satisfied as long as the Negro's basic mobility is from a smaller ghetto to a larger one. We can never be satisfied as long as our children are stripped of their selfhood and robbed of their dignity by signs stating: "For Whites Only." We cannot be satisfied as long as the Negro in Mississippi cannot vote and the Negro in New York believes he has nothing for which to vote. No, no, we are not satisfied and we will not be satisfied until justice rolls down like the waters and righteousness like a mighty stream.

He appealed to the multitude: "Go back to Mississippi, go back to Alabama, go back to South Carolina, go back to Georgia, go back to Louisiana, go back to the slums and ghettos of our modern cities, knowing that somehow this situation can and will be changed."

King had a dream, a vision of racial justice and social harmony. Rhythmically, the words describing it rolled over the crowd, becoming more utopian and yet believable as the audience's antiphonal response rose tumultuously.

I have a dream that one day on the red hills of Georgia the sons of former slaves and the sons of former slaveowners will be able to sit down together at the table of brotherhood.

I have a dream that one day even the State of Mississippi, a state sweltering with the heat of injustice, sweltering with the heat of oppression, will be transformed into an oasis of freedom and justice. I have a dream that my four little children will one day live in a nation where they will not be judged by the color of their skin but by the content of their character. I have a dream today.

I have a dream that one day down in Alabama with its vicious racists, with its Governor having his lips dripping with the words of interposition and nullification—one day right there in Alabama, little black boys and black girls will be able to join hands with little white boys and white girls as sisters and brothers.

I have a dream today.

Spines tingled and eyes teared as King ended:

> When we let freedom ring, when we let it ring from every village and every hamlet, from every state and every city, we will be able to speed up that day when all God's children, black men and white men, Jews and Gentiles, Protestants and Catholics, will be able to join hands and sing in the words of that old Negro spiritual, "Free at last! Free at last! Thank God almighty, we are free at last!"

In less than fifteen minutes, King had transformed an amiable effort at lobbying Congress into a scintillating historic event. "The thundering events of the summer required an appropriate climax," King later wrote, and he had provided it. His dream, judged by its impact both on those in Washington and on those watching on television, had buoyed the spirit of blacks and touched the hearts of whites. Not all, to be sure. It changed neither votes in Congress nor the minds of those most opposed or indifferent to racial equality. But, for most, King's eloquence and vision offset the ugly images of black violence that the demonstrations had started to evoke, replacing them with an inspiring picture of the movement at its benevolent best. To the extent that any single public utterance could, this speech made the black revolt acceptable to white America. King's dream capped the wave of direct action starting in Birmingham which in 1964 resulted in the passage of the civil-rights act.

Some blacks, however, felt betrayed by King and those responsible for the March on Washington. As most in the crowd cried and cheered when King perorated, one young black shouted furiously: "Fuck that dream, Martin. Now goddamit, NOW!" Others mocked "De Lawd." Malcolm X called the demonstration the "Farce on Washington." "Who ever heard of angry revolutionists swinging their bare feet together with their oppressor in lily-pad park pools, with gospels and guitars and 'I Have a Dream' speeches?" Malcolm asked. James Farmer spent the day in a Louisiana jail, refusing bail. Annoyed at the moderating influence of Kennedy and King, he stayed in his cell to make the point that he did not consider the March on Washington sufficiently militant. SNCC staffers were livid that John Lewis, their chairman, had been forced to soften his words in deference to the demand of some of the white speakers. Lewis had prepared a speech describing the civil-rights bill as too little, too late, denouncing both Republicans and Democrats as frauds, threatening the South with a Sherman-like "scorched earth" march through the heart of Dixie, and demanding of Kennedy: "I want to know—which side is the federal government on?" Those words were laundered from the talk by Lewis, but the angry reactions to the March on Washington and King's leadership, largely hidden from view that serene August afternoon, forecast the divisions and differences that would one day wreck the movement.

Nevertheless, throughout 1963, the black struggle remained outwardly united. An end to segregation appeared at hand, although Congress dawdled. In November the sudden crack of a rifle in Dallas precipitated the overdue legislation. The assassination of the President immediately stirred sympathy for the attainment of the goals Kennedy sought and an abhorrence of violent fringe politics, like those associated with the Klan and other extreme white supremacists. Many considered passage of the civil-rights bill the most fitting memorial to their slain leader.

The House of Representatives acted quickly after the 1964 session began. It considered the measure for eleven days and passed it overwhelmingly. The Senate took nearly three months to debate before voting 73 to 27 for the bill. On July 2, President Lyndon Johnson signed the act which prohibited discrimination in most places of public accommodation, authorized the government to withhold federal funds to public programs practicing discrimination, banned discrimination by employers and unions, created an Equal Employment Opportunity Commission, established a Community Relations Service, and provided technical and financial aid to communities desegregating their schools. The movement barely had time to celebrate. It was in the midst of the Mississippi Freedom Summer and a mighty effort to secure the franchise for blacks, the final item on the established civil-rights agenda.

14

Legacies of Conquest

David G. Gutierrez

On February 2, 1848, delegates representing the governments of the Republic of Mexico and the United States met in the dusty village of Guadalupe Hidalgo on the outskirts of Mexico City to sign the treaty ending the Mexican War. After more than two months of negotiations, and after nearly two years of bloody conflict that had left more than 63,000 dead on both sides, the Treaty of Guadalupe Hidalgo ended what was at that time the bloodiest and costliest war in American history. With most of the terms dictated by the victorious Americans, the treaty established a new border between the two nations, provided official recognition of the United States' previous annexation of Texas, and provided for the payment by the United States of 15 million dollars to Mexico in exchange for Mexico's former northern provinces. It ceded to the United States one-third of Mexico's territory—including Texas, more than half—which now comprises all or part of California, Arizona, Nevada, Utah, Wyoming, Colorado, Kansas, Oklahoma, and New Mexico.

The treaty also forever transformed the destiny of the estimated 75,000 to 100,000 Mexicans who remained in what had become the American Southwest. Although the Treaty of Guadalupe Hidalgo formally extended the full protection of the U.S. Constitution and "all the rights of citizens" to those individuals who chose to remain in the territory north of the new international border, Americans' past actions toward the ethnic and racial minorities that composed part of their society made it unlikely that the new Mexican American minority would be afforded anything near equal rights in American society. Indeed, in the half century following the annexation of Mexico's former northern provinces, the ethnic Mexican population of the region was slowly but surely relegated to an inferior, caste-like status in the region's evolving social system. Mexicans were quickly outnumbered by American immigrants; and, facing pervasive ethnocentrism and racial prejudice in their own homelands, they were gradually divested of both political and economic influence in all areas except northern New Mexico and south Texas (where they continued to hold large numerical majorities until the late nineteenth century). By the turn of the century most Mexican Americans found themselves in a position in society not much better than that occupied by Indians and African Americans elsewhere in the United States.

Over the course of the nineteenth century, however, these hardships played an important countervailing role by laying the foundation for the eventual emergence of a new sense of solidarity among Mexican Americans in the Southwest. Before annexation Mexicans on the northern frontier had been isolated from the centers of Mexican civilization and society and from one another by the region's vast expanses of mountains and deserts. However, the combination of military conquest and the subsequent racial prejudice and social subordination helped pull Mexican Americans together by providing the political and social context in which a new sense of community and common purpose would develop. Although the fruits of these first stirrings of ethnic consciousness would not be seen until late in the nineteenth century, this rising level of ethnic awareness provided the basis on which Mexican Americans would later contest their political and socioeconomic subordination in American society.

The Ambiguities of Mexican American Citizenship

Given American arrogance and disdain toward Mexicans and their culture before the Mexican War, it is almost surprising that the United States extended such lenient terms toward the defeated Mexicans. In the years immediately preceding the outbreak of hostilities and during the war itself, many Americans had argued quite seriously that the United States should annex the whole of Mexico. With jingoist newspapers such as the *New York Herald* and the *New York Sun* and ultranationalists such as John L. O'Sullivan and William Walker leading the way, the most strident advocates of American expansionism argued that it was "God's will" that the United States eventually absorb all of Mexico—and perhaps South America as well.

Yet advocates of the "All Mexico" position faced some formidable challenges in selling their views to American political leaders and the American public. Clearly, the most troubling of these were the problems involved in incorporating into American society the peoples who already lived in the coveted territory. It was one thing to call for an aggressive American march to the west and to the south, but quite another to envision the potential incorporation of even larger numbers of non-white, non-English-speaking people into the United States. Given the antipathy many Americans felt toward Mexico and Mexicans, this was a particularly thorny issue.

At the height of the debate over American territorial aggrandizement in the 1840s, the issue of subject peoples would come to dominate discussion. Indeed, as historian Reginald Horsman argued in his study of racialism and Manifest Destiny, in the months preceding the outbreak of war, "the bitter dispute concerning the annexation of Mexican territory was primarily an argument not about territory but about Mexicans." "Though God might . . . guid[e] the Americans to the conquest of Mexico," Horsman observed, "He had not provided a detailed plan for American rule over Mexican people."

Americans advanced a number of views as to what was to become of the people who might be acquired with any annexed territory. Some attempted to argue that such persons would simply melt into American society as they experienced the benefits of American civilization. For example, in presenting his rationale for America's Manifest Destiny, John L. O'Sullivan asserted that an American conquest of Mexico—particularly of Mexico's northern provinces—would be welcomed by Mexican citizens who had come to despise the arrogance and neglect they had traditionally received from their government in Mexico City. In O'Sullivan's view the Mexican residents of the northern provinces would welcome the advance of American civilization because "an irresistible army of Anglo-Saxon[s]" would bring with them "the plough and the rifle . . . schools and colleges, courts and representative halls, mills and meeting houses." A journalist advanced a similar argument in a November 1847 article in the *New York Sun*, observing that "the [Mexican] race is perfectly accustomed to being conquered, and the only new lesson we shall teach is that our victories will give liberty, safety, and prosperity to the vanquished, if they know enough to profit by the appearance of our stars." "To *liberate* and *ennoble*," the *Sun* reporter editorialized, "not to *enslave* and *debase*—is our mission."

Other Americans were not nearly so optimistic about the possibility of absorbing into the American orbit hundreds of thousands, if not more, racially mixed, Spanish-speaking people. Indeed, throughout the war many Americans argued that the annexation of densely populated Mexican territory would help create a new, potentially disastrous "race problem" in the United States. Responding to word of the fall of New Mexico to General Kearny's army in 1846, the opposition *Richmond Whig* argued this point forcefully, asserting "We have far more to dread from the acquisition of a debased population who have been so summarily manufactured into American citizens than to hope from the extension of our territorial limits." The *Illinois State Register* made a similar point, arguing against any American attempt to assimilate a mixed race "but little removed above the negro." Not surprisingly, the firebrand racist senator from South Carolina, John C. Calhoun, added his objection to the possible incorporation into the Union of large numbers of Mexicans. Arguing that Mexicans represented a motley amalgamation of "impure races, not [even] as good as the Cherokees or Choctaws," Calhoun asked, "Can we incorporate a people so dissimilar to us in every respect—so little qualified for free and popular government—without certain destruction to our political institutions?" As the war wound down in Mexico in late 1847, most members of Congress answered Calhoun's rhetorical question in the negative. Indeed, as the American army made its final advance on Mexico City, most American political leaders seemed to have agreed with Michigan Senator Lewis Cass, who asserted, "We do not want the people of Mexico, either as citizens or subjects. All we want is a portion of territory, which they nominally hold, generally uninhabited, or, where inhabited at all, sparsely so, and with a population, which would soon recede, or identify itself with ours."

With such a broad range of people voicing opposition to plans to annex all of Mexico, American expansionists were forced to temper their desires for territory. Consequently, as American forces made their final push toward Mexico City, President James K. Polk and his cabinet scaled back their territorial aspirations to demand a Rio Grande border and the annexation of New Mexico and Alta California. Despite Senator Cass's predictions about the fate of the Mexican citizens who would come with any annexed territory, however, the issue of nationality and citizenship presented American negotiators with some nettlesome problems.

It is one of the ironies of Western history that the complex diplomatic and political issues raised by the impending American annexation of Mexican territory were ultimately resolved (to the extent they could be resolved) not in the Congress or in the court of American public opinion but by a State Department bureaucrat in Mexico City operating without the official sanction of his government. Nicholas P. Trist, the chief clerk of the U.S. Department of State, had been sent to Mexico by President Polk to negotiate a draft treaty after Gen. Winfield Scott had begun his march on the Mexican capital following the fall of Veracruz in March 1847. Polk, however, soon grew disenchanted with Trist's handling of the negotiations, thinking him too lenient with the Mexicans, and in October of that year ordered his representative to break off negotiations immediately and return to Washington. Trist decided that he was close to reaching an agreement with the Mexican government, so, largely on his own initiative, he ignored Polk's dispatches and continued to negotiate.

With the American army already occupying the capital, Mexican negotiators realized that buying time was about the best they could achieve in the treaty negotiations. Nevertheless, from the outset the Mexican delegation insisted that the United States provide guarantees with regard to the rights of the Mexican nationals who chose to remain in the annexed territories. Indeed, according to Trist's memoirs, despite the many other pressing issues facing the Mexican delegation, "the condition of the inhabitants of the ceded or transferred territory is the topic upon which most time [was] expended" during the treaty negotiations. Although the Mexican government clearly was in no position to wrest significant concessions from the United States, the Mexican delegates were instructed to press the Americans on the question of the fate of Mexican citizens who remained in the conquered territories.

Mexico did not achieve all it had hoped in negotiations with the Americans, but when the Treaty of Guadalupe Hidalgo was finally signed in February 1848 the Mexican delegation had achieved remarkable success in convincing the American government to accede to its essential wishes on the issue of its former citizens. Under the terms of the treaty initially agreed to by the negotiators in Mexico, Mexicans remaining in U.S. territory were to have three basic options. According to Section IX of the treaty, they could "remove" themselves south of the new international border, they could retain their Mexican citizenship in the United States with the status of permanent resident aliens by publicly announcing their intention, or, if they chose neither option within one year of the treaty's effective date, they would be considered to have "elected" to become citizens of the United States.

Although Section IX subsequently was amended by the U.S. Senate, the terms of the bilateral protocol signed by representatives of both nations at Querétaro, Mexico, in May 1848 concerning Mexican nationals in the annexed territory remained essentially unchanged. Under the terms of the amended, final version of the treaty, those former citizens of Mexico who remained in American territory and chose not to retain Mexican citizenship were to be

> *incorporated into the Union of the United States, and admitted as soon as possible, according to the principles of the Federal Constitution, to the enjoyment of all the rights of citizens of the United States. In the meantime, they shall be maintained and protected in the enjoyment of their liberty, their property, and the civil rights now vested in them according to the Mexican laws. With respect to political rights, their condition shall be on an equality with that of the inhabitants of the other territories of the United States. . . .*

In theory the signing of the Treaty of Guadalupe Hidalgo and the subsequent Querétaro Protocol seemed to solve the problems associated with the incorporation into the American polity of a large foreign population by extending to them rights similar to those enjoyed by other citizens of the United States. In practice, however, the newly "created" Mexican American population faced two major obstacles to the free exercise of their civil rights in American society. The more fundamental of these concerned their legal status in the United States. As Richard Griswold del Castillo points out, although the treaty seemed to extend to Mexico's former nationals in the annexed territory "all the rights of citizens" of the United States, the wording of the treaty actually left the decision as to the timing and conditions conferring citizenship to the U.S. Congress.

Over the long run the second set of obstacles confronting Mexican Americans proved to be even more important in shaping patterns of interethnic relations in the nineteenth-century Southwest. Although the treaty offered Mexican Americans at least nominal protection of their rights of person and property, it could do little to transform the biased views of Mexicans that Americans continued to entertain. Indeed, the bitterness and hatred toward Mexicans stimulated by the recent war in many ways intensified Anglo Americans' hostility toward "Mexicans"—including those who, at least in theory, had become members of American society. Horsman notes that, if anything, "The total Mexican defeat convinced the Americans that their original judgement of the Mexican race had been correct." The impact of these persistently negative attitudes toward Mexicans was felt by Mexican Americans throughout the annexed territories in the months and years following the end of the war, but the most dramatic manifestations of Americans' racist tendencies emerged in California and Texas.

Of course, as numerous scholars of nineteenth-century California have noted, Americans had developed negative impressions of Mexican California well before the Mexican War. In his popular adventure travelogue *Two Years before the Mast*, for example, Richard Henry Dana had painted an unflattering portrait of the Californios that strongly influenced American popular perceptions of northern Mexican society. Although Dana expressed qualified admiration of some aspects of Californio society and lifestyle, in general he dismissed Californios as "thriftless, proud, and very much given to gaming." As for Mexican women, Dana admired their "dark beauty" but also noted that they were "but of little education . . . and none of the best morality." He was enthusiastic, however, about the territory the Mexicans inhabited. Musing over the Californios' lackadaisical development of "California's four or five hundred miles of sea-coast, . . . good harbors, . . . fine forests, . . . and herds of cattle," Dana was moved to wonder, "In the hands of an enterprising people, what a country this might be!"

Following California's annexation and the discovery of gold soon thereafter, Americans' expressed attitudes about Mexicans and their lands quickly lost this tone of idle speculation. Drawn to California by the discovery of gold in the foothills of the Sierra Nevada in early 1848, nearly 200,000 immigrants poured into California over the next two years, reducing the Spanish-speaking population to a tiny ethnic minority virtually overnight. Among the initial immigrants to the goldfields were an estimated ten to twenty thousand Mexican prospectors from Sonora. Because they brought their expertise in precious-metal mining with them to California, they were at first welcomed by American prospectors eager to learn Mexican techniques. Once American prospectors learned these methods, however, and a pressure on the goldfields intensified, Mexican miners came to be seen as unwanted "foreign" competition. Thus, in 1849 and increasingly in the early 1850s, American prospectors forcefully expelled Mexican, Mexican American, and other Latin American "greasers" from the goldfields. In addition, responding to pressures exerted by American miners, in 1850 the California Legislature passed the so-called Foreign Miners Tax designed to discourage foreign prospectors—especially Mexicans—from gold mining. Those who persisted in the fields or refused to pay the tax were intimidated, beaten, or killed; throughout the 1850s violent crimes against Mexicans in California increased dramatically.

In Texas, large-scale American immigration and the legacy of fierce racial animosity left by the Texas Revolution and the Mexican War stimulated a process of ethnic polarization even earlier than in California. Ironically, much of this ethnic polarization occurred as a result of the "success" of Mexico's colonization law of 1824. Originally passed in an effort to encourage immigration to the sparsely populated Texas frontier, the law soon attracted thousands of American immigrants (and their slaves). Although the new immigrants were required by law to renounce their former citizenship and become loyal citizens of the Republic of Mexico, by the early 1830s the colonization law had created an extremely unstable situation in which American immigrants probably outnumbered Mexicans in Texas by as much as ten to one. This imbalance continued after Texas was annexed by the United States. With a population estimated at somewhere between fourteen and twenty-three thousand (no more than 17 percent of Texas's total population), by the early 1850s Mexican Americans in Texas had become a small minority of a rapidly growing population of American and European immigrants. Just as important, Mexicans had become a spatially segregated minority as well. As a result of the racial hatred inflamed by such incidents as the massacres at the Alamo and Goliad in 1836, most Mexicans had been forced out of their former strongholds in the San Antonio area and became concentrated in the southern reaches of the state between the Nueces River and the Rio Grande. As Texas historian Arnoldo de León noted in his work on the evolution of racial attitudes in nineteenth-century Texas, the mythology surrounding the Texas Revolution contributed to the emergence of lasting stereotypes of "Mexican depravity and violence, a theme which became pervasive once Anglos made closer contact with . . . the Hispanic population following the [Mexican] war. . . . Firebrands spoke alarmingly of savage, degenerate, half-civilized, and barbarous Mexicans committing massacres and atrocities."

As thousands more American immigrants (a majority of whom originated in slave-holding southern states) poured into Texas after the Mexican War, such negative views of Mexicans spread throughout the state. To many of these new immigrants Mexicans represented a primitive "mongrel race," little better than the "wild" Indian tribes who still controlled the northern areas of Texas. Indeed, in the view of some American settlers in the state, Mexicans were inferior even, as Brownsville resident Oscar M. Addison put it in 1854, "to common nig[g]ers."

The Socioeconomic Impact of Annexation in California

Combined with the pervasiveness of negative American attitudes toward Mexicans, the change in sovereignty over Mexico's former northern provinces deeply affected the lives of the nearly 100,000 ethnic Mexicans who had become American citizens under the terms of the Treaty of Guadalupe Hidalgo. Incorporated into the United States by conquest and soon overwhelmed in most areas of the Southwest by the rapid influx of Anglo American and European immigrants, most Mexican Americans found themselves occupying an extremely tenuous position in the rapidly changing Americanized Southwest. Generally perceived and defined by their American conquerors as an inferior, backward people, the vast majority of the Mexican American population faced serious obstacles to the free enjoyment of their new status as American citizens.

The most pressing issue facing Mexican Americans in the years following annexation was their weakened position in the changing regional economy. Despite having been guaranteed equal protection under the law by the Treaty of 1848, most Mexican Americans found that their opportunities for economic advancement in the new political economy were severely circumscribed. Indeed, within two decades of the American conquest it had become clear that, with few exceptions, Mexican Americans had been relegated to a stigmatized, subordinate position in the social and economic hierarchies.

In postwar California several developments contributed to the gradual erosion of Mexican Americans' socioeconomic position. The first of these stemmed from the massive influx of immigrants into the territory following the discovery of gold in early 1848. Most of the prospectors who entered California soon left the arduous work of the goldfields and began to settle in northern California, often on large tracts of land held by members of the Californio elite. The squatters placed intense pressure on Mexican landowners, who were attempting to hold on to their ranchos. As the mining boom subsided in the 1850s and 1860s and as Anglo American and European immigrants drifted away from the Sierra foothills, this process of displacement was replicated in the southern California "cow counties." Even a brief survey of demographic changes in California towns and cities underscores the magnitude and rapidity of these shifts. In Los Angeles, for example, the ethnic Mexican population dwindled from 82 percent of the city's population in 1850 to about 20 percent in 1880. In Santa Barbara the Mexican population dropped from 70 percent of the total in 1860 to less than 50 percent in 1870 and to 27 percent in 1880. In San Diego Mexican Americans' numbers dropped from 28 percent of the total in 1860 to only 8 percent in 1870.

Mass immigration into California set in motion a series of related developments that undermined Mexican Americans' position in the evolving economy. As the large numbers of immigrants encroached on existing Mexican American communities, patterns of residential and social segregation began to emerge. It is important to note, as numerous scholars have, that the trend toward segregation in California represented a complex set of social forces. On one hand, the gradual concentration of Mexican Americans into smaller ethnic enclaves clearly reflected a combination of population pressures on Mexican neighborhoods and the desire of Anglo Americans to live apart from the lower-class "greasers" they encountered. On the other hand, however, the process of ethnic enclavement evolving in the region also involved a strong desire among Mexican Americans themselves to maintain boundaries between their communities and the Norteamericanos. Their decision to live in separate areas stemmed in part from their effort to maintain some semblance of their former community life. As Griswold del Castillo argues, in some respects "the creation of . . . barrio[s] was a positive accomplishment. The barrio gave a geographic identity, a feeling of being at home, to the dispossessed and the poor. It was a place, a traditional place, that offered some security in the midst of . . . social and economic turmoil." And, as Albert Camarillo notes, withdrawal into segregated barrios allowed Mexican Americans to continue to function "within a closed Mexican social universe. Faced with their new-found status as a segregated minority and confronted by a hostile outside world, the Mexican community entered a phase of social change and adaptation . . . [that] ensured the continuity of Mexican society" in California.

The mass migration of American settlers and the emerging patterns of ethnic segregation in California were accompanied and intensified by the transplantation of a new political and legal system to Mexico's former province. Bringing with them an American tradition of elections, criminal justice, and law enforcement, American immigrants quickly imposed their system of law and government on California. Of all the changes wrought by the shift in legal systems, perhaps the most important involved land law. This issue was crucial in California and other areas of the Southwest because so much of the regional economy under Mexican rule had been based on agriculture and the raising of livestock.

Most of the clashes between the American and Mexican legal traditions derived from the problems associated with confirming Mexican land titles. An early draft of Article X of the Treaty of Guadalupe Hidalgo had stipulated that "all grants of land made by the Mexican government or by the competent authorities, in territories previously appertaining to Mexico . . . shall be respected as valid, to the same extent that the same grants would be valid, if the said territories had remained within the limits of Mexico. The U.S. Senate, however, refused to ratify this clause of the treaty. Fearing that Article X would throw the question of land titles in Texas (which, of course, had been annexed by the United States *before* the Mexican War) into a hopeless quagmire, the Senate simply deleted the offending article from the treaty. Secretary of State James Buchanan attempted to put the best face on the Senate's action by explaining to Mexico's Foreign Relations minister that Article X was "unnecessary" because, as he put it, "the present treaty provides amply and specifically in its 8th and 9th articles for the security of property of every kind belonging to Mexicans, whether acquired under Mexican grants or otherwise in the acquired territory." "The property of foreigners under our Constitution and laws," Buchanan concluded, "will be equally secure without any Treaty stipulations."

Buchanan's assurances to the contrary notwithstanding, the change in sovereignty over Mexico's former territories raised complex questions about legal titles to land, some of which remain in dispute to the present day. It was not so much that Americans ran roughshod over the legal rights of Mexican landowners as that different legal traditions of property rights came into conflict. Under Mexican law (and Spanish law before that), procedures regulating property ownership, boundaries, and transfers were based as much on tradition and respect for authority as they were on codified, uniform statutes. For example, under Spanish and Mexican law, it was not at all uncommon to mark property boundaries with cow skulls, rocks, trees, and other such ephemeral landmarks. Needless to say, such seemingly casual stewardship of private property was unfathomable to the notoriously litigious Americans. Nonetheless, the American Court of Land Claims set up in California in 1851 to adjudicate land-grant claims often ruled in favor of Mexican claimants. Yet the combined pressure of the extremely high cost of legal representation, the imposition of property taxes (as opposed to the Mexican ad valorem system of taxing goods produced on the land), the rapid collapse of the livestock market after the Gold Rush, and the unrelenting pressure of squatters on Mexican Americans' lands ultimately spelled doom for almost all of the Californio propertied elite. By the mid-1850s in the north and the early 1870s in the south, the Californios' real estate holdings had dwindled to a tiny fraction of what they had been during the "Golden Age of the Ranchos."

Combined with the rapid erosion of Mexican Americans' economic position in the 1860s and 1870s, existing patterns of American prejudice toward Mexicans created an environment in which the annexed ethnic Mexican population in the Southwest also lost political influence. It is important to recognize here that the rate at which Mexican Americans' influence in political affairs eroded in different areas varied substantially, depending on the presence or absence of such factors as the survival of local propertied elites, the ratio of Mexican Americans to Anglo Americans, and in the various states and territories. Thus, whereas Spanish-speaking propertied elites in New Mexico were able to continue in positions of political influence until well into the twentieth century, it was generally true that Mexican Americans in other areas of the Southwest steadily lost political clout following annexation.

Historians of the Mexican American experience in California have demonstrated that Mexican Americans' political disfranchisement stemmed from the rapid demographic and economic transformation of their society after 1848. Between 1848 and the 1880s huge influxes of white immigrants, increasing Anglo domination over local economies, and a corresponding decrease in the wealth and property holdings of the former Mexican elite combined to erode Mexican Americans' influence in politics, California's constitution reiterated many of the civil guarantees extended to the Mexican population by the Treaty of Guadalupe Hidalgo, and Mexican Americans continued to influence local politics by electing some of their own in areas (such as Santa Barbara and Los Angeles) where they retained sizable minorities, but by the

1870s, and certainly by the 1880s, unfavorable population ratios, combined with Americans' use of gerrymandering and other forms of ethnic exclusion, gradually forced Mexican American out of the political arena. Consequently, by the turn of the century Mexican Americans had lost virtually all direct voice in local and state political affairs.

The dramatic decline of the Californio elite was only one part of Mexican Americans' decline in economic, social, and political status in the society that evolved under American rule. On the broadest level, Mexican Americans experienced vast structural displacement as the local economy shifted rapidly from a pastoral one, based predominantly on ranching and subsistent farming, to a capitalist one, increasingly based on commercial agriculture, trade, and later, the large-scale infrastructural development of the region. Before 1848 the vast majority of Mexican American laborers had been employed by the Mexican landholding elite in skilled and semi-skilled jobs as blacksmiths, harness and saddle makers, leather workers, vaqueros, or *trasquiladores* (sheepshearers). When the ranch economy was rapidly supplanted by the more diversified market economy introduced by American immigrants after the Gold Rush, the traditional occupational structure of the region was transformed. In the two decades after California enter the Union in 1850, Mexican American workers found most of their traditional occupations rendered obsolete.

Displaced from their former occupations, Mexican Americans were forced to seek work in a transformed labor market in which higher-paying occupations were dominated by Anglo American workers. Finding their access to skilled occupations, professions, and service jobs severely restricted, Mexican American workers were compelled either to accept semi-skilled or unskilled occupations or to enter the growing stream of migrant agricultural workers. To make matters worse, the concentration of Mexican American workers in these low-status occupations in many ways helped to reinforce and perpetuate negative stereotypes about "Mexicans'" native abilities, for over time Americans in the Southwest came to associate Mexican Americans with unskilled labor. Indeed, this status became institutionalized in some ways by the emergence of an ethnic division of labor characterized by a dual wage structure, in which Mexican workers were consistently paid less than "white" workers performing the same work. By the turn of the century the dual wage system was a characteristic feature of virtually all industries employing Mexican and other ethnic workers throughout the Southwest.

Developments in Texas

As in California, the demographics of post-annexation Texas played a strong role in shaping the future status of Mexican Americans in the society that evolved in the state. Although a small number of the Texas land-holding elite (particularly in the border region) were able to retain some control over their property—and thus a degree of political influence—for decades following the Mexican War, Tejanos in general experienced patterns of land loss similar to those occurring elsewhere in the Southwest. As in California, most of the Mexican land grants held by Mexican American landowners were eventually confirmed in Texas courts, but high legal fees, unscrupulous lawyers, and unpredictable markets combined to displace Mexican

Americans from their former lands. Summarizing the various factors affecting the Mexican American ranching elite in Texas, one historian notes that although "a segment of the landed Mexican elite . . . successfully commercialized, assimilated a mercantile outlook, and [thus] retained a patrimony of land and workers," the vast majority of Tejano landowners did not, "either because they failed to acquire an export-related source of capital or because they retained a complacent attitude toward merchandising." "Eventually," he continues, "taxes, drought, and disastrous fluctuations of the cattle market, the need to sink wells and improve cattle stock, and the expense of surveying and defending land titles combined to displace the 'unproductive' [Mexican American] landowner." The result was that "by 1900 the Mexican upper class would become nonexistent except in a few border enclaves."

Mass immigration from other parts of the United States, together with the Mexican ranching elite's loss of land, deeply influenced the structural position of Mexican American workers in the evolving regional economy. As a number of Texas scholars recently demonstrated, working-class Tejanos steadily lost economic ground in the five decades following the Mexican War. Moreover, as control over the primary source of wealth became increasingly concentrated in the hands of the new immigrants, landholding Mexican Americans experienced a corresponding loss of property. And, again as in California, this shift in control of the local economy was accompanied by a clear trend in which Mexican Americans slipped into the lowest levels of the maturing capitalist labor market. Whereas in 1850 Mexican American workers in Texas had been fairly evenly distributed among the occupational classifications of independent ranch-farm owner-operator, skilled worker, and semiskilled and unskilled laborer, by the 1870s a disproportionate number of Mexican American workers were employed in the rapidly expanding "unspecialized labor" sector. By the turn of the century almost two-thirds of Texas-born Mexican American workers toiled in unspecialized, unskilled and semiskilled labor categories. As in other parts of the Southwest, by 1900 Mexican Americans in Texas made up part of a regional economy characterized by a clear ethnic division of labor in which they were trapped in the least-skilled and lowest-paid jobs.

The process of the political disfranchisement of Mexican Americans that accompanied these economic changes was somewhat more complex in Texas than in California. On one hand, the climate of racial enmity against Mexican Americans in Texas was generally much worse than in California. Although violence and legislative repression against Mexican Americans were not uncommon in California, in Texas racial animosities arising from the Texas Revolution of the 1830s and the Mexican-American War of the 1840s had been continually reinforced in subsequent years by intermittent violence between Anglos and Mexicans along the border. Interethnic tensions were exacerbated by the Texas Rangers, who often took it upon themselves to "keep the Mexicans in their place" through intimidation and violence. As one Texas scholar notes, by the 1860s and 1870s the Texas Rangers had become a paramilitary "corps that enjoyed the tacit sanction of the white community to do to Mexicans in the name of the law what others did extra-legally."

Despite endemic racial conflict and the periodic repression of Mexicans by the Texas Rangers, however, a few "Texas Mexicans" were able to retain a degree of influence in local political affairs, particularly in areas where Mexican Americans continued to hold large numerical majorities. In towns with large Mexican populations, such as El Paso, Laredo, Brownsville, or Corpus Christi, Mexican Americans remained active in the new political order until the late nineteenth century. In other cases Mexican American and social elites forged successful, if tenuous, coalitions with Anglo leaders that helped to perpetuate their influence until after the turn of the century. When the railroads opened South Texas to settlement and development, however, large-scale migrations of Anglo American and European immigrants quickly changed the demographic structure—and thus the political structure—of the region. By the 1910s Anglos had achieved political domination even in those areas that remained largely ethnically Mexican.

Anglo Texans further consolidated their growing political power in the state through various legislative means. For example, in a series of moves initially designed to exclude East Texas blacks from the franchise, Anglos also effectively constrained or eliminated many Mexican Americans from political participation. One of the most effective methods of limiting the franchise was the utilization of the so-called White Man's Primaries implemented in the last quarter of the nineteen century in several Texas counties (including Bexar County, which encompassed San Antonio), White Man's Primaries limited the franchise exclusively to "qualified, white" voters—a set of criteria which allowed local whites wide latitude in determining voter eligibility. In 1923 the Texas legislature established the white primary statewide. Another measure designed primarily to obstruct black voters, the poll tax, was enacted by the legislature in 1902. The poll tax, required of all voters except those over sixty years of age or "otherwise qualified," ranged from $1.50 to $1.75 per voter. Roughly equivalent to a full day's pay for black and Mexican workers, the poll tax effectively constrained thousands from participation in elections.

In those areas of Texas in which Mexican Americans constituted a vital swing vote, machine politics dominated the scene. Common in the border counties, the development of political machines reflected the need of Anglo immigrants to garner support of local Mexican elites in their attempts to gain control of local politics. As David Montejano explains in his study of South Texas society, "In the case of the Texas-Mexican border region and generally in the annexed Southwest the ability to govern in the immediate postwar period was secured through an accommodation between the victorious Anglos and the defeated Mexican elite, with the latter [left] in command of the Mexican communities." Building on existing patterns of paternalistic relations between the Tejano land-owning elite and the working-class Mexicans who worked for them during the Mexican era, Anglo political bosses attempted to adopt and refine traditional Mexican forms of deferential social relations in their efforts to extend control over the new political system. Allying themselves with Mexican American *patrones*, or local bosses, Anglo political bosses provided patronage and/or cash payments to these "sub-bosses" in exchange for the working-class Mexican American vote they delivered. At election time the patrones, after consultation with such Anglo bosses as James Wells, Archie Parr, or those associated with the infamous El Paso "Ring," would "instruct" the votes of their Mexican American constituents. In exchange for their votes, working-class Tejanos received considerations ranging from cash payments on election day to emergency loans or other assistance during the rest of the year. These inducements helped to perpetuate existing patterns of social relations in which working-class Tejanos were tied to Mexican and Anglo bosses by bonds of mutual dependence. Thus, for many Tejanos of the border region, voting and other forms of political activity were seen less as active participation in American politics than as an almost natural extension of the same mutually beneficial transactions that had characterized Tejano society prior to the Mexican American War. As one scholar of the Texas boss system notes,

> Lacking any tradition of participation in electoral politics, [Tejanos] did not view themselves as independent voters or as an aggrieved interest group with the potential power to organize and force their demands on public officials. Instead, the heritage of peonage conditioned the Hispanic workers and farmers to define their political roles in terms of political obligation. They voted for a particular candidate not because of his qualifications or campaign promises, but because they felt indebted to the candidate . . . or to their employers, who supported the machine ticket.

Early Manifestations of Ethnic Awareness

The military conquest, annexation, and subsequent racial prejudice and economic displacement experienced by Mexican Americans placed intense strains on the culture and style of life they had developed over two centuries of continuous residence in the Southwest. As American and other immigrants poured into the region, bringing with them their systems of government, social norms, and institutions, the resident Mexican population faced an extremely difficult set of challenges. Most of this first generation of Mexican Americans had little choice but to try to adapt and accommodate themselves to the changes confronting their society. For the majority of Mexican Americans the general climate of anti-Mexican prejudice and their withdrawal from extensive contacts with the Anglo American interlopers served as formidable barriers to achieving even the most basic forms of integration, much less full-blown assimilation into the society of which they had become a part.

On the other hand, the intense pressures that annexation exerted on the traditional northern Mexican social order had unforeseen effects on the Mexican American population. There is no question that Mexican Americans suffered from Anglo Americans' tendency to stigmatize them by generically defining and thus, to a large degree, dismissing them as inferior "Mexicans" in what had juridically become part of the United States. At the same time, however, Americans' prejudices and discriminatory practices helped lay the foundation for the gradual emergence and development of new forms of ethnic awareness among the Spanish-speaking population of the Southwest. Collective ethnic awareness developed slowly over a number of years and varied significantly in content and expression depending on local circumstances, including local economic conditions, the ratio of Anglo to Mexican residents in a given area, proximity to the border, the extent of interethnic contact, and other factors. But by the 1870s scattered evidence indicates that Mexican Americans in various locales had begun to forge an affirmative sense of themselves as an ethnic minority of a larger society. In some ways it was indeed the immense challenge of adapting to a new political and social order, combined with Mexican Americans' ongoing experience of prejudice and discrimination, that provided a basis for solidarity among a group of people who had previously had few bases of community or collective action. The experience of prejudice and discrimination helped Mexican Americans to create a self-conscious ethnic collectivity where one did not exist before.

Scholars have noted similar dynamics among a broad variety of peoples and cultures in many areas of the world. For example, in his broadly comparative work on the genesis and evolution of ethnic and/or national identities in minority populations in Europe, Africa, and the Middle East, the British scholar Anthony D. Smith details the complex nature of evolving interethnic or interracial relations in different societies. Smith notes that the common process of ascription—the act of a dominant or superordinate group assigning a priori characteristics and labels to another group—often serves unexpected or even contradictory functions, particularly in situations where the subordinate group has been involuntarily incorporated into a new society. Smith argues that it is common for such newly created minority populations to develop a new sense of identity as a natural defense mechanism or as part of a larger "oppositional strategy" against the prejudice and discrimination shown them by the majority or dominant group. As Smith points out, the process of forging a generally accepted collective self-identity in an ethnic minority population often "is simply the converse of [discrimination's] distancing role. Just as [discrimination based on] colour can point up dissimilarity and distance, so may it reveal similarity and proximity," among racial or cultural minorities. Similarly, discrimination by a dominant group over a subordinate group may serve as a catalyst, encouraging members of minority populations to overcome lines of internal stratification that divided them in the past. Seeking new areas of commonality, they often "invent" a new (or renewed) sense of community in an attempt to better conditions for their group as a whole (however that group or community is ultimately defined). As Smith notes, "This is particularly apparent where group conflicts polarise members of different colour [or cultural] communities. The need for self-defence, for organisation and leadership, in the face of threat or attack inspires a desire for some rationale for the community, some set of justifications and explanations for their need to unite and mobilise."

Although no one has yet produced a systematic study of the development of Mexican American ethnic identity after 1848, scholars of nineteenth-century Mexican American history have provided strong indications that a process similar to that which Smith describes was surfacing in different local contexts among the recently "created" Mexican American population in California, New Mexico, and Texas. By the 1850s Mexican Americans throughout the Southwest had begun to speak of themselves as members of a Mexican American community, or, more commonly, as members of a broader linguistic/cultural community that was distinct from the North Americans. More importantly, Mexican Americans in communities across the region had taken the first steps toward mobilizing and organizing themselves based on this nascent sense of collective identity.

This is not to assert, however, that Mexican Americans responded uniformly to the changes wrought by annexation. On the contrary, to achieve any level of collective ethnic awareness or solidarity, Mexican Americans first had to contend with the internal class, regional, and other differences that traditionally divided the Mexican population of the north. As David Weber, Ramón A. Gutiérrez, and other Southwest historians have argued, in the quarter century before annexation, many, if not most, Spanish-speaking residents of Mexico's northern provinces did not even identify themselves as Mexicans and instead probably thought of themselves first as Nuevomexicanos, Tejanos, or Californios. As Weber puts it, "Loyalty to one's locality, one's *patria chica* [little nation, or locale], frequently took precedence over loyalty to the patria, or nation as a whole."

Given their long isolation on the fringes of the Mexican nation, these local attachments are hardly surprising. Considering themselves *hijos del país* (sons of the country), Mexicans in the various northern centers of settlement had driven deep roots into the regions where their families had lived for generations. Indeed, regional loyalties were so strong that many natives of the far-flung northern provinces—particularly members of the local elites—tended to view Mexican colonial administrators, soldiers, settlers, and sojourners as *extranjeros* (foreigners or outsiders)—despite the fact that both Norteños and Mexicans from Mexico were technically Mexicans. In fact, during the early Mexican Republic the Norteñ)os' petulant attitude toward the patria was so strong that revolts periodically broke out against Mexican authority in Alta California, Nuevo Mexico, and Tejas. Weber notes that in California "even casual visitors . . . noted the hostility and 'deep hatred' that the Californios held toward Mexicans from 'la otra banda,' or 'other shore' as Californios termed central Mexico."

For their part, Mexicans who visited the northern provinces were also aware of the social distance that had grown between the Norteños and Mexicans from the fatherland. This was clear in the observations made by Lt. José María Sánchez, an artillery officer who traveled with Inspector General Manuel Mier y Terán on his tour of Texas in 1828. Commenting on the Mexican residents of Nacogdoches, Texas, Sánchez noted with regret that

> The Mexicans that live here are very humble people, and perhaps their intentions are good, but because of their education and environment they are ignorant not only of the customs of our great cities, but even of the occurrences of our Revolution, excepting a few persons who have heard about them. Accustomed to the continued trade with the North Americans, they have adopted their customs and habits, and one may say truly that they are not Mexicans except by birth, for they even speak Spanish with marked incorrectness.

Society in nineteenth-century northwestern Mexico was stratified in ways that militated against the development of a strong sense of ethnic or cultural community. It was hierarchically organized into a social pyramid ordered by a combination of factors, including accumulated wealth and claimed lines of descent. By 1800 Hispanic society in the north was dominated by a small minority of wealthy landowners who claimed descent from the original Spanish settlers of New Spain. The exact shape of the social pyramid varied from region to region in the northern provinces, but in general Hispanic society in the early nineteenth century was divided into three fairly distinct strata. At the bottom were the Christianized or, more accurately, detribalized Indians (known as *genízaros* in New Mexico and neophytes in California) who worked for large landowners in a status resembling indentured servitude or for the many Catholic missions that dotted the northern frontier. Smallholder mestizos occupied the next tier. Although most people in this stratum, like the Christianized Indians, toiled at subsistence agriculture, ranch labor, artisanal crafts, and, toward the end of the Mexican period, as paid day laborers, the mestizos could—and did—claim at least some Spanish blood and thus were considered to be *gente de razón* (people of reason) as opposed to the savage Indians, who were deemed *gente sin razón* (people without reason). The final and smallest stratum of Hispanic frontier society consisted of the large landowners, government and military administrators, merchants, and in some cases, Catholic church officials who dominated the political economy. As Gutiérrez noted in his richly detailed work on the colonial and Mexican-era north, the landed aristocracy maintained and extended its dominance of northern society through a complex system of claimed European descent, the accumulation of wealth, and the strict supervision of marriage and women's sexuality.

Many of the lines of internal differentiation that had evolved in northwestern Mexico persisted after the American conquest. As Gutiérrez and others have argued, although Anglo Americans may have seen the emerging patterns of ethnic relations in the Southwest as a question concerning Americans, Mexicans, and Indians, Mexican Americans continued to recognize important status distinctions among themselves, which they attempted to maintain even after the change in sovereignty. Indeed, Mexican Americans' attempts to grapple with the social status issues raised by their incorporation into American society closely mirrored the lines of internal stratification that traditionally had divided them.

Take, for example, the different ways the various strata of Mexican society reacted to the American takeover and to Americans' subsequent tendency to view Mexicans simply as "Mexicans." Upper-class Mexican Americans contested Anglo Americans' efforts to classify (and thus to denigrate) them as Mexicans by denying and/or reconstructing their ethnic heritage. Traditionally considering themselves to be of inherently higher status than the Mexican working masses by virtue of their class standing and their *calidad* and their sense of *limpieza de sangre* (that is, their social "quality" based on their supposed "pure" European blood), members of the Californio, Tejano, and Nuevomexicano elite tried to persuade incoming American immigrants to recognize and acknowledge these status distinctions. In the early part of the nineteenth century this strategy worked because many Americans found it in their interest to forge economic, political, and, in many cases, matrimonial alliances with members of the existing Spanish-speaking elite. Seeking to maximize their influence with the extant indigenous elite, the first American immigrants to the region tended to acknowledge the status distinctions the elite tried so hard to maintain between themselves and the Mexican working class.

After annexation these status distinctions remained crucial to the Spanish-speaking elite's attempts to insulate themselves from the stigma associated with the Mexican label. By referring to themselves as Spanish in their dealings with Anglo Americans, members of the indigenous elite hoped to escape the prejudice exhibited toward Mexicans in the Southwest. They accomplished this, in part, by meticulously laying the foundation for what Carey McWilliams wryly termed the "Spanish fantasy heritage" of the Southwest. Existing historical evidence demonstrates that only a tiny fraction of the original Hispanic Southwest could legitimately claim pure Spanish descent, the overwhelming majority being descended from Mexico's vast mesti-zo population. Nevertheless, many of the elite families insisted on referring to themselves as *españoles*, or Spaniards, to distance themselves from what they defined as the *gente corriente*, the common or vulgar working-class people. As the position of the ethnic Mexican population eroded in subsequent years, the descendants of the former elite *gente de razón* families clung to such status distinctions even more tenaciously. By the last decades of the nineteenth centu-ry their efforts in this direction had become almost comical. As McWilliams noted of this trend in California, "By a definition provided by the *Californios* themselves, [a Mexican American] who achieves success in the borderlands is 'Spanish,' one who doesn't is 'Mexican'."

This strategy of denying mestizo descent was not the only option available to Mexican Americans as they attempted to deal with the many contradictions inherent in being Mexican in what had become an American society. Members of the working-class majority also grappled with the ambiguities inherent in their new status as ethnic Americans. Consequently, some began to articulate a sense of identity that represented a conscious attempt to meld their Mexican/Spanish colonial cultural heritage with their new political status as American citi-zens. Although it is impossible to recreate a representative cross-section of Mexican American public opinion on the issue of ethnic or community identity in the decades following annexa-tion, scattered evidence does indicate that soon after the Mexican cession Mexican Americans were actively engaged in a process of assessing their new position in American society. As Griswold del Castillo notes in his study of the Los Angeles Mexican community, local attach-ments and loyalties continued to exert a strong influence on the social identity of Mexican Americans in the Southwest, but the transfer of sovereignty over their homelands stimulated a strong tendency "to move from particular [local] allegiances toward a more general group sol-idarity."

Much of the impetus for moving toward a more inclusive sense of community stemmed from Mexican Americans' need to assert a positive sense of "peoplehood" in the face of the Anglo Americans' attempts to denigrate them as racial and cultural inferiors. One strategy, as we have seen, involved withdrawal into the confines of the barrios. Painfully aware of how Americans felt about them, many working-class Mexican Americans simply attempted to avoid unnecessary contact with the American immigrants. More important, in a weak position to alter their ethnic heritage by constructing a myth of upper-class European descent, they took solace instead in observing their own variants of Mexican culture in the relative privacy of their neighborhoods or in the more isolated rural areas in Texas, northern New Mexico, and south-ern Colorado that the Americans had not yet overrun. By isolating themselves in segregated barrios, colonias, and rural *rancherías*, working-class Mexican Americans could, and largely did, continue to live their lives in a manner similar to that which existed prior to annexation. Although there is no question that life in their impoverished neighborhoods reflected Mexican Americans' eroding economic and social standing, segregation in some ways contributed to a process of community formation, or reformation, rather than the dissolution or fading away of Mexican American communities that many Americans had expected or hoped for.

To working-class Mexican Americans urban barrios and rural colonias functioned as sanc-tuaries from the bewildering changes occurring around them. Anglos may have gained control of the political and economic lifeblood of the Southwest, but within the boundaries of their own neighborhoods Mexican Americans protected many of their cultural practices and rituals. In their own enclaves Mexican Americans continued to converse in Spanish, observed Roman Catholic rituals and celebrations, and entertained themselves in the style to which they had grown accustomed, and largely without interference from the Norteamericanos. In addition, working-class Mexican Americans courted, raised families, and perpetuated their traditional practice of *compadrazgo*—the system of ritual godparent sponsorship which bound them to one another through complex fictive kinship networks—without interference from the American immigrants who were otherwise transforming their society.

Some Mexican Americans developed other, more activist, methods of contesting their subordination in the new society of the Southwest. One way they contested their ascribed inferior ethnic status was to form their own voluntary organizations. One of the earliest and most ubiquitous forms of association among Mexican Americans and Mexican immigrants was the *mutualista*, or mutual-aid association. Like mutual-assistance and fraternal associations formed by other immigrant groups in the United States, Mexican mutualistas provided the working class and poor with a broad range of benefits and services they otherwise could not afford. By pooling their limited resources, members provided themselves with a number of benefits and services including funeral, disability, and other types of insurance, credit, and cultural events and entertainment. Originating in Mexico during the early nineteenth century, by the 1870s similar organizations had been established throughout Mexico and the Hispanic Southwest.

Other Mexican Americans employed more extreme measures to contest challenges to their dignity and to the general process of social subordination they experienced. As several social historians have demonstrated, when local conditions became intolerable Mexican Americans across the Southwest resorted to violence and/or acts of social banditry in their efforts, as one scholar put it, to retain "some measure of self-determination in the face of an increasingly oppressive new regime."

Over the long run, however, the development among Mexican Americans of a sense of themselves *as* Mexican Americans provided a far more important defense against discriminatory practices than did armed resistance or the formation of formal voluntary organizations. One of the clearest reflections of the evolution of this new sense of collective identity is seen in the gradual changes in the various terms Mexican Americans used to describe themselves. As we have seen, prior to extensive American penetration into northwestern Mexico in the early nineteenth century, residents of that area identified primarily with their localities rather than with the Republic of Mexico. After the Mexican War, however, the common experience of military defeat, widespread discrimination, and increasing poverty created conditions under which many Mexicans in the annexed territories began, in effect, to turn inward. Recognizing that they clearly were not accepted as Americans, many logically began to think of themselves as Mexicanos or as members of a larger, pan-Hispanic community of *La Raza* (the race or the people).

Although La Raza is a term that today has come to mean the entire mestizo population of greater Latin America, in the last third of the nineteenth century Mexican Americans often employed the term to describe the Mexican "race" on both sides of the new border. Use of group terms such as La Raza varied widely from region to region, but given the historical heterogeneity of the Spanish-speaking population the use of such terminology by Mexican Americans to describe campaigns of protest and resistance in Texas, New Mexico, and California is remarkable. In California, for example, Mexican Americans ranging from Francisco P. Ramírez, editor and publisher of the Los Angeles Spanish-language weekly *El Clamor Público*, to the social bandit Tiburcio Vásquez, advocated the creation of a new sense of ethnic solidarity among members of what the newspaper variously described as *la población Mexicana* (the Mexican population [of California]), *nuestros compatriotas* (our compatriots), *nuestra población California y Mexicana* (our population of [Mexican] Californians and Mexicans [from Mexico]), *la raza española* (the Hispanic race or people), or *nuestra raza* (our people).

These terms were popularized by the rapid proliferation of Spanish-language newspapers and the fraternal, mutual-aid, and Mexican patriotic associations that sprung up in the Southwest after annexation. Their use marked the birth of an oppositional strategy that acknowledged the common oppression Mexican Americans suffered in American society while offering an alternative, positive label that countered the stigmatized status many Americans sought to impose on Mexicans. As Griswold del Castillo describes the emergence of the term in California,

> *The increasing use of "La Raza" as a generic term in the Spanish-language press was evidence of a new kind of ethnic consciousness. . . . La Raza connoted racial, spiritual, and blood ties with the Latin American people, particularly with Mexico. And La Raza emerged as the single most important symbol of ethnic pride and identification. There were many ways of using this term, depending on the context. "La Raza Mexicana," "La Raza Hispano-Americana" "La Raza Española" and "La Raza Latina" were all used to convey a sense of the racial, class, and national variety within the Spanish-speaking community. But in general the use of "La Raza" implied membership in a cultural tradition that was separate from the . . . "norteamericanos."*

According to de León and other historians of nineteenth-century Texas, an even more intense process of ethnic redefinition and boundary marking occurred among Tejanos after 1848. With the vast majority of the surviving Mexican American population pushed into ethnic enclaves hugging the new border after the Mexican War, the demarcation between Anglo and Mexican was more clearly marked in Texas than anywhere else in the Southwest. Consequently, in the Nueces Strip—the territory between the Nueces River and the Rio Grande—and in other communities along the Rio Grande where Mexican Americans and Mexican sojourners predominated, Mexican Americans doggedly retained a strong sense of Mexican identity for decades following their political incorporation into the United States. Although Tejanos suffered from the effects of discrimination and economic subordination as much, if not more, than did Mexican Americans in other parts of the Southwest, the Tejanos, as de León notes, "continued their own cultural patterns, making bearable their life as poor and marginal people." Despite their incorporation into American society and in many ways because of their annexation into a foreign nation, most Mexican Americans in nineteenth-century Texas continued, as de León notes, to emphasize what they called *lo mexicano* (a sense of Mexicanness) as the cornerstone of their collective identity. Indeed, as de León and other Texas historians have argued, "'*lo mexicano*' prevailed over '*lo americano*' [a sense of Americanness], manifested in the population predominance of Mexicans, in the use of the Spanish language and Mexican work patterns, in the persistence of Mexican social traditions, and in the influence, however subtle, that the northern states of Mexico had on the area." In short, although Mexican Americans in the border region of Texas were no longer citizens of Mexico, Texas largely remained "a place where Tejanos could move about as Mexicans instead of Americans, if they had to."

The success of Mexican Americans in maintaining a distinctive culture in the Southwest did not lie in the fact that they violently or even overtly resisted Anglo Americans' steady encroachments on their way of life. Rather, the ultimate political and social significance of the perpetuation of the distinct Mexican American communities throughout the Southwest lay in the fact that Mexican Americans were able to survive and persist as an ethnically distinct people despite the change in political sovereignty over their homeland. In technical, political terms, although Mexican Americans, by virtue of their new status as American citizens, were no longer Mexicans, American racism and Mexican Americans' de facto subordinate status in the new social order encouraged them to consider themselves Mexicans in a way they never had before.

The irony in this situation was that Mexican Americans confounded Anglo Americans' expectations in at least two ways. In developing a new sense of community based both on a common Mexican cultural heritage and the common experience of racial prejudice in the United States, Mexican Americans were able to transform Anglo Americans' efforts to stigmatize them as racial inferiors into a positive strategy of self-affirmation as Mexicans in American society. At the same time, Mexican Americans' success in generating such new bases for solidarity went a long way toward guaranteeing the survival and growth of a distinct, if syncretic, variant of Mexican culture in what had become part of the United States. This was the last thing the proponents of Manifest Destiny had in mind when they had predicted the eventual fading away of the region's ethnic Mexican population.

The evolution of a society bifurcated in this manner spoke to a fundamental contradiction with which most Americans had yet to come to grips—a contradiction that would ultimately raise serious questions about the nature of the society the Americans had transplanted in the Southwest.

For in formally granting the ethnic Mexican population in the Southwest all the rights of American citizens in 1848, and yet denying them the possibility of exercising those rights, Americans planted the seeds of continuing ethnic discord in the region. As the ethnic Mexican population suddenly exploded in the last decades of the century due to the large numbers of immigrants that began to pour into the region from Mexico, the contradiction between the promise of the Treaty of Guadalupe Hidalgo and the American Constitution and the reality of American interracial and interethnic relations in the Southwest would take on even greater significance.

15

The American Southwest

John R. Chavez

World War II contributed significantly to the eclipse of the Mexicans' image of the Southwest as a lost homeland and of themselves as dispossessed natives. The intense "Americanism" during the war and the postwar period, together with the increased "Americanization" of the region's Spanish-speaking, led to that people's wide acceptance of the Anglo image of the Southwest as a new land, initially populated by Anglo settlers, followed by immigrants, including Mexicans. The eclipse, however, was not total; the traditional image occasionally shone behind the Americanized surface.

By the beginning of the 1940s a sizable new group of Mexicans was taking its place along-side the Hispanos (a term by then usually applied to the earlier Spanish-speaking residents of New Mexico only) and the early twentieth-century newcomers from Mexico. This group was largely composed of the children of those who had arrived during the Mexican Revolution. By the beginning of the war, the members of the second generation, who were usually U.S. citizens by birth, were becoming increasingly Americanized, and their service in the military hastened this process. Having reached draft age by the time of the war, the young men of the second generation entered the armed forces in great numbers, especially since they qualified for few of the deferments available to the upper classes. The intense patriotism in the United States during that period made Mexican Americans (a term popularized by the second generation) feel more a part of their country than they ever had before. Those in the military, but also the many civilians who participated in the war effort, felt that by working together with the rest of the nation on this task, they had earned full citizenship. Also, since defense work and the service had allowed Mexican Americans to see other regions of the United States, and indeed the world, they began to perceive their communities in the Southwest as part of the nation as a whole, rather than primarily an extension of Mexico and Latin America.

Of course, Mexicans had willingly participated in earlier U.S. wars, notably in the conflict with Spain, but World War II was different; it furthered the acculturation of the massive new group that now made up the majority of Mexicans in the United States. Because of their long contact with Anglo culture and also because of their praiseworthy records in earlier wars, Hispanos had previously laid claim to full citizenship, yet the results, as we have seen, had been ambiguous. While Hispanos had come to feel increasingly "American," they were still considered foreigners by their Anglo fellow citizens. Even though it never incorporated them fully into U.S. society, this Americanization had the important effect of separating Hispanos from Mexico. Americanization during World War II had the same effect on the children of the exiles who left Mexico during the revolution. Interestingly, the break that had separated the relatively Anglicized Hispanos from the newcomers for several decades began to close during World War II. As we have already noted, though Hispanos considered themselves more Spanish than the newcomers, what really separated the two groups was the Hispanos' relative Americanization. With the Americanization of the children of the newcomers, Mexicans in the United States were again brought together. After the Second World War, Mexican Americans found themselves separated from Mexico, unaccepted by the United States, but culturally reunited as an increasingly homogeneous group unique to the Southwest.

After their participation in World War II, the members of the second generation sought their rightful place in U.S. society, sometimes desperately so. Just as the "Spanish Americans" (Hispanos) had earlier tried to secure a place in that society by renouncing or rewriting their past, many of the second generation tried to forget their unique position in the Southwest and the country as a whole. Wanting desperately to be like other "Americans," ingredients in the mythical melting pot, they came to call themselves Mexican Americans, a term they hoped might put them on the level with such groups as Irish or Italian Americans. The use of the term was unfortunate, however, because with it came attached the myth of "the nation of immigrants," the complex of beliefs that surrounded the idea that the people of the United States had all originated in foreign lands. Despite the fact that the ancestors of Mexicans had been in the Americas and had regarded the Southwest as their homeland for thousands of years, many Mexican Americans came to accept the belief that their parents were immigrants simply because they had stepped over a line artificially drawn across Mexico.

Thus, what we might call the Mexican American image of the Southwest became common during and after World War II, and it was not set aside until the coming of the Chicano movement in the late 1960s. The region was increasingly seen as an integral part of the United States, and less as an extension of Mexico; the mental boundary between the Spanish-speaking Southwest and other U.S. regions became lighter, as the boundary with Mexico darkened. In extreme cases, when some Mexican Americans tried to completely assimilate with Anglos, they refused to see any special tie at all between themselves and the region that had once been northern Mexico. They accepted the idea that the Spanish and the Anglos had settled the land, that the Southwestern barrios were simply the equivalents of the immigrant ghettos of the East. The person who could shed his ethnic background, move out of the barrio, even out of the Southwest, was to be regarded as a success. Unfortunately for all Mexican Americans, those who adopted the new attitude were often those who were most talented and who could have provided badly needed leadership in their communities.

This abandonment was the greatest harm to result from the intense Americanism of World War II. Just as the working class had earlier been deserted by the Hispano elites, it was now surrendered to Anglo exploitation by the successful children of the Mexicans recently settled in the Southwest. Successful Mexican Americans were often embarrassed by their "foreign" parents and the "alien customs" of their working-class compatriots. Trying to escape the discrimination aimed at their group, these Mexican Americans disassociated themselves from anything Mexican, at times even boasting of their inability to speak Spanish. Under such circumstances, ideas such as bilingual education or biculturalism were seen as "un-American," an extremism that reached its peak during the McCarthyism and Cold War of the 1950s.

During the 1940s, however, Mexican Americans had not yet taken their new Americanism to the extremes. They were just beginning to enjoy their newly acquired confidence as U.S. citizens and were not yet feeling threatened by reactionary movements. While their participation in the war effort led to their new-found confidence, they also felt encouraged by the gradual change in North American policy toward Mexico and the rest of Latin America, a change that had begun in the late 1920s, gained momentum during the 1930s, and culminated with the military alliance formed by most of the countries of the Western Hemisphere against the Axis powers. After decades of openly aggressive activities toward Latin America, the United States had instituted what came to be known as the Good Neighbor Policy. The salient point of this policy was the decision to reduce North American military interventions in Latin America. Finding that open imperialism only created a poor atmosphere for its political and economic interests, the United States sought, at least in public, to deal with its neighbors as equals rather than inferiors. Also, by showing greater respect for the peoples and cultures of that part of the world, the United States hoped to improve its overall relations with Latin America. These efforts naturally had an important impact on that portion of Spanish America that penetrated into the southwestern United States because Mexican Americans, despite their deepening anglicization, to some degree still retained that dimension of their traditional image that depicted the region as an extension of Latin America.

After its victory over Spain at the turn of the century, the United States had become the major imperial power in the Caribbean, exercising that power with little restraint. In 1903 President Theodore Roosevelt instigated a revolution in Colombia, creating the Republic of Panama that in turn allowed the United States to build a canal across its territory. Protecting this right of way then became the rationale for most of the subsequent interventions in countries near the canal site. Although the United States had commendably rejected the temptation to annex Cuba after the Spanish-American War, it made a protectorate of the island and repeatedly sent troops to maintain the peace and North American interests. To prevent European powers from collecting their debts by occupying bankrupt nations uncomfortably close to the Panama Canal, the United States itself occupied those nations and forced them to pay their bills. The Dominican Republic and Nicaragua were two countries that experienced major, lengthy occupations by the military forces of their northern neighbor. That Southwest Mexicans were aware of U.S. activities in places such as Panama, even in 1903, can be seen from the fact that even small community newspapers, such as *El obrero* of Morenci, Arizona reported these activities regularly.

The United States first intervened in the Dominican Republic in 1905 out of fear of German penetration into the Caribbean. North American troops occupied the republic between 1916 and 1924, and the protectorate did not end until 1941, well after the beginnings of the Good Neighbor Policy. Because Nicaragua provided the best route for a potential rival to the Panama Canal, that country was occupied by Marines almost continuously for two decades. The withdrawal of troops from Nicaragua in 1933 was the first major act of the new policy toward Latin America. In accordance with the new policy, in 1936 the United States also gave up the "right" to intervene in Panama, which had been a protectorate since its separation from Colombia in 1903. Only against this historical background of repeated North American invasions of Hispanic-American lands (not to mention Haiti) can we fully appreciate the impact of the Good Neighbor Policy on Mexican Americans in the Southwest.

Latin Americans bitterly resented the incursions of the United States; and Mexicans, having the longest history of confrontation with the "colossus of the north," were more bitter than most. Not only had they early lost half of their homeland to the North Americans; during the Wilson administration they had experienced the occupation of Veracruz and General Pershing's punitive expedition. The 1920s had also been difficult years for relations between Mexico and the United States. The revolution not yet consolidated, continuing turmoil in Mexico kept the border between the two countries in a state of unrest, especially along the Texas boundary.

But a more serious difficulty was the conflict arising from the provisions of the new Mexican constitution that demanded the expropriation of foreign holdings in Mexico, especially those of oil companies. In the Southwest support for the Mexican position was especially strong in *La prensa*, a Los Angeles newspaper that described itself as constitutionalist. In the early stages of the disagreement over oil, *La prensa* in issue after issue condemned U.S. intervention, both military and economic. One article, interestingly enough by an Anglo-American journalist, John Kenneth Turner, clearly expressed the Mexican point of view, "from the beginning to the present, [President Woodrow Wilson] has spoken against [Mexico's] program of nationalization and land distribution . . . he has opposed all efforts toward an adequate control of . . . large industries, [and] the conservation of natural resources—especially oil. . . ." Moreover, the article's headline read, "Wall Street Has Gone Insane in Its Ambition to Despoil Mexico of Its Riches. . . ." This controversy continued through most of the 1920s and intensified whenever the Mexican government threatened to enforce the letter of the law. According to historian Thomas A. Bailey, between 1925 and 1927 the situation became so critical that "a new clamor for war with Mexico arose in the United States. The oil companies released tons of propaganda, in which they demanded armed intervention for the protection of their alleged rights." However, in late 1927, Mexico was persuaded (temporarily) to allow foreign companies which had begun work before 1917 to retain ownership of their subsoil properties.

This constant conflict between Mexico and the United States of course did nothing to improve the situation of Mexicans who arrived in the Southwest before 1930. With war threatening during the 1920s, Mexicans were not only considered foreigners but potential enemy aliens. Thus, unlike most other Latin Americans, Mexicans living in the Southwest faced North American aggression on a personal level. As a result, they were more than casually concerned with international relations between the Americas, seeing any decline or improvement in those relations reflecting on their own lives. Of course, a Mexican national culture that had been anti-American at least since 1836 and emphatically so since the revolution had conditioned them to consider the United States an enemy. During the oil crisis of the 1920s, for example, a popular corrido recalled Mexico's oldest grievance against its northern neighbor, arguing for Mexico to ally itself with an increasingly powerful Japan against the northern colossus:

> Mexico allied with the brave Japanese,
> Will recover the territory lost in the time of Santa Anna;
> Keep harassing her with your complaints,
> And tomorrow you will see what Mexico is worth.

Given this background of hostility and suspicion, Mexican community leaders in the Southwest, especially in the Spanish-language press, carefully followed relations between the two countries. After the oil controversy of the late 1920s, they noticed a mellowing in these relations (despite the deportations of Mexicans then being carried out by the United States). Once Mexico had agreed to allow North American companies to keep their oil holdings, the atmosphere between the two nations cleared somewhat. Furthermore, President Herbert Hoover, finding that open imperialism was increasingly counterproductive, began a public relations campaign in Latin America that eventually developed into the Good Neighbor Policy championed by Franklin D. Roosevelt. As a result, the early 1930s were characterized by a steadily improving climate in the Americas, highlighted in 1933 by the withdrawal of U.S. Marines from Nicaragua. Since Mexico had in the 1920s supported Nicaraguan rebels against the United States, the withdrawal of North American troops greatly improved U.S. relations not only with Latin America in general but with Mexico in particular.

Mexicans in the Southwest were naturally gratified by this turn of events. *La opinion* of Los Angeles reminded its readers that intervention had always been opposed by Mexicans because of their own exploitation at the hands of foreigners: "In our already independent republic, problems confronted us, such as . . . the first war against Texas and the North American invasion of 1847. Then, came the tripartite intervention [by Spain, Britain, and France in the 1860s) in which only France persisted. . . ." The newspaper accurately predicted: "The withdrawal of North American marines from that country (Nicaragua) will contribute greatly, . . . to secure intercontinental concord." During the following decade the United States withdrew troops from other Caribbean lands, giving up its "right" of intervention in such countries as Cuba.

The depression and the election of Franklin D. Roosevelt helped advance the Good Neighbor Policy because North American capitalism was forced into retreat on both domestic and international fronts. Potential investors from the United States had much less money to put into Latin America, and since previous investments had already been lost because of the worldwide depression, these investors had less reason to pressure Washington to intervene south of the border. Moreover, Franklin Roosevelt, elected on an antibusiness platform, saw little advantage in supporting any especially exploitive business adventures, particularly since by 1935 the rise of dictatorships in Europe made neighborliness in the Western Hemisphere increasingly advisable for the security of the United States. Roosevelt's position was severely tested in 1938 when Mexico finally nationalized its entire oil industry. When Mexico refused to compensate North American companies to their satisfaction, they once more clamored for armed intervention, but with the situation in Europe looking more and more grim, Roosevelt decided to acquiesce to Mexico's wishes. This proved to be a wise decision, as Mexico subsequently became an ally during the Second World War rather than the unfriendly neighbor it had been during World War I. As a sign of this new friendship, Mexican school maps that referred to the Southwest as "territory temporarily in the hands of the United States" were in the early 1940s gradually removed from Mexico's classrooms.

While the Good Neighbor Policy and World War II hastened the Americanization of the children of the Mexicans who had arrived in the Southwest during the twentieth century, manifestations of the new, "American" outlook had appeared earlier. In 1929, before the Good Neighbor Policy had gained much momentum, Mexicans in Texas met at Corpus Christi and organized the League of United Latin American Citizens (LULAC), a coalition of several groups that had formed after World War I. The League's name exhibited the break that its members were trying to make between themselves and Mexico. Since "Latin," like "Spanish," called to mind the members' European rather than Indian ancestry, that term was thought less offensive than "Mexican." In fact LULAC, which soon had chapters throughout the Southwest, was the first major organization dedicated to the assimilation of the Mexican into the "American" melting pot.

According to its constitution, the goal of the League was "to develop within the members of our race the best, purest and most perfect type of a true and loyal citizen of the United States of America." Unlike previous Mexican groups, LULAC abandoned Spanish: "The English language, which is the official language of *our country* [emphasis added] . . ., we declare it to be the official language of this Organization, and we pledge ourselves to learn, and speak and teach same to our children." LULAC also aimed "To assume complete responsibility for the education of our children as to their rights and duties and the . . . *customs of this country* [emphasis added]." The perspective of the Mexican with regard to the Southwest was clearly changing. The founders of LULAC now saw the region as the "American Southwest," an integral part of a country whose language and customs were Anglo, a region that was only theirs insofar as they were true U.S. citizens. This, of course, was the way Anglos saw the region, and the way liberal Anglos thought Mexicans should see it.

Yet, the older Mexican image of the homeland persisted even as LULAC tried to expunge it. Arguing for Americanization, an article in the *Lulac News* (1932) commented:

> *We can migrate to the south, leaving the land of our forefathers [emphasis added] to our energetic neighbors, and going to a land [Mexico] where our customs are not out of place, thereby holding our own; or we can accept our neighbors' customs, educate our children, and gain their respect. . . . Let us educate out children, enabling them to . . . unquestionably pride themselves citizens of the United States, and owe fealty and allegiance to one flag.*

Thus, though Mexicans were not foreign immigrants in the Southwest, the article's author was suggesting they play the part and assimilate as had "all other Americans." Interestingly, the author did not say that Anglo ways were better per se, but that they had to be adopted because

> *The gulf [between Anglos and Mexicans] has grown so, in the years, that still you [Mexicans] are a different people, and merely tolerated as citizens of a nation in which you resided even before you joined the union [emphasis added]. . . . Conditions have reached a point where your neighbors say, "a white man and a Mexican!"*

Of course conditions had always been such, but now many Mexicans, becoming Americanized, were more sensitive to racial prejudice. Ironically they felt that more Americanization would solve the problem.

Even though the founders of LULAC declared that they would "maintain a sincere and respectful reverence for our racial origin of which we are proud," they put little or no emphasis on maintaining Mexican culture itself. Individual members were more likely to follow the dictum repeated by one LULAC leader: "If you talk English you will think and act like Americans." This same leader stated: "We tell our people 'if you have not been treated like you should or have not the standard of living it is your own fault. Before asking for your rights you must be prepared.'" In other words, if Mexicans refused to give up the old ways and adopt the new, they themselves were responsible for the racial and economic oppression they experience. On the other hand, for those who accepted Anglo-American ways, the United States would be the land of opportunity. It should be no surprise that most of LULAC's members were businessmen, professionals, and other U.S.-born, English-speaking members of the middle class. LULAC tried to reach the laboring class, whose un-American ways were often seen as the cause of discrimination against U.S. Mexicans as a whole, but the League's policies had little success because, as LULAC members complained, "100 uneducated Mexicans come in for every one we teach."

The LULAC members' espousal of Americanization met with opposition from the more traditional sectors of Southwest Mexican communities, especially from the first generation:

> *The average non-political American of Latin descent calls us [the members of LULAC] "renegades." He says, "you are Mexicans, not Americans." Mexican citizens even in their*

press attack us. We are called renegades and anti-Mexicans. We call them visitors. They tell us, who are trying to tell them [Mexicans in Texas] to be more loyal to the United States, "But your forefathers are all of Mexican origin and you should continue to be Mexican." We say he is a visitor and it is none of his business.

Despite this division within Mexican communities and despite the League's program of Americanization, LULAC members complained: "We have not been able to convince some people that there is a difference between us. To the average American we are just Mexicans."

The members of LULAC rejected the image of the Southwest as a special place for the Mexican because they believed their people would benefit by conforming to the myth of the "nation of immigrants" and the "land of opportunity." In renouncing their people's traditional image of the Southwest, however, the LULAC members abandoned the old struggle for bilingual/bicultural education, an issue even the "Spanish Americans" had never surrendered. Also, in denying the special ties between the Southwest and Mexico (as had Hispanos), the "Latin Americans" not only minimized their Indian ancestry, they also denied that Mexicans had any special rights of entry into the Southwest. Since continued migration from Mexico increased competition for jobs and hindered LULAC's Americanization efforts, the League sought to restrict further migration from the south. Although LULAC's position on these issues weakened the chances for their people's cultural survival in the Southwest, League members did make a great effort to secure the rights of their people as citizens of the United States.

Although LULAC members believed in the assimilation of U.S. Mexicans into the Anglo world, they were not so busy assimilating themselves as individuals that they forgot their people as a whole. Rather than proceeding on their own, changing their surnames, pretending they were Italian or French in order to melt more easily into the majority, LULAC members insisted on the acceptance of their ethnic group as an equal among other immigrant groups in the United States. With this as an ideological base, the League fought for the civil rights of Mexicans throughout the Southwest and was especially concerned with segregation in the public schools. (Mexicans, they believed, could never become Americanized if they were given separate schooling.) On this front LULAC was strong enough by the 1940s to gain two important victories. In 1945 it brought four southern California school districts to court for *de facto* segregation of Mexican Americans; the districts were subsequently enjoined from continuing this practice, a decision that was upheld on appeal in 1947. And in Texas the intentional segregation of Mexican American school children was challenged by LULAC and declared unconstitutional by state courts in 1948. Through such efforts, the League's philosophy of Americanization helped Mexicans rise above their subordinate status, even though that philosophy weakened their culture in the Southwest.

With the implementation of the Good Neighbor Policy and the coming of the Second World War, gradually more Mexican Americans came to see themselves and the Southwest as did the members of LULAC. With the repatriation of so many Mexicans during the 1930s, Mexico's influence in the southwestern barrios abated somewhat, causing a rise in the general level of Americanization. When the League was founded in the late 1920s, the adult children of the Mexicans who had settled in the Southwest during the twentieth century were a small group, but by the 1940s the second generation, with its increasingly Anglo ways, had become much larger, more influential, and more likely to see its own region as the American Southwest. However, despite its increasing attachment to the United States, this group never completely abandoned the traditional image of the region even at the most patriotic times. In *Among the Valiant* (1966), an account of the Mexican American military contributions to World War II and the Korean conflict, Raúl Morín has written that, upon hearing the news of Pearl Harbor, two Los Angeles youths jokingly commented on the effects the war might have on Mexican Americans:

> "Ya estuvo *(This is it)*," said one, "Now we can look for the authorities to round up all the Mexicans and deport them to Mexico—bad security risks."
> Another excited character came up with, "They don't have to deport me! I'm going on my own; you're not going to catch me fighting a war for somebody else. I belong to Mexico. Soy puro mexicano *[I'm 100 percent Mexican]!*"

As Morín noted, the first comment was a reference to suggestions, made during World War I, that U.S. Mexicans be considered security risks since Germany had offered Mexico "all *[sic]* the territory that formerly belonged to the southern republic" in return for a victorious alliance against the United States. Both comments indicated that, because of their history as a subjugated and consequently distrusted population in the Southwest, the immediate reaction of Mexican Americans to Pearl Harbor was a feeling of insecurity and alienation. In spite of this feeling, the very two men who made the comments subsequently served in the army and the Marine Corps in the Pacific Theater. Morín, who himself served in Europe, explained the patriotism of Mexican Americans:

> We felt that this was an opportunity to show the rest of the nation that we too were also ready, . . . to fight for our nation. It did not matter whether we were looked upon as Mexicans . . .; the war soon made us all genuine Americans, eligible and available immediately . . . to defend our country, the United States of America.

Indeed Mexican Americans were almost immediately involved in the fighting. Two New Mexico National Guard units, composed mostly of Mexican Americans, were among the defenders of the Philippines, which were attacked by Japan after Pearl Harbor. At Bataan, they made up a quarter of the combat troops, and after the surrender of Corregidor, they were unfortunately well represented in the infamous Bataan Death March. During the rest of the war, Mexican Americans did more than their share of the fighting on all fronts. No other ethnic group, according to its percentage of the whole population, had as many men serving in combat divisions. No other ethnic group received as many decorations for valor. Significantly, in addition to the Mexican Americans who served were many Mexican nationals, residents of the United States, who enlisted with the encouragement of the president of Mexico. Also, after Mexico declared war, many more Mexican citizens crossed the border into the Southwest to volunteer for combat since they knew most of Mexico's own forces would see action only if the hemisphere were invaded.

Despite this overwhelming demonstration of support for the war on the part of Mexicans, they were nonetheless suspected of disloyalty and even treated as enemies on the home front. Anglo xenophobia, intensified by Pearl Harbor, first led to the internment of Japanese Americans as suspect aliens and soon after made Mexican Americans targets as well. For much of 1942 the United States was on the defensive in the Pacific, and the general public, fearing an invasion of the West Coast, worried about the possibility of quislings in its midst. With the Japanese Americans interned, the press in Los Angeles centered the public's attention on the Mexican American community where it suspected subversive activities among gangs of neighborhood youths. Like other poor urban neighborhoods, the Mexican American barrios on the east side of Los Angeles suffered from a relatively high crime rate due to the low socioeconomic position of their inhabitants, especially their often unemployed teen-agers. Segregated in schools and denied access to many public places of entertainment because of their race, Mexican American youths had to rely on each other for social interaction. A small number joined highly cohesive gangs that claimed and defended particular territories against their rivals, a situation that often led to violence. Such domestic violence, in time of war against foreign enemies, seemed nothing short of sedition to the public at large, especially once the press had exaggerated the problem.

From the spring of 1942 until the summer of 1943, the Los Angeles press headlined almost any crime connected with alleged gang members—"zoot-suiters" as they were dubbed after their distinctive and supposedly "un-American" dress. Subsequently, the police, feeling strong pressure from the press and consequently from the public, increased their surveillance of the barrios. This anti-gang campaign reached a climax in late 1942 when twenty-four youngsters were arrested for the apparent murder of a victim of alleged gang violence. The "Sleepy Lagoon Case," sensationalized by the press, became an opportunity for the society at large to express its hostility against zoot-suiters and all Mexicans. Seventeen of the youths were convicted on slight evidence, and though on appeal the convictions were in 1944 unanimously reversed, the trial had damaging effects on cultural relations in Los Angeles and on international relations with Latin America.

During the trial, racist statements concerning the character and loyalty of Mexican Americans were made in the press and by the police, statements so prejudiced that the federal government feared they would inflame opinion in Latin America against the United States. Shortly after the arrest of the Sleepy Lagoon defendants, the Los Angeles Police Department issued a document purporting to explain the crime wave in East Los Angeles. According to this report, Mexican Americans were biologically prone to crime and violence, a character inherited from their Indian ancestors, Mongoloid peoples from across the Bering Strait. Mexican Americans were thus portrayed as biologically linked with the vicious Japanese enemy, deserving treatment little better than that accorded the interned Japanese Americans. Such anti-Mexican rhetoric became so common during the trial that the Los Angeles County Sheriff (himself, ironically, a *californio*) suggested that before their evacuation Japanese Americans might have incited Mexican Americans to violence. With such statements filling the air, it was not surprising that in December 1942 the un-American activities committee of the California assembly began an investigation into possible connections (never substantiated) between gang violence, and a group of fifth columnists known as the *sinarquistas*.

The *sinarquistas*, Mexican reactionaries connected with the Falange of Spain, were a threat to the United States because they opposed Mexico's alliance with its northern neighbor and sought the return of the Southwest to Mexico. Feeling that country had always suffered in its dealing with North Americans, *sinarquistas* believed Mexico should have nothing to do with the United States. Also, since they regarded Franco's Spain as a model Christian state, which Mexico should emulate, the *sinarquistas* sympathized with the fascist powers that supported Franco and had, moreover, never harmed Mexico. Though opposed by the Mexican government, *sinarquistas* gained a substantial following south of the border and attempted to do the same north of it. In the spring of 1943, one press report claimed there were 50,000 *sinarquistas* within the Mexican barrios of California alone. Though the actual figure was only 2,000 for the entire United States, the first figure was frightening to a California Anglo population that had already been exposed in the press to an intense anti-Mexican campaign. The *sinarquistas* caused alarmed Anglos to recall Kaiser Wilhelm's courting of Mexico during World War I and the *sedicioso* troubles along the Texas border. Such Anglo fears, however, were no longer realistic because irredentism now had little appeal among Mexican Americans in the Southwest. The members of the second generation had become so Americanized that they could not see themselves permanently returning to Mexico as individuals, nor could they see their region politically reunited with the motherland.

That Mexican Americans, on the other hand, were hardly considered "Americans" is evident from events during and after the Sleepy Lagoon Trial. Police stepped up their patrols in the barrios, at one point blockading all the major streets, stopping and searching all cars with Mexican-looking occupants, and arresting over six hundred people on suspicion. Of these, less than a third were ever charged with a crime, let alone convicted. Police harassment of Mexican Americans continued along with inflammatory newspaper reports throughout the first half of 1943, until anti-Mexican riots erupted in early June of that year. Unfortunately, during that tense period, Los Angeles was filled with servicemen on leave from bases near the city. A number of fights involving servicemen and "zoot-suiters" were reported in the newspapers, which naturally sided with the men in uniform against the "unpatriotic" Mexicans. Incited by these reports, servicemen gathered in the city to get revenge against this "foreign enemy." For about a week of consecutive nights with the praise of the newspapers and the collaboration of the police, soldiers and sailors conducted raids on the east side, beat and stripped zoot-suiters of their "un-American" garb, and eventually attacked any Mexican or other member of a visible minority who happened to be in their path. Making no attempt to stop these raids, the police would instead appear on the scene of any particular incident just in time to arrest the victims of the crime. In response to all of this, the attitude of the press was best represented by the following headline from the *Los Angeles Times*: "Zoot Suiters Learn Lesson in Fights with Servicemen." The violence finally ceased only after the Mexican government asked the U.S. State Department to intervene. Worried over this threat to the Good Neighbor Policy,

Washington then ordered the armed forces to keep their men out of Los Angeles, and the trouble subsided.

The federal government was especially concerned about the racial conflict in Los Angeles because Mexico, as part of its contribution to the war, was sending thousands of its citizens to the Southwest to relieve the labor shortage caused by the draft. Furthermore, the Axis powers were making effective propaganda of the situation in Los Angeles; at one point, after the sentencing of the Sleepy Lagoon defendants, Axis radio broadcast the following to Latin America:

> The 360,000 Mexicans of Los Angeles are reported up in arms over this Yankee persecution. The concentration camps of Los Angeles are said to be overflowing with members of this persecuted minority. This is justice for you, as practiced by the "Good Neighbor," Uncle Sam. . . .

Mexico was indeed worried about the fate of its citizens and their descendants in the United States. Mexican newspapers constantly complained about Anglo racism, for attacks on and discrimination against Mexicans occurred in many parts of the United States. Before the disturbances in Los Angeles, there had been outbreaks in Oakland and Venice; during the Los Angeles riots, similar trouble had occurred in Pasadena, Long Beach, and San Diego; Beaumont, Texas, also experienced large-scale riots. Ultimately, the violence spread to several Midwestern and eastern cities where other minority groups were included among the victims. However, after the federal government had moved to calm the situation in Los Angeles, the local press, which had incited so much of the trouble, began to reflect Washington's neighborly concern for the victims of the riots: "No friendly government [such as Mexico's] must have just cause for saying that their nationals were mistreated." Sadly, even as the press called for an end to further violence, it refused to admit that most of the victims were U.S. citizens.

Racism at home led some Mexican Americans to wonder whether their group's high casualties overseas were actually the result of discrimination in combat assignments. If so, Mexican American servicemen as a whole did not complain. In the armed forces many for the first time experienced what it was like to be the equals of other citizens. After the war, veterans were proud of their new status, proud of their collective military record, and optimistic about the future, especially since many came home with practical skills learned in the service: "We learned new languages and trades and how other people lived, and we learned how Americans lived, too. So we came home with a lot of ideas and plans. . . . The war opened the doors for us." But when these veterans returned, they found things were not as equal at home as in the military. Throughout the Southwest, Mexican Americans were still refused service in many restaurants, theaters, and other public places; segregated in public schools; discriminated against in hiring; underrepresented in public office and on juries; and as a group still consigned to the lowest levels of society. Unfortunately, many Mexican American veterans personally experienced such discrimination on their return. Some of the most notorious cases occurred in Texas, where a deceased serviceman was refused burial in his home town and where winners of the Congressional Medal of Honor were denied service in restaurants.

Many Mexican American veterans found it painful to readjust to southwestern towns that expected them to return to subordinate status. The father of one South Texas veteran said of his son: "After he came home and found that things hadn't changed, he felt that he would rather be just another sailor than the kind of human being the Anglos treated him like." In 1946 a California leader, Ignacio L. López, commented concerning such men:

> *Every Southwest community has in it young men, formerly "little" Americans but who were able to act as complete Americans for three to four years. They know what it is to be released from the minority burden. They find it a heavy one to be asked to pick up again, on the other side of the tracks in a Southwest city. I am often tempted to say to them, "Go away! Go to another part of the United States!" There are places where there is no prejudice against the Mexican American, and where they could keep for the rest of their lives the precious feeling of integration and belonging.*

Indeed in the East and Midwest Mexican Americans were more readily accepted as ingredients for the melting pot because in those regions they were in a truer sense immigrants; in the Southwest, on the other hand, they remained the impoverished heirs of conquered natives. And being such, they could rarely heed López's "advice" to leave their native towns—as one former corporal put it:

> *The rest of the United States isn't like Descanso [a fictitious name for a California town], I've found out. I'd like to live in the East—I've got a girl there. But you couldn't move my mother, and I've got to help her until the kids are grown.*

Most Mexican American veterans were unable and unwilling to leave their southwestern communities, but instead sought to regain their rightful place in those communities. In doing so, they sometimes proceeded on the basis of both their new image of themselves as "Americans" *and* their older image of themselves as dispossessed natives of the Southwest. "How long had we been missing out on benefits derived as an American citizen?" asked veteran Raúl Morín. "Old times had told us and we had read in books how the early [Anglo] settlers had invaded our towns and had shoved us into the 'other side of the tracks.'" Now, along with other Mexican Americans who had participated in the war effort, veterans began to push back into the central life of their communities. In Edinburg, Texas (and elsewhere), this push met with resistance from the dominant group. For example, the wife of an Anglo veteran complained in a letter to the *Edinburg Valley Review*: "Edinburg has become complete Mexican— jobs, houses, everything. . . . let them [Mexicans] go back over where they were before the war. Give the American [Anglo] boys a chance; they gave their best to us." Predictably this letter drew angry responses from Mexican Americans; one relative of a veteran was especially upset at the suggestion that Edinburg be given back to the "Americans":

> *Texas was formerly a part of Mexico and Mexico is part of the North American conti-*
> *nent. So anyway you look at it, Mexicans whether U.S.-born or Mexican-born are*
> *Americans.*
> *So—the Mexicans to Mexico, Germans to Germany, Poles to Poland, etc. Let's do give*
> *this land back to real Americans—the Indians and the Mexicans.*

This exchange revealed that despite the emphasis on Americanism after World War II, Mexican Americans had not completely forgotten they were indigenous to the Southwest, and they were unlikely to abandon the towns and barrios of the region despite the oppression encountered there. Mario Suárez, one of the first Mexican Americans to publish short stories in English, described the particular attraction that the barrio (in this case a Tucson communi-ty) still had for the returning veteran:

> *. . . El Hoyo is something more [than its outward appearance]. It is this more which*
> *brought Felipe Ternero back from the wars. . . . It helped him to marry a fine girl named*
> *Julia. It brought Joe Zepeda back without a leg from Luzon and helps him hold more*
> *liquor than most men can hold with two. It brought Jorge Casillas . . ., back to compose*
> *boleros. Perhaps El Hoyo is the proof that those people exist who, while not being*
> *against anything, have as yet failed to observe the more popular [Anglo] modes of human*
> *conduct.*

The attraction of the southwestern barrio was its culture. There the returning veteran could still establish the kind of family he had always known; there he could feel himself a whole man despite the insults and injuries received in the outer world; there he could recreate his life from within his own cultural traditions. Moreover, from this corner of strength, he could move toward first-class citizenship.

When Mexican American veterans returned, they helped form a number of organizations whose goals were to eliminate discrimination in public places, in employment, in the legal sys-tem, in education, in all those areas where Spanish-speaking citizens received second-class treat-ment. In California the Unity Leagues and the Community Service Organization (the CSO) were formed soon after the war to help the Mexican American masses achieve full citizenship through Americanization programs. In Texas, Mexican American veterans and their families organized the American G.I. Forum to help secure their civil rights. The G.I. Forum appealed largely to the middle class and was in that way similar to the earlier League of United Latin American Citizens, which also gained strength after the war. Until the election of President Eisenhower, all these organizations relied heavily on the Good Neighbor Policy to influence the general public.

Though Mexican Americans now stressed their United States citizenship, they also found it advantageous to mention their Latin American heritage. For example, in *Are We Good Neighbors?* (1948), a collection of documents on discrimination against Mexican Americans, Alonso S. Perales, a diplomat to Latin America and a LULAC leader, argued that people of Latin descent in the Southwest, especially Texas, had to be treated with more dignity if Latin

America were ever to take the Good Neighbor Policy seriously. (Interestingly, Perales thus revived the image of his region as a subjugated outpost of Latin America, even as he argued for the full acceptance of his people into the society of the American Southwest.) As a result of such efforts, in a few years after the war Mexican Americans succeeded in eliminating some of the more openly racist practices against them, but as the 1950s advanced the postwar changes lost momentum.

During the conservative 1950s, Mexican Americans went out of their way to be "100 percent Americans," and many chapters of their organizations lost their fervor. LULAC and the G.I. Forum in many cases became nothing more than clubs, their middle-class members satisfied with their early victories and anxious not to endanger their improved status. Even the CSO, which remained more active than the other groups, turned to red-baiting activities to clear itself of charges that it was communist inspired. This was understandable considering that many Mexican and Mexican American leaders were harassed and sometimes deported by the federal government, usually for labor activities considered subversive. The Republican administration's deemphasizing of the Good Neighbor Policy also led to greater caution on the part of Mexican Americans. The Eisenhower administration took a belligerent attitude toward communism in Latin America, in 1954 indirectly intervening to topple a communist-supported government in Guatemala. While this alienated Latin America, Mexican Americans were either too intimidated or too "patriotic" to protest much. Since the federal government had violated the Good Neighbor Policy abroad, that policy was now certainly of little value to Mexican Americans in the Southwest.

The Mexican American emphasis on Americanism during the 1950s left all Mexicans defenseless when confronted by a new assault on their human rights, an assault known as Operation Wetback. Ever since the World War II labor shortage in agriculture, Mexico had been providing the United States with a worker called the bracero (hired hand), whom economist Ernesto Galarza has described as an "indentured alien . . ., an 'input factor' stripped of the political and social tributes that liberal democracy likes to ascribe to all human beings. . . ." Every year a stipulated number of Mexicans were sent to the farms of the Southwest where they were isolated, cheaply housed, fed, and paid while they worked the land. At the end of the season, they were returned to Mexico, thereby relieving the United States of responsibility for their care during the following period of unemployment. In essence the bracero program permitted the United States to obtain the labor it needed while granting the laborers few of the political and social benefits of life in the Southwest. The number of braceros grew year by year as the demands of agriculture increased; however, there never seemed to be enough, and after 1949 huge numbers of "illegal aliens" began to make up for the shortage.

Mexicans entered the United States illegally when the bracero program failed to accept them or because they wished to avoid the bureaucratic difficulties involved; they were hired by employers who were unable to obtain braceros or who wished to avoid the minimum wage and other restrictions imposed under the program. The "problem" with "illegals" was their tendency to remain in the Southwest. Unlike braceros, undocumented workers were more integrated into the Mexican American communities of the region; they were not merely a source of labor but participants in the life of the Southwest. This increasing "foreign" influence, however, threatened Anglo-Americans who in the 1950s were more fearful of subversive foreigners than usual. As a result, in 1954 the federal government initiated Operation Wetback, a massive deportation program that rivaled the repatriations carried out during the depression. The major reason for the operation was, according to the attorney general of the United States, to rid the country of political subversives. Once again regardless of their place of birth or citizenship, Mexicans were intimidated, separated from their families, and deported as if they were enemy aliens in the Southwest. And, unfortunately, little organized resistance was ever offered. Before the beginning of the operation, Mexican American organizations had supported restrictions on entrants from Mexico because of the competition given U.S.-born workers and because of the retardation of Americanization efforts. As a result, these organizations could hardly object to Operation Wetback, especially since Mexico, which could only welcome its own people, cooperated with the United States. Thus, satisfied with a bracero program that provided Mexican labor without increasing the local Mexican population, Anglo-Americans once again succeeded in using the artificial international boundary to the detriment of Mexicans on both sides of it.

By the end of 1956 Operation Wetback more or less ceased after well over a million Mexicans had been deported. The deportation of so many Mexicans left the Southwest and its barrios as "American" as they would ever be. It is not surprising that, during the late 1950s and early 1960s, persons who completely denied their ethnic background (a phenomenon never as common among Mexican Americans as among other groups) became more numerous among the Spanish-speaking. This trend did little to improve the condition of the weakened Mexican American organizations, since the *vendidos* or "sell-outs" (as the defectors were later called) wanted nothing at all to do with their group, not even to Americanize it. Among the defectors, unfortunately, were some of the most talented of Mexican Americans. One example of this type was a successful doctor respected in the Anglo society of South Texas: "When asked about Mexican American problems, he bristled. 'How should I know about them?' he countered. 'I don't even speak their language.'" Another example was a businessman who complained, "I wish I could get every drop of Mexican blood out of my veins and change it for something else." To their chagrin, such Mexican Americans could rarely blend into the Anglo background as easily as could members of European ethnic groups:

> *I think like an Anglo and I act like an Anglo but I'll never look like an Anglo. Just looking at me, no one could tell if I am an American or one of those blasted Mexicans from across the river. It's hell to look like a* foreigner in your own country [emphasis added.

This statement, with its ironic use of so significant a phrase, reflected extreme change in one aspect of the image the Spanish-speaking had of themselves and the Southwest, and yet that aspect remained somehow the same. In the past Mexicans had been made to seem like foreigners in the country of their ancestors by the invading Anglos; now Mexican Americans were made to seem like foreigners in the country of their citizenship by incoming Mexican nationals—in both cases Southwest Mexicans were seen as, and consequently felt like, aliens.

Furthermore, responses to these feelings of alienation had changed. In the past Southwest Mexicans had reacted by strengthening their own culture in the region, but in the 1940s Mexican Americans began to react to those feelings by trying to adopt Anglo ways. Though some, trying desperately to avoid Anglo prejudice, went to the extreme of denying their race, most Mexican Americans tried to think of themselves as proud members of one more immigrant group attempting to solve its problem of alienation through Americanization. Their new self-image revealed itself clearly in the first novel about themselves written by one of their own: "If we live in this country," remarked the protagonist of *Pocho* (1959) by José A. Villarreal, "we must live like Americans." Even in New Mexico and Colorado where the myth of the Spanish Southwest persisted, this drive for Americanization began in the 1940s to challenge hispanization as the preferred way of adjusting to the dominant society.

Fortunately for the survival of Southwest Mexican culture, however, many members of the Spanish-speaking population continued to view the region as they traditionally had. At the University of New Mexico in 1942, for example, a Hispano professor recalled the image of the Southwest as a frontier of Latin America, while arguing for bilingual education: "Many believe that English and Spanish should be taught so perfectly to all the citizens of New Mexico, as to equip them to be the bilingual intermediators of the Americas." And in 1958, at the other end of the period of intense Americanization, Mexican-American novelist John Rechy recalled the image of Southwest Mexicans as a conquered people: "The Mexican people of El Paso . . .—are all and always and completely Mexican, and will be. They speak only Spanish to each other and when they say the Capital they mean Mexico DF." Thus, Southwest Mexican nationalism quietly persisted until the radicalized world of the late 1960s roused that pride and channeled it into a forceful political movement demanding the economic, social, and cultural rights of a disinherited people. The image of the lost homeland and its dispossessed native Mexicans would once again come to the fore.

16

The Origins and History of the Chicano Movement

Roberto Rodriguez

Some mark the beginning of the Chicano resistance movement when Columbus was met by a fusillade of arrows in his first attempt to land in the Americas. Others set its beginning at the time of the defense of Tenochtitlán (now Mexico City) in 1521—pitting the Cuauhtemoc-led forces against the Spanish invaders. Others set it at the end of the Mexican-American War in 1848, when Mexico lost half of its territory to the United States and its Mexican residents became "strangers in their own lands."

The modern Chicano political movement, most scholars agree, began during the mid-1960s—a time coinciding with the Black Power Movement.

"It was a time of de-colonization struggles around the world and global revolution," says educator Elizabeth Martinez, author of various books, including *500 Years of Chicano History*.[1]

In the 1960s, the Chicano Movement was both a civil and human rights struggle, and a movement for liberation. In this realm, universities became one of the focal points of protest in the movement. Some of the principal demands were to open up universities to people of color and the establishment of Chicano studies, which was envisioned—through "El Plan de Santa Barbara"—as a place where the intellectual work of the movement could take place, at the service of the Chicano community.

Ada Sosa-Riddell, director of the Chicana/Latina Center, University of California at Davis, says that Movimiento Estudiantil Chicano de Aztlán (MEChA) and Chicano studies represent two of the long-lasting legacies of the Chicano Movement. However, with the advent of the antiaffirmative action mood of the country, we may well see the death of ethnic studies, she says.

"But you can't destroy Chicano studies" she continues, "You would have to burn the literature."

Chicano and Chicana Movements

In terms of the Chicano Movement, perhaps it's more appropriate to speak of movements in the plurality because the struggles in the different parts of the country were many, with separate goals and visions and unique histories. Some of them included: the struggle to improve the lives of farmworkers, the effort to end Jim Crow-style segregation and police repression, the land-grant struggles to recoup land lost as a result of the Mexican-American War, the struggle to improve educational opportunities, and the struggle for political representation and self-determination.

In time, other movements blossomed, specifically, the struggle for gender equality, access to higher education and immigrant rights, and a literary and artistic revolution that spoke to cultural rebirth and a rediscovery of mestizo/indigenous roots and self-definition.

This was brown power. It was also the building of Aztlán. For some, building Aztlán (the U.S. Southwest—or the lands stolen from Mexico during the Mexican-American War) literally meant fighting for a sovereign nation, while for others, it was the spiritual building of a people.

Each of these movements spawned hundreds of organizations, such as the United Farm Worker's Union, La Raza Unida Party, La Alianza de Pueblos Libres, the Brown Berets, the National Chicano Moratorium, CASA–Hermandad General de Trabajadores, the Crusade For Justice, the Mexican American Youth Organization, MEChA, the August 29th Movement, and Commision Femenil Nacional Mexicana. This succeeded a period in history in which the Mexican community was perceived by society as politically dormant.

During this time of great social upheaval, political fervor, and cultural rebirth, the Chicano Movement was hardly unified. The reasons: lack of historical memory, regionalism and sectarianism, but also government and law enforcement efforts to destroy this nascent movement, which was viewed as divisive and separatist.

The 1960s and 1970s were an exciting time, says Lea Ybarra, associate provost for academic affairs at California State University at Fresno. "We felt we could make a difference."

At Fresno State, where she began her studies, there was only a handful of Chicano and Chicana students. Today, there are more than four thousand. Now, students take things for granted: "We are witnessing a new phenomenon: the professors are more radical than the students," she states.

Luis Arroyo, professor and chair of Chicano and Latino studies at California State University at Long Beach, says that the Chicano Movement began as a movement for dignity and self-respect. During that phase—of struggling to be recognized as a people—there was a sense of unity. Yet, once an attempt was made to define the movement and give it an ideology, "We began to develop competing definitions as to what the movement was" says Arroyo.

To this day, those competing definitions continue to shape how scholars define what the movement was or wasn't, when it started, when and if it ended, and what it should be. A spillover of that conflict included what to call people of Mexican origin and whether the words Chicano and Chicana included people with origins other than Mexico.

Teresa Cordova, a feminist Chicana scholar at the University of New Mexico, says that an analysis of the Chicano Movement cannot be reduced to a European "great men in history" model (or great women), because it was a social movement. Those who say the Chicano Movement is dead, she adds, reveal their own disconnection: "Anyone saying the movement is dead means he's dead!"

A number of the past activists—many of whom were students—are today part of the environmental justice movement, work with youth, work in health or legal clinics, or teach in schools, she says. Many are also now senior scholars. "When we focus on the big names, we're missing the point. It didn't function that way," says Cordova. "There were lots of soldiers."

To the thesis that the Chicano Movement is dead, Ada Sosa-Riddell replies: "No, but there's a lot of people trying to kill it."

Precursors and the Missing Generation

What differentiates the Chicano Movement from earlier Mexican civil rights struggles is its national character, its mass nature, and its strong student base at colleges and universities.

Indeed, the role of students was unique in the 1960s and 1970s. The university became both a political battleground and a focal point of protest regarding its elitist nature in keeping people of color and working-class students outside of its doors.

While there had been political resistance ever since the Mexican-American War, and while there had been student activism on a smaller scale during the 1930s and 1940s, it was not until after World War II that Mexican Americans began to be visible on college campuses. However, it was not until the 1960s—as a result of educational opportunity programs—that Chicanos/Chicanas streamed onto campuses in unprecedented numbers. The exception, particularly in the nineteenth century, were the children of landed elites.

Their prior absence was generally due to segregation/discrimination in the educational system, says Carlos Muñoz, professor at UC Berkeley and author of *Youth, Identity and Power*, a book that chronicles the Chicano Movement.[2]

As such, there was no intellectual tradition in the Mexican American community in higher education similar to that which has existed in the African American community. The reason, says Muñoz, is that after the Mexican-American War, Whites did not feel a responsibility to educate Mexican Americans. Thus, there was never a push to create Mexican American colleges similar to the Black colleges.

Absent a large presence in higher education, Mexican American public scholars debated the issues of the day in newspapers, as opposed to lecture halls. As an example, *El Clamor Público*, published by Francisco P. Ramirez in Los Angeles in the 1850s, provided a forum for the discontented Mexican community in the United States.

Arturo Madrid, the Murchison Distinguished Professor of Humanities at Trinity University, says that contrary to popular belief, there is an untapped wealth of literature in Mexico about the Mexican-origin population in the United States prior to 1960. This was the era of McCarthyism and large-scale deportations of Mexicans that were both indiscriminate and also selectively targeted against Mexican political, labor, and community leaders—"against anyone that was suspect," he says. With a few exceptions, the effect was to leave in place a less combative Mexican American intellectual leadership, says Madrid.

Luis Arroyo agrees, saying that in his research he has uncovered a wealth of information regarding writings, books, and writers by immigrants prior to the 1960s. One such writer was Ramon Welch, he says, who wrote political commentaries and was a social activist in the 1950s prior to being deported.

Felix Gutierrez, director of the Freedom Forum's Pacific Media Center and whose parents were journalists and student activists during the 1930s–50s, says that political activism has always been a part of the Mexican American community. "What people were talking about in the 1960s, we were living in the 1950s," he says.

Gutierrez himself represents a link between the "Mexican American Movement" of the 1930s–50s, whose motto was "Progress through Education," and the 1960s movement. He, along with Ralph Guzman, were the faculty advisors for the first United Mexican American Student organization at California State University at Los Angeles.

Incidentally, Gutierrez followed in his parents' footsteps, obtaining a masters degree in journalism from Northwestern University. Yet at a time when Whites could obtain jobs in newsrooms without degrees, Gutierrez could not obtain a job in mainstream media. After a career in academe, he is now considered one of the nation's top media experts.

While Gutierrez sees the birth of the Chicano Movement as a resurgence of the earlier 1930s–50s movement, he distinguishes the 1960s as "a period of turbulence."

One of the principal parts of the country where that turbulence manifested was in Crystal City, Texas, where in 1963, Chicanos took over the city council in a part of the country that had long been dominated by agricultural patrons. The program of activists there, which is documented in the book *Avant-garde of the Chicano Movement in Texas*, by UC Riverside professor Armando Navarro,[3] "was to eliminate and replace the gringo," says Jose Angel Gutierrez, a professor at the University of Texas at Arlington.

Struggling against Jim Crow institutions, Chicano activists also won school board elections in South Texas but found out that Anglos remained embedded in power, as power brokers, teachers, and administrators. This knowledge, says Angel Gutierrez, is what triggered the creation of La Raza Unida Party—the first and only political party for Chicanos: "We became the electoral arm of the Chicano Movement."

Links to the Black Civil Rights Movement

Elizabeth Martinez, a past director of the New York chapter of the Student Nonviolent Coordinating Committee (SNCC) and affiliated with the organization since 1960, says that the Chicano Movement had not simply symbolic links with the civil rights movement, but actual ties. Martinez, who is of Oaxacan indigenous ancestry, grew up riding the back of the bus in the nation's capital. That experience is what created a bond with her to the civil rights movement.

SNCC was one of the principal groups involved in sit-ins at lunch counters and voter education in efforts to desegregate the South. In 1963, after four little girls were killed by a Ku Klux Klan bomb in Birmingham, Alabama, Martinez was enraged to the point where she joined the organization as a full-time member. In the Freedom Summer of 1964, shortly after the bodies of three murdered civil rights workers were found, Martinez recalls driving through the Mississippi Delta, thinking that the place was "stained with so much blood of so many black people who just tried to register people to vote."

Martinez notes that in 1965, as a member of SNCC, she delivered a speech at the historic farmworker march from Delano, California, to Sacramento, in solidarity with the United Farm Worker's Union. In 1968, on behalf of SNCC, she traveled to Albuquerque, to connect with the Chicano land struggle associated with New Mexico and to help found *El Grito del Norte* newspaper. "I went for two weeks and I stayed for eight years," she says.

New Mexico had drawn the attention of SNCC because in 1967, members of the Alianza land grant organization had staged an armed raid on a courthouse, protesting the Anglo theft of New Mexican land grants. Prior to the courthouse raid, the farmworker's movement—begun in 1963—had drawn the support of Martin Luther King Jr.

In 1966, aware of the uneasy race relations within the civil rights movement, Martinez began writing articles about being neither Black or White. Even then, she pointed to a problem that Latinos today often observe: when it comes to race, Latinos don't matter.

Many other Chicanos and Chicano organizations, such as Denver's Crusade for Justice and the National Brown Berets, were involved with the Black civil rights movement. Many of them later became instrumental in forming linkages between the Chicano, the Black Power, and the American Indian Movements.

The Development of Chicano Studies

In the late 1960s, as the struggle over access to higher education became increasingly important, high schools, colleges, and universities became not simply focal points of protest but also recruitment grounds for the different movements.

Carlos Muñoz, one of the many principals involved in the political development of the 1960s movement, says that the relatively large influx of Chicano students into universities unleashed both a political movement focused on civil and human rights, and an intellectual movement that both challenged historical knowledge and created the discipline of Chicano studies.

UCLA professor Juan Gómez-Quiñonez, author of various books including *Roots of Chicano Politics, 1600–1940* and *Chicano Politics: Reality and Promise, 1940–1990*, says that while resistance has always been present in the Chicano community, "Something different did happen in the 1960s that wasn't there before. It was an attitude."

That attitude was reflected in the concepts of Chicanos belonging to a community and that they were not foreigners, but indigenous to the Southwest. Gómez-Quiñonez notes that the placard, "This is our Land," first appeared at a rally at UCLA in 1967. Prior to the Chicano Movement, many people of Mexican origin privately spoke of the Southwest as Mexican/indigenous land, but it was not until the Chicano movement that this was done in a public or political manner.

Books such as *Occupied America*, by CSU Northridge professor, Rodolfo Acuña[4]—which was widely used in Chicano studies classes—created the intellectual underpinnings that rejected the notions, accepted by previous generations, that Chicanos were immigrants or foreigners, that they wanted to assimilate, and that they were docile.

When Chicano studies was created, its purpose was to give intellectual support to the movement and to listen to the voices of both men and women and the community organizations. The community produced the ideas and Chicano studies provided the intellectual support, says Gómez-Quiñonez.

Prior to the development of Chicano studies as a discipline, very little knowledge existed about the Chicano, says Refugio Rochín, former director of the Julian Samora Research Institute (JSRI) at Michigan State University. Neither was there a Chicano studies curriculum, and there were very few Chicano professors.

Julian Samora, who taught at Notre Dame from 1959–85, along with folklorist Americo Paredes and scholar labor activist Ernesto Galarza, was one of the few scholars who studied Mexican Americans and the Mexican-American community. Today, the JSRI, founded in 1989, carries on the work that Samora pioneered, the study of Latinos in the Midwest.

In the 1950s and early 1960s, because the scholarship of those three and a few others was not widely known, students like Rochín who were interested in studying Mexicans had to rely on Anglo scholars. After a stint with the Peace Corps in Colombia in the early 1960s, Rochín says his experience in Latin America reaffirmed his interest in his roots. Yet there was nowhere to study Mexican Americans except in the Latin American departments, he says. "Anglos were teaching us about ourselves," he says. It was the same mentality that Peter Skerry, author of *Mexican Americans: The Ambivalent Minority*, writes about today: "the Anglo model of wanting us to assimilate," says Rochín.[5]

With the advent of Chicano studies programs, for the first time, Chicano and Chicana scholars began to produce knowledge about their own community.

"Chicano studies changed the way we viewed the land we lived on," and it also allowed Chicanos to see U.S. imperialism, says Rochín. It also connected Chicanos to their indigenous roots and to Native American studies, he says.

The movement also created the idea of "sin fronteras"—"the concept of no borders," says Rochín.

Rochín notes also that while there are a few Chicano research centers or departments in the Midwest, such as at Michigan State University, Wayne State University, the University of Minnesota, and the University of Wisconsin, most were developed in California, where Chicanos were numerous, but still in the minority. This contrasts with a general lack of Chicano studies programs along the U.S./Mexico border, where Chicanos are in the majority.

The body of knowledge, and the resultant vast and growing literature, produced and recovered by a generation of Chicano and Chicana scholars, has proved that Chicano studies is a discipline, not a subdiscipline, adds Rochín. "Chicano studies has its own merit and its literature is unique."

Chicano and Chicana studies has pioneered immigrant studies and the study of the family, bilingual issues, and mestizaje, or cultural and racial mixture, says Rochín. The study of living and dealing with duality can be helpful to societies that are now having to deal with similar populations and ethnic tensions, he says.

Despite this, Chicano and Chicana studies is not on safe ground, and the reason for this has more to do with political attacks and back door attacks against their budgets than it does with scholarship.

Rochín says that multiculturalism has actually "killed interest [on the part of universities] in Chicano studies." Additionally, the notion of grouping all Latinos under the rubric "Hispanic" has also weakened and diluted the intent of Chicano studies and Puerto Rican studies, he says. Now, professors with little or no connection to Chicano studies get hired simply by the fact that they are from Spain or South America. "We're still suffering from that," he says.

Jose Angel Gutierrez, of the University of Texas at Arlington, whose Mexican American studies center was recently created, says that Chicano studies centers and departments have stopped being advocates. The exception, he says, are campuses such as CSU Northridge. Unlike other departments around the country, CSUN's Chicano studies department has historically been connected to political action, not simply quaint and disconnected ideological theories that focus on the self, he says. His center's contribution to the discipline, he says, will be to teach how to win an election and how to take community control. With his long experience in organizing, he says he will also contribute advice on how not to make mistakes. "I'm not a footnote."

Arturo Madrid states that after the initial phase of Chicano studies, Chicano and Chicana scholars not by their choosing generally confined their studies to the university. This is what motivated a number of scholars, including himself, to create the Tomas Rivera Center (TRC) think tank in 1984.

"It [TRC] was the first place where on a sustained basis, the intellectual research on the Chicano/Latino community was connected with persons who shape and influence public policy," says Madrid. As opposed to leaving the research on a university shelf, the idea was "to bring intellectual firepower [to public policy debates]," he says.

Maria Herrera Sobek, a professor at UC Santa Barbara is the kind of scholar who was both a product of and a participant in the Chicano Movement. Born of farmworker immigrant parents, Sobek grew up in a shack, attended segregated schools in Texas, and also picked cotton. Today a renowned scholar and poet, she says her background helped shape her academic studies. Her work on folklore and *corridos*–or ballads–comes directly from her upbringing, she says.

She says that while Chicano studies has been great for the university and the community, she agrees that Chicano scholars have not been successful at presenting their research to the public. This is particularly true on the issue of bilingual education. Despite the fact that all major research shows that bilingual education works, "The opposition has shaped the debate," she says.

Antonia Castañeda, a history professor at St. Mary's University in Texas, says that Chicano studies challenged the structure of the university. Yet because it is relatively a new field, it has historically been engaged in a struggle for survival. That's part of the reason why many scholars did not take part in public policy debates outside of the academy. "Linkages [still] need to be made," she says.

"The issues of housing, health, education, and child welfare have not gone away," says Castañeda. "Some of us have made it, but power will always make room for individuals."

The Rise of Chicana Feminist Scholars

Lea Ybarra was present when the National Association of Chicana and Chicano Scholars (NACCS) was formed. "By the time NACCS was created in 1974, women had to be taken into account," she says. For example, as an undergraduate, she had been the chair of the Third World Coalition at UC Berkeley, where women were in many leadership positions.

Despite this, men had to be constantly challenged for their lack of attention to women's issues. The women of NACCS did not allow themselves to be walked upon, she says: "There were so few of us, we were assertive. We had to be."

However, NACCS did not have a conference dedicated to women until 1983. Castañeda says that the Chicano Movement–which was a movement for liberation–was fraught with internal contradictions: "It was male-defined. It was sexist, misogynistic, and homophobic. The movement was about economic, educational and political equality, but fundamentally, it was not about gender equality."

Contrary to the picture of the ideal Mexican family–promoted by Chicano scholars–in which the woman stays at home to raise the children, Mexican women have always worked, at both waged and unwaged labor, says Castañeda. The challenge for Chicana scholars is not only to dispel such myths, but also to continue to examine the intersection of class, race, and gender, she adds. "For instance, Chicano scholars have examined police brutality, but not internal [domestic] violence directed at women."

Just as importantly, the anti-affirmative action mood of the country has Castañeda "terrified," because she fears it will shut off the pipeline of Chicana and Chicano scholars currently being trained at universities. "That is their [foes'] intent."

Chicana feminist scholars are exploring issues ignored by Chicanos, such as the role of women and gender in colonial society; early labor organizing efforts by Chicanas; and the role of women in community, civil, and human rights organizations. Chicana lesbians are also at the forefront of literature and other critical issues that affect all of the Chicano/Chicana community, says Castañeda.

At the end of the 1970s, Ada Sosa-Ridell, who was part of the early Chicana Caucus within NACCS, helped confound Mujeres Activas en Letras en Cambio Social (Active Women in Letters for Social Change [MALCS]), to deal with specific Chicana feminist issues. Prior to the time when Chicana feminists stepped forward, dealing with feminist issues had been "seen as White women stuff," she says.

This emphasis on examining women's issues caused a big conflict. "The biggest conflict was internal—among Chicanas," says Sosa-Riddell. "We were passionate." When Chicanas debated Chicanos, Chicanas didn't take their male counterpart's arguments seriously. "What do you expect, they're men," was the attitude Chicana scholars had.

Some of the issues that created heavy conflicts were lesbian concerns. "At stake was what it meant to be woman-centered," says Sosa-Riddell. Yet, to this day, many of the same issues continue to cause intense conflict, she adds.

MALCS has allowed for a full articulation of feminism, says Sosa-Ridell. For instance, Cynthia Orozco, a professor at the University of New Mexico, has challenged the 1969 "El Plan de Santa Barbara," the document that laid the foundation for Chicano studies, as excluding women.

A Resurgence of the Chicano/Chicana Movement

Many scholars maintain that ever since the death of farm labor leader Cesar Chávez in 1993, there has been a resurgence in the Chicano Movement, particularly at colleges and universities nationwide.

This new activism peaked in 1994 when hundreds of thousands of junior and senior high and college students across the country walked out of schools and held marches and rallies in opposition to California's anti-immigrant Proposition 187. "The mass mobilization against 187 reaffirmed the need to be unified," says Angela Acosta, an organizer with the Willie Valesquez Research Institute in Los Angeles. "The Chicano Movement shaped my life," says Acosta. Yet as someone who worked against 187, she believes the new movement isn't limited to Chicanos, but includes Latinos and other immigrants as well.

This new activism is also being manifested in the current multiracial movement to defend affirmative action, in which men and women and members of all races are struggling jointly to fight off the anti-affirmative movement.

Lea Ybarra says that despite the continuing attacks against Latinos and other people of color, "We [the 60s generation] have to be proud. There's still a lot to do, but we have to remember that we did accomplish a lot." Ybarra concludes: "'There will always be a need for Chicano studies. It is a discipline, it's not taught in high schools, and our color's not going to change."

Genevieve Aguilar, a student at Stanford, says that the Chicano Movement is definitely not dead—that it lives in students like herself who battle against those who believe that racism no longer exists and who don't see a need for Chicano or Latino programs. When students ask Aguilar, who has been in a number of Chicano and Chicana education organizations since she was in the ninth grade, why there isn't an institute for Whites, she responds: "There is: It's called government."

Maria Jimenez, a long-time human rights activist and director of the Immigration and Law Enforcement Monitoring Project with the American Friends Service Committee in Houston, says that the October 12, 1996, Latino march on Washington was the culmination of twenty-five to thirty years of struggle of the Chicano Movement: "It was the culmination of a historical experience" she says.

She views the march as "a maturation of political forces." While acknowledging that there have been thousands of Raza marches throughout the country, none had ever been staged in Washington. Latinos and Latinas have always had local marches because they've responded to the local conditions in which they live. The march demonstrated a national presence, she says. The message the marchers delivered, she says, is: "We're here, we've always been here, and we're not going away."

Notes

1. Elizabeth Sutherland Martinez, *Viva La Causa!; 500 Years of Chicano History* (Collision Course Video Productions, 1995).
2. Carlos Muñoz, *Youth, Identity, Power: The Chicano Movement* (London: Verso, 1989).
3. Armando Navarro, *Mexican American Youth Organization: Avant-garde of the Chicano Movement in Texas* (Austin: University of Texas Press, 1995).
4. Rodolfo Acuña, *Occupied America: A History of Chicanos*, 2d ed. (New York: Harper & Row, 1981).
5. Peter Skerry, *Mexican Americans: The Ambivalent Minority* (New York: Free Press; Maxwell Macmillan Canada; Maxwell Macmillan International, 1993).

References

Acuña, Rodolfo. *Occupied America: A History of Chicanos*, 2d ed. (New York: Harper & Row, 1981).

Martinez, Elizabeth Sutherland. *Viva La Causa!; 500 Years of Chicano History* (Collision Course Video Productions, 1995).

Muñoz, Carlos. *Youth, Identity, Power: The Chicano Movement* (London: Verso, 1989).

Navarro, Armando. *Mexican American Youth Organization: Avant-garde of the Chicano Movement in Texas* (Austin: University of Texas Press, 1995).

Skerry, Peter. *Mexican Americans: The Ambivalent Minority* (New York: Free Press; Maxwell Macmillan Canada; Maxwell Macmillan International, 1993).

17

The History of Asians in America

Timothy P. Fong

A Brief History of Asians in America

Immigration

The historical experience of Asian Americans in the United States is not at all atypical of other minority groups. As a distinct racial minority group, and as immigrants, Asian Americans faced enormous individual prejudice, frequent mob violence, and extreme forms of institutional discrimination. But Asian Americans have not merely been victims of hostility and oppression; indeed, they have also shown remarkable strength and perseverance, which is a testimony to their desire to make the United States their home. Between 1848 and 1924, hundreds of thousands of immigrants from China, Japan, the Philippines, Korea, and India came to the United States. While this period represents the first significant wave, these immigrants were by no means the very first Asians to come to America.

Recent archaeological finds off the coast of Southern California have led to speculation that the West Coast of America may have been visited by Buddhist missionaries from China in the fifth century. While direct evidence of this claim is still being debated, it is known that the

Spanish brought Chinese shipbuilders to Baja California as early as 1571, and later Filipino seamen were brought by Spanish galleons from Manila and settled along the coast of Louisiana. Chinese merchants and sailors were also present in the United States prior to the discovery of gold in California in 1848. Most people are unaware that Asian Indians were brought to America during the late eighteenth century as indentured servants and slaves.[1]

The California gold rush did not immediately ignite a mass rush of Chinese immigrants to America. In fact, only a few hundred Chinese arrived in California during the first years of the gold rush, and most of them were merchants. However, large-scale immigration did begin in earnest in 1852 when 52,000 Chinese arrived that year alone. Many Chinese came to the United States not only to seek their fortunes but also to escape political and economic turmoil in China. As gold ran out, thousands of Chinese were recruited in the mid-1860s to help work on the transcontinental railroad. Eventually more than 300,000 Chinese entered the United States in the nineteenth century, engaging in a variety of work. During this same period Chinese also immigrated to Hawaii, but in far fewer numbers than to the continental United States.[2]

Large capitalist and financial interests welcomed the Chinese as cheap labor and lobbied for the 1868 Burlingame Treaty, which recognized "free migration and emigration" of Chinese to the United States in exchange for American trade privileges in China. As early as 1870 Chinese were 9 percent of California's population and 25 percent of the state's work force.[3] The majority of these Chinese were young single men who intended to work in this country a few years and then return to China. Those who stayed seldom married because of laws severely limiting the immigration of Chinese women and prohibiting intermarriage with white women. The result was the Chinese were forced to live a harsh and lonely bachelor life that often featured vice and prostitution. In 1890, for example, there were roughly 102,620 Chinese men and only 3,868 Chinese women in the United States, a male-female ratio of 26:1.[4] Despite these conditions, Chinese workers continued to come to the United States.

Following the completion of the transcontinental railroad in 1869, large numbers of unemployed Chinese workers had to find new sources of employment. Many found work in agriculture where they cleared land, dug canals, planted orchards, harvested crops, and were the foundation for successful commercial production of many California crops. Others settled in San Francisco and other cities to manufacture shoes, cigars, and clothing. Still others started small businesses such as restaurants, laundries, and general stores. Domestic service such as houseboys, cooks, and gardeners were also other areas of employment for the Chinese. In short, the Chinese were involved in many occupations that were crucial to the economic development and domestication of the western region of the United States.[5] Unfortunately, intense hostility against the Chinese reached its peak in 1882 when Congress passed the Chinese Exclusion Act intended to "suspend" the entry of Chinese laborers for ten years. Other laws were eventually passed that barred Chinese laborers and their wives permanently.[6]

The historical experience of Japanese in the United States is both different yet similar to that of the Chinese. One major difference is that the Japanese emigrated in large numbers to Hawaii and were not significant in United States until the 1890s. In 1880 there were only 148 Japanese living in the U.S. mainland. In 1890 this number increased to 2,000, mostly merchants and students. However, the population increased dramatically when an influx of 38,000 Japanese workers from Hawaii arrived in the U.S. mainland between 1902 and 1907.[7] The second difference was the fact the Japanese were able to fully exploit an economic niche in agriculture that the Chinese had only started. The completion of several national railroad lines and the invention of the refrigerator car were two advancements that brought forth tremendous expansion in the California produce industry. The early Japanese were fortunate to arrive at an opportune time, and about two thirds of the Japanese found work as agricultural laborers. Within a short time the Japanese were starting their own farms in direct competition with non-Japanese farms. By 1919 the Japanese controlled over 450,000 acres of agricultural land. Although this figure represents only one percent of active California agricultural land at the time, the Japanese were so efficient in their farming practices that they captured 10 percent of the dollar volume of the state's crops.[8]

The third major difference was the emergence of Japan as an international military power at the turn of the century. Japan's victory in the Russo-Japanese War (1904–1905) impressed President Theodore Roosevelt and he believed a strategy of cooperation with the Japanese government was in the best interest of the United States. Roosevelt blocked calls for complete Japanese exclusion and instead worked a compromise with the Japanese government in 1907 known as the "Gentleman's Agreement." This agreement halted the immigration of Japanese laborers but allowed Japanese women into the United States. With this in mind, the fourth difference was the fact that the Japanese in the United States were able to actually increase in population, start families, and establish a rather stable community life.[9]

Filipino immigration began after the United States gained possession of the Philippines following the Spanish-American War in 1898. The first Filipinos to arrive were a few hundred pensionados, or students supported by government scholarships. Similar to the Japanese experience, a large number of Filipinos went directly to Hawaii before coming to the U.S. mainland. Between 1907 and 1919 over 28,000 Filipinos were actively recruited to work on sugar plantations in Hawaii. Filipinos began to emigrate to the United States following the passage of the 1924 Immigration Act, which prohibited all Asian immigration to this country and there was a need for agricultural and service labor.[10]

Because Filipinos lived on American territory, *they* were "nationals" who were free to travel in the United States without restriction. In the 1920s over 45,000 Filipinos arrived in Pacific Coast ports, and a 1930 study found 30,000 Filipinos working in California. These Filipinos were overwhelmingly young, single males. Their ages ranged between 16 and 29, and there were 14 Filipino men for every Filipina. Sixty percent of these Filipinos worked as migratory agricultural laborers, and 25 percent worked in domestic service in Los Angeles and San Francisco. The rest found work in manufacturing and as railroad porters. Unlike the Japanese, Filipinos did not make their mark in agriculture as farmers, but as labor union organizers.[11] Both Filipino farm worker activism and Japanese farm competition created a great deal of resentment among white farmers and laborers.

Koreans and Asian Indians slightly predated the Filipinos, but arrived in much smaller numbers. Between 1903 and 1905 over 7,000 Koreans were recruited for plantation labor work in Hawaii, but after Japan established a protectorate over Korea in 1905, all emigration was halted.[12] In the next five years, Japan increased its economic and political power and formally annexed Korea in 1910. Relatively few Koreans lived in the United States between 1905 and 1940. Among those included about 1,000 workers who migrated from Hawaii, about 100 Korean "picture brides," and a small number of American-born Koreans. The Korean population in the United States during that time was also bolstered by roughly 900 students, many of whom fled to their home country because of their opposition to Japanese rule. Like other Asian immigrant groups, Koreans found themselves concentrated in California agriculture working primarily as laborers, although a small number did become quite successful farmers.[13]

The first significant flow of Asian Indians occurred between 1904 and 1911, when just over 6,000 arrived in the United States. Unlike the other Asian groups, Asian Indians did not work in Hawaii prior to entering the American main-land, but they worked primarily in California agriculture. Similar to the Chinese, Filipinos, and Koreans, they had an extremely high male to female ratio. Of the Asian Indians who immigrated to the United States between 1904 and 1911, there were only three or four women, all of whom were married.[14] Eighty to ninety percent of the first Asian Indian settlers in the United States were Sikhs, a distinct ethno-religious minority group in India. Despite this fact, these Sikhs were often called Hindus, which they are not. Sikhs were easily recognizable from all other Asian immigrant groups because of their huskier build, they wore turbans, and they kept their beards. But like other Asians in the United States at the time, they also worked primarily in California's agricultural industry. Asian Indians worked first as farm workers, and like the Japanese, also formed cooperatives, pooled their resources, and began independent farming.[15] Immigration restrictions, their relatively small numbers, and an exaggerated male-female ratio prevented Asian Indians from developing a lasting farm presence. One major exception can be found in the Marysville-Yuba City area of Northern California, where Asian Indian Sikhs are still quite active in producing cling peaches.[16]

Anti-Asian Laws and Sentiment

The United States is a nation that proclaims to welcome and assimilate all newcomers. But the history of immigration, naturalization, and equal treatment under the law for Asian Americans has been an extremely difficult one. In 1790 Congress passed the first naturalization law limiting citizenship rights to only a "free white person."[17] In 1870, during the period of reconstruction following the end of the Civil War, Congress amended the law and allowed citizenship for "aliens of African nativity and persons of African descent."[18] For a while there was some discussion on expanding naturalization rights to Chinese immigrants, but that idea was rejected by politicians from western states.[19] This rejection is exemplary of the intense anti-Chinese sentiment at the time.

As early as 1850 California imposed a Foreign Miners Tax, which required the payment of $20 a month from all foreign miners.[20] The California Supreme Court ruled in *People v. Hall* (1854), that Chinese could not testify in court against a white person. This case threw out the testimony of three Chinese witnesses and reversed the murder conviction of George W. Hall, who was sentenced to hang for the murder of a Chinese man one year earlier.[21] In 1855 a local San Francisco ordinance levied a $50 tax on all aliens ineligible for citizenship. Since Chinese were ineligible for citizenship under the Naturalization Act of 1790, they were the primary targets for this law.[22]

The racially distinct Chinese were the primary scapegoats for the depressed economy in the 1870s, and mob violence erupted on several occasions through to the 1880s. The massacre of 21 Chinese in Los Angeles in 1871 and 28 Chinese in Rock Springs, Wyoming, in 1885 are examples of the worst incidents. It is within this environment that Congress passed the 1882 Chinese Exclusion Act. The act suspended immigration of Chinese laborers for only ten years, but it was extended in 1892 and 1902. The act was eventually extended indefinitely in 1904.[23] The intense institutional discrimination achieved the desired result: The Chinese population declined from 105,465 in 1880 to 61,639 in 1920.[24]

Anti-Chinese sentiment easily grew into large-scale anti-Asian sentiment as immigrants from Asia continued to enter the United States. During the same period that the Chinese population declined, the Japanese population grew and became highly visible. As early as 1910 there were 72,157 Japanese Americans compared to 71,531 Chinese Americans in the United States.[25] The Japanese farmers in California were particularly vulnerable targets for animosity. One of the most sweeping anti-Asian laws was aimed at the Japanese Americans, but affected all other Asian American groups as well. The 1913 Alien Land Law prohibited "aliens ineligible to citizenship" from owning or leasing land for more than three years. Initially the Japanese Americans were able to bypass the law primarily because they could buy or lease land under the names of their American-born offspring (the Nisei), who were U.S. citizens by birth. The law was strengthened in 1920, however, and the purchase of land under the names of American-born offspring was prohibited.[26]

Several sweeping anti-immigration laws were passed in the first quarter of the twentieth century that served to eliminate Asian immigration to the United States. A provision in the 1917 Immigration Act banned immigration from the so-called "Asian barred zone," except for the Philippines and Japan. A more severe anti-Asian restriction was further imposed by the 1924 National Origins Act, which placed a ceiling of 150,000 new immigrants per year. The 1924 act was intended to limit Eastern and Southern European immigration, but a provision was added that ended any immigration by aliens ineligible for citizenship.[27]

Asian Americans did not sit back passively in the fact of discriminatory laws; they hired lawyers and went to court to fight for their livelihoods, naturalization rights, and personal liberties. Sometimes they were successful, oftentimes they were not. In the case of *Yick Wo v. Hopkins* (1886), Chinese successfully challenged an 1880 San Francisco Laundry Ordinance, which regulated commercial laundry service in a way that clearly discriminated against the Chinese. Plaintiff Yick Wo had operated a laundry service for 22 years, but when he tried to renew his business license in 1885 he was turned down because his storefront was made out of wood. Two hundred other Chinese laundries were also denied business licenses on similar grounds, while 80 non-Chinese laundries were approved—even those in wooden buildings. The Supreme Court ruled in favor of Yick Wo, concluding there was "no reason" for the denial of the business license "except to the face and nationality" of the petitioner.[28]

The inability to gain citizenship was a defining factor throughout the early history of Asian Americans. The constitutionality of naturalization based on race was first challenged in the Supreme Court case of *Ozawa v. United States* (1922). Takao Ozawa was born in Japan but immigrated to the United States at an early age. He graduated from Berkeley High School in California and attended the University of California for three years. Ozawa was a model immigrant who did not smoke or drink, he attended a predominantly white church, his children attended public school, and English was the language spoken at home. When Ozawa was rejected in his initial attempt for naturalization, he appealed and argued that the provisions for citizenship in the 1790 and 1870 acts did not specifically exclude Japanese. In addition, Ozawa also tried to argue that Japanese should be considered "white."

The Court unanimously ruled against Ozawa on both grounds. First, the Court decided that initial framers of the law and its amendment did not intend to *exclude* people from naturalization but, instead, only determine who would be *included*. Ozawa was denied citizenship because the existing law simply didn't include Japanese. Second, the Court also ruled against Ozawa's argument that Japanese were actually more "white" than other darker-skinned "white" people such as some Italians, Spanish, and Portuguese. The Court clarified the matter by defining a "white person" to be synonymous with a "person of the Caucasian race." In short, Ozawa was not Caucasian (though he thought himself to be "white") and, thus, was ineligible for citizenship.[29]

Prior to the *Ozawa* case, Asian Indians already enjoyed the right of naturalization. In *United States v. Balsara* (1910), the Supreme Court determined that Asian Indians were Caucasian and approximately 70 became naturalized citizens. But the Immigration and Naturalization Service (INS) challenged this decision, and it was taken up again in the case of *United States v. Thind* (1923). This time the Supreme Court reversed its earlier decision and ruled that Bhagat Singh Thind could not be a citizen because he was not "white." Even though Asian Indians were classified as Caucasian, this was a scientific term that was inconsistent with the popular understanding. The Court's decision stated: "It may be true that the blond Scandinavian and the brown Hindu have a common ancestor in the dim reaches of antiquity, but the average man knows perfectly well that there are unmistakable differences between them today."[30] In other words, only "white" Caucasians were considered eligible for U.S. citizenship. In the wake of the *Thind* decision, the INS was able to cancel retroactively the citizenship of Asian Indians between 1923 and 1926.

Asian Americans also received disparate treatment compared to other immigrants in their most private affairs, such as marriage. In the nineteenth century, anti-miscegenation laws prohibiting marriage between blacks and whites were common throughout the United States. In 1880 the California legislature extended restrictive anti-miscegenation categories to prohibit any marriage between a white person and a "negro, mulatto, or Mongolian." This law, targeted at the Chinese, was not challenged until Salvador Roldan won a California Court of Appeals decision in 1933. Roldan, a Filipino American, argued that he was Malay, not Mongolian, and he should be allowed to marry his white fiancée. The Court conceded that the state's anti-miscegenation law was created in an atmosphere of intense anti-Chinese sentiment, and agreed Filipinos were not in mind when the initial legislation was approved.

Unfortunately, this victory was short-lived. The California State legislature amended the anti-miscegenation law to include the "Malay race" shortly after the Roldan decision was announced.[31]

World War II and the Cold War Era

For Asian Americans, World War II was an epoch; but the profound impact was distinct for different Asian American groups. For over 110,000 Japanese Americans, World War II was an agonizing ordeal soon after Japan's attack of Pearl Harbor on December 7, 1941. The FBI arrested thousands of Japanese Americans who were considered potential security threats immediately after the Pearl Harbor bombing raid. Arrested without evidence of disloyalty were the most visible Japanese American community leaders, including businessmen, Shinto and Buddhist priests, teachers in Japanese language schools, and editors of Japanese language newspapers. Wartime hysteria rose to a fever pitch, and on February 19, 1942, President Franklin Roosevelt issued Executive Order 9066. This order established various military zones and authorized the removal of anyone who was a potential threat. While there were a small number of German and Italian aliens detained and relocated, this did not compare to the mass relocation of Japanese Americans on the West Coast of the United States.[32]

The order to relocate Japanese Americans because of military necessity, and the threat they posed to security, was a fabrication. There was considerable debate even among military leaders over the genuine need for mass relocation, and the government's own intelligence reports found no evidence of Japanese American disloyalty. "For the most part the local Japanese are loyal to the United States or, at worst, hope that by remaining quiet they can avoid concentration camps or irresponsible mobs," one report stated. "We do not believe that they would be at least any more disloyal than any other racial group in the United States with whom we went to war."[33] This helps to explain why 160,000 Japanese Americans living in Hawaii were not interned. More telling was the fact that Japanese Americans in the continental United States were a small but much resented minority. Despite government reports to the contrary, business leaders, local politicians, and the media fueled antagonism against the Japanese Americans and agitated for their abrupt removal.[34]

With only seven days' notice to prepare once the internment order was issued, and no way of knowing how long the war would last, many Japanese Americans were forced to sell their homes and property at a mere fraction of their genuine value. It is estimated that the Japanese Americans suffered economic losses alone of at least $400 million. By August 1942 all the Japanese on the West Coast were interned in ten camps located in rural regions of California, Arizona, Utah, Idaho, Wyoming, and Arkansas. Two thirds of the interned Japanese American men, women, and children were U.S. citizens, whose only crime was their ancestry; even those with as little as one-eighth Japanese blood were interned. The camps themselves were crude, mass facilities surrounded by barbed wire and guarded by armed sentries. People were housed in large barracks with each family living in small cramped "apartments." Food was served in large mess halls, and toilet and shower facilities were communal. Many of the camps were extremely cold in the winter, hot in the summer, and dusty all year round. The camps remained open for the duration of the war.[35]

After the first year of the camps, the government began recruiting young Japanese American men to help in the war effort. The military desperately needed Japanese Americans to serve as interpreters for Japanese prisoners of war and translators of captured documents. But to the military's incredulity, most American-born Japanese had only modest Japanese language skills and had to take intense training in the Military Intelligence Service Language School before they could perform their duties.[36] It was, however, the heroic actions of the 100th Infantry Battalion, which later merged with the 442nd Regimental Combat Team, that stand out the most among historians. The two segregated units engaged in numerous campaigns and served with distinction throughout Europe. By the end of the war in Europe, for example, the Nisei soldiers of the 442nd suffered over 9,000 casualties, while earning over 18,000 individual decorations of honor. The 442nd was the most decorated unit of its size during all of World War II.[37]

Compared to the Japanese American experience, other Asian American groups fared far better during and after World War II. Changes for Chinese Americans were particularly dramatic. Prior to the war, the image of the Chinese was clearly negative compared to the Japanese. A survey of Princeton undergraduates in 1931 thought the top three traits of the Chinese were the fact they were "superstitious, sly, and conservative," while Japanese were considered "intelligent industrious, and progressive."[38] Immediately after the bombing of Pearl Harbor, Chinese store owners put up signs indicating they were not Japanese, and in some cases Chinese Americans wore buttons stating, "I am Chinese." To alleviate any further identification problems, *Time* magazine published an article on December 22, 1941, explaining how to tell the difference between Chinese and "Japs." The article compared photographs of a Chinese man and a Japanese man, highlighting the distinguishing facial features of each.[39] Just months later, a 1942 Gallup Poll characterized the Chinese as "hardworking, honest, and brave," while Japanese were seen as "treacherous, sly, and cruel."[40]

Employment opportunities outside of the segregated Chinatown community became available to Chinese Americans for the first time during the war, and continued even after the war ended. Chinese Americans trained in various professions and skilled crafts were able to find work in war-related industries that had never been open to them before. In addition, the employment of Chinese American women increased threefold during the 1940s. Leading the way were clerical positions, which increased from just 750 in 1940 to 3,200 in 1950. In 1940 women represented just one in five Chinese American professionals, but by 1950 this increased to one in three. On another level, Chinese actors suddenly found they were in demand for film roles—usually playing evil Japanese characters. Shortly after the war, writers such as Jade Snow Wong and Pardee Lowe discovered the newfound interest and appreciation of Chinese Americans could be turned into commercial success through the publication of their memoirs.[41]

On the military front, Asian Americans also distinguished themselves. Over 15,000 Chinese Americans served in all branches of the military, unlike the Japanese Americans who were placed only in segregated infantry units and in the Military Intelligence Service. Similarly, over 7,000 Filipino Americans volunteered for the army and formed the First and Second Filipino Infantry Regiments. About 1,000 other Filipino Americans were sent to the Philippines to perform reconnaissance and intelligence activities for General Douglas MacArthur.[42] Equally significant was the War Bride's Act of 1945, which allowed war veterans to bring wives from China and the Philippines as nonquota immigrants. This resulted in a rapid and dramatic shift in the historic gender imbalance of both groups. For example, between 1945 and 1952, nine out of ten (89.9 percent) Chinese immigrants were female, and 20,000 Chinese American babies were born by the mid-1950s. Similarly, between 1951 and 1960 seven out of ten (71 percent) Filipino immigrants were female.[43]

On the broad international front, alliances with China, the Philippines, and India eventually began the process of changing the overtly discriminatory immigration laws against Asians: The Chinese Exclusion Law was repealed in 1943 and an annual quota of 105 immigrants from China was allotted; in 1946 Congress approved legislation that extended citizenship to Filipino immigrants and permitted the entry of 100 Filipino immigrants annually; also in 1946, the Luce-Cellar Act ended the 1917 "Asian barred zone," allowed an immigration quota of 100 from India, and for the first time permitted Asian Indians to apply for citizenship since the *United States v. Thind* case of 1923. Though these changes were extremely modest, they carried important symbolic weight by helping to create a favorable international opinion of the United States during and immediately after the war.[44]

Geopolitical events during the Cold War era of the 1950s and 1960s immediately following World War II continued to have important ramifications for Asian Americans. After the 1949 Communist Revolution in China, about 5,000 Chinese students and young professionals were living in the United States. These "stranded" individuals were generally from China's most elite and educated families, and were not necessarily anxious to return to China because their property had already been confiscated and their livelihoods were threatened. These students and professionals were eventually allowed to stay in the United States.[45] Several other refugee acts in the late 1950s and early 1960s allowed some 18,000 other Chinese to enter and also stay in the United States. Many of these refugees were well-trained scientists and engineers who easily found jobs in private industry and in research universities. These educated professionals were quite distinct from the vast majority of earlier Chinese immigrants because they usually were able to integrate into the American mainstream quickly, becoming the basis of an emerging Chinese American middle class.[46]

The Cold War affected immigration from Asian countries as well, but in a very different fashion. During and after the Korean War (1950–1953), American soldiers often met and married Korean women and brought them home to the United States. Between 1952 and 1960 over a thousand Korean women a year immigrated to the United States as brides of U.S. servicemen. At the same time, orphaned Korean children, especially girls, also arrived in the United States in significant numbers. Throughout the 1950s and up to the mid-1960s, some 70 percent of all Korean immigrants were either women or young girls. While Korea was the site of the actual conflict, large numbers of troops were also stationed in nearby Japan. Even higher numbers of Japanese women married American soldiers, left their home country, and started a new life in the United States. Roughly six thousand Japanese wives of U.S. servicemen annually immigrated to the United States between 1952 and 1960, which was over 80 per-cent of all immigrants from Japan. These Korean and Japanese war brides and Korean orphans were spread throughout the United States and, as a result, had very little interaction with other Asian Americans already living in this country.[47] These war bride families were, however, a sig-nificant part of the biracial Asian American baby boom. . . .

Post-1965 Asian Immigrants and Refugees

Asian immigration and refugee policies have clearly been influenced by a number of factors, including public sentiment toward immigrants, demands of foreign policy, and the needs of the American economy. While World War II and the Cold War years were epochal for Asian Americans, the period since the mid-1960s has proven to be even more significant. An overview of U.S. immigration statistics shows just how important recent immigration reforms and refugee policies have affected Asian Americans.

Official records on immigrants entering the United States did not exist before 1820, but since that time it is quite obvious that the largest number of immigrants to this nation have come from European countries. Between 1820 and 1996 over 38 million Europeans immigrat-ed to the United States (see Table 1). In contrast, there were only 7.9 million immigrants from Asia during the same period of time. Looking at this figure more closely, however, we find over 5.6 million immigrants from Asia arrived in the United States in the brief period between 1971 and 1994. Though the Chinese and Japanese have the longest histories in the United States, the largest group of Asian immigrants since 1971 has come from the Philippines. Over 1.3 million Filipino immigrants entered the United States between 1971 and 1996. It is also significant to note that over 90 percent of Filipino, Asian Indian, Korean, and Southeast Asian refugees entered the United States since 1971.

This section of the chapter will focus on three broad events that have directly influenced both the numbers and diversity of Asians entering the United States since 1965. These events are (1) the passage of the 1965 Immigration Reform Act, (2) global economic restructuring and (3) the Vietnam War.

The 1965 Immigration Reform Act

Why did the dramatic increase in Asian immigration take place? What changes in the law or public attitudes facilitate such a rapid influx of immigrants from Asia? One important rea-son was the civil rights movement of the 1960s, which brought international attention to racial and economic inequality in the United States—including its biased immigration policies. This attention is the background for the passage of the 1965 Immigration Reform Act, the most important immigration reform legislation. This act, along with its amendments, significantly increased the token quotas established after World War II to allow the Eastern Hemisphere a maximum of 20,000 per country, and set a ceiling of 170,000.

Table 1

Immigration to the United States by Region, Fiscal Years 1820–1996

Region	Total 1820–1996	Between 1971–1996	% of Immigrants Since 1971
All countries	63,140,266	17,975,628	28.4
Europe	38,008,781	2,469,639	6.5
Asia	7,909,713	6,216,867	78.6
China*	1,161,767	718,464	61.8
Hong Kong**	383,906	285,358	74.3
India	684,690	643,894	94.0
Japan	505,026	139,642	27.7
Korea	753,349	712,485	94.6
Philippines	1,382,019	1,259,117	91.1
Vietnam	652,477	647,802	99.2
North America Canada and Newfoundland	4,436,540	443,194	9.9
Mexico	6,223,123	3,838,330	61.6
Caribbean	3,795,048	1,705,048	44.9
Central America	1,163,319	906,162	77.9
South America	1,595,418	1,102,703	69.1
Africa	538,190	461,717	85.8

*Beginning in 1957, China includes Taiwan.

**Data not reported separately until 1952.

Source: U.S. Immigration and Naturalization Service, Statistical Yearbook of the Immigration and Naturalization Service (Washington, D.C.: Government Printing Office, 1999), Table 2, p. 9, and Bureau of the Census, Statistical Abstract of the United States: 1998 (118th edition) Washington, D.C., 1998.

This act created the following seven-point preference system that serves as a general guide-line for immigration officials when issuing visas: (1) unmarried children of U.S. citizens who are at least 21 years of age; (2) spouses and unmarried children of permanent resident aliens; (3) members of the professions, scientists, and artists of exceptional ability; (4) married children of U.S. citizens; (5) brothers and sisters of U.S. citizens who are at least 21 years of age; (6) skilled or unskilled workers who are in short supply; and (7) non-preference applicants.

United States immigration policy also allowed virtually unrestricted immigration to certain categories of people including spouses, children under 21, and parents of U.S. citizens. These provisions served to accelerate immigration from Asia to the United States. While the primary goal of the 1965 Immigration Reform Act was to encourage family reunification, a much higher percentage of Asian immigrants initially began entering the United States under the established occupational and non-preference investment categories. In 1969, for example, 62 percent of Asian Indians, 43 percent of Filipinos, and 34.8 percent of Koreans entered the United States under the occupational and investor categories. By the mid-1970s, however, 80 to 90 percent of all Asian immigrants entered the United States through one of the family categories.[48] Still, studies clearly show that most post-1965 Asian immigrants tend to be more middle-class, educated, urbanized, and they arrive in the United States in family units rather than as individuals, compared to their pre-1965 counterparts.[49]

The framers of the 1965 law did not anticipate any dramatic changes in the historical pattern of immigration, but it is clear that Asian immigrants have taken advantage of almost every aspect of the 1965 Immigration Reform Act. Asians were just 7.7 percent of all immigrants to the United States between 1955 and 1964; this rose to 22.4 percent between 1965 and 1974, and increased to 43.3 percent between 1975 and 1984. The percentage of Asian immigrants remained steady for several years but declined sharply in the late 1980s and early 1990s (see Table 2). This decline was due to the sudden increase of mostly Mexicans who were able to apply for legal status following the passage of the Immigration Reform and Control Act of 1986 (IRCA). By the early 1990s, 2.67 million aliens received permanent residence status under IRCA.[50]

This "amnesty" provision was only a part of IRCA, which was fully intended to control illegal immigration into the United States. IRCA also required that all employers verify the legal status of all new employees, and it imposed civil and criminal penalties against employers who knowingly hire undocumented workers.[51] While IRCA closed the "back door" of illegal immigration, another reform, the Immigration Act of 1990, was enacted to keep open the "front door" of legal immigration. Indeed, this law actually authorizes an *increase* in legal immigration to the United States. In response to uncertain economic stability at home, growing global economic competition abroad, and the dramatically changed face of immigration, the 1990 law sent a mixed message to Asian immigrants.

First of all, the law actually authorized an increase in legal immigration, but at the same time placed a yearly cap on total immigration for the first time since the 1920s. For 1992 to 1995, the limit is 700,000 persons, and 675,000 thereafter. While this appears to be an arbitrary limit, it still allows for an unlimited number of visas for immediate relatives of U.S. citizens. This may not have a negative effect on Asian immigration since, as a group, Asians have the highest rate of naturalization compared to other immigrants.[52] Second, the law encourages immigration of more skilled workers to help meet the needs of the U.S. economy. The number of visas for skilled workers and their families increased from 58,000 to 140,000, while the number for unskilled workers was cut in half to just 10,000. This may prove to be a benefit to

Table 2
Percent of Immigrants Admitted by Region, Fiscal Years 1955–1994

Region	1955–1964	1965–1974	1975–1984	1985–1990	1991–1994
All	100.0	100.0	100.0	100.0	100.0*
Europe	50.2	29.8	13.4	8.9	14.9
North/West	28.6	11.0	5.2	4.0	4.6
South/East	21.6	18.7	8.1	4.9	10.3
Asia	7.7	22.4	43.3	33.5	33.0
North America	26.4	19.0	14.8	28.8	27.0
Caribbean	7.0	18.0	15.1	12.0	10.4
Central America	2.4	2.5	3.7	7.2	5.9
South America	5.1	6.0	6.6	6.2	5.5
Africa	.7	1.5	2.4	2.6	2.0
Oceania	.4	.7	.8	.5	.5

*May not add to 100 due to rounding.
Source: U.S. Immigration and Naturalization Service, *Statistical Yearbook of the Immigration and Naturalization Service* (Washington, D.C.: Government Printing Office, 1996), Table C, p. 21.

Asians who, since 1965, have been among the best-educated and best-trained immigrants this nation has ever seen. Third, the 1990 immigration law also seeks to "diversify" the new immigrants by giving more visas to countries who have sent relatively few migrants to the United States in recent years. This program has been popular with lawmakers who want to assist emigrants from Western European countries, at the expense of Asians. For example, up to 40 percent of the initial visas allocated for the diversity category were for Ireland. Noted immigration attorney Bill Ong Hing found sections of the Immigration Act of 1990 "provide extra independent and transition visas that are unavailable to Asians."[53]

The lasting legacy of the civil rights movement on immigration policy was the emphasis on fairness, equality, and family reunification. But the increased emphasis on highly skilled immigrants found in the 1990 immigration law indicates some loosening of those ideals and priorities. It is clear from the above descriptions of Asian American history that the conditions for the post-1965 Asian migrants are quite distinct from pre-1965 migrants. This seemingly obvious observation reflects the fact that international migration is not a simple, stable, nor homogeneous process. Even with this in mind, the most popular frame of reference for all movement to the United States continues to be the European immigrant experience throughout the nineteenth and early twentieth centuries. The popular European immigrant analogy is highlighted in the words of welcome written on the Statute of Liberty:

> Give me your tired, your poor
> Your huddled masses yearning to breathe free
> The wretched refuse of your teeming shore.
> Send these, the homeless, tempest-tost to me,
> I lift my lamp beside the golden door!

The European immigrant experience, however, is by no means universal, and is only part of what scholars today see as a much broader picture of the international movement of people and capital. Understanding the broader dynamics of global economic restructuring is useful in comparing and contrasting post-1965 Asian immigrants with other immigrants and minority groups in the United States.

Global Economic Restructuring

What makes people want to leave their home country and migrate to another country? The most commonly accepted answer is found within what is known as the push-pull theory. This theory generally asserts that difficult economic, social, and political conditions in the home country force, or push, people away. On the other hand, these people are attracted, or pulled, to another country where conditions are seen as more favorable. Upon closer examination, however, this theoretical viewpoint does run into some problems. Most significantly, the push-pull theory tends to see immigration flows as a natural, open, and spontaneous process, but does not adequately take into account the structural factors and policy changes that directly affect immigration flows. This is because earlier migration studies based on European immigration limited their focus on poor countries that sent low-skilled labor to affluent countries with growing economies that put newcomers to work. The push-pull theory is not incorrect, but is considered to be incomplete and historically static. Recent studies have taken a much broader approach to international migration and insist that in order to understand post-1965 immigration from Asia, it is necessary to understand the recent restructuring of the global economy.[54]

Since the end of World War II, global restructuring has involved the gradual movement of industrial manufacturing away from developed nations such as the United States to less developed nations in Asia and Latin America where labor costs are cheaper. This process was best seen in Japan in the 1950s through 1970s, and accelerated rapidly in the 1980s to newly industrialized Asian countries, namely Taiwan, Hong Kong, Singapore, and South Korea. Other Asian countries such as India, Thailand, Indonesia, Malaysia, and the Philippines also followed the same economic course with varying degrees of success. In the 1990s mainland China has increased its manufacturing and export capacity dramatically, and is steering on the same economic path of other Asian nations.

Among the effects of global restructuring on the United States is the declining need to import low-skilled labor because manufacturing jobs are moving abroad. At the same time, there is an inclining need to import individuals with advanced specialized skills that are in great demand. According to research by Paul Ong and Evelyn Blumenberg (1994), this phenomenon is evidenced in part by the increasing number of foreign-born students studying at U.S. colleges.[55] In the 1954–1955 academic year the United States was host to just 34,232 foreign exchange students; this number increased to over 440,000 in 1994.[56] Over half of all foreign students in the United States are from Asian countries, and most major in either engineering, science, or business. A 1993 report by the National Science Foundation found that over half of the doctorate degrees in engineering, mathematics, and computer science were earned by foreign graduate students.[57] Many of these foreign graduate students planned to work in the United States and eventually gained permanent immigrant status. Companies in the United States have, of course, been eager to hire foreign-born scientists and engineers. Not only are highly skilled immigrants valuable to employers as workers, many also start their own high-tech businesses. For example, Subramonian Shankar is the co-founder and president of American Megatrends, Inc., a company that manufactures personal-computer motherboards and software in Norcross, Georgia. AMI started business in 1985 and now has a work force of 130 people, made up of native-born Americans and immigrants. "I couldn't have done this in India," Shankar says proudly.[58]

The medical profession is another broad area where Asian immigrants have made a noticeable impact. Researchers Paul Ong and Tania Azores (1994) found that Asian Americans represented 4.4 percent of the registered nurses and 10.8 percent of the physicians in the United States in 1990. Ong and Azores estimate that only a third of Asian American physicians and a quarter of Asian American nurses were educated in the United States. Graduates of overseas medical and nursing schools have been coming to the United States since the passage of the 1946 Smith-Mundt Act, which created an exchange program for specialized training. While this exchange was intended to be temporary, many medical professionals were able to become permanent immigrants. A physician shortage in the United States during the late 1960s and early 1970s, coupled with the elimination of racial immigration quotas in 1965, brought forth a steady flow of foreign-trained M.D.s from Asian countries. A 1975 United States Commission on Civil Rights report found 5,000 Asian medical school graduates entered the United States annually during the early 1970s. But, under pressure from the medical industry, Congress passed the 1976 Health Professions Educational Act, which restricted the number of foreign-trained physicians who could enter the United States. Despite the passage of this law, almost 30,000 physicians from Asia immigrated to the United States between 1972 and 1985, and data up to 1990 show roughly half of all foreign-trained physicians entering the United States have come from Asia.[59]

Asia is also the largest source for foreign nurses. In particular, over half of all foreign-trained nurses come from the Philippines. One 1988 study conservatively estimated 50,000 Filipino nurses were working in the United States at the time. Filipino nurses find work in the United States attractive because they can earn up to 20 times the salary they can make in the Philippines, and their English-speaking abilities make them highly desired by employers.

Filipino nurses are also attracted to the United States because of liberal policies that eventually allow them to stay permanently. While most foreign-trained nurses are brought to work initially on a temporary basis, the passage of the Immigration Nursing Relief Act of 1989 allows nurses to adjust to permanent status after three years of service.[60]

The general explanations for the origins of migration found that the push-pull theory continues still to have some value today. Opportunities for large numbers of professionals in Asian countries are still difficult and limited, while opportunities and relatively high salaries are available in the United States. Political instability throughout Asia also continues to be an important push factor for Asian immigrants and refugees. At the same time, this immigration process is not totally natural or spontaneous, as witnessed by foreign student and immigration policies encouraging well-trained individuals to come to the United States. Overall, the changing character of the push and pull in terms of the types of migrants entering the United States and the new skills they bring are very much a result of dynamic global economic restructuring. Global economic restructuring is an important context for understanding not only why Asian immigrants have come to the United States but also how well they have adjusted and been accepted socially, economically, and politically. It is important to note that not all Asian immigrants are middle-class and successful professionals; there is also a sizable number of other Asian immigrants, especially refugees, who have found their lives in America extremely difficult. The extreme diversity among Asian Americans is due in large part to the third major event affecting migration from Asia—the Vietnam War.

The Vietnam War and Southeast Asian Refugees

Since 1975 large numbers of Southeast Asian refugees have entered the United States, and today California is the home for most of them (see Table 3). Roughly three quarters of all Southeast Asian refugees are from Vietnam, with the rest from Laos and Cambodia. Unlike most other post-1965 Asian immigrants who came to the United States in a rather orderly fashion seeking family reunification and economic opportunities, Southeast Asian refugees arrived as part of an international resettlement effort of people who faced genuine political persecution and bodily harm in their home countries. Southeast Asian refugees to the United States can be easily divided into three distinct waves: the first wave arrived in the United States in 1975 shortly after the fall of Saigon; the second wave arrived between 1978 and 1980; and the third entered the United States after 1980 and continues to this day. The United States has accepted these refugees not only for humanitarian reasons but also because of a recognition that U.S. foreign policy and military actions in Southeast Asia had a hand in creating much of the calamity that has befallen the entire region.

U.S. political interests in Southeast Asia actually began during World War II, although for years efforts were limited to foreign aid and military advisers. Direct military intervention rapidly escalated in 1965 when President Lyndon B. Johnson stepped up bombing raids in Southeast Asia and authorized the use of the first U.S. combat troops in order to contain increasing Communist insurgency. The undeclared war continued until U.S. troops withdrew

Table 3
States with the Largest Southeast Asian Populations

State	Vietnamese	Cambodian	Laotian	Hmong	Total
California	280,223	68,190	58,058	46,892	453,363
Texas	69,634	5,887	9,332	176	85,029
Washington	18,696	11,096	6,191	741	36,724
Minnesota	9,387	3,858	6,381	16,833	36,459
Massachusetts	15,449	14,050	3,985	248	33,732
Virginia	20,693	3,889	2,589	7	27,178
Pennsylvania	15,887	5,495	2,048	358	23,788
Wisconsin	2,494	521	3,622	16,373	23,010
New York	15,555	3,646	3,253	165	22,619
Florida	16,346	1,617	2,409	7	20,379

Source: U.S. Bureau of the Census, *1990 Census of the Population, General Population Characteristics, United States Summary* (Washington, D.C.: Government Printing Office, 1993), CP-1-1, Table 262.

in 1973 at the cost of 57,000 American and one million Vietnamese lives. The conflict also caused great environmental destruction throughout Southeast Asia, and created tremendous domestic antiwar protests in the United States.[61]

As soon as the U.S. troops left, however, Communist forces in Vietnam regrouped and quickly began sweeping across the countryside. By March 1975 it was clear that the capital of South Vietnam, Saigon, would soon fall to Communist forces. As a result, President Gerald Ford authorized the attorney general to admit 130,000 refugees into the United States.[62] In the last chaotic days prior to the fall of Saigon on April 30, 1975, "high-risk" individuals in Vietnam, namely high-ranking government and military personnel, were hurriedly airlifted away to safety at temporary receiving centers in Guam, Thailand, and the Philippines. This group marked the first wave of Southeast Asian refugees, who would eventually resettle in the United States. The first wave is distinct in that they were generally the educated urban elite and middle class from Vietnam. Because many of them had worked closely with the U.S. military, they tended to be more westernized (40 percent were Catholics), and a good portion of them were able to speak English (30 percent spoke English well). Another significant feature is the fact that roughly 95 percent of the first wave of Southeast Asian refugees were Vietnamese, even though the capitals of Laos and Cambodia also fell to Communist forces in 1975.[63]

Once these first wave refugees came to the United States, they were flown to one of four military base/reception centers in California, Arkansas, Pennsylvania, and Florida. From these bases they registered with a voluntary agency that would eventually help to resettle them with a sponsor. About 60 percent of the sponsors were families, while the other 40 percent were usually churches and individuals. Sponsors were responsible for day-to-day needs of the refugees until they were able to find jobs and become independent. The resettlement of the first wave of refugees was funded by the 1975 Indochinese Resettlement Assistance Act and was seen as a quick and temporary process. Indeed, all four reception centers closed by the end of 1975 and the Resettlement Act expired in 1977.

The second wave of Southeast Asian refugees was larger, more heterogeneous, and many believe even more devastated by their relocation experience than the first wave. The second wave of refugees were generally less educated, urbanized, and westernized (only 7 percent spoke English and only about 7 percent were Catholic) compared to their predecessors; at the same time they were much more ethnically diverse than the *first* wave. According to statistics, between 1978 and 1980, about 55.5 percent of Southeast Asian refugees were from Vietnam (including many ethnic-Chinese), 36.6 percent from Laos, and 7.8 percent from Cambodia. The second wave consisted of people who suffered under the Communist regimes and were unable to leave their countries immediately before or after the new governments took power.[64]

In Vietnam, the ethnic-Chinese merchant class was very much the target of resentment by the new Communist government. Many of the Chinese businesses in Vietnam were nationalized, Chinese language schools and newspapers were closed, education and employment rights were denied, and food rations were reduced. Under these conditions, about 250,000 left North Vietnam and sought refuge in China. Roughly 70 percent of the estimated 500,000 "boat people" who tried to escape Vietnam by sea were ethnic-Chinese. The treacherous journey usually took place on ill-equipped crowded boats that were unable to withstand the rigors of the ocean or outrun marauding Thai pirates. The U.S. Committee for Refugees estimates at least 100,000 people lost their lives trying to escape Vietnam by boat.[65] Along with the Chinese, others in Vietnam, particularly those who had supported the U.S.-backed South Vietnamese government, and their families were also subject to especially harsh treatment by the new Communist leadership. Many were sent to "reeducation camps" and banished to work in rural regions clearing land devastated by 30 years of war.

The holocaust in Cambodia began immediately after the Khmer Rouge (Red Khmer) marched into the capital city of Phnom Penh on April 17, 1975. That same day the entire population of the capital was ordered to the countryside. After three years it has been broadly estimated between 1 and 3 million Cambodians died from starvation, disease, and execution out of a population of less than 7 million. In 1978 Vietnam (with support from the Soviet Union) invaded Cambodia, drove the Khmer Rouge out of power, and established a new government under its own control. Famine and warfare continued under Vietnamese occupation, and by 1979 over 600,000 refugees from Cambodia fled the country, mostly to neighboring Thailand.

In Laos, the transition from one government to another was initially rather smooth compared to Vietnam following the fall of Saigon. After over a decade of civil war, a coalition government was formed in April 1974 that included Laotian Communists, the Pathet Lao. But shortly after Communists took power in Vietnam and Cambodia, the Pathet Lao moved to solidify its full control of the country. It was at this time that troops from both Laos and Vietnam began a military campaign against the Hmong hill people, a preliterate ethnic minority group that lived in the mountains of Laos who were recruited by the U.S. government to serve as mercenaries against Communist forces in the region. The Hmong were seen as traitors to the Communist revolution, and massive bombing raids were ordered against them that included the dropping of napalm and poisonous chemicals. Thousands of Hmong were killed in these fierce assaults, and those who remained had little choice but to seek refuge in neighboring Thailand. While the Hmong were not the only people in Laos who were persecuted, by 1979 roughly 3,000 Hmong were entering Thailand every month, and as late as 1983 an estimated 75 percent of the 76,000 Laotians in Thai refugee camps were Hmong people.[66]

The world could not ignore this massive outpouring of refugees from Southeast Asia, and in 1979 President Jimmy Carter allowed 14,000 refugees a month to enter the United States. In addition, Congress passed the Refugee Act of 1980, which among other things set an annual quota of 50,000 refugees per year, funded resettlement programs, and allowed refugees to become eligible for the same welfare benefits as U.S. citizens after 36 months of refugee assistance (this was changed to 18 months in 1982). The third wave of Southeast Asians are technically not considered refugees, but are in actuality immigrants. This has been facilitated by the 1980 Orderly Departure program (ODP), agreement with Vietnam that allows individuals and families to enter the United States. ODP was a benefit for three groups: relatives of permanently settled refugees in the United States, Amerasians, and former reeducation camp internees. By the end of 1992, over 300,000 Vietnamese immigrated to the United States, including 80,000 Amerasians and their relatives, as well as 60,000 former camp internees and their families.[67] . . .

It is obvious that Southeast Asian refugees/ immigrants have been a rapidly growing and extremely diverse group. According to the 1990 census, there were 1,001,054 Southeast Asians in the United States, or 13 percent of the total population of Asian Americans. Individually, the census counted 614,547 Vietnamese, 149,014 Laotians, 147,411 Cambodians, and 90,082 Hmong. Some have argued that these census figures are an undercount of the actual numbers of people from Southeast Asian countries. Researchers point to the fact that the total number of arrivals to the united States from Southeast Asia is roughly the same as census figures. This is an anomaly because the census figure should be about 20 percent larger to reflect the number of American-born Southeast Asians. There are, however, several reasons for this disparity. First of all, new arrivals from Southeast Asia who have little knowledge of the English language may simply not have responded to census questionnaires. This certainly is a general concern for all Asian American groups. Second, and probably most important, it is estimated that between 15 and 25 percent of those from Vietnam, Cambodia, and Laos are actually ethnic-Chinese. It is quite possible that many ethnic-Chinese from Southeast Asia answered the appropriate census question of ethnicity without regard to their nationality. Third, no one is exactly sure how Amerasians identified themselves on the 1990 census, or if they even participated at all. While a factor, it is important to note that most of the Amerasians from Vietnam did not actually enter the United States until after the 1990 census was taken. All references to the Southeast Asian population should keep these considerations in mind.[68]

Conclusion

This reading briefly describes the history and recent growth of the Asian population in the United States. It also highlights the significance of the 1965 Immigration Reform Act, global economic restructuring, and the Vietnam War as three broad events that profoundly impacted both the number and type of migrants who have come to the United States from Asian countries. In order to examine post-1965 Asian Americans comprehensively, it is particularly important to look not only at the rapid growth of the population but also at a multitude of other factors, such as personal history, nativity, length of time in the United States, pre-migration experiences and traumas, education, socioeconomic class background, and gender. . . .

Notes

1. Shih-shan Henry Tsai, *The Chinese Experience in America* (Bloomington: Indiana University Press, 1986), p. 1; also see Stan Steiner, *Fusahang: The Chinese Who Built America* (New York: Harper & Row, 1979), pp. 24–35; Elena S. H. Yu, "Filipino Migration and Community Organization in the United States," *California Sociologist* 3:2 (1980); 76–102; and Joan M. Jensen, *Passage from India: Asian Indian Immigrants in North America* (New Haven: Yale University Press, 1988). pp. 12–13.
2. Sucheng Chan, *Asian Californians* (San Francisco: MTL/Boyd & Fraser, 1991). pp. 5–6.
3. Ronald Takaki, *Strangers from a Different Shore* (Boston: Little, Brown and Company, 1989), pp. 79, 114.
4. Stanford Lyman, *Chinese Americans* (New York: Random House, 1974), pp. 86–88.
5. Chan, *Asian Californians*, pp. 27–33.
6. Lyman, *Chinese Americans*, pp. 63–69.
7. Yuji Ichioka, *The Issei: The World of the First Generation Japanese Immigrants, 1885–1924* (New York: The Free Press, 1988), pp. 64–65.
8. Roger Daniels, *Concentration Camps: North America Japanese in the United States and Canada During World War II* (Malabar, FL: Robert A. Kreiger, 1981), p. 7.
9. Bill Ong Hing, *Making and Remaking Asian America Through Immigration Policy, 1850–1990* (Stanford, CA: Stanford University Press, 1993), pp. 28–30.
10. Chan, *Asian Californians*, p. 7.
11. Edwin B. Almirol, *Ethnic Identity and Social Negotiation: A Study of a Filipino Community in California* (New York: AMS Press, 1985), pp. 52–59; and H. Brett

Melendy, "Filipinos in the United States," in Norris Hundlkey, Jr. (ed.), *The Asian American: The Historical Experience* (Santa Barbara: Cleo Books, 1977), pp. 101–128.

12. Takaki, *Strangers from a Different Shore,* pp. 53–57.

13. Chan, *Asian Californians,* pp. 7, 17–19, 37; and Warren Y. Kim, *Koreans in America* (Seoul: Po Chin Chai Printing Co., 1971), pp. 22–27.

14. Joan M. Jensen, *Passage from India: Asian Indian Immigrants in North America* (New Haven: Yale University Press, 1988), pp. 24–41; and Rajanki K. Das, *Hindustani Workers on the Pacific Coast* (Berlin and Leipzig: Walter De Bruyter & Co., 1923), p. 77.

15. Das, *Hindustani Workers,* pp. 66–67.

16. Bruce La Brack, "Occupational Specialization Among Rural California Sikhs: The Interplay of Culture and Economics," *Amerasia Journal* 9:2 (1982): 29–56.

17. Naturalization Act of 1790, I Stat. 103 (1790).

18. Act of 14 July 1870, 16 Stat. 256.

19. Roger Daniels, *Asian Americans: Chinese and Japanese in the United States* (Seattle: University of Washington Press, 1988) p. 43.

20. Chan, *Asian Californians,* p. 42.

21. Robert F. Heizer and Alan F Almquist, *The Other Californians: Prejudice and Discrimination under Spain, Mexico, and the United States to 1920* (Berkeley: University of California Press, 1971), p. 129.

22. Takaki, *Strangers from a Different Shore,* p. 82.

23. Lyman, *Chinese Americans.* pp. 55–85.

24. Takaki, *Strangers from a Different Shore,* pp. 111–112.

25. Juan L. Gonzales, *Racial and Ethnic Groups in America,* second edition (Dubuque, Iowa: Kendall/Hunt Publishing Co., 1993), p. 136; and Juan L. Gonzales, *Racial and Ethnic Families in America,* second edition (Dubuque, Iowa: Kendall/Hunt Publishing Co., 1993), p. 3.

26. Chan, *Asian Californians,* pp. 44–45.

27. Hing, *Making and Remaking Asian America,* pp. 32–39.

28. *Yick Wo v. Hopkins,* 118 U.S. 356 (1886); and Lyman, *Chinese Americans,* p. 79.

29. *Takao Ozawa v. United States,* 260 U.S. 178 (1922); Heizer and Alquist, *The Other Californians,* pp. 192–193; and Ichioka, *The Issei,* pp. 210–226.

30. *United States v. Bhagat Singh Thind,* 261 U.S. 204 (1923); Jensen, *Passage from India,* pp. 255–260; and Gurdial Singh, "East Indians in the United States," *Sociology and Social Research* 30:3 (1946): 208–216.

31. Megumi Dick Osumi, "Asians and California's Anti-Miscegenation Laws," in Nobuya Tsuchida (ed.), *Asian and Pacific American Experiences: Women's Perspectives* (Minneapolis: Asian/Pacific American Learning Resource Center, University of Minnesota, 1982), pp. 1–37; and Takaki, *Strangers from a Different Shore,* pp. 330–331.

32. William Petersen, *Japanese Americans* (New York: Random House, 1971), pp. 66–100; Roger Daniels, *Concentration Camps: U.S.A.* (New York: Holt, Rinehart & Winston, 1971), pp. 75, 81–82; and Jacobus tenBroek, Edward N. Barnhart, and Floyd W. Matson,

Prejudice, War, and the Constitution (Berkeley: University of California Press), pp. 118–120.

33. Cited in Commission on Wartime Relocation and Internment of Civilians, *Personal Justice Denied* (Washington, D.C.: Government Printing Office, 1982), pp. 52–53.

34. Takaki, *Strangers from a Different Shore,* pp. 379–392.

35. Commission on Wartime Relocation and Internment of Civilians, *Personal Justice Denied,* p. 217; tenBroek, Barnhart, and Matson, *Prejudice, War, and the Constitution,* pp. 155–177, 180–181; and Daniels, *Concentration Camps: North America.*

36. Chan, *Asian Californians,* p. 101.

37. Petersen, *Japanese Americans,* p. 87.

38. Cited in Marvin Karlins, Thomas L. Coffman, and Gary Walters, "On the Fading of Social Stereotypes: Studies of Three Generations of College Students," *Journal of Personality and Psychology* 13 (1990): 4–5.

39. *Time,* December 22, 1941, p. 33.

40. Cited in Harold Isaacs, *Images of Asia: American News of China and India* (New York: Harper & Row, 1972), pp. xviii–xix.

41. Chan, *Asian Californians,* pp. 103–104; and Lyman, *Chinese Americans,* pp. 127, 134.

42. Takaki, *Strangers from a Different Shore,* pp. 357–363, 370–378; Manuel Buaken, "Life in the Armed Forces," *New Republic* 109 (1943); 279–280; and Bienvenido Santos, "Filipinos in War," *Far Eastern Survey* 11 (1942): 249–250.

43. Harry H. L. Kitano and Roger Daniels, *Asian Americans: Emerging Minorities,* second edition (Englewood Cliffs, New Jersey: Prentice Hall 1995), p. 42, Table 4–2; and Monica Boyd, "Oriental Immigration: The Experience of Chinese, Japanese, and Filipino Populations in the United States," *International Migration Review* 10 (1976): 48–60, Table 1.

44. Chan, *Asian Californians,* pp. 105–106.

45. Diane Mark and Ginger Chih, *A Place Called Chinese America* (San Francisco: The Organization of Chinese Americans, 1982), pp. 105–107.

46. Chan, *Asian Californians,* pp. 108–109.

47. Ibid., pp. 109–110.

48. Hing, *Making and Remaking Asian America,* Appendix B, pp. 189–200; Table 9, p. 82.

49. Hing, *Making and Remaking Asian America,* pp. 79–120; Luciano Mangiafico, *Contemporary American Immigrants: Patterns of Filipino, Korean, and Chinese Settlement in the United States* (New York: Praeger Publishers, 1988), pp. 1–26; James T. Fawcett and Benjamin V. Carino (eds.), *Pacific Bridges: The New Immigration from Asia and the Pacific Islands* (Staten Island, NY: Center for Migration Studies, 1987); and Herbert R. Barringer, Robert W. Gardner, and Michael J. Levine (eds.), *Asian and Pacific Islanders in the United States* (New York: Russell Sage Foundation, 1993).

50. U.S. Immigration and Naturalization Service, *Statistical Yearbook of the Immigration and Naturalization Service, 1993* (Washington, D.C.: Government Printing Office, 1994), p. 20.

51. Roger Daniels, *Coming to America* (New York: Harper-Collins Publishers, 1990), pp. 391–397.

52. U.S. Immigration and Naturalization Service, *Statistical Yearbook of the Immigration and Naturalization Service, 1994* (Washington, D.C.: Government Printing Office, 1996), p. 126, Chart O.

53. Hing, *Making and Remaking Asian America,* pp. 7–8.

54. Paul Ong, Edna Bonacich, and Lucie Cheng (eds.), *The New Asian Immigration in Los Angeles and Global Restructuring* (Philadelphia: Temple University Press, 1994), pp. 3–100; and Edna Bonacich, Lucie Cheng, Norma Chinchilla, Nora Hamilton, and Paul Ong (eds.), *Global Production: The Apparel Industry in the Pacific Rim* (Philadelphia: Temple University Press, 1994), pp. 3–20.

55. Paul Ong and Ewelyn Blumenberg, "Scientists and Engineers," in Paul Ong (ed.) *The State of Asian Pacific America: Economic Diversity, Issues & Policies* Los Angeles: LEAP Asian Pacific American Public Policy Institute and UCLA Asian American Studies Center, 1994), pp. 113–138. It is important to note that I am distinguishing between foreign exchange students who are overseas nationals from Asian American students who happen to be foreign born.

56. Ibid. p. 173; and U.S. Department of Commerce, *Statistical Abstract of the United States, 1995* (Washington, D.C.: Government Printing Office, 1995), p. 188. Table 295.

57. Cited in *Statistical Abstract,* 1995, p. 619, Table 997.

58. Michael J. Mandel and Christopher Farrell, "The Immigrants: How They're Helping to Revitalize the U.S. Economy," *Business Week,* July 13, 1992, pp. 114–120, 122.

59. Paul Ong and Tamia Azores, "Health Professionals on the Front-Line," in Paul Ong (ed.), *The State of Asian Pacific America: Economic Diversity, Issues & Policies,* pp. 139–164.

60. Paul Ong and Tania Azores, "The Migration and Incorporation of Filipino Nurses," in Ong et al. (eds.), *The New Asian Immigration in Los Angeles and Global Restructuring,* pp. 166–195; and Mangiafico, *Contemporary American Immigrants,* pp. 42–43.

61. Literature on the Vietnam conflict is voluminous. For an excellent and readable overview see Stanley Karnow, *Vietnam: A History* (New York: Penguin Books, 1991).

62. The quota for refugees under the 1965 Immigration Reform Act was only 17,400, so President Gerald Ford instructed the attorney general to use his "parole" power to admit the 130,000 refugees. The use of parole was also used to bring European refugees to the United States during the 1950s. For more details, see Hing, *Making and Remaking Asian America,* pp. 123–128, and Paul J. Strand and Woodrow Jones, Jr., *Indochinese Refugees in America: Problems of Adaptation and Assimilation* (Durham, NC: Duke University Press, 1985).

63. Chan, *Asian Californians,* p. 128; and Chor-Swan Ngin, "The Acculturation Pattern of Orange County's Southeast Asian Refugees," *Journal of Orange County Studies* 3:4 (Fall 1989–Spring 1990): 46–53.

64. Ngin, "The Acculturation Pattern of Orange County's Southeast Asian Refugees," p. 49; and Ngoan Le, "The Case of the Southeast Asian Refugees: Policy for a Community 'At-Risk,'" in *The State of Asian Pacific America: Policy Issues to the Year 2020* (Los Angeles:

LEAP Asian Pacific American Public Policy Institute and UCLA Asian American Studies Center, 1993), pp. 167–188.

65. For more details see Strand and Jones, *Indochinese Refugees in America;* Barry I. Wain, *The Refused: The Agony of Indochina Refugees* (New York: Simon & Schuster, 1981); and U.S. Committee for Refugees, *Uncertain Harbors: The Plight of Vietnamese Boat People* (Washington, D.C.: Government Printing Office, 1987).

66. Chan, *Asian Californians,* pp. 121–139; Kitano and Daniels, Asian Americans: Emerging Minorities, pp. 170–191; U.S. Committee for Refugees, *Cambodians in Thailand: People on the Edge* (Washington, D.C.: Government Printing Office, 1985); and U.S. Committee for Refugees, *Refugees from Laos: In Harm's Way* (Washington, D.C.: Government Printing Office, 1986).

67. U.S. Committee for Refugees, *Uncertain Harbors,* pp. 19–20; and Ruben Rumbaut, "Vietnamese, Laotian, and Cambodian Americans," in Pyong Gap Min (ed.), *Asian Americans: Contemporary Trends and Issues* (Thousand Oaks, CA: Sage Publications, 1995), p. 240.

68. Ruben Rumbaut and J. R. Weeks, "Fertility and Adaptation: Indochinese Refugees in the United States," *International Migration Review* 20:2 (1986): 428–466; and Rumbaut, "Vietnamese, Laotian, and Cambodian Americans," pp. 239–242.

18

Filipino Americans: Historical Overview

Linda A. Revilla

Introduction

Filipino Americans are currently the second largest Asian group in the United States, yet comparatively little is known about them. Although Filipinos have settled in the United States for over two hundred years, it was not until the changing immigration law in 1965 that their numbers started to increase dramatically. Filipino Americans in 1990 numbered over 1.4 million.

Because of the Philippine's history as a Spanish colony and an American colony, the experience of Filipinos in the United States was somewhat different from that of the Chinese and Japanese. Historically, Filipino immigrants have been perhaps the most Westernized among the Asian immigrant groups. Many immigrants spoke English and were familiar with the American lifestyle. During the era of Asian exclusion, Filipinos alone were eligible to freely immigrate. However, their status as "American nationals," not eligible for citizenship, was an example of the second-class status they were relegated to in the United States, a status similar to that of other Asian immigrants. World War Two and then the 1965 Immigration Act were events that significantly impacted the Filipino American community. Today, Filipinos are the second largest immigrant group to the U.S. annually. The majority of these new Filipino immigrants are well-educated. This is in contrast to the American-born Filipinos who tend to have less education. As this example indicates, Filipino Americans are a heterogeneous population, with varying regional, linguistic, social class, and generational backgrounds. Although there are many successful Filipino Americans, such as politicians, nurses, and entertainers, the majority find themselves under employed. Filipino Americans, like other American ethnic groups, face a myriad of social issues related to their minority status. This article will focus on the Filipino American history and introduce some contemporary issues facing Filipino Americans today.

Early History of the Philippines

The Philippines is an archipelago of more than 7,000 islands of varying sizes, most of which are uninhabited. The Philippines is surrounded by the Pacific Ocean and the North China Sea. The people are considered to be Malay, intermixed with many different ethnicities, such as Spanish, Chinese, Indian, European American, Indonesian, German and others. There are at least eight distinct languages, and over 70 different dialects, which some linguists argue are separate languages themselves. The national language, based mostly on the Tagalog language, is called "Pilipino" (Alcantara, 1975a; Pido, 1986).

Philippine society in the early 16th century had as its basis the *barangay,* a kinship-based settlement led by a chief, or *datu.* Barangays varied in size, and could range from having 10 to 100 households. Barangays had their own social organizations and often their own languages or dialects. Barangays were involved in agriculture, fishing, hunting, and trade with other barangays throughout the islands, and with Chinese and other traders. Trade with outsiders brought many changes, one of the most significant being the spread of Islam. The influence of Islam expanded, especially in the southern islands, and provided the impetus for more sophisticated social and political systems to be developed by the 15th century (Van Niel, 1992).

In pre-colonial Filipino culture, women were considered equal to men. They could own and inherit property, engage in trade, become leaders of barangays, and hold high positions as priestesses (Domingo-Kirk, 1994). Colonization by the Spanish and the Americans was to drastically change the status of women.

Spanish Colonization of the Philippines

Ferdinand Magellan's expedition landed in Samar, in what is now the Philippines in 1521, and claimed the islands for Spain. On the island of Mactan, Magellan insulted a native leader, Lapu-Lapu, and was killed. Magellan's forces were driven off the island. It took almost fifty years for Spanish conquistadors to annex the islands, which they named *Las Islas Filipinas,* after King Philip II of Spain. The Spanish set out to convert the native population to Christianity. Spanish colonists controlled vast tracts of land and the political and economic systems of the islands. The Catholic Church, which succeeded in converting the majority of the population, also owned vast tracts of land and controlled the educational system. Manila became an important port for the Spanish galleon trade between Asia and the New World. Under Spanish rule, many native people were reduced to being landless peasant sharecroppers (Crouchett, 1982; Karnow, 1989). Aquino (1992) describes Spanish colonization of the Philippines as follows,

> For the next three hundred years, this "sovereign light" would lead to not only one of the longest but also one of the most cruel colonial regimes in the world. The Spanish regime systematically destroyed native communities and their institutions. It brutalized the indios, making them work as forced labor in the government's various projects, or as indentured servants to friars or public officials. Above all, the Spaniards imposed an alien religion, Catholicism, on the population whose sacred native beliefs and shrines had to be destroyed. The vanquished were viewed as savages or pagans who had to be civilized. In many cases, the indios would simply be killed outright. Genocide was a tool of conquest . . . For three centuries, the Filipinos were prisoners and slaves in their own country, subject to every conceivable kind of exploitation and abuse . . . (p.3).

The Spanish colonizers sought to destroy vestiges of indigenous Filipino culture, which they saw as inferior. The Jesuit priest Chrino destroyed hundreds of manuscripts written in ancient Tagalog script in Batangas, Philippines (Enriquez, 1994). This, and other willful acts of destruction by the Spanish are the reasons why there are few remaining manuscripts written in this indigenous language.

During the Spanish reign, the Filipinos mounted more than 200 rebellions at different places, under different leaders, and with varying degrees of success. Finally, rebel leadership and troops were strong enough to launch the Philippine Revolution in August, 1896. Later that year, Jose Rizal, a Filipino intellectual who called for governmental reforms, was executed by the Spanish. His death inflamed the revolution. At the same time the Filipinos under the leadership of Andres Bonifacio and then Emilio Aguinaldo fought to drive the Spanish out of the Philippines, the United States was engaged in the Spanish-American War. American Commodore Dewey sailed into Manila Bay to fight the Spanish fleet. At this time the Spanish were under siege in Manila, surrounded by Filipino forces that they refused to surrender to. The Spanish fought a mock battle with the Americans and surrendered to them. The U.S. eventually won the war. The Treaty of Paris ceded the Philippines to the U.S. for 20 million dollars. Six months earlier, the Filipinos had claimed an independent republic on June 12, 1898, and set up a government. The fledgling Filipino government, however, was not recognized by western powers. The Americans responded to the Filipinos' claim of independence by heeding "manifest destiny," and established a military government. Fighting between the Filipinos and Americans begins in early 1899. The forgotten war that resulted is known in the United States as the "Filipino Insurrection." A total of 126,000 American troops were involved. The Filipinos, who call this war the "Philippine-American War," fought for their country for over 3 years, eventually losing in 1901, although some Filipinos continued fighting for years. The civilian population greatly suffered during the war, which saw some American commanders following a "scorched earth" policy of burning villages, storehouses, and crops and killing "everything (sic) over ten." This war, which some have referred to as "America's first Vietnam," resulted in Filipino deaths which have been estimated to have been as high as 1 million. Thus, the Philipines became an American colony, beginning an American presence in the Philippines that still exists (Alegado, 1992; Francisco, 1973; Pido, 1986).

American Colonization of the Philippines

American colonial rule in the Philippines has been described as "benevolent despotism." The Americans continued the western tradition of exploiting the Philippines for the benefit of the United States. For example, the Payne-Aldrich Act of 1909 allowed American products into the Philippines duty free, in exchange for some Philippine agricultural products allowed into the U.S. under a quota (Alegado, 1992). However, the Americans also embarked on some modernization of the Philippines, setting up education, public health, and public works programs.

Strobel (1994) quotes the United States Philippine Commission report of 1905, which discusses the use of English in the Philippines, "If we can give the Filipino husband man (sic) a knowledge of the English language and the most elemental acquaintance of English writings, we will free him from that degraded dependence upon the man of influence of his own race." English was the primary means of communication used by the American colonizers in the Philippines. In the American-style schools, taught by white Americans, Filipino children learned in English about George Washington, Thomas Jefferson, and the U.S. Civil War. They learned to dream of a white Christmas and what apple pies are, but never learned about their own history as a people, and never learned in their native tongues. This "Americanization" of the Philippines was to have broad implications for Filipino immigration to the United States.

Although relatively few elite Filipino families were able to benefit from Spanish and then later American colonization, the bulk of the populace remained poor. Land problems, which had their genesis under Spanish colonization, continued under the Americans. The problem was especially acute in the northern part of the Philippines, in Ilocos Norte and Ilocos Sur, where there was not enough available land to support the people who lived on it. These regions have had a tradition of people leaving for other parts of the Philippines in search of better economic opportunities. This region also supplied the most immigrants to the United States during the first three decades of the twentieth century.

Despite the changes in the Philippines brought about by the American colonizers, little was done to alleviate the land problem. This was to have consequences for Filipino migration to the United States. During the period of U.S. colonial rule, Filipinos were legally considered to be "American nationals" and as such were able to enter the United States freely. Although the Philippines became formally independent from the United States in 1946, the U.S. has continued to exercise a powerful military, economic, and cultural influence on her former colony. The trade relation between the two countries has taken the colonial pattern: the Philippines providing raw materials for, and importing manufactured goods from, the United States. Until the early 1990s, the United States kept large military and naval bases in the Philippines. Moreover, English is still commonly used in public schools and the overall American cultural influence is still powerful.

Filipinos in the United States

The first recorded date of a Filipino presence in what is now the United States happened in 1587. Under the Spanish, the Philippines was an important stop of the Spanish Galleon trade between Asia and Mexico. Spanish galleons were often built in the Philippines, and crewed by Filipinos, who served as common seamen, navigators, marine officers, and boatmen. *Nuestra Senora de Esperanza,* a galleon charged with exploring the California coast, dropped anchor in what is now Morro Bay, California. A landing party, which included Filipino crewmen ("Luzon Indians," as they were called then), got into a skirmish with the local American Indians, and fled back to the ship. The galleon probably sailed away to a Spanish port in Mexico. Other Spanish ships were more successful in exploring California, and the galleon trade flourished between Manila and Acapulco and California. After sailing to "the New World," many Filipinos ended up staying, and became part of the Spanish settlement of Mexico and California (Crouchett, 1982).

Significantly, the first permanent Filipino settlements in the United States began in the late eighteenth century, long before the American involvement in the Philippines. Filipinos forced to build and crew Spanish galleons jumped ship in Mexico and Louisiana and made their way to the bayous outside New Orleans. They established settlements there as early as 1763. They built villages on stilts, and fished and shrimped for a living. These men, who often had families in New Orleans, were the first Asians to settle in what is now the U.S. (Espina, 1982; Cordova, 1983). Other early Filipino pioneers were the "war brides" of Spanish-American War and Philippine-American War veterans, who married their soldier husbands in the Philippines, and settled with them back in the United States (Cordova, 1983). Most of the early twentieth century Filipino immigration to the United States was focused on Hawai'i, the west coast, Alaska, and scattered cities throughout the midwest and the east coast.

The First Wave: Students

Filipinos did not immigrate to the United States in large numbers until the beginning of the twentieth century. The first wave of Filipinos began arriving in 1903. The Pensionado Act, passed by the U.S. Congress, provided support for young Filipinos to be sent to the United States for education about American life. The "pensionados," as they were called, matriculated in such institutions as Harvard, Stanford, Cornell, and the University of California at Berkeley. They founded Filipino student organizations, some of which are still in existence, produced Filipino newsletters, and sent glowing reports back home of the educational opportunities to be found in the United States (Cordova, 1983; Melendy, 1977). Following completion of their studies, the Pensionados returned to the Philippines to be social, political, and economic leaders. However, their pioneering efforts were continued as thousands of young Filipinos, inspired by the success stories of the Pensionados, went to the United States in search of education. Between 1910 and 1938 almost 14,000 Filipinos were enrolled as students around the United States (Crouchett, 1982).

The Second Wave: Workers

Many would-be students found the cost of education prohibitive, especially during the Depression, and thus turned instead to obtaining jobs. They, along with other young men who had come to the United States seeking employment, comprised the bulk of the second wave of Filipino immigrants. From 1905 to 1935, when the Philippines became semi-independent, there was unlimited immigration of Filipinos to the United States, since Filipinos as U.S. citizens could freely travel to the U.S. without obtaining visas. The second-wave Filipino immigrants were mostly men, the would-be students, and also laborers recruited to fill the growing cheap labor demands in Hawai'i, Alaska, and the western United States. Previously, the Chinese and Japanese had been used to fill those labor demands. The Chinese Exclusion Act of 1882 put an end to Chinese immigration, and the 1907–1908 Gentlemen's Agreement with Japan severely restricted Japanese immigration. These restrictive measures against other Asian immigrant groups created the need for a new cheap labor source, which Filipino laborers met. During this time the Philippines was experiencing growing poverty. Many peasants turned to foreign employment as a way to regain economic control over their lives.

Life in Hawai'i

Filipinos, like the other Asians in Hawai'i, immigrated to Hawai'i under the auspices of the Hawai'i Sugar Planters' Association, as contract labor for the sugar plantations. Plantation and mill workers were given three year contracts that provided transportation to Hawai'i, housing, food, fuel, and medical care. The first group of Filipino workers in Hawai'i arrived in 1906. Between the years 1906 to 1935, when Filipino immigration to Hawai'i was stopped for a decade, about 125,000 Filipinos were recruited or otherwise immigrated to the islands. The high point of such immigration occurred in 1925, when 11,621 Filipinos disembarked in Honolulu. After that year, the HSPA did not need to recruit workers; enough Filipinos were volunteering to make the trip to Hawai'i (Cordova, 1983; Kitano and Daniels, 1988; Melendy, 1977; Pido, 1986).

After their contracts expired, an estimated one third of the immigrants moved on to the mainland, one third returned to the Philippines, and the rest stayed in the territory (Cariaga, 1937). By 1940, the Filipino population in Hawai'i numbered 52,569 (Nordyke, 1989, p. 188). The community was overwhelmingly made up of single men. The conditions of the contract, restrictive immigration laws, lack of financial and other resources, and cultural reasons, compelled many Filipino women to remain in the Philippines.

Alcantara (1981) describes the motivations of some of the people who chose Hawai'i as the place to make a new life. "Caridad," one of the relatively few women who came to Hawai'i during the early years of Filipino immigration tells her story:

> My husband Mario and I grew up in the same barrio. My grandmother and my parents did not like me to marry him because he was very poor . . . We got married nonetheless and we depended on my grandmother because we did not have any land to farm. For three years Mario sought jobs around Talisay, a larger town 25 miles away, but he could find no regular job. By then we had our daughter. In 1916 he left for Davao, on the island of Mindanao, where he found a regular job as a plowboy on a Spaniard's plantation. My daughter and I joined him there. Work on that plantation was hard and Mario made barely enough to support us, so when I got pregnant again in 1918 we returned to my grandmother's house.
>
> One day in 1919 Mario rushed home to tell me we were going to Hawai'i. There was this former barrio man and he attracted a crowd because he was wearing good clothes, new shoes, and he had a gold watch on a chain. He told everybody how he got his money planting and harvesting sugar cane. There was an American with him who signed up people who wanted to go to Hawai'i.
>
> Within a month we left by truck for Cebu City and boarded the ship to Hawai'i (p. 7).

Caridad's story illustrates the willingness of the Filipinos to move to find work. In this example, her husband looked for work first in a nearby city, then on another part of the Philippines, and finally to Hawai'i.

During the peak years of Filipino immigration to Hawai'i (1909–1932) the ratio of male to female arrivals was at best 3 to 1, in 1923 and 1924, and at worst, 95 to 1, in 1927, when almost nine thousand men and fewer than 100 women arrived (Nordyke, 1989). Thus, the Filipino American second generation was relatively small, especially when compared to other ethnic groups in Hawai'i. The world of these second generation Filipinos was most often one on a plantation. Alcantara (1975b) describes this lifestyle:

> The plantation fostered ethnic competition and divisiveness through such devices as residential segregation, structural stratification by ethnicity, ethnic preferential treatment in wages, perquisites and mobility, and breaking up racial strikes by introducing other ethnic groups. In this situation, ethnic group life had a strategic importance in plantation work and was made viable through the retention of the group's traditional culture; ethnic identification was important inasmuch as the individual's fate as a worker depended on the status of his group (pp. 3–4).

Forman (1980) describes the first life goal of these immigrant Filipinos to be "neighborliness," "feeling and behaving with responsibility and good will towards one another."

Neighborliness was enhanced with the development of ethnic community organizations and family and kinship networks. Ethnic community organizations of the era included mutual aid associations, labor unions, Masonic societies, and women's groups (Okamura, 1981). According to Forman (1980), the second life goal of the Filipinos was "to establish a family of which one may be justifiably proud." This goal was made almost impossible by the handicap that most immigrants faced of having a salary too small to support a family, and by the lack of Filipino women in Hawai'i. Despite the presence of relatively few women, Filipino family and kinship networks developed that played an important role in the social calendar of the plantations (Alegado, 1991). HSPA officials wanted second-generation plantation youngsters to forego education, and instead, follow in the footsteps of their laboring parents (Daws, 1968). The inadequacy of the public school system can be ascertained by the fact that in 1930, three out of every ten Filipinos, including children, were illiterate, only three teachers in the territory were Filipino, and only 24% of the eligible 16 and 17 year old Filipinos attended school (Fuchs 1961). Nevertheless, there were some Filipinos who went through the public school system and then continued on to college. Alegado (1991) notes that the dearth of young Filipinos meant that whenever a Filipino youth graduated from college, or even high school, large celebrations commemorated the event. These and other large celebrations were important for reinforcing neighborliness, which is said to have taken the place of the Filipino alliance system of a network of family and friends (Forman, 1980).

Forman (1980) states that the third life goal for the immigrant Filipinos was "to improve one's socioeconomic condition." This, too, was all but impossible during the plantation era. The "divide and control" tactics of the HSPA, including long hours of labor for very little pay, price gouging at the plantation stores, a strict system of fines and punishments, and a myriad of other harsh working and living conditions made it extremely difficult for Filipinos and other plantation employees to improve their working and living conditions. Filipinos in Hawai'i at this time had little recourse. As "nationals" they were considered wards of the U.S. Government, and as such, complained to an American-controlled Philippine government that was impotent to help improve their conditions.

In 1919, Prudencio Remigio, member of the Philippine Assembly and Filipino Commissioner in Hawai'i, wrote a report to the Governor General and Secretary of Commerce and Communication of the Philippines. Remegio had visited 22 plantations on the islands of Oahu, Maui, and Hawai'i. At the time, most of the male Filipinos had emigrated under three-year contracts paying them either $18 or $20 for a 26-working-day month. Women were paid $12 a month under the same contracts. Remegio's report spelled out a number of complaints that the workers had regarding articles of the contracts that were not honored by the plantations, among them, issues concerning living quarters, availability of medical care, access to firewood or cooking fuel, and inability to fulfill the terms of the contract by working 26 days per month. Other complaints that the workers had concerned the inadequacy of their salaries, given the cost of living in Hawai'i, and poor treatment by the lunas. According to Remegio,

Attracted by the exaggerated propaganda of the agents with respect to better opportunities that, according to them, would be found in a foreign country, they sign contracts, accepting the conditions, without knowing in advance the circumstances in the place where they will go.

Although their hopes are raised in this manner, when they reach the destination, it turns out from rude experience, that circumstances do not permit their desires and aspirations to improve themselves to be fulfilled, and the supposed opportunities that have impelled them to leave their own country are not found. The situation becomes odious for some, forced for others, and desperate for all . . .

Besides the applications for return passage received from the different workers . . . and the constant complaints and reports from particular persons that I have received during my stay in the Hawaiian Islands, there are hundreds of workers, not to say more, who anxiously await from the Government of the Philippines a measure that can extract them from their lamentable condition (Remegio, 1919; p. 180).

The main form of fighting back against oppressive plantation conditions that the Filipinos used was through striking and unionizing. The earlier Filipino Immigrants were instrumental in the unionization of plantation workers in Hawai'i. As early as the 1910s Filipinos in Hawai'i were organizing themselves into unions. They were involved in several strikes during the 1920s and 1930s with other ethnic unions, most notably the Japanese. Labor historian Edward Beechert (1979) describes one strike,

In the 1924 strike which was just a Filipino strike, largely Visayan, the same tactic was used. This time they [HSPA] hired people to cause trouble between Visayas and Ilokanos—so they'd fight each other. All we read in books is that 16 people were killed in Kauai, in Hanapepe. They don't tell how some 4,000 Filipinos camped in Hilo for six months . . . Filipinos realized that they had to be very careful or they'd be arrested. Planters told the Board of Health, Look at the nuisance—no toilets, they're camped on the streets. But the Board of Health said, we have inspectors. Police got tired of the planters and arrested the strikers anyway—over 1000—charged with menace to public health and vagrancy. But the Filipinos held out for six months! . . . I know of no other case in American labor history where people could feel themselves and maintain the community for that length of time . . . The Filipinos had a very strong community of a kind that is not supposed to exist (pp. 13–14).

The first major success of multi-ethnic unions occurred in Kauai in 1940, by 1950 Hawai'i plantation workers were among the best paid in the world (Takaki, 1989).

Life on the West Coast and in Alaska

During the 1920s approximately 45,000 Filipinos arrived on the West Coast (Melendy, 1977). The majority of them stayed on the West Coast, although some went east to big cities like Chicago, New York, and Philadelphia. In California, Washington and Oregon Filipinos were in the unenviable position of competing with white men for jobs and women. Discriminatory laws, coupled with language barriers, and the Depression made it virtually impossible for most Filipinos to get any better jobs than in the service industries or a migrant labor. The earlier Filipino immigrants on the West Coast, like those in Hawai'i, were for the most part a bachelor society. They traveled from season to season, from one farming community to another, following crop harvests.

In the 1930s, approximately 25,000 Filipinos worked in the bread basket of California, the San Joaquin Valley. Stereotyped as good for "stoop labor," Filipinos harvested crops such as asparagus, grapes, lettuce, carrots, and beets. They were used especially in the asparagus growing industry, because it was believed they were not bothered by the peat dust in which asparagus grew. Additionally, since they were smaller than white men, it was believed that they could stoop more easily. The typical working schedule was ten hours of work each day, for 26 days, with few Sundays or holidays off (Cordova, 1984). As two men remember,

> I worked in the fields and orchards during the summer . . . when I graduated from Stockton High after completing a four year curriculum in three years, I had to turn down a scholarship to Stanford University to go to the fields to work . . . I picked hops in Elk Grove, peas in Greenfield and Salinas, grapes in Fresno, Selma, and Delano, bunched carrots and covered cantaloupe in Yuma and El Centro, and packed lettuce in Soledad, sorted potatoes on MacDonald Island, and picked tomatoes in Tracy and walnuts in Concord . . . It was hard work . . . we endured insecticide and sulfur. We migrated like birds to harvest the crops (p. 26).

> In 1932 I worked in Santa Clara, picking peas for one dollar a day, ten cents an hour. Then we had to pay 65 cents for expenses. So how much was left? Thirty-five cents . . . If you were on the farm the wages were all the same wherever you go . . . The average was then 10, 15 cents an hour during those days in the Depression. If you get 15 cents an hour, you work 10 hours and get a dollar and a half minus 75 cents for board. Then maybe you'd get 200 hours a month. Sometimes you don't have enough hours to pay your board. I used to pay during the winter. But from October November, January, February we didn't have much work. I used to owe the labor contractors sometimes 75 or 80 dollars. Until May, I'd have to pay that. Yes, that was really my life and the lives of other men who lived then. I was glad that at least we have our three meals a day (Cordova, 1984; p. 18).

Organized by labor contractors, who would negotiate contract terms with the farmers, it was difficult for the Filipino laborers to improve their abysmal working conditions. American labor unions provided no recourse. The labor unions were against immigration, and worked instead to have Filipino laborers excluded from the United States. Growers often used "divide and control" techniques to keep wages down. Different ethnic groups were used for different types of farm labor and were used to break each other's strikes. Nevertheless, Filipino laborers managed to organize themselves into unions and staged one of their first strikes in Watsonville in 1930. Although the strike was not successful, it had a major impact on the fledgling Filipino unions, providing the impetus for the 1934 successful strike against the lettuce growers of Salinas (DeWitt, 1978). Filipinos continued their legacy of striking and unionizing when they led the 1965 grape boycott that culminated in the partnership with Mexican laborers and the formation of the United Farmworkers Union.

Many of the Filipinos involved in organizing the agricultural unions were also active in organizing the unions for the Alaska cannery workers. Filipinos were a presence in Alaska canneries since 1909 (Masson and Guimary, 1981). Recruited by contract laborers in the West Coast cities, thousands of young Filipino immigrant men made the journey to Alaska to work for the short season of three months or the long season of six months. The contractor, who had negotiated with the cannery, was responsible for the workers' transportation to and from Alaska, their food, and the wages. The canneries were usually responsible only for housing the workers. Workers were often exploited by contractors. For example, in order to maximize profits for themselves, contractors often skimped on the food, feeding the workers poorly (Cordova, 1983).

Despite many difficulties stemming from in-fighting and lack of support from American unions, in 1937 Filipino cannery workers were able to organize themselves into a union that successfully bargained with canneries to improve wages and abolish the labor contractor system of cannery workers (Masson and Guimary, 1981).

Discrimination against Filipinos

Anti-Filipino sentiment was rampant on the West Coast. The history of Filipinos here followed the same pattern of the Chinese and Japanese immigrants before them; large-scale agricultural labor importation, racial discrimination in the forms of isolation and occasional exploitation, and explicit efforts at deportation and exclusion (Wallovits, 1972). Resentment over Filipino laborers' competition for jobs and white women grew as the region's economic situation worsened with the Depression. Because they were not eligible to become citizens in California, Filipinos could not own or lease land and could not obtain many professional licenses. In 1943, Filipinos were able to lease land in California, especially that vacated by interned Japanese Americans, but were still unable to own land. Filipinos faced discrimination in a number of venues, including housing, hotels, restaurants, barbers, pools, cinemas, tennis courts, and even churches (Melendy, 1977). Filipinos recall being spat upon, shoved off of sidewalks, and called racial slurs. In 1928, Filipinos were run out of the Yakima Valley in Washington. Anti-Filipino disturbances and riots were reported in other towns, among them Exeter, California, in October 1929 and Hood River and Banks, Oregon, in January 1930. The violence culminated in the 1930 riots in Watsonville, California. A mob of white vigilantes raided a dance hall leased by Filipinos and harassed Filipinos in farm labor camps. Fermin Tobera, a 22 year old laborer, was shot and killed in his bunk (Cordova, 1983, Wallovits, 1972). One incident was reported in this newspaper account,

> *Dozens of Filipinos were hurled from their beds in the Filipino Center, a Club home, early this morning when a bomb exploded on the front porch of the structure, carried away the facade and shattered windows of dwellings within a block's radius. No one was reported seriously hurt. The bomb was hurled, police said, from a speeding automobile. . . . An instant later there was a terrific detonation and the entire front of the club was literally blown to bits. Police declared the bombing an aftermatch (sic) of anti-Filipino riots and demonstrations in San Jose, Watsonville, and San Francisco ("Islanders driven out by explosion," 1930, as cited in Wallovits, 1972; p. 70).*

One man remembers how he felt during those times,

> *It shocked me there for a while because Americans didn't seem to respect us. So right away I knew what I learned in school when I was back home was not really true. The Americans would disregard us and put us down. I didn't know why. But I could tell by the way they looked at you, or sometimes when they hollered at you, you know, "Hey goo-goo" or "Look at those Filipino monkeys" and "Why don't you go back to where you came from?" That didn't really hurt my feelings very much because I thought they were just the lower class Americans. I thought that if they were really educated and were living the democratic way of life, they wouldn't say things like that. So I figured as long as they didn't physically bother me, I wasn't going to let their remarks hurt me. But it kind of demoralized my feelings for a while because they didn't respect us, as if we were trash (Cordova, 1984; p. 34).*

Carlos Bulosan, a Filipino writer, depicts a scene in a restaurant where a Filipino man, his white American wife, and their child were refused service. When the Filipino man asked the owner if he could buy a bottle of milk for his hungry child, the owner responded by pushing him outside, shouting, ". . . you goddam brown monkeys have your nerve, marrying our women. Now get out of town!" (Bulosan, 1943). Bulosan was illustrating life for the young Filipino men in the 1920s and 1930s. The majority of Filipino men at that time were bachelors ranging in age from 16 to 30. In 1930 immigrant Filipino men outnumbered Filipino women by approximately 23 to 1 (Empeno, 1976). California was just one of the many states prohibiting marriages between white Americans and "unassimilable aliens." California's anti-miscegenation law had been in existence since 1901. "Negroes, mulattos, and Mongolians" were not allowed to marry whites according to California Civil Codes. Interpretation of the law, however, was often up to the county clerk who issued marriage license. Generally, Filipinos were considered to be "Mongolians." In 1933 the court case of Roldan vs. Los Angeles County was heard before the California Supreme Court. The Court ruled that immigrant and American-born Filipinos were considered members of the "Malay" race and were thus eligible to marry whites. However, the California legislature quickly changed the civil code to include persons of the "Malay" race in the list of those groups whose members could not marry whites. Other states, including Nevada, Oregon, and Washington, followed the suit. California's anti-miscegenation law was ruled unconstitutional in 1948 (Cordova, 1983; Empeno, 1976; Melendy, 1977). It took another two decades before anti-miscegenation laws in other states were ruled unconstitutional.

As early as 1927, Congressman Welch and Senator Johnson, both from California, had tried to get legislation passed in Congress declaring Filipinos eligible for immigration exclusion. They were supported by local and national "patriotic" societies such as the Immigration Restriction League, and organizations such as the American Legion, Native Sons of the Golden West, and the American Federation of Labor (Wallovits, 1972). The secretary of another exclusion organization, the California joint Immigration Committee stated,

> It has been shown that continued Filipino immigration to the United States is unwise for both peoples; that Filipinos themselves concede to it; that in addition to unassimilibility, absence of women adds a danger to the Filipino situation; that immediate remedy must be applied if conflict in California is to be avoided . . . This situation is acknowledged that no effective remedy has been suggested by either party except (1) independence, which would convert Filipinos into aliens and automatically bar them as immigrants, and (2) an exclusion measure . . . Restriction of immigration is the only effective plan since the situation demands immediate remedy . . . California in this matter is seeking to protect the nation, as well as itself, against the peaceful penetration of another colored race (Wallovits, 1972; p. 6).

Opposition for the Filipino exclusion movement came from Filipinos themselves and the farmers who depended upon them for labor. One farm manager stated,

> There are some complaints about Mexicans and Filipinos taking work away from the white men, but these complaints are practically without foundation in fact, for the white or American laborers will not do this class of work . . . The fact is that instead of taking work away from American laborers, the Mexicans and Filipinos actually create work for them (Wallovits, 1972; p. 41).

Despite vocal opposition to the exclusion movement, the exclusionists prevailed in 1934 when Congress passed the Tydings-McDuffie Act. In this Act the Philippines was granted commonwealth status and the immigration of Filipinos to the United States was restricted to 50 persons a year. The "American nationals" suddenly became "aliens" ineligible for federal assistance and many jobs (Manzon, 1938). The Filipino Repatriation Act, passed in 1935, provided Filipino immigrants with free transportation back to the Philippines (Mozon, 1938). However, once back in the Philippines the returnee would only be able to return back to the United States under the 50 per year quota. It is estimated that only about 2,200 Filipinos returned to the Philippines under the terms of this act, and it was acknowledged to have been a failure (Melendy, 1977, Wallovits, 1972). During the World War II years immigration was suspended for all but the Filipinos serving in the U.S. Armed Forces.

Loyal Americans: The First and Second Filipino Infantry Regiments, U.S. Army

A turning point for the Filipino American population was the bombing of Pearl Harbor and the entry of the United States into World War Two. At the start of the war, immigrant Filipinos were denied entry into the American Armed Forces, because they were aliens ineligible for citizenship." Within a few weeks, however, Washington authorized creation of the "First Filipino Infantry Battalion," whose troops would comprise Filipinos in the United States. The "First Battalion" saw so many volunteers that it was upgraded to the "First Filipino Infantry Regiment," on July 13, 1942. The influx of volunteers continued, and the "Second Filipino Infantry Regiment" was formed a few months later. At top strength, the regiments contained more than 7,000 men. This number is quite significant, given that the total Filipino American population has been estimated to be about 100,000 in 1940.

Most of the regiment comprised immigrant Filipinos, the men who had traveled to America in the 1920s and 1930s, relegated to manual field labor or canneries or, in the cities, service occupations. These men were usually in their 30s, much older than the usual Army recruit. Many joined for altruistic reasons; to fight for the adopted country, and to help free the homeland, which was invaded by the Japanese. Still, for others, joining up was a combination of altruism and realism; few good jobs were available for Filipinos in the 1940s, although the situation improved with the war economy. However, part of the regiment was made up of young men from Hawai'i, second-generation Filipino Americans.

The Regiments underwent basic training in California. During basic training hundreds of men volunteered for specialized units and missions, so that the strength of the units were always in flux. One thousand of these volunteers became members of the specially formed First Reconnaissance Battalion, which became Commanding General Douglas MacArthur's "eyes and ears" in the Philippines and gathered the intelligence that paved the way for the American re-invasion of the Philippines in October 1944. The First Filipino Infantry went overseas in April 1944. Their first stop was New Guinea, where they continued advanced combat training. Some of the men became members of the initial wave of American re-invasion forces and landed at Leyte Gulf with General MacArthur. The bulk of the troops finally landed in the Philippines in February 1945. Their main mission was to eliminate the remaining Japanese troops in the islands, otherwise known as "mopping up the enemy." Because of the unique abilities of the men, including familiarity with the terrain and the ability to speak Philippine languages, throughout the duration of the war the regiments supplied personnel for other units. After the war, most of the men stayed in the Philippines for more than half a year before returning to the United States. The regiments were disbanded a few months after the war's end. They made their mark in the Filipino American community in many ways. In 1943 when Congress allowed Filipinos serving the U.S. Armed Forces to become citizens, 1200 men of the Regiments were naturalized in one ceremony, the largest group of Asians ever to become American citizens. Eventually, more than half of the regiments became citizens. Their heroism, and that of the Filipino soldiers in the Philippines during the war helped change American attitudes toward Filipinos for the better and provided the impetus for the 1946 Act which enabled all eligible Filipino immigrants the right to American citizenship. Many of the veterans married "war brides" in the Philippines, and brought them back home, creating for the first time a large community of Filipino American families. Finally, the veterans took advantage of the G.I. Bill, went to college, and became business and community leaders. The First and Second Filipino Infantry Regiments were the catalyst for change in the Filipino American community. As one veteran eloquently describes, "serving in the regiments was our emancipation" (Cordova, 1982; Fabros, 1993; Markrich, Revilla, & Castillo, 1995).

Contemporary Issues

In 1946, when the Philippines gained independence, the immigration quota was doubled to allow 100 persons a year to immigrate. Finally, with the passage of the Immigration and Naturalization Act in 1965, Filipino immigration accelerated. Besides the descendants of the Louisiana settlers, there exist four sizable generational groups of Filipinos in the United States, the first generation of early immigrants, their second and third-generations, and the new wave of the post-1965 immigrants.

Since the passage of the 1965 Immigration and Naturalization Act, Filipino immigration has rapidly increased. Since the late 1980s more than 50,000 Filipinos have been annually admitted to the United States as formal immigrants. The Philippines has sent more immigrants to the United States than any other Asian country over the two decades and has been the second largest source country of U.S. immigrants next to Mexico.

Post-1965 Asian immigrants consist largely of the urban, middle-class segment of the Asian population. This urban, middle-class background of Asian immigrants may be most conspicuous among Filipino immigrants. The high socioeconomic background of the Filipino immigrants in the 1970s can be explained by the fact that a large proportion of them were professionals, particularly medical professionals such as nurses, physicians, surgeons, and pharmacists. The Philippines sent more professional immigrants to the United States in the late 1960s and the early 1970s than any other country in the world. The departure of well-educated Filipino professionals is a brain drain from the Philippines, which is a concern for researchers and policy makers (Minocha, 1987). However, due to revisions of the 1965 Immigration Act, the vast majority of the post-1976 immigrants have come to the United States based on family unification. Filipino immigrants admitted through family unification categories are likely to represent lower socioeconomic status than the earlier occupational preference immigrants.

Despite the high educational achievements of many new Filipino immigrants, Filipino Americans today are often "under employed," that is, *in* an occupation that does not fully utilize their educational background. Additionally, Filipinos are usually found in the "secondary labor market," where the pay is low and opportunities for advancement is limited (Cabezas, Shinagawa, & Kawaguchi, 1986–87). Filipinas, like other women of color, face a "glass ceiling," which limits their opportunities to advance to management positions. A recent newspaper article quotes Filipinas describing their work experiences. One Filipina remarks on the changes she has seen regarding racism in the workplace.

> *The only change I saw as far as racism is that it's a little more clever now. It's not like you walk into an office and people are flinging racial epithets at you. It's more a kind of tension you may have when dealing with some people ("Multicolored glass ceiling," 1993; p. E1).*

Filipinas are encouraged to attend workshops for women that address workplace issues that identify barriers to advancement and strategies for overcoming those barriers.

Filipinos in the United States are sometimes victims of "accent discrimination." A well documented case was that of Manuel Fragrante, in Honolulu, Hawai'i. As Enriquez (1994) comments,

> *A most curious form of denigration has to do with the notion that 'Filipinos have an accent.' The truth is, everyone speaks with an accent characteristic of his ethnic background, whether Chinese, Japanese or Indian. American accent varies from the Northeastern seaboard, the deep South, the Midwest and the West Coast. Meanwhile, French accent is perceived as 'charming' or 'sophisticated.' What makes Filipino accent any different begs for a theory. In the Fragrante case, a Filipino in Hawai'i was denied a job because of his accent even though the job does not involve dealing with the public. Never mind if he topped the examination given to all applicants for the position (p. 15).*

Filipinos have been making headlines by challenging "English only" policies at the workplace ("Racism and English," 1989). For example, in January 1990 Harborview Medical Center in Seattle, Washington implemented a policy dictating that English should be the only language used for business purposes with the General Accounting Department. Disciplinary actions for violating the policy could have included job termination. The policy was aimed primarily at seven Filipino workers in the Accounting Department. The Filipino workers filed a grievance that was supported by union representatives and the local community. Eventually, the policy was rescinded ("English-only policy," 1990). Unfortunately, however, many more "English only" policies in the workplace still remain intact.

Regarding education, Azores (1986–87) found that as many as 25% of young Filipino Americans drop out of high school in California. Those who do stay in school and aspire to a college education are often unable to attain that goal. Filipino Americans who attend college also have high drop rates. At the University of Washington in Seattle, Filipino American undergraduate students have one of the highest attrition rates, similar to African American and Hispanic students (Judal, 1992). Data from the University of California, Los Angeles (Office of Budget, 1987) shows that Filipino Americans have a graduation rate of only 40%, much lower than those of other Asian groups. Almirol (1988) notes that in Autumn 1985 only 0.6% of the master's students in the U.C. system were Filipino Americans.

A recent report on Filipinos in Hawai'i emphasizes the education and employment issues that are representative of the Filipino American community as a whole. In Hawai'i, where Filipinos represent 15.2% of the population, according to the 1990 Census,

> *Filipinos represent 18% of Department of Education pupils, less than 5% of teachers, less than 4% of principals/vice principals, 13.5% of educational assistants, and 23% of general laborers and custodians. At the University of Hawai'i [system], Filipinos comprise 14% of 1993 enrollment. Seventy percent of Filipinos within the University of Hawai'i system are in community colleges and only 219 are in graduate programs. There are very few Filipino faculty members (Weygan-Hildebrand, 1995; p. i).*

Relatively few studies focusing on Filipinos in education have been conducted. Thus it is difficult to explain why Filipinos are not doing as well as other Asian American counterparts in education. In general, reasons for this lack of success in employment and education may range from culture shock to racism (Flores, 1994; Kitano & Daniels, 1988

Conclusion

The Filipino American experience is unique. It is a history of colonization in the Philippines and racism in the United States. Filipinos encountered the same pattern of race relations that other Asian immigrant groups experienced in the U.S.: first, welcomed and even recruited for their labor, then being victimized as "unassimilable aliens," isolated from mainstream America, and finally excluded from further immigration. What is different about Filipinos from the other Asians is that Filipinos were American 'nationals," taught back home in the Philippines about the American ideals of freedom and democracy, but in reality being treated as second-class citizens in the U.S. World War Two marked the beginning of change for the Filipino American community in terms of social and economic issues. The 1965 Immigration Act transformed the Filipino American community from one of old-timer bachelors and baby boom families, to one with many Philippine-born highly educated professionals and their families. Despite these changes, Filipinos somehow remain "forgotten" Asian Americans, their successes and problems unknown, under researched, and ignored. It remains to be seen whether the number of immigrants from the Philippines will continue to seek out the American dream at the current high levels annually. If so, Filipinos should be the largest Asian American group by the turn of the century.

References

Alcantara, R. (1975a). *A guided study course—American subcultures; Filipino Americans.* Honolulu: University of Hawai'i.

Alcantara, R. (1975b). Ethnic identity: The Asians in Hawai'i. Unpublished manuscript, University of Hawai'i, Hamilton Library, Honolulu.

Alcantara, R. (1981). *Sakada: Filipino adaptation in Hawai'i.* Washington, D.C.: University Press of America.

Alegado, D. (1991). The Filipino community in Hawai'i: Development and change. *Social Process, 33,* 12–38.

Alegado, D. (1992). Philippine chronology up to 1946. In B. Aquino & D. Alegado (Eds.), *The Age of Discovery: Impact on Philippine culture and society (2nd ed).* Honolulu, HI: Center for Philippine Studies, University of Hawai'i at Manoa.

Almmirol, E. B. (1988). Exclusion and institutional barriers in the university system; the Filipino experience. In G. Okihiro, S. Hune, A. Hansen, and J. Liu (Eds.), *Reflections on shattered windows: promises and prospects for Asian American Studies* (pp. 59–67). Pullman, WA: Washington State University.

Aquino, B. (1992). Rethinking Magellan and rediscovering the Philippines. In B. Aquino & D. Alegado (Eds.), *The Age of Discovery: Impact on Philippine culture and society (2nd ed).* Honolulu, HI: Center for Philippine Studies, University of Hawai'i at Manoa.

Azores, T. (1986–87). Educational attainment and upward mobility: prospects for Filipino Americans. *Amerasia Journal,* 13, 39–52.

Beechen, E. (1979). Humanist in "Changing stereotypes of the Filipino worker in Hawai'i." In T. Hernandez (Ed.). *Sadinno To Papanam? Proceedings.* Honolulu: Hawai'i Committee for the Humanities.

Bulosan, C. (1943). *America Is in the Heart* (pp. 144–145). Seattle: University of Washington Press.

Cabezas, A., Shinagawa, L., & Kawaguchi, G. (1986–87). New inquiries into the socioeconomic status of Pilipino Americans in California. *Amerasia Journal,* 13, 1–21.

Cariaga, R. (1937). *The Filipinos in Hawai'i.* Honolulu, HI: Filipino Public Relations Bureau.

Cordova, F. *(1983). Filipinos: Forgotten Asian Americans* (pp. 1–8, 22–115, 123–134). Dubuque, IA: Kendall/Hunt Publishing Company.

Cordova, J. (ed.) (1984). *Voices: A Filipino American oral history.* Stockton, CA: Filipino Oral History Project, Inc.

Crouchett, L. (1982). *Filipinos in California: From the days of the galleons to the present.* El Cerrito, CA: Downy Place.

Daws, G. (1968). *Shoal of time.* Honolulu, HI: University of Hawai'i.

DeWitt, H. (1978). The Filipino labor union: The Salinas lettuce strike of 1934. *Amerasia Journal,* 5, 1–21.

Domingo-Kirk, C. (1994) Victim's discourses: Filipina domestic workers in Germany. *Journal of the American Association for Philippine Psychology,* 1, 24–36.

Empeno, H. (1976). Anti-miscegenation laws and the Pilipino. In J. Quinsaat (Ed.), *Letters in exile: An introductory reader on the history of Pilipinos in America* (pp. 63–71). Los Angeles: UCLA Asian American Studies Center. "English-only policy at Harboview withdrawn." (1990, April 4). *International Examiner*, p. 1.

Enriquez, V. (1994) Indigenous psychology: From traditional indigenous concepts to modern psychological practice. *Journal of the American Association for Philippine Psychology, 1*, 4–23.

Espina, M. (1982). *Readings on Filipinos in Louisina.* An Unpublished Manuscript.

Fabros, A., Jr. (1993). *In honor of our fathers: The Filipino American Experience in World War II Research Project.* Fresno, CA: 'R Kids Kollege Fund.

Flores, P. (1994). The Philippine American youth between two expectations; Filipino and U.S. parenting standards. *Journal of the American Association for Philippine Psychology, 1*, 55–68.

Forman, S. (1980). Hawai'i's immigrants from the Philippines. In J. McDermott, W. Tseng, & T. Maretzki (Eds), *People and cultures of Hawai'i: A psychological profile* (pp. 163–178). Honolulu, HI: John A. Burns School of Medicine and University of Hawai'i.

Francisco, L. (1976). The first Vietnam: The Philippine-American war, 1899–1902. In J. Quinsaat (Ed.), *Letters in exile: An introductory reader on the history of Pilipinos in America* (pp. 1–22). Los Angeles: UCLA Asian American Studies Center.

Fuchs, L. (1961). *Hawai'i Pono. A social history.* New York: Harcourt, Brace, and World.

"Islanders driven out by explosion." (1930, January 29). *Oakland Tribune.*

Judal, D. (1992). Conversation between Ms. Judal, a University of Washington Educational Opportunity counselor, and the author.

Karnow, S. (1989). *In our image: America's empire in the Philippines.* (pp. 3–116). New York: Random House.

Kitano, H. and Daniels R. (1988). *Asian Americans: Emerging minorities.* Englewood Cliffs, NJ: Prentice Hall.

Manzon, M. (1938). *The strange case of the Filipinos in the United States.* New York: American Committee for Protection of the Foreign Born.

Markrich, M., Revilla, L., & Castillo, S. (1995). *An untold triumph: America's Filipino soldiers.* Documentary preview videotape. Honolulu, HI.

Masson, J. and D. Guimary. (1981). Pilipinos and unionization of the Alaskan canned salmon industry. *Amerasia Journal, 8*, 1–30.

Melendy, H. (1977). *Asians in America: Filipinos, Koreans, and East Indians* (pp. 17–108). Boston: Twayne.

Minocha, U. (1987). South Asian immigrants: trends and impacts on the sending and receiving societies. In James Fawcett and Benjamin Cariao (Eds.), *Pacific bridges: The new immigration from Asian and Pacific Islands* (pp. 347–376). Staten Island Center for Migration Studies.

"Multicolored glass ceiling." (1993, September 12). *San Francisco Chronicle*, pp. El, E4.

Nordyke, E. (1989). *The peopling of Hawai'i* (2nd ed.). Honolulu: University of Hawai'i.

Office of Budget, Institutional Planning, and Analysis, UCLA. (1987, November 12). Retention and graduation rates of entering cohorts. Unpublished report.

Okamura, J. (1981). Filipino organizations. In Hawai'i Filipino News (Eds.), *The Filipinos in Hawaii: The first 75 years. 1906-1981.* Honolulu: Hawai'i Filipino News Speciality Publications.

Pido, A. (1986). *The Pilipinos in America: Macro/micro dimensions of immigration and integration* (pp. 23-24). Staten Island: Center for Migration Studies.

"Racism and English only in Ramona." (1989, November 19). *Pacific Ties,* p. 21.

Remegio, P. (1919). "Report of the Filipino Commissioner in Hawai'i to His Excellency, the Governor General and the Honorable Secretary of Commerce and Communication, Government of the Philippine Islands." Honolulu: Filipino Historical Society of Hawai'i, reprinted 1982 (Translated from Spanish by Edgar C. Knowlton).

Strobel, L. (1994) The cultural identity of third-wave Filipino Americans. *Journal of the American Association for Philippine Psychology,* 1, 37-54.

Takaki, R. (1989). *Strangers from a different shore: A history of Asian Americans* (pp. 132-176, 315-354). Boston: Little, Brown and Company.

Van Niel, R. (1992). The Philippines before 1521 A.D. In B. Aquino & D. Alegado (Eds.), *The Age of Discovery: impact on Philippine culture and society* (2nd ed.). Honolulu, HI: Center for Philippine Studies, University of Hawai'i at Manoa.

Wallovits, S. (1972). *Filipinos in California.* San Francisco: R & E Research Associates.

Weygan-Hildebrand, C. (1995). *A snapshot about Filipinos in Hawai'i.* Honolulu: Hawai'i Community Foundation.

Portions of this article appeared, in "Filipino Americans" by Pauline Agbayani-Siewert and Linda A. Revilla, in P. Min (Ed.) (1995). *Asian Americans: Contemporary Trends and Issues,* Thousand Oaks, CA: Sage. Acknowledgments to Greg Mark, Bryan Man, and Maria Pangilinan.

Questions

1. Compare and contrast important laws and policies that have impacted the Native American population in the United States.

2. How do Robinson and Sitkoff describe forms of resistance and the struggle for Black equality?

3. What is the relationship between the Treaty of Guadalupe Hidalgo and the rise of a Mexican American identity?

4. In what specific ways have U.S. immigration laws shaped the Asian American experience?

5. What conclusions have you drawn from these readings in history? Is it possible to construct a racial justice agenda that incorporates lessons from the past? What would it look like?

SECTION THREE

Resistance, Discontent and . . .

Introduction

An important part of our study is an attempt to analyze the rebellions of colonized people, the overt, covert, and everyday articulation of discontent, the ways in which people have attempted to overcome systems of exploitation and subordination. The last section of this book brought together a group of readings that generally described events, characters, and conflicts in history. In this section, we are concerned with the various ways in which people move from being victims to agents for change. Resistance has had many faces. The national independence movements of the 1960s were often expressed in terms of self-determination: the essential democratic demand that a free people must be able to control their own political and economic systems. But the break with the old colonial structures also called into question the cultural underpinnings of the colonial relationship. Whose stories would be privileged? Was there a master language? By what standard were cultures found to be barbaric or sophisticated, infantile or civilized? The first selection, Howard Winant's *Durban,* discusses the significance of the U.N.-sponsored World Conference Against Racism in the shadow of the World Trade Center Tragedy in September, 2001. Although the Bush administration deflected the questions raised at Durban, a growing international movement for racial justice is challenging the position of the U.S. The conference urged the recognition of the connection between sex/gender and race in its analysis of poverty, AIDs, and the trafficking in women and children. Winant suggests that the fact of a "diasporic world" can be the basis for undermining authoritarian and religious fundamentalism wherever it appears. As an alternative, he offers the recognition of global interdependence, debt relief, and "antiracism as practice" as central features of a radical democratic agenda that can move people beyond a vague and perpetual war against terror.

In *Science and the Oral Tradition*, Vine DeLoria challenges students to think outside the mechanistic "objectivity" of western culture. He asks students to resist western arrangements of truth and acknowledge the rich meanings found in the oral tradition.

Understanding resistance requires students to look beneath standard forms of organization to see the terrain and political struggles of everyday life. Robin Kelly's *Writing Black Working Class History* describes this "infrapolitics" as an underexamined fabric of cultural conflicts. It is a politic that does not rest upon unions, coalitions, or charismatic leaders. In his analysis, music, hairstyles, and language are examples of contested sites of power where people produce their own politics of resistance. For Kelly, cultural rebellion should not be seen as simple false consciousness or immaturity, but instead as a possible diagnostic tool for evaluating power relations in society. In *Logic of Black Urban Rebellions*, Daryl B. Harris rejects the position that black violence should be understood simplistically in terms of criminality or "riff raff" theory. Instead, he situates these rebellions within a larger tradition of freedom struggles.

In *Warriors for Gringostroika*, Guillermo Gomez Pena discusses how traditional forms of cultural domination are being undermined by the energy and vitality of border culture. For Gomez Pena, the border represents an evolving fusion of languages, histories, and cosmologies that are melting traditional notions of authentic and high culture. Deborah Woo's *Inventing and Reinventing the Model Minority* considers some of the factors that encourage the public to associate Asian Americans with success. To better understand the concept of the model minority is to disaggregate census data, recognize media distortions, and acknowledge the reality of more recent highly educated immigrants. Woo also suggests that explaining success as a product of culture is both simplistic and problematic. The popular emphasis on "rags to riches" myths and model minorities may in fact serve as an entertaining distraction from structural problems in the U.S. economy.

19

Durban, Globalization, and the World After 9/11: Toward a New Politics

Howard Winant

The UN World Conference Against Racism was a very American event. About 40% of the delegates accredited to the NGO forum were North American; at Durban, one had the constant experience of running into old movement comrades and friends, as well as seeing a new and younger generation of U.S. activists coming together.

The WCAR was American in another way, too: It was anti-American. Just as the first two WCARs (1978 and 1983) were focused on anathematizing and ending the South African apartheid regime, the 2001 Durban conference sought to challenge the U.S. empire, the hegemonic position the U.S. occupies in a post-colonial, post-Cold War, post-apartheid and post-civil rights world.

Of course, the U.S. government was well aware of this situation. The ostensibly pro-civil rights Clinton Administration coquetted with the conference throughout its planning stages, worrying about the oppositional and activist orientation being developed in its various "Prepcoms" and NGO statements, but at the same time hoping to moderate and coopt the conference, to secure a role for the U.S. as a reform-oriented official participant. Aware of the malign implications of turning their back on the conference, especially among their already estranged domestic constituents on the Democratic Party's left, the Clintonites were unwilling entirely to repudiate the conference. That task was left to the Bush Administration, whose domestic political priorities were the converse of Clinton's. Bush was a creature of the Republican right, a Southern president (in the U.S. sense of the word), a usurper who owed his office in large part to anti-black voting rights fraud. He sought by attacking the conference to shore up his key lower-strata "socially conservative" constituencies—for he had already assured the loyalty of the corporate fat cats by enacting massive regressive income and wealth redistribution. Disowning the conference had an extra benefit for the Bushies, too: it provided a "wedge issue" to divide two key Democratic Party constituencies, blacks and Jews.

Then came September 11, and Durban was swept into the dustbin of history. What had seemed to us—the NGO delegates—such a crucial event was now yesterday's news, if people could remember it at all. A massive world crisis will do that to you.

And indeed, the 9/11 event was a rupture in U.S. politics and world politics. The actual assaults—horrifying and tragic as they were—were not themselves the source of such dramatic political shifts. Rather, the U.S. government's response to the attacks, the reactionary counteroffensive that Bush and his minions have undertaken against civil society both within the U.S. and against a range of perceived and real enemies around the world, was decisive in kicking off the political crisis that democratic and egalitarian social movements now face. The emergency conditions confronting our movements derive from several sources:

- The widespread fear of "terrorism," a panicky response that the Bush regime has effectively abetted and cultivated, much as its right-wing progenitors fomented anti-communist hysteria in the Cold War years (and before that in the 1920s as well);
- A resurgent reactionary nationalism that continues to garner widespread popular adherence by drawing on familiar old tropes: "fortress America," "the land of the free and the home of the brave," the emergency measures necessitated by "wartime," etc.;
- A racially-based identification of "the enemy" as Arab or Arab-American, Muslims in general (even those, whether Muslim or not, who resemble Arabs), and beyond this, the incipient demonization of the Islamic world, which hints at a series of very old scores: the Crusades, the "clash of civilizations," the Reconquista, etc. A thus far minor but interesting wrinkle in this ideological complex is the Bush Administration's selective cooptation of feminist criticism of the repression of women in some (but certainly not all) fundamentalist Islamic regimes.

As a result of these developments, we confront a very disturbing political situation: the near-paralysis of oppositional politics. The movements that seemed renascent before 9/11—notably the anti-globalization, anti-WTO movement and the resurgent anti-racist movement represented by Durban, by reparations initiatives, by resistance to racial profiling, and by critiques of the prison-industrial complex—have now been put on hold. Though not completely stymied, they have been set back considerably. Denying this is whistling in the dark.

Current support for the Bush regime is driven by two factors: the sense of crisis and the failure of any credible political alternative. Rather than sinking into the slough of despond, we should be working on developing a movement-oriented explanation of the present situation. In the absence of mass opposition, ideas really count. In fact, if there were available to us a radical democratic, anti-racist, anti-apocalyptic alternative account—alternative to the standard rhetoric of the "A Nation Challenged" sort, I mean—the apparent "common-sense" of much of the Bushies' rhetoric would be much easier to challenge.

So here are some contributions toward that alternative political stance. I hope that these ideas, in concert with those of many other radical activists and intellectuals, will help reinvigorate the movement we so desperately need.

Radical Globalism In the era of the internet, of diaspora, of AIDS and resurgent tuberculosis, of tidal waves of migration, globalization is not the domain only of corporations and capital; it is also a popular domain. Exclusivist concepts of citizenship are over. "Fortress" America (or Fortress Europe, or Fortress anywhere else) is an unworkable and repressive political construct. Interdependence should be recognized as a potential source of strength, not weakness. Ethnoglobality has replaced ethnonationality. Huge expatriate and post-colonial populations in the world's North represent a tremendous resource for development and democratization, if they can be afforded full citizenship rights, not demonized and super-exploited. Already private remittances from "developed" countries to poor ones constitute a major source of "foreign aid," totalling about $75 billion/year.

Greed Kills One message of both Durban and 9/11 is that the world's North, for its own security, needs to terminate its ceaseless exploitation of the global South. The consumerism of "McWorld" is built on a planetary sweatshop. The global "debt trap" now engulfs not only impoverished nations, but fairly developed ones like Argentina, Mexico and South Korea. African debt/GNP ratios have reached the obscene level of 125 %, and debt service in many Southern countries amounts to more than 50% of state revenue per year. Assaults on the world's poor via the global financial system—notably, the debt and its policing by the IMF through "structural adjustment policies"—result in the deaths of tens of millions every year. This can readily be understood in terms of racism and terrorism: The world's poor are largely peasants and super-exploited workers, dark-skinned sharecroppers and peons of a global corporate plantation. Transnational Simon Legrees now seek to sell their Southern darkies the water they drink, the crops they have traditionally planted and harvested, and the weapons their corrupt governments will use to kill the peons of bordering countries. Health care or AIDS medicines for these subhumans? Not unless they can pay our fees at the country club!

Colonialism Is Not Over The European colonial powers could not sustain their empires after WW II, a fact they sometimes had to be taught the hard way, through armed revolutions. But they learned by the 1960s that indirect rule works better than explicit empire anyway. Setting up spheres of influence throughout the now-"independent" global South allowed for a level of pillage and depredation unimaginable during the bad old days of overt colonialism. After WWII, the U.S. became the chief neocolonialist power, carrying on its decades-long schizophrenia about whether it was more properly the "big stick" imperialist or the isolationist avoider of "foreign entanglements." Defeat in Vietnam and the regime's subsequent difficulty in mounting interventions (the so-called "Vietnam syndrome") show that this conflict continues in our own day, although after 9/11 and the Afghanistan triumphs, the "Vietnam syndrome" may well be dead: further cause for worry.

Proxy colonialism also should be mentioned, notably in the Middle East, where Israel operates as the favorite U.S. gendarme. Israel seems to have decided that this is the proper moment for an all-out war with the Palestinians, and Bush seems to have signed on. At Durban, I thought, laudable condemnation of Israeli colonialism was vitiated by real anti-semitism. That the Bushies used this as a poor excuse for leaving the conference doesn't mean that it wasn't a real problem.

Racism and Anti-Racism as Practice In a recent book (*The World Is a Ghetto: Race and Democracy Since World War II*), I have argued that racism must be understood in terms of its consequences, not as a matter of intentions or beliefs. Today, racism has been largely—though not entirely, to be sure—detached from its perpetrators. In its most advanced forms, indeed, it has no perpetrators; it is a nearly invisible, taken-for-granted, "common-sense" feature of everyday life and global social structure. This is the situation that allows U.S. courts and mainstream political discourse to overturn affirmative action, to proclaim the U.S. a "color-blind" society, etc. But if we define racism as *the routinized outcome of practices that create or reproduce hierarchical social structures based on essentialized racial categories,* then we can see better how it extends from the transnational to the national to the experiential and personal, from the global debt burden to racial profiling, from Negrophobia to Islamophobia. Racism is a deeply entrenched social structure, largely congruent with the rise of capitalism, the rise of democracy (for some), and the triumph of Enlightenment concepts of identity and culture.

Since racism is so large, combating it must also be a large-scale practice. The reparations idea provides a valuable guidepost here. Reparation means repair, making whole, making good what was evil. As a sociopolitical project, reparations can be seen to extend from the large to the small, from the institutional to the personal. Clearly, abolishing the debt (not "forgiving," for who is to forgive and who is to be forgiven?) fits within the reparations logic, as does affirmative action.

Redistribution fits as well, but here we must be careful: The politics of income and wealth distribution are "double-entry" bookkeeping items. Not only the allocation of resources is involved, but also the derivation of revenues. Thinking about the problem on the U.S. (national) level, for example: If reparations were to be paid for the crime against humanity (an important point from Durban) that was African slavery, it would be important to look at both the inflow and the outflow side of the process. On the outflow side, reparations should take the form of social investment (for example, a "Marshall Plan for the cities" or something similar). Payments to individuals or families would be problematic: Slavery was far more centrally a collective wrong than an individual depredation. Its historical outcome in structural racism is the main evil we want to annul, and the negative effects of past slavery for present-day individuals are hard to assess. On the inflow side, there is a danger that reparations would be paid out of general revenues, unduly assessing present-day working people for the crimes of past colonialists and elites, perpetuating rather than attenuating racial conflicts, and allowing new variants of the "color-blind" argument to loom up in the future. An alternative revenue-oriented strategy would raise the money by means of a wealth tax, thus recognizing how many present-day capital hoards had their origins in slavery. Insurance companies indemnified slaveowners if their slaves escaped or shipbound Africans revolted, for example. British slaveowners were compensated for their "losses" in 1833 when Parliament abolished slavery, and North American slavocrats regained their autarchic local autonomy in the "Compromise" (which Du Bois called a counterrevolution) of 1877.

Beyond reparations, anti-racist practice can be understood macro-politically in terms of social citizenship and micro-politically in terms of acculturation and socialization. Very briefly, the concept of *social citizenship* was proposed by T. H. Marshall as the obligation of the post-WWII welfare state, the proximate stage in the achievement of popular sovereignty. Rights, Marshall argued, had been acquired by the populace in stages: first economic, then political. The time had now come for the achievement of social rights. Of course, this formulation was offered when the British flag still flew over Lagos and Singapore and Jim Crow still flourished in the U.S.; it was proposed when postmodern criticism of the limits of "rights talk" (in critical race theory, for example) had not yet been made; and it certainly did not encompass the diasporic and globalized issues anti-racists face today. Yet we can make use of it to think of political inclusion, social provision, even world citizenship.

By *acculturation and socialization* I mean the reawakening of the 1960s concept that "the personal is political" as a key principle of anti-racist personal practice. No one—no matter what their racial identity is—can be free of racism in their heads or hearts; as I have said, it is too deeply ingrained a social structure. Yet a great deal of thought and action has been devoted to the problem of fostering anti-racist practice at the individual and experiential level. Developing these skills, fostering the interruption and interrogation of racism, and extending its reach in family, school and cultural work, is an important dimension of the practice we want to foster.

Democracy Is Inseparable from Pluralism Both Durban and the current world crisis (of 9/11, globalization, and the Afghan war) teach us once again that hegemony is inherently unstable and conflictual. But they also demonstrate that embattled hegemonies demonize their oppositions. The standard practice here is to rely upon racial and religious differences to unify supporters and stigmatize critics: You're either with us or against us, a loyal subject or a "terrorist." These tactics remain effective, especially during "wartime," but they are also newly vulnerable to internal divisions. The diasporic world, the many millions of post-colonial immigrants now in the Northern countries, and the legacy of anti-racist and civil rights movements, all potentially undermine such authoritarian appeals. The dimension of religious pluralism is especially important now. Why? Because racial and religious profiling are converging. Because Islamophobia is threatening to polarize the globe once again, this time in a nuclear age. And because religious fundamentalism—North and South, East and West—is itself a direct threat to democracy.

The Body Is the Person The body was a key topic at Durban, because racial identity is always about the body. At Durban, there was discussion about enslavement (ownership of one's body by another) past and present, about trafficking in women's and children's (particularly girls') bodies, AIDS and other diseases as racial phenomena, and about the multiform linkages between sex/gender and race. It is not news that racism derives much of its energy from sexism, from the efforts of men to possess and control women's bodies. Nor is it surprising that authoritarian and anti-democratic rule takes women as its first hostages. Whether traditional or modern, whether religious or corporate, whether opposing the burqua, demanding the right to abortion, or resisting the maquilas and sweatshops that dot the globe, a central thread of democratic movements—anti-racist, anti-globalization and anti-authoritarian—is the liberation of women. The right of all human beings to control over their own bodies is a fundamental democratic demand.

In Lieu of a Conclusion These are only tentative thoughts on the enormous challenge we—our movement, our radical democratic commitments—face in the post-Durban, and especially post-9/11, era. But this work will continue; it is part of a larger project. Numerous activists and writers are struggling with these issues. Not through any one set of ideas, but through the aggregation and synthesis of many efforts to make sense of the current crisis, will we advance toward a new politics. Ultimately, while ideas may be important, what we all rely upon most is the great unfulfilled desire for freedom that exists in human beings. Our task as a movement is to interpret and help organize that desire.

20

Red Earth, White Lies: Native Americans and the Myth of Scientific Fact

Vine Deloria, Jr.

Every human society maintains its sense of identity with a set of stories that explain, at least to its satisfaction, how things came to be. A good many societies begin at a creation and carry forward a tenuous link of events, which they consider to be historical—which is to say actual experiences of the group that often serve as precedents for determining present and future actions. Sometimes these stories incorporate moral teachings and what we have come to call religious traditions, the actions of the higher spiritual powers or invisible forces that were important actors in the more spectacular and memorable events of their history. A good many societies speak of catastrophic events or of the movement of their people from one planet to another. Monsters and strange creatures also appear in stories and beg credibility when these tales are recited.

Of those societies that found a way to create a written record of the past, the Hebrews have been most influential, since it was the adoption of the Hebrew version of ancient events that came to be accepted, through the spread of Christianity, as the valid and incontestable explanation of how this planet came to be. Arguments about the great flood of Noah and the presence in geological strata of skeletons of animals not seen today opened the floodgates of controversy about the age of the Earth and directed the attention of Western thinkers toward the proposition that our planet might have a much different past. Eventually, the believers in biblical accuracy were put to rout by secular thinkers who substituted a seemingly infinite amount of time during which everything "evolved" in place of the shorter time scale of creation and religious history as it was represented in the Bible.

Most Americans do not pause to look back at the developments of the past two hundred years that make our society and time unique. With the triumph of Darwinian evolution as the accepted explanation of the origin of our Earth—indeed, of the whole universe—we are the first society to accept a purely mechanistic origin for ourselves and the teeming life we find on planet Earth. Science tells us that this whole panorama of life, our deepest experiences, and our most cherished ideas and emotions are really just the result of a fortunate combination of amino acids happening to coalesce billions of years ago and that our most profound experiences are simply electrical impulses derived from the logical consequence of that first accident. We thus stand alone against the cumulative memories and wisdom of all other societies when maintaining this point of view. We justify our position by accusing our ancestors and existing tribal societies of being superstitious and ignorant of the real causes of organic existence. Do we really have a basis for this belief?

Unfortunately, the discussion of the age of the Earth and the nature of past events has been conducted wholly within the confines of Western civilization. Consequently, the traditions of all other peoples have been shunted aside, since, if the Bible were shown to be mythical fairy tales, and it was the confirmed word of God, the accounts of other peoples, non-Westerners, would be even less reliable. When secular science defeated Christian fundamentalism, in its victory it was able to promulgate the belief that all accounts of a creation or of spectacular catastrophic events were superstitions devised by ignorant peoples to explain the processes of the world around them. The defeat of Christianity foreclosed the possibility that any other tradition that had accounts of past Earth events could join in the enterprise to explain to an increasingly global society the origins of the planet and of our race. Since Christianity was regarded as the only true religion, all traditions were seen as folklore and myth.

Religious people did not surrender easily and, indeed, even today we have a surprising number of people who believe the literal truth of Old Testament accounts and reject or grudgingly admit the possibility of the secular scientific explanation. The scientific view of Earth history is a rather simple thing depending more on the status of secular science than on the validity of its tenets. Science simply demanded an infinite amount of time during which minute changes in both organisms and geological strata could occur. Given an infinite amount of time, and then promulgating the thesis that all change was incremental, indeed almost infinitesimal, generations of scientists were able to convince us that we "evolved" from apes, that our geological strata, the large limestone and sandstone mountains that we love so much, were the product of changes so small that they could not be detected by present-day observations. No good overview of scientific beliefs has been presented since the defeat of the fundamentalists. Consequently, the belief in infinitesimal change has received little critical examination and contains numerous errors of both logic and interpretation.

Inconsistencies abound, but we are so brainwashed by science that we do not even ask the relatively simple questions about ordinary things. We have shifting continents attached to sliding gigantic "plates' and we also have continents rising and falling to allow for the deposition of limestone and marine sediments. Exactly how both processes can occur at once is not clear, and it is only our trained belief that an infinite amount of time has passed that allows both processes to be held as literal truths. Species both evolve and stop evolving during this time period. Read any book on evolution and you will discover a surprising number of modern species that stopped evolving millions of years ago. In addition, even the most sophisticated of modern scientists, in explaining the fossil remains, finds that species in the rocks are distant relatives to each other, not direct lineages.

Our modern scientists, led by Stephen Jay Gould, have devised a new explanation of evolution that reverses Darwin's original ideas completely. Where secular science once pointed at fossil formations as evidence that evolutionary changes occurred over time, Gould and his friends point out the *absence* of transitional fossils as evidence that evolution occurred, but in rapid spurts. Apparently somewhere, and at a time unknown, when species were ready to evolve they went offstage, made their changes, and then rushed back into the geologic strata to leave evidence of their existence.

Thus millions of years are believed to have passed between species of similar body form although no real evidence of the passing of years is available. The Grand Canyon of Arizona, touted as one of the locations where we can see this infinite time pass, lacks two major geological formations—the Ordovician and Silurian—and we have no explanation for these profoundly long missing periods of geological time. We are told that dinosaurs lived 65 million years ago, and yet from Roy Chapman Andrews forward our scientists continue to find the dinosaur skeletons on top of the ground or very near the surface. So 65 million years of sediment apparently was insufficient to bury these monsters from our sight

Any group that wishes to be regarded as the authority in a human society must not simply banish or discredit the views of their rivals, they must become the sole source of truth for that society and defend their status and the power to interpret against all comers by providing the best explanation of the data. As priests and politicians have discovered, it is even permissible to tell lies in order to maintain status, since the most fatal counterattack against entrenched authority will not be directed against their facts but against their status. As Americans, we have been trained to believe that science is infallible in the sense that, while science does not know everything, its processes of investigation and experimentation are the best available so that, given time and resources, the truth will eventually be discovered. This belief has degenerated into a strange form of religious belief because the technology that science provides us, best exemplified in the "instant replay" in sports, encourages us to cede all critical faculties to science in exchange for creature comforts.

Like any other group of priests and politicians, however, scientists lie and fudge their conclusions as much as the most distrusted professions in our society—lawyers and car dealers. In recent years we have seen several instances of false or doctored research reports, one a very serious manipulation of cancer research on women's breasts. It appears that, earlier, Charles Darwin liberally borrowed the ideas of Alfred Wallace to become the father of evolution.

Johannes Kepler fudged his math in order to get the scientists of his day to take his theories seriously, and it appears that Gregor Mendel's plants did not always follow the genetic doctrines that he later articulated. Louis Pasteur, a giant of science, apparently "lied about his research, stole ideas from a competitor and was deceitful" in some fundamental ways, according to a recently published book, *The Private Science of Louis Pasteur,* by Gerald L. Geison. Lawrence K. Altman, in a review in *The New York Times Book Review,* observed that disclosures made by the book ". . . are revealing that science is not as objective, neat and scrupulously honest as it is portrayed."

Perhaps the epitome of scientific fraud was the work of Sir Cyril Burt on twins. Fearful of peer criticism of his work, Burt simply performed the peer-review process by himself, writing glowing reviews of his work using pseudonyms. This deceit, and the manipulation of statistical data in the studies, was eventually exposed, but in the interim most fellow scientists simply followed the party line and supported him because he was one of the old-boy network. And severe questions arise whether or not Teilhard de Chardin was a part of the Piltdown fraud that substantially affected articulation of theories of human evolution for half of this century.

We are taught to visualize the scientist as a cheerful fellow clad in a white smock, working in a spotless lab, and asking the insightful questions that will eventually reach us at K-Mart in the form of improved vitamins, new kinds of audiotapes, and labor-saving devices. On reaching the end of his experiment, which has featured a set of daring questions that he is forcing Mother Nature to surrender, our scientist publishes his results. His peers give serious critical attention to his theory and check his lab results and interpretations, and science moves another step forward into the unknown.

Eventually, we are told, the results of this research, combined with many other reports, are digested by intellects of the highest order and the paradigm of scientific explanation moves steadily forward, reducing the number of secrets that Mother Nature has left. Finally, popular science writers—Stephen Jay Gould, Carl Sagan, Jared Diamond, Robert Ardrey, and Jacob Bronowski—and others take this mass of technical scientific wisdom and distill it for us poor ignorant lay people so we can understand in general terms the great wisdom that science has created.

The actual situation is much different. Academics, and they include everyone we think of as scientists except people who work in commercial labs, are incredibly timid people. Many of them are intent primarily on maintaining their status within their university and profession and consequently they resemble nothing so much as cocker spaniels who are eager to please their masters, the masters in this case being the vaguely defined academic profession. Scholars, and again I include scientists, are generally specialists in their field and are often wholly ignorant of developments outside their field. Thus, a person can become an international expert on butterflies and not know a single thing about frogs other than that they are disappearing— a fact more often picked up in the Sunday newspaper science section than from reading a scientific journal. Scientists and scholars are notoriously obedient to the consensus opinions of their profession, which usually means they pay homage to the opinions of scholars and scientists who occupy the prestige chairs at Ivy League and large research universities or even dead personalities of the past.

Scientists do work hard in maintaining themselves within their niche in their respective disciplines. This task is accomplished by publishing articles in the journals of their profession. A glance at the index of any journal will reveal that the articles are written for the express purpose of generating mystique and appear to be carefully edited to eliminate any possibility of a clear thought. Editors of journals and editorial boards are notoriously conservative and reject anything that would resemble a breath of fresh air.

Any idea that appears to challenge orthodoxy and is published is usually accompanied by copious responses from the names in the profession who are given an opportunity to quash any heretical conclusions that the article might suggest. Many subjects, no matter how interesting, are simply prohibited because they call into question long-standing beliefs. Prestigious personalities can determine what is published and what is not. Journals do not reflect science or human knowledge; they represent the subjects that are not prohibited in polite discussion by a few established personalities in the larger intellectual world.

We often read newspaper accounts of new scientific theories. Too often we have been trained to believe that the new discoveries are proven fact rather than speculative supposition within a field that is already dominated by orthodox doctrines. Quite frequently the newspaper accounts will contain the phrase "most scientists agree," implying to the lay person that hundreds of scientists have sincerely and prayerfully considered the issue, reached a consensus, and believe that the theory is reliable.

Nothing could be further from reality. In all probability a handful of people have read or heard of the article and, because it is written by a "responsible scholar," have feared to criticize it. But who is the responsible scholar responsible to? Not to the public, not to science, or history, or anthropology, but to the small group of similarly situated people who will make recommendations on behalf of his or her scholarship, award the prizes which each discipline holds dear, and write letters advocating his or her advancement. Unless a "scientist" is speaking specifically about his or her field, the chances are very great that he or she does not know any more about the subject than your average well-read layperson.

Since it is possible for a prestigious personality to dominate a field populated with fearful little people trying to protect their status, some areas of "science" have not progressed in decades and some scientific doctrines actually have no roots except their traditional place in the intellectual structure of the discipline. For more than a century scientists have labeled unknown animal behavior as "instinct," which simply indicated that they did not know the processes of response. And instinct was passed off as a responsible scientific answer to an important question. "Evolution" is used to cover a multitude of academic sins.

Samuel Eliot Morison was a singularly devoted worshipper of Columbus, and while he was alive it was virtually impossible to discuss pre-Columbian expeditions to the Western Hemisphere in any academic setting. It is still anathema to give the topic serious consideration. Ales Hrdlicka, longtime anthropologist at the Smithsonian Institution, was a zealous foe of early dates for the populating of North America, and even today most anthropologists and archaeologists immediately run to their computers to discredit any digs that would suggest a date earlier than 12,000 B.C.– 50,000 B.C. The recent findings at Monte Verde in Chile were actually the reluctant admission by the dinosaurs of archaeology/anthropology who grudgingly agreed to add 1,300 years to the acceptable date of human occupation of the Western Hemisphere—not a notable "advance" in scientific thinking considering the inaccuracies of C-14 dating techniques.

I came to academia believing the traditional picture of the scholar after nearly two decades of political activism. Joining the University of Arizona Department of Political Science, I was very interested in learning more about political theory, since I had heard good arguments made during the civil rights movement on the implications of social contract theory. For over a year I patiently went to lunch with my colleagues hoping to engage in heated analyses of the central tenets of our profession. I learned mostly about the politics of getting an edge with the administration for more benefits, a great deal about the adjustments being made in the athletic program, and a bit about the campus affairs of the more active administrators and professors. I do not recall any conversation in which anything of substance dealing with our discipline was forthcoming.

Arriving at the University of Colorado, I was stunned to hear from my students that some of my history colleagues were beginning their courses on American history with a mindless recitation of the Bering Strait theory of the peopling of the Western Hemisphere. Basically, they were simply repeating scholarly folklore, since there is, to my knowledge, no good source which articulates the theory in any reasonable format. Indeed, this "theory" has been around so long that people no longer feel they have to explain or defend it—they can merely refer to it. I will deal with this issue in another chapter. It is important here simply to note that the immense knowledge and factual proof of many scientific theories does not exist. Many theories and facts recited by scholars and scientists today are merely academic folklore which professors heard in their undergraduate days and have not examined at all.

Some forty-five years ago, Immanuel Velikovsky published his classic work *Worlds in Collision,* in which he suggested that the Earth had been subjected to several catastrophes of an extraterrestrial nature that had involved Mars and Venus. He based these ideas on the Old Testament memories of the Hebrews and added an immense number of footnotes referring to the memories of other peoples. A significant number of his suggestions regarding the nature of our solar system and the geological features of the planets have been proved accurate in the decades since he wrote. By and large, however, scientists rushed to attack his books and threatened a boycott of Macmillan, his publisher, which made it necessary to move the book to Doubleday to keep it in print

A sufficient literature has evolved since then to argue the case for Velikovsky, but I would like to illustrate the scientific response in just one instance because it demonstrates the tenacity with which the academic community holds on to its beliefs. Velikovsky said that Venus at one time had been a comet and had disrupted Earth. On the basis of this identification he suggested that the surface temperature of Venus would be something approaching incandescence. Orthodox science at the time believed that Venus had a surface temperature of 25°C.

With the space probes able to gather considerably more information on Venus, the surface temperature when measured was estimated at around 800°C—a substantially radical difference. When Velikovsky pointed out the difference in measurement, his critics replied that heat was a "relative" term. Today, this high temperature is explained by an ad hoc "greenhouse" theory which suggests that clouds can raise the temperatures of planets to incredibly high measurements by a natural process.

Much of the documentation used by Velikovsky relied on the recorded beliefs of non-Western peoples in every part of the globe. Often his technique was to seek traditions that would involve some discernible physical change in a local environment that might be anticipated if a much larger and more violent event affected the whole planet. An example of this practice was to take the Long Day of Joshua and look at the other side of the Earth and find a tradition in Central America in which the night was extended for a prolonged duration. He found corresponding evidence for several of the events of his interplanetary collisions in the traditions of tribal peoples.

Some evidence, and I will review these traditions in a later chapter, did not offer much support for the cometary disruption as he conceived it. Nevertheless, by incorporating these non-Western traditions into a theory in which events having a planetary scope could be suggested and evidence for such an event could be examined, Velikovsky offered a scenario in which a truly planetary history could be constructed.

Orthodox science has done just the reverse. It accepts non-Western traditions to the degree to which they help to bolster the existing and approved orthodox doctrines. The vast majority of the time, the non-Western interpretations of Earth history and the history of human beings are rejected as Stone Age remnants of human societies that could not invent or accept the mechanistic and later industrial interpretation of the natural world. The evolutionary framework we presently have does not represent human experiences of the past and present, but simply Western doctrinal arrangements of selected bits of evidence of those experiences.

Respect for non-Western traditions is exceedingly difficult to achieve. Not only did secular scientists rout the Christian fundamentalists, they placed themselves in the posture of knowing more, on the basis of their own very short-term investigations, than the collective remembrances of the rest of humankind. Social science, in particular anthropology, preserved information about the remnants of tribal cultures around the world, most particularly in North America, but it also promulgated the idea that these tribal cultures were of Stone Age achievement and represented primitive superstitions which could not be believed.

It was with a certain degree of satisfaction, therefore, that I watched the comet crash into Jupiter during the summer of 1994, since it has been orthodox science for over a century that our solar system is immune to radical disruption by outside cosmic bodies—one of the charges made against Velikovsky. The new chaos theory, now one of the popular ways of examining phenomena, suggests that constant uniformity is probably not a characteristic of any system in this universe. The event and the new theory lend considerable support for a re-examination of the insights and knowledge of tribal peoples when trying to understand the nature of our world.

Some efforts have already been made in a number of fields to investigate the knowledge of tribal peoples and incorporate it into modern scientific explanations. Thor Heyerdahl was one of the first people to show, by repeating the event, that ancient peoples could well have traveled by sea to various parts of the globe. I think partially as a result of his voyages a small group of anthropologists have now allowed that Indians, instead of marching four abreast over the mythical Bering land bridge, might have come by boat on a bay and inlet basis from the Asian continent to North America.

Recognizing that Indians may have been capable of building boats seems a minor step forward until we remember that for almost two centuries scientific doctrine *required* that Indians come by land because they were incapable of building rafts. Polynesian voyages of considerable distances have now been duplicated, giving credence to the idea that Hawaiian tales of sea voyages were not superstitious ways of discussing ocean currents. Critical in this respect is the fact that Hawaiians would not be believed until a white man had duplicated the feat.

In methodological terms there is a major problem in bringing non-Western traditions within the scope of serious scientific perspective, and that is the inherent racism in academia and in scientific circles. Some of the racism is doctrinaire and unforgiving—for instance, the belief that, for a person and/or community possessing any knowledge that is not white/Western in origin, the data is unreliable. A corollary of this belief is that non-Western peoples tend to be excitable, are subjective and not objective, and consequently are unreliable observers.

Other attitudes encompass the idea that the non-Western knowledge, while interesting, is a lucky correspondence between what science has "proved" and what these people discovered by chance. Even with tribal peoples now entering academic fields, there is bias, and most academics deeply believe that an Indian, or any other non-Western person, cannot be an accurate observer of his or her own traditions because that individual is personally involved. It follows, to listen to the apologists for many university departments, that an urban, educated white person, who admittedly has a deep personal interest in a non-Western community but who does not speak the language, has never lived in the community, and visits the people only occasionally during the summer, has a better understanding of the culture, economics, and politics of the group than do the people themselves. When this attitude is seen in religious studies it is appalling: white scholars truly believe that they know more about tribal religions than the people who actually do the ceremonies.

The bottom line about the information possessed by non-Western peoples is that the information becomes valid only when offered by a white scholar recognized by the academic establishment; in effect, the color of the skin guarantees scientific objectivity. Thus, ethnic scholars are not encouraged to do research in their own communities—studies done by whites are preferred. Many scholars with ethnic backgrounds are even denied tenure because they are ethnic and their studies and publications relate to that background. Particularly in the arts and social sciences, supposed bastions of liberalism, minority scholars are simply run out of the professions unless they are totally submissive to prevailing doctrines of the discipline and their writings do not clash with established authority.

We come then to examine the content of "science" and the "oral tradition," which is to say the traditions of non-Western peoples. Arnold Toynbee in *A Study of History* criticized his discipline for its parochial perspective. He wrote that it was "as though a geographer were to produce a book entitled 'World Geography' which proved on inspection to be all about the Mediterranean Basin and Europe." By analogy, "science" is pretty much the same. It is that collection of beliefs—some with considerable evidence, some lacking any proof at all—which reflects data gathered by a small group of people over the past five hundred years with the simple belief that phenomena have been objectively observed and properly described because they have sworn themselves to sincerity. Unfortunately the assumptions and presuppositions which these people bring to the interpretation of phenomena are regarded as "normal"—as the way that people validly view the world.

Anomalies, facts that cannot or do not fit into the complete edifice, are simply ignored, their champions discredited. Validity and verification in science primarily consist of a willing conspiracy among scientists not to challenge the authorities in the field and to take the sincerity of colleagues as insight. Consequently, there are literally millions of observed facts which simply do not appear in scientific writing because they would tend to raise doubts about the prevailing paradigm.

The non-Western, tribal equivalent of science is the oral tradition, the teachings that have been passed down from one generation to the next over uncounted centuries. The oral tradition is a loosely held collection of anecdotal material that, taken together, explains the nature of the physical world as people have experienced it and the important events of their historical journey. The Old Testament was once oral tradition until it was written down. Sagas and Eddas form part of the European oral tradition. Some romance has attached to Indian oral traditions in recent times due to the interest in spirituality, and consequently some people have come to believe that oral traditions refer *only* to religious matters. This description is not true. The bulk of American Indian traditions probably deal with commonsense ordinary topics such as plants, animals, weather, and past events that are not particularly of a religious nature.

Until Indian tribes, and by extension other tribal peoples, were submerged by the invasion of Western colonizing peoples, the oral tradition represented not simply information on ancient events but precise knowledge of birds, animals, plants, geologic features, and religious experiences of a particular group of people. Sometimes the visions of different tribes would match and describe a particular event, experience, or condition and sometimes they would not.

Tribal elders did not worry if their version of creation was entirely different from the scenario held by a neighboring tribe. People believed that each tribe had its own special relationship with the superior spiritual forces that governed the universe. The task of each tribe was to remain true to its special calling without worrying about what others were doing. Tribal knowledge was not fragmented data arranged according to rational speculation. It was simply the distilled memory of the People describing the events they had experienced and the lands they had lived in. Black Elk, talking to John Neihardt, explained the methodology well: "This they tell, and whether it happened so or not, I do not know; but if you think about it, you can see that it is true." The oral tradition, people felt, was serious; it was knowledge, and even the most unlikely aspects might be understood as true.

Fragmentation of human knowledge by science means that most explanations must be constructed on an ad hoc basis with the hope that use of the scientific method will guarantee that all bits of data are ultimately related. Unfortunately, the day of the philosopher in Western society has passed and no single group today serves the function of surveying the totality of knowledge and trying to bring it into a coherent and simple explanation which can be made available to the rest of society. Earlier in this century, scientific philosophers such as Alfred North Whitehead, P. W. Bridgman, R. G. Collingwood, Hans Margeneau, and Werner Heisenberg attempted to frame coherent explanations of the whole, relying primarily on their knowledge of physics, mathematics, and astronomy to describe the rest of the data that other disciplines of science had gathered.

In the old days, elders performed a similar function and recited the oral traditions of the tribe during the wintertime and as a regular part of camp or village life. Religious ceremonials generally involved the recitation of the origin and migration stories, and most of the accumulated wisdom of the tribe was familiar to everyone. Special knowledge regarding other forms of life, if revealed in visions or dreams, was made available to the larger community on a "need-to-know" basis, since it was generally regarded as personal knowledge.

Storytelling was a precise art because of the nature of Indian languages. Some tribal languages had as many as twenty words to describe rain, snow, wind, and other natural elements; languages had precise words to describe the various states of human emotion, the intensity of human physical efforts, and the serenity of the land itself. If the stories began "Once upon a time . . ." they quickly gave the listener a completely accurate rendering of a specific experience which Western languages could not possibly duplicate. In this context, everyone understood the philosophical overview, and ad hoc explanations were treated as facts that must be understood but whose time for understanding had not yet come.

In some of the larger Indian nations, elders functioned pretty much as scientists do today. That is, no one person could remember all the information about the trivial past, the religious revelations, and the complex knowledge of the physical world. Consequently, people specialized in certain kinds of knowledge. Specialization occurred most frequently at vision quests or puberty ceremonies when young people sought help and guidance from birds, animals, and spirits. Often their careers would be shown to them and special information, roots, symbols, and powers given. This information would usually be shared with the spiritual leaders who had supervised the ceremony, but sometimes the person was told to bring a certain medicine, dance, or a bit of information to the rest of the community. The difference between non-Western and Western knowledge is that the knowledge is personal for non-Western peoples and impersonal for the Western scientist. Americans believe that anyone can use knowledge; for American Indians, only those people given the knowledge by other entities can use it properly.

Education, in the American system, is a function of class and economics, and with some rare exceptions the scientific-academic community is self-perpetuating. Middle- and upper-class peoples have a significantly better chance to become scientists than do average citizens simply because they can afford to continue in school until they receive a Ph.D. While graduate school education does provide further training in one's chosen field, its primary purpose is to ensure that people wishing to become scholars and scientists are rendered socially acceptable to people already entrenched in the respective professions.

Originally, graduate theses were supposed to be creative and original scholarly work which advanced the knowledge of the world in some significant way. In recent decades this requirement has lapsed completely, and in order to receive an advanced degree today a student need only demonstrate to the committee that he or she will not embarrass the sponsoring professors by being outspoken or taking radical positions that would disrupt the discipline. Rarely do MA theses or Ph.D. dissertations contribute anything to our knowledge.

With the Plains Indian tribes, and I suspect with the vast majority of the Indian groups, the most revered person was the scout. On his knowledge and powers of observation the rest of the community vested their survival. His task was to search out herds of game animals, report the presence of enemies, analyze the weather, and be aware of the slightest change in the environment. If he was wrong, or even slightly inaccurate, the community might perish or decide on a course of action that would have detrimental effects. People sometimes decided against the course of action recommended by a scout, but they never doubted his veracity. Lying by a scout was a dreadful act punished by death or banishment.

A remarkably high percentage of scouts also became the great storytellers and were repositories of the oral tradition. They might vary some of the descriptions of events to entertain their audience, but these editing devices were recognized by everyone, since all the stories were known in their basic outline. Sometimes, in the storytelling, people vied for the chance to introduce puns and humorous variations on words which would transform the story into a multileveled account. Becoming a respected articulator of the knowledge of the tribe was not a status dependent upon economic or even military prowess. Indeed, like modern fishermen measuring fish they once caught, people tended to look suspiciously at the versions of experiences told by individuals whose accomplishments were not in the field of observation. Some tribes prohibited a person from lauding his own accomplishments for fear of exaggeration, requiring friends and relatives to describe exploits.

Comparing the two ways of gaining a position of authority in society, then, the oral tradition clearly had many more guarantees that its knowledge would not become the subject of personal bias. The possessor of the oral traditions had nothing that would encourage him or her to change the meaning or emphasis of the information except, as already noted, the desire to entertain. People had no vested interest in wealth or prestige by becoming knowledgeable and, lacking any concept of tenure, storytellers maintained their status only to the degree that they represented information and wisdom. Any suspicion that they didn't know a subject would eliminate them as a serious and reliable source of knowledge.

Within the scientific establishment, on the other hand, immense rewards are made available to the individual who stands out among his or her colleagues. Consequently, in today's academic setting, with the impact of the television personality cult, advocating popular theories or making a theory popular is a requirement of academic success, regardless of the truth of the situation. In some instances, the more bizarre and outlandish the theory, the more useful it is in bringing economic rewards to its creator. Sensationalism often substitutes for truth, and that is one reason why we have so many popular psychologists and sociologists.

The major difference between American Indian views of the physical world and Western science lies in the premise accepted by Indians and rejected by scientists: the world in which we live is alive. Many scientists believe this idea to be primitive superstition and, consequently, scientific explanation rejects any nuance of interpretation that would credit the existence of any activities of the natural world as having partial intelligence, or sentience present. American

Indians look at events to determine the spiritual activity supporting or undergirding them. Science insists, albeit at a great price in understanding, that the observer be as detached as possible from the event he or she is observing. Indians know that human beings must participate in events, not isolate themselves from occurrences in the physical world. Indians thus obtain information from birds, animals, rivers, and mountains, which is inaccessible to modern science.

Again, however, there are certain kinds of correspondences between the Indian way and modern scientific techniques. We know from meteorology that seeding clouds with certain chemicals can bring rain. This method of dealing with natural forces is wholly mechanical and can be described as the power to force nature to do our bidding. Indians performed the same function by conducting ceremonies and asking the spirits for rain. Science is severely limited, however, since it cannot affect winds, clouds, and storms except by certain kinds of alterations. Luther Standing Bear recounts an instance in which a Sioux medicine man drastically changed the weather with his powers because he had become a friend to the forces that stood behind the meteorological phenomena:

> Some of my band, the Oglalas, went to visit the Brule band and by way of entertainment preparations were made for a dance and feast. The day was bright and beautiful, and everyone was dressed in feathers and painted buckskin. But a storm came up suddenly, threatening to disrupt the gathering, so of course there was much unhappiness as the wind began to blow harder and rain began to fall. Last Horse walked into his tipi and disrobed, coming out wearing only a breechclout and moccasins. His hair streamed down his back and in his hand he carried a rattle. Walking slowly to the center of the village he raised his face to the sky and sang his Thunder songs, which commanded the clouds to part. Slowly but surely, under the magic of the song, the clouds parted and the sky was clear once more.

Acting in concert with friendly thunder and storm spirits is rather commonplace in many Indian tribes and demonstrates the more comprehensive scope of the oral tradition in comparison to both scientific knowledge and powers.

Indians came to understand that all things were related, and while many tribes understood this knowledge in terms of religious rituals, it was also a methodology/guideline which instructed them in making their observations of the behavior of other forms of life. Attuned to their environment, Indians could find food, locate trails, protect themselves from inclement weather, and anticipate coming events by their understanding of how entities related to each other. This knowledge is not unique to American Indians. It would be available to anyone who lived primarily in the natural world, was reasonably observant, and gave other forms of life respect for intelligence and the power of thought.

Western science also has the idea of relativity, but the concept was initially applied only in theoretical physics to explain the relationship of space, time, and matter. Gradually, scientists have moved from philosophical physics to apply the concept of relatedness to biological phenomena and environments. Now many scientists believe that all things are related, and some articles, primarily coming from people in physics, now state flatly that all things really are related. The proposition, however, still seems to be an intellectual concept that lacks the sense of emotional involvement. If scientists really believed in the unity and interrelatedness of all things, their emphasis would shift dramatically and they would forswear using animals for lab research, change their conception of agronomy entirely, do considerably different studies of water and landscapes, and begin to deal seriously with the by-products of their experiments. Hopefully that day is coming.

When the sciences became divided, our knowledge of the world became badly fragmented. Scientists, in creating narrow classifications of disciplines, developed more precise focus and were able to articulate the substance of the discipline and its goals. They were also able to simply discard phenomena and data which did not fit into their specialist subject area. Rejected data were called anomalies, and no single discipline assumed responsibility for including anomalies in any of the smaller disciplinary paradigms. Thus there are literally millions of irrefutable facts which science simply dismisses, even though they go to make up entities and events which composed our world.

Some areas of interdisciplinary work cause great controversy because of previous excesses by the discipline which originally had the interpretive franchise. A great many of the ancient Indian ruins in the United States were once classified as religious sites by anthropologists who never did know what they were, but imagined many early cultures to be dictatorial theocracies and therefore supposed that people spent their lives building temples. Many of these same ruins are now interpreted by archaeoastronomers as primitive but sophisticated computers which can scan the horizon if properly used, and they are seen as providing proof of a complicated Indian star knowledge. At the present time we really don't know what some of these ruins represented. It is obvious that the two different interpretations simply reflect fads within Western scientific disciplines, and religious interpretations have faded for the moment. But even labeling a site as astronomical is an improvement, since it partially sidesteps the old stereotype of Indians being primitive and ignorant savages.

At the American Association for the Advancement of Science annual meeting in Chicago in 1992, there was a panel presentation of a new field called "zoopharmacognosy," which is a term describing the use of medicinal plants by animals. The panel got a laudatory review in a *Newsweek* article, which described fearless scientists spying on sick animals and observing them using certain plants to cure themselves. A Duke University primatologist was quoted as saying, "If these work for primates, then they are potential treatments for humans," this insight apparently being a startling departure from ordinary scientific logic. The article quoted Harvard ethnobotanist Shawn Sigstedt suggesting that bears may have taught the Navajos to use a species of the *Ligusticum* plant, just as they had claimed!

For Western peoples, the announcement of zoopharmacognosy may be an exciting breakthrough on the frontiers of science, but getting information from birds and animals regarding plants is an absurdly self-evident proposition for American Indians. It gives substance to the idea that all things are related, and it is the basis for many tribal traditions regarding medicinal uses of plants. The excitement illustrates a point made above: Why didn't people take Indians seriously when we said that animals and birds give us information on medicinal plants?

Why is such knowledge only valid and valuable when white scientists document and articulate it?

About twenty years ago a very popular book summarized some of the information being retrieved about plants—*The Secret Life of Plants* by Peter Tompkins and Christopher Bird. The book covered the various experiments done by scientists to measure what appeared to be the emotional life of plants, including the famous Backster effect in which plants' emotions were registered on a meter. A casual reference in the book to Indians using music to ensure greater plant growth was followed almost immediately by reference to a white man in Wauwatosa, Wisconsin, a florist who piped music into his greenhouses to make plants grow better.

No real discussion was ever presented regarding American Indian knowledge of plant life, even though it is well known that Corn Dances are one of the chief religious ceremonies of the southwestern Indians. In the schizophrenia that we know as America, Indians using songs and dances to improve crops is not significant, but a florist piping music into a greenhouse is astounding and illustrates a hidden principle of the universe.

We should not be too critical if some scientists are lurking in the bushes trying to discover bears eating unusual plants or if people talk to their plants, pray over them, or serenade them with music. These things do help expand the frontiers of science away from the stuffy and sterile materialistic perspective and begin to open up new ways of approaching nature. What is it, however, that blocks any possibility of dialogue between Western science and the tribal peoples who know these things, and more, as a matter of course?

Two things need to be done, in my opinion, before there can be any exchange of views between American Indians and Western science. First, corrective measures must be taken to eliminate scientific misconceptions about Indians, their culture, and their past. Second, there needs to be a way that Indian traditions can contribute to the understanding of scientific beliefs at enough specific points so that the Indian traditions will be taken seriously as valid bodies of knowledge. Both changes involve a fundamental struggle over the question of authority, since even when Indian ideas are demonstrated to be correct there is the racist propensity to argue that the Indian understanding was just an ad hoc lucky guess—which is perilously close to what now passes for scientific knowledge.

Writing Black Working-Class History from Way, Way Below

Robin D. G. Kelley

Against this monster, people all over the world, and particularly ordinary working people in factories, mines, fields, and offices, are rebelling every day in ways of their own invention. Sometimes their struggles are on a small personal scale . . . Always the aim is to regain control over their own conditions of life and their relations with one another. Their strivings have few chroniclers. They themselves are constantly attempting various forms of organization, uncertain of where the struggle is going to end.

   —C.L.R. James, Grace C. Lee, and Pierre Chalieu, *Facing Reality*

"**M**cDonald's Is a Happy Place!"

I really believed that slogan when I began working there in 1978. For many of us employed at the central Pasadena franchise, Mickey D's actually meant food, folks, and fun, though our main objective *was funds.* Don't get me wrong; the work was tiring and the polyester uniforms unbearable. The swing managers, who made slightly more than the rank-and-file, were constantly on our ass to move fast and smile more frequently. The customers treated us as if we were stupid, probably because 90 percent of the employees at our franchise were African Americans or Chicanos from poor families. But we found inventive ways to compensate. Like virtually all of my fellow workers, I liberated McDonaldland cookies by the boxful, volunteered to clean "lots and lobbies" in order to talk to my friends, and accidentally cooked too many Quarter Pounders and apple pies near closing time, knowing fully well that we could take home whatever was left over. Sometimes we (mis)used the available technology to our advantage. Back in our day, the shakes did not come ready mixed. We had to pour the frozen shake mix from the shake machine into a paper cup, add flavored syrup, and place it on an electric blender for a couple of minutes. If it was not attached correctly, the mixer blade would cut the sides of the cup and cause a disaster. While these mishaps slowed us down and created a mess to clean up, anyone with an extra cup handy got a little shake out of it. Because we were underpaid and overworked, we accepted consumption as just compensation—though in hindsight eating Big Macs and fries to make up for low wages and mistreatment was probably closer to self-flagellation.

That we were part of the "working class" engaged in workplace struggles never crossed our minds, in part because the battles that were dear to most of us and the strategies we adopted fell outside the parameters of what most people think of as traditional "labor disputes." I've never known anyone at our McDonald's to argue about wages; rather, some of us occasionally asked our friends to punch our time cards before we arrived, especially if we were running late. And no one to my knowledge demanded that management extend our break; we simply operated on "CP" (colored people's) time, turning fifteen minutes into twenty-five. What we fought over were more important things like what radio station to play. The owner and some of the managers felt bound to easy listening; we turned to stations like K-DAY on AM or KJLH and K-ACE on the FM dial so we could rock to the funky sounds of Rick James, Parliament, Heatwave, The Ohio Players, and—yes—Michael Jackson. Hair was perhaps the most contested battle ground. Those of us without closely cropped cuts were expected to wear hairnets, and we were simply not having it. Of course, the kids who identified with the black and Chicano gangs of the late seventies had no problem with this rule since they wore hairnets all the time. But to net one's gheri curl, a lingering Afro, a freshly permed doo was outrageous. We fought those battles with amazing tenacity—and won most of the time. We even attempted to alter our ugly uniforms by opening buttons, wearing our hats tilted to the side, rolling up our sleeves a certain way, or adding a variety of different accessories.

Nothing was sacred, not even the labor process. We undoubtedly had our share of slowdowns and deliberate acts of carelessness, but what I remember most was the way many of us stylized our work We ignored the films and manuals and turned work into performance. Women on the cash register maneuvered effortlessly with long, carefully manicured nails and four finger rings. Tossing trash became an opportunity to try out our best Dr J moves. The brothers who worked the grill (it was only *brothers* from what I recall) were far more concerned with looking cool than ensuring an equal distribution of reconstituted onions on each all-beef patty. Just imagine a young black male "gangsta limpin'" between the toaster and the grill, brandishing a spatula like a walking stick or a microphone. And while all of this was going on, folks were signifying on one another, talking loudly about each other's mommas, daddys, boyfriends, girlfriends, automobiles (or lack thereof), breath, skin color, uniforms; on occasion describing in hilarious detail the peculiarities of customers standing on the other side of the counter. Such chatter often drew in the customers, who found themselves entertained or offended—or both—by our verbal circus and collective dialogues.

The employees at the central Pasadena McDonald's were constantly inventing new ways to rebel, ways rooted in our own peculiar circumstances. And we never knew where the struggle would end; indeed, I doubt any of us thought we were part of a movement that even had an end other than punching out a time card (though I do think the "Taylorizing" of McDonald's, the introduction of new technology to make service simpler and more efficient, has a lot to do with management's struggle to minimize these acts of resistance and recreation). But *what* we fought for is a crucial part of the overall story; the terrain was often cultural, centering on identity, dignity, and fun. We tried to turn work into pleasure, to turn our bodies into instruments of pleasure. Generational and cultural specificity had a good deal to do with our unique forms of resistance, but a lot of our actions were linked directly to the labor process, gender conventions, and our class status.

Like most working people throughout the world, my fellow employees at Mickey D's were neither total victims of routinization, exploitation, sexism, and racism, nor were they "rational" economic beings driven by the most base utilitarian concerns. Their lives and struggles were so much more complicated. If we are to make meaning of these kinds of actions rather than dismiss them as manifestations of immaturity, false consciousness, or primitive rebellion, we must begin to dig beneath the surface of trade union pronouncements, political institutions, and organized social movements, deep into the daily lives, cultures, and communities which make the working classes so much more than people who work. We have to step into the complicated maze of experience that renders "ordinary" folks so extraordinarily multifaceted, diverse, and complicated. Most importantly, we need to break away from traditional notions of politics. We must not only redefine what is "political" but question a lot of common ideas about what are "authentic" movements and strategies of resistance. By "authentic" I mean the assumption that only certain organizations and ideologies can truly represent particular group interests (e.g., workers' struggles must be located within labor organizations, or African American concerns are most clearly articulated in so-called "mainstream" civil rights organizations such as the NAACP or the Urban League). Such an approach not only disregards diversity and conflict within groups, but it presumes that the only struggles that count take place through institutions.

If we are going to write a history of black working-class resistance, where do we place the vast majority of people who did not belong to either "working-class" organizations or black political movements? A lot of black working people struggled and survived without direct links to the kinds of organizations that dominate historical accounts of African American or U.S. working-class resistance. The so-called margins of struggle, whether it is the unorganized, often spontaneous battles with authority or social movements thought to be inauthentic or unrepresentative of the "community's interests," are really a fundamental part of the larger story wait-ing to be told.

Race Rebels begins to recover and explore aspects of black working-class life and politics that have been relegated to the margins. By focusing on the daily lives of African American work-ing people, strategies of resistance and survival, expressive cultures, and their involvement in radical political movements, this book attempts to chronicle the inventive and diverse struggles waged by black workers during the twentieth century and to understand what they mean for rethinking the way we construct the political, social, and cultural history of the United States. I chose the title *Race Rebels* because this book looks at forms of resistance—organized and unorganized—that have remained outside of (and even critical of) what we've come to under-stand as the key figures and institutions in African American politics. The historical actors I write about are literally *race rebels* and thus have been largely ignored by chroniclers of black politics and labor activism. Secondly, the title points to the centrality of race in the minds and experiences of African Americans. Race, particularly a sense of "blackness," not only figures prominently in the collective identities of black working people but substantially shapes the entire nation's conceptions of class and gender. Part of what *Race Rebels* explores is the extent to which black working people struggled to maintain and define a sense of racial identity and solidarity.

Some of the questions *Race Rebels* takes up have their roots in works by an older genera-tion of radical scholars who chose to study slavery and its demise when fascism was on the rise in Europe and the future of colonialism was uncertain. The two most influential books in this respect were written nearly three decades before E. P. Thompson's *The Making of the English Working Class*—namely, W.E.B. DuBois's *Black Reconstruction* (1935) and C.L.R. James's study of the Haitian Revolution titled *Black Jacobins* (1938). These majestic histories of revo-lution, resistance, and the making of new working classes out of the destruction of slavery anticipated the "new" social historians' efforts to write "history from below." They also con-tributed enormously to revising the history of Western revolutions by placing race, culture, and the agency of African people—the slaves and ex-slaves—at the center of the story. Neither author viewed the newly created black proletariat as merely passive products of economic exploitation and dislocation. In DuBois's account freedpeople are on the move, undermining slavery at every halting step. The men and women who fought to reconstruct the South were more than servants and cotton pickers; they were Negroes with a capital *N*, they belonged to families and churches, and they brought with them a powerful millenarian vision of fairness and equality. And the white poor who supported efforts to stop them, the folks whose most valuable pos-session was probably their skin, put the noose around their own neck in exchange for mem-bership in the white race. *Black Reconstruction* may still be the most powerful reminder of how fundamental race is for understanding American culture and politics. For C.L.R. James the slaves' memories of Africa, the world they created in the quarters bordering the cane fields, the social meaning ascribed to skin color, the cultural and religious conflicts *within* African-descended communities, were as critical to creating and shaping the Revolution as were back-breaking labor and the lash.

The "new labor" or "new social historians," who set out to write "history from below" in the early to mid-1960s, traveled even further down the road opened up by their predecessors. Unlike DuBois and James, whose work on black "labor" entered the scholarly world either quietly or amid vehement opposition, this new generation of historians caused a revolution. The story of its origins is so familiar that it may one day be added to the New Testament. The late E. P. Thompson was the Moses of it all, along with his British ex-Communist comrades and fellow travelers like Eric Hobsbawm and Africanists like Terrence Ranger; across the Channel were prophets like George Rudé, and across the Atlantic were disciples like Herbert Gutman, David Montgomery, Eugene Genovese, and so on. They differed in time, place, and subject matter, but they all shared the radical belief that one could, indeed, write history "from below." Of course, there were those critics who felt the new genre failed to take on the state or ignored political economy. And for all of its radical moorings "history from below" started out very manly and very white (or at least Euroethnic), though that changed somewhat with the emergence of women's and ethnic studies.

Yet, as old as the "new" labor history is, "history from below" in its heyday had a very small impact on the study of African Americans. Certainly, there are those who might argue that all black history is "from below," so to speak, since African Americans are primarily a working-class population. This view has its problems, however. Aside from the fact that every racial or ethnic group in the United States was primarily working class, it denies or minimizes diversity and conflict within African American communities. Unable to see a world that left few written records, many scholars concerned with studying "race relations" folded the black working class into a very limited and at times monolithic definition of the "black community." By overlooking or playing down class and gender differences, mainstream middle-class male leaders have too often been regarded as, in historian Nell Painter's words, "representative colored men."

The chapters in part I not only question whether a handful of "representative Negroes" can speak for the mass of working-class African Americans, but also suggest that some of the most dynamic struggles take place outside—indeed, sometimes in spite of—established organizations and institutions. All four chapters explore the political significance of everyday forms of resistance at work and in public space, the pleasures and politics of culture, and community institutions that are usually not defined as "working-class" organizations. In other words, I sought to dig a little deeper, beneath "below," to those workers whose record of resistance and survival is far more elusive. I'm referring here to evasive, day-to-day strategies: from footdragging to sabotage, theft at the workplace to absenteeism, cursing to graffiti.

These chapters also explore the double-edged sword of race in the South, which is why I called part I "We Wear the Mask" from Paul Laurence Dunbar's poem of the same title. The mask of "grins and lies" enhanced black working people's invisibility and enabled them to wage a kind of underground "guerrilla" battle with their employers, the police, and other representatives of the status quo. Although the South certainly had its share of militant African American and interracial movements, and the status quo was sufficiently afraid of rebellion to expend a tremendous amount of resources on keeping the peace and surveilling black communities, the mask worked precisely because most Southern whites accepted their own racial mythology; they believed that "darkies" were happy and content, and that any open, collective acts of defiance were probably inspired from the outside. On the other hand, the "mask" exacted a price from black folks as well. The inner pain generated by having to choke back one's feelings in the face of racism could create tensions. Writer Gloria Wade-Gayles, who grew up in a Memphis housing project and came of age on the eve of the civil riots movement, beautifully captured this dilemma: "As teenagers, many of us were caught between our anger at white people and our respect for our black elders; between a need to vent our rage in the light of day and a desire to remain alive; and between two images of our people: one for downtown and the other for ourselves." As I suggest in my discussion of black resistance during World War II and during the civil rights movement, the "mask" was no longer viable; evasive strategies continued, to be sure, but often with a militant face.

No matter what we might think about the "grins and lies," the evasive tactics, the tiny acts of rebellion and survival, the reality is that most black working-class resistance has remained unorganized, clandestine, and evasive. The driving questions that run through this book include: how do African American working people struggle and survive outside of established organizations or organized social movements? What impact do these daily conflicts and hidden concerns have on movements that purport to speak for the dispossessed? Can we call this politics?

"History from below" clearly pushed me to explore the politics of the everyday. The approach I take is deeply influenced by scholars who work on South Asia, especially political anthropologist James C. Scott. Scott maintains that, despite appearances of consent, oppressed groups challenge those in power by constructing a "hidden transcript," a dissident political culture that manifests itself in daily conversations, folklore, jokes, songs, and other cultural practices. One also finds the hidden transcript emerging "onstage" in spaces controlled by the powerful, though almost always in disguised forms. The veiled social and cultural worlds of oppressed people frequently surface in everyday forms of resistance—theft, footdragging, the destruction of property—or, more rarely, in open attacks on individuals, institutions, or symbols of domination. Together, the "hidden transcripts" created in aggrieved communities and expressed through culture, and the daily acts of resistance and survival, constitute what Scott calls "infrapolitics." As he puts it, "the circumspect struggle waged daily by subordinate groups is, like infrared rays, beyond the visible end of the spectrum. That it should be invisible . . . is in large part by design—a tactical choice born of a prudent awareness of the balance of power."

Like Scott, I use the concept of infrapolitics to describe the daily confrontations, evasive actions, and stifled thoughts that often inform organized political movements. I am not suggesting that the realm of infrapolitics is any more or less important or effective than what we traditionally understand to be politics. Instead, I want to suggest that the political history of oppressed people cannot be understood without reference to infrapolitics, for these daily acts have a cumulative effect on power relations. While the meaning and effectiveness of various acts differ according to the particular circumstances, they do make a difference, whether intended or not.

One measure of the power and historical importance of the informal infrapolitics of the oppressed is, the response of those who dominate traditional politics. Daily acts of resistance and survival have had consequences for existing power relations, and the powerful have deployed immense resources in order to avoid those consequences or to punish transgressors. Knowing how those in power interpret, redefine, and respond to the thoughts and actions of the oppressed is just as important as identifying and analyzing resistance. The policies, strategies, or symbolic representations of those in power—what Scott calls the "official" or "public" transcript—cannot be understood without examining the infrapolitics of oppressed groups. The approach I am proposing will help illuminate how power operates, and how seemingly innocuous, individualistic acts of survival and resistance shape politics, workplace struggles, and the social order generally. I take the lead from ethnographer Lila Abu-Lughod who argues that everyday forms of resistance ought to be "diagnostic" of power. Instead of seeing these practices merely as examples of the "dignity and heroism of resisters," she argues that they could "teach us about the complex interworkings of historically changing structures of power."

Writing "history from below" that emphasizes the infrapolitics of the black working class requires that we substantially redefine politics. Too often politics is defined by *how* people participate rather than *why*; by traditional definition the question of what is political hinges on whether or not groups are involved in elections, political parties, or grass-roots social movements. Yet the how seems far less important than the why, since many of the so-called real political institutions have not always proved effective for, or even accessible to, oppressed people. By shifting our focus to what motivated disenfranchised black working people to struggle and what strategies they developed, we may discover that their participation in "mainstream" politics—including their battle for the franchise—grew out of the very circumstances, experiences, and memories that impelled many to steal from their employer, join a mutual benefit association, or spit in a bus driver's face. In other words, I am rejecting the tendency to dichotomize people's lives, to assume that clear-cut "political" motivations exist separately from issues of economic well-being, safety, pleasure, cultural expression, sexuality, freedom of mobility, and other facets of daily life. Politics is not separate from lived experience or the imaginary world of what is possible; to the contrary, politics is about these things. Politics comprises the many battles to roll back constraints and exercise some power over, or create some space within, the institutions and social relationships that dominate our lives.

When people decide that they want to devote their life or part of their life to rolling back those constraints, then many choose to support movements or institutions that speak to their concerns. But given the multiplicity of constraints and the wide range of issues black working people have dealt with (as African Americans, wage laborers, women, men, consumers, neighbors, creative persons, victims of police brutality, etc.), what kinds of organizations were they drawn to and why? How have they reshaped those movements to incorporate more of their concerns and how have they been changed in the process? Although I cannot promise to answer these questions in any broad and comprehensive way, and I doubt that they can be answered in any single volume, they are the main themes in part II: "To Be Red and Black." I chose to explore African American involvement in the Communist Party because it challenges any easy assertions about what political movements are "authentic" or marginal to black working-class experience. I am not suggesting that the Communist Party is a better representative of black working-class politics than a more familiar organization like the NAACP. But during the interwar period, thousands of African Americans were drawn to Communist circles, and they entered not as malleable vessels ready to be molded by Party ideology. They put their own stamp on the Party, especially locally, and turned it into an important site of black working-class politics.

The questions this section takes up grow out of my first book, *Hammer and Hoe: Alabama Communists during the Great Depression*, which locates a distinctive black radical tradition within the larger scope of working-class politics. But by looking at black working-class radicalism within the context of an international movement, I soon realized that whatever "traditions," beliefs, or ideologies these largely illiterate industrial, agricultural, and service workers brought with them, they ultimately changed. The Communist Party was not simply a neutral vehicle for the darker proletariat to realize some predetermined agenda. Nor did the black rank-and-file Communists check their racial politics at the door. For example, the first chapter in part II ("'Afric's Sons With Banner Red'") argues that a lot of the poetry and songs written by African American rank-and-file Communists bore a closer resemblance to Garveyism than to proletarian literature—a rather odd development given the CP's vigilant battle against all forms of "petty bourgeois racial chauvinism." In the chapter on the experiences of African American volunteers in the Spanish Civil War, I suggest that what motivated almost ninety predominantly working-class black men and one black woman to risk life and limb to fight fascism abroad was a kind of race-conscious, Pan-Africanist internationalism. Awakened by Italy's invasion of Ethiopia, these Black Communists and sympathizers fought Franco as a backhanded response to Mussolini. But their unexpected experiences in the Spanish Republic and as members of a radical International Brigade changed them forever. In both cases, these black radicals created a kind of hybrid movement that combined Garveyism, Pan-Africanism, African American vernacular cultures and traditions, and Euro-American Marxist thought. Their actions and the ways in which they constructed their identities should lead us to question categories that we too frequently regard as mutually exclusive in African American communities: nationalism and communism, religion and communism, Pan-Africanism and internationalism.

The kind of redefinition of politics I am calling for has been one of the main projects of cultural studies scholars, whose insights have deeply influenced my recent work, especially in part III: "Rebels Without a Cause?" These last two chapters examine black working-class male youth culture in two periods: the 1940s and the 1980s and 1990s. Through an examination of Malcolm X's teenage years, chapter 7 tries to unravel the cultural politics of the zoot suit, bebop, and the hipster ethic. Chapter 8 explores the aesthetics and politics of gangsta rap, from its irreverent and misogynist roots in early vernacular traditions to its dark rendering of black life in the postindustrial ghetto.

By including a section on black youth culture, I wanted to make a case for placing young people's experiences squarely within the context of working-class history. Of course, there are issues unique to studying youth that we must consider: unlike more mature adults, young people are in the process of discovering the world as they negotiate it. They are creating new cultures, strategies of resistance, identities, sexualities, and in the process generating a wider range of problems for authorities whose job it is to keep them in check. Nevertheless, because the young black men who strolled down Harlem's 125th Street in the 1940s, or "gangsta limped" along LA's Crenshaw Boulevard in the 1990s, were partly products of dramatic economic transformations, they are central to telling the story of the black working class. Thus I try to place Malcolm X's teenage years, his politics, style, and the significance of the hipster culture, within the context of race, class, and gender relations and the changing political economy during World War II. Similarly, the transformation of South Central Los Angeles as a result of deindustrialization and recent developments in policing is important for understanding the prevalence of gangsta rap in L.A. That chapter looks at what the transformation of L.A. has meant to—not just for–African American youth.

This last section of *Race Rebels* brings us closer to the present but further away from the world we traditionally think of as the "working class." We travel to the darkest recesses of "history from below," to the cultural world beneath the bottom. Both chapters engage aspects of culture regarded by some on the Left (and all on the Right) as nihilistic, apolitical, or simply worthless. These are people—in this case, young urban black males—whose behavior has been regarded by many critics within African American communities as well outside the mainstream. They are race rebels very much like Richard Wright's "Bigger Thomas," products of capitalist transformation, urban decay, persistent racism, male pathos, and nihilistic imaginations, struggling to create a collective identity that reflects their race, gender, class, and location in the city.

Increasingly, I have come to see that the global restructuring of the economy during the last three decades or so has marked a significant moment in the history of the black working class. In fact, in the public and scholarly discourse on the contemporary urban crisis, the term "working class" has somehow disappeared. In its place is a fairly new and amorphous category called the "underclass." Of course, we hear of the successful black middle class, and, on occasion, the phrase "stable black working class" appears in the texts of some left-leaning scholars— but the latter is used as a moral category to distinguish the people we like from the people we don't like, the good Negroes from the bad apples, the Amos's from the Andy's. As my friend and brilliant historian of Atlantic labor history Peter Linebaugh has said on many occasions, the working class occupies many different locations: sometimes they're at work, sometimes they're at home, sometimes they're in jail, and sometimes they're drunk lying in a gutter. They are neither devils nor angels, selfish individuals nor socialists. They don't share a common worldview or even a single culture (especially when you compare across time, space, race, and gender). They are simply people whose very survival depends on work or some form of income (i.e., public assistance, charity, unemployment insurance, crime). This is what the African American working class looks like from way, way below, and it is not always a pretty sight.

Race Rebels is less concerned with giving readers heroic role models or romantic stories of triumph than with chronicling and rethinking black working-class politics, culture, and resistance. More than anything, these chapters try to make sense of people where they are rather than where we would like them to be. This book is just a small and very incomplete step toward suggesting ways to connect everyday struggles to formal politics; to break down the iron triangle by refusing to privilege race, class, or gender; to reject formulaic interpretations in favor of the complexity of lived experience; to erase the boundaries between social, cultural, and political history, to pay attention to cultural hybridity; and reject the kind of subtle essentialism that treats African American culture in the singular. If we want to make sense of those McDonald's workers, or the rebellions written about by C.L.R. James, Grace Lee, and Pierre Chaulieu almost four decades ago, those of us committed to writing working-class history must look way, way, way below, to the places where the noble and heroic tradition of labor militancy is not as evident.

22

The Logic of Black Urban Rebellions

Daryl B. Harris

Although the breadth of African American political behavior covers a broad range of possibilities, an inordinate amount of analytic attention has been paid to those that mirror traditional forms at the expense of other forms. Strongly influenced by mainstream standards, this fixation invariably results in deference being given to democratic theory and behavioralism as analytical guides. Although quite limited in their ability to capture the dynamics of African American phenomena, democratic theory and behavioralism still are routinely used as guides in the study of Black folk.

This explanatory bias notwithstanding, the extensive Black protest activities of the 1950s and 1960s *caused* a dramatic increase in interest in explaining nontraditional Black phenomena. Social scientists, especially sociologists, subsequently scrambled to present innovative theories to account for these supposedly new phenomena, including many that focused on the more than 300 Black uprisings that have engulfed America's cities. By the late 1960s, a deluge of theories on Black urban rebellions had emerged. Each one offered to illuminate our understanding of these destructive and deadly societal events. This outpouring of analyses, however, rather than providing clarity about Black violence, did more to muddle, misconstrue, and even limit the conceptual terrain by effectively restricting what we ask and what we understand about such events.

Daryl Harris, *Journal of Black Studies* (Volume 28, Number 3), pp. 368–385, copyright © 1998 by Sage Publications. Reprinted by permission of Sage Publications, Inc.

Because of the conceptual deficiencies that are prevalent in much of these analyses, this project is an attempt to develop more useful conceptualizations so that Black urban rebellions might be better understood. I begin with a critique of the existing knowledge on Black rebellions, primarily because so much mystification has been sown and perpetuated by that knowledge. I then propose an alternative perspective that is grounded in the historical and cultural experiences of African Americans. In so doing, I contend that the occurrence of Black urban rebellion is, on one level, a tactical response to contemporary forms of White domination and, on another level, an act in which key core values of the African American experience are sustained. The value of this approach is twofold. First, it allows for a distinct appraisal of the systemic and societal constructs that create and perpetuate the African American predicament in urban America. Second, in referencing African American core values, such as resistance, freedom, and self-determination, we have a much broader conceptual base from which to assess the significance and limitations of urban rebellion as a stratagem to achieve justice and freedom. Whereas some previous studies have at least recognized the element of protest in Black rebellions, this analysis differs from those in that it contextualizes Black violence as a contributory component to the long-standing African American freedom movement. In looking to the core values of the African American experience as key referents to examine Black urban rebellions, we are better positioned to forge new ground in the construction of knowledge and theory. In fact, the proper appraisal of all African American phenomena begins with placing African ideals and values at the center of inquiry (Asante, 1990).

The Perils of Knowledge on Black Being and Rebellions

I have already indicated that the outpouring of analyses on Black rebellions has impeded our capacity to discern the meaning of such events. What accounts for all this misunderstanding? The answer is that what we ask about social phenomena and what we ultimately come to understand about them are invariably guided by the assumptions and values we hold (Mannheim, 1936; McKee, 1993). These assumptions and values dilute the objectivity of an analysis. Sometimes they are openly divulged by the researcher; other times they are masked in intricate methodological procedures and techniques. Either way, assumptions and values are integral to whatever perspective is being promulgated. In turn, the perspective, in its dependence on its own assumptions and values, winds up affirming them. If one understands these preexisting mind-sets, the conceptual limits of existing knowledge on Black rebellion vividly appear.

In the American context, what undergirds social relations (including especially their intellectual components) between African Americans and Euro-Americans is the idea (evolved into a full-blown mythology) that Africans are inferior beings, that they are an uncultured segment of the human family incapable of advanced thought, and that they have no heritage worthy of reverence. This is an erroneous notion, contrived by European and Euro-American theorists to facilitate and rationalize European domination over Africa's progeny and riches, which does not diminish its capacity to have far-reaching social import. But the mythology does not end there. What purpose is there in claiming (or believing) African inferiority without having a concomitant mythology of European superiority? The two notions of relative worth are flip sides of the same narrative from which sundry perspectives about Black urban rebellion have evolved. It stands to reason that any perspective emerging from this foundation is problematic and pernicious. Let us consider why.

I have chosen to critique the theorizing done on Black rebellion based on the Black inferiority/White superiority mythology for several reasons. First, I want to expose the ways in which this mythology, so central to the idea and practice of White racial domination, underlies and contaminates the process of theorizing. Entangled in a maze of negative assumptions about the nature of Black being, the theorist on Black rebellion is driven to demonstrate that African Americans are in one way or another unprincipled and uncultivated. Second, this mythology tells us that the very *essence* or quality of American race relations extends well beyond vast measurable factors, such as socioeconomic status and number of elected and appointed positions. All over the Earth, forms and structures of governance and economy are modified and extended, while simultaneously preserving and perpetuating fundamental ideas and values. In the United States, for example, slavery as a form of White racial domination ended in 1865 only to be replaced by another form of White racial domination, Jim Crow segregation. So the acquisition of freedom from enslavement, the procurement of the franchise, and even the eventual ascension to elected and employment positions by African Americans, commonly regarded as racial progress and betterment, did not abrogate the core ideas and values that have determined the nature of American race relations. Third, because the construction of knowledge on Black rebellion has been thoroughly contaminated by the assumption of Black inferiority and leads theorists headlong into generating fallacies, we have sufficient cause to look for or to devise innovative explanatory paradigms devoid of this defect. Gaining clarity on Black rebellion, therefore, necessarily entails a critique of existing knowledge.

The Populist Manifesto: Refrains from the Riffraff Genre

The simplest and most pervasive explanation of Black urban rebellions contends that they are engineered by small bands of malcontents intent on furthering their illicit endeavors. Commonly referred to as the riffraff or the criminality theory, an imaginary 1% or 2% of the urban Black population is credited with fomenting Black anger and insurrection. Right away, we observe that this theory makes a judgment about the morality of Black people merely by calling the rebellions festivals of criminality. The morality judgment is plain: Blacks are immoral and vile. More than a few public officials and social elites promulgate this view as they are untroubled in depicting African Americans in absolute, immoral and negative ways. For instance, regarding the 1980 Black rebellion in Miami, *The Miami Herald* told its readers that the "looting and burning is a by-product—perpetuated by hoodlums, thugs and punks looking for excuses to rip off people" (Oglesby, 1980, p. 1A).

Although lacking at the level of empiricism, the riffraff theory has nonetheless garnered widespread acceptance among the general populace, particularly among Whites. In this regard,

Fogelson (1971) believes that the general acceptance of the riffraff theory by bewildered and terrified Whites is reassuring in that it tells them that widespread Black discontentment is more illusionary than real (p. 28). But with the Black urban rebellions of the 1960s numbering more than 300 and with indisputable evidence showing a broad cross-section of African American involvement and commiseration (Sears & McConahay, 1973; U.S. National Advisory Commission on Civil Disorders, 1968), we have reason to examine other causes for why most Whites remain sanguine about the riffraff definition.

The riffraff argument does not need nor want an empirical basis to substantiate it. Its existence or attractiveness to Whites is entirely independent of such matters. Nor does the riffraff argument seek to delude Whites about the nature and extent of Black discontentment. When Whites give thought to the term riffraff, they do not restrict their conceptions to the small percentage of African Americans whose lives are preoccupied with wrongdoing. Rather, the term riffraff acts as a cognitive cue, alerting Whites to think in racial-spatial relationships. Such relationships allow for the entire Black urban community, including women and children, to be perceived as an incorrigible riffraff. In this way, the theory derives meaning and force from Euro-American hegemonic assumptions about Black being from ignoble assumptions on which forms of racial domination are constructed.

Among the various theories on Black rebellion, the riffraff theory is most explicit and forthright in calling for enhanced repressive and social control measures to contain the Black urban masses. This is the real value to the riffraff perspective—it provides the necessary rationalization for an enhanced police presence in urban America to protect the Whites and their establishments from the Blacks. Alarmed Whites fearing for their lives and property see preventative and, when need arises, repressive measures as absolutely indispensable to their peace of mind. The reassurance that Whites might feel about the riffraff theory stems from their understanding of it as a pretext for proposed repressive sanctions, which are ultimately aimed at quelling even the very idea of Black rebellion.

During the 1960s, for instance, the United States Army developed specific programs to prepare military and police personnel for direct confrontations with the Black urban masses. These measures included providing high-tech weapons and training to the National Guard and some local police units. Coupled with this strategy of meeting Black urban rebellion with open, massive force, the Departments of Justice and Defense intensified their clandestine operations in cities with substantial Black populations, focusing specifically on African Americans they suspected of fomenting Black discontent and rebellion (O'Reilly, 1989).

The repressive, social control policy approach (commonly called White backlash) also proved to be a significant issue in electoral politics, particularly in the presidential election of 1968 (McAdam, 1982, pp. 194–201). The Republican presidential candidate, Richard Nixon, seized on the anxiety and fears of the masses of Whites and promised, if elected, to quell Black urban rebellion and restore stability to the nation through the use of force. With law and order the policy choice of the victorious Nixon administration and with the Viet Nam war eclipsing other national issues in prominence during the latter part of the 1960s, Black urban rebellion was effectively muzzled.

Furthermore, the riffraff theory coincides neatly with democratic (pluralist) theory and ideology, which posit "orderly, peaceful, and systemic" behavior as the only legitimate and valid form of social and political behavior (Dahl, 1967). Democratic theory contends that all groups, including those most disillusioned in American society, have ample opportunities to present their issue claims for negotiation and, ultimately, for processing within the political system. Based on that assumption, the politics of American democracy is portrayed as a relatively stable project wherein a multiplicity of competing groups peacefully impress their will on the political process. The very fact that Black urban rebellions are spontaneous, violent, and short in duration has been sufficient for theorists of American democracy to declare them unintelligible aberrations that are devoid of political significance. Opposed to ascribing substantive political meaning to Black rebellions, democratic theory becomes dependent on the riffraff definition as a default rejoin*der* for Black antisystemic and nonsystemic behavior. In this way, the riffraff definition serves as an invisible yet vital pillar for democratic theory and ideology, summoned expeditiously by theorists of American democracy whenever African American behavior deviates from the core tenets.

Extension of civil and voting rights to African Americans in the 1960s bolstered this conviction and left most Whites and a good number of African Americans believing that these advances heralded the complete eradication of systemic evils arrayed against Black people. A new beginning in race relations thus began, democratic theorists might say, wherein the slate of racial hatred was made clean, the rough spots of discrimination smoothed over, and the crooked edges of police brutality straightened out. Armed with this conception of an alleged racial conciliation, Black rebellions as riffraff-inspired bedlam is not only plausible but predictable.

Other explanations of Black rebellion bear stark resemblance to the riffraff theory, modified in such a way as to mask their negative assumptions about Black being. The first of these is the rabble-rouser theory. This holds that only a handful of rabble-rousers conspire to initiate Black urban rebellion as a means of advancing their narrow political agendas. Almost always, these rabble-rousing conspirators are thought to belong to some fringe group of Communist radicals or Black Power militants. Again, we are admonished that an otherwise contented and listless Black urban community is readily susceptible to engaging in destructive and deadly actions, this time merely by being summoned by a small group of political dissidents. The Black urban community, however, is far from feeling content and does not need to be instructed by political agitators of whatever political disposition to harbor discontentment. The dynamics of White racial domination, as expressed most acutely in deplorable socioeconomic conditions, political powerlessness, and constant assaults on Black being (both physically and psychically), guarantee that discontent will be a part of the African American sensibility.

Another theory resembling the riffraff perspective is the recent migrant theory. This contends that Black urban rebellion results from the inability of Black migrants from the rural South to adjust to the living arrangements and cultural mores of the urban North. Implicit in this perspective is that Black people do not possess the cultural fortitude to surmount the rigors of urban life and that there is cultural degeneracy among them. Epitomizing this view are the remarks from the McCone Commission on the 1965 Watts rebellion:

> *Many have moved to the city only in the last generation and are totally unprepared to meet the conditions of modern city life. At the core of the cities where they cluster, law and order have only tenuous hold; the conditions of life itself are often marginal; idleness leads to despair and finally, mass violence supplies a momentary relief from the malaise. (California Governor's Commission on the Los Angeles Riots, 1965, p.3)*

In the same vein, mass society theory stresses the presence of weak or ineffective intermediate relations among social members that filter their intervening relationships, thereby inviting the prospect for widespread mass behavior. Minus the strong, binding cultural networks that serve as representation mechanisms and stabilizing influences on social members, participation in the larger social system escapes the filtering process and becomes direct, unstructured, and unconventional (Kornhauser, 1959). Ultimately, with respect to African Americans, the recent migrant/mass society paradigm is more interested in their cultural and social adaptability into White cultural and societal modes of behavior than with systemic issues.

Finally, the teenage rebellion theory attributes Black urban rebellion to wild youths easily excited by the thought of tossing stones and bottles at symbols of a constraining, heavy-handed social order. Although the young tend to be more involved in rebellion, most studies (Sears & McConahay, 1973; U.S. National Advisory Commission on Civil Disorders, 1968) have indicated that Black urban insurgents come from every age group.

All of the above theories constitute the riffraff genre of theorizing, and all are comparable to the extent that each attributes Black urban rebellion to a small number of mischief makers within the urban community or to malcontents coming from without. In either case, the baseline assumption of Black people being uncultured and troublesome, so central to the idea and practice of White racial domination, is affirmed. In the end, the staying power of riffraff theorizing and its prominence as an option in informing public policy choices are firmly rooted in nefarious images Whites hold about Black being. This negative imaging process, said sociologist James McKee (1993), serves as the fundamental starting point for sociological studies of Black people (p. 342). More troubling is that these theories ultimately function either to reinforce the racial status quo or to admonish African Americans to adjust their behavior to conform to Euro-American styles of conduct.

Before moving on to the social science segment, we should note that social scientists have not been impervious to the allure of populist refrains. For example, indicative of the riffraff genre of theorizing is the work of sociologist Edward Banfield (1970). In fact, Banfield tips his hand at the outset by titling one of his chapters "Rioting Mainly for Fun and Profit." After rejecting all possibilities that Black rebellion stems from substantive social and political grievances held by African Americans, Banfield predictably and proudly tells us that Black urban violence is nothing more than "outbreaks of animal spirits and of stealing by slum dwellers" (pp. 197–198). To argue that Banfield willfully misconstrues and muddles the conceptual terrain of this phenomenon is an understatement. In his total disregard for the burdensome experiences of African Americans, he resorts to casting epithets that portray the African American psyche as bestial and infantile, incapable of even generating indignant feelings about police beatings and killings and deplorable living conditions. Banfield's invidious reasoning corresponds perfectly to the mythology of Black inferiority, trapping him in such a way that he can only see amusement and low-caste criminality in Black rebellion.

Social Scientists and the Problem of Objectification

A related problem engendered by the mythology of Black inferiority is that it generates views of African Americans as objects existing on the *margins* of the Euro-American experience. The presumption here is that the Euro-American experience, projected through its particular cultural mores and institutional arrangements, is the paragon of existence and is universally applicable to the whole of humanity. But to the extent that African Americans, as are all objects, are lacking in identity and agency, they presumably would be incapable of shaping any historical moment as independent, self-conscious, social actors. Two modes of explaining Black urban rebellion emerge from this Eurocentric viewpoint. One, the sociopsychological approach, constitutes a more or less rarefied version of riffraff theorizing. The other, the protest approach, does perceive the element of protest in Black rebellious behavior. But because it is anchored in the Euro-American experience, it is limited, at best, to viewing such protest merely as an attempt to gain a place in that experience.

Subsumed under the sociopsychological category are a range of models that underscore frustration and aggression as catalysts for violent behavior. The most celebrated of these are the relative deprivation and rising expectations models. Like its more candid riffraff counterpart, however, this category of theory sees Black rebellious behavior as nothing more than depraved reactions to the strains and fissures of nonracist, if sometimes harsh, societal processes such as urbanization, technological changes and economic cycles (Smelser, 1962). These benign societal processes, it is thought, beget frustration and anger, which in turn beget Black rebellion. One might wonder why Black rebellions do not occur more frequently or even why there are no White rebellions in the contemporary period because such societal processes are commonplace manifestations in American society (Lupsha, 1969, p. 284). Nevertheless, in objectifying African American phenomena, sociopsychological models foster an analytical approach that favors individuation; that is, individual Blacks are lifted out of the African American collective experience so that their personal frustration (and contentment) levels can be gauged. As reductionist methods of inquiry, sociopsychological approaches are forced to project individual (personal) statuses as the decisive catalysts for group behavior. But with the individual (as peripheral object) being the primary unit of analysis, the common experiences of African Americans—their shared feelings, hardships, and collective expressions of struggle against abhorrent conditions and treatment are conspicuously ignored.

Such explanations ultimately continue the legacy of regarding Black urban rebellion as the primary resolve of those who resort to unacceptable means of expression, and therefore, their claims and grievances are not worthy of consideration in the political system. Lacking political legitimacy, as some of these arguments suggest they do, Black insurgents really distort reality and sabotage the correct, normal avenues for the redress of grievances. Irrationality and all of its ominous connotations are subsequently used to describe Black rebellious actions. Furthermore, when irrationality, a code word for abnormal or bizarre social expression, is used to interpret violent actions, it becomes convenient to dismiss African Americans altogether as deviants. Thus, when singularly applied, psychic strain as the impetus for the emergence of rebellion runs the risk of portraying such actions as only efforts to relieve mental anxieties and not to reform, remove, or replace the systemic and societal constructs that create the anxieties.

Also, in ignoring the injurious effects of Euro-American domination on African Americans in a wide range of life activities, the Black freedom movement and struggle against injustice and racism (individual and institutional) as contextual foundations are noticeably excluded from consideration. The consequences are that Black nontraditional and antisystemic behavioral responses to racial domination are appraised without considering the historical and situational forms of racial domination. Willhelm (1971) has noted that the absence of a historical perspective within the sociopsychological approach leads to wrongly blaming African Americans for their feelings of discontentment: "To place blame for discontentment on the Negro minority while simultaneously ignoring the white society of which this minority is a part is to ignore reality and indict an already overly abused people" (pp. 150–151).

A bigger flaw in these theories is that by reducing the Black collective experience to personalized mental statuses, the theories impede the development of meaning about Black violence that can be derived from considering the collectivist ethos of African American history and culture. With the Black-White situation being one in which Whites occupy the dominant position and Blacks occupy the subordinate/submissive position (Jones, 1972), we are assured that the interactive affairs between the two groups will be primarily conflictual rather than harmonic. This thereby ensures an array of oppositional and emancipatory efforts on the part of African Americans. This leads us to consider the protest theory.

Although some previous studies have at least recognized the element of protest in Black rebellions (Fogelson, 1971; Skolnick, 1969; Tomlinson, 1970), they do not go far enough. They observe, rightly, that violence is an expression of protest against the indignities of racial discrimination and exploitation. However, without the core values of the African American experience as key referents, developing a more complete explanation of Black violence cannot occur. This is what Fogelson does when, instead of looking to the African American heritage for cultural symbols and principles, he looks only to the vaunted Euro-American cultural symbol—the American Dream—as the definitive and solitary aspiration for African Americans (p.13). But, in so doing, he fails to discern that the interposition of White supremacist domination in Black-White relations makes this symbol a mere abstraction for substantial numbers of African Americans. For good reason, principles not adhered to are turned on their head.

To support his proposition, Fogelson (1971) must first contest the idea that African Americans are colonized/dominated. Yet, in reproaching the colonial model, which is but one form of domination, he gets mired down in comparing the particulars of materiality rather than specifying the essence of Black-White relations. With the colonial and neocolonial domination of continental Africa not being perfectly analogous in all of their material particulars with the Black-White situation in the United States, Fogelson winds up dismissing the comparison altogether. Hence, the inference is that African Americans are not really dominated.

This view, however, artificially severs and constricts the meaning of domination in such a way that material conditions are given priority over essence. But domination is much more than material conditions. Domination involves thematic propensities in intergroup relations where the material and psychocultural spheres of reality intersect. One does not exist without the other. Yet, it is the psychocultural sphere that gives the material world its form, structure, and systematized functioning. Fogelson (1971) ignores the psychocultural dimension of domination and, in so doing, ignores the psychocultural process of resistance against domination. This leads him to insinuate that African Americans experience only exploitation and discrimination, not domination. There is no good reason to make such a leap in logic. In fact, what Fogelson wants to assure us of is that the African American experience is but an appendage of the Euro-American experience and that all Black people wanted after six summers of uprisings in the 1960s was for White society to honor its egalitarian principles. But in rejecting the colonial model, Fogelson dismisses the possibility that Black indigenous values and concepts have anything to do with the violence. Only Euro-American values, most notably the celebrated American Dream, form the basis for analysis. In conceptualizing the African American experience in this way, he denies subject status to Black people. In other words, he does not see Black people as self-conscious actors fashioning their own history and destiny.

Contrary to Fogelson's (1971) views, it is not simply "matters of the heart" of White society that are at issue. What is important are the self-generative values and motifs cultivated by Blacks, first among themselves and then in their interactive relations with others. Without these values and motifs, there is no genuine movement for Black freedom and self-determination but only reactionary impulses to the interposition of Euro-American cultural and political formations.

To examine Black urban rebellion, we must look to the African American heritage for concepts and values. Doing so leads to new ground that can be explored in the construction of knowledge and the development of a theory of Black collective violence. Let us now explore key issues in the African American experience for a more appropriate conceptual framework to guide our analysis.

The Heritage of African Americans: Basis for a New Perspective

Two levels of explanation—one historical, the other contemporary—will assist in gaining clarity on Black urban rebellion. Combined, these offer a more comprehensive basis for exploring the situational factors and cultural processes leading to Black urban rebellion. The appropriateness of this approach is based on its holism.

The historical level of analysis enables one to look beyond current conditions and events to examine Black violence as an outgrowth of key core values derived from the African American historical experience. As such, we are talking about more than mere protest against contemporary forms of Euro-American domination. The task lies in demonstrating that Black violence is properly regarded as a contributory component to the long-standing African American freedom movement. From this vantage point, the 20th century's urban Black uprisings are not isolated events without meaning. Nor are they disconnected from the ebb and flow of African American history. Instead, like their 17th- through 19th-century counterparts (the slave revolts), Black urban rebellions constitute displays of violent resistance against the dynamics of Euro-American domination.

The inception of resistance as a cultural symbol and its evolution into an emancipatory motif among African Americans has been well noted by numerous writers. In a magnificent story of the African American freedom movement, Harding (1981) first reminds us that Black resistance to European impingements has its origins in Africa, where the African

> struggle was to resist the breaking of our nations, our families, and the chain of our existence. Our struggle was to free ourselves from the already obviously brutal captivity which was spreading over the people like some cloud of foreboding and death, to free ourselves for the life that our forebears had willed to us and our children. (p. 9)

Harding (1981) adds that "it was on the edges of our continent—where some of us gulped down handfuls of sand in a last effort to hold the reality of the land—that the long struggle for black freedom began" (p. 3). With African nations and culture being disrupted by European enslavement and colonization, resistance through the expressive forms of music, song, and dance would become the principal means of revitalizing Black being (Richards, 1992). In the African diaspora, these creative cultural forms serve to promote group solidarity, sustain hope, build self-confidence, and provide ways of expressing and verbalizing aggression.

It was during the slaveocracy period that an ideology of Black resistance to White racial domination was explicated. With the publication of David Walker's *Appeal* in 1829, we have the first sustained critique by an African person of White racism and slavery as systemic, societal evils (Walker, 1829/1993, p. 9). Walker's polemic scrutinizes the religio-political creed of the United States, pointing out in graphic and erudite detail the sordidness with which Euro-Americans adhered to its precepts. But Walker did more than criticize. His *Appeal* provoked immense trepidation among Whites, particularly the slaveholding classes, because of its urgent call for Africans to resist White domination in every possible way. Interestingly, just two years after the first edition of Walker's *Appeal*, Nat Turner launched one of the most dreadful slave revolts in American history. Many believe that Walker's influence was instrumental in urging Nat Turner and his comrades to make their move.

Other Black theorists, such as Henry Highland Garnet in 1843 and Frantz Fanon during the watershed *years* of African anticolonial struggle, have also explained the indispensable and contributory role of violent resistance to domination in the process of achieving freedom. Speaking at the 1843 National Negro Convention in Buffalo, New York, the Reverend Garnet exhorted enslaved Africans to rebel. "Let your motto be resistance! resistance! resistance!" the spirited Garnet declared. "No oppressed people have ever secured their liberty without resistance. What kind of resistance you had better make, you must decide by the circumstances that surround you, and according to the suggestion of expediency" (as cited in Aptheker, 1973, p. 233). For Fanon (1963), violent resistance to colonial domination is essential to the process of decolonizing the African psyche, of ridding African consciousness of an imposed inferiority complex.

As an emancipatory motif and core principle of the African American heritage, resistance is the obligatory means by which the goals of freedom, self-determination, and justice might be actualized. In its expression, resistance can be both individual and collective, calculated and spontaneous, and nonviolent and violent. Although resistance itself is not exclusively an African value (presumably other subjugated groups would value resistance as well), when explaining its functional worth to African Americans, their interests and goals must be the reference source. This cultural and sociopolitical groundedness expands the conceptual base, thereby allowing for a proper assessment of the significance and limitations of various types of Black resistance. From this vantage point, for instance, we can readily observe one limitation of Black urban rebellion: It does not revitalize the cultural and educational lives of Black people (Asante, 1990, p. 179). All told, however, Black defiance, including collective violence, has been part of the historical and historic movement for Black freedom and justice.

The contemporary level, on the other hand, encompasses what can be called the primary determinants underlying Black violence. Of particular importance is the situational context of contemporary Euro-American domination over and oppression of African Americans in which Black resistance, including violence, takes shape. In this context, it is possible to see Black violence as a behavioral response to the distressing and circumscribing effects of Euro-American dominance. This facilitates a distinct appraisal of the systemic and societal constructs that have created and perpetuated African American subordination in urban America.

The contemporary level of analysis is also flexible enough to take into consideration the situational variations or circumstances one might expect to find in different cities. But the primary concern must be on systemic, societal issues and must concentrate on the essence of Black-White intergroup relations. By focusing on systemic, societal issues, we find that there are thematic propensities that pattern the reality of intergroup relations. These represent the central forces shaping racial conflict in the United States. Foremost among these thematic forces is the practice of White supremacist domination circumscribing and depreciating Black being in all areas of life activity. The Black response has been a variety of resistance endeavors, seeking ultimately to bring to an end White domination and to bring into being freedom and justice.

References

Aptheker, H. (1973). *A documentary history of the negro people in the United States:* From colonial times through the Civil War. Secaucus, NJ: Citadel Press.

Asante, M. K. (1990). *Kemet, Afrocentricity and knowledge.* Trenton. NJ: Africa World Press.

Banfield, E. C. (1970). The unheavenly city: *The nature and the future of our urban crisis.* Boston: Little, Brown.

California Governor's Commission on the Los Angeles Riots. (1965, December 2). *Violence in the city—An end or a beginning?* Los Angeles: Author.

Dahl, R. A. (1967). *Pluralist democracy in the United States: Conflict and consent.* Chicago: Rand McNally.

Fanon, F. (1963). *The wretched of the Earth* (Trans. by Constance Farrington). New York: Grove Weidenfeld.

Fogelson, R. M. (1971). *Violence as protest: A study of riots and ghettos.* Garden City, NY: Doubleday.

Harding, V. (1981). *There is a river: The Black struggle for freedom in America.* New York: Harcourt Brace Jovanovich.

Jones, M. (1972). A frame of reference for Black politics. In L. Henderson Jr. (Ed.), *Black political life in the United States* (pp. 7-20). San Francisco: Chandler.

Kornhauser, W. (1959). *The politics of mass society.* Glencoe, IL: Free Press.

Lupsha, P. A. (1969). On theories of urban violence. *Urban Affairs Quarterly, 4,* 272-296.

Mannheim, K. (1936). *Ideology and utopia: An introduction to the sociology of knowledge.* New York: Harcourt, Brace.

McAdam, D. (1982). *Political process and the development of Black insurgency, 1930-1970.* Chicago: University of Chicago Press.

McKee, J. B. (1993). *Sociology and the race problem: The failure of a perspective.* Urbana University of Illinois Press.

Oglesby, J. (1980, May 19). Blacks can't cure travesty with rioting. *The Miami Herald,* p. 1A.

O'Reilly, K. (1989). *Racial matters: The FBI's secret file on Black America, 1960-1972.* New York: Free Press.

Richards, D. M. (1992). *Let the circle be unbroken: The implications of African spirituality in the diaspora.* Lawrenceville, NJ: Red Sea Press.

Sears, D. O., & McConahay, J. B. (1973). *The politics of violence: The new urban Blacks and the Watts riot.* Boston: Houghton Mifflin.

Skolnick, J. H, (1969). *The politics of protest.* New York: Simon & Schuster.

Smelser, N. J. (1962). *Theory of collective behavior.* New York: Free Press.

Tomlinson, T. M. (1970). Determinants of Black politics: Riots and the growth of militancy. *Psychiatry: Journal for the Study of Interpersonal Processes, 33,* 247-264.

U.S. National Advisory Commission on Civil Disorders. (1968). *Report of the National Advisory Commission on Civil Disorders.* New York: Bantam.

Walker, D. (1993). *David Walker's Appeal* (Introduction by James Turner). Baltimore, MD: Black Classic Press. (Original work published 1829)

Willhelm, S. (1971). *Who needs the negro?* Garden City, NY: Anchor.

23

Warrior for Gringostroika

Guillermo Gómez-Peña

I live smack in the fissure between two worlds, in the infected wound: half a block from the end of Western civilization and four miles from the beginning of the Mexican/American border, the northernmost point of Latin America. In my fractured reality, but a reality nonetheless, they cohabit two histories, languages, cosmologies, artistic traditions, and political traditions which are drastically counterposed. Many "deterritorialized" Latin American artists in Europe and the United States have opted for "internationalism" (a cultural identity based upon the "most advanced" of the ideas originating out of New York or Paris). I, on the other hand, opt for "borderness" and assume my role: my generation, the chilango (slang term for a Mexico City native), who came to "El Norte" fleeing the imminent ecological and social catastrophe of Mexico City, gradually integrated itself into otherness, in search of that other Mexico grafted onto the entrails of the et cetera . . . became Chicano-ized. We de-Mexicanized ourselves to Mexi-understand ourselves, some without wanting to, others on purpose. And one day, the border became our house, laboratory, and ministry of culture (or counterculture).

We witness the borderization of the world, by-product of the "deterritorialization" of vast human sectors. The borders either expand or are shot full of holes. Cultures and languages mutually invade one another. The South rises and melts, while the North descends dangerously with its economic and military pincers. The East moves west and vice versa. Europe and

North America daily receive uncontainable migrations of human beings, a majority of whom are being displaced involuntarily. This phenomenon is the result of multiple factors: regional wars, unemployment, overpopulation, and especially the enormous disparity in North/South relations.

The demographic facts are staggering: the Middle East and Black Africa are already in Europe, and Latin America's heart now beats in the United States. New York and Paris increasingly resemble Mexico City and Sao Paolo. Cities like Tijuana and Los Angeles, once sociourban aberrations, are becoming models of a new hybrid culture, full of uncertainty and vitality. And border youth—the fearsome "cholo-punks," children of the chasm that is opening between the "First" and the "Third" worlds, become the indisputable heirs to a new mestizaje (the fusion of the Amerindian and European races).

In this context, concepts like "high culture," "ethnic purity," "cultural identity," "beauty," and "fine arts" are absurdities and anachronisms. Like it or not, we are attending the funeral of modernity and the birth of a new culture.

Our experience as Latino border artists and intellectuals in the United States fluctuates between legality and between partial citizenship and full. For the Anglo community we are simply "an ethnic minority," a subculture, that is to say, some kind of pre-industrial tribe with a good consumerist appetite. For the art world, we are practitioners of distant languages that, in the best of cases, are perceived as exotic.

In general, we are perceived through the folkloric prisms of Hollywood, fad literature, and publicity; or through the ideological filters of mass media. For the average Anglo, we are nothing but "images," "symbols," "metaphors." We lack ontological existence and anthropological concreteness. We are perceived indiscriminately as magic creatures with shamanistic powers, happy bohemians with pretechnological sensibilities, or as romantic revolutionaries born in a Cuban poster from the 1970s. All this without mentioning the more ordinary myths, which link us with drugs, supersexuality, gratuitous violence, and terrorism; myths that serve to justify racism and disguise the fear of cultural otherness.

These mechanisms of mythification generate semantic interference and obstruct true intercultural dialogue. To make border art implies to reveal and subvert said mechanism.

Despite the great cultural mirage sponsored by the people in power, everywhere we look we find pluralism, crisis, and non-synchronicity. The so-called dominant culture is no longer dominant. Dominant culture is a meta-reality that only exists in the virtual space of the mainstream media and in the ideologically and aesthetically controlled spaces—of the monocultural institutions.

Today, if there is a dominant culture, it is border culture. And those who still haven't crossed a border will do it very soon. All Americans (from the vast continent America) were, are, or will be border-crossers. "All Mexicans," says Tomas Ybarra-Frausto, a Chicano theoritician in New York, "are potential Chicanos." As you read this text, you are crossing a border yourself.

Intercultural Dialogue

The social and ethnic fabric of the United States is filled with interstitial wounds, invisible to those who didn't experience the historical events that generated them, or who are victimized by historical amnesia. Those who cannot see these wounds feel frustrated by the hardships of intercultural dialogue. Intercultural dialogue unleashes the demons of history.

Arlene Raven, an artist and writer in New York, once told me, "In order to heal the wound, we first have to open it." In 1989, we are just opening the wound. To truly communicate with the cultural other is an extremely painful and scary experience. It is like getting lost in a forest of misconceptions or walking on mined territory.

The territory of intercultural dialogue is abrupt and labyrinthine. It is filled with geysers and cracks; with intolerant ghosts and invisible walls. Anglo-Americans are filled with stereotypical notions about Latinos and Latino-American art. Latin Americans are exaggeratedly distrustful of initiatives toward binational dialogue coming from this side/el otro lado. Bicultural Latinos in the United States (be they Chicanos, Nuyorricans, or others) and monocultural citizens of Latin America have a hard time getting along. This conflict represents one of the most painful border wounds, a wound in the middle of a family, a bitter split between two lovers from the same hometown.

Fear is the sign of the times. The 1980s are the culture of fear. Everywhere I go, I meet Anglo-Americans immersed in fear. They are scared of us, the other, taking over their country, their jobs, their neighborhoods, their universities, their art world. To "them," "we" are a whole package that includes an indistinct Spanish language, weird art, a sexual threat, gang activity, drugs, and "illegal aliens." They don't realize that their fear has been implanted as a form of political control; that this fear is the very source of the endemic violence that has been affecting this society since its foundation.

Border culture can help dismantle the mechanisms of fear. Border culture can guide us back to common ground and improve our negotiating skills. Border culture is a process of negotiation towards utopia, but in this case, utopia means peaceful coexistence and fruitful cooperation. The border is all we share/La frontera es lo único que compartimos.

My border colleagues and I are involved in a tripartite debate around separatism. Some Chicano nationalists who still haven't understood that Chicano culture has been redefined by the recent Caribbean and Central American immigrations feel threatened by the perspective of intercultural dialogue and Pan-Americanism. Meanwhile, sectors of the Mexican intelligentsia, viewing themselves as "guardians of Mexican sovereignty," see in our proposals for binational dialogue "a disguised form of integration" and pull back. Ironically, the conservative Anglo-Americans who are witnessing with panic the irreversible borderization of the United States tend to agree with Chicano and Mexican separatists who claim to speak from the left. The three parties prefer to defend "their" identity and culture, rather than to dialogue with the cultural other. The three parties would like to see the border closed. Their intransigent views are based on the modernist premise that identity and culture are closed systems, and that the less these systems change, the more "authentic" they are.

The Border Is . . . (A Manifesto)

Border culture is a polysemantic term.

Stepping outside of one's culture is equivalent to walking outside of the law.

Border culture means boycott, complot, ilegalidad, clandestinidad, contrabando, transgresión, desobediencia binacional: en otros palabras, to smuggle dangerous poetry and utopian visions from one culture to another, desde allá, hasta acá.

But it also means to maintain one's dignity outside the law.

But it also means hybrid art forms for new contents-ingestation: spray mural, techno-altar, poetry-in-tongues, audio graffiti, punkarachi, video corrido, anti-bolero, anti-todo: la migra (border patrol), art world, police, monocultura; en otras palabras y tierras, an art against the monolingües, tapados, nacionalistas, ex-teticistas en extinción, per omnia saecula speculorum.

. . .

But it also means to be fluid in English, Spanish, Spanglish, and Ingleñol, 'cause Spanglish is the language of border diplomacy.

But it also means transcultural friendship and collaboration among races, sexes, and generations.

But it also means to practice creative appropriation, expropriation, and subversion of dominant cultural forms.

But it also means a new cartography; a brand-new map to host the new project; the democratization of the East; the socialization of the West; the Third-Worldization of the North and the First-Worldization of the South.

But it also means a multiplicity of voices away from the center, different geo-cultural relations among more culturally akin regions: Tepito—San Diejuana, San Pancho—Nuyorrico, Miami—Quebec, San Antonio—Berlin, your home town and mine, digamos, a new internationalism ex centris.

But it also means regresar y volver a partir: to return and depart once again, 'cause border culture is a Sisyphean experience and to arrive is just an illusion.

But it also means a new terminology for new hybrid identities and métiers constantly metamorphosing: sudacá, not sudaca; Chicarrican, not Hispanic; mestizaje, not miscegenation; social thinker, not bohemian; accionista, not performer; intercultural, not postmodern.

But it also means to develop new models to interpret the world-in-crisis, the only world we know.

But it also means to push the borders of countries and languages or, better said, to find new languages to express the fluctuating borders.

But it also means experimenting with the fringes between art and society, legalidad and illegality, English and español, male and female, North and South, self and other; and subverting these relationships.

But it also means to speak from the crevasse, desde acá, desde el medio. The border is the juncture, not the edge, and monoculturalism has been expelled to the margins.

But it also means glasnost, not government censorship, for censorship is the opposite of border culture.

But it also means to analyze critically all that lies on the current table of debates: multicul-turalism, the Latino "boom," "ethnic art," controversial art, even border culture.

But it also means to question and transgress border culture. What today is powerful and necessary, tomorrow is arcane and ridiculous; what today is border culture, tomorrow is insti-tutional art, not vice versa.

But it also means to escape the current co-optation of border culture.

But it also means to look at the past and the future at the same time. 1492 was the begin-ning of a genocidal era. 1992 will mark the beginning of a new era: America post-Colombina, Arteamérica sin fronteras. Soon, a new internationalism will have to gravitate around the spinal cord of this continent—not Europe, not just the North, not just white, not only you, compañero del otro lado de la frontera, el lenguaje y el océano.

24

The Inventing and Reinventing of "Model Minorities": The Cultural Veil Obscuring Structural Sources of Inequality

Deborah Woo

With but a few changes in detail, the same fable can be—and has been—told about the Japanese, Irish, Jews, Italians, Greeks, Swedes and many more. Its form is always the same: a people beset by hardships and oppression in their own country bravely cross the seas to America, a land which promises freedom and opportunity. Once arrived, however, they encounter prejudice, oppression, and difficult times. However, they never lose faith in the dream that originally compelled them. They work hard, refuse to be discouraged by the abuses that harm their lives and hinder their progress, and eventually—usually in the second, or sometimes the third generation—succeed. History is, thus, nicely encapsulated within the American Protestant ethic . . . (Lyman, 1973: 71)

Sociologist Stanford Lyman thus indicated how success stories about Chinese in America were part of "America's perpetual morality tale about its minorities." This imagery has not only been extended to other Asian Americans but been firmly implanted through the recitation of statistical data.

During the 1970s when the Asian American population was largely Japanese Americans and Chinese Americans, gross statistical profiles of these groups pointed to their high educational and occupational achievement (Varon, 1967). Conversely, one found relatively low rates of divorce (Sanborn, 1977; Barringer et al., 1995: 136–144), unemployment (Jaco and Wilber, 1975), crime[1] and delinquency (Beach, 1932; Kitano, 1969; Takagi and Platt, 1978; Strong, 1934), and mental illness (Jew and Brody, 1967). As the fastest growing of minority groups in the United States (O'Hare and Felt, 1991; Gardner et al., 1985; Bureau of the Census, 1993),[2] Asian Americans are the most highly educated of all groups, including white males, and are projected in the next decade to make up a disproportionate share of the professional workforce (Ong and Hee, 1993; Fullerton, 1989).

While supporting facts for the morality tale are often based on census data, the myth is kept alive by media accounts. It is here, in fact, where demography is aligned with culturally appealing explanations. A strong work ethic, high value placed on educational achievement, and stable family relations are routinely cited as among the most influential factors promoting upward mobility. Underlying it all is a theme of hard work and determination that echoes the stories told by Horatio Alger (1832–1899). A Harvard educated man and ordained minister, Alger had penned hundreds of stories about penniless boys who pulled themselves out of poverty by their own "bootstraps." As works of fiction intended to inspire, they valorized honesty and diligence, the heroes representing not so much extraordinary individuals but ones who made modest though significant efforts. The "Asian" Horatio Alger myth can be seen as an extension of such tales woven around aspiring immigrants in this country. In the more recent period, the substance of the narrative has been slightly altered to incorporate high-tech success, but the form of these stories remains very much the same.

This presentation discusses how the *cultural* assumptions underlying the thesis ignore certain *structural* or *class* issues. In doing so, it calls into question a fundamental premise of model minority logic—namely, that cultural factors are the primary ingredients for success. Apart from Horatio Alger's legacy, a culturalist approach to understanding social issues has enjoyed great favor in the United States, whereas a long history of class analysis has dominated European thought on stratification.[3] The controversy between cultural and class analyses came to a head in the United States during the unrest and agitation of the 1960s, with the emergence of the "culture of poverty" idea. American leftists saw this idea as "victim-blaming," as the social problems of American blacks were attributed to a "culture of poverty," an "unstable family structure" and way of life that promoted failure or low achievement (Moynihan, 1965; Valentine, 1968). By the same logic, discriminatory actions on the part of employers and a host of institutions could be dismissed as causes of continuing racial segregation and its consequences for employment (Massey and Denton, 1993; Wilson, 1997).

As a result, cultural explanations in general become politically suspect among that generation of scholars and activists, particularly as the melting pot ideal, along with culturally-based mobility assumptions, were empirically contradicted by research evidence (Glazer and Moynihan, 1963; Steinberg, 1982).[4] Culture of poverty ideas, however, would resurface in a new form, namely, through an inverted discourse that premised achievement on an enabling cultural repertoire of values associated with Asian Americans as "model minorities."

By the 1980s and 1990s the model minority thesis was being used as a wedge in arguments against affirmative action (*Asian American Policy Review,* 1996). With the publication of *The Bell Curve* in 1994, genetic twist was added to these racial explanations, as social inequalities were reduced to "natural" differences in inherited intelligence between the races. The relatively inferior status of blacks vis-a-vis whites and Asians was reframed as one of basic intelligence, and by implication, a problem that could not be remedied through government intervention (Herrnstein and Murray, 1994).

For these reasons, where issues of social inequality in matters of race and ethnicity are concerned, Asian Americans occupy a critical place in our thinking about ethnic politics. They are not only a common empirical reference point for evaluating relative progress and achievement among different groups but an ideological one as well. Critics of the ideological agenda have disputed the statistical facts themselves, along with the cultural theory purporting to explain them. The concept of "model minority" has been criticized as simplistic, masking extreme inequalities within and between different Asian American groups, as well as deflecting attention from structural issues that might better account for success or failure. Although such critiques have produced a certain retreat from uncritical use of the term in public discourse,[5] in the larger public arena the image of a successfully assimilating minority continues to be seductive, forming an inescapable backdrop for a wide array of issues where Asian Americans have been drawn into broader social and political analyses of American society.

An analysis of the various factors responsible for the persistence of the model minority thesis therefore has significant theoretical implications. The basic argument in this chapter is that model minority theory has withstood counterevidence and counterarguments by ushering available facts under its own umbrella, and that this has been possible due to inattention to the problematic aspects of doing so. In a review and analysis of images in the popular press in the 1960s and 1980s, Keith Osajima pointed out how subsequent versions of the thesis have been based on "remarkably pliable constructs," enabling critical research findings to be embraced and subsumed under the core thesis of success, though the fundamental thesis remained largely unchanged (Osajima, 1988). In this way, simplistic portrayals became slightly more "complex" in the 1980s. The bulk of the following analysis is aimed at reviewing some of the major critiques of the thesis, introducing others which deserve attention, and thereby explaining how the thesis has survived into the 1990s.

Asian Americans as "Model Minorities": A Legacy of the 1960s

Up until the late 1960s, the Asian population in the United States was a fraction of what it is today and still largely invisible. The introduction of national immigration quotas in the 1920s had sharply curtailed Asian immigration, reducing it to a trickle. Until the abolishment of these quotas in 1965, the maximum annual immigration permitted from Asia was 2,990, compared to a total allowance of 149,667 for Europe (Chan, 1991:146). Subsequent immigration would fundamentally transform the social composition of Asian American communities by increasing the dominance of the foreign-born population and the presence of a large proportion of professionals (Hing, 1993). It was the experiences, however, of native-born Chinese and Japanese Americans, who formed the large majority of the Asian American population prior to 1965, that would be the original stimulus for media stories of success.

There is no question that this nation has absorbed immigrants with extraordinary differences in history, religion, race, class, and national origin (Levine, 1996). As evidenced by the acculturation of subsequent generations and increasing rates of outmarriage,[6] a certain degree of assimilation or acculturation occurs simply as a matter of time and increasing social contact, with relations of power setting the term for that contact. Yet, it has been the persistence of racial inequalities that has served as an ongoing challenge to faith in the inevitability of assimilation, as well as a catalyst to demands for change.

During the 1960s, the need to reexamine and address issues of racial inequality was pronounced. Racial unrest was one of several sources of societal discontent, which together with the war in Vietnam, led to demands for government reforms that had not been equaled since the Great Depression of the 1930s. Over and against such moves towards fundamental institutional change were competing attempts to recast the causes of social inequality in terms of individual effort and hard work.

Thus, for example, on December 26, 1966, *U.S. News and World Report* printed an article entitled "Success Story of One Minority in the U.S.," in which it was suggested that blacks and other minorities were making unreasonable demands for government assistance. At a time when it is being proposed that hundreds of billions be spent to uplift Negroes and other minorities, the nation's 300,000 Chinese-Americans are moving ahead on their own, with no help from anyone else" (p. 73). Earlier in the year, *The New York Times* had published a piece called "Success Story, Japanese American Style," in which the emphasis upon self-help was implicitly, if not explicitly, a point of admiration. "By any criterion we choose, the Japanese Americans are better off than any other group in our society, including native-born whites. They have established this remarkable record, moreover, by their own almost totally unaided effort" (p. 25).

Such news coverage quickly caught the attention of Asian Americans in the scholarly community, who have been sharply critical of such portrayals ever since (Kitano and Sue, 1973[7]; Kim, 1973; Suzuki, 1977; Kim and Hurh, 1983; Osajima, 1988; Suzuki, 1989). The concern was twofold: (1) that there were unwarranted assumptions made about the progress of Asian Americans, and (2) that the comparisons with other racial groups were invidious and insidious, generating ill feelings with the moral injunction that underachievers, particularly "certain" minorities, "re-form" themselves after this "model."

While the 1980s would generate research and objective evidence countering unqualified accounts of Asian American success, the print media continued to promote a picture of extraordinary accomplishment. Thus, for example, in 1982 the *Oakland Tribune* noted that Chinese Americans had among the highest per capita incomes, echoing the impressive accomplishments which have marked overseas Chinese communities.

They have been inordinately successful on both sides of the Pacific. U.S. census fig-
ures indicate that Asian Americans, including 705,000 of Chinese extraction, now have
the nation's highest per capita income, echoing the achievements that have made Hong
Kong, Singapore, and Taipei nodal points of booming Asia. (Oakland Tribune, *May 26,*
1982)

As the Immigration Act of 1965 introduced new ethnic dimensions into the Asian American population, making it more diverse than ever before,[8] success stories have been reproduced for other Asian ethnic groups as well, including Japanese, Koreans, and Southeast Asians (Caudill and DeVos, 1956; Kim and Hurh, 1983; Osajima, 1988; Caplan et al., 1985, 1992, 1994). Even diverging cultural values did not undermine the popular view that had brought this population center stage, namely, Horatio Alger dreams and belief in a "cultural formula for success."

The Persistence and Elasticity of the "Model Minority Thesis"

Insofar as they represent living embodiments of certain ideals and their related ethical injunctions, Asian Americans have enjoyed a certain status as prima facie testimonials to these myths. The model minority thesis has persisted, however, for other reasons. It is in the face of a cumulative body of contradicting evidence that a closer examination is called for. Five reasons are offered to explain this tenacity: (1) media celebration of a few dramatic examples of "rags-to-riches" stories, (2) the existence of a sizable and visible group of highly educated professionals, (3) failure to disaggregate census data, (4) unexamined assertions about the relationship between culture and mobility, including a dearth of studies on the relative role of culture and social class background, and (5) the specific political or ideological purposes served by the thesis.

The thread throughout this discussion is that the thesis was never based on careful, systematic analysis but rather has been a loose grab-bag of assumptions. Expediently put together, there is a flexibility to the reasoning which is stretched to accommodate contradictions, both empirical and logical. The major crutch supporting the thesis is itself ideological—the myth of the American Dream.

Media Celebration of a Few Dramatic Examples of "Rags-to-Riches" Stories

Good journalism minimally implies careful coverage and documentation of the facts on some topic. At its very best, it goes beyond the mere reporting of facts and brings an analysis, critical perspective or comprehension of the issues. Where Asian Americans have walked onto the stage, it is the way in which they have been cast as players that has made their appearance "newsworthy." The stories of individuals here are rarely simply about individuals but about a racial set or cultural mold. This is true whether the subject is an imbroglio as serious as campaign finance contributions with an "Asian Connection" (Wu and Nicholson, 1997) or "human interest stories" which are told for their broad popular appeal as morality tales. This section speaks to the latter, with the particular goal of showing how the value of such cultural narratives derives less from representations that conform with some objective reality than from how they function to support the dominant ideology that fits the American Dream (Hsu, 1996).

In April of 1998, the *Washington Post* retold a familiar fable, now rendered in the form of high-tech success. The opening line thus read: "The classic dream of entrepreneurial America came true in Landover yesterday: Jeong Kim, a Korean-born immigrant who once worked the night shift at 7-Eleven to put himself through school, sold his company—for $1 billion." In selecting this news account for his "Osgood Files," radio commentator Charles Osgood similarly opined: "This is a story that Horatio Alger would love to tell." The impetus for the report was the merger of Jeong Kim's company Yurie with Lucent Technology, and Kim's appointment as president of Lucent's Carrier Networks division, making him one of the 100 richest high-tech executives in the country. Such mergers reflect the timbre of our time, though what is considered unmistakably noteworthy and thereby "newsworthy" was the more personal narrative of bootstrap success, matched only by the company's "rocket ascendancy."

At 14, Kim had come to the United States from Seoul with his Korean-born parents, and eventually attended Johns Hopkins University, where he studied electrical engineering and then went on to the University of Maryland, where he received his Ph.D. in engineering. After serving seven years in the navy, where he was the officer of a nuclear submarine, he went to work as a contract engineer at the Naval Research Laboratory. It is here where he began to develop the idea for a multimedia technology that would enable reporters to pipe almost instant voice, data and video feeds from action taking place at international "hot spots," battlefields or elections. Founded on this technology in 1992, his company Yurie made its impact almost immediately, soon marketing to federal agencies and later to [the] world-wide market.

Although initially framed as a "classic" story of entrepreneurial success, the *Washington Post* account later reveals that Kim had not pulled himself entirely up by his bootstraps. Yurie had, like other companies, been "born from government contracts," having received $305,000 Defense Department money through a separate program for small, minority-owned businesses (*Washington Post*, April 18, 1998). The coherence of the story as a cultural narrative is affected by this last observation, and it is to the credit of the writers that they sought to explore this issue. Nevertheless, in the end, it is the original framing of the report that will be remembered.

Over the years, the media has been saturated with stories about individual dreams which are realized through sheer perseverance. On July 16, 1998, CBS News' *48 Hours* dedicated an entire program, "Making It," to this theme, where the dream now encompasses individual aspirations that surpass even Horatio Alger's expectations in terms of the pot at the end of the rainbow: "Only in America: a place where you can reach for your dreams and make it big, against all odds, aiming for that million dollar payday." Stories about Asian Americans which have been tailored to mirror the ethos of the American Dream generally attribute this population's resourcefulness and resilience to cultural values (Osajima, 1988). This culturally-based perceptive is also given legitimacy by academics (Caudill and DeVos, 1956; Petersen, 1971; Sowell, 1981). Whether because of a general public thirst that remains unquenched, or because of particular circumstances surrounding their own condition, ethnic insiders, in turn, have relished success stories where desperate circumstances, back-breaking or mind-numbing work, are transcended through pluck, ingenuity, and above all, the ability to endure and persevere.

The story of David Tsang is illustrative of how such accounts derive their appeal as inspirational stories. A successful entrepreneur and founder of three high-technology companies in the Bay Area, his life is told in a style that conforms with the contours of the fabled climb from rags-to-riches. A "shy young man of 19," he arrives with only "$300 in his pocket and a shabby suitcase" in a country which "seemed like an intimidating, unfriendly land." Despite being alone (with his only contact a "distant friend of his father") and facing obstacles that include corporate politics and his having "just the barest knowledge of English," Tsang "persevered." In the end, this discipline pays off, and after some thirty years, Tsang is described as someone who continues to work 10- to 12-hour days and 6-day weeks, who "prides himself in never giving up," and now offers himself as a role model to "younger, potential Asian American entrepreneurs" (*Asian Week,* March 8, 1996).

In yet another news account, Chong-Moon Lee, also a Silicon Valley entrepreneur, is described as one who persisted despite desperate circumstances which forced him to live on "21-cent packages of Ramen noodles," near bankruptcy, and frequenting pawn shops in order to pay a $168 phone bill (*Asian Week,* November 3, 1995). Lee eventually not only recoups but becomes a major benefactor. Thus, the *San Francisco Chronicle's* coverage of his story underscored his meteoric rise as follows: "From the depths of longing for a hamburger he couldn't afford and contemplating suicide, this entrepreneur rose to such success he was able to give $15 million to S.F.'s Asian Art Museum. Chong-Moon Lee makes Horatio Alger look like a slacker" (*San Francisco Chronicle,* November 5, 1995).

Although such journalism pieces serve as inspirational stories, the problem occurs when they are elevated to the level of social analyses and models for others to emulate, without there also being a commensurate effort to integrate and analyze the role played by other pertinent factors. What these accounts often fail to do is draw the link between biography, history, and society, which C. Wright Mills saw as necessary for escaping the entrapment created by framing the problems in everyday life as individual "troubles," rather than as public "issues."

> *Troubles occur within the character of the individual and within the range of his immediate relations with others; they have to do with his self and with those limited areas of social life of which he is directly and personally aware. Accordingly, the statement and the resolution of troubles properly lie within the individual as a biographical entity and within the scope of his immediate milieu—the social setting that is directly open to his personal experience and to some extent his willful activity. A trouble is a private matter. . . .*
>
> Issues *have to do with matters that transcend these local environments of the individual and the range of his inner life. They have to do with the organization of many such milieux into the institutions of an historical society as a whole, with the ways in which*

various milieux overlap and interpenetrate to form the larger structure of social and historical life. An issue is a public matter. . . . (Mills, 1959: 8)

Individuals who have worked their way up from poverty to wealth are the anomaly, not the rule (Domhoff, 1998: 100–101), though the afterglow left from media attention directed at these anomalies belies the more sociological truth of advantage due to social class privilege. The celebrated success story of Chong-Moon Lee might itself, on closer examination, be qualified in important ways. As a first-generation Korean-born immigrant, Lee certainly faced difficulties a native-born American would not have. He also had, however, certain social advantages and connections, including royal descent. One of his ancestors had been a king who invented the Korean language in the fourteenth century and whose family ruled the country until the Japanese take-over in 1905. Prior to his own immigration and founding of Diamond Multimedia Systems in 1982, Lee had been a university professor as well as successful pharmaceuticals executive in the family business of manufacturing antibiotics. In other words, while his personal success itself is not at issue, his particular biography deviates significantly from the typical Horatio Alger one of humble beginnings. If it is to be treated as a morality tale, then it would seem that the moral of the story is that "making it" in American society is unlikely, given the formidable odds for someone even from such an elite background as Lee. Conversely, the more poignant social commentary is the fact that many who adhere to an ethic of hard work have faced hurdles that are insurmountable. This is not to say that exceptions to this larger pattern cannot be found, but the point is that they *are* exceptions.

Whether or not details about social origins are omitted or included, narrative as ideology is crafted to suggest that the all-important factors were individual character, high moral standards. and motivation. The contradictions in Chong-Moon Lee's life were bracketed discursively, so that by the end of the narrative, an extraordinary history of privilege, with all of its tangible and intangible resources, recedes into the background. In other biographies, we know little about whether or not *other* factors were relevant in propelling such individuals out of desperate circumstances. David Tsang's background, for example, is not fully revealed. We are told that his father was a teacher, which one might infer provided at least a certain level of status, security, and economic means, but this background is otherwise sketchy. Even when there are facts contradicting the idea of humble beginnings or of individual "bootstrappers," the major theme of the American Dream is preserved. Those who identify with this dominant ethos generally buy into the model minority assumption that education will bring with it equality and achievement (Lee, 1996). The life trajectories of those on the bottom, however, are rarely examined for the purpose of empirically specifying the limits of cultural determinism. An implicit assumption or hope is that it will be simply a matter of time and cultural fortitude before those less fortunate close the gap between themselves and their more successful counterparts.

A. Magazine's cover story a few years ago was similarly opaque about the backgrounds of those individuals identified in the title of the article as "Power Brokers: The 25 Most Influential People in Asian America." Directed towards a young Asian American audience, the magazine did not intend any serious coverage of these personages. As the editors themselves state in the paragraph below, they wanted merely to spotlight those they believed to be having a significant influence not simply on "Asian America" but on the country as a whole.

> *The powerful are artists of the social canvas: agenda-makers, trendsetters, and gate keepers. As a result, the process we followed in choosing these individuals as the nation's 25 most powerful Asian Americans relied less on science than instinct. What we sought was a list of those Asian Americans who had touched more people and done more to alter the cultural fabric than any others. Some of those included are symbolic figures— pioneers who have made historic breakthroughs; others are behind-the-scenes decision- makers, whose effects are quieter, but no less important. Some are young faces just begin- ning the upward arcs of their contributing careers; others are veterans whose notable achievements are a matter of record. There are familiar names included, and there are some which are surprising. But, like power itself, we know how mutable this list is and how arbitrary. By this time next year, this order will have changed, and some new names will have replaced old. Until then, we'll be watching these 25 closely. Because they aren't just influencing the direction of Asian America. They're setting the pace for America as a whole. (A. Magazine, 1993: 25)*

Given that such profiles are offered up decontextualized, the omission of a frame leaves the door open to their being seen as Asian-spun versions of the American Dream. As pointed out in another article in this same issue, the value is in having such individuals as role models, especially where there appear to be barriers to achieving the American Dream. The reference here is to glass ceiling barriers, where the rare few who make it are seen as exemplars for other aspirants: "an Asian who demonstrates talent for leadership at an important American organ- ization sends out the message that Asian Americans *can* do the job, and ultimately empowers the entire community" (Chen, 1993:71). Despite the hopefulness behind this conclusion, the viability of role models may be contingent, however, upon other factors as well, ones not so easily emulated.

In their own review of "Asian Americans in the Power Elite," Zweigenhaft and Domhoff (1998) argue that social class plays a critical role in mobility. When looking into the family backgrounds of the Asian Americans in the corporate elite, they found that many did not make the climb from the very bottom of the social ladder but rather from already high rungs of that ladder. Thus, they reported that:

> *. . . Chang-Lin Tien, former Chancellor of the University of California, Berkeley, and a director of Wells Fargo Banks, reports that he arrived in the United States at the age of 21 as a penniless immigrant, unable to speak the language, but he also was born into a wealthy banking family in Wanchu, and his wife's father was a high-ranking officer in Chiang Kai Shek's army. . . .*
>
> *Perhaps the best-known Chinese American—best known because she is a television "personality"—provides yet another example. Connie Chung is the daughter of a former intelligence officer in Chiang Kai Shek's army. . . .*

> *Pei-Yuan Chia, former vice chair of Citibank, was the highest ranking Asian-American executive and corporate director at a world-class American corporation until his unexpected retirement in 1996 at age 56. He also was a prototypical Chinese-American member of the power elite. Born in Hong Kong in 1939, he grew up in a family with a "long line of bankers." . . .*

Zweigenhaft and Domhoff's book is replete with such examples for other groups, women as well as other ethnic minorities, where the biographical details alone contradict Alger's moral message. Indeed, the true moral behind such life stories seems to be that the American Dream is primarily open to those who come with certain material advantages and social connections.

The Existence of a Sizable and Visible Groups of Highly Educated Professionals

A rosy portrait of structural assimilation into American society has been made by pointing to major inroads which Asian Americans have made into both higher education and professional work. There is no denying the existence of a sizable and visible group of highly educated professionals. Rather, it is the conceptual or theoretical leaps from such observations that need to be reexamined, especially the view that they are the contemporary Horatio Alger's heroes.

To remain true to the myth of humble beginnings, one would have to ignore the fact that the 1965 Immigration Act contained special provisions that specifically recruited professionally trained personnel to these shores. As a select group of immigrants, they arrive either already educated and trained, or from sufficiently affluent social class backgrounds which enable them to pursue their education abroad. In fact, the vast majority of Asian students who receive postgraduate degrees from American institutions are foreign-born (Escueta and O'Brien, 1991), with many choosing to remain in the United States after they have graduated. In their study of diversity in America's "power elite," Zweigenhaft and Domhoff acknowledge that there were few "authentic bootstrappers" among Asian Americans, especially Chinese who formed the majority of Asian American directors in Fortune 1000 Boards (Zweigenhaft and Domhoff, 1998:144): "Unlike most Chinese immigrants to the United States before the 1970s, who came from low-income backgrounds, the great majority of Chinese Americans at the top levels of American society are from well-to-do or well-educated families in China, Taiwan, and Hong Kong" (Zweigenhaft and Domhoff, 1998:141).

In general, those in the upper echelons, especially corporate executives, board members, and directors, tended also to be overwhelmingly from the upper strata of society as well. This generalization was found to be true for Jews, women, blacks, Latinos, Asian Americans, and gays and lesbians. Women and minorities who found their way into the power elite were also likely to have to be "better educated than the white males already a part of it." For this reason, the authors state that class was not the only factor that would explain the composition of those in the power elite. One had to also have cultural capital in the form of degrees from high-status institutions. (Zweigenhaft and Domhoff, 1998:179).

Other studies have similarly noted that those from elite universities and colleges were best groomed or primed for the high-status track (Kingston and Lewis, 1990), and that wealth, social connections, and elite educational credentials went far towards explaining disparities in social mobility (Useem and Karabel, 1990).

Whether it is education or social class which has the greater [influence] on mobility, the convergence of high educational and social status among the sizable and visible group of Asian professionals in the United States obscures this distinction. In other words, the lateral mobility of such immigrants to the United States is premised on their affluence, as is any subsequent vertical rise up the ladder.

Failure to Disaggregate Census Data

Of all the criticisms brought to bear on the model minority thesis, the most common one is directed towards the glib and facile generalizations that gloss over important internal differences within this population. At one time, German Americans were blanketly viewed as a rapidly assimilating minority because their internal diversity was overlooked. In a 1996 publication entitled "German Americans: Paradoxes of a 'Model Minority,'" Walter Kamphoefner said that by the 1970s, different sources had already commented on the rapid and complete assimilation of German Americans into American society. Yet, this perception of complete assimilation was erroneously based on the fact that the public made no distinction between "old immigrants" and "new immigrants."[9]

Like German Americans, Asian Americans include many "old" as well as "new immigrants."[10] The native-born descendants of these old immigrants are more likely to be more culturally assimilated than recent immigrants from Asia. Length of time in the U.S., in fact, was found to have an important hearing on *both* income and acculturation. Income levels tended to increase while poverty levels decreased, the longer Asian Americans had been in the United States. All *native* Asian Americans, in fact, with the exception of Vietnamese, did better than blacks or Hispanics in terms of both income and poverty levels (Barringer et al., 1995:154-155).

There are *other* aspects of internal diversity within the Asian American population which also undermine the notion of uniform cultural or structural assimilation. Like earlier German Americans, there are segments of this population which are more accustomed to rural life[11] and more likely than their urban counterparts to resist the pulls of mainstream American society (Knoll, 1982; Walker-Moffat, 1995).

Analysts, furthermore, have noted that Asian American populations tend to concentrate at the extremes of various indicators of social status—i.e., at both the high and low ends, creating what is called a "bimodal" distribution.[12] Statistical "averages" obscure this fact, and the continuing failure to disaggregate these data perpetuates a picture of high achievement, whether we are talking about educational achievement or occupational mobility.

In the case of education achievement, there are large clusters of Asian Americans who are high achievers and the college-bound. In addition, however, there are students whose high school records are not only less promising, but indicative of retention problems, including delinquency (Hune and Chan, 1997; Trueba et al., 1993).

Failure to disaggregate statistical data in other ways has also resulted in spurious comparisons with the white population that suggest Asian Americans are not only doing well but "outdoing whites." (Suzuki, 1989). The common belief that they earn more than other groups, including majority males, was significantly qualified once other factors were "controlled for." These included the number of wage earners per family, region of residence, the nature of managerial work, and whether income calculations are based on mean or median income.

National income averages are misleading since Asian Americans tend to reside in metropolitan areas of high-income states, whereas the general population or non-Hispanic whites are more geographically dispersed. In 1990, three-fifths of Asian Americans lived in just three states—California, Hawaii, and New York (Lott, 1998:59). Thus, if we look at the median annual income for Asian Americans *nationwide* for that year, it was $36,000, whereas that for non-Hispanic whites was $31,100. Disaggregating *national income data* for this same year *reverses* this very picture. From comparisons based on four metropolitan areas: specifically, the median annual income for Asian Pacific Americans was $37,200, compared to $40,000 for non-Hispanic whites (Ong and Hee, 1994:34). Not only are Asian American incomes lower but when one recalls where they live, their dollars also have lower buying power.

Like national income figures, the use of "mean income" can similarly obscure. Given the bimodal character of the Asian American population, median income rather than mean income is the preferred measure, the median being that point above and below which 50 percent of all cases fall. When such adjustments in calculation were made, the median incomes of Japanese, Chinese, Filipino, Koreans, Asian Indians, and Vietnamese, were invariably lower than the mean (Barringer et al., 1995:152–153).

Even when median income is utilized, other crucial differences are still camouflaged. Thus, median family incomes were reported in 1979 to be "considerably higher for all Asian Americans than for whites" (with the exception of Vietnamese). Taking into account such factors [as] the number of wage-earners per household and geographical area of residence sharply alters the comparative picture. The U.S. General Accounting Office explicitly drew attention to this fact when it reported on 1985 incomes. Specifically, it reported that while Asian American households earned $2,973 a month, 28 percent more than the average U.S. household income of $2,325, this difference *disappeared*, once one looked at *per capita* income (U.S. General Accounting Office, 1990:20–21). In other words, Asian Americans did not necessarily *earn more*, but household incomes tended to be higher because they were more likely to have *more income earners*, including unpaid family members.

Where census data are used to gauge the existence of glass ceiling barriers, managerial data are seldom disaggregated to distinguish between fundamentally different managerial levels in the corporate hierarchy or between different sectors of the economy.[13] The distinction between managers in mainstream corporate America and those in ethnic enclaves is especially critical for Asian Americans, since these managerial structures are not comparable. As the following chapter will discuss at greater length, managerial status for Asian Americans often takes the form of self-employment, which may be an indicator not so much of an entrepreneurial spirit but of downward mobility and disaffection with mainstream employment. Even if this propensity for small business involvement is considered a viable opportunity structure, participation in it does not occur across all Asian Americans groups.[14]

In sum, these general methodological issues have critical theoretical implications when assessing the relative progress of Asian Americans vis-a-vis other racial or immigrant groups. While there have been some moves to achieve a better picture of the existing demographic diversity among Asian Americans in census data, analyzing these patterns is another matter.

Unexamined Assertions about the Relationship between Culture and Mobility

Although Asian cultural values have been credited for much individual or group success, it would seem critical to examine the relationship between culture and mobility. There has, however, been a dearth of studies in this regard. One cannot, in other words, *assume* the operation of certain values, or assuming their existence, predict where they will lead.

For one, census data are not a good source of cultural data, except perhaps for language. Thus, sociologist Herbert Barringer and his associates (1995:168) noted in their comprehensive review of the literature on the status of Asian Americans: "census data offer precious little in support of cultural theories." This state of affairs, of course, has not kept people from reading into such data—from assuming, inferring, or imputing the influence of culture as a causal factor. As noted at the outset of this chapter, statistical data provide a certain profile of successful adjustment among Asian Americans. For each statistic, a cultural value can be invoked to explain the rate in question: high educational attainment rates (e.g., value placed on learning, on the scholarly tradition), low employment rates (e.g., strong work ethic), low divorce or delinquency rates (e.g., a strong value placed on the family), low rates of psychiatric hospitalization (e.g., a philosophical attitude of acceptance), and so on.

Notwithstanding that cultural values may be operating at some level, cultural theorizing and empirical research has not kept pace with demographic changes in the population. Second, despite the implied determinism to cultural explanations of mobility, they are unable to explain notable exceptional patterns of deviations even where the values in question are not at issue. The cultural motivation that is often assumed to underlie educational achievement and entrepreneurial activity falls short in both regards.

With respect to the first point, most critiques of the model minority thesis have acknowledged diversity in the Asian American population and have repeatedly pointed to the fact that "not all" Asian Americans have made similar progress.[15] Only by ignoring this cultural diversity as well as the differential within these populations is it possible to exclusively posit success on an enabling body of cultural values. During the 1960s, Chinese and Japanese were the two largest Asian ethnic populations in the United States, and Confucianism was a major part of their cultural orientation, which also included Buddhism, as well as elements of American culture. Since then, the Asian American population has become much more diverse. While the 1970 census included four designated census categories for Asian groups (Chinese, Japanese, Filipino, and Koreans) and one Pacific group (Hawaiians), by the 1980 census, the number of

Asian American groups had increased to twelve, with as many as six Pacific groups (Lott, 1991:58).

A comparison of select Asian subgroups in terms of value orientation and objective status would seem to support the idea of Confucian as this enabling body of values. Where the Confucian tradition has been strongest (e.g., among the Chinese and Japanese), one finds greater clustering of these individuals at the upper end of the income, educational, and occupational ladders. Conversely, those groups where the historical and cultural trail to Confucianism is moot or absent (e.g., among Hmong, Khmer, and Cambodians) are ones where poverty is also higher (Trueba et al., 1993:44).

When still other Asian ethnic groups are brought into the picture, however, it is questionable whether Confucian values themselves can be credited. Thus, for example, Korean Americans fall somewhere between Chinese and Japanese in terms of educational attainment. Despite a strong Confucian tradition in Korea, a significant portion of those who immigrated to the United States in the early 1900s as well as in recent years have been Christian (Abelman and Lie, 1995:198, fn 7; Kim, 1981:187–207; Knoll, 1982:116–121). In the case of both Asian Indians and Filipinos, college completion rates exceed that of other Asian ethnic groups, including the Chinese and Japanese, and yet "neither Filipinos nor Asian Indians can be said to be influenced by Confucianism and they equal or surpass East Asians in educational attainment" (Barringer et al., 1995:164). In other words, there is no single overarching cultural umbrella that satisfactorily explains these similarly high achievement levels.

The model minority thesis has managed to survive because it has managed to stretch or reinvent itself *discursively*, as opposed to through new empirical research (e.g., that which shows how different subcultural tendencies achieve the same ends). Thus, where Confucian values have not fit the picture, the picture of success has been repainted with broader brush strokes positing values related to "hard work" as the key differentiating factor between the poor and the successful.

Yet a second reason why such broad cultural generalizations are insufficient lies in exceptions to their implied determinism. Values alone—seen as "wants," "preferences," or subjective inclinations—are inadequate for understanding action or conduct. Yet given that such assertions continue to be made, it is hard to explain why those who adhere strongly to the same values are not similarly positioned in life.[16]

Some of the relatively greater educational progress of Asian Americans over blacks can be linked not simply to cultural values but to preexisting experiences or structures of support. These include pre-immigration work experiences, either prior professional training or commercial involvement, as well as access to capital for investment (Carnoy, 1995). Money for educational pursuits or business adventures came through family borrowing, rotating credit associations, and more recently, for a select group of entrepreneurs, through large-scale venture capital firms (Park, 1996). For those with little education or English fluency, entrepreneurialism established an economic *floor* for pursuing educational ambitions. In other words, while first-generation immigrant parents might themselves be uneducated and illiterate, their ability to set up small shops makes it possible for their children to climb out of poverty.

While both education and entrepreneurialism offer ways out of poverty, the ability to take advantage of such opportunities is itself influenced by factors other than culture. In the case of Korean Americans, for example, it has been suggested that the relative contribution to mobility played by Confucian or Christian cultural traditions may be less important than situational or structural factors (Min, 1996). If culture were the determining factor, they would have gladly foregone commercial pursuits in favor of government or academic jobs.[17] As Abelmann and Lie explain, among immigrants to the U.S., entrepreneurialism represents a form of downward mobility:

> *Commercial pursuits, especially shopkeeping were less prestigious, if not frowned upon. . . .*
>
> *. . . many 1970s immigrants had graduated from college, including extremely prestigious universities such as Seoul National University (SNU) . . . For an SNU graduate to "make it" as a greengrocer or a dry cleaner in the United States is akin to an elite U.S. university graduate's succeeding as a convenience store owner in opulent Japan. . . .*
>
> *. . . The incongruous image of a college-educated European American opening up a shop in a poor inner-city neighborhood should make us question the idea that Korean Americans are somehow naturally inclined toward opening and running small businesses.*
>
> *. . . Korea immigrant entrepreneurship should . . . be seen as a concatenation of conscious decisions, albeit made under strong structural constraints. (Abelmann and Lie, 1995:123–125, 129)*

Instead, self-employment was taken up because of negative factors, such as language barriers, the nontransferability of professional credentials or college degrees, and other structural constraints to white-collar and professional employment, including racial discrimination (Abelmann and Lie, 1995:126–147).

As long as culture is viewed simply as a property of individuals (rather] than of structures, cultural explanations will give short shrift to structural explanations. Attributing the *absence* of small business activity among American descendants of slaves to the absence of entrepreneurial values is one such example. For the absence of such values can themselves be linked to the disappearance of such *structures* as the esusu, an African form of the rotating credit association.[18] As a result, blacks have been more dependent upon white employers and government policies for establishing the economic floor from which educational gains can be made. The educational progress of black children, in turn, has been most rapid when public policy measures were directed towards improving schools and alleviating poverty (Carnoy, 1995).

The presumption of entrepreneurial values among Koreans could be seen as an error of imputation, and not a weakness with theories of cultural endowment. If so, it is a recurring error of no small consequence. Yet, the problems with cultural explanations have less to do with the substance of the logic than with how they are invoked. As Portes and Rumbaut (1990:77) pointed out, they are "always *post-factum*," i.e., invoked after a group has already achieved success, but are otherwise unable to predict success. Moreover, the numerous empirical exceptions to the theory cannot be neatly encompassed by such explanations.[19]

Finally, although education is now almost a *prerequisite* for mobility, culture need not be. In their book *Inequality by Design*, sociology professors at the University of California, Berkeley (Fischer et al., 1996) drew upon a cumulative body of research to show how social inequalities are significantly affected by social class background as well as by social or national policy arrangements. Social status was shown to have direct implications for IQ. For example, even though Koreans have achieved high levels of education in the United States, their lower, minority status in Japan is manifested in lower IQ scores. In the United States, however, IQ differences between Koreans and Japanese fade (Fischer et al., 1996:172, 191–193, 199). Rather than being a direct measure of innate intelligence, IQ was more a measure of how academic performance was contingent upon social background and circumstances. Again, as we saw earlier, social class background might better explain important differences among Asian Americans, as well as between Asian Americans and other racial-ethnic groups.

To return to the point about census data raised at the beginning of this section, census data are not designed to address cultural theories. Despite this limitation, we might make the best of this situation were we to approach such statistics as a basis for *generating* theories. Besides cultural explanations, one might posit a range of structural explanations for the rates in question. For example, even when student achievement can be traced to parental pressures to perform, the motivation need not be culturally-based. Parental exhortations to "work hard," for example, may be derived from the realization that discrimination makes it necessary for a minority to work "twice as hard" in order to succeed. This alternative, structural perspective has yet to get the attention it deserves, even in the educational context where the model minority thesis prevails. In the occupational sphere, there is some research which has noted that the motivation behind ongoing education among Asian Americans is not cultural but "structural"—a response to blocked mobility (Sue and Okazaki, 1990).

Specific Political or Ideological Purposes Served by the Thesis

As pointed out in different ways throughout this chapter, cultural explanations obscure structural conditions, institutional policies, and particularly the relative social class privilege that has assisted the large majority of those who "make it." Insofar as the model minority view has lent itself towards obscuring these issues, it has served to maintain the status quo. As such, it has not been subject to careful study, but has persisted because of this ideological purpose.[20] Were there not blacks and other minorities who form a prominent part of the picture of sustained economic disadvantage, the thesis would not exist.

Given the value placed on social equality in the United States, gross inequities have been a source of national embarrassment, ill ease, and the source of social if not *ideological* crisis. In this context, "model minorities" serve as a sign of the ongoing viability of the American Dream. Where there are inequities, these are largely reduced to matters of individual will or choice: If Asian Americans can apparently make it, then why not blacks, other minorities, or other groups? Thus, for example, success on the part of individual Jews has occasioned some to wonder aloud why blacks do not imitate or emulate those strategies.

Jews have moved up in American life by utilizing middle-class skills—reason, orderliness, conservation of capital, and a high valuation and use of education. . . . Finding that playing by the "rules of the game"—reward based on merit, training and seniority—has worked for them, many Jews wonder why Negroes do not utilize the same methods for getting ahead. (Friedman, cited in Steinberg, 1982:88)

The Jewish Horatio Alger story itself has been critiqued in ways which parallel some of the analysis in the previous pages. Sociologist Stephen Steinberg made several pointed criticisms in this regard: (1) that success was not uniformly distributed throughout the Jewish population, (2) that even those who had managed to climb the occupational hierarchy still found their mobility limited, (3) that Jewish cultural values have limited explanatory power, and (4) that structural considerations had a vital bearing on the degree to which preimmigration skills interfaced well with the needs of the American economy. For these reasons, he said "the popular image of Jews as a middle-class monolith tends to be overdrawn," and that even by the mid-1960s, one still found that "almost a quarter of all employed Jewish males in New York City were manual workers, and another unspecified number worked in low-paying white-collar occupations" (Steinberg, 1982:90). Those who manage to escape from the "working class" into the professions were far from being an "economic elite."

The most important qualification of the Jewish success story is that American Jews by no means constitute an economic elite. The Jewish middle class has been concentrated mostly in small business and the professions; Jews are conspicuously absent from the managerial hierarchies of major corporations. This was first established in 1936. . . . Only two industries had significant Jewish representation—the apparel industry and the movie and broadcasting industries. (Steinberg, 1982: 90–91)

Zweigenhaft and Domhoff's more recent study partially supports Steinberg's earlier findings. As late as the 1970s there were few Jews in the executive ranks of large *Fortune*-level companies. Unlike Gentiles, they were more likely to be in smaller Fortune-level companies, to have joined as "outsiders with expertise" rather than coming up through the ranks, or to be in companies "owned or founded by Jews."

. . . Jews were well represented in the corporate elite but were more likely to be in small Fortune-level companies rather than large ones. We also found that they had traveled different pathways in getting to the corporate elite than had their Gentile counterparts. Whereas Gentile executives were most likely to have advanced through the managerial ranks of the corporation, the Jewish directors were more likely to have joined the boards as outsiders with expertise in such areas as investment banking, corporate law, or public

relations—unless they had risen through the ranks of companies owned or founded by Jews. (Zweigenhaft and Domhoff, 1998:20).

Since the 1970s, however, Jews have made such significant inroads into the largest Fortune-level boards that the authors conclude they are now "most certainly overrepresented in the corporate elite" (Zweigenhaft and Domhoff, 1998:23).

Despite the ideology of a classless society, Zweigenhaft and Domhoff (1998:176–181) specified four factors they believe to be critical to the assimilation of Jews (as well as to the assimilation of other minorities and women): identity management, class, education, and light skin. Steinberg, for his part, directly questioned the viability of the Jewish Horatio Alger myth as *cultural* ideology. While acknowledging that cultural values certainly played an important role in promoting literacy, study, and intellectual achievement, he emphasized the fact that preimmigration skills were also critical. Jews from Eastern Europe arrived with industrial skills which intersected well with the needs of the burgeoning American industrial economy. In this respect, they were different from other immigrants, including Asians who arrived at the turn of the century,[21] though they share certain similarities with those Asian immigrants in the post-1965 who would also be included as part of the model minority picture.

Ironically, although the small business endeavors of both Jewish and Asian American merchants have been similarly attributed to cultural traits, in both instances what is frequently omitted in such accounts is the fact that these ventures do not necessarily conform with the respective occupational ideals of these groups. Many Korean American businessmen are from the ranks of the college-educated, who have been unable to make it in mainstream America. East European Jews, for their part, were motivated to become merchants and shopkeepers, primarily because of discriminatory laws which restricted their ability to own land. For these reasons, rather than any cultural predilection, they ended up in livelihoods such as moneylending and liquor trades, occupations in which they might not otherwise have engaged. The enmity which they thereafter attracted to themselves led to programs which eventually forced their emigration (Cowan and Cowan, 1989:14, 21–27; Steinberg, 1982:94; Schwarz, 1956:296).

Although the casting of Asian Americans as "model minorities" has temporarily supplanted the standard reference point for assimilation, which has been the European immigrant experience on this continent (Steinberg, 1982), the persuasiveness and appeal of such logic—as ideology—is contingent on several factors. However empirical studies may challenge the *validity* of the model minority thesis, it has persisted because it serves both an ideological and political purpose. On the one hand, it is couched in values consistent with middle-class American values and taps into familiar cultural beliefs and myths associated with Horatio Alger and the American Dream. On the other hand, the dominant attitude towards Asian Americans has depended on whether they represent a greater or lesser threat than other groups to the existing hierarchy. While dubbed a "model minority," Asian Americans have rarely, if ever, been seriously elevated as a model for majority whites, especially where competition between the two has been direct. It is precisely in these situations where the thesis is no longer considered tenable that ideology and politics become most salient and apparent to those who run up against a new logic, if not new, unexpected barriers.

Thus, where Asian American admissions to colleges and universities have been associated with declining white enrollments, praise is at best faint and more often likely to be accompanied by concerns about Asian American "overrepresentation" and by unflattering characterizations of them as "nerds," who are "academically narrow" or lacking in socially desirable qualities (*San Jose Mercury,* February 23, 1998; Woo, 1996, 1990; Takagi, 1992:58, 60-61). In work spheres where Asian American professionals have appeared in significant numbers, their mobility has been impeded by "glass ceilings" and negative assessments of their managerial potential. Whatever the justifications for their exclusion, the idea of them as "model" no longer surfaces.

Cultural Ideologies and Their Social-Historical Contexts: The Limits of Ideology

The analysis in this chapter has suggested that cultural explanations are at best only partially accurate in accounting for what we know about Asian Americans as an aggregate. In fact, the social soil from which the idea of a model minority germinated may say more about the politics of power than it does about the factors underlying achievement. The questions concerning us here are of a different order than those which motivated the original formulation of the thesis. Instead of asking, "What are the cultural factors behind success?" the appearance of a glass ceiling prompts one instead to ask: "What are the rationales or justifications offered to explain differential progress? If cultural factors are inadequate, to what extent are structural factors at issue? What place, if any, do cultural explanations occupy within this structure or scheme of things?" For the moment, let it suffice to say that these questions themselves can be seen as a product of a social, historical context that breathes life into these questions.

Historically specific, the model minority thesis is premised on the fundamental assumption that educational achievement is the *sine qua non* of success. For this reason, it is unlike its Horatio Alger counterpart, which was created earlier in the nation's history when higher education served as finishing schools for the elite. For the masses of ordinary people then, both agrarian and new emerging industrial sectors of America were still able to provide opportunities to make a living without so much as a high school diploma. It is only in postwar decades that the nation has firmly embraced an ideology that links education achievement with occupational mobility. The postwar economy was an expanding one and the GI bill made it possible for education to be widely pursued. In this way, structural opportunities were created for educational achievement to become a form of social or cultural capital that could be converted into job security, greater socioeconomic benefits, professional autonomy or authority. In this new ideological formulation, education would substantially counter and overcome the effects of racial discrimination and racial privilege. However, . . . the prerequisites for mobility go beyond education. Glass ceilings, specifically, point to the limits of ideology by suggesting ongoing "artificial" barriers.

Notes

1. Between the years 1870–1890, when the anti-Chinese movement gained momentum, until it ultimately led to the 1882 Exclusion Act, Chinese were incarcerated in California State Prisons at a rate higher than their proportion of the population, particularly for crimes involving economic gain (e.g., burglary and larceny). For example, while only 8 percent of the California population in 1870, they were 14 percent of those imprisoned. By 1890, the Exclusion Act had clearly had its effect: not only did the Chinese population drop to 5 percent but the prison rate fell to 2 percent (Shimabukuro, 1980).

2. While the Census Bureau has published different population estimates for Asian and Pacific Islanders, there is little question that their rate of growth has surpassed other groups, including blacks, Hispanics, and non-Hispanic whites. Now the third largest minority, after blacks and Hispanics, they are expected to approximate 9.9 million by the year 2000, or 4 percent of the U.S. population. By 1990, they were already 7.3 million, having doubled their size since 1980. The 1980 figures themselves represent a doubling of the population since 1970. In 1970, the Asian American population numbered 1.4 million. By 1980, that population had more than doubled to 3.5 million, or 1.5 percent of the total U.S. population of 226.5 million.

3. Part of this difference can be attributed to the relative diversity—or lack thereof—in these respective countries or continents. Given the racial homogeneity of Great Britain during Marx's time, inequality was largely reflected in social class differences.

4. Chapters from Steinberg's book were based on materials published in the 1970s.

5. Reference to the term "model minority thesis" is most commonly made in Asian American academic circles where the construct survives as a short-hand way of referring to the hidden cultural assumptions which continue to underlie social or political debates where Asian Americans figure as a successful minority.

6. Insofar [as] interracial marriage with the white, mainstream majority of Americans is the result not only of greater contact in both business and social affairs but also of greater social acceptance, such rates have been treated as an important indicator of assimilation (Kitano and Sue, 1973). More recent interpretations, however, suggest that trends towards intra-marriages among Asian Americans point to an alternative view of acculturation, namely, the assimilation of ideas in the context of social and economic experiences associated with the experience of "race" in America (Shinigawa and Pang, 1996).

7. This volume was a special issue devoted to "Asian Americans: A Success Story?"

8. The 1990 census contains information not only on nine major subcategories of "Asian or Pacific Islanders," but on at least twenty "other" Asian ethnic groups.

9. Germans had arrived as early as the eighteenth century and their mass migration to the United States during the 1840s and 1850s was such that by World War I German Americans already included many second-generation descendants. Descendants of older immigrants could be expected to be completely assimilated and invisible by the 1970s simply because they had arrived so much earlier. Another reason offered, however, for the overall perception of complete assimilation was "Anglo Saxon race ideology at the turn of

the century," which, according to Kamphoefner, "caused people to see what they wanted to see." The allusion here was to the "anti-German hysteria of World War I" and some psychological need to counter negative attitudes towards Germany as an enemy nation with positive attitudes towards German Americans as "easily Americanized."

10. The German American population, however, suffered few curbs on its numbers through restricted immigration. Unlike Asian immigration, national immigration quotas in the 1920s had had little effect on German immigration because aliens from the western hemisphere were exempted from such quotas and specifically classified as "nonquota" immigrants.

11. According to Kamphoefner, those German Americans who were less assimilated were geographically isolated in rural areas. Patterns of cultural survival were most evident here. These included use of the German language, social resistance to prohibition and anti-alcohol legislation, and other signs of cultural preservation, including a "locational persistence" associated with peasant attitudes towards landownership as a major form of security. Attitudes in this regard were so tenacious that sacrifices on behalf of landholding might well be pursued at the expense of children's education.

12. The "modal" tendency simply refers to the "frequency" of an occurrence on any given measure or indicator.

13. Dual labor or split labor market theorists have referred to these respective sectors as "primary" and "secondary," or as "core" and "periphery."

14. Filipinos, for example, have been underrepresented in small business, whereas Koreans are heavily concentrated here, more so than other Asian Americans and/or other immigrant groups. According to Min, "the Korean group shows the highest rate of self-employment among seventeen recent immigrant groups classified in the 1980 Census, while the Filipino group ranks fifteenth, ahead only of the Portuguese and Haitian groups . . ." Min theorized about a number of differences between Filipino and Korean immigrants that might explain their differential distribution. For one, there is a higher representation of Filipino immigrants as professional or white-collar workers in non-Filipino firms, which itself might be traced to the fact that the Philippines is an English-speaking country. By contrast, Koreans would have had greater language barriers than Koreans to entering the U.S. general labor market. In addition, as immigrants they have had more of a previous history of working in an industrial business economy, which can be seen as giving them an "advantage" when it came to starting up small businesses (Min, 1986–87:56).

15. Even among Japanese and Chinese Americans, who were the original inspiration for the model minority thesis, one can find high poverty levels among recent immigrants (Barringer et al., 1995:155).

16. Culture of poverty theories notwithstanding, blacks themselves have highly valued education as a path to mobility, leading some researchers to explore the gap between these abstract and concrete attitudes, and their different implications for predicting achievement or mobility outcomes (Zweigenhaft and Domhoff, 1998:186, 190). For this same reason, sociologist Ann Swidler argued against this conventional view of culture in favor of

defining culture as a repertoire of skills, habits, or styles that organize action (Swidler, 1986).

17. Kwoh (1947:86–87, 114) has similarly explained the paucity of businessmen among American-born Chinese graduates to the low prestige and lack of real opportunity for mobility afforded by such work, along with the expectations associated with their college training.

18. The particular form which slavery itself took in the United States led to the disappearance of the esusu. Specifically, its disappearance has been attributed to the patriarchal relationship between the American plantation owners and their slaves. In contrast to West Indian slaves, whose absentee owners permitted them to develop their own subsistence economy (if only out of necessity, because the slave population here was much larger relative to slaveowners), American slaves were discouraged from independently cultivating their own plots of land or else devoting themselves to trades and crafts. Moreover, they were legally denied the right to maintain their own traditions, customs, and language, and otherwise positioned to "absorb the culture of the slaveowner" (Light, 1987). In his study of the Mississippi Chinese, James Loewen discusses and explains in detail how a variety of situational and structural factors positioned the Chinese so that they were able to become prosperous in the grocery business because they were able to enter a "ready-made niche" that was unavailable to blacks. The importance of situational factors is also underscored by the fact that Mississippi Chinese were more concentrated in the grocery business to an extent not found in other Chinese immigrants ("with identical geographic and class origins") elsewhere in the United States (Loewen, 1988:32–57).

19. Portes and Rumbaut (1990:77–78) also noted several other weaknesses associated with cultural theories of small business success: Given flourishing businesses among a diverse range of ethnic groups, there is a "theoretical untidiness" in isolating "unique entrepreneurial 'values'" for groups from a wide range of religiocultural backgrounds. The problem of explanation, moreover, is compounded by the fact that others from the same backgrounds are not entrepreneurially inclined (e.g., why Chinese Buddhists and not Buddhist Cambodians?). Similarly, sojourner theories of entrepreneurship might explain why some temporary residents might be motivated to accumulate profits in order to return home but the exceptions to this theory are also numerous (e.g., entrepreneurial activity among Eastern European Jews intending to stay in the U.S. or among Cuban refugees with little prospects of return). Finally, situational theories of disadvantage do not fully explain why some Asian minorities (Chinese and Japanese) have high rates of employment while other groups (Filipinos and Mexicans) are underrepresented in self-employment.

20. According to Karl Mannheim dominant groups, given that the existing order supports their own group interests, will be particularly invested in an ideology that supports the status quo.

The concept "ideology" reflects the one discovery which emerged from political conflict, namely, that ruling groups in their thinking become so intensively interest-bound to a situation that they are simply no longer able to see certain facts which would undermine their sense of domination. There is implicit in the word "ideology" the insight that in cer-

tain situations the collective unconscious of certain groups obscures the real condition of society both to itself and to others and thereby stabilizes it (Mannheim 1936:40).
21. These included Koreans, Asian Indians, Japanese, and Filipinos, although the last two groups contributed to the bulk of this immigration.

References

Abelman, Nancy, and John Lie. *Blue Dreams: Korean Americans and the Los Angeles Riots.* Cambridge, MA and London, England: Harvard University Press, 1995.

"Arts Philanthropist." *Asian Week* November 3, 1995.

Asian American Policy Review. Vol. VI. "Affirmative Action," 1996.

Barringer, Herbert, Robert W. Gardner, and Michael J. Levin (eds.). *Asians and Pacific Islanders in the United States.* New York: Russell Sage Foundation, for the National Committee for Research on the 1980 Census, 1995.

Beach, W.G. *Oriental Crime in California.* Palo Alto, CA: Stanford University Press, 1932.

Bureau of the Census. *We the American Asians.* Washington, D.C.: U.S. Government Printing Office, Population Reference Bureau, September 1993.

Caplan, Nathan. "Study Shows Boat Refugees' Children Achieve Academic Success." *Refugee Reports* VI (10): 1–6, October 11, 1985.

Caplan, Nathan, Marcella H. Choy, and John K. Whitmore. *Children of the Boat People: A Study of Educational Success.* Ann Arbor: The University of Michigan Press, 1994.

Caplan, Nathan, Marcella H. Choy, and John K. Whitmore. "Indochinese Refugee Families and Academic Achievement." *Scientific American* 266 (2): 36–42, February 1992.

Carnoy, Martin. *Faded Dreams: The Politics and Economics of Race in America.* New York: Cambridge University Press, 1995.

Caudill, William, and George DeVos. "Achievement, Culture and Personality: The Case of Japanese Americans." *American Anthropologist* 58: 1102–1126, 1956.

Chan, Sucheng. *Asian Americans: An Interpretive History.* Boston: Twayne, 1991.

Chen, Joanne. "The Asian American Dream?" *A. Magazine* 2(3): 16–17, 70–71, Fall 1993.

"Chinese in a Global Economy." *Oakland Tribune* May 26,1982.

"Chong-Moon Lee." *San Francisco Chronicle* November 5, 1995.

Cowan, Neil M., and Ruth Schwartz Cowan. *Our Parents' Lives: The Americanization of Eastern European Jews.* New York: Basic Books, 1989.

Domhoff, William. *Who Rules America? Power and Politics in the Year 2000.* Mountain View, CA: Mayfield Publishing Company, 1998.

"East, West Teaching Traditions Collide." *San Jose Mercury* February 23, 1998.

Escueta, Eugenia, and Eileen O'Brien. "Asian Americans in Higher Education: Trends and Issues." *Research Briefs, American Council on Education* 2 (4): 1–11, 1991.

Fischer, Claude S., Michael Hout, Martin Sanchez Jankowski, Samuel R. Lucas, Ann Swidler, and Kim Voss. *Inequality By Design: Cracking the Bell Curve Myth.* Princeton, New Jersey: Princeton University Press, 1996.

Fullerton, Howard N., Jr. "New Labor Force Projections, Spanning 1988 to 2000." *Monthly Labor Review* 3–12, November 1989.

Gardner, Robert W., Bryant Robey, and Peter C. Smith. "Asian Americans: Growth, Change, and Diversity." *Population Bulletin* Vol. 40, No. 4: 1–44, October 1985.

Glazer, Nathan. and Daniel Patrick Moynihan. *Beyond the Melting Pot: The Negroes, Puerto Ricans, Jews, Italians, and Irish of New York City.* Cambridge, MA: The M.I.T. Press and Harvard University Press, 1963.

Herrnstein, Richard J., and Charles Murray. *The Bell Curve: Intelligence and Class Structure in American Life.* New York: Free Press, 1994.

Hing, Bill Ong. "Social Forces Unleashed after 1969." Chapter Three in *Making and Remaking Asian America Through Immigration Policy: 1850–1990.* Stanford, CA: Stanford University Press, 1993.

Hsu, Ruth. "Will the Model Minority Please Identify Itself? American Ethnic Identity and Its Discontents." *Diaspora* 5 (1): 37–64, Spring 1966.

Hune, Shirley, and Kenyon S. Chan. "Special Focus: Asian Pacific American Demographic and Educational Trends," pp. 39–67 in Deborah J. Carter and Reginald Wilson, *Minorities in Higher Education, Fifteen Annual Status Report, 1996–1997.* Washington, D.C.: American Council on Education, April 1997.

"For Immigrant, A Billion-Dollar High-Tech Deal: Maryland Entrepreneur to Sell Firm He Founded." *Washington Post* April 28, 1998.

Jaco, Daniel E., and George L. Wilber. "Asian Americans in the Labor Market." *Monthly Labor Review* 33–38, July 1975.

Jew, Charles C., and Stuart A. Brody. "Mental Illness among the Chinese: I. Hospitalization Rates over the Past Century." *Comprehensive Psychiatry* 9 (2): 129–134, 1967.

Kamphoefner, Walter D. "German Americans: Paradoxes of a Model Minority," pp. 152–160 in Silvia Pedraza and Ruben Rumbaut (eds.), *Origins and Destinies: Immigration, Race, and Ethnicity in America.* Belmont, CA: Wadsworth, 1996.

Kim, Bok Lim. "Asian Americans: No Model Minority." *Social Work* 18: 44–53, 1973.

Kim, Chung, and Won Moo Huth. "Korean Americans and the Success Image: A Critique." *Amerasia Journal* 10 (2): 3–21, 1983.

Kingston, Paul William, and Lionel S. Lewis (eds.). *The High-Status Track: Studies of Elite Schools and Stratification.* Albany, New York: SUNY, 1990.

Kitano, Harry. *Japanese Americans: The Evolution of a Subculture.* Englewood Cliffs, New Jersey: Prentice-Hall, 1969.

Kitano, Harry H.L., and Stanley Sue. "The Model Minorities." *The Journal of Social Issues* 29: 1–9, 1973.

Knoll, Tricia. *Becoming Americans: Asian Sojourners, Immigrants, and Refugees in the Western United States.* Portland, Oregon: Coast to Coast Books, 1982.

Lee, Stacy. *Unraveling the "Model Minority" Stereotype: Listening to Asian American Youth.* New York: Teachers' College Press, 1996.

Levine, Larry. *The Opening of the American Mind.* Boston: Beacon Press, 1996.

Light, Ivan. "Ethnic Enterprise in America: Japanese, Chinese, and Blacks," pp. 83–93 in Ron Takaki (ed.), *From Different Shores: Perspectives on Race and Ethnicity in America*. New York: Oxford University Press, 1987.

Loewen, James W. The Mississippi Chinese: Between Black and White. Prospect Heights, Illinois: Waveland Press, 1988.

Lott, Juanita T. "Policy Implications of Population Changes in the Asian American Community." *Asian American Policy Review* II: 57–64, Spring 1991.

Lyman, Stanford Morris. Review of Betty Lee Sung, *The Story of the Chinese in America*, in *Journal of Ethnic Studies* 1 (1): 71–72, Spring 1973.

Mannheim, Karl. *Ideology and Utopia*. New York: Harcourt, Brace & World. 1936.

Massey, Douglas S., and Nancy A. Denton. *American Apartheid: Segregation and the Making of the Underclass*. Cambridge, MA: Harvard University Press, 1993.

Mills, C. Wright. *The Sociological Imagination*. New York: Oxford University Press, 1959.

Min, Pyong Gap. "The Entrepreneurial Adaptation of Korean Immigrants," pp. 302–314 in Silvia Pedraza and Ruben Rumbaut (eds.), *Origins and Destinies: Immigration, Race, and Ethnicity in America*. Belmont California: Wadsworth, 1996.

Min, Pyong Gap. "Filipino and Korean Immigrants in Small Business: A Comparative Analysis." *Amerasia Journal* 13 (1): 53–71, 1986–87.

Moynihan, Daniel Patrick. *The Negro Family: The Case for National Action*. Washington, D.C.: U.S. Department of Labor, 1965.

O'Hare, William P., and Judy C. Felt. *Asian Americans: America's Fastest Growing Minority Group*. Washington, D.C.: Population Reference Bureau, No. 19 in a series of occasional papers, Population Trends and Public Policy, pp. 1–16, February 1991.

Ong, Paul, and Suzanne J. Hee. "Economic Diversity," in Paul Ong (ed.), *The State of Asian Pacific America: Economic Diversity, Issues and Policies*. Los Angeles: LEAP Asian Pacific American Policy Institute and UCLA Asian American Studies Center, 1994.

____. "Work Issues Facing Asian Pacific Americans: Labor Policy," pp. 141–152 in *The State of Asian Pacific America: Policy Issues to the Year 2020*. Los Angeles: LEAP Asian Pacific American Policy Institute and UCLA Asian American Studies Center, 1993.

Osajima, Keith. "Asian Americans as the Model Minority: An Analysis of the Popular Press Image in the 1960s and 1980s," pp. 165–175 in Gary Y. Okihiro, Shirley Hune, Arthur A. Hansen, and John M. Liu (eds.), *Reflections on Shattered Windows*. Pullman, Washington: Washington State University Press, 1988.

Park, Edward Jang-Woo. "Asian American Entrepreneurs in the High Technology Industry in Silicon Valley." pp. 155–177 in Bill Ong Hing and Ronald Lee (eds.), *Reframing the Immigration Debate: a Public Policy Report*. Los Angeles: LEAP Asian Pacific American Public Policy Institute, 1996.

Petersen, William. *Japanese Americans*. New York: Random House, 1971.

Portes, Alejandro, and Ruben G. Rumbaut. *Immigrant America: A Portrait*. Berkeley and Los Angeles: University of California Press, 1990.

"Power Brokers: The 25 Most Influential People in Asian America." *A. Magazine*, Vol. 2 (3): 25–34, Fall 1993.

Sanborn, Kenneth O. "Intercultural Marriage in Hawaii," pp. 41–50 in Wen-shing Tseng, John F. McDermott, and Thomas W. Maretzki (eds.), *Adjustment in Intercultural Marriage.* Honolulu: University of Hawaii Press, 1977.

Shimabukuro, Milton. "Chinese in California State Prisons, 1870–1890," pp. 221–224 in Genny Lim (ed.), *The Chinese American Experience: Papers from the Second National Conference on Chinese American Studies.* San Francisco: The Chinese Historical Society of America and The Chinese Culture Foundation of San Francisco, 1980.

Shinigawa, Larry Hajime, and Gin Yong Pang. "Asian American Panethnicity and Intermarriage." *Amerasia Journal* 22 (2): 127–152, 1996.

"Silicon Valley Pioneer." *Asian Week* March 8, 1996.

Sowell, Thomas. "The Chinese" and "The Japanese," Chapters 6 and 7 in Thomas Sowell, *Ethnic America: A History.* New York: Basic Books, 1981.

Steinberg, Stephen. *The Ethnic Myth: Race, Ethnicity, and Class in America.* Boston: Beacon Press, 1982.

Strong, Edward K. *The Second-Generation Japanese Problem.* Palo Alto, CA: Stanford University Press, 1934.

"Success Story, Japanese American Style." *New York Times* January 9, 1966.

"Success Story of One Minority in the U.S." *U.S. News and World Report* December 26, 1966.

Sue, Stanley, and Sumie Okazaki. "Asian American Educational Achievements: A Phenomenon in Search of an Explanation." *American Psychologist* 45 (8):913–920, August 1990.

Suzuki, Bob. "Education and Socialization of Asian Americans: A Revisionist Analysis of the Model Minority Thesis." *Amerasia* 4: 23–51, 1977.

Suzuki, Bob H. "Asian Americans as the 'Model Minority': Outdoing Whites? or Media Hype?" *Change:* 13–19, November/December 1989.

Takagi, Dana Y. *The Retreat from Race: Asian-American Admissions and Racial Politics.* New Brunswick, New Jersey: Rutgers University Press, 1992.

Takagi, Paul, and Tony Platt. "Behind the Gilded Ghetto: An Analysis of Race, Class, and Crime in Chinatown." *Crime and Social Justice:* 2–25, Spring-Summer 1978.

Trueba, Henry T., Lilly Cheng, and Kenji, Ima. *Myth or Reality: Adaptive Strategies of Asian Americans in California.* Washington, D.C.: Falmer Press, 1993.

U.S. General Accounting Office. *Asian Americans: A Status Report* GAO/HRD-90-36FS, March 1990.

Useem, Michael, and Jerome Karabel. "Pathways to Top Corporate Management," pp. 175–207 in Paul William Kingston and Lionel S. Lewis (eds.), *The High-Status Track: Studies of Elite Schools and Stratification.* Albany, NY: SUNY, 1990.

Valentine, Charles A., *Culture and Poverty: Critique and Counter-Proposals.* Chicago and London: University of Chicago Press, 1968.

Varon, Barbara F. "The Japanese Americans: Comparative Occupational Status, 1960 and 1950." *Demography* 4:809–819, 1967.

Walker-Moffat, Wendy. *The Other Side of the Asian American Success Story.* San Francisco: Jossey-Bass, 1995.

Wilson, William Julius. *When Work Disappears: The World of the New Urban Poor.* NY: Vintage, 1997.

Woo, Deborah. "Asian Americans in Higher Education: Issues of Diversity and Access." *Race, Gender & Class* 3 (3):11–37, Spring 1996.

Woo, Deborah. "The 'Overrepresentation' of Asian Americans: Red Herrings and Yellow Perils." *Sage Race Relations Abstracts* 15 (2), May 1990.

Wu, Frank, and May Nicholson. "Racial Aspects of Media Coverage on the John Huang Matter." *Asian American Policy Review* VII: 1–37, Spring 1997.

Zweigenhaft, Richard L., and William Domhoff. *Diversity in the Power Elite: Have Women and Minorities Reached the Top?* New Haven: Yale University Press, 1998.

Questions

1. How does Winant frame the significance of the United Nations World Conference Against Racism? Is there evidence that the United Sates is an empire? In what ways would that be related to racism?

2. Why can't people just be colorblind? Why can't people just be individuals or just Americans? Why do people want to identify with groups based on race or ethnicity? Isn't that racism?

3. How have we been taught to be ethnocentric in the United States?

4. Describe some of the ways in which people express racial discontent?

5. What is the significance of the term mestizo? How does this relate to the border between the United States and Mexico?

6. Why would Model Minorities need to be invented?

SECTION FOUR

Organizing for Social Justice

Introduction

It is easy to retreat into the mind, into forms of fantasy and representation as an alternative to confronting such persistent problems as poverty, homelessness, health care, and hunger. But prophets and reasonable people recognize that if you are hungry, you have to make a sandwich, and power does not concede much if you do not develop a specific set of demands. It is not enough to be Hamlet-like, wandering about the castle ruminating on the meaning of life—sometimes you need to make a plan and organize.

Generally speaking, the only lasting strength of subordinated people rests in organized mass movements that express those people's interests. Organizing such movements can be a daunting task, particularly in a country that pushes people towards radical forms of individualism disconnected from solidarity and community. But creating a new legal and social reality through mass democratic pressure is an important part of our past and present. If workers appreciate weekends off, paid holidays, child labor laws, the eight-hour workday, antidiscrimination laws, voting rights, unemployment insurance and occupational safety regulations, they need look no further than the struggles that have occurred in the streets, in the fields, by the river, and in the factories across this nation. It is the connection between theory and practice, between abstract ideas and the world of social justice struggles, that animates ethnic studies. Ethnic studies provides a non-fantasy-based ideological framework through which students can grapple with the meaning of race, class, and gender. Students are not asked to mimic ideas according to a convention, but instead to think critically about power and supremacy in all their forms. Because the effects of power have been etched so deeply onto the bodies of the subordinated, ethnic studies keeps an eye on power. But the emphasis on power and knowledge is a troubling approach because it acknowledges the vulnerability of all things to criticism. It strips the vitality from long-held truths, undermining vast reservoirs of certitude and questioning the very order of things. On the positive side, it is rooted in an emerging global understanding that human health is connected to critical thinking skills and the rejection of all forms of antisocial socialization.

In the following set of readings, the authors propose strategies and tactics on issues confronting people of color at both the national and international levels. In *Responding to Hate*, the Center for Democratic Renewal in Atlanta, Georgia, recommends careful research, community education, and a well-thought-out action plan for confronting hate groups. Well-intentioned campaigns based on love and tolerance are not enough. Understanding the conditions in your community that give rise to hate is essential to any effective plan.

In the reading entitled *The Truth about Racial Profiling*, the American Civil Liberties Union describes a racial history of surveillance and harassment in this country. Indeed, the phrase "rounding up the usual suspects" takes on an ominous racialized meaning, including seeing people of color as criminals and enlisting the state in a campaign of constant surveillance—and ugly consequences. The ACLU dispels myths associated with racial profiling and describes the campaign to stop racial profiling in California.

The next essay in this section, *View from the Ground* by Francis Calpotura and Bob Wing, asks racial justice organizers to comment on their work. They emphasize the importance of creating movements that are constructed by the people most affected by racist policies. Their vision includes a strategic understanding of building alliances, recognizing globalization, not retreating from race analysis, and promoting social justice values in community education. Developing a racial justice analysis for the immigrant rights movement is equally important and timely given the climate of suspicion and fear in the nation since the tragic events of September 11, 2001. As discussed by the National Network for Immigrant and Refugee Rights in *Immigrant Rights: Striving for Racial Justice, Economic Equality, and Human Dignity*, the domestic emphasis on security has severely limited all discussion of immigration reform and accelerated the rhetoric of anti-immigrant activists. The network nevertheless emphasizes two important factors in their work. The first is the increasingly obvious fact that immigration is not just a domestic issue, but is tied to global economic forces. By extension, strategies for reform need to reflect an understanding of immigrants as the focus of human rights and not as the subject of criminal laws.

—— 25 ——

Responding to Hate Groups
Ten Points to Remember

The Center for Democratic Renewal

1. Document the problem and stay informed. Your first step should be to conduct thorough research about hate group activity and bigoted violence in your community. ◆ Develop a chronology of incidents drawing on newspaper accounts, victim reports, and other sources. Stay informed about developments by clipping your local newspaper, subscribing to other publications, and networking with other individuals and agencies.

2. Speak out and create a moral barrier to hate activity. Communities that ignore the problem of hate group activity and bigoted violence can sometimes create the impression that they don't care. ◆ This silence is often interpreted by hate groups as an invitation to step up their activities. Through press conferences, rallies, community meetings, and public hearings, you can create a climate of public opinion that condemns racism and bigotry right from the start.

3. Match the solution to the problem. Whatever strategy you use to respond should be tailored to the specific situation you are dealing with; don't rely on rigid, formula-type ◆ solutions.

4. Build coalitions. Hate violence and bigotry against one targeted group helps to legitimize activities against other groups. If you involve a wide spectrum of people representing diverse constituencies, you will have a better chance of achieving a unified, effective response.

5. Assist victims. Providing support and aid to hate violence victims is central to any response strategy. Don't get so busy organizing press conferences and issuing proclamations that you forget to make a housecall and express your personal support.

6. Work with constituencies targeted for recruitment. People who join hate groups usually do so out of frustration, fear, and anger; they might even be your neighbors next door. By offering meaningful social, economic, spiritual, and political alternatives you can discourage participation in hate groups by the very people most vulnerable to recruitment.

7. Target your own community as well as the hate group. Organizations like the Ku Klux Klan don't create social conflict out of thin air; they have to feed off existing community tensions in order to exist. The enemy of community harmony is not always the hate group itself, but the existing bigotry and division the group can exploit. For these and other reasons it is also essential to conduct anti-bigotry education programs on an ongoing basis, after the hate group has left your community.

8. Encourage peer-based responses among youth. Young people respond best to leadership that comes from within their peer group. While adults can provide valuable resources and insight, it is essential that youth groups develop and cultivate their own leaders and implement programs of their own design to combat bigotry.

9. Remember that hate groups are not a fringe phenomenon and their followers don't always wear white sheets. Although the number of active white supremacists and neo-Nazis probably totals no more than 25,000 in the United States, as many as 500,000 Americans read their literature. This movement is complex and made up of numerous sometimes competing and sometimes cooperating organizations. Hate groups impact the mainstream of society in a variety of ways, including: running candidates for public office; publishing sophisticated propaganda; buying radio time and media outlets; distributing cable television programs; manipulating the media; and building alliances with more respectable conservative groups, including some fundamentalist and evangelical Christian organizations.

10. Broaden your agenda. The problem is more than criminal. Hate activity is a political and social problem requiring a range of responses beyond those initiated by police. Citizen advocacy groups, religious agencies, and others should develop a public policy agenda that addresses a wide range of issues, including appropriate legislation, mandatory school curricula, expanded victim services, etc.

--- 26 ---

The Truth about Racial Profiling

American Civil Liberties Union

The experience of being viewed by law enforcement as suspicious, dangerous, or out of place, is all too familiar to thousands of African Americans, Latinos and Asian Americans, many of whom can easily recall being stopped, interrogated, detained, or searched for no apparent reason other than the color of their skin. Trading stories of biased police encounters resulting in humiliation or terror is commonplace in juvenile detention centers, on street corners, in barber shops, as well as at fancy functions hosted by minority professionals. A Latino teenager in baggy pants on a street corner is presumed to be a drug dealer; a black lawyer in his new Mercedes is presumed to be a thief. The stories are legion.

Until recently, these biased encounters with the police had no special name, though the experience of being viewed as suspicious and treated like a criminal for no reason has always been understood in communities of color to be a special experience, not shared by whites.

Today, the terms "racial profiling" and "driving while black or brown" are widely used by the media, in political campaigns, and within communities of all colors. Yet the public and political debates regarding the extent to which racial profiling occurs and what, if anything, should be done to stop it, reveals a continued lack of understanding regarding what racial profiling is, how it began, why it has thrived, and the serious harm it causes.

Numerous myths regarding racial profiling have infected the public policy debate. The most damaging, perhaps, is the myth that African Americans and Latinos are more likely to be carrying drugs or other contraband in their vehicles than whites. Law enforcement officials will often point to the racial composition of our prisons and jails in an attempt to justify racial profiling, under the theory that it makes sense to target African Americans and Latinos for traffic stops because they are more likely than whites to be guilty of some other crime. The New Jersey Attorney General dubbed this phenomenon the "circular illogic of racial profiling."

Contrary to popular belief, however, every comprehensive study of racial profiling has shown that people of color are not more likely than whites to be carrying drugs or other contraband in their vehicles. In fact, recent studies in New Jersey and Maryland revealed that whites were more likely than African Americans or Latinos to be carrying drugs or other contraband. And in California, Latinos are more likely than any other racial or ethnic group to be stopped, searched and then released by the California Highway Patrol without a ticket or arrest, because they are innocent of any crime.

Myths have consequences. The racist myth that motorists of color are more likely to be guilty of something when driving down the road has resulted in thousands of innocent people of color being detained by the police on their way to work, church, school, or the grocery store. Countless motorists have found themselves stranded curbside, fielding questions about their personal life while their car is being searched, or even dismantled, by officers who hold a futile hope of finding drugs or other contraband.

The myth has created a vicious cycle. Because police look for drugs primarily among African Americans and Latinos, a disproportionate number of those groups are arrested, prosecuted, convicted and jailed. The fact that our prisons and jails are filled to capacity with African Americans and Latinos serves to reinforce the false perception that those groups are primarily responsible for drug trafficking. White drivers, by contrast, receive far less police attention, are far less likely to be searched for drugs or other contraband, and are therefore far less likely to be arrested. As a result, only a small percentage of whites find themselves behind bars for drug-related offenses, thus perpetuating the false perception that whites are less likely than other groups to commit drug-related crimes.

The myth has also helped to create a political environment in which politicians can get away with offering little more than rhetoric in response to the problem. Governor Gray Davis, for example, has aligned himself with extremist police unions opposed to meaningful reform, and has refused to sign a mandatory data collection bill that would make it possible to track, monitor and prove discrimination by the police.

The time is long overdue for the public, and our politicians, to know the truth about racial profiling. When the truth is known, no excuses for inaction remain.

What It Is

Racial profiling is the use of race by law enforcement in any fashion and to any degree when making decisions about whom to stop, interrogate, search, or arrest except where there is a specific suspect description. That exception aside, racial profiling occurs whenever police view someone as more likely to be a criminal at least in part because of the color of their skin.

The term "racial profiling" is traceable to the drug courier profiles created by the U.S. Drug Enforcement Agency (DEA) in the early 1970s that purported to describe likely drug couriers based on a number of characteristics, such as whether the person seemed nervous, was traveling between certain cities, or paid for travel in cash.

Although the so-called "indicators" of criminal activity were race-neutral on their face, African Americans and Latinos complained that they were regularly being told by law enforcement that they "fit the profile." They were stopped, questioned, and searched while minding their own business and engaged in perfectly lawful behavior in airports, on trains, or walking down the street. The indicators were so broad they could be applied to huge numbers of innocent people. It soon became apparent that police officers were routinely using race as a major factor in deciding who should be viewed as a suspected drug courier. The emergence of the term "racial profiling" reflected the growing awareness that the profiles had more to do with race, than any evidence of criminal activity. As explained by Milton Reynolds, a recent victim of racial profiling in the San Francisco Bay Area: "If you're black or brown, you fit the profile."

Drug courier profiles continue to be used today in virtually every state law enforcement agency in the country. Even beyond drug enforcement, police officers have become accustomed to viewing and treating people differently on the basis of race. Young black kids, hanging out and laughing with their friends on a street corner, are viewed as potential troublemakers. The police may stop, question and frisk them, based on the assumption that they are probably carrying guns or dealing dope. White kids, hanging out in their neighborhood and laughing with their friends, are viewed as good kids, having a good time. Unconscious and conscious stereotypes regarding who the likely criminals are influence officers' perceptions of identical innocent conduct.

Unfortunately, many within law enforcement continue to insist that race can and should be used as a factor in developing "probable cause" or "reasonable suspicion" of criminal activity. They argue that officers should be allowed to consider race as one of many factors in deciding whom to stop and search. Indeed, some advocates of biased police practices argue that racial profiling should be defined as stopping or searching someone "solely" on the basis of race or ethnicity, thus leaving officers free to rely on race in part.

Race has no place in determinations regarding who seems "suspicious." Whenever law enforcement uses race at all—even as one factor—in deciding whom to stop, interrogate or search, race is being used as a proxy for criminal activity.

If the police have no reason to suspect that criminal activity is occurring without considering someone's race, they should not stop or search someone after considering the color of his or her skin. Race is not an indicator of criminality. If the officer would not have stopped or searched someone who is white based on the same facts or under the same circumstances, the officer should not treat an African American or Latino differently.

The only situation in which it is appropriate for the police to consider someone's race is when a specific suspect has been identified as having committed a specific crime. Under those circumstances, race may well be relevant. Obviously, it does not make sense for the police to stop and interrogate an African American man who is 6 feet, 5 inches tall, when looking for a suspected thief identified by a witness as an Asian American man who is 5 feet, 7 inches tall.

Federal law supports this view. In *United States v. Montero-Camargo,* the U.S. Court of Appeals for the Ninth Circuit held that it was unlawful for the Border Patrol, when searching for illegal immigrants, to use racial or ethnic appearance as a factor in deciding whom to stop or search. Hispanic appearance is of "such little probative value that it cannot be considered a relevant factor," the Court stated.

Treating people differently based on their race, rather than on actual evidence of criminal activity, is what racial profiling is all about. Police should make decisions based on the evidence, not on race.

How It Began

Racial profiling is nothing new. The practice of viewing people of color as likely criminals dates back to the days when slavery was alive and well in Southern states. African Americans who were legal residents in the North were often viewed as run-away slaves, seized on the streets and detained by slave catchers, city officials, and the police. Many lost their freedom and were returned to Southern plantation owners based on the false assumption that they had escaped their owners.

Following slavery and Reconstruction, the police enforced segregation laws through racial profiling, viewing African Americans in white neighborhoods as "out of place" and targeting them as potential criminal suspects. In the early part of this century, vigilante justice in the form of brutal beatings, cross burnings and lynching was carried out against African Americans while law enforcement officials turned a blind eye. In the West, Mexican Americans were subjected to wholesale police round-ups, and often deported. By the 1960s and 70s, widespread complaints of racially biased police abuse and harassment fueled riots and spurred the formation of groups like the Black Panthers and the Brown Berets to organize resistance to police misconduct.

During the past twenty years, a new form of racial profiling has emerged, known as "DWB" or "driving while black or brown." This new form of profiling is more sophisticated—and sometimes more subtle—than its predecessors, but it threatens to undermine the integrity of the criminal justice system as a whole.

The term "DWB," like the term "racial profiling," is traceable to the DEA and the war on drugs. In 1986, the DEA rolled out a federally funded highway drug interdiction program, known as Operation Pipeline. This program trains officers at state highway patrol agencies nationwide to use minor traffic violations as an excuse to pull people over and attempt to search their cars for drugs based on a racially biased drug courier profile.

Tens of thousands of officers have been trained by the DEA to use these pretext stops to stop, detain, interrogate and search primarily African American and Latino motorists. Through Operation Pipeline, the drug courier profiles developed in the 1970s were taken to the roads and highways in virtually every state in the country, including California. The DEA has trained more than 30,000 officers in 48 participating states in Pipeline tactics and techniques, and countless local law enforcement agencies have embraced the DEA's philosophy and training, adapting it to suit their own agencies. Pretext stops are now regularly used outside the drug interdiction context to detain, interrogate and search "suspicious" looking people—even when there is no evidence of criminal activity.

People of color have long complained about race-based traffic stops, but the war on drugs and the influence of the DEA have literally made "driving while black or brown" a crime. People of color no longer have the freedom to get in their car and drive down the street without fear that they might be viewed as a potential criminal or drug courier. On their way to work or running an errand, the sight of a police car brings a ripple of fear that they might be stopped, interrogated and possibly searched for driving a car that is too fancy, or a car that needs repairs, or for driving with out-of-state license plates, or driving a rental car or simply driving while black or brown. The war on drugs, taken to the roads and highways, has deprived thousands of innocent motorists of color of the basic freedom to drive down the street without fear of the police.

Why It Thrives

The War on Drugs

Racial profiling has thrived during the past twenty years, thanks in large part to the war on drugs. Despite its name, casualties of this domestic war understand that the war has little to do with solving the problem of drug abuse, and much to do with creating an environment in which people of color can be lawfully targeted for incarceration.

The best evidence of this fact is that twenty years after the war was declared, the problem of drug abuse remains unsolved, yet a huge proportion of the African American and Latino communities have been forced behind bars. Although African Americans and Latinos are not any more likely than whites to be carrying drugs or other contraband in their vehicles, they have been the main targets of the drug war. No official announcement by our elected leaders has been made that African Americans and Latinos are the enemy in the drug war, but the message has been heard loud and clear. Ask any ordinary, mainstream voter to picture in his or her mind a criminal, or a drug offender, and the odds are they will imagine someone who is black or brown.

The message has also been heard by law enforcement. In March 1999, the Chief of Troopers for the New Jersey State Police, Carl Williams, was fired by then Governor Christine Todd Whitman soon after a news article appeared in which he defended the targeting of African American and Latino motorists because, he said, "mostly minorities" trafficked in marijuana and cocaine. Williams' comments were met with shock and outrage, yet in making those remarks he was doing little more than stating explicitly what the DEA has been training officers to think and do for nearly two decades. Federal funding has been flowing into state and local law enforcement agencies to do precisely what Williams described.

The drug war has created a political environment in which politicians have everything to gain and nothing to lose by cracking down on a supposed enemy that is easily identifiable, and which mainstream white voters understand is not them. The get-tough-on-crime rhetoric sells because white America understands that nobody is talking about getting tough on their children. Not really. Harsh drug laws and mandatory minimum sentences sail through legislatures because white America understands whom those laws are intended for. The black and brown faces by the side of the road, and the black and brown youth spread eagle on the sidewalk while being frisked, are presumed guilty by those who happen to pass by and are quickly forgotten.

The Missing Fourth Amendment

As the drug war escalated in this country, the U.S. Supreme Court's commitment to enforcing Fourth Amendment protections against unreasonable searches and seizures dissipated to the vanishing point. In a series of stunning decisions, the Supreme Court granted law enforcement nearly unfetted discretion to stop, detain, interrogate, search and arrest motorists—even when there is no evidence of criminal activity beyond a minor traffic violation. Most significantly, pretext stops and consent searches—the primary tools of discrimination in the war on drugs—were upheld by the Supreme Court as reasonable exercises of law enforcement discretion.

A pretext stop, simply stated, is a traffic stop made by a police officer not for the purpose of enforcing traffic laws but rather for the purpose of investigating imaginary criminal activity for which the officer has no evidence. Officers trained to conduct pretext stops use extremely minor traffic violations—such as a burned out license plate light or the failure to use one's turn signal at precisely the right time—as an excuse to stop, interrogate and search motorists, even when there is no good reason to believe the person is involved in criminal activity.

This practice was challenged in 1996 in a case called *Whren v. United States.* The question before the Court was whether the police can use a minor traffic violation as an opportunity to go on a fishing-expedition for drugs, interrogate a motorist and ask for consent to search, even when there is no evidence of illegal drug activity. The Supreme Court, in a 5-4 decision, concluded that, yes, officers could do precisely that without violating the Fourth Amendment prohibition against unreasonable searches and seizures.

In practice, the *Whren* decision has given the police virtually unlimited authority to stop and search any vehicle. Every driver violates some provision of the vehicle code at some point, because state traffic codes identify so many different infractions. Even when driving a very short distance, it is likely that a motorist will fail to use his or her turn signal at precisely the right time, fail to track properly between the yellow lines, fail to stop the proper distance from the pedestrian walkway, or will drive a little too slow or too fast. Vehicle equipment is also highly regulated. A small light bulb must illuminate the rear license plate. Taillights must be visible from a particular distance. Tire tread must be a certain depth. And all equipment must be in working order at all times. In order to stop someone who "looks" suspicious or out of place, or who looks like a criminal or a drug courier, all the police have to do is wait for the person to commit some minor traffic violation and then pull them over to check them out, interrogate them, or get consent to search for purely imagined criminal activity.

Because officers hold conscious and unconscious stereotypes regarding who the likely criminals are and because the drug war creates a climate in which people of color are viewed as the enemy, it is not surprising that African Americans and Latinos are subjected to pretext stops far more frequently than whites. Generally speaking, whites are stopped because the officer actually wants to enforce the traffic code. The motorist is ticketed or warned and allowed to go on their way. For people of color, every traffic stop carries with it the real likelihood that they may find themselves interrogated, detained, searched—and even arrested—for doing nothing more, for example, than failing to use their turn signal at precisely the right time.

Since *Whren,* the Court has extended police power over cars and drivers even further. In *Maryland v. Wilson* (1997) the Court gave police the power to order passengers out of their vehicles, regardless of whether there is any basis to suspect they are dangerous or involved in criminal activity. And in *Ohio v. Robinette* (1996) the Court held that when a motorist refuses consent to search, the officer is not required to tell the driver that he or she is free to leave. Few motorists refuse consent to search, either because they do not know they have a right to refuse, or because they fear that if they refuse they will arouse the officer's suspicions further or provoke the officer to violence The Supreme Court ruled that officers have no duty to dispel these fears or inform a motorist that dares to refuse consent to search that they are free to go.

Perhaps the most shocking Supreme Court decision in recent years, however, is *Atwater v. Lago Vista* (2001). That case held that officers may arrest motorists and put them in jail for minor traffic violations, such as failing to wear a seat belt—even if the maximum penalty for the traffic violation is a fine, not jail time. In Atwater, a white woman who was driving with her children in a pick-up truck without her seat belt was stopped, arrested, and thrown in jail, even though a seat belt violation is punishable only by a fine. The Supreme Court ruled that the officer's actions did not constitute an unreasonable seizure under the Fourth Amendment, thus opening the door to the possibility that any and every traffic violation may culminate in arrest.

While the victim in *Atwater* was white, there can be no doubt that the overwhelming majority of motorists who find themselves behind bars for committing a minor traffic violation will be black or brown. Studies of racial profiling have consistently shown that African Americans and Latinos are far more likely to be treated harshly in the course of an ordinary traffic stop than whites. Indeed, the U.S. Supreme Court appears content to eviscerate Fourth

Amendment protections against unreasonable searches and seizures in large part because the justices understand that their sons and daughters are not likely to be arrested for a minor traffic violation, or stranded on the side of the road while their car is dismantled in the hopes of finding drugs.

The One in the Blue Is Always Right

One of the main reasons racial profiling continues to thrive, aside from the political environment and the evisceration of the Fourth Amendment, is that victims of racial profiling are rarely deemed credible, and rarely have the time, money or other resources to challenge a discriminatory traffic stop. Most victims of racial profiling are so relieved when the encounter is over, they want nothing more than to forget the incident ever occurred. Those who do challenge race-based traffic stops find that they are discouraged from filing complaints, and even when they manage to file a complaint, the police are generally trusted to police themselves. After an internal investigation, police departments routinely conclude that the officer's version of events and stated intent is more credible than the victim's. So the complaint is often dismissed or ignored.

Victims of racial profiling also fear retaliation. Stories abound of police harassment of innocent motorists increasing, rather than decreasing, following the filing of a complaint. In addition, California—law provides that police officers have a special right to sue people who file false complaints against them, and seek monetary damages. Thus, any victim who worries that his or her story might not be believed is unlikely to file a complaint out of fear they will become the target of a lawsuit filed by the police officer who discriminated against them.

These practical and legal barriers make victims extremely distrustful of the legal system, and make lawyers reluctant to represent people who have valid complaints. As a result, another vicious cycle is created, in which judges come to believe that racial profiling affects only the guilty. Because few victims of racial profiling file lawsuits, the only cases of racial profiling judges tend to see involve the "guilty ones." And because the police target primarily African Americans and Latinos, judges are constantly confronted with African American and Latino defendants who are guilty of something, thus reinforcing their predisposition to believe that racial profiling may well be justified.

Undocumented immigrants who are targeted on the basis of race by law enforcement, are perhaps the most vulnerable to discrimination and abuse by the police, because they risk deportation if they complain of mistreatment. For example, in February 2001, the *Los Angeles Times* reported that Orange County police departments had detained more than 4,000 suspected illegal immigrants during the previous two years, driving many straight to the INS checkpoint in San Clemente for deportation. The suspected immigrants are stopped for minor infractions, asked about their immigration status, and then taken to the border if the officers think they might not be in the country legally.

An 18-year-old Anaheim woman was taken into police custody following a traffic stop for expired registration. An INS agent determined that she may be in the country illegally, and suddenly a minor traffic violation turned into a deportation proceeding. In another incident, a 16-year-old Latino boy was arrested for jaywalking. Although he was in the country legally, he couldn't produce identification. The police turned him over to the Border Patrol and he was wrongly deported. The Border Patrol does not keep statistics on the legal residents wrongly taken to San Clemente for deportation. An INS spokesman in Washington, D.C., said that it is common for local police to say "he looked illegal," and make judgments about legal residency based on appearance alone.

Although thousands of Latinos have been victims of racial profiling by local law enforcement, the INS, and Border Patrol, few people will file complaints with law enforcement out of fear that the police could retaliate by deporting them, or someone in their family, who happens to be an immigrant.

The invisibility of innocent victims of racial profiling is one of the reasons it remains critically important for all law enforcement agencies to collect data regarding the race and ethnicity of motorists who are stopped and searched. Without data tracking the rate at which people of color are stopped, searched, and released because they are innocent, racial profiling remains hidden from view and individual complaints can be easily dismissed as "isolated incidents." Data recently released by the Oakland Police Department, for example, showing that African Americans were more than three times as likely to be stopped and searched as whites, lent considerable credibility to claims of victims such as Reggie Williams, who had been stopped more than 10 times in two years, and searched on more than half of those occasions. "When that data came out," he said, "I felt like finally somebody is going to have to take this seriously. I know they won't take me seriously 'cause I don't have an education, and I don't have any money, and so I know I can't fight this thing. They can write me off, and they can write off each of us one-by-one, but now they have to explain why all of us are being treated this way. Now they've got to give some answers."

The Harm It Causes

Being stopped, interrogated or searched by the police on the basis of race is an experience that is often remembered for a lifetime. The humiliation of being ordered out of your car, hands and feet spread apart, frisked while neighbors or strangers pass by, having your car searched or torn apart in a futile search for drugs, being interrogated about your personal life, whether you live in the neighborhood or what business you have in this part of town—these experiences are hard to forget, and they color one's view of law enforcement and the criminal justice system for the rest of one's life.

Racial profiling is particularly damaging to youth. It sends the powerful message that no matter how hard you try in school, no matter whether you play by the rules and obey the law or not, no matter what your dreams and goals might be, because of your race—because of who you are—you will always be viewed as and treated like a criminal. Young people generally strive to fulfill the expectations of others. Racial profiling tells young people that nothing more than criminal activity is expected from them.

Far from deterring juvenile crime, racial profiling eliminates a major incentive for law-abiding behavior. If it becomes obvious at an early age that no matter what you do, you are likely to be "jacked up" by the police and land in jail, the perceived benefits of playing by society's rules fade from view. It stands to reason that in low-income, racially segregated neighborhoods, where youth of color are denied adequate education and are exposed to few opportunities or examples of success, the police should be particularly careful to treat young people with respect, and stop and search them only when there is actual evidence of criminal activity. Allowing officers to make stops and searches based on stereotypes sends the message that there's no way to avoid being viewed and treated like a second-class citizen.

Frustration, rage and cynicism are the predictable by-products of racial profiling. These justifiable emotions render healthy police-community relations impossible. Why should a young Latino man who was stopped, searched, and held at gunpoint for no apparent reason be willing to trust the police? Would he be willing to come forward as a witness to a crime? If called to serve on a jury, could he trust a police officer who takes the stand? Would. he be willing or interested in working collaboratively with law enforcement to address any issue in his community?

Riots and uprisings in communities of color—including the explosions in Los Angeles, New York, D.C., Cincinnati, and Philadelphia—are usually triggered by a fatal shooting of an unarmed African American or Latino man. The rage and violence that follows is a testament to the powerful impact pervasive, racially-biased police harassment has on communities of color. During every race-based stop, search, or interrogation, the victim knows, in the back of his mind, that if he makes a wrong move or gesture the police may respond with deadly force. A cell phone, wallet or candy bar might be mistaken for a gun; a sudden move might be interpreted as threatening. And he may not get through the encounter alive.

Perhaps the most pervasive effect of racial profiling is the grossly disproportionate number of African American and Latino men arrested for nonviolent drug offenses. Every comprehensive study has shown that people of color are no more likely than whites to be carrying drugs or other contraband in their vehicles. However, because they are stopped and searched for drugs at grossly disproportionate rates, they are also arrested and incarcerated at grossly disproportionate rates. The racial composition of our prisons and jails today is, in large part, a product of racial profiling.

Ultimately, the question is not whether racial profiling harms communities of color or the criminal justice system as a whole—it unquestionably does. The important question we, as a society, face today is whether we care enough about the victims—the real people behind the profiles—to do what is necessary to bring this sordid chapter in our nation's history to an end.

The Struggle to End Racial Profiling in California

Although racial profiling has come to be recognized as a national disgrace by elected officials and civil rights leaders from President Bush and President Clinton to Jesse Jackson and Dolores Huerta, California's Democratic Governor, Gray Davis, has placed himself firmly on the wrong side of the issue.

As the leader of the country's most populous and racially diverse state, Governor Davis has become the most visible and stubborn opponent of meaningful reform. Davis has refused to sign bills of the type eagerly supported by other governors from both parties. His "do nothing" approach to racial profiling has led to litigation and profound disillusionment in communities of color.

Governor Davis Vetoes Data Collection Legislation

The controversy for Davis started in September 1999 when the California Legislature passed a modest data collection measure that would have required the state's law enforcement agencies to collect less than one third of the data required by the bills enthusiastically signed in to law by the governors of Rhode Island and Missouri. The vote in the Legislature was overwhelmingly bipartisan: 29-0 in the Senate and 61-16 in the Assembly. The bill was supported not only by the civil rights community but also by national minority police associations and the state Attorney General.

The bill was carried on the Assembly floor by Rod Pacheco, the first Latino Republican elected to the California Legislature in nearly a century, and a former prosecutor who had been named "legislator of the year" by law enforcement. Pacheco gave a passionate speech on the floor about his own experience with racial profiling growing up in East Los Angeles.

Nonetheless, on September 28, 1999, Governor Davis stunned California by vetoing the bill on the ground there was "no evidence the practice is taking place statewide." The Governor claimed it was not "appropriate" for government to require local police agencies to address this civil rights issue with data collection, but "encouraged" the state's law enforcement agencies, if they chose, to address racial profiling with data collection on a voluntary basis. He ordered the California Highway Patrol to begin collecting data, but he told local law enforcement agencies that it was up to them to decide whether they wanted to collect data or not. As civil rights advocates pointed out, Davis's position harkened back to the days when Southern politicians claimed that the enforcement of the nation's civil rights laws should be a local option. Ironically, the only other governor to veto a racial profiling bill was Davis's predecessor, Republican governor Pete Wilson.

Within hours of the veto, outrage spread through communities of color and civil rights organizations mobilized in response. The backlash against Davis's refusal to take this simple step of tracking traffic stops, so that it would be possible to identify and prove discrimination, was so swift and vehement that within 24 hours the Governor felt compelled to engage in damage control. The day after the veto, he released a befuddling statement saying that he had written the Mayor of Los Angeles and the Los Angeles County Board of Supervisors asking them to collect the data required in the bill he had vetoed the day before. While the targets of the letter openly expressed irritation at the governor's stunt, communities of color fumed.

Press conferences were held in San Jose, Oakland and Los Angeles in the days that followed at which civil rights leaders from the NAACP, ACLU, LULAC, and MALDEF, as well as elected leaders—including the former mayor of Oakland—blasted the governor for turning his back on communities of color and not taking their concerns seriously. The bill's sponsor, Senator Kevin Murray, explained to the *Sacramento Bee,* "He's done something harmful and maybe even insulting to the minorities of this state."

Governor Davis, elected with the overwhelming support of communities of color, had not only minimized his gubernatorial obligation to protect civil rights on the local level, he insulted and betrayed key constituencies.

Grassroots Uprising

Four months after Davis's veto, not a single major law enforcement agency had volunteered to collect data. In response, what the *Bee* described as a "determined group of nearly a dozen state legislators" challenged their Governor in January by re-introducing the data bill he had vetoed. They spoke of their own experiences with racial profiling and insisted that data was necessary. Senator Maria Escutia and Assemblyman Edward Vincent talked about being stopped for no reason—in Vincent's case when he was working as a probation officer. "This is something that particularly male Hispanics and African Americans have contended with very quietly . . . (This) has happened to me over the years," said Sen. Richard Alarcon, D-San Fernando. "This issue has reached critical mass in communities of color . . . We will not let this issue die," said Sen. Kevin Murray, D-Culver City, the lead author of the bill.

The response from Governor Davis? "The Governor's position on this hasn't changed an inch," said his spokesman Michael Bustamante. (*Sacramento Bee,* January 27, 2000.)

The Governor was not only ignoring legislators of his own party, but thousands of people who stepped forward to speak out about their own experiences of "Driving While Black or Brown." The ACLU advertised its English and Spanish DWB hotlines on billboards, radio stations and ethnic publications around the state. Thousands of people of color who had been racially-profiled, stopped and searched by the CHP, local police departments and sheriffs' departments called to report their stories, and express their desire to take part in a movement that would stop the practice.

Civil rights and grassroots organizations throughout California came together to form the Racial Justice Coalition (RJC). Immediately on the heels of Governor Davis's veto, the coalition called its first meeting and vowed to launch a major statewide campaign against racial profiling in California with the primary goal of securing statewide mandatory data collection.

From the beginning, the RJC merged traditional civil rights groups like the NAACP, MALDEF, LULAC, Lawyers' Committee for Civil Rights and the ACLU with local, grassroots, and immigrant rights groups like Ella Baker Center for Human Rights, La Raza Centro Legal, PUEBLO, Californians for Justice, and the National Center for Immigrant and Refugee Rights. It also attracted labor unions like the United Farm Workers and SEIU locals, among others. Most importantly, the Coalition provided a means by which victims of racial profiling could join a large-scale organizing campaign against biased police practices.

The RJC was united in its view that the time was long overdue for racially biased police practices to come to an end. "The veto was an insult to people of color in California," stated

Michelle Alexander, Director of the Racial Justice Project of the ACLU of Northern California. "If Governor Davis doesn't know that racial profiling is a serious problem in California, then he doesn't know the people he claims to represent."

"Racial profiling is not a figment of our imagination, said Walter Wilson, then-Political Action Chair for the Western Region of the NAACP. "If Governor Davis thinks that we are going to forget this veto, he's wrong. We won't rest until discriminatory police practices are part of the distant past. The question is what side of history Governor Davis wants to be on."

A strong commitment to organize with, and on behalf of, those most affected by biased police practices emerged as central to the RJC's philosophy. Marcos Contreras, then-State Director of LULAC, explained, "The Latino community in California is gravely concerned about racial profiling. In front of our families and loved ones, we are being humiliated and interrogated for no good reason. We joined this coalition because these practices have to stop, and it is up to us to make them stop."

The RJC's determination to mobilize against racial profiling quickly attracted a wide spectrum of public support. In California alone, over 50 organizations endorsed the call for a major demonstration on April 27, 2000, at the State Capitol to demand that Governor Davis sign the new data collection bill. Eight town hall meetings were organized by the RJC across the state attracting thousands of people, and hundreds related poignant testimony describing incidents of racial profiling and brutality by law enforcement. A racial justice constituency that had been separated and frustrated in their efforts to achieve change, joined to flex their collective political muscle. Compelling testimony at the town hall meetings generated local and statewide media coverage of discrimination by the police. "DWB" became a part of California's vocabulary.

Fraudulent Racial Profiling Bill

Less than an hour before the statewide April 27th demonstration in front of the State Capitol began, the Governor issued a press release stating that he had agreed to sign a bill "outlawing" racial profiling. The area was bristling with TV cameras, satellite trucks and microphones. The news media expected the crowd and the Coalition speakers to respond with elation.

It was immediately apparent, however, that the new racial profiling bill was no cause for celebration. Davis had cut a deal with the sponsor of the legislation, Senator Kevin Murray, in which Davis agreed to sign a bill that would supposedly "outlaw" racial profiling in exchange for Murray's promise to abandon his data collection bill. The deal also included diversity training for police officers and a requirement that the police hand out their business cards to people who are stopped but not ticketed. The Los Angeles Police Department (LAPD) issued a press release congratulating Davis and Murray, noting that the new racial profiling bill "will require all law enforcement agencies to conform to long-standing LAPD practice." The LAPD—an agency notorious for its own racial profiling practices—had not even begun to solve its own problem, yet pursuant to the new bill all officers in California would be expected follow the lead of the LAPD.

Weeks later, the actual language of the new racial profiling bill was finally released. As it turned out, the deal was worse than anyone had imagined. The new bill did not "outlaw" racial profiling or create any new civil or criminal penalties for race discrimination by the police. Instead, the bill simply defined racial profiling as "detaining a suspect, . . . without any individualized suspicion." That has been the law for more than 200 years—the Fourth Amendment to the U.S. Constitution. There was no new law in the bill.

The so-called "diversity training" was also a fraud. The bill eliminated all of the substantive training provisions that had existed in an earlier diversity training bill, and gave nearly unfettered discretion to establish the curriculum and standards to Peace Officers Standards and Training—a group adamantly opposed to data collection and other meaningful police reform.

The business cards included in the new bill did not provide any means for motorists who suffered discrimination to report complaints. The bill merely required the business card to provide a phone number that "may be used, if necessary, to report any comments, positive or negative." It did not require the phone number to be connected to the complaint system already required by state law. The bill, in effect, required agencies to create a "suggestion line" while leaving agencies free to completely ignore the "suggestions." The bill would actually reduce police accountability, by making it more difficult for complaints to be filed, investigated and tracked.

In the months that followed, civil rights leaders and community members held press conferences at the State Capitol denouncing the watered-down bill and explaining why it would do more harm than good. Hundreds of concerned community members and advocates lobbied legislators and testified at numerous hearings on the new bill, exposing its inadequacies and demanding data collection. The Governor had hoped to throw the Coalition in disarray by signing the fraudulent bill, but the Coalition held together and pressed for mandatory data collection.

Every major newspaper in California issued editorials acknowledging that the new racial profiling bill would do little or nothing except give Governor Davis the opportunity to claim false credit for addressing racial profiling. The bill was labeled a "fraud" by the *Sacramento Bee,* "a flimsy bill that meekly ambles between compromise and pandering," by the *San Jose Mercury News,* and "less than a compromise than it is a cop-out" by the *Oakland Tribune.* The *Los Angeles Times* pointed out that, since Davis supports the tracking of school scores to spot problems that need to be solved in education, "the same should go for law enforcement."

With the Democratic National Convention coming to Los Angeles, it fell to national civil rights leaders to try to convince California's governor of the need for mandatory data collection. Numerous other states had already enacted laws requiring data collection, including Rhode Island, North Carolina, Connecticut, Kansas, Missouri, Tennessee and Washington. Four of those bills were signed by Republican governors; three were signed by Democrats. Governor Davis was the only sitting governor to veto a data collection bill, and his opposition threatened the positive momentum that was building across the country.

In an August 7, 2000, press release, members of the Congressional Black Caucus urged Davis to drop his opposition to data. The release quoted Congressman John Conyers saying, "Nothing is more important to developing a solution to this problem than gathering meaningful data." With the Convention opening locally that day, Congresswoman Maxine Waters said, "Los Angeles is a city that has been plagued by problems of racial profiling and police abuse. We have to address racial profiling on the battleground where it is a particular problem."

The next day, the Racial Justice Coalition ran a full page ad in the *New York Times* under the headline, "Governor Davis: Why Are You the Only Sitting Governor to Veto a Racial Profiling Bill?" with an open letter to the governor signed by 18 key, national civil rights figures and organizations ranging from Rev. Jesse Jackson, Sr. of Rainbow/Push and Martin Luther King III of the Southern Christian Leadership Conference to Raul Yzaguirre of the National Council of La Raza, Ira Glasser of the ACLU, Karen Narasaki of the National Asian Pacific American Legal Consortium and Elaine Jones of the NAACP Legal Defense and Education Fund.

Finally, on August 24, 2000, the broad coalition of civil rights groups and elected officials succeeded in getting its message across. Legislators on the Senate Public Safety Committee made clear that they were not fooled by the new racial profiling bill and would not pass it out of committee. When Senator John Vasconcellos was asked by the *Los Angeles Times* what he thought of the Governor's racial profiling bill, he replied: "It's b.s. Business cards are a cover for doing nothing." Senate President Pro Tem John Burton made it clear that the fraudulent racial profiling bill was dead. "Every civil rights leader in the country is opposed to it," Burton said. The bill was promptly withdrawn.

Civil rights leaders applauded the demise of the bill, and vowed to continue the fight for data collection and police accountability. Liz Guillen, MALDEF's Legislative Director, breathed a sigh of relief: "I'm glad to see that the legislators came to understand that Latinos and others who are racially profiled would still have no way of documenting the problem. We will continue to work toward enacting a meaningful racial profiling bill that includes data collection."

But the collective sigh of relief came too soon. In the final days of the legislative session, another racial profiling bill backed by Governor Davis was introduced and swept through the Legislature with no meaningful hearing and little debate. There was no time to mobilize or respond. The bill included diversity training and an empty ban on racial profiling. The business cards were dropped. The new bill was a recycled version of the profiling bill that had just been withdrawn.

Governor Davis signed the new bill on September 26, 2000, and issued a press release congratulating himself. In the release, Davis acknowledged that the bill did not include mandatory data collection or any other form of police accountability, stating "I believe that local mayors, supervisors, and law enforcement officials, not the state, are best positioned to decide whether or not to collect data on racial profiling. And I strongly urge them to do so. . . . In addition, the City of Los Angeles will soon join the ranks of law enforcement agencies collecting data on racial profiling."

What Davis failed to point out is that Los Angeles would be collecting data not because of the Governor's encouragement but because the federal government was forcing them to do so. In fact, ever since Davis's veto of the data bill the prior year, the LAPD and the Mayor had continued to vigorously resist instituting data collection. In February 2000, the ACLU of Southern California filed a federal lawsuit on behalf of three African American and two Latino men who had been followed, stopped and detained by Los Angeles Police officers for no valid reason. Eventually, the Civil Rights Division of the Justice Department had to step in and insist that a traffic stop data program be made part of the consent decree it was forcing on the department, because Governor Davis and local officials had abdicated their responsibility to protect motorists of color from discrimination. Had Davis been willing to sign a data collection measure, this part of the decree would have been unnecessary.

The Failure of Voluntary Data Collection

Governor Davis's "all optional, all the time" approach to racial profiling data collection and reporting has proven to be a failure—even with respect to the agencies that have volunteered.

Under the bill Davis vetoed in 1999, all law enforcement agencies in the state would have been required to collect and report several key, specific categories of data on their stop and search practices and send that information to the California Highway Patrol (CHP) for inclusion in a statewide report to be released each July for at least four years. Davis rejected that approach, and instead instructed the CHP to produce a report annually for three years on the CHP's voluntary data collection efforts and to include in the report "information from any agency willing to voluntarily submit their data to the CHP." (Governor Davis's letter to CHP Commissioner D. O. "Spike" Helmick, September 28, 2000.)

The CHP's first report was dated July 1, 2000, but was not made public until months later when it was leaked to the *Stockton Record*. The report was grossly inadequate. To begin with, it aggregated all the stop data, making it impossible to make the relevant comparisons and measure stop and search rates of each CHP division and office as compared to the surrounding geographic areas. In addition, the report failed to include any race data on the search practices even though search rates are generally the best indicator of whether racial profiling is occurring in an agency. The CHP report simply stated in passing, with no data or documentation: "Hispanics were most often represented in searches resulting in a verbal warning." The CHP Commissioner claimed the failure to include the search data was an oversight. If Governor Davis had signed the mandatory data collection bill, all of the relevant data would have been reported by the CHP as required by law.

As for data from local agencies, the report revealed that only a small handful of agencies in California reported their data to the CHP. There are more than 350 law enforcement agencies in California, but only 16 agencies in the entire state reported data. Only one agency south of the Bay Area, the San Luis Obispo County Sheriff's Department, reported data. Dozens of California agencies engaged in data collection efforts declined to report their data to the CHP—apparently because of the lack of standardization and consistency in the program.

The data that was forthcoming from these 16 agencies was extremely limited, and rarely included highly relevant data about searches and the reason for the stop—information that is critical to determining whether racial profiling is a problem in any agency. The few agencies that reported search data by race didn't seem to understand its significance. The San Leandro Police Department, for example, reported that Latino drivers were twice as likely to be searched after traffic stops than whites. With young male drivers often thought to be the most likely target of profiling practices, Latinos were three times more likely to be searched and African Americans were 80% more likely to be searched than their white counterparts. Yet, notwithstanding these glaring disparities, the San Leandro Police Department's reaction was to suspend the data collection program citing the lack of direction from Governor Davis's program.

Although Davis's call for volunteerism in law enforcement has proven to be an abysmal failure, Davis has given no indication that he ever plans to show leadership and require law enforcement to do what is necessary to protect motorists' civil rights. Quite to the contrary, Davis refused to support yet another racial profiling bill in 2001, this one introduced by Assemblymember Marco Firebaugh with broad support from the Latino and Black Caucuses. The bill correctly defined and prohibited racial profiling, provided a cause of action for victims, and mandated statewide data collection. It was supported by more than 100 organizations, including every major civil rights organization and minority law enforcement associations, such as the National Organization of Black Law Enforcement Executives (NOBLE). After Davis vowed to veto the bill if it reached his desk, the bill stalled and never reached a floor vote.

Adding insult to injury, on July 26, 2001, Governor Davis wiped out key voluntary data collection provisions from the annual budget, thus allowing local law enforcement agencies to qualify for special funding to support data collection programs, even if those agencies are not collecting the basic data that is necessary to determine whether racial profiling occurs in their departments.

The 2001 state budget included $1 million in special grants to local law enforcement agencies that agreed to collect data voluntarily to track racial profiling, in addition to approximately $2 million rolled over from last year's budget. The budget language stated that the funds would be available only to those law enforcement agencies that required its officers to collect the five essential categories of data necessary to track racial profiling. Governor Davis eliminated the key provisions, including the reason for the stop, whether a search was conducted, whether drugs or other evidence of illegal activity was found and the result of the stop.

On behalf of the NAACP, LULAC, victims of racial profiling and taxpayers, the ACLU immediately sued the Governor, charging that he usurped the Legislature and exceeded his authority under the state constitution when he struck all of the relevant data provisions for the 2001 Budget Bill. As governor, Davis has the power to sign or veto bills, but not rewrite them by striking provisions that he does not like.

Before the court had the opportunity to hear the case, Davis switched his position and announced that all law enforcement agencies would now be required to collect the specified data in order to qualify for funding to support their voluntary data collection programs.

Recognizing that he was about to lose a major racial profiling lawsuit, Davis cut his losses and made the necessary changes.

While this is a significant victory, the reality remains that only a small percentage of law enforcement agencies are collecting any racial profiling data, and the vast majority of agencies that are collecting data, are not collecting the essential elements of data that are necessary to determine whether racial profiling is occurring, such as search data.

Search data is critical to determining whether and to what extent racial profiling occurs in any law enforcement agency, because it indicates the extent to which motorists of color are viewed and treated as potential criminals in the course of an ordinary traffic stop. Search data revealed through discovery in the class action lawsuit, *Rodriguez, et al. v. California Highway Patrol,* showed that Latinos were three times as likely as whites to be searched by drug interdiction officers in the Central and Coastal Division, and African Americans were twice as likely to be searched. In response to these discriminatory search rates, the CHP issued a six-month moratorium on consent searches (the practice of seeking consent to search a vehicle even when there is no evidence of criminal activity). The CHP is the only law enforcement agency in the country to ban this controversial drug interdiction tactic; the moratorium on consent searches is still in effect.

Search data has proved critical in uncovering patterns of racial profiling in other agencies in California as well. For example, the Oakland Police Department recently released data showing that African Americans were three times as likely to be searched as whites. Similarly, the Stockton and San Diego Police Departments released data showing that Latinos and African Americans were more than twice as likely as whites to be searched in the course of an ordinary traffic stop.

There are more than 350 law enforcement agencies in California. According to a Public Records Act survey conducted by the ACLU during the summer of 2001, fewer than 50 agencies have agreed to collect some data voluntarily. Only a small handful of agencies have agreed to collect the five essential elements of data that were outlined in the original budget language, including the Sacramento Police Department, the San Francisco Police Department, the San Diego Police Department, and the Oakland Police Department. These agencies clearly recognize that positive police-community relations is impossible if law enforcement is unwilling to take the basic step of collecting the information necessary to monitor and protect people's civil rights. As long as communities of color experience pervasive discrimination by law enforcement, the police will be viewed in those communities as the enemy, rather than as an ally in the fight against crime.

Reluctance to Change

Although a few departments have begun to collect the necessary data, few departments have been willing to make any policy changes to remedy the severe disparities in stop and search rates. Law enforcement still clings to the notion that it makes sense to employ tactics that have the purpose or effect of targeting motorists by race.

For example, the Sacramento Police Department has arguably the best data collection program in California. The department collects all of the necessary data and has demonstrated a genuine commitment to gathering accurate data. However, after a year of collecting data, the department released a biased and misleading report by an "independent analyst," Howard Greenwald, a management and policy professor from the University of Southern California.

Greenwald's report showed that African Americans were twice as likely as whites, and Latinos were 1.75 times as likely, to be ordered out of their cars, detained for prolonged periods of time, and searched following routine traffic stops. The data also revealed highly disparate stop rates. For example, in two neighborhoods where African Americans comprised only 7.2% and 8.6% of the population, they accounted for 22.4% and 27.7% of the drivers stopped respectively.

The report concluded that, despite these gross racial disparities, there was no reason to believe that the Sacramento Police Department was engaged in "inappropriate" racial profiling. According to Greenwald, it made sense for officers to rely on race as a factor in making decisions about whom to stop and search in high crime areas or during certain times of the night. He further reasoned that since a higher percentage of African Americans are reported as perpetuators of certain types of crime, disproportionate traffic stop and search rates make sense. He arrived at this conclusion despite the fact there is no evidence whatsoever that African Americans are more likely to commit traffic offenses than whites. His analysis proceeded by first asserting that it is appropriate to target African Americans and Latinos for traffic stops based on the assumption that they are more likely to be guilty of some unrelated crime, and then he concluded that the data revealed no "inappropriate" racial profiling. He reached this remarkable conclusion notwithstanding the fact that motorists of color were no more likely to be carrying drugs or other contraband in their vehicles than whites.

The Greenwald report sparked outrage among community groups. Yet, instead of condemning Greenwald's explicit approval of racial profiling, or correcting the impression created by the report that it is "appropriate" to target motorists on the basis of race, Chief of Police Arturo Venegas put the report on the department's website, congratulated himself for the department's data collection efforts before the Sacramento City Council, and convened a committee of community groups to consult with Greenwald on how to analyze data in the future.

It seems that even in progressive departments, there remains considerable reluctance to confront the problem of racial profiling and implement meaningful reforms. Unfortunately, the overwhelming majority of law enforcement agencies are following Governor Davis's lead and doing nothing to address the serious problem in California. Historically, the voluntary enforcement of people's civil rights has proven to be utterly unworkable. The same remains true today.

Data Collection in California

Who Is Being Stopped and Searched?

California Highway Patrol

Latinos are the most likely racial or ethnic group to be stopped, searched, and then released without a ticket or citation because they are innocent of any crime.

Latinos are three times as likely as whites to be stopped and searched by drug interdiction officers in the Central and Coastal Divisions, and African Americans are twice as likely as whites to be stopped and searched.

In 1997, the CHP's drug interdiction canine units stopped nearly 34,000 people, but less than 2% of them were actually carrying drugs.

San Diego Police Department

Latinos represented 20% of the *city's driving population, but 28% of stops, and 50%* of searches.

African Americans represented 8% of the city's driving population, but comprised 11.6% of vehicle stops, and nearly 20% of searches.

In more than 90% of all vehicle searches, officers found no drugs or contraband of any kind. Less than 2% of vehicle stops resulted in arrest for any offense.

Sacramento Police Department

In every neighborhood except one, the percentage of African Americans who were stopped exceeded the percentage of African Americans in the neighborhood's population. In one neighborhood, African Americans accounted for only 8.6% of the population, but accounted for 27.7% of the stops.

African Americans comprise only 14% of the driving population, but 34% of those stopped for non-hazardous violations.

African Americans were twice as likely as whites to be ordered out of their vehicles, and Latinos were 1.74 times al likely to be ordered out of their cars.

African Americans were twice as likely as whites to be searched in the course of a traffic stop, Latinos were 1.75 times as likely to be searched.

San Leandro Police Department

Latino drivers are twice as likely to be searched as whites.

Among young men, Latinos are three times as likely to be searched, and African Americans are 80% more likely to be searched.

Oakland Police Department

African Americans are 3.3 times more likely than whites to be searched in the course of a traffic stop.

More than 14% of all stops of African American motorists resulted in a search, while only 4% of stops of white motorists resulted in a search. African Americans were 65.8% of motorists searched.

Whites are far less likely to be stopped than motorists of color. According to the 2000 census, whites comprise 31.3% of Oakland's population, yet they account for only 16% of vehicle stops.

The New Threat to Accountability

Today, there is a new, extraordinary threat to fair and equitable police practices, as well as racial justice in virtually all spheres. This new threat is dubbed by its sponsors, the Racial Privacy Initiative. This initiative is sponsored by Ward Connerly, the African American businessman who led the campaign to prohibit affirmative action at the University of California in 1995, and then took his campaign statewide to secure passage of Proposition 209.

Despite its name, this initiative has nothing to do with protecting people's privacy, and everything to do with turning the clock back to a time when laws against discrimination did not even exist. The so-called Racial Privacy Initiative would prohibit state agencies from collecting racial data, and thus keep secret from the public basic information about race and ethnicity so that it would be nearly impossible to enforce anti-discrimination laws, or make policy reforms that are in the best interests of the communities those laws are designed to serve.

Since the passage of the Civil Rights Act of 1964—which outlawed racial discrimination in housing, employment and other key areas of public life—data collection and reporting has been a critical feature of civil rights enforcement. Without mandatory data collection and reporting by employers, for example, it would impossible to know whether an employer is engaging in a pattern of discrimination in hiring, promotion or discipline. Accordingly, data collection has been a key enforcement mechanism in state and federal civil rights laws for decades. The fact that law enforcement has been exempt from data collection requirements to identify and track possible discrimination in its operations reflects a glaring loophole—a loophole which the ACLU, NAACP, LULAC, MALDEF and dozens of other civil rights organizations have been struggling to close through the DWB Campaign.

Ironically, Connerly's initiative would create an exception for law enforcement, thus allowing police departments to continue to create crime statistics and identify suspects by race. Yet the initiative also includes a provision specifically prohibiting the California Legislature from enacting any law that would require local law enforcement agencies to collect data, including data to track racial profiling. Thus, the initiative specifically allows law enforcement to continue identifying suspects by race and engaging in racial profiling, but prevents the public from passing any laws that would have the effect of uncovering that discrimination.

Because the Connerly initiative would have the effect of nullifying any mandatory data collection bill enacted by the Legislature, and would permanently thwart any effort to identify and address race discrimination by state and local law enforcement agencies (or any other public agencies), the ACLU and numerous other civil rights organizations in the state have made defeating the Connerly initiative a top priority.

The Road to Reform

In the era of the war on drugs, African American and Latino men have been identified as the "enemy" and presumed guilty by law enforcement, politicians, and the media. As a result, racial profiling has become part of the culture of law enforcement and our society as a whole. In this report, we have tried to deepen the public understanding of this problem and document the ongoing efforts to eradicate racial profiling.

We have heard the voices of some of the thousands of black and brown motorists who have been stopped merely because of the color of their skin. We have reported the difficult, complex—and as yet, unsuccessful—political struggle to secure the passage of a data collection bill in California. Where do we go from here?

Bringing an end to racial profiling will not be easy, but it is possible. The ACLU calls on state, federal, and local legislators, as well as law enforcement officials to pursue the following five-point plan for eliminating racial profiling. This plan should be implemented through (a) state legislation; (b) city council ordinances; (c) amendments to city charters; and (d) voluntary action by law enforcement.

Define and Prohibit Racial Profiling

A clear definition and prohibition against racial profiling should be adopted and implemented at the federal, state and local level. Law enforcement should be prohibited from relying on race in any fashion and to any degree when making decisions about whom to stop, detain, interrogate or search except where there is a specific suspect description.

This definition and prohibition was originally promulgated by the U.S. Justice Department and included in the consent decree resolving the racial profiling lawsuit against the New Jersey State Police. It is a model definition, and is the standard against which all police conduct should be judged.

Some law enforcement agencies and advocates of biased police practices argue that officers should be free to rely on race, in part, when developing reasonable suspicion or probable cause of criminal activity. They argue that illegal racial profiling should be defined as occurring only when police rely "solely" on race or ethnicity, thus leaving officers free to rely on race in part.

If the police have no reason to suspect that criminal activity is occurring without considering someone's race, they should not stop or search someone after considering the color of his or her skin. Motorists should not be treated differently based on their race or ethnicity to any degree.

Quite simply, there is no excuse for the use of race by law enforcement, except when there is a specific suspect description identifying a particular suspect by race. Every law enforcement agency should have a clear policy prohibiting racial profiling in accordance with this definition.

Secure Comprehensive Mandatory Data Collection

Without comprehensive data, it is impossible to track, monitor or prove discrimination by the police. Every law enforcement agency in the state should be required to collect, at a minimum, data regarding: (a) the race and ethnicity of the motorist; (b) the reason for the stop; (c) whether a search was conducted; (d) what, if anything, was found in the course of the search; and (e) the result of the stop—i.e., whether a ticket was issued or an arrest was made. These five categories of data are absolutely essential to determining whether and to what extent racial profiling is a problem in any community. Because Governor Davis has abdicated his responsibility to protect people of all colors from discrimination, local city councils (and county boards of

---

What Data Should be Collected?

Any law enforcement agency that fails or refuses to collect the five categories of data listed below is NOT collecting the basic data that is necessary to determine whether a problem exists. In fact, the decision by a law enforcement agency to collect some, but not all, of this data may be an attempt to conceal—rather than uncover—racial profiling by their officers.

1. **Race/Ethnicity of Motorist.** Without this information, it is impossible to determine whether and to what extent people of color are stopped at a disproportionate rate.
2. **The Reason for the Stop.** People of color are often stopped for extremely minor traffic violations, such as burned out license plate lights, overly worn tire tread, failure to use the turn signal properly, etc. Without information regarding the reason for the stop, it is impossible to know whether motorists of color are being singled out and stopped for minor violations that are ignored when committed by whites.
3. **Whether a Search Was Conducted.** Search data is absolutely essential. In some jurisdictions, people of color may be stopped at similar rates as whites, but people of color are searched at dramatically higher rates. If data is collected only regarding who is stopped, it may seem like no discrimination is occurring, when in fact discrimination is rampant.
4. **Whether Drugs or Other Evidence of Illegal Activity Was Found.** It is not enough simply to learn that a search was conducted. Without information regarding whether drugs or other evidence of illegal activity were actually found during the search, it is impossible to determine whether officers are searching extraordinary numbers of innocent people, or generally wrong in their assumptions about certain racial or ethnic groups.
5. **Whether a Citation Was Issued or Arrest Was Made.** This information is critical to determine whether there are discriminatory ticketing patterns, or whether certain racial and ethnic groups are being subjected to "status checks"—stopped, interrogated, possible searched, and then released without a ticket or citation.

supervisors) should pass resolutions and amend local city charters to require collection of the five essential elements of data. Of course, any agency that is seriously committed to ending racial profiling will agree to collect this data voluntarily.

Ban Pretext Stops

Pretext stops should be banned. Pretext stops occur when police officers use minor traffic violations as an excuse to stop drivers when the real reason for the stop is that officers—without any reasonable suspicion of any criminal activity—want to conduct a fishing-expedition for illegal drugs or other criminal activity.

Police officers should be prohibited from using minor traffic violations as an excuse or "pretext" for investigating imaginary criminal activity for which there is no evidence. Motorists of color are far more likely to be viewed as "suspicious," stopped for minor traffic violations and then detained for questioning regarding some imaginary criminal activity that has nothing to do with the supposed traffic violation.

Although the U.S. Supreme Court has held that police officers do not violate the Fourth Amendment when they use minor traffic violations to engage in fishing expeditions for drugs or other criminal activity (*Whren v. United States*), pretext stops are bad police policy. They operate to discriminate and they destroy trust in law enforcement.

If there is no evidence of criminal activity, police should not be allowed to use minor traffic violations to stop people who "look like" they might be guilty of something. Pretext stops were recently outlawed in the State of Washington, and they should be made illegal here in California as well.

Ban Consent Searches

Consent searches should also be banned. Consent searches are the police practice of seeking consent to search a vehicle even when there is no evidence of criminal activity. The U.S. Supreme Court has said that it is permissible to search completely innocent people, even where there is no evidence of criminal activity, as long as they are persuaded to give their consent. Although the U.S. Supreme Court has said this practice is constitutional, this practice is bad policy and should be prohibited.

Police officers should not be allowed to search people's vehicles without probable cause of criminal activity. People of color are far more likely than whites to be viewed as likely drug couriers and asked for consent to search their vehicles for no good reason. Actual evidence of criminal activity—not race—should be the sole justification for a search. Without probable cause, there should be no search.

On April 19, 2001, the California Highway Patrol issued a six-month moratorium on consent searches following release of data showing that Latinos were three times as likely to be searched as whites by drug interdiction officers, and African Americans were twice as likely as whites to be searched. No law enforcement agency should be permitted to request consent to search someone's vehicle without actual evidence that they are engaged in criminal activity.

Enact State Legislation on Racial Profiling

The California State Legislature should pass, and the Governor should sign, a racial profiling bill that correctly defines and prohibits racial profiling, and requires statewide mandatory data collection, including, at a minimum, the five essential elements of data described above. Democratic and Republican governors have signed mandatory data collection bills in numerous other states, including Connecticut, Kansas, Maryland, Massachusetts, Missouri, North Carolina, Rhode Island, Tennessee and Washington. California is one of the most racially and ethnically diverse states in the country. It should not be slow to prohibit and protect its residents from racial discrimination by the police.

Mandate Proper Training

Because racial profiling is based on ingrained practices, assumptions and stereotypes that have been learned and practiced by officers for decades, it is essential that every department institute a program to retrain officers. Officers must be taught the value of data collection, and the reasons why pretext stops and consent searches are discriminatory and ineffective. Officers must also be trained about the harmful effects of racial profiling and its ineffectiveness as a law enforcement tool. The training needs to deal with profiling, not just in the abstract, but also as it affects individuals in their community.

It is worthy of emphasis, however, that a "diversity training" program—in the absence of data collection, a proper ban on racial profiling, and the elimination of discriminatory tactics such as pretext stops and consent searches will not be effective. Attempting to change discriminatory attitudes or stereotypes without changing discriminatory policies and practices is futile. In order for a training program to be meaningful, it must be designed to get officers to unlearn many of the biased tactics, as well as the biased ideas, they have been taught to believe are appropriate. Training should be mandatory and implemented at the academy as well as in individual departments.

Establish Meaningful Accountability

Any serious effort by a department to confront racial profiling must address the manner in which people can lodge complaints about individual officers. Victims of racial profiling must have confidence that their complaints will be thoroughly and aggressively investigated by an independent agency that has the authority to investigate and act upon complaints, as well as influence department policy.

The oldest civilian review board in the country is in Berkeley, California. There, the Police Review Commission hears complaints at public meetings brought by individual members of the community and addresses broad policy issues recommending changes in departmental procedures and practices. In San Francisco, the Office of Citizen's Complaints functions as the department's internal affairs division, but is located in a separate building and is run and staffed entirely by civilians.

Independent civilian oversight allows victims of racial profiling to voice their complaints about police in an environment where they have a reasonable chance of being heard. It leads to more vigorous investigations, brings a non-police perspective into the process, and increases credibility in the community. Victims of racial profiling rarely file complaints with the police department because of lack of trust and fear of retaliation. The existence of an independent civilian review process helps to ensure that victims feel more confident filing complaints, thus making it easier to identify, retrain, and discipline officers engaging in racial profiling.

---- 27 ----

The View from the Ground:
Organizers Speak Out on Race

Francis Calpotura

Bob Wing

At ground zero of today's racial and class conflicts stands a staunch and determined band of racial justice organizers who are organizing with low-income communities of color. Because they deal daily with the people who bear the brunt of racism, they are in a unique position to understand its workings and impacts. Their experiences tell the tale of how race not only matters, but matters centrally in shaping people's lives.

Racial justice organizers spend their lives trying to figure out how to work with their constituents and attack racism most effectively. Their confrontation with racism, and the struggle against it, is absolutely practical. For them, theory is truly a guide to action rooted in concrete experience, and action constantly calls for deepening theory.

This is why we've asked a panel of kick-ass, cutting-edge, anti-racist organizers to reflect on the lessons they have learned at the intersection of race and organizing in our time. We've asked them how they navigate these dangerous political waters and assertively develop strategies to advance racial justice. In response, they address some of the most provocative issues facing organizers today: the impact of globalization, the limits of multiculturalism, how differences between various racial and ethnic groups shape organizing in different communities and building unity, the difference between "equity" and "justice," the limitations of focusing on immediate victories, the importance of political education, and many others.

The participants are: Jane Bai out of New York City's Committee Against Anti-Asian Violence–Organizing Asian Communities (CAAAV); Jeanne Gauna of the SouthWest Organizing Project (SWOP) in Albuquerque; Maria Jiménez of the American Friends Service Committee's Immigration Law Enforcement Monitoring Project (ILEMP) in Houston; Janet Robideau of Indian People's Action (IPA) in Missoula, Montana; Anthony Thigpenn of Los Angeles' Environment and Economic Justice Project and AGENDA; Jerome Scott of Project South in Atlanta; and Steve Williams of San Francisco's People Organized to Win Employment Rights (POWER).

These organizers are diverse in personal profile, organizing style, constituencies, and geographical location. But all are at the epicenter of racial justice activities that not only bring their communities together but also articulate, for people within their organizations and for those outside, an understanding of what's going on in a racialized social and economic order and what needs to be done to turn it around.

Q. How does your organizing work deal with race and racism?

Janet: The work of Indian People's Action (IPA) focuses on institutional racism in education, employment, and law enforcement, and how these systems affect the lives of urban Indians in Montana. For example, we're fighting with the school district to address the high suspension and drop-out rates for Indian students. We're demanding that they address why, out of 750 certified teachers in the Missoula school district, there are only three Native American teachers and seven teachers of color, total. Race plays a big part in how our kids get treated, what they're taught, and who gets to teach them.

Jane: The work of the Committee Against Anti-Asian Violence centers around race and how it plays out in Asian and Pacific Islander communities in New York City. Specifically, we deal with how state violence issues like police brutality and Immigration and Naturalization Services (INS) enforcement are connected to the prison industrial complex and how they affect Asian communities and other communities of color.

Anthony: AGENDA is trying to do a couple of things in our organizing work in communities of color in the Metropolitan Los Angeles area. One is to work on a large enough scale so that we have the power to really make a difference on issues facing our communities. The other is to develop models for advancing political consciousness that move people beyond their immediate community self-interest to becoming social change activists pushing for a different vision of society.

Jeanne: The environmental justice (EJ) movement is a direct response to the fact that people of color are being routinely poisoned, and that we are not being protected by the agencies that are supposed to protect us: the Environmental Protection Agency (EPA), local governments, the health department, you name it. SWOP coined the term "environmental racism" to spotlight this reality because no one, including the mainstream environmental organizations, was doing anything about it. In fact, sometimes these organizations were contributing to environmental racism. So the EJ movement put everyone on notice that this couldn't go on. Early on, we decided that the movement would be defined by the people most affected by these policies, and that people would speak for themselves. These became the central principles of the EI movement.

Steve: POWER organizes with low- and no-wage workers who have a non-traditional relationship to the work force. Our first campaign has been with welfare workers who are forced to do some form of work in exchange for a welfare check. I think our particular contribution to this area of organizing has been to develop real political education among welfare workers so that they understand that this is not just a fight for equal pay for equal work, but that it takes place in the context of international capital, white supremacy, and patriarchy. When you see the attacks on people of color around the globe, it sharpens the focus in understanding what is taking place in communities of color here in the United States—a Third World workforce forced to work in hyper-exploited conditions.

Q. What are some of the key lessons from your organizing work that could help others deal with and understand race?

Jerome: At Project South, we believe that white supremacy is still the leading edge of oppression in this country. We also believe that you can't just concentrate on white supremacy without bringing up issues of class as well. But having said that, when we look at organizing efforts in the South, there are folks who just want to deal with economic issues—increase wages and that sort of stuff. They ignore the racism and white supremacy that is the very foundation of the wage issues. We have to look at issues of class in relationship to white supremacy, or else we're missing the boat.

Maria: Proposition 187 in California, which got replicated around the country, is the most recent watershed event in terms of immigrants and native-born Latinos responding to racism. It wasn't so much the proposition, but what it signified: the institutionalization of racist attitudes against all undocumented immigrants masked as public policy by government entities and politicians. Latinos' resistance to another generation of our people being subjected to these attacks sparked activity and organization in Latino communities across the country: the huge march in Washington, D.C., organizing drywall workers in Los Angeles, the effort of hundreds of thousands of people to become naturalized citizens, and getting out to vote. This has changed the landscape in anti-racist organizing for immigrants.

Anthony: At AGENDA, we think that self-organization of a particular ethnicity or racial community can often be a legitimate form because the cultures and/or conditions of a particular community warrant that. But I think these efforts have to be placed in a broader context. We cannot limit ourselves to organizing just one group of people, because our vision of society is broader than that. And, if we're trying to organize on a large scale to gain real power, I don't believe there's any one ethnicity that can do it by themselves. Alliances have to be built between different communities and we need to create multicultural organizations and multiracial movements.

Jane: CAAAV understands that different communities are segregated, policed, repressed, and exploited in different ways. For example, when we talk about policing in an Asian immigrant community, we don't just go out there and say, "Hey, it happens to us, too, and here are all the people who have been brutalized by the police in our communities." Each Asian immigrant community experiences state violence in different ways. Violence against the Cambodian community in the Bronx is different from violence in the largely undocumented Fukienese community that lives in Chinatown. The harassment of Cambodian youth by the New York City Police Department is a different experience than INS raids in Chinatown, even though both are acts of state repression. Therefore, organizing in each community needs to be different.

Janet: IPA uses the school district's own numbers to show how institutional racism works, that it's not the individual prejudice of a teacher, or a principal even the superintendent. It's the system that produces higher suspension rates for Indian students: it's the district's policies that discriminate against our children and reinforce individual prejudice.

Q. Do you see any negative trends in how organizations deal with issues of race and organizing?

Jeanne: One of the key tensions that has existed in the EJ movement from the start has been between those who were calling for "equity" and those of us who demanded "justice." Earlier, it was the national white environmental organizations who were pushing for "environmental equity." Nowadays, mainstream national organizations of color—like the Hispanic Environmental Network, which goes around and gets major corporate sponsors—are using that language. The term "equity" was a government creation pushed onto the EJ movement by the Environmental Protection Agency. SWOP doesn't want "equal opportunity pollution." We want to reshape the whole table. We want a fundamental reordering of our priorities and commitments, and that starts with corporate and government accountability to the community. We want justice. There are those of us who use race as a driving force to change society, and there are those in our own communities who use it to drive opportunities for themselves. And then they wonder why they're being shunned by the movement.

Maria: Some people think that bringing multiple cultures together in the name of diversity means that there's anti-racist organizing going on. I think it is important for various cultures to interact and engage in political projects together because these become laboratories for breaking down barriers and finding strategic unity. But I think the more difficult task of "political integration" is to identify what it is about the current historical political moment that creates the need for immigrants from Mexico and Central America to get together with Nigerians and Indians to overcome this country's racist immigration policies. ILEMP believes that the very presence of immigrants is the most concrete manifestation of the global integration of communities, and race plays a huge part in global development. The disparate experiences of immigrant and refugee communities must be integrated to craft a long-term strategy based on this analysis. Just pushing "multiculturalism" without political content is not helpful.

Janet: People want us to use pretty words like "diversity" and "multicultural awareness" instead of calling it what it is. At IPA, we know it is institutional racism. It's like we're all in the same room, and there's this huge pink elephant in the middle of the room. That pink elephant is racism. But nobody wants to look at it; people walk around it; they don't want to see it. But we can't begin to move forward until we name it and get other folks to actually see it. Until we can do that, we can't really change anything, we can't get the pink elephant out of the room. People are too busy running around proclaiming, "I am not a racist." Either they get over their blindness and see the pink elephant, or they'll get run over in a stampede they don't see coming.

Jerome: When people talk about multiculturalism in the South, they are basically talking about black and white: the growing Latino population is left out. Another thing that gets glossed over in our language and practice is the difference between "white supremacy" and "racism." When people say "racism," it conjures up people's attitudes, or that white people have a bad attitude about people of color, or that people of color have a bad attitude about white folks, or each other. But the real deal, I think, is "white supremacy," because it's an institutionalized thing with long historical roots that goes beyond individual bad attitudes and shapes the development of the policies and cultures of institutions. The term "white supremacy" indicates more of a structural phenomenon than "racism."

Jane: When people are fighting for jobs, they are really talking about jobs for the "enfranchised"—people who either are citizens or are documented. CAAAV believes that race is centrally embedded in the whole construct of citizenship and all the systems that emanate from it—public services, jobs, opportunities. When we're fighting for jobs or better housing, we want to reframe the issue—whose interests are being served by these demarcations and incredible enforcement structures that delineate citizens from non-citizens?

Q. What are the key challenges and opportunities in advancing racial justice in the coming period?

Maria: I think the basic challenge actually lies within the progressive movement itself. As a longtime organizer, I've observed this perception that immigrants can't form their own organizations, can't lead their organizations, can't speak for themselves, can't build organizations with enough power to make a real difference. An immigrant rights organization like ILEMP will not look and feel like a traditional community organization, and therefore will not act like one. It combines services with national advocacy, and its grassroots organizing practice is influenced by experiences from its members' countries of origin. Most immigrant rights activities are concentrated in major urban centers and the border region. Immigrant communities blend domestic and homeland issues, and make the experience of globalization painfully real. To meet these challenges, one of the key areas of concentration is developing an infrastructure for a new, emerging leadership in immigrant communities.

Steve: People on welfare are all poor and are overwhelmingly women of color. What has been important for POWER in organizing with them is to pinpoint the intersections of white supremacy, patriarchy, and capitalism. The fight is not simply one for racial justice, but also for economic justice and for gender justice. One of the major trends is to try to focus on one particular lens of oppression as opposed to the complexity of the intersections. Some may attempt to deal with racial justice to the exclusion of dealing with the broader system of capitalism, or vice versa. Neither approach advances our work significantly. The other tendency is to focus exclusively on tactical skills development, because doing analysis is just too complicated or even unnecessary. This approach assumes that the system we currently have is an acceptable system, and all we need to do is to tweak or modify it in some way so that welfare workers receive a slightly higher wage. That approach really gets us nowhere.

Jerome: Project South believes that one of the main challenges in the next period is how well we as a movement promote the leadership of low-income people. Central to that leadership development is a systematic education process about how white supremacy functions as the leading oppressive tool in this country. The key is to organize with low-income people, to develop them as leaders in the process, and to develop education around the centrality of white supremacy. If you're fighting for leadership by low-income people in this country, and you're fighting side-by-side with those people, then you are doing some serious anti-racist, anti-white-supremacist work.

Jane: The next challenge CAAAV faces is to link issues of citizenship, immigration, and immigrants of color with the African American community by showing how INS detention and enforcement policies are linked to the prison industrial complex. This project challenges us to deepen our understanding of the way that race operates. Dealing with racism is much more complicated than just saying that the black and Latino communities are disproportionately incarcerated in the prison system, and that immigrants are in the INS detention system. One point of commonality is an economic one, another is the strategies and tactics employed by both types of incarcerated populations. CAAAV is trying to get into that nexus.

Jeanne: We need to develop our own institutions, strengthen our organizations, and build an infrastructure to support them. We have to write down our own history, our own training manuals, our own models of doing this work. The EJ movement has set up many regional and racially specific networks in the past 15 years, and there's much we all can learn from that experience. We're having the second People of Color Environmental Leadership Summit next year, ten years after the first one, to see what lessons we've learned, and what challenges lie ahead for the Movement. Right now is the calm before another major storm.

Janet: People who have been very successful organizing in other communities of color want to use the same type of strategies and tools and tactics in Indian country, but they don't meet the same success. They don't know our culture, and they expect our people to react to similar agitations, exhibit the same interest level in traditional organizing methods, and engage in similar tactics that they see in other communities of color. We don't respond well to cookie-cutter organizing. We adhere to our own cultures and traditions, and our own rhythm of building towards action. For example, we don't focus on the treatment of ourselves; as Indian people, the number one priority has always been our children. We're the kind of people that say: "Do whatever you want to me, I'll endure. But mess with my child, then I'll have to kick the shit out of you." Our numbers may be small, but that doesn't mean that we can't be powerful.

Anthony: AGENDA believes that one of the biggest obstacles to advancing the practice of community organizing is the traditional fixation on the campaign and the basic organizing premise that you have to win something concrete to motivate and keep people involved. While there is some truth to that, one of the things we're trying to do is not just talk to people about the immediate campaign, or the immediate impact it will have on their family, but also to engage them on broader social and political issues. What is our vision of society? Of community? Our values? Clearly, the development of a more consistent political education program strengthens that engagement. But how do we combine political education with organizing on a large scale? We've done good work, and built a solid membership structure, but we're still organizing on too small of a scale to challenge the power structures in L.A. What would it take to challenge for power in the whole country?

28

Immigrant Rights:
Striving for Racial Justice, Economic
Equality and Human Dignity

National Network for Immigrant and Refugee Rights

Over the last two years, the possibility of a broad legalization program for undocumented immigrants living and working in the United States has emerged as not only a potentially achievable goal for the immigrant rights movement, but as a political issue taken up by anti-immigrant groups, employers hungry for profits, and high profile political figures. Legalization itself has always been a long-term objective for many immigrant rights groups, some of which fought for more than a decade for the 1986 legalization that had allowed more than two million undocumented immigrants to gain legal status. Preparing for this newest struggle, immigrant rights activists anticipated strong and well-funded opposition from the anti-immigrant movement, which was expected to invest hundreds of thousands of dollars in media campaigns to influence public opinion. Over the years, immigration restrictionists have attempted to drive wedges between groups of immigrants based on differences such as legal status or national origin; have argued that legalization and family reunification would contribute to harmful population growth; and have opposed even limited guest worker programs.

What the immigrant rights movement could not anticipate was the severe backlash against immigrants, particularly the undocumented, that occurred in the wake of the terrorist attacks of September 11. In the days and weeks following the national tragedy, the anti-immigrant movement seized this "opportunity" to bring longstanding arguments, particularly those labeling immigrants as criminals, to the forefront of "breaking news." In this moment of shock and terror, in which thousands of lives were lost, including immigrant workers from around the world, anti-immigrant groups moved quickly to blame "illegal aliens" for not only this act of violence, but for a host of social ills. Unfortunately, such anti-immigrant and anti-immigration arguments resonated with a growing audience. Immediately following September 11, racist vigilante activities began to target Arab Americans and people perceived to be of Middle Eastern descent, including threats and attacks on mosques, temples and schools, harassment by police and security guards, and other acts of racist violence. Despite official statements against such violations, rapid federal enactment of anti-terrorism legislation fixated on immigrants, particularly noncitizens and the undocumented, establishing new and potentially permanent restrictions on civil liberties.

Moving Forward after September 11, 2001

In this changed climate, the immigrant rights movement, while still working to ensure that issues of legalization and expanded rights for immigrants remain on the national agenda, clearly faces new challenges, especially when coupled with the economic downturn, historically a breeding ground for anti-immigrant hysteria.

We must create new strategies that address the current context and which work towards long-term goals, such as creating immigration policies that uphold the civil and human rights of all immigrants, regardless of status. For example, the aftermath of Sept. 11 has reinforced the need for immigrant rights activists to build or strengthen alliances to address anti-immigrant violence, hate crimes, and racial profiling against Arab Americans, people of Middle Eastern descent, and other immigrants of color. Activists have also been confronted with immediate concerns arising in the wake of the attacks, and some have moved to the forefront of emerging global anti-war movements, efforts to fight fast track legislation, such as the USA PATRIOT Act that sacrifice civil rights to "fight terrorism," and growing resistance to increased scape-goating of immigrants, such as the new acceptance of racial profiling as a "counter-terrorism" measure. At an international level, U.S. attacks on Afghanistan have displaced hundreds of thousands of people, creating even more refugees with few places to go. Through all of this, immigrant rights groups must walk a careful line between challenging U.S. policies and practices, and dealing with the very tangible effects of the events of September 11.

The violent and widespread anti-immigrant response to the attacks, however, is no surprise. For years, the conservative Right has helped create a climate in which immigrants—particularly the undocumented—are seen as undeserving of human rights. Immigrants have been portrayed as criminals, terrorists, and welfare cheats—and accused of everything from increasing crime and invading communities to stealing the jobs of hardworking citizens to destroying the environment. At the same time, the movement for immigrant rights in the United States has faced serious obstacles in developing effective strategies to resist or transform either the public debate or its policy impact.

Creating new ways of talking about immigration, immigrant rights, and human rights is one of the primary challenges of today's immigrant rights movement, regardless of how current events may change the political climate. Ensuring the human and civil rights of all people, regardless of immigration status, involves more than just responding to anti-immigrant groups and policies. It means bringing immigrant rights into the larger movement for racial justice, labor rights, global economic equality, and human rights—something which is equally critical both during periods of increased support for immigrant rights, and during times of heightened nativism and anti-immigrant sentiment.

Framing Immigration—Where We Are Today

The impact of the anti-immigrant Right on the current immigration debate cannot be overemphasized. In fact, up to this point, the immigration debate has largely been shaped by the anti-immigrant movement. Relying on a number of appealing and exclusionary arguments, the anti-immigrant Right has tapped into the public imagination in a way immigrant rights activists have yet to match. Because of this, discussions around immigration have centered around the themes of race relations and conflict, economic displacement, environmental destruction and overpopulation, urban sprawl, and crime.

During the past few years, these arguments have had less impact, and during this time, immigrant rights organizers and advocates have been able to steadily build up alliances and engage greater numbers of immigrant community members around direct issues.

But the real impact of anti-immigrant arguments is evidenced in the drastic shift in the discussion of legalization proposals since September 11. Some policymakers and advocates have begun to argue that legalization is a way to improve national security—reasoning that by bringing people out of the shadows, their activities can better be monitored. Unfortunately, such arguments deflate the need for legalization as a means of providing safety and security for all people.

In a period dominated by national security concerns and the presumed sacrifice of civil liberties, there is all the more reason to ensure that the most vulnerable are provided with basic protections. The United States will hardly be "safer" by locking out those who have migrated to the United States for a safe and secure life, to work, to go to school, to be reunited with family. Legalization programs embedded in a national security framework actually threaten to create a new class of noncitizens who, while documented, are nevertheless ineligible for the same civil rights protections as citizens and who are subject to the same violations legalization proposals were intended, at least by immigrant rights groups, to prevent. Challenging this framework raises many issues, including what the ultimate goal of the immigrant rights movement is, what we expect to gain from legalization, and the role of immigrant rights in a larger struggle for civil and human rights for all people. While such issues and conflicts are not new, they must be vigorously questioned to avoid compromising our overall vision for immigrant rights.

Immigration as a Racial Justice Issue

Whether proposing that there be a moratorium on immigration because of crime or urban sprawl or national security, anti-immigrant groups have relied strongly on racist arguments and sentiment to boost their position. Rapid demographic changes in the United States have played a significant role in defining the recent wave of anti-immigrant sentiment. Migrants from Latin America, Asia, and Africa now comprise the majority of newcomers to the United States. Today, 8.5 percent of arriving migrants are people of color. In four of the country's five largest cities—New York, Los Angeles, Chicago and Houston—Latinos and Asians already collectively form a majority of the population, while in California, people of color are now the majority. The changing demography of the United States, particularly in regions with increased immigration, has aroused racial anxieties in many White communities and some communities of color. While some communities have responded positively to these changes, there are an even greater number of highly publicized incidents of tension and hostility between newcomers and other residents.[1]

The Immigrant rights movement has faced several formidable obstacles to forging a successful alliance with a broad movement for civil rights and racial justice. At an institutional level, White supremacy continues to define access to education, employment, community resources, *and* other opportunities for communities of color. Within the movement, distrust and/or lack of relations among and between groups of color remain principal obstacles to building a broad anti-racist movement inclusive of an immigrant rights agenda. With a lack of meaningful communication, points of conflict and tension often erupt over the allocation of material resources among economically marginalized groups of color. In order to expand and preserve civil and human rights for immigrants, the immigrant rights movement must build a strong base of multiracial support and articulate a distinctly anti-racist agenda. Immigrant rights groups must also begin to reach out to communities with which they have not previously worked, including Arab, South Asian and Muslim communities which have recently become the targets of both racist and anti-immigrant policies and violence.

Pitting Workers against Each Other

Economic arguments against immigration often rely on racist ideologies to justify immigration restrictions, as well as to divide workers and prevent a unified movement for economic justice. Fueled by racial, ethnic, and economic tensions, anti-immigrant sentiment has been extremely effective at pitting low-wage workers of color against each other. Many communities have also been divided around the question of immigration and its impact on job availability for native-born people of color. In response to such concerns, the immigrant rights movement has often dismissed the possibility of job displacement impacting established communities of color, particularly African Americans. This approach has only exacerbated existing tensions. Instead, the immigrant rights movement needs to support research examining the structural conditions limiting access to decent jobs and resources for all workers.

The labor movement itself has also been divided on its position in regard to immigrant workers. Some progressive unions, such as the Service Employees International Union (SEIU) and the Hotel and Restaurant Employees Union (HERE), have supported immigrant workers and opposed policies such as employer sanctions, and in the process have proven to be crucial allies for immigrant rights advocates. Until recently, the AFL-CIO itself had supported employer sanctions in an effort to "protect" the jobs and interests of U.S.-born workers. In early 2000, however, the AFL-CIO shifted its position, speaking out strongly in support of immigrant workers rights and calling for a broad legalization program and an end to employer sanctions. Such action may help broaden support for immigrant workers on a number of levels, from the workplace to the political arena, and is now all the more critical, considering both the national security framework being applied to immigrants and the economic downturn. The AFL-CIO recently reaffirmed its support for immigrant rights in a post-September 11 resolution acknowledging the increased scapegoating of immigrants following the terrorist attacks.

The Specter of Population Explosion

In recent years, some anti-immigrant groups and population restrictionist advocates have promoted surprisingly effective claims that population increases due to migration pose the greatest threat to the environment. Arguments blaming immigrants for dwindling resources can be very powerful to people frustrated with traffic jams, overcrowded classrooms, and long unemployment lines in their communities. More recently, restrictionists have played to environmental concerns over urban sprawl, citing immigration as a major source of urban overcrowding. Such arguments have generally not swayed the environmental movement to side against immigration. However, they have not helped to build better relations between the environmental movement and immigrant communities.

While there has been some progress in breaking down the barriers between the predominantly White traditional environmental movement and communities of color through the environmental justice movement, these attacks threaten our ability to address serious environmental issues in migrant communities. In the United States, communities of color, including immigrant unities, have overwhelmingly been the victims of environmental degradation, not its cause. Furthermore, if immigrants and other people are unable to exercise their human and civil rights, they cannot be equal partners in defending and shaping a safe and healthy environment for the benefit of all people.

Criminalization of Immigration

Finally, whether at the U.S.-Mexico border or in the interior of the United States, immigration has been framed as an issue about breaking the law, not about participation in a global economic system. Linking immigration and crime justifies a heightened law enforcement approach to immigration control, as demonstrated in the fact that immigrants are now the fastest-growing incarcerated population. Portraying immigrants as criminals has proven to be an effective public relations strategy for the INS and for anti-immigrant groups, making it easier to deny basic rights of privacy and due process, as well as human and civil rights, to immigrants. This practice has recently been taken to a new level with the labeling of immigrants as terrorists and has included such violations as secret detention and the creation of military trials for non-citizen civilians.

In the United States, debates around the question of immigration usually do not take into account its global dimensions. Restrictionists and immigrant advocates alike have often failed to consider the sources and patterns of international migration when formulating policy and strategy. A global perspective sheds light on the limitations of restrictive immigration policies. Although the stated aim of U.S. immigration policy is to control immigration, that policy framework fails to address the root causes of international migration, including economic pressures, ethnic and social conflicts, and environmental degradation. Significantly, the United States has often played a central role in creating the global conditions which lead to migration, from Structural Adjustment Policies that ravage national economies and social systems, to U.S.-based corporate policies, and to military intervention.

Messages of the Immigrant Rights Movement— A Closer Look

Recognizing the impact of the anti-immigrant movement on the immigration debate, however, is not enough. Because the anti-immigrant Right has been very skillful in convincing the public that immigrants cause social and economic problems, it is easy to name the anti-immigrant arguments: "there are too many immigrants;" "they take away jobs;" "the United States can't *take* in all the world's poor;" "there are too many Mexicans;" "we are losing our culture." In contrast, the immigrant rights movement has often failed to clearly articulate what *our* message is.[2] Of course, those who advocate for immigrant rights have advanced certain arguments to defend against changes in immigration law or increases in enforcement. Advocates have often resorted to quick defenses without opportunity to analyze the implications of some arguments that are commonly employed. For example, following September 11, some advocates for legalization have argued for a legalization program to help national security, disregarding the possible impact such a "legalization" may have on the civil and human rights of all noncitizens. By examining the limitations of some of these arguments, we can lay the groundwork for some more effective ways to reframe the debate—and also to avoid falling into similar traps in the future.

Splitting "Illegal" and Legal Immigration

In the past, Washington-based political negotiations have sometimes pushed advocates to compromise their position on what many see as an untenable or politically vulnerable stance—the defense of the undocumented. Scrambling to win public support in a period of heightened nativism, some advocacy groups have conceded to the rhetoric of anti-immigrant lawmakers. By agreeing that illegal immigration is a problem, some advocates had hoped to preserve at least a few rights for immigrants, even if only for a limited constituency.[3] In their view, energies need to be focused on portraying legal immigrants as hardworking, law-abiding, and deserving of rights, in contrast to their undocumented counterparts.

However, some of the concessions made in the name of political pragmatism have only served to further demonize and criminalize undocumented immigrants. In the absence of any visible public defense of their rights, the undocumented have become scapegoats for both the anti-immigrant and "pro-immigrant" agenda. The media further portrays undocumented immigrants as underground drug dealers, criminals, and lazy welfare cheats.

The danger of such negative characterizations of undocumented immigrants became apparent in the debate over Proposition 187 in California. Some advocates projected that stopping illegal immigration was necessary, but that the proposition was a misguided strategy. Playing on the fears of many White voters, anti-187 ads evoked the dangerous threat of disease spreading among "illegals" who "handle your food supply," the possibility of gangs of youth roaming the street after being expelled from school, and the bureaucratic costs of implementing the measure.[4]

Emphasizing the difference between "legal" and "illegal" immigrants also perpetuates a false divide in immigrant communities. Many immigrants exist in "transnational families" which include members of varying legal status.[5] One household may include U.S. citizen children, permanent resident parents, and an undocumented cousin, sibling, or grandmother.

Conceding to the documented/undocumented divide obscures the very reasons why people are forced to migrate without documents. While violent conflict and repression exist in many parts of the world, only migrants from certain countries have been granted refugee status in the United States. This distinction usually reflects the bias of U.S. foreign policy: migrants from countries considered to be U.S. adversaries such as Cuba have gained refugee or asylee status far more easily than Salvadorans or Guatemalans fleeing U.S.-backed military repression. In addition, long waits for family visas make it very difficult for migrants from countries such as the Philippines or Mexico to obtain legal entry to the United States. For poor immigrants without a sponsoring relative who meets certain income requirements, the chances of obtaining a permit for legal entry are even more slim. In contrast, a millionaire can obtain residency in the United States with few obstacles. Because of such biased policies, there are few avenues open to migrants from certain areas—particularly Latin America and Asia—other than to migrate without authorization.

The attempt to maintain public support by contrasting one set of immigrants to another has weakened the immigrant rights movement. Not only has it alienated mainstream advocacy and lobbying groups from the grassroots, but it has failed to maintain a reasonable degree of protection for either undocumented or legal immigrants. For example, the strategy to "split the bill" (into provisions dealing with undocumented and "legal" immigrants) adopted by many advocates in the 1996 round of legislative negotiations may have proved successful in its short-term goal of derailing Congressional proposals to reduce legal immigration. But it also guaranteed the passage of a bill which contained numerous damaging provisions—and by no means spared legal immigrants from harm. Now, immigrants intending to apply for political asylum *must* do so at the airport, often without the aid of an attorney. Many longtime legal permanent residents who have been convicted of crimes (including minor drug offenses) are now immediately subject to deportation, even if they have resided in the United States since infancy, and have no family or other ties to their native country. While the 1996 legislation initially made it easier for the U.S. government to deport permanent residents for their political beliefs and affiliations, in June 2001 two Supreme Court rulings determined that deportation provisions in the law could not be applied retroactively and that the INS could not indefinitely imprison immigrants.[6] Unfortunately, in the wake of the events of September 11, such moves to uphold the *civil* and human rights of immigrants have been challenged once again, this time in the name of anti-terrorism measures, leaving all noncitizens, including permanent residents, additionally vulnerable to rights violations. The combined impact of these laws on many immigrant families is devastating.

The Perils of Cost-Benefit Analysis

The question of whether immigrants are a net fiscal benefit or drain to the United States often distorts the debate with reports quantifying immigrants' contributions and costs cited by both immigrant-rights advocates and those opposed to immigration. These arguments are deeply problematic on both empirical and moral grounds.

The debate over Proposition 187 in California provides a good example of how cost-benefit arguments result in confusion. Supporters of the measure often cited Donald Huddle's 1993 report, "The Net Costs of Immigration to California," which argued that immigrants incurred $18.1 billion more in public assistance costs to California taxpayers than the $8.9 billion immigrants paid in taxes. This figure includes $4.2 billion for costs of assistance to 914,000 California residents who were unemployed "because of immigration."[7] However, the Urban Institute report *Setting the Record Straight,* more often cited by immigrant rights activists, reported that immigrants in California contributed $30 billion in taxes and received only $18.7 billion in government services, resulting in a $12 billion net contribution in taxes to California.[8]

As these comparisons demonstrate, cost-benefit arguments ultimately become a confusing numbers game. By crafting arguments that evaluate the contributions of immigrants as opposed to their costs, immigrant rights advocates have engaged in a slippery battle. While highlighting the positive role that immigrants can play as economic actors, the immigrant rights movement cannot rely on cost-benefit arguments as a main argument. One study's data on the costs and taxes paid by immigrants can easily refute another's, and the accuracy of such data is difficult to ascertain.[9] Subtle methodological distinctions between various studies often fail to translate into effective arguments. They usually boil down to ideological differences in the sponsoring organizations' or authors' perspectives.[10]

Some cost-benefit studies have determined that immigration is a benefit to the economy because immigrant workers provide a supply of cheap labor. The problem with this aspect of the cost-benefit strategy is that it has sometimes conflated the immigrant-rights message with the interests of big business. Is the real message of the immigrant rights movement that immigrants are willing to work for cheap?

During the legislative battle over immigration in 1996, national and local immigrants rights organizations forged tactical alliances with business interests to defend employment- and family-based legal immigration. The Silicon Valley computer industry, for example, rallied around the protection of high-tech jobs as part of the "split the bill" strategy championed by some immigrant rights groups. Although some industry representatives were specifically working to relax restrictions on mobility for educated, professional immigrants, many immigrant advocates saw this as an opportunity to build a case on behalf of immigrants in general.[11] Other advocates, even if they did not actively ally themselves with business interests, tacitly accepted involvement of these powerful firms as confirmation of their claims that immigrants are vital to the U.S. economy. Today, a similar dynamic has emerged in the debate over legalization, as business interests have allied themselves with efforts to create an expanded guest worker program under the guise of "legalizing hard-working Mexicans." In reality, businesses are more interested in developing new opportunities to legally exploit workers and increase profits, though it is unclear how this agenda may play out in the current climate focused on national security and economic decline.

In 1996, the weight of large business interests like Microsoft and the National Association of Manufacturers undoubtedly bolstered the split-the-bill strategy. But their high-profile defense of immigration has cost the immigrant rights movement other allies: namely, some who are concerned about protecting the interests of American-born workers. Author Michael Lind, for example, has argued that the immigrant rights movement is actually working to protect the interest of big business at the expense of U.S. workers. Lind claimed in a *New Republic* editorial that reducing immigration "is a perfectly legitimate liberal cause—if 'liberal' means protecting the interests of ordinary wage-earning Americans." He writes that those truly concerned about the interests of the working poor should note that the greatest income gains for both Black and White Americans have been noted during periods of immigration restriction. He also asserts that union membership is disrupted when "mass immigration produces a workforce divided by ethnicity."[12] Similarly, a 1997 brief issued by the progressive Institute for Policy Studies encourages labor advocates to give serious consideration to a national worker identification card and to guest worker programs to fill "jobs that U.S. residents don't want."

Some of the economic benefits immigrants bring are rooted in the fact that they are often a cheap, and pliable labor force. Organized labor and many working people understandably bridle when immigrant rights activists speak in this vein. We should instead point out that the real goal of restrictive legislation is to keep immigrants, and others, from gaining labor rights they deserve by maintaining an underground workforce. Big business's interest in protecting immigration in order to maintain a cheap, pliable labor force is distinct from an agenda which advances labor and civil rights for all workers, regardless of immigration status, in the interest of economic justice. Part of evaluating the "cost-benefit" strategy is to ensure that immigrant-rights advocates do not perpetuate the notion that immigrants are "good for the economy" because they are easily exploitable, low-wage workers. In other words, just because the *Wall Street Journal* calls for open borders does not mean that it is a natural ally of a progressive immigrant rights movement.

Even more fundamentally, by relying on cost-benefit arguments, the immigrant rights movement remains rooted in a framework that construes immigration policy narrowly as a matter of what is "good for the United States" according to simple numeric calculations. We lose an opportunity to focus attention on the global economic phenomena that affect immigrants and native-born residents alike.

We also lose a chance to challenge assertions about standards used to determine human and labor rights. If rights are simply accorded in order to correspond with economic success or contributions, what does that say about the elderly, the disabled, or children? Should they not have rights because they may not contribute economically? All people make contributions in different ways at different times to the communities and societies they live in. Our focus should not be whether an individual has earned certain rights, but why basic standards for human rights should apply to everyone, regardless of immigration status.

Do cost-benefit arguments have any place in the arguments advanced by the immigrant rights movement? Clearly, there is a need to refute erroneous accusations about the drain immigrants pose to society. However, instead of relying on simple cost-benefit calculations, we need to point out who really benefits when immigrants are denied rights: unscrupulous employers seeking profit while ignoring occupational and, frequently, environmental standards. The deep conflict of interest in such positions is evident in the recent debate around legalization and employer sanctions. Some employer interests have actually expressed support for legalization and an end to employer sanctions as part of a move to advocate for expanded temporary worker programs. Employers are increasingly willing to make concessions that workers may eventually become permanent residents in exchange for what is essentially a captive and exploitable work force.

The "Nation of Immigrants" Argument

Appealing to a long and rich history of immigration to the United States, many voices in the struggle for immigrant rights have used the argument that the country has always been "a nation of immigrants" in order to build support for immigrant communities today. Indeed, a majority of the U.S. population can trace its ancestry to immigrant roots. Cartoons depicting Native Americans asking, "Who's the Illegal Alien, Pilgrim?" highlight the fact that the first European settlers didn't obtain authorization before arriving and decimating the indigenous population.

Appeals to a history enriched by immigration are effective. The Statue of Liberty, which has historically served as a symbol of welcome to immigrants, is an icon of national importance. However, anti-immigrant factions have also used its symbolism to argue that the United States can no longer afford to be so generous. A 1996 cover story in the *Atlantic Monthly* depicting a weary Lady Liberty asked, "Can We Still Afford to be a Nation of Immigrants?" The article implied that the country has reached its limit of how much immigration it can absorb and, even more insidiously, that today's immigrants are "mostly Mexicans" whose ethnic separatism threatens traditional patterns of assimilation. In light of post September 11 national security concerns, this issue has been re-raised and expanded to include other ethnic groups, and will likely continue to be a growing thread in both anti-immigrant arguments and "anti-terrorism" discussions.

In reality, immigrants have always been present in the United States, and an accurate historical perspective reveals that periods of nativism and anti-immigrant sentiment almost always reflect economic trends and are rooted in racist ideology. The Chinese Exclusion Act, enacted in response to fear of Chinese competition and the Depression-era deportation of more than 500,000 people of Mexican descent (including U.S. citizens) through "Operation 'Wetback'" are just a few examples.

Finally, the notion that the United States "was built on immigrant labor" should be expanded to account for the roles of non-immigrant (or forcibly migrated) groups like Native Americans and African Americans. To simply assert that immigrants constructed the nation obscures the fact that U.S. colonizers and settlers stole Native American lands, practiced genocide, and through the enslavement of Africans, built the foundations of a U.S. economic empire. A more effective alternative should acknowledge the exploitation and sacrifice of many groups, including immigrants, who are deserving of rights, protection, and recognition.

Conclusion: Creating Arguments that Work

Many of the arguments used by immigrant rights advocates are not effective tools for advancing our long-term goals. Cost-benefit, documented-undocumented, or "nation of immigrants" arguments are limited in that they are reactive, rather than proactive. They are rooted in a framework which still sees immigration as a law enforcement problem, and not as an issue about human rights. This is even more evident in the current move to sacrifice civil liberties, particularly those of noncitizens, for national security.

Looking at the state of the debate, it is clear that we can learn some important lessons from our adversaries: the anti-immigration movement is a broad coalition which encompasses sectors of the Far Right, population groups, politicians, lobbyists, and community-based anti-immigrant organizations. Their messages are simple and rhetorically compelling. Their strategy has been to build effective local, grassroots alliances in order to tap into key concerns in communities and channel frustration or dissatisfaction into anti-immigrant sentiment. For example, in 2001 Sachem Quality of Life, a local, Farmingville, New York, based anti-immigrant group, utilized the backing and support of the nationally recognized FAIR, combined with on-the-ground community organizing to not only defeat a local proposal to create a hiring hall for immigrant day laborers, but to construct Farmingville as representative of the national immigration debate and its impact on middle-class, suburban communities.

While the immigrant rights movement also needs to formulate simple and convincing messages that reflect the concerns of a broad, grassroots base, our challenge is more formidable. Rather than urging people to scapegoat an already vulnerable population, we need to encourage people to think outside of the current confines of the debate. We must work consciously and collaboratively to avoid falling back on arguments that do not support the rights of all immigrants or that divide immigrants based on legal status or national origin. In order to do this, the immigrant rights movement needs to develop strategies that help us to reframe our messages based on a shared set of principles which uphold the rights of all people. We must work to defend and expand human rights (which include labor, cultural, civil, social, environmental, and economic rights) for everyone, regardless of immigration status, and to recognize racial equality and justice as critical to expanding a progressive immigrant rights movement. We need to assert that wealth should not determine a person's ability to move across borders and that, in a globalized economy, the concept of the "equality or mobility" is key to creating equity for working people. The immigrant rights movement should also defend full and equal access to education and public benefits, and to other rights guaranteed by the U.S. Constitution, the Universal Declaration of Human Rights, and international law, for all immigrants. Finally, we must continue to pursue coalition politics that link challenges faced by immigrants to other sectors, including welfare recipients, low-wage workers, police accountability groups, prison reform groups, and communities of color.

Messages and objectives based on these principles can be formulated and utilized in a number of ways. For example, by offering a critique of global economic restructuring and its impact on migration, groups can call attention to migration as an issue intrinsically related to inequities in wealth and power. Similarly, we can challenge the framing of immigration as a law enforcement problem by explaining how approaching immigration exclusively as an issue of enforcement is not only inhumane, but ineffective because it fails to address the root causes of migration. As we continue to strive to integrate our struggle with a struggle for racial justice, the immigrant rights movement should also be both on the front lines of building a movement against racism, and encouraging civil rights leaders to promote immigrant rights in their own work. By framing migration as a labor issue, we can build active alliances with labor, expose how immigration law promotes sweatshop conditions, and link our efforts with emerging movements for immigrant workers' rights. Finally, we should not only actively integrate a human rights framework into our own work, but promote alliances with other sectors who use a human rights framework as a tool to analyze conditions in the United States and to achieve racial, economic, and social justice. This means building alliances with groups focused on issues such as police accountability, environmental justice, labor rights, civil rights, and women's rights. Fundamentally, these principles are inseparable, and are crucial to developing an international movement against racism, which is influenced by globalization, migration, and changing demographics.

Pursuing alliances and developing messages based on these basic principles, however, doesn't mean disengaging from the discussion over current policies and practices. In fact, engagement with legislative threats and policy debates is essential to ensure that immigrants' rights are not further compromised. Legislatively-focused strategies can also contribute to movement-building and immigrant community empowerment, and can be the basis for establishing crucial, long term alliances. Recent xenophobic measures have already catalyzed formidable mobilizations, with recent restrictions on noncitizens in particular highlighting the links between struggles for immigrant rights and movements for racial justice and human rights. As a movement, we have the potential to galvanize significant efforts by immigrant community groups and larger entities, such as the labor movement and civil rights institutions. Immigrants, people of color, and working-class people together form a majority in the United States—and have the power to change both popular opinion and public policy. If we can frame immigrant rights as an issue about human dignity, economic parity, and racial justice, then we can begin to lay the groundwork for transforming the immigration debate.

Notes

1. For examples of positive instances of intergroup organizing, see Julia Teresa Quiroz, *Together in Our Differences: How Newcomers and Established Residents are Rebuilding America's Communities,* (Washington D.C.: National Immigration Forum, 1995).

2. It is on precisely this point that organizations like the Federation for American Immigration Reform are able to base their strategies. See FAIR, *How to ~~Survive~~ Win the Immigration Debate,* (Washington, D.C.: by the author, 1997).

3. A D.C.-based lobbying organization, for example, took the explicit position that "legal immigration is not the same as illegal immigration" and asserted that "the American people want the federal government to take decisive and effective action to control illegal immigration." National Immigration Forum, "What's Wrong with the House Immigration Bill," November 1995.

4. Quotes from Arturo Vargas, co-chair of Taxpayers Against 187, from "Beyond Proposition 187: Strategies for Community Change" conference, Northeastern University, Boston, MA, March 31, *1995.*

5. Leo Chavez, "Proposition 187: The Nationalist Response to the Transnationalist Challenge" (Paper presented at Ernesto Galarza Public Policy Conference, Riverside, CA, January 1995).

6. The Anti-Terrorism and Effective Death Penalty Act (AEDPA) was largely responsible for these changes.

7. Donald Huddle, "The Net Costs of Immigration to California," Carrying Capacity Network, November 4, 1993; Rafael Alarcón, *Proposition 187: An Effective Measure to Deter Undocumented Migration to California?* (San Francisco: Multicultural Education, Training, and Advocacy, October 1994).

8. Michael Fix and Jeffrey S. Passel, *Immigration and Immigrants: Setting the Record Straight* (Washington, D.C.: Urban Institute, 1994); and Passel, Clark, and Griego, *How Much Do Immigrants Really Cost?* (Washington, D.C.: Urban Institute, February, 1994). A 1997 study by George Vernez and Kevin F. MacCarthy of the Rand Corporation suggests that certain groups of immigrants benefit the economy more than others, and that a point system should be used to evaluate an immigrant's potential contribution versus his or her cost.

9. In testimony before a House of Representatives subcommittee on human resources, economists Michael Fix and Jeffrey Passel refuted studies which attribute high economic costs to undocumented immigrants by arguing that such studies have been produced by government agencies interested in "recovering" the costs of immigrants and receiving economic compensation. Their review found that, although such studies vary in quality, the results frequently overstate the negative impacts of immigrants in several ways; they systematically understate tax contributions of immigrants, overstate service costs for immigrants, and exaggerate the impacts and costs of job displacement. Most importantly, Fix and Passel claimed that these studies inflate the size of the immigrant population, particularly the undocumented immigrant population. See Fix and Passel, op. cit.

10. Some studies diverge from the taxes and services balance-sheet approach by trying to distinguish the fiscal impact of immigrants (in terms of their use of government resources) from their net impact on the economy (or their overall impact on wages and productivity). But even these reports, which seem to draw positive conclusions about immigrants, can sometimes work against the long-term interests of the immigrant-rights movement. The National Academy of Sciences issued a 1997 report, which concluded that immigration produces "substantial economic benefits for the United States as a whole" but nevertheless "slightly reduces the wages and job opportunities of low-skilled American workers, especially high school dropouts." The report assessed the costs "imposed" by immigrants, including public education and social services. Its authors concluded that most Americans are enjoying a healthier economy because of the benefits of immigration, including an increased supply of labor and resulting lower consumer prices.

11. Some think tanks developed studies of their own to support such arguments. A 1997 study by the Rand corporation, for example, lauded the benefits of immigrant business executives proposed changing the family-based visa system and instead developing a point system to favor skilled and well-educated workers. "How to Make Immigration Better for America: Favor Aliens with Job Skills," *U.S. News and World Report,* Dec. 29, 1997–Jan. *5, 1998.*

12. Michael Lind, "Huddled Excesses," *The New Republic,* vol. 214 no. 14 (April 1, 1996):6. In fact, the most restrictive period for immigration was World War II when wartime conditions upset usual migration patterns. The U.S. economy was enhanced by massive government investment in creating employment and enhancing industry. The fact that U.S. workers experienced great income gains in this period had to do with government investment in the domestic infrastructure, not with immigration levels.

Questions

1. How would you supplement the list of ways to respond to hate groups?

2. What are some of the negative trends that racial justice organizers have observed in different community struggles?

3. What is racial profiling? Why do many people find this concept difficult to understand? In a time of war, should racial profiling be permitted?

4. How would you distinguish a law enforcement approach to immigration from a labor/human rights perspective? How has the tension between these two approaches been articulated in law and policy?